The Engine
That Could

The Engine That Could

Seventy-Five Years of Values-Driven Change at Cummins Engine Company

JEFFREY L. CRUIKSHANK
DAVID B. SICILIA

HARVARD BUSINESS SCHOOL PRESS
BOSTON, MASSACHUSETTS

Printed in the United States of America

01 00 99 98   5 4 3 2

Library of Congress Cataloging-in-Publication Data

Cruikshank, Jeffrey L.
    The engine that could : seventy-five years of values-driven change at
Cummins Engine Company / Jeffrey L. Cruikshank, David B. Sicilia.
        p.   cm.
    Includes bibliographical references and index.
    ISBN 0-87584-613-0 (alk. paper)
    1. Cummins Engine Company—History. 2. Internal combustion engine
industry—United States—History. 3. Diesel motor industry—United
States—History. I. Sicilia, David B. II. Cummins Engine Company.
III. Title.
    HD9705.5 I574C853 1997
        338.7'629506'0973—dc21   97-2746
                                                          CIP

The paper used in this publication meets the requirements of the
American National Standard for Permanence of Paper for Printed Library Materials Z39.49-1984.

To Joe Cruikshank and Anna Bella Sicilia,
born with this project

Contents

Preface

In 1993, Cummins hired us to research and write a history of the company—partly to commemorate the company's seventy-fifth anniversary, but also to help the company understand itself better as it emerged from a particularly trying episode in its history. We spent more than three years talking with scores of people in and around Cummins, studying the company's records, and reviewing pertinent materials in other historical collections. We had access to the entire written record, which turned out to be far more complete than the company knew.

With three exceptions, we were not steered away from any subjects. Those exceptions were: the individual foibles and failings that cropped up at Cummins (as in all human organizations) but had little or no impact on the company's fate; one legal proceeding, the final settlement of which committed Cummins not to talk publicly about the case; and proprietary information about emerging technologies.

Within these loose boundaries, we were free to explore. In fact, we were challenged regularly to push harder, dig deeper, and analyze more vigorously. Initial drafts of the manuscript, including those that included some of the more painful and difficult episodes in the company's history, were met with a consistent and encouraging reaction: Tell us more.

Cummins responded energetically to our many drafts, and the book is better for it. In some cases, we have included dissenting opinions as footnotes. Final editorial control, however, rested with us.

Jeffrey L. Cruikshank
Boston, Massachusetts

David B. Sicilia
College Park, Maryland

The Engine
That Could

1 | The Engine That Could

By MOST CONVENTIONAL RECKONINGS, THE Cummins Engine Company should not exist. It is, as one Cummins CEO phrased it several years ago, an improbable company.

After its founding era, the company's principal business was selling diesel engines to truck manufacturers, many of whom already made their own gasoline engines. And these customers, engaged in intense competition with each other, were fiercely jealous of the key vendor that they shared. For Cummins, it was an unending balancing act—something like forever juggling a dozen different lovers, always taking care to make each feel more beloved than the rest.

Today, in 1997, the company—a worldwide manufacturer of diesel engines and related equipment, based in Columbus, Indiana—is a vastly bigger, more complex, and more stable company. But in many ways, it is still improbable. The only survivor in a once crowded field of independent engine makers, it is a tough competitor in a dynamic and unforgiving marketplace. This toughmindedness is a trait that has contributed in important ways to the company's survival.

At the same time, Cummins is known for its extensive and innovative programs in corporate philanthropy, and for its enduring commitment to team-based work practices. These features, too—seemingly at odds with toughmindedness—have helped the company survive and prosper.

In this book, drawing extensively on the history and current practices of Cummins, the authors attempt to provide an in-depth look at a model of doing business that is creative, flexible, and realistic. We explain how that model has evolved over time, and how it has survived the pressures of dramatically changing competitive contexts.

Cummins' managers are quick to say that nothing in business ever is certain or final. We agree. But the Cummins model has proven to be remarkably durable. Working within that model, Cummins has set high standards for itself, and for the most part it has met them.

The company's seventy-five-year history also recapitulates much of what is interesting and important about the evolution of American business between the 1920s and the 1990s. For these reasons, we are convinced that the story of Cummins deserves to be discovered, scrutinized, and interpreted.

Toward the end of our story, we draw on the history of Cummins to distill some broadly applicable lessons. Companies that are improbable, tough-minded, and humane have, it turns out, important lessons to teach.

Why Cummins?

There are six compelling themes that emerge from an in-depth look at the Cummins Engine Company. They are:

- The history of American business in the context of what aptly has been called "the American Century"
- The evolution of a unique and durable technology: the diesel engine
- The struggle within one company to maintain focus in a changing world
- The paradoxical struggle to adjust that focus (from technology oriented to customer oriented)
- The consequences (mostly positive) of adopting and maintaining a long-term perspective
- The need to respond to accelerating and intensifying change in the marketplace (including Japanese competition and the threat of takeovers) with both short-term measures and long-term strategies

Let us introduce each of these themes in turn. First, this is a story of American business in the twentieth century. Our story illustrates most of the archetypes and icons of recent American industrial history. It captures some of the excitement and enthusiasm of the Age of the Inventor, although that era already was coming to a close when the company was born. It spans speculation, depression, mobilization, and Pax Americana. It captures both the optimism and immodesty of America as it set out to repair a world that had been devastated by war, and—in the wake of that dramatically successful reconstruction—the nation's long decades of disillusionment, during which a hard-won wisdom finally supplanted the innocence of an earlier era.

This is also the story of a remarkable machine: the diesel engine. Rudolf Diesel's invention proved incredibly difficult to commercialize, in part because diesel engine makers in the early years of this century tried to produce a design that would work equally well across the incredibly diverse spectrum of applications in which diesels can be used. Clessie Cummins, the self-taught mechanical genius for whom the Engine Company was named, finally sidestepped this trap by designing a high-speed automotive diesel that was particularly suited for use in trucks. This necessitated crucial breakthroughs in the systems that would supply fuel to his engines. When the Cummins engine and injection system finally came together in the early 1930s and was used to repower trucks originally equipped with gasoline engines, it represented a dramatic leap forward in the evolution of diesel technology. Clessie Cummins had done what no one else in the world had yet been able to do.

This is the story, too, of a company that has retained its focus and identity over many decades. Most single-product industrial companies that were organized in the United States at the end of the nineteenth century or the beginning of the twentieth century have long since gone out of business or been subsumed in larger conglomerates. Electric Boat—the Connecticut-based progenitor of the submarine—was swallowed up by General Dynamics. The faceless United Technologies is a collection of formerly independent and focused companies: Otis Elevator, Sikorsky Helicopters, and others. St. Louis-based Emerson Electric, an industrial powerhouse, consists of literally dozens of small, single-product (or limited product-line) companies that have been stitched together into a more or less coherent whole.

Cummins avoided this fate for several reasons. Perhaps most important, Clessie Cummins' breakthrough technology proved astonishingly durable and—with extensive modifications—suitable for a wide range of applications. The basic engine block that Cummins (and his chief engineer, Hans Knudsen) designed in the late 1920s was still in production a half-century later. There are few parallels in the entire landscape of twentieth-century American manufacturing.

Cummins is also unique for having managed to grow without blurring its focus. One inescapable lesson of American business history is that for most companies, in most contexts, there are only two choices: Grow or die. Cummins' leaders learned this lesson early and applied it relentlessly. But for Cummins, this first meant growth within the truck industry—both through increased market share and "dieselization" of heavy-duty trucks—and subsequently growth in international markets, new classes of trucks (light- and medium-duty), and an increasingly broad range of applications (marine, industrial, power generation, etc.). The product line grew outward organically from its core.

This strategy has its risks, including commitment to a technology that lacks or loses a market. Cummins began its existence as an experimental machine shop, and—through genius and persistence—came up with a remarkable technology. The technicians were appropriately proud of their work. But there was no *market* for this product. It took Cummins decades to learn to sustain an appropriate focus on cutting-edge technology (to ensure that it could lead its industry) while also paying careful attention to the customer base (to ensure that it would have someone to sell its engines to). This is a creative tension, and it continues to the present.

The Engine Company also warrants a sustained inquiry because it consistently has adopted a long-term perspective. This is a perspective that legions of scholars and business leaders in recent years have identified as a prerequisite for America's manufacturing competitiveness. At Cummins, this perspective is captured in the phrase "patient capital." The patient-capital tradition at Cummins was established by the members of the founding Irwin-Sweeney-Miller family, who infused money into the business continuously for twenty years (including the most trying years of the Great Depression) before their diesel-making venture finally managed to turn a profit. As recently as the 1960s, the founding family (especially J. Irwin Miller and his sister, Clementine Tangeman) owned more than half of the capital stock of the Engine Company, and provided an important steadying influence. Even today, the family's influence—paradoxically conservative and venturesome, as we shall see—is pervasive at Cummins.

One of the places this influence has been felt most strongly is in the realm of corporate citizenship, as indicated above, and this is yet another reason for an in-depth look at Cummins. The company's unique approach to its social responsibilities is due in large part to the singular influence of J. Irwin Miller. Again, there are virtually no parallels in recent American business history to Miller, who joined the company in 1934 and still has a powerful voice in its affairs today, more than sixty years later. Largely at his urging, Cummins in the 1950s began allocating 5 percent of its pretax domestic profits to charitable causes—the highest allowable rate, and one that was matched consistently by only one other American company. Also beginning in the 1950s, the Cummins Engine Foundation started paying the fees of promising young architects who were commissioned by Cummins' home city of Columbus to design public buildings, with an initial focus on public schools. The result has been the transformation of Columbus into a small-scale showcase of twentieth-century American architecture.

Corporate citizenship at Cummins has had many faces. In marked contrast to its industry cousins in Detroit, Cummins acknowledged relatively early (during the mid-1960s) that its products were contributing to America's air-pollution problems. In the 1970s, the Engine Company designed and played a unique role vis-à-vis the regulatory community. Rather than seeking delays or reversals of ever-tightening pollution controls, Cummins tried to ensure that the Environmental Protection Agency, the California Air

Resources Board, and other key agencies would promulgate sensible and effective rules. The Health Effects Institute—a highly unusual joint venture between the EPA and the nation's engine manufacturers—was the direct result of Cummins' efforts to ensure that the regulatory process would promote fairness, efficiency, wisdom, and stability.

In recent decades, Cummins has been deeply immersed in the dominant trends in American business. These include several subplots that the company definitely would have preferred to avoid. But even when Cummins found itself under siege, it responded in creative ways. The contrast with the American automobile industry again is instructive. When Detroit realized belatedly that Japanese imports represented a mortal threat, the industry sought protection through trade barriers. As a result, the industry wound up surrendering market share in exchange for short-term profits. When Cummins' time came— that is, when the Japanese began making exploratory forays into the U.S. heavy-duty diesel market in the early 1980s—the Engine Company tightened its belt and cut its new-engine prices between 20 and 40 percent.

The immediate result was a flood tide of red ink at Cummins. But in the medium term, the Japanese challengers decided that they could not compete on Cummins' home turf. Meanwhile, Cummins was learning a great deal about manufacturing practices from its Japanese competitors (who, as we will see, served as willing instructors). In the wake of this most intense period of competition, moreover, Cummins rebuilt productive partnerships with key Japanese companies.

"Internationalize!" has been a call to arms for American businesses in recent decades as champions of foreign expansion have touted it as a solution to a host of problems. Cummins has an interesting and colorful record in this field as well. Arriving fairly late on the international scene (the company's first foreign outpost was established in Scotland in the late 1950s), Cummins has grown rapidly into a significant international manufacturer, with roughly half of its sales coming from outside the United States. Ranked number 121 on the 1995 Fortune 500 list of the largest U.S. manufacturers, Cummins in the same year was fortieth on the list of top-ranking exporters. (Many companies that ranked above Cummins on that list were exporters of commodities, such as grain and paper pulp, rather than manufacturers.)[1] Today, Cummins seems well positioned for continued international growth.

The most important business story in the 1980s was the great wave of takeovers and mergers, which—depending on one's point of view—either crippled or rationalized American industry. Some of these consolidations were mutually agreeable; others were shotgun weddings. In this drama, too, Cummins played a small but highly visible role. In 1989, a British company acquired almost 9 percent of Cummins, in what may or may not have been a move toward takeover. And, within a week of the day that this first overture ended, a second company announced that it had acquired a large block of Cummins stock. This initiated a strange tug-of-war for control over the Columbus-based manufacturer. For all practical purposes, the episode ended when Cummins succeeded in setting up partnerships with three of its key customers, each of whom bought large blocks of stock in the company.

The history of Cummins includes some lessons that its managers wished they had never been required to learn, and which speak to the concerns of many American manufacturers. Despite a consistent policy of significant investment in research and development, for example, there were long dry spells for the company's Research and Engineering (R&E) group. More than once, Cummins has bet on the wrong technological horse. And by its own reckoning, Cummins' management sometimes came up short. In part due to spectacular rates of growth in the postwar decades—the company doubled in size roughly every five years—Cummins' management structure was consistently thin, sometimes bordering on the rickety. New ventures often were undertaken well before the management resources needed to support them were in place. This led, at times, to mistakes on both strategic and tactical levels.

Nor has Cummins escaped the painful downsizings and other dislocations of recent decades. The company's Columbus-based manufacturing force was reduced (both through layoffs and attrition) by almost 50 percent during the turbulent 1980s, as the company struggled very visibly in its small-town setting to restructure and regroup for the future. More than forty Cummins plants, warehouses, and office facilities were closed between 1983 and 1992. Between 1979 and 1989, the company's Southern Indiana shop-floor work force declined from 6,800 to 3,700. Thousands of people—line workers and executives alike—lost good jobs.[2]

As this book goes to press, Cummins has recently experienced yet another cyclical rebound. On the eve of the twenty-first century, and in the context of an economy that is increasingly integrated on a global basis, creating and protecting good jobs remains a prime concern of many at Cummins. It is a challenge that faces most other American manufacturing firms as well.

Change and culture

At regular intervals in the last four or five decades, J. Irwin Miller has made the point that Cummins is not a charity. The company, says Miller, must compete toe-to-toe with the best companies in the world. It must provide returns on investment that are comparable over the long run to the best alternatives, or investors (including Miller and his family) will be fully justified in taking their money elsewhere.

Diesel making historically has been a highly capital-intensive industry, and the Engine Company has had little choice but to reward its investors if it hoped to keep attracting the funds necessary to support its continued growth. And given the fact that Cummins has sat squarely in a highly cyclical industry—the heavy-duty truck business—the company has had to be doubly profitable in good years to make up for the deep troughs.

Perhaps it is these harsh economic fundamentals that have fostered the change-oriented culture that is a Cummins hallmark. "Obsolete your own products" is a Miller maxim that is cited regularly at Cummins. Change will certainly come; the only question is: Who will be driving it? Miller's successor as chief executive officer, Henry B. Schacht, once attributed his company's success to its willing embrace of change:

> *Change is a way of life. An industrial company should seize upon change as opportunity. It should look forward to change; it should thrive on change; but most of all, it should create and force change rather than react to change created by others. . . .*
>
> *Change is healthy. Creating and forcing change is the prime job of any management, no matter what the institution or group, no matter where the location.*[3]

It is important to note, however, that Cummins' commitment to change lives side-by-side with a tradition-rich corporate culture. There are many reasons why the Cummins culture is both pervasive and durable. Several already have been mentioned: the sheer longevity of Cummins' core technologies, and the six decades of service by J. Irwin Miller. Few companies ever get the opportunity to present a sixty-year service award, as Cummins did for Miller in 1994. (A special pin had to be designed for the occasion.)

Another is the wide-open Midwestern charm of Clessie Cummins himself. This has been preserved in oral lore, in Clessie's breezy autobiography, and in the 16mm Bell and Howell movies that he made of his "Barnum and Bailey" marketing exploits in the 1930s: cross-country bus trips, truck endurance runs, demonstration races, and the like, which successfully brought the Cummins Engine Company to the attention of a public otherwise uninterested in the diesel industry. Even after Clessie himself stopped making home movies, the trials and triumphs of Cummins engines continued to be well documented. The company's first four trips to the Indianapolis 500 (two in the 1930s, and two in the 1950s) were captured on film. And the romance of trucking, as glorified in countless Hollywood films and country-and-western songs, extended easily to Cummins, which as recently as 1983 powered more than 60 percent of the heavy-duty trucks in America. Most of the old-timers at Cummins delight in oft-told stories about trucks getting into trouble—beset by freezing fuel, overloaded with thawing chickens or melting strawberries—and then getting back out of trouble with the help of a Cummins distributor.

The worldwide Cummins distributor network is another reinforcer of the corporate culture. Technically, Cummins' domestic and international distributors are independent of the company: They buy their businesses from the company on a three-year, not-necessarily-renewable basis; and when they retire, they are required to sell those businesses back to Cummins. But Cummins distributors tend to think of themselves (and are strongly encouraged by the company to think of themselves) as family members. Dating back to the 1930s, the fate of the domestic distributors—who are allowed to distribute *only* Cummins products—was joined to the fortunes of the parent company. But the reverse was also true. Cummins would only survive if it could train its end users to specify Cummins engines in their White, Reo, PACCAR, Sterling, or Autocar trucks. Much of this educational salesmanship was carried out by the distributors, and most of the follow-up service that would persuade a trucker that he had made the right choice was performed by the local distributor. Many of the relationships thus formed are decades old.

Two contradictory ingredients, therefore, exist comfortably side-by-side at Cummins. A company that is absolutely committed to change is also a company that guards its traditions jealously. To an unusual extent, Cummins has prospered because it has succeeded in defining what is negotiable and what is not.

This success has endless implications for the way the company does business, particularly in the realm of ethical conduct. One day in the summer of 1994, a Cummins engineer received the first in what turned out to be a series of four innocuous-looking packages from a city in Illinois. Upon opening this first package, the engineer realized that he was looking at partial plans for a new engine then under design by Cummins' arch-rival, Caterpillar. This was vital industrial intelligence, slipped to Cummins by a disgruntled Caterpillar employee. (Caterpillar was then in the midst of a prolonged and rancorous strike.) The Cummins law department rewrapped the package and sent it back to Caterpillar. As the next three packages arrived in Columbus, they too were routed back to Illinois. These events came to the attention of Caterpillar's general counsel, who wrote a note of thanks to his counterpart at Cummins. "I find it gratifying," the Caterpillar executive noted, "when ethical behavior overshadows the temptation for a competitive edge."[4] *

Perhaps this can be attributed in part to the relative isolation of Cummins' headquarters, forty miles south of Indianapolis in the mostly rural environs of south-central Indiana. (At the Indianapolis airport's car-rental desks, the computers give directions to Columbus, *Ohio*, some three hundred miles away, but not to Columbus, Indiana.) Bartholomew County, Indiana,

---

*Several years later, Henry Schacht recalls, Cat reciprocated by returning unopened a listing of all Cummins product margins, slipped to Cat by an ex-Cummins employee looking (unsuccessfully) for a job from Cat.

doesn't attract the highest rollers and most flamboyant personalities in American business—a fact that occasionally has concerned the Engine Company's leaders. (Briefly in the mid-1960s, the company considered putting its major research facility on one of the coasts, suspecting that top-flight engineers were turning up their noses at provincial Columbus.) But most of the time, Cummins considers its insulated surroundings to be a blessing. It is a judgment with which Howard H. Stevenson, a Harvard Business School professor and an authority on entrepreneurship, agrees. "It's a very effective presorting mechanism," he explains. "People who want to drive in the fast lane don't volunteer for service in Columbus, Indiana."[5]

And when they do, they tend to either adapt or leave. "If somebody is outside of our value system," explains Tim Solso—named the company's seventh president in 1994—"the culture sheds that person immediately."[6] Self-promotion and egotism aren't well tolerated at Cummins, and people who can't break these habits generally move on. Several Cummins "alumni" have achieved outstanding success in corporations where idiosyncrasies of ego are accommodated more easily.

The Cummins culture, both straight-laced and democratic, has relaxed somewhat with changing times. But it is still true that the nail that sticks up gets hammered down. There are no assigned parking spaces or private dining rooms (other than for entertaining clients). The open architecture at Cummins' headquarters emphasizes the team and de-emphasizes the individual. Hierarchies are relatively flat, and organization charts are hard to find. Consensus is prized, and it is pursued aggressively—sometimes to an extreme—by decision makers on many levels. Cummins has been called the "most Japanese" of American companies by some of the company's most aggressive and successful Japanese competitors.

And all of this is thoroughly and sometimes hotly debated. Perhaps this is the single best measure of the strength of the Cummins corporate culture: The culture is distinctive enough and vigorous enough to stimulate a spirited debate, both inside and outside the company. Most people who engage with the company wind up holding strong opinions about it.

Three leaders

We have introduced the idea that culture defines the individual at Cummins. Now we must add the notion that there are three living individuals who have defined much of what is special about the culture of the company.

The first of these we have already introduced. J. Irwin Miller is one of the remarkable figures in twentieth-century American business. Born in 1909, he was the scion of the wealthiest family in Columbus, Indiana, and easily could have lived out his life as the biggest fish in a small pond. But Miller escaped this fate, in part by allying himself with Clessie Cummins—some twenty years his senior, but nevertheless a close friend from the days of Miller's boyhood—and in part by taking full advantage of the rare opportunities afforded to him by his unconventional and exacting family.

Again, the blend is rich and paradoxical. Clessie Cummins gave Miller access to life as it was lived by ordinary people (although Cummins, a self-taught genius, was anything but ordinary). At the same time, the extended Irwin-Sweeney-Miller family, consisting of six adults and two children living together in an ornate Italianate mansion, provided a window on much broader worlds. Irwin Miller was one of two Columbus, Indiana-based students of the violin who practiced on a Stradivarius; his sister Clementine was the other.

Soon, the call of those other worlds took Miller far away from Columbus. As an undergraduate at Yale, Miller performed well academically, but remained in what he later called an "adolescent fog."[7] During his graduate studies at Oxford, he began to emerge from that fog. He studied the American Revolution as seen through English eyes, met Gandhi, and was steeped in the intellectual ferment that characterized Great Britain and Europe in the early 1930s.

After a brief apprenticeship with a family-owned grocery chain in San Francisco, Miller went to work for Cummins in 1934 as the company's second general manager. There is some truth in Miller's self-deprecating statement that the family stashed him away in the Engine Company to keep him from disrupting their bread-and-butter businesses (the local bank and a starch refining company, among others). And at first, Miller had a difficult time defining a meaningful role for himself. Clessie Cummins and others at the company were skeptical of Miller's business abilities. Miller shared these doubts. It was not until he completed a stint in the Navy during World War II, far from the eyes and influence of his family, that he overcame his reluctance to assert himself at Cummins.

But Miller "took over" Cummins only on his own terms. Except for one brief interlude, he never maintained an office at the Engine Company's headquarters. Instead, he located himself in the Irwin Bank building, the original wellspring of the family fortune, from which he exerted a strong but oblique influence over Cummins. In the 1950s and 1960s, Miller installed a sequence of two presidents who attempted to run the company within the broad guidelines that he himself established.

Through the early 1960s, Miller's time was spread across a broad range of activities, including a three-year stint as the first lay president of the National Council of Churches. As a result of this and other activist associations, Miller—an intensely private man—found himself to be increasingly a public figure. Ironically, this activism earned Miller, a lifelong Republican, the trust of the Kennedy and Johnson administrations and the enmity of the

Nixon White House. In 1968, *Esquire* magazine put Miller on its cover, with the accompanying headline: "This man should be the next president of the United States." Almost despite himself, Miller was a celebrity, and a person to whom Americans in many walks of life looked for leadership.

But it was an idiosyncratic kind of leadership that Miller offered. The point was underscored in 1969, when Miller elevated a young Cummins executive to the presidency of the company. This was Henry B. Schacht, who—despite a solid grounding in the financing and international aspects of the business—knew relatively little about manufacturing diesels. Schacht, like other young executives whom Miller championed, was a recent graduate of the Harvard Business School. Schacht was anything but a child of privilege, but he was bright, articulate, and an extremely quick study. With Miller and other senior colleagues providing cover for him, Schacht educated himself retroactively in the core aspects of the business, and simultaneously began planning future directions for the company.

Schacht was first the beneficiary of good times, and then the victim of bad times. A sustained strike in 1972 cost Cummins market share, and made Schacht and his colleagues think more rigorously about their company: What did it stand for? Where was it going? In an explicit effort to sustain the company's long-standing target of 15 percent return on shareholders' equity, Schacht's team made a series of colorful forays into unrelated diversification, buying a bank, a ski manufacturer, and a piece of an Irish cattle-raising company. But a severe recession in 1975, combined with astounding growth in the base business at the beginning and the end of the 1970s, foredoomed these efforts.

Schacht emerged as a corporate statesman in his own right, involving himself (like Miller before him) in issues ranging far beyond the parochial affairs of Cummins. But this emergence was severely restricted until Schacht had a colleague to whom he could entrust the day-to-day operations of the company. He found such an ally in James A. Henderson, another Miller protégé, who received his MBA from the Harvard Business School the year after Schacht. During the roller-coaster decades of the 1970s and 1980s, Schacht and his alter ego Henderson—whom Schacht refers to simply as his "partner"—experienced both exhilarating highs and demoralizing lows. They brought forth the company's first significant new technologies in more than a decade. They effected a painful restructuring of the company, cutting costs and shedding thousands of jobs, in an effort to cut prices and fight off competitors. They refocused the company on issues of cost, quality, and responsiveness.

This effort consumed a full decade, and ultimately was successful. But in the short term, it led to huge operating losses, which in turn depressed Cummins' stock price and made the company a tempting takeover target. As it turned out, the division of labor established at Cummins some twenty years earlier—a broad-gauged Mr. Outside complemented by a hands-on Mr.

Inside—may have been a corporate lifesaver. Schacht spent nearly two full years in the late 1980s fighting off unwelcome corporate suitors. Meanwhile, Henderson ran the shop back in Columbus, recasting the Engine Company's manufacturing practices, tightening up its planning and reporting functions, and working to stanch the flow of red ink.

It was a strange, paradox-laden existence for Schacht, Henderson, and their fellow managers at Cummins. Financial analysts complained that the company was sacrificing the interests of its shareholders in favor of other goals.[8] In 1987, Schacht was excoriated for presiding over a "profitless prosperity."[9] Within two years, he was hailed on the cover of *Business Week* as "Mr. Rust Belt"—the industrial statesman who had cracked the puzzle of manufacturing competitively in the United States.

The improbable antidote

"I question whether any other corporation would have allowed the top management to survive in their positions as long as Cummins did," says a trucking industry executive (and former employee of a Cummins distributor).[10] But Schacht and Henderson had invested heavily in educating their board and their stockholders. As a result, they were reasonably confident that these key constituencies would stand by them long enough to allow them to act in the company's long-term interests. They also had the unqualified support of Irwin Miller, and this made many things possible.

For example, they were able to surmount the intense ups and downs of their highly cyclical industry, even turning that cycle to the company's advantage. John McArthur, former dean and professor at the Harvard Business School, argues that Cummins rides the business cycle more effectively than any other American manufacturer—slashing operations dramatically when necessary, and investing heavily at that point in the cycle when investment presents the most potential.[11]

At the same time, cutting across this clear-eyed and hard-nosed approach to business was a tenacious adherence to *principle*. Cummins in the late 1970s held a 20 percent share of the diesel engine market in South Africa, and was being encouraged by the government to build manufacturing facilities there. The company agreed, on condition that it be permitted to do business in South Africa the same way it did business everywhere else in the world: Cummins South Africa would have an integrated work force, supervisors of all races, and so on. Quickly, the word came back from the South African authorities. No; that would not be acceptable, and if Cummins should choose to stand on principle, a European diesel maker would be happy to go into South Africa in Cummins' place.[12]

"And that's what happened," Henry Schacht later remembered. "We lost all the business. Our view was that you don't need to have all the business in the world. You have certain fundamental principles—and if they can't be followed, then it's not business you want."[13] Schacht also recalls that it "didn't take five minutes of the board's time" to make this decision.

Today, all corporations talk about mission, culture, and identity, but only a small subset of companies "walk the talk." After several years of sustained inquiry, the authors are convinced that Cummins is one of them. Cummins has put its values on the table. People inside the company take those values fully into account when they act on its behalf. People outside the company fully expect to encounter those values when they do business with Cummins. The South African episode illustrates the perils inherent in a principled stance: *We lost all the business.* But it also illustrates a strength which has helped the company at crucial junctures. In the same period when Cummins' arch-rival, Caterpillar, was engaged in a bitter labor dispute, for example, Cummins negotiated a remarkable eleven-year agreement with the independent, Columbus-based Diesel Workers Union.

In 1989, the Harvard Business School Press published *When the Machine Stopped*, an account by journalist Max Holland about a now-defunct company that once was one of the largest machine-tool manufacturers in the United States. *When the Machine Stopped* was billed as a "cautionary tale." To our eyes, the book was a depressing catalog of errors. The once proud and innovative company was driven into the ground—to some extent by Japanese competition and other larger economic trends, but fundamentally through a sustained, crippling dose of mismanagement. Holland made no unwarranted extrapolations to American industry in general, but at least two of his readers were left with a great sense of disquiet. Holland's subject company went off the rails quickly and fatally, despite the fact that management's mistakes were so blatant (at least in retrospect). Was this the future of American industry?

Our answer is, "Not necessarily." In the following pages, we tell the story of a company that took a very different route. Our book, as it turns out, is a complement to Holland's, offering an antidote to many of the maladies he diagnosed. In that spirit, we suggest in our final chapter how we think the Cummins experience—the story of an "engine that could"—applies beyond the confines of Columbus, Indiana.

2 | A Tenuous Venture, 1919–1929

IN THE EARLY EVENING OF February 20, 1919, thirteen men assembled to launch a new business venture in the south-central Indiana city of Columbus. The meeting took place at the local Chamber of Commerce, and held few surprises for its participants. The men arrived ready to endorse the bylaws of a seventeen-day-old corporation named the Cummins Engine Company. The new company's mission: "to manufacture and sell internal combustion engines, engine accessories, attachments, tools, machinery or appliances" and to take out, acquire, or transfer related patents.[1]

All but two of the men played relatively minor roles in the organization and financing of the company. These two—the moving forces behind the meeting—were William Glanton Irwin, one of the community's leading businessmen and the source of nearly all of the company's $50,000 starting capital; and Clessie Lyle Cummins, a mechanic-inventor whose idea it had been to build and sell engines. A third force behind the meeting that evening was the technology itself. Cummins proposed to build diesels, a type of internal combustion engine that was still rare in the industrialized world, more so in America than in parts of Europe.

Entrepreneurship is the act of combining existing resources in an original way. According to economist Joseph Schumpeter, the entrepreneur succeeds—and transforms society in the process—by "exploiting an invention or, more generally, an untried technological possibility for producing a new commodity or producing an old one in a new way."[2] This definition aptly suits Clessie Cummins and his new firm; in 1919 the diesel engine still was essentially an untried technological possibility in the United States. The Cummins Engine Company was created to harness a variety of resources in service to a common goal: producing and selling compression ignition oil engines.

This chapter explores the origins and nature of Cummins' original assets—human, financial, and technological—and its first tentative decade in business. Central to this story are the careers of co-founders W. G. Irwin and Clessie Cummins, and their urgent search for a viable market for diesel engines in the 1920s.

Marshalling resources

In several ways, and in several different eras, the state of Indiana has defined "middle America." In the mid-1800s, the Hoosier state stood at the geographical center of the nation; and between 1880 and 1920 it was the nation's population center. In the 1920s, the sociologists Robert and Helen Lynd picked Muncie—which they called Middletown—for an ambitious study of "typical" American life.

Predominantly rural Indiana industrialized in ways that often deviated from broader national patterns. Indiana was especially aggressive, for example, at constructing transportation networks. First came a web of state-owned turnpikes: toll roads for wagon haulage. Steamboats enjoyed a heyday between 1815 and 1855, around the same time that a canal-building mania swept the state. The railroad arrived in mid-century, and by 1880 there were 4,373 miles of track, including eight cross-state systems.[3]

The steam railroad's first important challenger, in the 1890s, was the electric interurban railroad. Hoosiers built traction roads as zealously as they had dug canals, with similar results. Indiana laid more miles of interurban track (1,825) than any state except Ohio; and Indianapolis featured more interurban spokes (thirteen in 1903) than any other American city.[4] The Irwin family of Columbus built the first interurban to enter the state capital: the Greenwood & Franklin, which reached Columbus in 1902. But soon the proliferation of internal combustion cars and trucks would vanquish the great interurbans, a process largely complete by the end of the 1920s.[5]

Large-scale manufacturing followed on the heels of these transportation improvements. Between 1860 and 1900, the number of factories in Indiana tripled, and in the next two decades the number of people employed in the state's factories doubled, power utilized tripled, capital grew fourfold, and wages and total value of product increased fivefold. By the end of World War I, Indiana was the third leading producer of iron and steel in the nation.[6]

Indiana manufacturing flourished in part by shifting toward new and growing industries, most notably automobiles. In the industry's formative decade (1895–1905), automaking was centered in the major eastern seaboard cities of Boston, Philadelphia, and New York. Production then shifted to the Great Lakes and the grain belt. At one time or another, more than fifty Indiana cities boasted automobile plants, which produced hundreds of models as well as parts and accessories. Production peaked in 1908–1911, but the state benefited thereafter from its proximity to Detroit. In 1920, Indianapolis still was a leading center for automaking, which was then the state's second largest manufacturing industry.[7]

But Indiana's considerable economic achievements in this period concealed some troubling undercurrents. Growth was not as robust as in several other states within the new "industrial heartland," bordered roughly by Chicago, the Great Lakes, Pittsburgh, and the Ohio River. Before 1920, manufacturing grew more slowly in Indiana than in Ohio, Illinois, and Michigan.

Furthermore, development within the state was spotty. In 1920, most manufactured goods came out of a handful of regions: Lake County, a leading center of auto and agricultural machinery making; the oil- and steel-making Calumet cities; the central state gas belt communities of Muncie, Kokomo, and Anderson; and, of course, Greater Indianapolis. As one historian has noted, "The [state's] industrial future after World War I seemed to belong to central and northern Indiana."[8]

The Cummins Engine Company was born in one of the state's industrially marginal regions. Columbus was founded in the Hawpatch district (near the confluence of the Driftwood and Flatrock Rivers) in 1821, the same year Indianapolis was established as the new state capital forty-five miles to the north-northwest.[9] But the two communities followed markedly divergent paths. While Indianapolis emerged as a bustling commercial center, Columbus' handful of white settlers struggled with treacherous conditions. There were thick forests to clear, fetid swamps to drain. At one point in the summer of 1821, every resident of Columbus except one was ill (many with malaria), and then the lone healthy resident drowned in a flatboat accident.

Nevertheless, during that first year, the village's undaunted settlers erected a post office, a general store, and a tavern. Soon, mills were built, and flatboat traffic linked Columbus with the wider world of commerce. Those ties strengthened considerably with the coming of the railroad, beginning with the Madison & Indianapolis Railroad in 1844. By the early 1850s, rail connections linked Columbus with Jeffersonville, Shelbyville, and Greensburg.[10]

Factories sprang up downtown in the decades following the Civil War, transforming Columbus into a modest but ambitious industrial town. Most prominent was Reeves and Company, successor to an agricultural implements firm established by several brothers in 1875. By the 1880s, the factory occupied an entire block on the east side of town and employed several hundred workers. The brothers also built a successful business in wooden pulleys and variable speed transmissions (Reeves Pulley Company), and they constructed several experimental automobiles.[11]

Reeves apparatus was sold widely, but the first Columbus manufactory to gain a national and international reputation was the Cerealine Manufacturing

Company, which produced a corn product used in food preparations and beer making. Other sizable companies were W. W. Mooney & Sons (tannery), American Starch Company, Moore & Tilton (staves and barrels), Saxony Woolens, and Orinoco Furniture.[12]

In spite of these advances, the citizens of Bartholomew County witnessed industrialization mainly from a distance. In the southern portion of the state, only Vanderburgh County, far to the southwest, possessed a notable manufacturing base. Bartholomew bordered Brown County, which ranked last in the state in manufacturing. Noted for its output of furniture, wagons and carriages, agricultural implements, and wood products, Bartholomew County possessed little of the state's capacity for iron and steel making, automobile or railway equipment manufacturing, flour milling and baking, or meat packing.[13]

Opportunities in Columbus were limited—for merchants, laborers, skilled artisans, and aspiring industrialists alike. Cerealine left town in 1892, and failed the following year. Reeves and Company closed its doors in 1905 (although its offspring, Reeves Pulley, survived, and eventually became Reliance Manufacturing). Reflecting the slowdown, the population of Columbus increased by a mere 860 persons in the first two decades of the new century.

The year Cummins was founded, Columbus had fewer than 9,000 residents, making it the thirty-sixth largest community in the state.[14] It boasted a small cadre of industrial enterprises, but no giant manufacturing complexes comparable to the Studebaker plant at South Bend, the Haynes auto plant at Kokomo, the GE factory at Fort Wayne, or U.S. Steel's behemoth Gary works.[15]

Capital and commitment: the Irwin family

Among the original settlers of Columbus were two Irish-American brothers, Hans and John Irwin, who began farming around 1821. Fifteen years later, John relocated to nearby Johnson County with his wife, Vilinda Finley, and their twelve-year-old son, Joseph Ireland Irwin (b. August 16, 1824).[16] Joseph returned to Columbus a few years later, and there he began a remarkable career that was to establish the Irwins as one of Indiana's most influential families. Beginning with Joseph's achievements in the mid-nineteenth century and continuing to the present day, the Irwins and their relatives have played key roles in the religious, political, business, and cultural affairs of their community and beyond.

One facet of the family's far-ranging endeavors—the business side—was remarkably diverse and complex. Early Irwin ventures were successful enough to spawn others. By the time the Engine Company was founded, the Irwins were part of a tightly knit extended family that included Sweeneys and Millers. Within the extended family, business interests shaped and supported religious and political activities, just as those, in turn, molded the way the Irwins conducted business. To understand the history of Cummins Engine, therefore, one must first understand the origins of Irwin values and Irwin capital alike.

The first Irwins to set foot on American soil were Joseph Oliver and Elizabeth Ireland, who emigrated from Ireland to Kentucky near the end of the Revolutionary War. In 1828 they joined their relatives in Columbus. Their grandson, Joseph (John Irwin's son), was born on the family farm four miles north of Columbus. As in the previous two generations of Irwins in the New World, the Irwin name was carried forward by a single male offspring.[17]

Soon after the family moved to Johnson County, Joseph's father died of pneumonia. The boy was eager to leave the farm, but remained there until the age of twenty-one to assist his mother and three sisters. In 1846, he set out for Columbus. At Edinburg, he pocketed the thirty cents his mother had given him for train fare and walked the remaining distance. This meager savings was the sum total of his stake.[18]

He soon found work at Snyder & Alden's dry goods store, where he put in long hours and saved much of what he earned. Within three years he had accumulated $150, which he combined with a $500 loan from a local farmer to purchase thirty acres of land in Columbus (north and east of present-day Fifth and Washington). This land speculation—Joseph's initial foray into business—paid off well. He sold off portions of the tract at a profit and reinvested the money in more land. In 1850, Joseph Irwin opened a general store at 317 Washington Street. (It later moved, and remained open until 1891.)

Merchandising was the key that unlocked other Irwin businesses. Noticing that his retail trade fell off during the fall and spring when road conditions were at their worst, Irwin began to invest in toll roads in 1867. Ultimately he completed nearly fifty miles of the throughways, mostly in Bartholomew County. It was a tough business. Shippers often refused to pay tolls, erected "shut pikes," and sometimes even attacked toll collectors. (This may explain why Irwin decided to install the county's first telephone line between his store and a tollgate.) But Irwin proved as tough as the business. On one occasion, he took a dispute over a three-cent toll all the way to the state supreme court—and won. Still, the business was unprofitable—only his roads feeding the Driftwood River Bridge operated in the black—and Irwin sold his last turnpike in 1890.

By then, the Irwin general store had spawned another, more lucrative, enterprise: private banking. Joseph Irwin's store had two relatively rare assets: a trustworthy proprietor and a safe. As a courtesy, Irwin sometimes allowed regular customers to hoard their cash in the strongbox. Some even wrote purchase orders against their holdings. During the Civil War, Irwin opened a banking "department" within the general store. The sideline expanded gradually, but most likely it was the harrowing collapse of the local McEwen and Sons Bank in 1871 that inspired the formation of "Irwin's Bank" later that year. (The bank remained private until its merger with Union Trust, as Irwin-Union Trust, in 1928.)[19]

The country bank prospered. Informally, it was a clearinghouse of information about potential future investments, and generated the capital the Irwins needed to pursue such opportunities. Joseph Irwin's influence grew, not only because of his prominence in business, but also thanks to his increasing involvement in state politics. Originally a Whig, he evolved into a staunch supporter of Indiana's new Republican party. From the 1860s to the 1880s, he held key positions in the state G.O.P., including county chairman and delegate, and forged friendships with leading politicos.[20] When Indiana's Benjamin Harrison occupied the White House in 1888, he asked Irwin to serve as his Secretary of the Treasury. (The banker declined.) In politics, Joseph Irwin supported causes that dovetailed with his economic interests. He vehemently supported the tariff—like a good Republican, but also like a self-interested owner-investor. As an Irwin family biographer concludes, "There can be no doubt as to the economic motivation for [Joseph Irwin's] political career."[21]

In the 1890s, J. I. Irwin entered his late sixties. Having created an Indiana business empire, he now pondered its future management. Although women within the extended family were ahead of their time as business investors and advisors, Joseph and Clementine Irwin, like most of their contemporaries, looked to men for business leadership. Of the couple's two surviving children (three girls and a boy had died in early childhood), only one was male. Following Linnie (b. February 25, 1859) came William Glanton Irwin, born in Columbus on November 24, 1866.

W. G. had been a transportation pioneer of sorts since boyhood, when he owned the first bicycle in Columbus and convinced a local hardware dealer to stock the item for his friends. In 1885 he entered Butler University at Irvington, on the board of which his father had served for years. After graduating with a B.S. in 1889, he became manager of the Irwin bank. Five years later, W. G. made his first business investment, sinking $5,000 of his own capital (along with $20,000 of his father's money) into the National Tin Plate Company of Anderson, Indiana. W. G.'s sister, Linnie, and her husband, Z. T. Sweeney, invested additional family money in the enterprise. They sold the business at a handsome profit in 1899. With that windfall in hand, the family promptly undertook their ambitious interurban project.

Joseph increasingly placed business responsibility in W. G.'s hands. But he looked to the next generation as well. At the turn of the century, W. G. was thirty-four years old and unmarried. In Linnie's family, however, Joseph saw a promising candidate for future business leadership. Along with two girls (Nettie, b. 1876, and Elsie, b. 1888), the Sweeneys gave her father a grandson and namesake: Joseph Irwin Sweeney (b. 1880). As a young man, Joe Sweeney showed considerable charm and talent, and followed the family path into Butler College. But on a lazy August day in 1900, while frolicking in the White River, he dove off the high bank, surfaced briefly, and sank to his death. His twentieth birthday was two months away.[22]

The tragedy affected the family deeply, and its repercussions echoed for many years. Clementine Miller, born of the next generation, recalls how she "always heard a lot about Joseph" in family discussions, and that his death "changed everything because they were all pinning their hopes on Joe." Linnie Sweeney, Joe's mother, was hit the hardest. Though never again as outgoing as she had been, she resolved to make good come of adversity. For the rest of her life, she dedicated herself to helping young men succeed.

Neither an Irwin nor a Sweeney now stood in line behind W. G. Still, the banker forged ahead in business, expanding the scale and scope of his activities in the first decade of the new century. Joseph Irwin, meanwhile, increasingly spent his days at the family's summer home on Lake Rosseau, Ontario, although he remained active in the family business. He died of bronchitis on August 13, 1910—the tenth anniversary of his grandson's fatal accident.

W. G. now reigned as the family's business patriarch. But he was hardly alone. Year by year, the Irwin house at Fifth and Mechanic Streets (now Fifth and Lafayette) accommodated a growing extended family, as a new branch of the family tree sprouted from Linnie's marriage. In time, the in-laws became insiders, involved intimately in the family's business, political, and religious affairs.

Linnie's husband, Zachary Taylor Sweeney (1849–1926), an ordained minister in Disciples of Christ church, had lived in the mansion for years, and he became its senior member after Joseph's death. Hugh Thomas Miller, the son of a Johnson County minister of the same church, joined the household after his marriage to Nettie Sweeney in 1900. A scholar of French and history trained at Butler University and in Europe, Hugh had met Nettie while teaching at Butler, and accepted a post at Irwin's Bank a year before their marriage. The couple soon produced a new generation: Elizabeth Clementine Miller (b. 1905) and Joseph Irwin Miller (b. 1909).

With several family members descended from Disciples of Christ ministers, the household had a strong religious culture. The Disciples were one of several American-born restorationist groups that arose in the expansionary and egalitarian atmosphere of the Jacksonian era. Inspired by former Presbyterians Barton Stone, Thomas and Alexander Campbell, and Walter Scott, the "Campbellites" (as some were known) emphasized Christian union and sought the restoration of the New Testament. Members of the church believed strongly in free will, liberty of opinion, and the importance of written and oral debate—values prevalent in the Irwin-Sweeney-Miller household. These traditions also prompted many church members to patronize academies and universities, including Butler University, which the Irwins supported financially and administratively for decades.[23]

Among the male in-laws, politics forged strong bonds. Following in the footsteps of his father—who convinced Benjamin Harrison to appoint Z. T. Sweeney as general consul in Turkey—W. G. helped advance Hugh Miller's political career. Miller was elected to the Indiana General Assembly in 1902, and served as lieutenant governor between 1905 and 1909. Though he lost in his bids for the Indiana governorship in 1908 and for the U.S. Senate in 1914, he planned an aggressive second try for the Senate in 1916. W. G. lobbied the business community energetically on Hugh's behalf. And it was Irwin who (on December 10, 1915) had to inform an inner circle of Republican leaders that their candidate was too ill to finish the race for the Senate. Hugh had been diagnosed with tuberculosis. After a sanitorium rest cure, he retired from the hurly-burly of politics to a quieter life at the Irwin bank.

Religion, business, and politics are a volatile mix in most circumstances, but they blended smoothly in the Irwin-Sweeney-Miller household. Though Z. T. Sweeney and Hugh Miller exerted the strongest religious influence, W. G. conformed to the same strict moral code and personal habits of his father. On one occasion, he refused to purchase wine for his sister even though a doctor prescribed it to settle her nerves. W. G., for his part, dominated in business, but often called upon his relatives for guidance and capital.

The women in the household combined the worldly and the spiritual through community and philanthropic works, as well as in the upbringing of their children. For their day, they enjoyed an uncommon degree of independence. Linnie Sweeney and Nettie Sweeney Miller served actively on the boards of the bank and a large starch company controlled by the Irwins. The men in the home supported the women's suffrage movement; the women, ironically, opposed it, choosing instead to spend their time working on behalf of the poor and promoting employment opportunities for young men of the community. As J. Irwin Miller recalls, "The females were equally strong, equally influential—in some ways more influential. Everything was talked out together. Whether in church, community, or business, no move would be made unless there was family consensus."[24]

Perhaps more than any of the adults, Irwin and Clementine Miller were shaped by the rich environment within the grand Fifth Street house. Born in the first decade of the new century, the two children were raised by six accomplished adults. They were included in family discussions and introduced to visitors.[25] They absorbed the wide-ranging discourse that flowed around the dinner table—and, as Clementine later recalled, "we never felt intimidated."

Her brother similarly remembers the engaging ambiance of their childhood home. Young Irwin enjoyed his escapes to Clessie's workshop—a grimy seat of mechanical ingenuity[26]—but his worldview was forged mainly at home, where the tenets of social tolerance and Christian service were a daily staple. These influences in J. Irwin Miller's life surfaced more than a generation later, when he assumed the leadership of his family's businesses.

During the first two decades of the new century, W. G. restructured the family's investments. In 1904 he bought the starch works of the Corn Products

Company of Edinburg, Indiana (twelve miles north of Columbus). Eight years later, he leased the interurban to the Interstate Public Service Company, controlled by Midwestern electric utility magnate Samuel Insull. In 1914, W. G. bought a large interest in the Van Camp Packing Company, based in Indianapolis. Along with Irwin's Bank, the starch and packing companies became the highest profit producers in the Irwin investment portfolio.

W. G. Irwin was not a passive investor. In most ventures, he demonstrated not only an acute sense of timing, but also an ability to discern the dynamics of new industries and to compete successfully. The first trait can be seen in his divestiture of the interurban. By 1907, the road extended south from Indianapolis to Seymour, and each month carried well over 50,000 passengers and grossed nearly $30,000. But in 1912, the Indianapolis, Columbus, & Southern suffered a poor year, and Irwin cannily entertained approaches from Insull. The Chicago Edison head controlled the interurban lines of northern and central Indiana, and was seeking a connection for a line he was building north from Louisville, Kentucky. When Irwin proposed a lease—in part due to his sentimental attachment to the I, C & S—Insull glibly stated that it did not matter whether the lease ran for 99 or 999 years. Irwin replied that 999 years would be fine, and negotiated the deal for $616,000 (financed with 5 percent notes).

The move was prescient. American interurban railroads began a downward spiral in 1915. Competition from automobiles, combined with declining productivity and falling returns in the interurban industry, set off a wave of abandonments that led to a wholesale collapse in the 1930s. Few foresaw the coming debacle. Industry leaders paid scant attention to the automobile threat before 1913, and many remained optimistic about their industry's prospects well into the early 1920s. Though the Irwin line (merged into Interstate Public Service, later Public Service Company of Indiana) fared better under Insull than most other interurbans, it slipped toward default, and ceased operations altogether after a spectacular wreck on September 8, 1941. Irwin magnanimously agreed to cancel the remaining 969 years of the lease for approximately $2.5 million. He could have lost money on a grand scale as a result of his interurban venture; instead, he earned a satisfactory return. Few of his counterparts in the business could claim as much.

In the case of the starch company, W. G. assessed opportunities and mastered the dynamics of an industry unfamiliar to him in a fashion typical of his eventful career. The Irwins originally purchased the ramshackle Cutsinger Starch Works from the Corn Products Company for its generating capacity.[27] Located a dozen miles north of Columbus, the factory featured a power plant large enough to supply much of the Irwin interurban's energy needs. When Irwin offered the factory's owners $10,000, they replied that the plant was worth $500,000. Irwin got the factory at his price. After a careful study of the starch-making business, W. G. resuscitated the old works as the Union Starch and Refining Company and transformed it into a profitable enterprise.

The Irwins sought opportunities along the rapidly shifting terrain of American business in the Gilded Age. They combined a banker's prudence with an unusual openness to new technologies. They blended the search for profits with a sense of community mission and a desire to help local entrepreneurs. Their next venture was entirely in this spirit.

Man and machines: Clessie L. Cummins

On the warm and windy Friday afternoon of July 22, 1911, the citizens of Bartholomew and Jackson Counties were treated to an unusual sight. Along the nineteen miles of Indianapolis, Columbus & Southern track that connected Columbus and Seymour, onlookers watched as a bizarre vehicle barrelled down the tracks: a Packard sedan, bedecked with colored flags, atop four wood-and-steel railroad wheels. The car was carrying its normally staid owner, W. G. Irwin, along with several of the interurban's officials. At the wheel sat the Irwin family's young chauffeur, Clessie Lyle Cummins.

Cummins served as the de facto motorman of the "Extra P" in part because of his driving skills—which were considerable—and in part because he worked occasionally as a motorman on the traction railroad, and knew the route. He also was the inventor of this curious transportation hybrid.

The Packard had derailed during a test run two days earlier, and Clessie had promised to maintain a conservative 25 mph speed on the demonstration ride. But Cummins pressed the Packard hard into a head wind on his way to Seymour, occasionally hitting 50 mph. The return trip was faster still. Communicating with dispatchers through an on-board telephone, Clessie averaged nearly 60 mph. (He stopped once when the railroad general manager's hat blew off.) The day ended with relaxed celebration. W. G. Irwin invited several of his friends for a late afternoon swim in Big Sand Creek. Again, they rode the Extra P. Along the way, reported the local paper, "Mr. Irwin acted as conductor . . . and flagged the railroad crossings like a veteran conductor."

Cummins announced in the press that he had great plans for the Extra P. He hoped to make longer runs, perhaps a trip to the East. Staying off the roads made sense; in fact, it was Clessie's frustration with the poor condition of Indiana's roads that reportedly inspired him to convert the Packard to ride the rails in the first place. In later runs, following the heady successes of that July day, the banker's car was plagued with mechanical troubles, from slipping wheels to inadequate brakes. But it was a near miss with a traction railroad train one day that ended the short, thrilling career of the auto-railcar.[28]

This was neither the first nor the last time Clessie Cummins would test an intriguing invention in a public venue. His most revolutionary trial—

which also was to involve a converted Packard—was still eighteen years in the future. Even so, the Extra P embodied much that was typical in the colorful and inventive career of Clessie L. Cummins. Like many inventors, Clessie spent much of his time developing labor-saving devices, hoping to apply mechanical power to ease human burdens—often his own. Less typically, most of Clessie's innovations involved engines, or automobiles, or both.

Two aspects of the episode are especially telling. First, it suggests something about the special nature of the relationship between the young mechanic and the middle-aged banker. In mid-1911, Clessie was twenty-two, W. G. Irwin forty-five. The Irwins were among a small handful of county residents affluent enough to own such a deluxe automobile. Still, W. G. was no spendthrift. It was surely a vote of confidence for the frugal, respectable banker to place his expensive automobile—which he and his father used daily for their banking business—in the hands of a young inventor known for his push-to-the-limits experimentation. W. G. Irwin had abundant confidence in Clessie Cummins. Often they collaborated in this way, with Irwin donating capital—the equipment, facilities, materials, or funds—and Cummins contributing ideas and mechanical know-how.

Just as notable in the Extra P story is Clessie's flair for promotion. After testing the machine just enough to give himself a reasonable chance of success, he took to the rails. He and Irwin loaded the vehicle with railroad officials. He traversed two cities and several small towns. He ran the car at top speeds, in part to test its mechanics, but also because speed was exhilarating to riders and spectators alike. The story was covered enthusiastically in the local newspaper before and after the big day. Someone, evidently, was talking to the press.

The two points are interrelated. Clessie was his own biggest fan; the ceremony and speed of July 1911 were as much for his own benefit as for anyone else's. But the excitement of the afternoon also enthralled and ensnared W. G. Irwin. The banker joined in the festivities, rode the rails, flagged trains, and served as proud host to his friends and business associates. (It was he, after all, who had sponsored all the excitement.) Clessie's enthusiasm was infectious, and few were ever as thoroughly infected as W. G. In the banking trade, risk taking was rendered routine. Clessie made risk taking a great adventure.

When Clessie Cummins was born two days after the Christmas of 1888, there were no automobiles. Few American cities had electric lights. In rural settings like Clessie's birthplace—Henry County, Indiana—indoor plumbing was rare. The pre-industrial era was ending quickly, though, for this was the age of giant corporations like Carnegie Steel, American Telephone & Telegraph, and J. D. Rockefeller's "octopus," the Standard Oil Company. In short order, these and other companies transformed the lives of millions of Americans, providing them with increased comfort, convenience, mobility, and prosperity.[29]

The late nineteenth century was the age of the giant "trusts," but it also was the era of the heroic inventor. The life of Clessie Cummins spanned, and in many ways typified, this remarkable era. In the year that Clessie was born, Thomas Edison patented the first phonograph, which earned him international fame and the sobriquet of "wizard." And although Edison's small workshop evolved into the mammoth General Electric, the inventor's quirky independence was heralded as much as his genius.

Clessie's parents, Francis Marion Cummins (1864–1946) and Almira Josephine Edleman (1868–1964)—known as Frank and Josephine—were married in 1885. Clessie was born on a farm that had been cleared and settled by his paternal grandfather. Despite those family ties, his childhood was far from rooted. When he was two, his father, along with an uncle, Henry Adams, launched a cooperage business. Since only a choice variety of elm made good barrel hoops, the business drove the family across the Indiana and Ohio countryside in search of virgin elm stands.

Clessie's childhood was shaped by his intense curiosity and fascination with things mechanical. He loved machines. As he later reflected, "I never suffered any indecision about my real objectives in life." He often tinkered with gadgets to ease the burden of his household chores, like the crude device he designed for opening bean pods. In Clarksville, Ohio, where the Cummins family lived for part of the 1890s, Clessie spent many hours helping and learning at the side of a local blacksmith. At age eleven, with guidance from a clockmaker, he built a miniature steam engine—the first evidence of his lifelong passion for engines—which he rented to classmates. The parents of Clarksville put a stop to the practice after a series of miniature boiler explosions.

Along with his mechanical talent, Clessie's knack for persuading adults to work with him and to help him—a skill no doubt reinforced by his genuine enthusiasm for his projects—helped him flourish as an apprentice. The boy needed this outside support. His family's nomadic lifestyle provided him with only sporadic schooling, and his parents were mainly indifferent to his relentless experimentation. "To my knowledge," recalls his brother Don, "he never went to Mother or Dad for anything. In fact, they never knew what he was up to." Though Clessie's projects often caused a commotion, he was not a problem child. He helped his older sister, Irene Henrietta (b. 1891), raise the growing Cummins clan: Nell (b. 1893), Charles Deloss (b. 1898), and Donovan Joel (b. 1902). By the time Don arrived, Clessie, then age fourteen, possessed an adultlike independence and focus.

Around that time, the family migrated to Mt. Vernon, Ohio, where Clessie's involvement in mechanics deepened. After school, he first worked in a bicycle shop, and then began to hang around the Cooper-Corliss Engine Company, a manufacturer of giant steam engines. His fascination with the machines grew so powerful that, as he later recalled, it "acted almost like a drug." In typical fashion, he ingratiated himself with the foreman. When Clessie decided to build a small steam engine on his own, Cooper-Corliss cast the boy's hand-carved wooden parts without charge. Clessie then stealthily traded one of his mother's kitchen cabinets for a boiler tank and built the engine in his backyard. It ran for a while, and then—when pushed too hard—exploded.[30]

In 1904, the Cummins family moved their cooperage business to Columbus, Indiana. Clessie entered a new school for the thirteenth time in his short life. By force of circumstance, he was now enrolling in the eighth grade for the third time. When he turned sixteen halfway through the fall term, he defied his parents' wishes and dropped out. (In that period of American history, only about six out of ten children attended school at all, and a larger percentage never completed high school.)[31] By this time Clessie was, he later wrote, "thoroughly disgusted with the entire educational system." He was eager to join "the practical classroom," as he deemed the world of work and wages.

Over the next four years, working for a succession of Indiana machinists and automakers, Clessie acquired an impressive hands-on education in the art of building steam and automotive engines. His first job was repairing farm equipment and steam engines for a local machine shop owned by Harry and Lynne Benefield. (There he met Quentin Noblitt, who soon left to establish the Indianapolis Pump and Tube Company, but returned to Columbus years later to set up the predecessor to Arvin, one of the nation's largest suppliers of automotive accessories.) After a year, Clessie joined Reeves Pulley. By this time, the giant pulley manufacturer also was producing auto parts and engines, so Clessie gained his first practical experience with automotive engineering.

Reeves held other fascinations as well. Like Clessie, the Reeves brothers dabbled in unorthodox technologies—although they had considerably more resources at their disposal, and a much more respectable track record. Milton Reeves' "Motocycle" (1896), for example, was one of the nation's first automobiles. Around the time Clessie joined their company, the brothers converted a railroad car to run on gasoline, and staged a trial run that was witnessed by W. G. and Joseph Irwin. Perhaps this transportation hybrid inspired Clessie's "Extra P" of 1911 (by which time Milton Reeves was experimenting with bizarre multi-axled cars dubbed "Octoauto" and "Sextoauto").

Clessie's interest in automotive marketing grew in parallel with his mechanical expertise. He was especially captivated by the impresarios of promotion. One who made a vivid impression on Clessie was Carl Fisher, an Indianapolis Stoddard-Dayton distributor, who suspended a car from a hovering balloon to lure in customers. "His talent for sales promotion never ceased to amaze me," Clessie later wrote.

Cummins left Reeves for American Motor Car of Indianapolis in 1906, then moved to Teetor-Hartley Motors in Hagerstown when the Panic of 1907 wiped out American. A year later, back in Indianapolis, he joined Nordyke-

Marmon. Clessie held a range of jobs at these automakers, from tool shop worker to final test inspector. Each manufacturer gave him a new perspective on the emerging industry. American was developing a unique "underslung" car, for instance, while Teetor-Hartley was conducting pioneering work on piston rings. By 1908, although still only a teenager, Clessie was remarkably well schooled in the art of automaking. Now he advanced another level in the "practical classroom."

While at Nordyke-Marmon, Clessie had begun working as a part-time driver for T. S. Blish, who owned a flour-milling business in Seymour. Cars still were so rare and temperamental that their owners often doubled as mechanics, tinkering constantly with their machines to keep them in running order. (Ford's Model T, released in 1908, came with a tool kit.) Those without such aptitude sought the help of mechanics, for there was as yet no network of automobile filling stations and repair shops. Affluent automobile owners like Blish generally hired driver-mechanics. The work suited Clessie perfectly.

In the fall of 1908, Clessie learned that a new position of this kind might be available. His mother provided the lead. While attending church with Linnie Sweeney (W. G. Irwin's sister), Josephine Cummins heard that the Irwins were looking for a driver. Wanting to keep her teenage son closer to home, she urged Clessie to interview for the job. He agreed, but then ducked out of an initial meeting with W. G. because he was intimidated by the banker's stern demeanor. (He also had learned why the position was available: Joseph Irwin had abruptly fired his previous driver for smoking.) But W. G. pursued Clessie, and arranged for him to demonstrate his skills on a test drive.

There was one problem: Clessie's size, relative to the car. The Irwins owned a giant Packard, one of the largest cars on the market. They stored it on blocks in a converted barn near their mansion. Clessie, small in stature, managed to lower the huge automobile to the ground, but then faced a much more difficult challenge. The electric self-starter was not commercially available in the United States until 1912. It was reasonable to wonder—as both W. G. and Clessie did that day—whether a slight, 110-pound teenager could hand-crank the heavy Packard engine. After several tries, the answer was obvious. He could not.

Starting the car surely was a job requirement. In desperation, Clessie resorted to a trick he knew from boating. He dipped a rag into the gas tank, squeezed a few drops of fuel into each cylinder priming cup, rocked the engine back and forth to draw fuel into the cylinders, closed the cups, rocked the engine again, and fired the ignition spark. It worked. Much later, when Clessie knew more about engine mechanics, he noted the "astronomical odds against such a procedure being successful with a big engine." It was luck, as much as ingenuity, that won him his first job with the Irwins. Clessie started work on October 8, 1908, pleased with his salary of $85 per month, and proud to navigate the fancy Packard through the modest streets of Columbus.

Clessie's occupational wanderings did not end that day. His formal role as chauffeur to the Irwins lasted only two years. (In another sense, it was a lifetime appointment: Until his death in 1943, W. G. Irwin never learned to drive, and continued to call on Cummins.) During this same two-year period, moreover, Clessie put in additional stints at Reeves in Columbus and Marmon in Indianapolis. But day by day, a growing network of ties was binding the young inventor-mechanic to Columbus and to the Irwins.

One set of ties was personal. Josephine Cummins was pleased to have her eldest son home again, and urged him to stay. At the same time, Clessie was becoming romantically involved with Ethel Mildred McCoy, who worked as Z. T. Sweeney's secretary in an office the floor above Clessie in the Irwin garage building. (Sweeney was then state fish and game commissioner.) The romance blossomed into marriage. The Reverend Sweeney performed the ceremony on May 18, 1910, a few hours before Halley's Comet streaked across the sky.

By that time, Clessie's work for the Irwins ranged widely. As driving assignments tapered off for the winter, W. G. suggested that Clessie fill in the gaps as a part-time motorman on the interurban. Soon he was helping at the corn starch company and the bank, while still handling mechanical repairs at the Irwin household. He also developed a growing number of personal ties with members of the family. In particular, he spent many hours with Hugh and Nettie Miller's two children, Clementine and Irwin. Clessie sometimes was asked to keep an eye on Clementine when she was a toddler, a task he apparently found embarrassing. While driving the family's electric wagon—considered a "ladies' car"—with Clementine in tow, he preferred to stow the three-year-old on the floor of the vehicle, out of sight from his teenage friends. Clessie also established a close bond with Irwin, even though the Miller boy was his junior by twenty-one years.

Linnie Sweeney took a special interest in Clessie, an attachment intensified by the loss of her own son. "Because I was . . . apparently of a similar temperament [to Joe]," Clessie wrote in his autobiography, "Mrs. Sweeney seemed to derive considerable comfort from my presence. I liked to whistle to myself as I worked on the family car or at other chores around the Irwin home. 'Sometimes I can almost believe it's Joe I hear,' Mrs. Sweeney confided."

Clessie was a regular at the Fifth Street mansion. He often dropped in for the midday meal, when the Irwins, Sweeneys, and Millers who were in town assembled for food and conversation. Clessie could be counted on to entertain his fellow diners with talk of his latest ideas and inventions. The Reverend Sweeney was probably the most skeptical of Clessie's best-laid plans—"Clessie's got it again" he often said when the young man appeared at the door—but family members were generally supportive. Although he was only one of several young men encouraged by this family of influential bankers, ministers, and politicians, Clessie clearly occupied a special place. In the Irwin household, recalls his brother Don, Clessie was "like a member of the family."[32]

Clessie's ties with his family, the Irwins, and the community were strong and growing stronger. But they never overcame his wanderlust for long. Clessie was not only an inveterate tinkerer, but also an incessant traveler. In 1912, he decided to take a long boating expedition to New Orleans, and convinced his brother-in-law, Brainard McCoy, to come along. It was a harum-scarum voyage, but it focused Clessie's attention on oil-burning engines, and thus had a great impact on his life.

Clessie loved boats as much as he loved engines. He often took to the water when he needed to think, and he acquired much of his mechanical knowledge by troubleshooting marine engines, which were notoriously fickle. Often he sailed on the White River in the sixteen-foot motor craft he had built by hand.

On November 9, 1912, he and McCoy shoved off from Jeffersonville, Indiana, destined for New Orleans via the Ohio-Mississippi river system. "Every day brought a new and usually terrifying experience," Clessie later recalled of the six-week trip. Near the end of the journey, for instance, the two men found themselves stranded on a mud bar for five days with a severely damaged boat and no food.

Because gasoline was not readily available along the rivers, the travelers from Indiana were plagued by fuel shortages throughout the voyage. On the other hand, kerosene (then also known as oil or fuel oil), which was used widely for interior illumination, was in plentiful supply. In typical fashion, Clessie jury-rigged the boat's engine to run on kerosene, in part by preheating the fuel with the boat's muffler to aid combustion. The engine ran roughly, at best. But Clessie remained intrigued by the question of how to design a combustion engine that could run on oil instead of gasoline.

From New Orleans, Clessie proceeded on to Tampa, where he found work at an engine machine shop. Some of the engines he worked on there were oil-fueled. A voracious reader throughout his adult life, Clessie now began to read intensively about this "diesel"-type oil engine—a technology named for German inventor Rudolf Diesel. Clessie soon became convinced of two things. First, diesels held enormous potential as a way to "meet operational demands with minimum maintenance attention and maximum economy." Second, existing diesel engine designs were inadequate, mainly because they were "unnecessarily complicated." Perhaps, Clessie reasoned, an entirely new theory of diesel operation was needed.[33]

After returning to Columbus in mid-1913, Clessie zealously promoted diesel engines to W. G. Irwin. The banker seems not to have shared the inventor's enthusiasm for the unproven technology, but he nevertheless proposed an attractive deal. If Clessie would return as driver-mechanic for the Irwin family, W. G. would let him use a vacant forge building as an auto repair shop. (The run-down building was on Fifth Street, just west of the present-day Irwin-Union Bank building.)[34] Irwin would even supply some tools, for which Clessie could pay out of future earnings from the shop. In this way, the Irwins would regain access to Clessie's mechanical talents, while Clessie could take on additional jobs to earn money, still pursuing his inventive impulses in his spare time. Clessie jumped at the chance. He soon secured a steady stream of auto repair jobs, and he also found time to work on his own inventions.

The growing operation moved when W. G. replaced the old forge building with a new structure. The Irwins were just completing an elaborate renovation and expansion of the Fifth Street mansion, so W. G. decided to convert the former stable behind his home (on Sixth Street) into a garage. This would provide enough space for the two family cars and Clessie's shop. He let Clessie design and use the facility free of charge, and also agreed to a salary of $30 per month for Clessie's part-time services as driver, mechanic, and general household repairman. Clessie dubbed the modest operation the "Cummins Machine Works."

In the cluttered Sixth Street garage, Clessie indulged his inventive interests. In 1915 he produced a marine "stuffing box" for readjusting motorboat drive shafts. The following year, he fashioned a propeller-driven bobsled, which he piloted through the streets of Columbus on the day after Christmas. He earned modest profits from a few of these devices. But the machine shop took up increasing amounts of his time.[35]

Within its first year, the business employed four men and was netting Cummins as much as $600 per month. As the business grew, it changed direction. Machine work steadily replaced auto repair, which was phased out by 1916. With America's entry into World War I the following year, the shop secured its first government contract from an existing customer. The Stenotype Company of Indianapolis hired the Works to fashion a large number of cast-iron hubs for artillery wagon wheels. Soon Cummins crews were working overtime producing parts for British and American war contractors. When the Sweeneys and Millers returned from a summer sojourn at their Canadian home in 1917, they found the garage crammed with men and equipment, working around the clock. Their own cars had been parked in a public garage. "They jokingly remarked to friends," Clessie recalled, "that they'd soon be forced to move out of their house to make room for my work."[36]

That didn't happen, but the operation soon was moved to a larger facility, a former warehouse adjacent to the Pennsylvania Railroad Station. The brick structure at Seventh and Jackson Streets, known as the Ben C. Thomas Building, had once served as one of Cerealine's factories. Cummins Machine Works occupied the portion of the building connected to the taller section, at the opposite end from the train depot.[37] (Today this non-Cummins portion of the Cerealine Building, as it is now known, comprises part of the company's Columbus headquarters.) At the new facility, government work grew to include a variety of Army and Navy ordnance jobs, and Cummins' work force expanded to fifty men.[38]

The Works' heavy reliance on war contracts had brought prosperity in wartime. But by the middle of 1918, peace seemed imminent. Would the company shrink to its prewar size? Clessie undoubtedly felt the press of his new responsibilities—not only his many new employees, but also his first two children: Brainard (b. May 14, 1914) and Beatrice (b. July 7, 1917).

Casting about for a new direction, Clessie revived his long-standing interest in diesel technology. Though Rudolf Diesel had patented his discovery in Germany nearly a generation earlier, the technology came late to the United States, and evolved slowly after its arrival. Information about oil engines was scarce, as were prototypes of the engines themselves in the smaller sizes Clessie hoped to produce. Not surprisingly, therefore, Clessie Cummins entered the diesel engine business by securing manufacturing rights from an American licensee of a Dutch technology. In a sense, Clessie was about to relive the history of the diesel, including the bizarre tale of its transfer to America, and its halting early development on both sides of the Atlantic.

Unproven technology: the early diesel

When Clessie Cummins was still a toddler in central Indiana, Rudolf Diesel was conceptualizing a new kind of internal combustion engine in Augsburg, Germany. Over the next generation, Diesel's technology was commercialized throughout the industrialized West, thanks to the efforts of scores of entrepreneurs like Cummins. But the diesel's diffusion was neither simple nor triumphant. Rudolf Diesel's pivotal invention brought him fame and fortune, but also financial instability, personal and professional heartache, and serious health problems, all of which contributed to his suicide in 1913. It fell to other inventors, notably Jan Brons in the Netherlands, to design the more efficient diesel engines sold in the United States during and after World War I.

Rudolf Diesel's Failed Promise

The diesel's troubled childhood was partly the result of bad timing. When Rudolf Christian Karl Diesel was born in Paris (to German parents) in 1858, engine making was still a practitioner's craft, rather than a scientist's specialty. But that changed quickly, and Diesel embodied the change. Devoted to engineering from an early age, he graduated from the Augsburg industrial school in 1875 at the top of his class and won a two-year scholarship at the Munich Technical School (Technische Hochschule München), a rigorous engineering school. There he became thoroughly familiar with the principles of thermodynamics and studied under Carl von Linde, founder of the liquid-gas (refrigeration) industry.[39]

In 1890, Diesel began to conduct theoretical work on internal combustion engines. He envisioned a four-stroke machine in which the fuel would burn without ignition and at a constant temperature. On the first (downward) stroke, the engine's piston would draw air into the cylinder. The piston's upward, return stroke would compress the air to very high pressure and thus high temperature. With the next downward stroke, fuel would be introduced into the piston at such a rate that the heat generated from its combustion would counterbalance the natural temperature decline that accompanied the expansion of the gases as the piston retracted. No external cooling would be required, allowing the engine to operate, Diesel theorized, at a remarkable 70–80 percent thermal efficiency. The fourth, upward stroke would expel the exhaust gases.[40]

The key innovation in Diesel's design was its *isothermal* feature—that is, the engine's ability to achieve combustion at constant temperature. (Diesel's breakthrough was not, as is commonly believed today, the notion of compression ignition.)[41] But Diesel's design promised to achieve greater efficiency by operating over a broader range of temperatures and by converting heat fully into mechanical power.[42]

An engine operating according to these principles would have several attributes. It could use a variety of fuels—from crude oil to coal dust to peanut oil—which would give it a flexibility especially valuable in remote operating locales. Unlike gasoline ignition models, the engine would require no ignition system or carburetor. This much simpler design presumably would give the diesel more trouble-free operation. Most important, Diesel's invention promised to consume much less fuel per horsepower than gas-powered engines. Though engine oil was relatively inexpensive at the time, economical operation always would be a competitive advantage, especially among commercial and industrial customers. For these reasons, Diesel referred to his creation as a "universal engine" or an "economical heat motor."[43]

In 1892, Diesel laid out these ideas in a manuscript, took out his first patents, and gained the financial backing of Friedrich Krupp and former employer Heinrich Buz, president of the Augsburg Engine Works (Maschinenfabrik Augsburg A.G.). The following year, to raise additional research capital, he published his manuscript as the *Theory and Construction of a Rational Heat Engine*, and formed a syndicate with both Augsburg and Krupp.[44]

In spite of this substantial backing, it took Diesel four years and 600,000 marks to produce a working model of his invention. The central problem—which would continue to plague diesel makers for decades—was injection. After experimenting with "solid injection" systems, which relied on pumps or pistons, Diesel came to employ a compression system to achieve "air injection." This system, which atomized fuel in the piston chamber, worked better than solid injection methods. But with compression injection came higher fuel consumption and, in turn, higher temperatures. Cooling was needed. Thus, in the process of developing a working model, the inventor was compelled to modify key components of his original theory. Diesel's working engine operated at constant pressure—which came to be known as the "Diesel cycle"—but not at constant temperature, as called for in his original design. Moreover, the compression equipment required for the new cycle was expensive and heavy.[45]

Theory had collided with practice. Unlike earlier engines—from the steam engine to Otto's gas-fueled design—the diesel was a product born of the pencil rather than the workbench. Earlier technologies had been fashioned at the hands of machinists and other mechanically oriented craftsmen. Some of those inventors, of course, were well versed in the relevant theory, but most were "cut and try" empirical problem solvers. By the end of the nineteenth century, however, theoretical science was making dramatic gains in the industrialized West. This was especially true in Germany, with its heavy concentration of chemical and machinery works and its unparalleled system of technical education. In short, before Diesel's time, practice outran theory, and was hindered as a result. Now the opposite was true, with unhappy consequences of a different sort.[46]

While refining his technology in the mid-1890s and concurrently struggling to defend the originality of his invention, Diesel was also forging arrangements to profit from it.[47] His plan was to make money through royalties—that is, by licensing manufacturing rights to leading firms on several continents. Between 1892 and mid-1897, he awarded licenses in Germany (to M.A.N. and Krupp), France, Sweden, Denmark, Switzerland, Great Britain, Belgium, Austria-Hungary, Russia, and Egypt. Conspicuously absent from the list was the United States. Diesel fretted about the omission, for he saw America as the greatest potential market for his machines.[48]

On September 6, 1897, Diesel met the man who was about to become the first licensee of his technology in North America: Adolphus Busch (1839–1913). A German immigrant to America in 1857, Busch had built a business empire by combining a brewery supply company he inherited from his father with a brewery established by his father-in-law, Eberhard Anheuser. By 1897, Anheuser-Busch commanded the largest share of the U.S. beer market (2.5 percent), and Busch was one of the richest men in America. Although no longer a young man, he continually prospected for new business opportunities. Often he relied on the close ties he maintained with his homeland, through yearly excursions and a network of German friends and associates.[49]

Busch had learned of Diesel's breakthrough in the summer of 1897, and enthusiastically bought temporary rights to the technology the day after he was introduced to Diesel at Baden-Baden. Before making a bigger commitment, however, Busch hired an engineer to investigate further. The engineer soon caught the diesel bug, calling the purchase of American rights to Diesel's technology "as promising an investment as the purchase of any patent claim could be." Almost immediately, Busch agreed to pay Diesel one million marks (about $238,000) plus a 6 percent royalty for the sole U.S. and Canadian rights to the engine.[50]

Like Rudolf Diesel, Adolphus Busch hoped to profit by selling diesel manufacturing rights, and not by building and selling engines himself. To this end, he organized the Diesel Motor Company of America in New York, capitalized at $1 million, on January 4, 1898. Busch now seemed to possess a winning combination: monopoly rights—in the world's leading industrial market—to an enormously promising technology developed by a renowned German engineer; substantial capital reserves; and, under the terms of his agreement with the inventor, access to all diesel developments emerging from an international network of licensees.[51]

But Busch's hopes for the diesel never materialized. After two corporate reorganizations and millions of dollars in additional investment, he failed to build a viable diesel business by the time his monopoly expired completely in 1912. This conspicuous failure severely hampered diesel development in America.

The central problem was that diesel licensees vastly underestimated the amount of development work still required for the technology. This contributed, in turn, to a damaging breakdown of cooperation among licensees worldwide. The young technology never received the collaborative development it so urgently required. In Europe, diesel licensees encountered serious problems with the technology within months of Diesel's widely heralded 1897 lecture. No manufacturer was able to produce a working machine.[52] In late 1898, several leading diesel interests in Germany, including the Augsburg Engine Works, consolidated into the Augsburg-Nuremberg Engine Works (Maschinenfabrik Augsburg-Nürnberg), known as M.A.N., an organization that ostensibly represented Diesel's interests, but that in fact increasingly shunted aside the inventor and monopolized the development of his technology.[53]

Back in the United States, Busch was kept ignorant of the M.A.N. merger until after the fact. M.A.N. then cut off Busch's direct access to Rudolf Diesel. Isolated and frustrated, Busch pushed ahead with his plans to build a diesel specially suited for American conditions. As with other diesel licensees, his frustration gradually turned to anger at the inventor. "I often feel like giving Diesel a good thrashing. . . ," he complained in 1899. "What did he do—nothing for two years, pocketed my money, lived well and pretended to be overworked." By 1900, Busch licensees had constructed a handful of engines, but they worked poorly, some running so hot that their lubricating oil ignited, causing explosions and injuries.[54]

In 1901, Busch merged his company with the International Power Company (New Jersey) and reorganized it as the American Diesel Engine Company. American Diesel managed to produce an engine model that sold reasonably well after it was exhibited at the 1904 St. Louis World's Fair.

Relations between the Americans and Rudolf Diesel began to mend (they forged a new agreement in 1908), and Busch remained enthusiastic, in spite of the bankruptcy of American Diesel in 1909. "We must . . . become the greatest industrial company in the world," he declared, "a second Standard Oil Company."[55]

It was, in fact, the beginning of the end for the Busch diesel monopoly. As its patents began to expire in 1907 and 1909, competitors moved in. The Electric Boat Company (New Jersey) entered the business in 1909 and, through an alliance with the New London Ship and Engine Company made in the following year, secured access to M.A.N. diesel technology. Meanwhile, Adolphus Busch, now seventy years old, suffered a serious illness in 1909, and responsibility for the family's diesel business (among others) passed to his son, August. The younger Busch struggled to revive the floundering oil engine business, which he reorganized as the Busch-Sulzer Brothers-Diesel Engine Company. But it was too late. In May 1912, Rudolf Diesel sagely warned Busch to "find a factory _at once_" and form a trust or "the competition will swamp us like an irresistible ocean wave." That year alone, five rivals entered the U.S. diesel market.[56]

Between 1902 and 1912, Busch's diesel company (in its various guises) had sold a mere 260 diesel engines (for a total of 47,000 hp), mostly to industrial customers in the Northeast. The company turned a profit in some years during the decade, but on the whole Busch lost money in the business.[57]

Rudolf Diesel's fate was even more lamentable. He lost much of his wealth through speculation in real estate, oil fields, and other investments, and though he owned or leased many companies, their failure meant that he never received the anticipated millions of additional dollars in dividends and royalties. By 1913, he faced financial ruin. While en route from Antwerp to England aboard the ship _Dresden_, he disappeared into a calm sea sometime on the night of September 29–30. "If only my friend Diesel had said something to me," Busch later said. "I knew that things were not going well with him."[58]

The diesel engine's inept and stifled introduction into the U.S. market had many causes. Corporate mismanagement by the Busch firm surely played a role, as did the lack of German cooperation. Also damaging was Busch's misplaced optimism about the marketability of the product. In that misapprehension, however, the brewery baron was hardly alone. Historians agree that the acceptance of the 1897 diesel as a workable, marketable invention was an error shared by engineers, businessmen, mechanics, and other experts alike. "It is extraordinary," writes one scholar, "that so many good people could be so wrong."[59]

The problem persisted into the early twentieth century. Because of its fuel flexibility and efficiency, the diesel remained a seductive technology. The challenge facing its makers and promoters was not simply how to perfect this technology, but also how to refine it for specific market applications. Throughout Europe and the United States, entrepreneurs searched hard to identify and exploit markets for the diesel engine. Just as there was no universally applicable diesel engine, there also was no monolithic diesel market.

Almost from the start, Rudolf Diesel had envisioned many applications for his invention, ranging from automobiles and aircraft to locomotives.[60] (He supported efforts to develop Sulzer's "Thermo-Locomotive," for example.) However, the diesel engine—hobbled in the marketplace by its relatively high weight per horsepower, but advantaged in fuel economy—gained a secure place in the stationary power market, where it filled a niche (generally in the 20–100 hp range) between much larger steam engines and smaller gasoline-powered engines.[61]

In the first decade of the twentieth century, diesel makers in Europe and Russia began to focus on marine applications, where the diesel's poor weight-to-power ratio was far outweighed by its economy of operation and its reliance on fuels less volatile and dangerous than gasoline. In 1912, Copenhagen launched the first diesel-powered ocean-going vessel, *Selandia*, which was powered by two 1,000 hp diesels. During World War I, the world's leading navies featured diesel-powered submarines, and Germany outfitted most of its notoriously deadly U-boats with M.A.N. and Krupp diesels.[62]

In America, the technical refinement of the diesel lagged. ("American engines were slow, overweight dowagers compared with the latest European models," notes one authority.)[63] Not surprisingly, American entrepreneurs focused on somewhat different markets. The models Busch sold were used in power plants, mines, mills, retail operations, and manufactories, while production of the first marine diesels was stalled by the Busch patent monopoly until about 1910.

Migration of the Brons Engine

The ill-fated Diesel-Busch collaboration was not the only conduit through which diesel technology came to America. Although Rudolf Diesel sustained good patent protection of his developments, several other inventors succeeded in patenting similar machines—some intended to skirt the German engineer's patents, and others to overcome what they perceived to be fundamental weaknesses in his design. In the latter group, several inventors strived to eliminate Diesel's cumbersome air compression system, which crippled its usefulness in the small horsepower market. The first to make strides in this area was Friedrich August Haselwander, who received a patent for his improvement within months of Diesel's crucial 1897 lecture.[64]

But the first company to successfully address this critical problem—and to do so by developing "a new form of compression ignition engine"—was a small Dutch company named N. V. Appingedammer Bronsmotorenfabriek. Submerged in this unwieldy title are the words for the firm's namesake— Jan Brons (1865–1954)—and its factory location, the town of Appingedam, on the far northern coast of the Netherlands. A self-educated mechanic, Brons had been encouraged to tinker with internal combustion engines by his father, Tjako, a master builder who was looking for a mechanical means of powering threshing machines. Since Diesel had no patent in Holland, Brons & Sons was free to develop diesel-type oil engines, a task it undertook in 1892.[65] The first Brons "Safety Engines," rated at ten and twelve brake horsepower, were sold three years later. In 1899, Brons demonstrated his device by using it to power a large buslike vehicle. His firm was reorganized the following year as Brons & Timmer, which, although still primarily a machine shop, produced a small vertical diesel for auxiliary sailboat power.[66]

In the spring of 1902, an accident led to the critical Brons innovation. While Jan was testing a new engine design, its compressor failed. Remarkably, the engine continued to operate. After making additional modifications, most notably the addition of a special vaporizing "cup" at the end of the fuel valve, Brons began producing compressorless engines in 1904, and received German patent protection on his birthday, January 20, 1906. In the unique Brons cycle, the preliminary explosion of a small quantity of fuel would draw the remaining and main charge of fuel from the sprayer into the working cylinder for combustion. But getting the preliminary explosion to initiate the (main) secondary one through the tiny sprayer holes proved difficult.

Brons solved this problem by adding an adjustable bleed valve to admit a controlled quantity of air into the cup, where it would mix with the fuel admitted by the throttle. He was less successful in confronting another difficulty: the Brons engine operated poorly on lower grade fuels, which contained fewer of the light fractions that readily vaporized in the fuel cup for pre-ignition. Despite this flaw, the company moved ahead in the business. It was reorganized and relocated in 1906, and in the next thirteen years produced just over 1,000 oil engines.[67] They were best suited to applications that called for low horsepower at constant speed and drag, such as in marine cargo and fishing vessels.[68]

The story of the migration of the Brons engine to America is somewhat convoluted. The catalyst for the move was Rasmus Martin Hvid (pronounced "veed"), born in Denmark in 1883 but a naturalized U.S. citizen. Hvid applied for an engine design patent in early 1912 (it was awarded April 6, 1915), and founded the R. M. Hvid Co. in Battle Creek, Michigan, on July 12, 1912. Like Diesel, Hvid hoped to profit not by manufacturing engines but by licensing his technology to American engine producers.[69]

Hvid's patent rested on an ingenious feature—a series of upper cup orifices adjoining a thin air annulus chamber—which set it apart from the Brons engine. In operation, however, these holes and the air space adjacent to them clogged with carbon, and many (possibly all) of Hvid licensees failed to drill them in the first place. Recognizing that, without working air holes, his engine was effectively identical to the Brons device patented in 1906, Hvid took out a Brons license in August 1914, the month that World War I erupted in Europe.[70]

By that time, Clessie Cummins was convinced that compression ignition oil engines were the "best and safest in which a manufacturer could engage," an opinion based on years of experience with internal combustion engines, most recently his experiences along the Mississippi and in a Tampa engine shop.[71] The first oil engine began operating in Clessie's hometown in the summer of 1915. In July, the *Columbus Evening Republican* announced (and Clessie also probably learned through word of mouth) that the proprietors of Schaefer & Schwartzkopf's flour mill on Third Street had installed a 60 hp diesel engine.[72] The machine was manufactured by the St. Mary's Engine Co. of St. Mary's, Ohio, one of the earliest Hvid licensees. It was designed by an engineer at St. Mary's named Hans L. Knudsen.[73]

During the First World War, the ranks of Hvid engine makers grew (there were eleven by 1916), with the Hercules Gas Engine Co. of Evansville, Indiana, emerging as the largest.[74] Clessie recorded in one account that a description of the Hvid engine "came to my attention . . . in the spring of 1918."[75] In another, he explained how he "personally investigated three or four plants in which engines of this type were being operated" and received "very favorable" reports at each locale.[76] Hercules probably was among the facilities that Clessie visited, for the giant Evansville company was a key wartime customer of Clessie's machine shop.

As he contemplated entering the diesel business, Clessie was heavily influenced by the prior entry into the Hvid clan of such large manufacturers. "At least eight or ten large and well known corporations that had large engineering departments" had thoroughly investigated Hvid technology before deciding to invest, Clessie explained. The fact that Hvid licensees agreed to share production, engineering, and sales information "to the best interest of everyone concerned" was another incentive to new entrants.[77]

The signing of the World War I armistice on November 11, 1918, must have infused Clessie's plans to enter diesel manufacturing with a new sense of urgency. He had long anticipated the cessation of lucrative wartime machine work; now it was a reality. Nor was Clessie alone in his rush to remobilize for peacetime work. As a local reporter, who probably gleaned his information from Clessie, noted after Cummins Engine was founded: "Immediately after the armistice was signed and shops were released to peace work, there was a scramble among manufacturers for the right to make the Hvid engine and Mr. Cummins is to be congratulated on being one of the first to succeed."[78] The Cummins contract with Hvid called for a one-time license fee of $2,500 plus royalties of $5.00 per engine.[79]

The Cummins Engine Company was born fourteen weeks after the armistice, when the press of postwar need and opportunity came together with more personal and individual forces. These included Clessie's lifelong passion for internal combustion engines, his perception that the diesel represented a significant growth industry, and his willingness to devote his considerable mechanical and promotional talents to the cause. Just as important were the traditions of the Irwins, whose family business empire was erected on twin pillars of astute investment and community service, and whose backing of Clessie's venture reflected a tradition of support for local entrepreneurs. And finally, as Clessie Cummins and W. G. Irwin revealed often in their writings and actions, theirs was a special relationship, and one that extended beyond the bounds of rational business decision making.

Like all entrepreneurial ventures, launching the Cummins Engine Company entailed risks. "No one in the immediate organization has ever built oil engines," Clessie later acknowledged in his first report to shareholders.[80] For the time being, the risks were relatively minor for both key players. Clessie channeled his creativity and seemingly boundless energy in a single direction, while W. G. invested a modest amount of capital and added a new challenge to his diverse business domain. Before long, however, the scale and complexity of the operations would grow. So, too, would the commitment of its founders, and the risks each had to assume.

The Cummins Engine Company was entrepreneurial in another sense as well. Unlike the businesses founded by Rudolf Diesel, Adolphus Busch, and Rasmus Hvid, Cummins was established to *manufacture* oil engines. Its ultimate success would depend on its ability to produce commercially viable products. "The inventor produces ideas," Joseph Schumpeter reminds us, "the entrepreneur 'gets things done.'"[81] At Cummins, it was time to get things done.

The venture begins: the early 1920s

At the organizational meeting of the Cummins Engine Company (February 20, 1919), Clessie Cummins was elected president of the new corporation. Present at the meeting were Cummins, W. G. Irwin, Ernest Snider, Jarastus R. Dunlap, John E. Northway, Frank Richman, J. H. Dunlap, L. B. Newby, H. L. Rost, Fred J. Meyer, Cecil H. Smith, Ray Henderson, Isom Ross, Dean Bottorff, Robert Seward, A. Tross, and Joseph Kroot. After a quick reshuffling, the group elected the corporation's first set of directors—Cummins,

Snider, Dunlap, and Bottorff—as well as its other officers: Dunlap as vice president, Snider as secretary, and Bottorff as treasurer.*

The directors planned to assemble at Irwin's Bank every few weeks or months, as needed, and to host annual shareholders' meetings each January.[82] Little is known about the hopes and expectations of this original group of diesel enthusiasts, although W. G. recorded that "the people of our town were very much interested in" Clessie's activities before and during the war, so that when he "decided that he wanted to be a manufacturer . . . of Diesel engines, a considerable number of people joined with him in . . . the Cummins Engine Company."[83]

The first task at hand was to size up the company's physical assets. The Cummins Engine Company was being created through a metamorphosis of the Cummins Machine Works. Although W. G. Irwin had purchased the original equipment for that business years earlier, Clessie also had purchased additional equipment out of retained earnings to expand the business. The directors of the new company voted to hire D. E. Lewellen and Quentin Noblitt, Clessie's long-time friend, to set the "fair cash value of the machinery, tools and equipment now owned by Clessie L. Cummins that will be useful to the corporation." Cummins received $19,350 in stock for these assets, although he estimated their worth at $25,000. "I much preferred to take a personal licking on the equipment," he later explained, "than to have a company with too little capital."[84]

More was needed. In March, the directors required shareholders to pay in capital on 40 percent of the stock issued in order to buy equipment and to cover operating expenses. The next month, they called in another 30 percent of outstanding capital and bought a Beaman & Smith milling machine and a Binsee boring mill.[85] With the Hvid engine diagrams in hand, work progressed quickly. By May, Clessie and his crew were putting the finishing touches on the company's first engine: a single-cylinder, 6 hp, horizontal engine designed for use on the farm and in the shop. Its hopper-cooled piston had a seven-inch stroke and five-inch bore, and it turned the crankshaft at 600 rpm.[86]

Now the onus shifted to sales. Although the shop began to turn out Hvid engines in modest numbers as it geared up, there was no ready market for the product. Nor could the machines be tested thoroughly—or improved—without the benefit of customer experience in the field. The situation was critical, for the business did not have the capital to carry it for very long without a revenue stream. "After we had taken out a license and started to produce engines," Clessie recalled a few years later, "we found that without an outlet for our engines we would have little or no chance to succeed."[87]

—————————————————————————

*By coincidence, the Cummins organizational meeting followed by a month a similar meeting in Indianapolis, at which the Indianapolis Air Pump Company was born. This company—later called Noblitt-Sparks Industries, Inc., and still later Arvin Industries, Inc.—relocated to Columbus in 1931, and was a much more significant force in the local economy than Cummins for many years.

Adventures with Sears and Hvid

A break came a few months later, in the fall of 1919, when the nation's largest retailer, Sears, Roebuck & Company, approached Cummins to discuss an engine contract. The deal was so large—4,500 engines—that it promised to transform the company. This ultimately happened, but in unexpected and unhappy ways.

Sears was still a mail-order business in 1919. (Its first retail store did not open until 1925.) The Sears catalogue was a cornucopia of merchandise, supplying to rural customers the same variety of low-priced goods available to urban dwellers. The Sears "wish book" included everything from clothing and household notions to houses and automobiles. Among its extensive farm equipment offerings was a line of "Thermoil" oil engines in 1.5, 3, 5, and 7 hp sizes. These were Hvid models manufactured by the Evansville, Indiana-based Hercules Engine Company.[88]

Established in 1913, Hercules had farmed out work to Clessie's shop during the war, and now boasted annual sales of $2.4 million. Even with a newly completed plant, Hercules could not satisfy Sears' large demand for low-horsepower Hvid engines. V. E. "Mac" McMullen, the Evansville factory manager, suggested to W. M. Tippet, manager of the farm equipment division at Sears, that the retailer consider using Cummins as an engine supplier. Tippett paid a visit to Columbus in the fall of 1919, accompanied by his assistant, B. F. Watson, and a consulting engineer named E. B. Blakely.[89]

The men approved the budding operation, and they offered Cummins a contract to produce 4,500 1.5 and 3 hp engines. "The proposal," Clessie recalled, "nearly took my breath away." There were concerns, as well as excitement. Clessie wondered whether the Hvid design would work well in such small sizes, a point on which he received assurances from Watson. He also examined the terms of the contract carefully and consulted with associates. "I cannot possibly see where he has made any mistake in his figures," Noblitt told W. G. the day Clessie left to meet with Sears. And Irwin optimistically endorsed the offer that Clessie brought back from Chicago. "I cannot but feel," the banker confided to Noblitt, "that [Cummins Engine] now [has] a prospect for a good future."[90]

To meet the terms of this contract, Cummins Engine had to expand. With W. G.'s approval, Clessie met with company directors two weeks after his return from Chicago and approved a plan to double the company's capitalization to $100,000—a move endorsed at a special shareholders' meeting on November 7, 1919. One-fifth of the 500 new shares issued were made available to Clessie, collectable in installments. With 200 shares, Clessie became the largest stockholder; W. G. was second with 100 shares; and others each held between one and ten shares.[91]

Even so, Irwin's financial role in the company grew increasingly important. In January 1920 he (and Noblitt) joined the board. In March, Cummins' directors voted to borrow $10,000, then another $26,000 "at once" in April, followed by $15,000 "for the continuation of the business" in June. Irwin provided these funds, interest free. Moreover, it was only with his backing—as one of the state's wealthiest and most reputable bankers—that Cummins Engine could obtain credit from its suppliers.[92]

The Sears contract and Cummins' subsequent expansion came at an inauspicious time. Early in 1920 the United States economy began a dizzyingly rapid decline, which ended in a short-lived but crippling economic depression. To most outside observers, the Cummins Engine Company was happily oblivious to the downturn. Throughout the year, the company purchased additional equipment and added some fifty mechanics and assemblers to its payroll. The Seventh Street building became so cramped with machines and men that a one-story attached "shed" was built to house additional facilities for assembly, final testing, administration, and drafting. Late in the year, the *Columbus Evening Republican* ran a story titled, "Workmen Busy in Engine Factory: Cummins Company Not Affected by National Industrial Depression." The article described eighty-five workmen "rush[ing] to their tasks" within the plant.[93]

Thanks mainly to the Sears contract, Cummins had ample work. But insiders were worried. The engine maker was plagued by a host of troubles that prevented it from producing a regular stream of high-quality products. Month by month, the company fell further behind on its Sears production schedule, and an embarrassingly large portion of the machines that were completed were found to be defective or inoperable. By September, Cummins was holding 400 Thermoil orders, some as old as nine months. Not surprisingly, the retailer sent Watson and Blakely back to Columbus for a firsthand look.[94] Their reports to Tippett reveal much about the very early days of the Cummins operation.

Watson found Clessie's "excuse" for the delays—poor quality pistons purchased from an outside supplier—to be wholly inadequate, and was amazed at the inventor's casual attitude toward the problem. "I don't believe he realizes the importance of the position he is in. . . . [T]his condition does not seem to worry him in the least." Watson recommended that Tippett "omit these engines from our Spring books" to prevent further dissatisfaction among Sears customers.[95]

Blakely's report portrayed Cummins Engine as unsystematic and under-equipped. Item 1 of his report read: "Management weak. Not enough attention paid to detail. No definite manufacturing plan. Don't seem to realize importance of getting out engines at any cost, leaving profit making for future." But despite all of his criticisms, Blakely concluded that "there seems to be a general improvement in tone and looks of plant."[96] Tippett himself arrived at a more generous verdict after speaking with Clessie Cummins soon thereafter. "I feel that Mr. Cummins has had a long hard pull," he told W. G. Irwin, ". . . and as he is just now about ready to go over the top, there is no use in talking about what might have been done."[97] Like many who encountered the company's namesake, Tippett was turned around by Clessie's persuasiveness. As another Indianapolis businessman noted after meeting Clessie a few months later, "one couldn't resist Mr. Cummins' whole-hearted enthusiasm."[98]

Clessie could not smooth the ruffled feathers of every Cummins customer, however. Nor were many problems easily reparable. The company's machinists had much to learn about the basic art of engine making. At the same time, they were struggling to master the special manufacturing requirements of compression ignition engines. Oil engine manufacture demanded a unique set of stresses, tolerances, and other metallurgical characteristics; materials best for making gasoline engine bearings and valves, for instance, failed inside oil engines. To complicate matters further, Cummins outsourced the manufacture of many critical engine components—including valves, pistons, and rings—and suffered the predictable consequences when these parts were flawed or incompatible. In short, virtually every early Cummins engine was a case study in real-time learning and troubleshooting.[99]

Still, these manufacturing problems do not explain fully why Thermoil engines were being returned to the retailer—and, in turn, to Cummins—in a torrent by late 1921. It was then that Sears sent a representative to the farm regions of Wisconsin and Minnesota, where most of the returns originated. The agent discovered that groups of farmers were abusing the retailer's generous, money-back guarantee. Liberal warranties were a business necessity for mail-order retailers such as Sears and Montgomery Ward; without them, customers would not purchase goods sight unseen. The terms of the guarantees differed according to classes of products. For its "Thermoil" line, Sears offered a full refund, plus shipping and handling, within sixty days of purchase. It was not unusual, Sears was now discovering, for a group of farmers to pool capital to purchase an engine, share it among members of the group to cut wood and perform other tasks, and return the machine within sixty days for a full refund. As a result of this ploy and the numerous manufacturing problems, Cummins was soon receiving nearly as many engines per day as it was shipping out.[100]

With losses mounting for both Sears and Cummins, the Thermoil contract was canceled in 1922, with about 1,400 engines still undelivered. But the two parties could not reach terms on a final settlement, and litigation loomed. For Cummins, the key point of contention was the huge inventory of parts it was left holding for the never-to-be-built engines. Fortunately, Clessie had stowed in the company safe a letter in which Tippet agreed to reimburse Cummins for any inventory-related costs. With this in hand, he and John Niven, a business associate of W. G. Irwin, visited Tippet at his Chicago office and recovered $85,000.[101]

"The three-year association [with Sears]," Clessie wrote in his 1967 auto-biography, "cost Cummins Engine Company several hundred thousand dollars."[102] In that account, Clessie emphasized the farmers' abuse of the Sears guarantee as the root cause of the Thermoil debacle. But in his address to Cummins shareholders three years after the fact, he alluded to a larger factor: the depression of 1920–1921. After the downturn began, he explained, "prices had to be slashed to get business at all, and we were caught with a heavy inventory on our hands."[103]

The recession had a devastating effect on Sears and its customers. Following an unprecedented surge in sales and profits in 1919, Sears began cutting prices in mid-1920 to boost sagging sales, and ended the year with tiny growth but huge inventories. In 1921—a year dubbed "uniformly bad and nearly disastrous" by Sears historians—the retailer cut its work force by 16 percent and posted a $16.4 million loss. Durable goods were the hardest hit. Sales of Sears gasoline engines, for example, plunged 78 percent in 1920–1921. The postwar depression struck agriculture harder than any other sector, leaving farmers unable to afford catalogue purchases—especially expensive durable goods like oil engines. Linked by the Thermoil engine, the American farmer, the world's largest retailer, and Indiana's youngest diesel producer suffered alike.[104]

Still, the Thermoil episode taught Cummins Engine valuable lessons about development, manufacturing, and marketing. As Blakely had pointed out, Cummins needed tighter management and higher-quality equipment. Disgruntled Sears customers had signaled weaknesses in Hvid technology. A better product was needed, and Cummins—if it was to survive—would have to pay far more attention to customer service.

From Licensee to Diesel Developer

Modern industrial corporations, no matter how diverse, perform four basic functions: research and development, manufacturing, marketing, and finance. Between 1921 and 1925, the Cummins Engine Company redefined its role in each of these areas. The company began the decade as a licensed manufacturer of low-horsepower Hvid engines for stationary power. But it quickly evolved into a cooperative effort of two corporations: one devoted to manufacturing; the other—the Oil Engine Development Company—to research and development. Together, these companies developed and produced their own line of oil engines mainly for marine applications. This transformation did not come smoothly, nor did it provide enduring solutions to the company's challenges. The early 1920s were a critical stage in the maturation of the budding enterprise.

With each passing month at Cummins, the Hvid name increasingly became associated with deception and failure. Echoing the sentiments of

Adolphus Busch and other diesel licensees, Clessie later explained: "We were assured that in taking out a license to build this engine we would be getting a highly refined and profitable design, and that there were numerous economies that would be possible, due to standardization of design, and of which we would all be able to partake." Instead, he groused, "we were all more or less misled as to the practicability of the engine which we had decided to build." As was so often the case in his life, Clessie had his own ideas about the technology. "During the time in which we were building the Hvid type engine," he recorded, "I constantly had in mind an engine that would not be subject to the weaknesses in principle that were developing in the Hvid type engine."[105]

To prevent his Chicago licensor from reaping the fruits of his research, Clessie consulted with company lawyers about voiding the Hvid license, but found to his disappointment that the contract offered no such provisions. Cummins was captive to a flawed technology, one that seemed to be driving it relentlessly toward "receivership or bankruptcy."[106] This left only one hope for survival: developing a technology that would bypass the Hvid patents.

In July 1921, Clessie sat down with an attorney to review Hvid's patents.[107] After giving the documents "a pretty good study," the two men saw a way out of the snare. They discovered that the injector air holes in the Hvid engine (as patented in 1915) were the critical feature that set it apart from the Brons engine. Fortunately, Clessie's fuel system did not include the essentially useless Hvid injector holes, and thus seemed usable "without interference from Hvid." Clessie filed a patent application—his first in the field of compression injection oil engines—on September 27, 1921.[108]

It was a turning point in the company's history. The Cummins Engine Company would transform itself from a licensed manufacturer into an originator and builder of its own diesel-type engines. The strategy was born of necessity as much as opportunism. "We had convinced ourselves," Clessie later told stockholders, "that there was no possible chance to work out our salvation as long as we continued with the Hvid engine."[109]

The First Engineer and the Oil Engine Development Company

Not long before his death in 1943, W. G. Irwin recorded his memories of the early years of the Cummins Engine Company. The resulting "history" is brief (barely four typewritten pages long) but is filled with interesting detail and insight. One of the most moving and illuminating passages recalls a discussion he had with Clessie "something like a year" after Cummins Engine began operations.

> *Mr. Cummins came to me in my office and told me that the engine he was building was not a good one and that his venture was not a success; in fact that all of the money that had been put into it had been*

*lost and that he had little to show for what he had done. I felt sorry for
him and asked him if there were no salvage to be had from the wreck.
He said there was nothing but an idea. He tried to explain the idea to
me with the result that when he told me it would cost $10,000 to
prove the idea, I told him I would furnish the money.*[110]

This critical meeting probably took place in the second half of 1921. It
was then that W. G. and Clessie put concrete plans in motion to transform
Cummins from licensee to diesel developer. The application for Clessie's
patent in September—not an inexpensive process—was one step. But two
more ambitious moves in early 1922 set the new strategy firmly in motion:
the hiring of the company's first formally trained engineer, Hans L. Knudsen,
and the formation of the Oil Engine Development Company. Both required
the new infusion of capital to which Irwin referred in his history.

Knudsen would serve as one of Cummins Engine's leading technicians
for nearly twenty-six years. The details of his early life remain sketchy. He was
born in Denmark, served in the merchant marine, and entered a technical
school at Mittweida, Germany (near Dresden). While in school, Knudsen
spent his evenings learning French—the language in which the curriculum
was taught—but devoted his days to engineering topics, including the study
of compression ignition engines. The training was purely theoretical;
Knudsen did not see a working diesel engine until he emigrated to the United
States soon after graduation.

His first employment in America was with General Electric, where he
conducted electrical rather than mechanical work. After about a year and a
half, Knudsen joined the St. Mary's Machine Company of Ohio. The firm's
products included engines that ran on generator gas and "semi-diesels" (oil
engines with less-than-diesel compression levels). In 1914, around the time
Knudsen joined the company, St. Mary's took out a license from Hvid. "It
was my first job there to convert all those engines into the Hvid engine system," Knudsen recalled.[111]

Demonstrating a special ability to diagnose and remedy engine operating
problems, Knudsen became a troubleshooter and engine designer for R. M.
Hvid himself. Hvid's modest office in Chicago desperately needed this kind
of technical assistance. Strictly a licensing operation, it was incapable of producing, testing, or modifying the machines. "I often spoke to [Hvid] about
. . . establish[ing] a laboratory there so that he knew all the problems with the
engine. . . ," Knudsen recalled. "But he wasn't interested." Knudsen traveled
widely within the Hvid licensee network. His clients included Evinrude
Motor Co. (Milwaukee) and Hercules, where he met the manager of Sears'
small-engine production, V. E. McMullen.[112]

Knudsen put in a two-month troubleshooting stint at Cummins in the
summer of 1921, investigating why Cummins could not properly govern its

engines. He soon identified the source of the problem: a fuel-governing valve designed for much larger engines. After correcting the flaw, and also learning more about Clessie's work, Knudsen returned to Chicago.

In December of 1921—following the crucial interval of disillusionment and strategy making at Cummins—Clessie telephoned the Danish engineer in Chicago and invited him to Columbus "to discuss . . . the design of an engine based on a patent of his own." Knudsen met with Irwin and Cummins at the bank, where (as he recorded years later in his own concise history of Cummins Engine), "C. L. disclosed his patent to me. I observed at once that [Clessie's patent] was a modification of the Hvid system introducing mechanical timing instead of relying solely on pressures and orifices in the fuel chambers to effect the injection. [They asked] my opinion . . . as to whether such a system would function. My reply was that there was no question about it operating but that it would require a lot of research to make it operate satisfactorily."

Clessie and W. G. must have agreed, for they asked Knudsen to "undertake the design of the engine and join the Cummins Engine Co. in charge of engineering." "To this," Knudsen wrote, "my answer was yes." The engineer wrapped up his affairs in Chicago, and then returned to Columbus to begin work in January 1922.[113]

The following month, Clessie Cummins and W. G. Irwin formed a new organization to carry out the required development work. The Oil Engine Development Company (OEDC) was organized on February 2, six days before application for its incorporation was filed in Bartholomew County. Although the company's mission statement was reminiscent of the engine company's—to "design, build, improve, develop, perfect, and sell oil and other engines, and, in connection therewith, to acquire, hold, sell, assign, and license to use patent and patent rights"—the OEDC's founders never intended it to manufacture engines. (That function was left entirely to Cummins Engine.) Instead, the OEDC would take over the research and development functions previously carried out by the engine company. It would apply for and own all oil engine patents. It would grant manufacturing rights to this technology to Cummins Engine in exchange for a $3 per horsepower royalty but no licensing fee. And it would reimburse Cummins Engine for the cost of labor, equipment, and other facilities it used in this developmental work. The company was capitalized at $20,000. Clessie owned 50 percent of its shares, W. G. 49 percent, and Linnie Sweeney (the swing vote) 1 percent.

Why was a separate company created to carry out functions hitherto performed by Cummins Engine? There is no simple answer. To begin with, few records pertaining to the OEDC's founding have survived. Second, both the scant evidence available and the event's historical context suggest that the OEDC served several ends. Finally, the organization's purpose seems to have changed over time, with the OEDC never fulfilling its primary mission in the first place. Even so, the matter is of consequence, not only for what it reveals of Cummins Engine's early history, but also because the OEDC would become the focus of a conflict between Clessie Cummins and W. G. Irwin two decades after its creation.

One rationale for the OEDC, both men acknowledged, was to insulate Cummins Engine shareholders from further losses. Recognizing the daunting and expensive development work that still lay ahead, W. G. was willing to invest more of his own money, but did not expect his fellow stockholders to do likewise. As Clessie told Cummins' owners in 1925, "Mr. Irwin said that under the circumstances, and in fairness to the stockholders, we could not consider advancing any further money to start in a long siege of development of a new type of engine."[114]

The Development Company also may have helped open the way for future technical developments clear of Hvid entanglements. Hvid's license, after all, was with Cummins Engine. For the Chicago firm, prosecuting the OEDC for patent infringement would have been harder than proving that Cummins had violated its contract. But if this was a motivating factor behind the OEDC, it quickly faded in importance. After four years of wrangling, Cummins Engine escaped the Hvid license by trading rights to Clessie's first patent plus $13,200.[115]

More to the point, the OEDC's founders had their own licensing in mind. According to a study made by J. Irwin Miller in 1941, the idea behind the OEDC was "that the Cummins Engine Company would never manufacture more than a small percentage of the types of engines to which the fuel system was applicable and that license arrangements for its use by others would be sought."[116] And in 1929 Clessie reminded W. G. Irwin that "our original understanding and agreement . . . was that the Development Company would license various other builders and gradually build up a profitable return from royalties."[117]

Why was the OEDC needed to carry out this function, given that Cummins Engine's articles of incorporation allowed it to license and transfer patents? The answer almost certainly involved Clessie. His portion of OEDC ownership was much larger than his share of Cummins. More royalties would find their way to him through the OEDC than through the virtually defunct original venture. The OEDC held out the promise that Clessie might one day reap generous financial rewards from the technology it controlled. But its more immediate—and critical—purpose was to keep the stream of Irwin money flowing and the doors of the company open.

The F Engine and the Marine Market

By early 1922, Knudsen had joined Cummins, the Sears contract was moribund, and Clessie was working on his own engine design. Throughout the first half of the decade, developmental work at Cummins was tedious and frustrating, though punctuated by moments of exhilaration. Expectations usually outran realities, and problems proved much easier to identify than to solve.

Clessie began to divide his time between the factory and the field. Hoping to move beyond low-horsepower stationary power sales at the same time he jettisoned the Hvid technology, he began to focus on a new market: marine power. For Clessie this was a predictable course. He had first experimented with adapting and using kerosene fuel aboard his own boat, and no doubt saw frequent references to marine diesel developments in the United States and Europe in his readings about the industry.

His interest in the marine market was encouraged when a large shrimp packer in New Orleans placed an engine order. Because the customer prudently demanded that Clessie supervise the installation as a condition of purchase, Cummins headed south. There he discovered exciting possibilities. If the Cummins-powered boat performed well, he reported to W. G. in the summer of 1922, fleet owners with hundreds of boats might switch to Cummins diesels. "There is some very keen rivalry here amongst the boat owners," he reported, "and no small amount of jealousy, which I see will work to our advantage." With characteristic determination, he concluded that marine power would be a lucrative, recession-proof market "if we go after it and from now on I am going after it and furthermore I am going to get it."[118]

Clessie spent half a year "going after it" along the shores of the Gulf and northeast Florida, touting the Cummins engine among fishing and shrimping fleet owners. The indefatigable promoter often met his match among the wily southern seamen. On one occasion, Clessie lost a trawling contest, only to discover that the net he had dragged was much heavier than his opponent's. He switched nets and won the rematch. But some boat owners, wary of the new technology, flatly refused to let Clessie install the smaller propellers suitable for higher-speed diesels.[119]

Clessie finished his southern tour with little to show for it. The main reason was not the toughness of the seafaring customers, however. It was, quite simply, that Cummins diesels were performing poorly. Injector cups became clogged with carbon after only a few hours of operation. Engines ran roughly, wearing out or shattering critical parts. The situation reached its nadir, Clessie recorded, when the "counterweights started flying off and cutting engines in two and taking out the sides of boats and the tops of cabins, [even causing] a few injuries to some of the crew." Meanwhile, W. G. was less than enthralled with Clessie's extended sales tour. "I cannot understand how you could be content to leave your business for so long a time," the Columbus-bound banker complained.[120]

He had a point. As Clessie learned again and again among the southern fishermen, the Cummins engine needed dramatic improvement. In spite of some early modifications, it remained fundamentally a Hvid product.

Clessie's new enthusiasm for the marine market provided another reason to free the company from the shackles of the Hvid license.

Early Cummins engines were plagued by two major weaknesses. First, poor timing caused pistons and cylinders to wear out inordinately fast. If an engine's fuel injection, compression, and explosion were not synchronized precisely, it ran roughly, placing undue stress on critical moving parts. The timing problem was exacerbated in multi-cylinder engines, with which Cummins began to experiment during this period. Clessie's initial solution was to control injection and combustion by mechanically linking the fuel inlet valve with a device that opened and closed injector spray holes. This ingenious scheme was not wholly satisfactory, however, and would be supplanted by a much superior system nearly a decade later. Nevertheless, Clessie exhibited his perennial optimism in the face of this problem. In late 1923, for instance—with months of work behind him and many more to come—he told W. G. that the "mechanical difficulty in the injector" was a problem "which can always be whipped."[121]

The second chronic mechanical difficulty was carbon buildup in the fuel cup. Preliminary combustion in the "hot cup" left carbon residue that began to clog the tiny spray holes after several hours of operation. If the apparatus was not cleaned regularly by operators, the engine would lose power. Cummins experimented with as many as 3,000 fuel cup designs, filling notebook after notebook with sketches and test data. "Our greatest trouble has been caused by following too closely old, accepted formulas," Clessie told W. G., sounding the classic inventor's theme. Finally, Cummins (with help from Knudsen) hit upon the idea of a much smaller, "volumeless" fuel cup—so small, in fact, that there was insufficient hot air available to cause an explosion or carbonization of the fuel.[122]

This modification greatly reduced the carbonization problem, although, as in the case of mechanical timing, critical improvements were still to come. With the hot cup eliminated as an inducement for injection, preliminary work began on using the timing valve as a plunger. These two modifications—virtual elimination of the fuel chamber and mechanical (plunger) injection—formed the basis of Cummins Engine's path-breaking injection technology.[123]

Other avenues of research were less fruitful. Probably the biggest technological dead end in the early 1920s was the company's effort to develop a presumably simpler and more trouble-free *two*-cycle engine. (Such engines require one upward and one downward stroke of the piston to complete the cycle of injection, ignition, and exhaust; four-cycle engines require two of each.) "We fell for this one," Clessie later reflected ruefully, calling the impulse to produce two-stroke engines a "bug which seems to affect nearly all beginners [in] the Diesel field." Cummins compounded the challenge by trying to incorporate innovative design features into its first two-cycles. The company produced a handful of step-piston "Model TC" (two-cycle) engines, but they were plagued with injection problems and, explained Clessie, "actually [had] more moving parts than in a good four cycle engine [but with] all the faults inherent in the two cycle."[124]

Out of this swirl of innovation and problem solving emerged, in 1924, the company's first distinctive engine line: the Model F (for four-cycle). Most early editions had one or two pistons, bolted as separate units to a common base. The Model F featured a 5.5-inch bore, 6-inch stroke, and developed 12.5 hp at 600 rpm. Some of the first units also featured Clessie's innovative mechanical injection system.

Now it was time to promote the new line aggressively. The F engine performed best when pulling heavy loads at constant speeds, the kind of performance demanded by fishing trawlers. (And, as with all diesels, its lack of electrical ignition was a distinct advantage over gasoline engines in marine settings.) The company had looked into supplying the U.S. Navy, but negotiations were moving slowly.[125] So Clessie took to the water once again. In the spring of 1924, he installed a brand-new Model F in a boat, mounted a conspicuous sign on the vessel that read, "This boat is driven with a New Cummins Oil Engine 12 1/2 H.P. for 50 cents a day," and again headed south.[126]

This time, Clessie's expedition generated sales. At New Orleans, he described the local Cummins agent as "walking on air," and he ordered the factory to produce a large batch of engines. Clessie also touted his engines in the Pacific Northwest, where he encountered customer resistance but still came away with sales. Irwin tried halfheartedly to apply the brakes. "We went too fast with Sears-Roebuck and we don't want another mistake of this kind," he cautioned. But he also took heart at the "wonderful results" down south.[127] The flurry of activity was a harbinger of things to come.

Searching for a market

The month of April 1925 was a period of intense change both for Cummins Engine and its president. On the 21st, Clessie delivered an "annual report" to Cummins shareholders, his first since the company's founding. He began with a candid assessment of the firm's brief but eventful history, reflecting upon why he and W. G. had entered the business and recounting the "innumerable disappointments" that had followed. "Time after time it appeared that we had found the answer to the problems confronting us," he recalled, "but sooner or later it always resulted in failure." As befit the occasion, however, Clessie concluded his speech with an upbeat view of the future, noting the company's "excellent engine" and "well equipped and organized" factory. The long siege, he suggested, was coming to an end.

Clessie also introduced Cummins shareholders to the Oil Engine Development Company. It had developed a fine new engine, he said, but "in place of the $10,000.00 which we figured might finish the job, it required close to $100,000.00 to finish the development." Given this financial burden, the OEDC would charge Cummins Engine no license fee and only a "nominal" royalty for manufacturing rights. However, "because it would take several years" for Cummins to repay the OEDC for its work, Clessie explained, "it is considered only fair" that the Development Company seek outside licensees. Still, he assured the stockholders, the OEDC would license only "such sizes as the Engine Company cannot or does not care to manufacture, and [would] protect the engine company through some sort of preferential royalty arrangement."

Although licensing opportunities may have partially inspired the OEDC's formation three years earlier, Clessie now made the strategy more explicit and pursued it aggressively for the next few years. This may have reflected uncertainty on the part of Clessie and W. G. that Cummins Engine could ever become a big player in diesel manufacturing or, conversely, their confidence in the salability of OEDC technology. Perhaps both sentiments were present to some degree. In either case, the licensing strategy signified the mounting pressure to earn profits and stanch the flow of red ink in both organizations. The push to license was merely one manifestation of the escalating opportunism that characterized Cummins in the late 1920s.

Clessie had a great personal stake in the business. So, too, did the Irwin-Sweeney-Miller family, which had continued to advance money to the company since the 1922 recapitalization. By 1925, these advances totaled some $90,000. On April 21, the board authorized the issuance of 900 shares of preferred stock at a par value of $100 per share, of which 886 were issued to members of the Irwin-Sweeney-Miller group. This represented the first time, although not the last, that the company's debts to its founding family were capitalized. Although this recapitalization significantly diluted Clessie's percentage of ownership in the company—from 28 percent down to 18 percent—a deal was struck whereby Clessie would receive an additional 200 shares of common stock per year until 1930, which would gradually restore his ownership position.[128]

In the week following this meeting, Clessie's personal life took dramatic turns. On April 24, his wife Ethel delivered a third son, a redhead named George Thomas. With Ethel and the baby apparently recovering well, Clessie boarded a train for Chicago two days later to meet with the company's patent attorney. But an urgent telegram summoned him back to Columbus on the 26th: Ethel was "seriously ill." He arrived at the hospital just in time to bid his dying wife goodbye.

Now a widower with five children, Clessie called on his mother-in-law to help at home. Business was expanding rapidly and was demanding more and more of his time. In fact, soon after the recapitalization, Clessie convinced Irwin that Cummins needed a new manufacturing facility. And although the floors within the Thomas Building were sagging under the weight of equipment and inventory, Irwin chose to wait until the old factory was "absolutely crowded" before investing in "bricks and mortar." He did not wait long. The next few months brought a bevy of orders and leads.

In May, Cummins Engine received its first order from the Northwest Engineering Co., a Wisconsin producer of construction equipment, which wanted to install a large number of F engines in its power shovels. Meanwhile, Clessie moved ahead on other fronts. In August 1925, he traveled to New York to meet with the United States Shipping Board. After picking up some tips about the Washington trade—"they load up their proposal with everything they can think of to protect themselves, but leave the manufacturer out in the cold," he reported to Irwin—he submitted a bid for fourteen auxiliary engines. There was a certain irony to this move, for "the Hvid crowd up in Lansing" had submitted a competitive bid.[129]

A more intriguing market possibility was railroad dieselization. The week after Clessie returned from New York, he was visited by a manufacturer named Butler, who was well connected with several American locomotive makers. After witnessing several engine tests, Butler expressed great enthusiasm about the "flexibility and simplicity" of the company's engine. There was a good chance, he told Clessie, that a leading locomotive maker would soon place an order with Cummins for 300 six- or eight-cylinder models. "According to Butler, the locomotive builders are all keenly interested, and also the more progressive of the rail heads," Clessie noted. "He feels this is a very big field and that whoever is able to get in on it will have some fine business."[130]

Butler's assessment of the industry was accurate. American railroads became seriously interested in dieselization for the first time in the mid-1920s. Competition from alternative forms of transportation (especially trucking) was becoming intense—track mileage was declining for the first time in history—and this placed a premium on fast and economical operation. At the same time, high gasoline prices inspired leading manufacturers of gasoline-electric railcars such as the Electro-Motive Company to consider switching to the more efficient diesel technology. In 1924, the American Locomotive Company, which controlled 40 percent of the American market, produced the nation's first diesel-electric switching locomotive, and it soon began work on lighter-weight passenger models.[131] Clessie and W. G. spent much of their time cultivating this emerging industry in the late 1920s.

By October of 1925, the Cummins factory was so busy that evening work shifts were a regular occurrence.[132] Now Irwin was ready to expand the plant. He considered buying the old Reeves factory, but balked at the asking price. Soon after that property sold to another suitor in October, W. G. secured a fourteen-acre tract between Central Avenue and "Irwin park" from its adjacent owner, J. T. Kitchen Lumber Company, and William H. Mobley.

Because Irwin already owned another twenty acres immediately to the south, there was now great potential for expansion. With the new parcel in hand, the banker began to secure rights of way across several small streets and alleys for a rail connection to the future plant.[133]

Then a more ambitious plan took shape. Within a month of the land purchase, W. G. and Clessie decided that Cummins Engine should expand production quickly. Accordingly, Irwin purchased part of the former Emerson-Brantingham facilities, a set of industrial properties that had sold at auction several weeks earlier to C. Russell Feldmann of New York. Feldmann retained the main plant and several buildings, while reselling to Irwin an assembly building south of Fifth Street (not including its foundry and railroad tracks), an office building north of Fifth, and some vacant lots and warehouses, the latter to be razed. Late 1925 and early 1926 found Cummins busily moving its main production facilities into the assembly building, erecting new structures, and installing tens of thousands of dollars' worth of new equipment.[134] The company's present-day Main Engine Plant sprawls across this Fifth Street site.

At this critical juncture, Irwin was cautiously optimistic about the engine company's future. "We are just out of the early experimental stage," he told an Indianapolis engineer. "We hope, though, that there will be sufficient proof within a comparatively short time to enable us to feel justified in undertaking the production on a much greater scale."[135]

As 1926 drew to a close, Clessie was optimistic as well. Not only was business booming in the new plant, but his domestic affairs were on the mend. By this time, Clessie had been helped at home by his mother-in-law, his mother, a hired assistant, and his sister Irene. The situation now stabilized as Clessie took a new wife. He had met Estelle Margaret Feldmann (Russell's sister) in New York during the Emerson-Brantingham negotiations, and they were married in the home of Stella's parents on the 8th of October.

New technologies for new markets

Strategic planning is a vital tool of large industrial corporations, often carried out in central offices by executives not burdened by the concerns of day-to-day operations. For many smaller companies, however, strategy making is an intermittent luxury. The press of daily affairs leaves little or no time for broad-gauge reflection and planning. Even the best-laid plans can be overwhelmed by the need to chase opportunities. Such was the situation at Cummins in the mid-1920s.

It is therefore not surprising that an outsider produced what was probably the only strategic analysis written about Cummins in the 1920s. On August 24, 1926, manufacturing consultant R. A. Millholland (of Millholland Sales & Engineering Co., Indianapolis) submitted an insightful "MEMORANDUM" that suggested a new course for Cummins. The surest path to manufacturing success, he suggested, was to invest in manufacturing facilities to lower production costs, and then to mass market. He recommended that Cummins focus on the market for smaller engines—diesels for "light plants, motor boats, concrete mixers, small pumps, small power applications, farm use, auxiliaries for small ships, construction camp lighting, store and garage lighting, country movie house lighting, etc." By mass-producing small units, Cummins would require less capital, encounter fewer competitors, and enter a larger potential market than if it custom-built large diesels. The second-best strategy for Cummins, he concluded, would be to both mass produce and customize, but that would "require several separate plants."[136]

Clessie liked the plan. He himself had been gathering ideas for a 6–7 hp engine similar to the original Sears model. "The beauty of this size is that there is absolutely no competition in it, except Hill," he told Irwin. Moreover, smaller engines were well suited for mass production. "If you do not agree with us on this . . . you might as well be ready to face a real session," he teased the banker, "as we have enough ammunition laid up here to snow you under."[137]

Then came a revealing afterthought. Small-engine production was needed to keep the shop busy, Clessie explained, because "it will be many more months before the big engine can be rolling." In fact, in the late 1920s Cummins would build—in a single plant—small, medium, _and_ large engines, following the lead of the rapidly shifting marketplace. Each new market demanded an appropriate technology. In some instances, the Engine Company inappropriately applied existing technology to new applications. In other cases, technologies modified for existing applications proved useful in new markets.

The Northwest contract exemplified both of these trends. The shovel maker learned quickly that Cummins' marine (F) engine was ill suited for construction work. Dirt and dust easily clogged many of the engine's critical moving parts—rocker arms, push rods, and camshaft bearings, among others—which were exposed outside of the engine housing. In addition, there were throttling problems. Clessie's unique fuel-metering system (in which the injector monitored the rate of injection) worked well under constant load, but poorly under variable conditions. Operators who pulled back from a full throttle found that fuel continued to pour into the fuel cup. This relative increase in fuel gave them an unexpected—and unwelcome—surge of horsepower and rpm.[138]

In response to these difficulties, Cummins Engine first developed the Model P engine. Approximately half of the moving parts exposed in the F were now enclosed in the crankcase, and its throttle adjusted automatically to meet variable speeds. Two other models followed shortly thereafter. The Model W, otherwise like the P, had a slightly larger bore and longer stroke. Similarly, the Model N mimicked the F, but with a larger, single cylinder.[139]

Relations with Northwest worsened despite these improvements. Nevertheless, this work demonstrated the company's ability to refine technology to meet specific market conditions, and led to more widely useful applications. Much of the mid-decade development came to fruition in 1928 with introduction of the Model U, possibly the world's first fully enclosed diesel engine. The evolution over a few short years from the Model F to the Model U was striking. The former had inclined valves and an innovative but problematic fuel pump; the newer model featured vertical valves and a more dependable single-disc pump that injected each fuel charge.[140] It was these features that began to garner industry attention for Cummins in the late 1920s.

By 1927 Cummins was losing interest in the shovel business (and Northwest proved to be a troublesome customer). It was earning higher margins elsewhere. More important, new markets were beckoning.[141] Clessie saw the prospect of building locomotive engines, for example, as a "tremendous" opportunity. One of the nation's leading industries, railroads offered a gargantuan replacement market if they chose to dieselize any significant portion of their rolling stock. Even beyond that, observed the ever-promotional Clessie, "when they plow a Diesel Engine into another, as they do the steam outfit occasionally, it surely means a new engine right off the bat." Clessie explained his approach to Irwin: "The first plan is to get engines out in some manner and establish ourselves." Cummins would build a single unit, charging a premium price of $23,000 or so ("due to the development work needed"), then sell subsequent units for around $18,000 once manufacturing methods were refined. The real challenge was getting started. "There are so many [diesel] failures that . . . they are all skeptical. . . . [I]t is pretty hard to sell anyone except a good friend on the oil engine idea at this time."[142]

Clessie found such a friend in James T. Wallis, the superintendent of motive power at the Pennsylvania Railroad. Wallis was interested in using diesels in the Pennsylvania's switchyards, and possibly on major interurban routes then being electrified. (Diesel locomotives are actually driven by electricity. The diesel engine powers a generator which in turn feeds an electric motor that moves the train.) Wallis had little support within his organization, but remained loyal to the cause. In 1927 he placed an order with Cummins for a single railroad diesel.[143] This project also generated some interest among other railroads, as Clessie hoped, although Cummins was in no position to take on more railroad business.

Meanwhile, the company was making headway in Washington. Orders from the U.S. Coast Guard, Shipping Board, and Lighthouse Service were pouring in, taking up most of the factory's output. A large number were used to power lighthouse generator sets. In early 1927, for example, Cummins engines were sent to lighthouses in Alaska, Hawaii, Dry Tortugas (near Key West), Staten Island, Duluth, Detroit, and Charlotte, North Carolina. These sales reflected the improving quality of the company's products. Bidding was competitive, and successful contractors had to meet the government's strict operating requirements.[144]

In the final years of the "Roaring Twenties"—when most businessmen enjoyed flush times and many Wall Street speculators made prodigious profits—Cummins Engine gravitated toward the luxury yacht market. Clessie, who had spurned "high grade, tricky yacht work" in late 1926, told W. G. one year later: "All in all, it looks like we can count on a nice share of business in this big yacht field, as they are playing with people who have plenty of money and the desire for high speed is such that they will go to any extreme to get it."[145] At the time, Cummins was making a variety of low horsepower engines, as well as the behemoth 300 hp machine for the Pennsylvania. Now it plunged ahead with 175 hp models for the attractive luxury boating market. Once again, opportunism carried the day.[146]

The locomotive and yacht work was exotic, but it did not pay the bills. Smaller engines for marine and generator applications remained the staple of the business. Of the 155 engines sold in 1928, 103 were Model Us, most in the six-cylinder size, with one- and four-cylinder units also popular. The remaining 52 engines were distributed among Fs, Ps, Ws, and Ns in sizes ranging from one to six cylinders.[147] That year—although Cummins sold an average of only 3 engines per week—was the best on record. Between 1927 and 1928, revenues more than doubled from $143,759 to $299,820, while losses declined from $56,669 to $40,627.[148]

It may have been this improving financial picture that prompted a revisiting of the company's capital structure in 1928. Since the 1925 restructuring, the Irwin-Sweeney-Miller family had continued to loan money to Cummins Engine. No interest had been paid on the 900 preferred shares issued in 1925; nevertheless, Linnie Sweeney and W. G. Irwin subscribed for all of the additional 2,500 preferred shares now being authorized by the board. In this case, as in 1925, Clessie's ownership position was reduced significantly: from 26.5 percent (up from 18 percent since 1925 due to annual additions to his common stock) down to 16.43 percent. This time, however, no mechanism was created to rebuild Clessie's share—a circumstance that would come back to haunt the company more than a decade later.[149]

In the meantime, however, Clessie again had the resources he needed to move forward. He also had ample reason to feel proud of the company's improving reputation throughout the industry. More and more technicians and businessmen were acknowledging the quality of the Cummins engine. Typical of this trend was a report from R. A. Millholland's brother, who surveyed diesel developments during a cross-country trip in 1928 and reported back that Cummins Engine's technology was "far ahead of the procession."[150]

Clessie also was gaining recognition in the field. When the Society of Automotive Engineers devoted a 1927 session to diesel developments, Clessie was among the small handful of featured speakers. The following year, General Motors, which was rapidly overtaking Ford as the world's preeminent automaker, showed an interest in Cummins' products as it contemplated a move into the diesel field. Clessie got an inkling of this effort, but never learned the full scope of GM's interest in Cummins Engine.

The General Motors Research Laboratories launched a diesel research program in 1928. In March the lab purchased a Cummins Model U, mounted it on a dynamometer, and began months of intensive testing. Cummins Engine was apprised of some of this work, and Clessie was invited to the facility in July, where he saw the Model U being tested alongside Cadillac and Buick models. He was pleased to discover that GM executive William S. Knudsen (no relation to Hans) knew of the Cummins test. "I told Mr. Knudsen that he might see one of our little engines running in the laboratory if he cared to," Clessie reported to Irwin, "and he said that he already had seen it, and smiled—so I guess the information is spreading around up there pretty well."[151]

GM's interest in Cummins ran much deeper, however—despite the fact that the lab's technicians were reporting problems with the Model U and GM's head of research, Charles F. Kettering, remained skeptical about the practicability of using diesels in the automotive field. In September, Kettering concluded that Cummins led the group of eight producers of smaller, high-speed engines that GM had investigated. "The Cummins Engine Company of Columbus, Indiana," he wrote to a GM vice president in September 1928, "have a slightly different type of injection which I think has greater possibilities than any of the rest." Accordingly, Kettering targeted Cummins for acquisition as part of his plan to bring GM into the diesel field. The first step, he explained to General Motors president Alfred P. Sloan, should be "to purchase or make some arrangements with the Cummins Engine Company . . . , [which] is now making what we consider the best small Diesel engine on the market."[152]

Clessie apparently never got wind of this scheme, which for unknown reasons was not pursued. It is likely he would have been interested. As the company's reputation spread, other suitors emerged in the early 1930s, and Clessie proved eager to negotiate. For in spite of the upswing in business in the late 1920s, Clessie was becoming increasingly frustrated by the company's probationary condition. Success bred in him a desire for much more success. Clessie wanted to join the big leagues.

Dark days

The overheated prosperity of the Roaring Twenties eluded both the Cummins Engine Company and Clessie Cummins himself. Despite Clessie's intense efforts to develop a new technology and create a successful enterprise in a new industry, he found himself at the helm of an unprofitable business that was still searching for a clear mission. And in spite of his hopes of growing rich on royalties and dividends, he supported his growing family on a comfortable but far from extravagant salary. For his part, W. G. Irwin—though hardly a speculator—must have contemplated paths not taken in the expansionary postwar economy. Since the beginning of the prosperous 1920s, he had sunk $650,000 into Cummins Engine without realizing a penny of profit.

And so, a decade into the struggle, Clessie Cummins and W. G. Irwin grew weary. At different moments, each man attempted to exit from, or even shut down, the business. The banker's patience and the inventor's optimism were reaching their limits. In the end, the company's survival depended on luck and timing as much as anything else.

On February 26, 1929—six days after the Cummins Engine Company's ten-year anniversary—Clessie typed a resignation letter to W. G. It was not his first, nor would it be his last. But it revealed much about Clessie's hopes and frustrations, his changing relations with his patron, and the state of the business.

In the first part of the letter, the company president sounded much like a frustrated middle manager. He complained of being second-guessed about "trivial" business decisions (such as the hiring of workers), and of the "awful handicap" of needing to wait "sometimes for days" to consult with Irwin about routine matters. These concerns were "of such minor importance as to be ridiculous," Clessie admitted. But to him they suggested something larger: Irwin's lack of confidence in his ability to handle "the many complicated and complex matters that develop from hour to hour."

Clessie went on to reveal the deeper wellspring of his dissatisfaction. "I have worked hard, put in long hours and have enjoyed most of it," he wrote. "My salary is about what I could make in a good machine shop with no responsibility and with the knowledge that when the whistle blew, I would be free until another day." His financial motivation had come from the promise of royalties and license fees paid to the OEDC. But Clessie felt stymied in his attempts to garner outside licenses. He wanted Irwin to pursue the matter more aggressively. One promising lead evaporated, he said, because Irwin canceled a New York meeting. "You can afford to wait" for these opportunities, Clessie told the affluent banker, but "[I cannot] pass up these opportunities to make a few much needed dollars."[153]

Irwin's response is unknown. Still, Clessie's perceptions were not without foundation. Within the constraints of his busy schedule, the banker took a strong hand in the management of the company. After all, he was a capable manager, and had more than a minor financial interest in the firm. Moreover, Clessie was away much of the time, and he and Irwin had not appointed a manager to serve in his absence.

As for licensing, Clessie indeed seems to have pursued the strategy more aggressively than Irwin. In 1926, when asked by a manufacturer to license head and valve devices, W. G. was circumspect. "This is a question to us that has many angles," he replied. "We have been giving this considerable thought but we feel that we are scarcely in a position to reach a satisfactory conclusion" in the near future. In contrast, Clessie wrote the same year: "I believe that by all means, we should do everything in our power to make these license connections as quickly as possible."[154]

His enthusiasm for licensing grew in mid-1927, after he met with the company's patent attorney, who was "very insistent that we are making a mistake if we do not grant one or two license[s] at least." Licensing would strengthen the company's position in the event of patent litigation, he told Irwin. With more capital involved, "the courts would not be inclined to tear up industry unless it was a pretty clear case of infringement." Moreover, even in the event of a successful patent challenge, "royalties are not subject to assessment for damages." Clessie held a letter of interest from the Mack Truck Company and was eager to approach Fairbanks-Morse as well.[155]

Clessie's interest in licensing, of course, extended beyond his concern for the company's legal standing. Because of his personal financial condition, the lack of royalties and license fees from Cummins Engine and the OEDC had dramatically different consequences for him than for Irwin. For that reason, his greater urgency about the matter is hardly surprising.

Clessie did not resign in early 1929, but he continued to grapple with his demons. His short-term financial needs pulled against his long-term commitment to the business. In a heartfelt letter he penned to Irwin in August, he asked for financial relief and expressed his ambivalence about staying the course. Irwin's recent caution against "being discouraged at the wrong time has kept me in a quandary," he said. "I am blowing hot one day and cold the next. I am trying to find out in my own mind if I am allowing my own personal needs of the moment to warp my judgement or whether I am up against a real for sure wall. I don't feel that I have a yellow streak or that I am a quitter but self preservation is a strong instinct and hard to dismiss."

With more bills coming in and the business unlikely to "give me relief for a long time to come," Clessie now asked for royalties due from the engine company. According to his calculations, these amounted to $33,141 from 1925–1927 and $13,146 from 1928, with nearly twice as much expected in the current year.[156] Indeed, Cummins was well on its way to another banner year. Sales for the first half of 1929 far outpaced the same period in the previous year. By this time, however, the engine company's cumulative loss exceeded $400,000. Irwin decided that Cummins still would pay no royalties to the OEDC.

Even so, Clessie must have reveled in the excitement and attention that came to the company in October. In the middle of the month, the company finally shipped the seven-ton locomotive engine to the Pennsylvania Railroad's Altoona works. Then, on the 24th, nearly two dozen railroad executives from the B&O, Pennsylvania, Baldwin Locomotive Works, American Locomotive, Union Pacific, and key firms toured the Cummins Engine plant.[157]

Five days later the hammer fell. Black Tuesday—October 29, 1929—saw the largest single-day drop in Wall Street history (although the market's decline actually began in early September). By the time the downward spiral ended in March of 1933, more than 80 percent of the value of NYSE stocks had been wiped out, and U.S. per capita income was cut in half.

More immediately, the depression hobbled Cummins Engine's present and prospective markets. Railroads, automaking, and other capital-intensive industries were especially hard hit. The Great Depression stifled railroad dieselization so severely that American industry produced fewer than 200 units per year before 1939. And if this was not enough to dash Cummins' hopes, the sympathetic Wallis died of a heart attack in November 1930, and Cummins never again found an executive at the Pennsylvania—or any other railroad—who was as interested in its products.[158]

Nor did the market for construction equipment and other durable goods fare well. The deflationary years that followed in the wake of the Great Crash were hardly a time to purchase such items. Expensive consumer goods, like automobiles, radios, washers, and especially yachts, also suffered. On every front, Cummins sales evaporated.

After waiting a decent interval, W. G. Irwin summoned Clessie Cummins to his office on December 15th to deliver the grim news. With the yacht market finished, Cummins Engine stood virtually no chance of success. It was time to cut their losses and liquidate the firm.

A Special Packard

Clessie's 1967 autobiography, *My Days with the Diesel*, hinges on a dramatic moment of inspiration. "As I sat alone in the gloom of my tiny office" the day after Irwin pronounced the death sentence on the company, he wrote, "I picked up the latest issue of a trade magazine." There he found yet another article about the diesel industry that failed to mention Cummins. Then "an amazing idea flashed before me." Clessie picked up the phone, called H. L. Knudsen, and told him to bring a U Engine down to the office. When the engineer asked why, Clessie responded, "We're going to Indianapolis to find an automobile that will take a Model U engine." Thus began a chain of events that ultimately drew Cummins Engine into the automotive market, saved the company, and charted a successful course for the future.

The fundamentals of the story are true. Clessie came up with the idea of installing a Cummins engine in an automobile. A used Packard was purchased for the experiment. The car ran, convincing Irwin to delay his liquidation plans. And Cummins eventually gained a foothold by serving the automotive market. However, many aspects of Clessie's account are apocryphal, apparently fashioned by him (or his ghostwriter) for dramatic purposes. Like many heroic accounts of invention, Clessie's book tells of a sudden "flash" of inspiration that transformed everything in its wake. The reality is more complicated and, in many ways, more interesting.

We cannot be sure precisely when the idea of automotive diesel power first crossed Clessie's mind. It is possible, although unlikely, that he read of Rudolf Diesel's notions about automotive diesels in the 1890s when he first began to study oil engines in 1913. Or perhaps it was in the spring of 1919, when the first Cummins engine made the paper, and Clessie prompted the local reporter—hardly an authority on oil engines—to conclude: "Should this type of engine prove successful it will be only a step further to produce it in multi-cylinder form and adapt it to the automobile and aeroplane."[159] Then there was Clessie's life-long interest in automobiles, and his propensity to combine vehicles and engines in unconventional ways (as in his automobile railcar and propeller-driven bobsled). The idea of installing a diesel in an automobile did not require a wild leap of imagination, especially for the likes of Clessie Cummins.

The mid-1920s were a fertile period for automotive diesel development. In 1923 M.A.N. and Benz became the first to successfully test diesel trucks, which they exhibited at the Berlin automobile show the following year. Also in 1924, Dorner Ölmotoren A.G. of Hanover, Germany, experimented with a diesel engine passenger car. Related experiments soon followed in Germany, France, Switzerland, Austria, and the United States.[160]

Perhaps inspired by news of these developments, Clessie devised a plan in the winter of 1924 to mount a special engine in an automobile and drive it to New York as a publicity stunt. He spoke of this scheme in a Columbus Rotary Club speech the following year. "Drawings of the engine were made and some of the other work done," reported the *Evening Republican*, "but the press of other things made it impossible for him to complete the project." Even so, Clessie remained enthusiastic about the potential efficiency of such a car.[161] In September 1925, two months before his Rotary speech, Clessie had met a "hard boiled German engineer" who also edited a diesel trade journal and had spent most of his life "trying to develop a small diesel engine that would be fit for automotive and kindred use." The German boosted Clessie's pride—and probably his interest in the automotive market—by raving about the Cummins engine.[162]

Automotive power therefore was one of several promising diesel markets that Clessie explored in the 1920s. At that time, his work did not progress to the prototype stage, most likely because other markets that he pursued—construction equipment, marine power, small-scale electrical generation, locomotives—were generating orders. Now that those businesses were languishing, Clessie returned to the automotive idea.

So Clessie and Knudsen headed for Indianapolis. They quickly found what they were looking for: a used 1925 seven-passenger Packard limousine. With a straight eight-cylinder engine, the limo featured the kind of huge engine compartment Clessie needed for his special installation. He paid $600 for the car, sent Knudsen ahead, and pointed the Packard toward Columbus.

It was night when he rolled into town. He stowed the vehicle in a steel shed, once used by Emerson-Brantingham to store oil, behind the Cummins plant. The project was to be kept secret until its completion. Only his brother Don and two other mechanics were told of the plan.

The crew went to work early the next morning. "All hell broke loose," recalled Don Cummins. Clessie was impatient for the diesel-powered car, but the work of converting the limousine to diesel occupied the crew around the clock for two days. The crew ordered Cummins machinists to fabricate special parts, while providing no explanations. Knudsen customized a flywheel to match the diesel engine with the car's transmission. The gear ratio on the limousine's transmission was adjusted to handle the diesel's lower rpm.

Once the gasoline engine was removed, the Model U would not fit in its place—blocked as it was by the Packard's steering apparatus. Breaking the tension, Don Cummins deadpanned that the steering gear could be removed, and that this solution would present no problems as long as the car was always driven in a straight line. Finally, the crew hoisted up the huge automobile and lowered it down over the engine. Only the radiator fan had to be removed to accommodate the diesel.

It was the early morning of Christmas 1929. Snow covered the streets of downtown Columbus as Clessie pulled out of the shed. The Irwin mansion was his ultimate destination (although he may have picked up his children along the way). The car ran smoothly. But Clessie found Irwin in no mood for a holiday joyride, especially in a newly purchased car. As W. G. grumbled about the extravagance, Clessie revealed his secret to Linnie and Nettie Sweeney, who cajoled the banker into joining them for a quick ride.

A few miles out of town the Packard began to overheat. (The problem was not the missing fan, but rather the diesel engine's high water outlet, which created an air pocket in the cooling system.) Clessie stood beside the car with the hood open to cool the engine. Eventually W. G. grew impatient and climbed out of the car. It was then that he discovered the Packard's unusual power source.

Irwin's spirits lifted as he mulled over the market possibilities of the Cummins automotive diesel. The gambit had worked, Clessie later wrote, because it "rejuvenated" Irwin's enthusiasm for Cummins Engine and put an end to his plans for liquidation.

Ironically, the same could not be said of Clessie. Although, in early 1930, he followed through with his six-year-old plan to stage an automotive diesel publicity stunt (described in the next chapter), Clessie continued to entertain the notion of selling the business. In this roller-coaster phase of the company's history, the two men switched roles. Irwin now assumed the part of the company cheerleader.

One day in early April 1930, for instance, Clessie discussed the sale of the company while demonstrating the diesel Packard in South Bend, Indiana. In the morning he took several engineers from Bendix for a demonstration ride. Late in the day he was joined by H. B. Vance, a vice president at Studebaker. The two men got along well. "He gets down to brass tacks quickly," Clessie noted. Even so, when Clessie spent the evening at Vance's home, the conversation drifted to classical music and other pleasantries, never to business.

That came, in spades, the following morning. If a "mysterious someone" were to ask Cummins Engine to name a selling price, Vance inquired elliptically, what would it be? Clessie said he doubted the possibility of an outright sale. To this Vance replied that "every man had his price." Clessie said that about $1.5 million was invested in the business. Reasonable enough, Vance responded. Encouraged, Clessie added that there was, of course, the matter of profits—perhaps another $500,000. When the car maker still didn't flinch, Clessie plunged ahead with more conditions: a percentage of profits out of future earnings for existing Cummins shareholders; further development of marine and industrial engines; assurances that the firm would remain in Columbus. Again and again, Vance concurred.

"I like Mr. Vance very much," Clessie wrote to Irwin, when reporting the encounter. It was time to arrange a meeting.

Perhaps Clessie was dazzled by this talk of big money. Yet he readily acknowledged the provisional nature of the figures. Moreover, his summary remarks to Irwin reveal his open attitude about this—and similar—propositions: "In general, it seems to me that some such plan . . . should accomplish everything desired"—a "handsome profit," the development of local industry, and a chance of future earnings from the business. "It may be that a better set-up can be worked out, but I sincerely hope that something will come to a head in the near future, while our popularity is at its peak and before too many other developments are dumped into the picture."[163]

Irwin's response is also illuminating. He promptly sent a letter of inquiry about Vance to an associate at Studebaker. What does he do "outside of the factory?" asked the banker. "Does he take any particular interest in church affairs; if so, with what church? Is he interested in the affairs of the town and does he try to make himself a part of the community?"[164] The answer was not what Irwin wanted to hear. Vance was "the keenest analyst I ever knew," Irwin's friend replied, but he "does not take any particular interest in church affairs" and contributes to his community financially but not "by personal service."[165]

W. G. eventually met with Studebaker's president, A. R. Erskine, to discuss a possible merger, but the negotiations ended quickly. For W. G., community service and religious conviction were not merely abstractions. Unless Cummins remained a local enterprise whose leaders embodied these values, then he would not do business.[166]

Still another opportunity to sell the company arose in the summer of 1930. On this occasion, C. Russell Feldmann put together a plan to sell Cummins Engine and the Winton Engine Company of Cleveland (on which Feldmann held an option) to General Motors. Once again, Clessie was eager to "find surcease from the long battle," but Irwin was uninterested.[167]

In spite of occasional rifts, W. G. Irwin and Clessie Cummins continued to function as a remarkably complementary team. In the dark days of 1929, they also demonstrated an uncanny sense of timing. John Niven, who became involved in the Cummins Engine Company's affairs during this period, said it best: "The saving fact was that W. G. and Clessie never weakened at the same time."[168]

For most new companies, the first years of existence are difficult. But at the Cummins Engine Company, they were especially tumultuous. The company's original technology proved to be unworkable. Its first large contract led only to acrimony and a huge financial loss. On several occasions, the company was compelled to reorient itself toward new markets. Losses were heaped upon losses. More than once, Cummins Engine skirted the edge of disaster.

Even so, the company made significant gains and learned important lessons in the 1920s. Although Cummins quickly joined the ranks of disillusioned diesel technology licensees, Clessie Cummins, Hans Knudsen, and other technicians made key innovations that moved the firm beyond its original, flawed technology.

On the marketing side, the company struggled to overcome its technology's novelty and poor reputation. In answer to the central issue of the decade—*which market?*—Cummins explored several possible directions: stationary power, construction equipment, marine power, government ships and lighthouses, locomotives, and automobiles.

To exploit these markets, the corporation needed to grow. Remaining in the diesel engine business required not only more technical and sales expertise than anyone at Cummins anticipated, but also considerably more capital for facilities and equipment than most investors were willing to risk. On this front, W. G. Irwin provided the necessary support, financing critical reorganizations and expansions.

The company's key assets—the technical and promotional ingenuity of Clessie Cummins and the financial support of W. G. Irwin—carried it through this tumultuous first decade in business. But ten years of losses and disappointments had taken their toll. Both men began to waver in their commitment to the business. Despite an interesting experiment with automotive power, Cummins Engine's options now seemed limited, its future as uncertain as ever, as the nation descended into severe economic depression.

3 | Gaining a Foothold, 1930–1939

WHEN THE GREAT DEPRESSION STRUCK America in 1930, Cummins still had not earned a profit. It continued to hemorrhage red ink throughout the protracted slump. Like a burgeoning number of firms, Cummins was a prime candidate for bankruptcy. The company's notable failure to license its proprietary technology in the early 1930s worsened its already grim prospects.

Yet the early Depression was an unusually creative, even pivotal, period for the Columbus-based diesel maker. As most firms retrenched in the face of the economic disaster, and thousands actually failed, Cummins built a national reputation for itself. The main reason was Clessie Cummins, who emerged not only as an intuitive genius at engine and component design, but also as a brilliant promoter, able to convince both industry experts and auto buffs that the automotive diesel was a practical option.

Cummins also assembled its first professional management team. John Niven and J. Irwin Miller, the company's first general managers; V. E. McMullen, the new production manager; and Paris Letsinger, the second head of marketing—all coordinated the company's key functions and defined them in enduring ways. Without their intervention, the company would have been rudderless in W. G. Irwin's and Clessie's frequent absences and unable to deliver on Clessie's optimistic promises to the public.

At the same time, the company made its first real headway in developing a reliable, popular product early in the decade. The H engine was a remarkably durable and resilient workhorse. Although far from perfect, it lent itself to endless improvements. J. Irwin Miller later concluded that Clessie Cummins may have oversold the company's products through his "Barnum and Bailey stunts." But throughout the decade, with the H engine and other technical improvements, Cummins began to close the gap between promise and reality.

The paramount change at Cummins in the early years of the Great Depression was its decision—in spite of a sustained dalliance with locomotive making—to focus on the automotive market. The decision was, quite literally, a defining moment. It set a clear goal toward which the company could direct its efforts in research, manufacturing, and marketing. More than that, the mission defined Cummins more clearly in the eyes of the outside world by focusing on automotive sales. It was a key strategic gambit. In the early 1930s, the automotive market was unexplored territory for the American diesel industry. Cummins was at the head of the expeditionary party. More and more of its fuel-efficient diesel engines—once confined mainly to ships, tractors, railroad switch cars, and power plants—now found their way into streamlined locomotives, trucks, and buses.

Because Cummins pioneered in opening the automotive diesel market in the early years of the Great Depression, its fortunes were improving when a second downturn hit in 1937. The company earned its first profit in 1937, and remained profitable for decades thereafter. Cummins escaped bankruptcy in the early 1930s only because W. G. Irwin stood firm as its financial backer. (By the end of the decade, the company owed the family almost $2 million in loan principal and interest.) But without the progress of the early decade—in research, manufacturing, and marketing—Cummins could not have held its financial footing when the second downturn struck.

Cummins and the automotive market

After the diesel-powered Packard's inaugural run in late 1929, Clessie Cummins made, in his words, a fateful "spur of the moment" decision. The National Automobile Show, a major annual event, was scheduled to open in New York City on January 6, 1930. Why not drive the Packard east to exhibit it in the show? In fact, there were several good reasons *not* to attempt such a stunt, not the least of which was the fact that the modified vehicle had logged a grand total of ten miles with its new power plant. But after a day or two of deliberations with W. G. Irwin, Clessie decided to plunge ahead.[1]

This adventure opened an important chapter both in Clessie's life and in the history of the Engine Company. For the next several years, Clessie spent much of his time on the road promoting automotive diesels. "We ran a three ring circus," he later noted, "with racing, transcontinental runs, endurance tests, bus and truck records, and what not." It was a time filled with color, excitement, danger, near-calamity, and triumph—an interlude that Clessie later aptly dubbed his "Barnum and Bailey days."[2]

Clessie's escapades on the road were not simply publicity stunts, however. They served important ends. First, they demonstrated the durability and reliability of the company's products. This was critical, given the diesel engine's dubious reputation in America. Second, they elevated the Engine Company's reputation from the local to the national level. This achievement was all the more remarkable—and significant to the struggling company—because it was done on a tiny budget. Finally, and most important, Clessie's promotions introduced the public to the notion that diesel engines were suitable for automotive power, a concept that was still novel in the United States. Taken together, these accomplishments built a strong three-way association: among diesels, Cummins Engine Company, and automotive vehicles. It was an association on which the company would build its future.

This success could not have been achieved without reliable products. Marketing and manufacturing complemented each other at Cummins. The company's growing reputation boosted sales, which encouraged new product developments, and in turn permitted still more impressive demonstrations. As a result of this self-reinforcing dynamic, Cummins Engine emerged solidly committed to the automotive market.

It is easy to conclude in retrospect that the rise of the diesel-powered vehicle was inevitable in the early 1930s. The Great Depression was placing a premium on economy of operation in transportation. Railroads were losing business to more versatile forms of ground transportation, especially trucks. Following the great strides made by the gasoline-powered vehicle in the 1920s, the time seemed ripe for the more efficient diesel to make its mark. This is all true, as far as it goes. But it is also true that most market innovations appear obvious in hindsight, and that every entrepreneurial opportunity needs human initiative to become a reality. Clessie Cummins played that critical role, and emerged as the preeminent spokesman for the automotive diesel in America.

The "Barnum and Bailey days" were Clessie's finest hour. He not only performed a needed function at a propitious time in history—he excelled at the task. His charisma and unflagging enthusiasm won over members of the press, industry experts, and automotive buffs alike. At the same time, his long-standing ability to solve mechanical problems and improvise in tight situations enabled him to avert disasters both on the road and on the racetrack.

He had another asset as well. Clessie and the American automotive industry had grown up together. Clessie had learned much about the art of automotive promotion from this eventful history.

Automobile pioneers invented more than self-propelled machines. They also found new ways to promote their strange contraptions. In the mid-1890s, Americans began to experiment with the kinds of "horseless carriages" that had been invented a few years earlier in Europe. Concurrently, auto enthusiasts on both sides of the Atlantic developed three highly effective ways of introducing the new technology to the public: automobile races, endurance runs, and auto shows.

In these formative years, there was no clear distinction between races and endurance runs. Automobiles were so unreliable, and road and track conditions so harsh, that high speed was not the main qualification for victory. The objective was, instead, to complete an entire race at a reasonable speed. Winners of track and cross-country races often reaped enormous benefits from their successes, in the form of increased sales and readier access to investment capital. These events also did much to foster the spread of automobility in general.

At the Paris-Bordeaux-Paris race of July 11, 1895, sponsored by the newly formed Automobile Club of France, only nine of the twenty-two starters completed the race. But those who finished helped establish both France's preeminence in the field and the superiority of the internal combustion engine over the steam engine. When word of the event spread to the United States, automobile-related inventions flooded into the Patent Office, and similar races were arranged. In 1895, only two cars finished the grueling *Chicago Times-Herald* Thanksgiving Day race, with the winner averaging just eight miles per hour. Even so, notes a leading automotive historian, the event "gave substantial impetus to automotive activity in the United States."[3]

No episode better illustrates the promotional value of endurance runs than the exploits of another engine maker, Alexander Winton of Cleveland.* After his first Cleveland–New York demonstration run in 1897 boosted sales for the company, Winton made plans to repeat the event two years later. This time, however, he arranged to bring along journalist Charles B. Shanks. Thanks largely to Shanks' reportage, an estimated *one million* spectators gathered along the route! James R. Doolittle, in his pioneering history of the auto industry, described this 1899 run as "the first real effort at intelligent publicity" and credited it with helping automobile sales spread from engineers to "the general public." Endurance races soon became a staple of the business. In 1903 there were three transcontinental runs, and between 1905 and 1913, Boston millionaire Charles Glidden regularly sponsored automobile "reliability tours."[4]

Track racing also was born in the mid-1890s, beginning with a Narragansett, Rhode Island, contest on September 7, 1896. While many auto enthusiasts viewed these events as useless and risky exhibitions of freakish technologies, races served to build the reputations and fortunes of upstart manufacturers. Henry Ford languished in the automobile business until he scored a dramatic upset against Winton in a 1901 race at Grosse Pointe, Michigan. (So confident was Winton in his more powerful machine—and so influential was he in the racing field—that he made sure a trophy was select-

*According to C. Lyle Cummins, his father Clessie and Alexander Winton were close friends. Cummins engines frequently were sold as auxiliaries on Winton-powered yachts.

ed that would complement the decor in his home.) The victory earned the upstart Ford a national reputation that enabled him to attract new financial backers and launch the Ford Motor Company in 1903.[5]

Automobile shows also came to America in 1896, when Charles Duryea's models were exhibited in circuses, and a Daimler was displayed at Madison Square Garden. By the turn of the century, exhibitions devoted solely to automobiles were being sponsored by new organizations such as the Automobile Club of America and the National Association of Automobile Manufacturers. Originally designed to sell cars, the shows soon evolved into venues for previewing new models.[6]

Clessie Cummins and the Art of Promotion

In planning his trip to the National Automobile Show, Clessie Cummins hoped to generate a good share of publicity for his company, its products, and the idea of the automotive diesel. Accordingly, he decided to combine two popular forms of automobile promotion—the show itself, and also the long drive to New York as a demonstration of economy and endurance. Taking a page from the book of Winton and other automotive pioneers, Clessie sought out journalists to accompany him on the expedition.

Clessie was aided in these efforts by W. G. Irwin. With his enthusiasm for the automotive diesel then running high, the banker contacted his friend Kent Cooper, a Columbus native who worked as general manager of the Associated Press (AP) in New York. Irwin asked Cooper to encourage his Indianapolis and New York associates to cover the story. Cooper's feature editor agreed, and contacted the AP's Indianapolis Bureau. Thus, when Clessie and his wife drove the diesel Packard to Indianapolis, they met with William F. (Bill) Sturm, a veteran journalist who specialized in automotive racing, and also with Claude Wolfe of the AP. Unlike Sturm, Wolfe was skeptical about Clessie's chances for success, but he nevertheless agreed to accompany Clessie on the first leg of the promotional trip.[7]

The run began on Saturday, January 4, 1930. Officials of the Hoosier Motor Club sealed twenty-two gallons of fuel oil in the Packard's tank and marked the official departure time: 10:00 a.m. Although Clessie had done little to prepare the experimental vehicle for the 800-mile trip, he nonetheless boasted to reporters that he would make the trip in just over two days (arriving in Manhattan by 4:00 p.m. Monday) without refilling the tank. Two escort cars accompanied the Packard as far as Greenfield, where Stella Cummins and Claude Wolfe turned back and Hans Knudsen joined Clessie and Sturm in the Packard. Soon, reports sent out by Wolfe (and later Sturm, who went ahead to New York from Zanesville) began to generate advance publicity—and welcoming crowds—along the route.[8]

For the first day, at least, the trip went smoothly. But on Sunday, conditions deteriorated rapidly. While crossing the Allegheny Mountains on Route 22 out of Pittsburgh, the men encountered frigid temperatures. Pushing forward, shivering in their unheated car, Clessie and Knudsen steered toward Harrisburg. Upon arrival, they stowed the mud-caked limousine for the evening. In the middle of the night, however, they were roused by a panicked knock on the door: the Packard was on fire! An electrical short had sparked a fire in the engine compartment. The damage seemed minimal, but once under way on Monday, Clessie and Knudsen discovered that the car's generator circuit had been rendered inoperative. Now, if the engine stalled—as it threatened to do whenever Clessie let the engine speed drop near idle—the men would be stranded, the promotional stunt thwarted. Moreover, the huge car was consuming more fuel than Clessie predicted. The twenty-two gallons he thought would get the car to New York were gone after 640 miles.[9]

The final miles—through the Holland Tunnel into Manhattan at rush hour—were the most suspenseful, as the huge vehicle lumbered toward its destination through dense traffic. Remarkably, Clessie and Knudsen rolled up to the Roosevelt Hotel at 4:45 p.m., less than a hour beyond Clessie's optimistic deadline—at which point the limousine promptly stalled.[10]

On the first long-distance automotive diesel run in American history, Clessie's Packard had traversed 792 miles on thirty gallons of fuel. This was a few gallons more than anticipated but—at an average of thirty-five miles per gallon—much more economical than even small cars of the day. Clessie had bought fuel at wholesale, which brought the total fuel bill for the trip down to a minuscule $1.38. Yet even at retail diesel fuel prices, the trip would have cost a mere $3, far below the $24.75 worth of gasoline needed to cover the same distance in a comparable vehicle. The savings resulted both from the lower cost of the fuel (compared with gasoline) and the diesel's greater efficiency per gallon.[11]

This exceptional fuel economy captured the attention of auto enthusiasts in New York and elsewhere in the Depression-weary nation. A phalanx of reporters, tipped off by Sturm, crammed into Clessie's hotel room, firing questions about the diesel trip. After this session, Knudsen and Clessie were escorted to a dinner hosted by the Indianapolis Motor Speedway and attended by some 120 automotive journalists. The Speedway's new owner, World War I flying ace and auto racing legend Edward V. "Eddie" Rickenbacker, told the audience of his friend Clessie's achievement. The exhausted promoter dozed in his seat as Rickenbacker introduced him, but the positive response to the grueling stunt inspired Clessie to look for new public relations opportunities.[12]

In the meantime, the sponsors of the Automobile Show were less than pleased with Clessie's unscheduled publicity-grabbing debut, and barred him from exhibiting the Packard in or near its exhibition space in the Grand

Central Palace. Even so, scores of spectators crowded around the special car for a look. The gawkers included industry notables. Walter P. Chrysler was among them, but his aides prevented the automotive mogul from being photographed alongside Cummins.[13]

When the show ended, the two Hoosiers drove the limousine on to Philadelphia and Baltimore, where they showed it to railroad officials, and then to the National Road Show at nearby Atlantic City.[14] There, again, the diesel car was denied access to the exhibition hall. This time, however, Clessie rented space in a nearby storefront, where he displayed the experimental Packard to crowds of curious onlookers for a week.[15]

Following a circuitous route back to Columbus, Clessie and Knudsen steered their publicity tour through several major cities. In Pittsburgh, as the diesel sat for three days with its hood open, the engine was blanketed during a snowstorm. When Clessie prepared to depart for Detroit—where the Society of Automotive Engineers was to hold its annual convention—three men approached the car, stated they worked for an automobile manufacturer that would remain unnamed, and challenged Clessie to start the Packard. Diesels had a well-deserved reputation as poor cold-weather starters, but the Model U fired easily. Clessie made sure this episode played prominently in the press.[16]

Already exhilarated by his growing celebrity, Clessie reached new heights in the Motor City. There, he met with the automobile industry's reigning sovereign, Henry Ford. (Clessie claimed to have been invited by Ford. His hometown newspaper asserted that the meeting "was a case of Mr. Cummins being introduced to high officials, then higher officials," until Ford himself was called to inspect the car.)[17] Clessie saw parallels between Henry Ford's origins and his own: two country boys enamored of cars and engines. But Cummins did not see himself as the future Henry Ford of diesel automobiles. Rather— as he explained to Ford during a test drive in the Packard—Clessie saw the diesel's future in trucks and tractors. Ford disagreed, arguing that the most promising diesel market was aeronautics. Still, the two men hit it off well, and the meeting left an indelible impression on Clessie, in part because of Ford's harsh treatment of his son, Edsel.[18]

Severe winter conditions and mechanical problems continued to bedevil Clessie on the last leg of the trip (from Detroit to Columbus). On several occasions, as moisture began to freeze in the car's fuel line, he pulled over and built a fire under the fuel tank—a risky solution, under the best of circumstances! But he reached home in one piece on January 25. Columbus celebrated the historic trip of its automotive hero with several days of festivities.[19]

Despite the many mechanical mishaps—none of which was related to the engine itself—the diesel Packard had performed remarkably well. In just under a month it had traversed 2,780 miles, many of them along unpaved roads, over mountains, through ice and snow. Just as important, Clessie, Irwin, Sturm,

Rickenbacker, and others ensured that the historic trip received plenty of notice. It was chronicled by reporters in magazines and newspapers, by Clessie in automotive industry journals, and by Sturm in the prestigious *Scientific American*.[20]

In the wake of this trip, Sturm learned of another opportunity for publicity. In late March, British race-car driver Kaye Don would attempt to drive his twenty-four cylinder "Silver Bullet" to a new land speed record on the hard sands of Daytona Beach, Florida. Official timekeepers from the American Automobile Association would be there, along with a sizable corps of reporters. If Clessie showed up in a diesel race car, Sturm reasoned, he would garner free publicity and perhaps even chalk up the first official speed record for a diesel-powered vehicle.[21]

The idea appealed to Clessie, who promptly predicted that he could set a record of 80–85 mph. For this, he would need a lighter car, albeit one with an ample engine compartment. Clessie bought a Packard roadster (which featured a chassis somewhat lighter than the limousine's), removed its fenders, modified its gear ratio, and installed the marine diesel, now stepped up to 84 hp. Clessie and his crew (Don Cummins, Jay Chambers, and a blind engineer from piston-ring manufacturer Perfect Circle named Ralph Teetor) then drove the experimental race car 1,060 miles to Daytona Beach on less than $2 worth of fuel. (Clessie documented the trip using his recently purchased Bell and Howell 16 mm camera.)[22]

Kaye Don was slated to make his run on March 20, but when the day arrived, the "Silver Bullet" was laid up with mechanical troubles. With spectators and the press eager for action, Clessie was invited to fill the breach. After several runs up and down the beach's measured mile, he clocked a top run at 80.398 mph. Running at around 1,800 rpm—double the norm for standard diesels—the roadster's engine confirmed Clessie's thinking about high-speed diesel performance. The story was picked up by the NEA wire service and fed to hundreds of newspapers across the country.[23]

A year later, Clessie returned to Daytona Beach under similar circumstances: British race champion Sir Malcolm Campbell was seeking a new speed record. This time, Clessie aspired to break the 100 mph barrier with a diesel race car. To help him achieve this ambitious feat, Cummins Engine invested approximately $10,000 (including special equipment) to custom build its first diesel race car, dubbed "Number 8." The car's body was fashioned by Fred Duesenberg, a friend of Clessie's and one of the leading makers of high-quality American automobiles. Its chassis was a giant Model A Duesenberg, sixteen feet long with a 116-inch wheel base, modified to handle a heavy marine diesel. Its engine was a Cummins Model U, manufactured out of strong, lightweight duralumin (an alloy of aluminum, copper, magnesium, and manganese), fully capable of producing up to 100 hp with a mere ten pounds of weight per horsepower—a ratio comparable to gasoline engines. Underscoring Number 8's novelty was its Indiana license plate number: "1,000,000."[24]

In several attempts on Friday, February 6, 1931, Clessie missed the 100 mph mark by as little as 2 mph. The following day, he relentlessly barreled down the beach in run after mile run, bucking along the small ridges of hard-packed sand while anxious officials signaled for him to stop. When he finally rolled to a halt, the obstinate inventor learned that he had beaten the 100 mph mark—by 0.775 of a mile per hour! Now, even the most die-hard skeptics of the diesel could not fairly characterize it as sluggish or unversatile. The achievement earned Clessie another round of national publicity; *Business Week*, for example, published a photograph of Clessie flashing a post-record-setting grin at Daytona Beach.[25]

Clessie then revealed his plans to enter the Indianapolis 500 Memorial Day race. From a promotional standpoint, this choice was eminently predictable. Constructed in 1909, the Indianapolis Motor Speedway had sponsored its first Memorial Day 500-mile race two years later, and soon emerged as the leading attraction for automotive professionals and fans. Eddie Rickenbacker, who bought the track in 1927, understood not only the Speedway's role in encouraging the popularity of auto racing, but also its significance as a proving ground for nascent automotive technologies. "The real gratification in operating the Speedway," he noted in his memoirs, "came from the realization that we were enabling the automotive and allied industries to make great strides in their art." In his estimation, one Indy 500 race was equivalent to 100,000 miles of ordinary driving, or as many as fifteen years of routine testing.[26]

Clessie's Number 8 presented classification problems at the Indy 500, just as the Packard limousine had at the automobile shows. The racetrack had no rules governing diesels. Also, Number 8 was too heavy, and its engine displacement too large, to qualify under existing rules. Once again, Rickenbacker—who not only owned the track but also headed the AAA's contest board—gave his Indiana friend a helping hand, convincing the board to allow the diesel car to race as a special engineering entry. Meanwhile, Clessie assembled his crew. Agreeing with associates not to race Number 8 himself ("They have me sewed up so that I can't have any fun," Clessie told reporters), he recruited race car driver Dave Evans. Thane Houser would ride with Evans as chief mechanic, and flying ace Jimmy Doolittle would serve as flagman.[27]

A pit crew also was assembled, but with the fervent hope that it would remain unnecessary. The Cummins team did not expect Evans to outpace his thirty-two gas-driven competitors. Rather, they hoped he would make headlines of a different sort: They wanted Number 8 to become the first car in history to race the Indianapolis 500 *nonstop*.

In the months leading up to the Memorial Day race (May 30, 1931), the Cummins crew modified Number 8 to suit its nonstop mission. The 2.5-mile brick Speedway had a reputation for punishing drivers and vehicles severely, even those that enjoyed periodic respite in the pits. Accordingly, the crew beefed up the Cummins race car's steering and suspension system, added special tires, and made numerous runs on the track. They also modified Number 8's cockpit to ease the long ride for Evans and Houser by adding special instrument dials, extra padding, and other amenities. Most important, they installed an airplane-like two-pedal system (for the throttle, clutch, and brake) that shifted the position of Evans' legs away from the transmission housing, which was sure to become unbearably hot during the nonstop race.[28]

Race day was overcast. Seated behind the giant, rumbling diesel just before the starting signal, Dave Evans handed Clessie his wallet and watch. "Whatever you do, C. L.," he said, "don't let them cremate me if anything happens." Evans was not aiming for theatrical effect. Everyone associated with the Speedway culture knew the very real dangers inherent in the event; many had seen its grisly consequences. The track was bumpy and slippery from oil thrown off by the race cars, which this day blended with rain to form an even more dangerous slick. Drivers wore leather helmets, which afforded little protection. Fatal crashes—which often picked off unfortunate spectators behind the track's weak retaining walls—were fairly common.[29]

Evans got off to a respectable start. But an hour or so into the race, Houser began signalling to Doolittle. The two men had arranged a system of signal codes so that Number 8 could receive assistance without stopping. Unfortunately, Doolittle found that he had misplaced his list of codes. The signalling continued, lap after lap, but the problem evidently was not serious enough to stop the racer. Evans and Houser finished the race—without stopping—in five hours, forty-eight minutes, and nine seconds. The car burned only thirty-one gallons of fuel. Just as remarkably, Number 8 averaged a speed of 86.17 mph (in spite of an hour-long rain slowdown) and finished in thirteenth place, beating nearly two-thirds of its gas-powered rivals.[30]

After the race, recalled the exhausted Evans, "several presidents of the big gasoline automobile companies came up and congratulated us. They didn't think it could be done. Well, I didn't either, at first." Even Chevrolet's president, William S. Knudsen, stopped by with a few words of congratulation. As for the signalling, Evans told the crew he had been calling for water ever since Number 8's aircraft temperature gauge had failed early in the race. In spite of this, the diesel consumed only three pints of water in the 500 miles, and never overheated. An embarrassed Doolittle later found his missing pit-crew codes—written on the inside of his belt.[31]

The nonstop run sparked another wave of publicity, and also yielded valuable technical know-how for Cummins. As the company moved ahead with plans to develop a diesel engine for trucks, it now aimed for an engine that delivered greater horsepower (about 125) at higher rpm (up to 2,200) with greater cooling capacity than its marine models. Knowing that this development work would take many months, Clessie continued to work toward keeping the automotive diesel concept—now increasingly associated with the Cummins name—in the public limelight.

The time seemed ripe for a "Barnum and Bailey" stunt targeted specifically at the trucking market. Once again, Clessie aspired to become the diesel pioneer within a well-established category of automotive competition. In this case, he planned to complete a cross-country endurance run in a diesel-powered truck.

Truck endurance runs dated back almost as far as long-distance automotive runs. The first commercial truck endurance test was sponsored by the Automobile Club of America in 1903, when fourteen entries from eleven companies competed for two days. Within a decade, truckers were completing transcontinental runs. According to *Scientific American*, a diesel-powered Reo Speedwagon operated by the Hill Diesel Engine Company (6,600 pounds gross weight) posted a 959-mile run from Lansing, Michigan, to New York City in February 1931, thereby becoming the "first American Diesel engine powered truck to make a long distance service run." General Motors had set a coast-to-coast record with a gasoline-powered truck (103 hours, 59 minutes running time). Clessie hoped to complete the first coast-to-coast diesel cargo truck run. The cargo: the Number 8 racer.[32]

The truck's body was fabricated in Indianapolis and mounted on a chassis made by the Indiana Truck Company of Marion. To accommodate the three driver-mechanics who would take shifts at the wheel—Clessie, Evans, and Ford Moyer—the truck's cargo hold was outfitted with two beds, a storage bin, and a stove. Even so, the three men had low expectations for their dining and sleeping comfort along the way, and arranged for the Continental Oil Company to supply both fuel oil and at least one hot meal per day. Plans to record and publicize the trek were made with equal care. At preassigned checkpoints, Western Union Telegraph officials would record official times and wire them to New York. Evans also arranged a Los Angeles reception to include the city's mayor and California's governor.

The truck rolled out of New York, bound for Los Angeles, in early August 1931, and the cross-country trip quickly turned adventurous. While crossing the Allegheny Mountains, the truck's brakes began to weaken. In southern Illinois, its cooling system sprang a leak, overheating the engine. The crew rigged a temporary repair (partially made of wooden shingles stolen from a shed along the road) and limped into St. Louis. Evans flew to Columbus, and soon returned with Doolittle, Jay Chambers, and a new fuel pump. Seventeen precious hours had been lost.[33]

As earlier endurance run truckers had discovered, bridges in remote locales posed a special problem. For example, a truck that completed a 3,710-mile coast-to-coast run in 1916 reportedly collapsed forty-three bridges and culverts along the way. The Cummins truck seems to have caused no such damage, but it was forced to make numerous detours because of washed-out bridges. It made at least one emergency stream fording near Amarillo, Texas.[34]

Further west, as the truck barreled across the scorching southwestern plains, the crises mounted. In one eventful day, the crew endured both a failed rocker arm and a cabin fire, which rattled nerves and burnt cabin seats, but caused no serious damage. But the real hair-raiser occurred on a harrowing downhill run, with failing brakes, through the Cajon Pass near Barstow, California. Clessie was driving as the truck gained speed on the long descent. As he later recounted, "I suddenly saw something moving across the road ahead. There was a long dark shadow, and then a red glow flared in the sky. I realized with new alarm that a freight train was cutting across our path." Racing toward a collision, Clessie frantically tried to slow the truck by downshifting. The train's caboose "cleared the highway just as we reached the tracks."

The transcontinental run, like Clessie's earlier stunts, yielded impressive performance statistics. With an average speed of only 33.02 mph, the diesel truck nevertheless completed the run in 125 hours, 52 minutes, with a running time of 97 hours, 20 minutes, beating GM's gasoline record. Replaying the story of the tortoise and the hare, the Cummins truck had triumphed through persistence. More important, fuel consumption averaged a mere 15.75 miles per gallon, or 0.1 cent per ton mile. Total fuel cost for the 3,214-mile trip: $11.22! Truck fleet owners, intensely cost-conscious even in the best of economic times, began to take notice.[35]

Once again, the stunt generated reams of publicity. Clessie and his colleagues drove on to San Francisco, where they unloaded Number 8 and drove it into the redwoods for some sightseeing (and moviemaking). In September 1931, Clessie left the truck and its celebrated cargo with Evans and Moyer, and took the train back to Columbus. There, he immediately set to work on the product that his company had been promising to the world: a high-speed diesel truck engine.[36]

Trials for the H Engine

After several months of intense developmental work, Cummins Engine released its first high-speed diesel engine designed specifically for the automotive market. The first Model H was demonstrated for the public (and more important, for members of the Irwin-Sweeney-Miller family) on November 19, 1931. "A babe was born in Columbus today," declared a local reporter who recognized the significance of the event. The six-cylinder Model H (with 4⅞-inch bore, 6-inch stroke pistons) delivered 125 hp but was smaller and lighter than comparably powered Cummins marine engines.[37]

With this new engine offering, and encouraged by a surge of interest in diesel transportation, Clessie felt that more publicity was needed to cultivate the trucking market. His next stunt combined endurance running, the Indianapolis Speedway, and the Cummins truck—powered by a new Model H engine. This time out, Clessie's goal was to set a nonstop truck mileage record. Continental boundaries would impose no limits, for the three-driver team (Clessie, Evans, and Moyer) planned to circle the Speedway track until either they, the truck, or the Cummins diesel gave out. As usual, Clessie peppered the press with predictions. With a little luck, he said, he hoped to reach the 10,000-mile mark. This distance was shorter than the 13,400-mile record set (also at the Speedway) by a Marmon-Roosevelt pleasure car, but it was much farther than any truck had ever gone without stopping.[38]

While customizing the truck to meet this challenge, the Cummins team kept in mind the Speedway's lenient rules governing nonstop runs. The vehicle had to remain in forward motion—however slowly—under its own power, and repairs could be made en route. Accordingly, the Cummins crew added handrails along the truck's front fenders and a platform on the front of the radiator; they installed special fuel and lubricating oil systems to permit in-motion refueling and oil changes; and they designed steering-system grease joints that could be hand-filled from outside the truck.

The grueling event began at 2:00 p.m. on December 12, 1931. Clessie drove from 6 a.m. to 6 p.m., while Evans and Moyer divided the night driving. After two days, with the truck completing 1,035 miles in hundreds of turns around the track, raceway officials noticed that the truck's right rear wheel was wobbling and called the run to a halt. Frustrated and determined, the Cummins team fixed the problem and started over.

Two days into the second attempt, Moyer gave out, abandoning the vehicle to escape the interminable bumping and droning. Clessie and Evans hung on, goading each other—playfully, yet seriously—toward their faraway goal. The truck proved to be weaker than the two determined men. First, the cooling system sprang a leak. Then, one night, the steering arm assembly began to disintegrate. As Evans reduced the truck's speed to a few miles per hour, Don Cummins climbed under the front of the truck with a flashlight to attempt the repair. Through dozens of laps, as an inspection car rode alongside, he completed the painstaking task. The truck never stopped.[39]

After several days of monotonous runs around the two-and-a-half-mile-long track, Clessie spotted a shiny object on the track which turned out to be one of the cap screws that held on the oil pan. Again, Don Cummins (this time working with Jay Chambers) made the repair. They rigged up ropes and a pole that allowed them to climb underneath the engine while the truck chugged along slowly. Clessie was furious with the shop that had installed the oil pan inadequately in the first place—thereby putting his brother at risk—

but the repair worked. With 7,200 miles behind them, Clessie and Evans decided to push for a new record.[40]

The truck surpassed the Marmon's 10,000-mile record without refilling its 800-gallon tanks, and pressed on. Once again, a Cummins diesel had demonstrated remarkable fuel economy. Clessie and Evans took on fuel about 500 miles later and summoned the will to push their brand-new record far beyond the old mark. Fog descended on the track, so thick at times that flares were needed to demarcate the route. The men fought on in semiconsciousness, battered by the seemingly endless jolting of the brick road surface. Two days before Christmas, Clessie and Evans told the press they were feeling "goofy" and might need to drive around the track 10,000 to 15,000 miles in the opposite direction to unwind. On Christmas Day, each man disembarked separately to spend a few hours with his family, but the truck droned on.[41]

The ordeal finally ended at 2:00 p.m. the day after Christmas, exactly two weeks and 13,535 miles after it began. After the truck rolled to a stop, the two men—sporting grizzled beards and coated with grime—stepped onto the track with wobbling legs. Despite the truck's numerous mechanical failings, the Cummins H engine had performed ceaselessly and flawlessly. It had operated continuously since the beginning of the first run, powering the vehicle around the oval track for a total of 14,600 miles (including the initial try) while averaging 43.397 mph. Clessie soon announced that the company would release a dozen or so automotive engines to be tested in different regions of the country.[42]

Carrying Hopes to Europe

Clessie was eager to carry his promotional campaign to Europe. In part, this reflected his conviction that Cummins' automotive technology already was better than what Europe had to offer. (Clessie enjoyed the irony of carrying diesel technology back to its continent of origin.) He also saw Europe, with its much higher fuel costs, as a fertile market for the diesel. Finally, there was the perennial stimulus of patent rights. Cummins Engine had applied for or secured patents on the injector and a novel "sneezer" in Japan, Australia, Canada, and more than a dozen nations in Western and Eastern Europe. But the company's patent attorneys continued to warn of the "complicated and troublesome problem" of sustaining protection across this broad geographic spectrum. As Clessie urged W. G. Irwin in the summer of 1931, "We should take immediate steps to make some manufacturing arrangements in the countries in which we have patent protection."[43]

W. G. remained reluctant to license in the United States, but he was open to the notion of selling manufacturing rights in Europe. In March 1930,

Irwin entertained the idea of taking a diesel car to Europe to "find people to take on manufacture under a royalty plan."[44] He, too, seemed anxious to protect the company's foreign patent positions, and perhaps garner some much needed revenues in the process. He evidently was not interested in taking the much more ambitious step of establishing a Cummins plant overseas. "We have not considered royalties for the United States," he wrote in late 1931, "but are working on the foreign rights which we have always felt should be handled by manufacturers in their own countries on a royalty basis."[45]

Months passed, but no definite plan took shape. Irwin began to investigate the European diesel scene, both on his 1931 vacation tour and through correspondence with associates and prospective licensees. Fiat of Italy expressed strong interest in licensing the Cummins injector. Citroën of France sent its chief engineer and his assistant to Columbus in late 1931, and these notables were favorably impressed with the Cummins technology, especially the new H engine. "I took notice of Mr. Cummins' letter giving his agreement in principle as to the license for your Diesel motors," André Citroën wrote to W. G. Irwin, who responded by stating that he hoped that the engine's "definitive perfection [will allow] us to have the happiest of technical and commercial relationships together." The French automaker ordered two Model H engines to be installed in military trucks, thereby becoming the first customer for what was destined to be Cummins' most successful product line.[46]

W. G. paid the greatest attention to England, where an associate named A. J. Yeats (who operated a London taxi service) kept the banker apprised of local diesel developments. Yeats served as a Cummins scout, visiting automobile exhibitions and testing the waters for possible licensing partnerships. At one major show, he learned that nearly all of the manufacturers used the Bosch fuel pump, and all but two had heard of Cummins. Cummins' reputation, it seemed, was spreading in Europe as well.[47]

Still, some British automakers were openly hostile to the notion of a licensing agreement with Cummins. Gardner, the oldest firm in the group, was "afraid of mass production methods flooding them out here," Yeats observed. Given the broader context, this was not surprising. Beginning with Ford in 1911, American automakers had invaded the British market with the full force of their newly developed mass-production techniques, and the local firms took several years to adapt.[48]

But others, including a leading maker of diesel trucks and buses named Thorneycroft, were eager to negotiate with Cummins. To help build this relationship, W. G. solicited help from his great-nephew, J. Irwin Miller, who recently had entered Balliol College at Oxford to study philosophy, politics, and economics. Miller gathered some information on Thorneycroft, but seems not to have interrupted his studies—nor much delayed his tour through Europe in a used Morris with his friend, Seymour Dribben—to conduct diesel business. Still, this modest task represented Miller's first work for the Cummins Engine Company. Miller had little inkling of how dramatically his level of involvement with the company was about to change.[49]

Plans for a European trip for Clessie Cummins finally came together in early 1932. The reports from London had taken on a new urgency: "There is no doubt but what the Diesel engine will be in general use in trucks and boats before so very long, it is coming on very fast," wrote Yeats. At the same time, the Wakefield Oil Company in London, which had sponsored Clessie's record-setting run at Daytona Beach, offered to cover the cost of transporting Number 8 to Europe.[50]

W. G. Irwin was eager to accompany Clessie. With the help of Albert Lasker, the banker booked passage for the two men and their vehicle on the SS *Leviathan* out of New York City. Meanwhile, Clessie painted the Indianapolis record on the side of the race car, modified the racer for street worthiness—adding a windshield, cloth top, and waterproof side luggage compartments—and set out for the port of New York. Along the way, Clessie encountered some troubles with Number 8, but he had no time to work on the car before shoving off on April 26.[51]

The *Leviathan* docked at Cherbourg, France, where Clessie and W. G. were met by members of England's Royal Automobile Club. The two men then began their expedition: a swing through Western Europe to call on prospective manufacturers, to stage demonstration races, and—for W. G.— to complete some banking business. But the trip quickly turned into an adventure. To begin with, Wakefield Oil's carefully prepared itinerary never arrived in the mail. Then W. G.'s French proved to be less than serviceable. As Clessie and W. G. muddled their way across the countryside, Number 8 began experiencing a string of mechanical failures.

The trip was punctuated by highs and lows. In Paris, the car's brakes failed. In desperation, Clessie called a local automobile distributor who had helped during the nonstop truck run. Soon an ornate limousine pulled up bearing the distributor, a mechanic, and several others whom Clessie engaged in conversation. When the car was repaired the following day, Clessie learned he had been joking around with Prince Nicholas of Rumania and his entourage. The Prince, thoroughly charmed by Clessie's informality, later asked the gregarious American to take him for a spin on the racetrack. Clessie happily obliged.

Meanwhile, meetings with manufacturers were encouraging. Citroën proudly showed the Americans a test truck in which they had installed a Cummins engine and suggested that more orders were sure to follow. From Paris, Clessie and W. G. drove through southern France, heading toward the Fiat works at Turin, Italy. Along the way Clessie found time to work on the racer. But during a harrowing demonstration run on Fiat's rooftop track—

which had been designed for much smaller vehicles—Number 8 failed to perform up to expectations. And at the next stop—Scintilla Magneto Company in Solothrun, Switzerland—the car's fuel pump failed, grounding Clessie for three days at a Swiss machine shop.

Now it was June, and the trip was drawing to a close. Clessie and W. G. headed back to London. Wakefield's sponsorship called for a series of demonstration runs. Race-car driver Don Kaye persuaded Clessie to let him test the car. But Kaye evidently pushed the machine too hard around the Brooklands Track, and the engine seized up completely. And so, despite being surrounded by the treasures and rich heritage of Europe, and being courted by officials from Rolls Royce and by Sir John Thorneycroft himself, Clessie Cummins once again found himself struggling under the hood of a car.

After a quick jaunt to Paris to witness Citroën's new Cummins diesel demonstration truck, Clessie returned to England to join W. G. and Number 8 for the return voyage on the *Empress of Britain*. They arrived home in early July 1932.[52]

This return to Columbus was less triumphal than others Clessie had enjoyed. There was no fanfare, no welcoming crowds. And worse, W. G. and Clessie had returned empty-handed. Clessie's income was supposed to be based in part on royalties, but there were no licensees in sight. Clessie had demonstrated his product in front of hundreds of manufacturers and reporters, and had made the first diesel run on several European tracks. He had again attracted a great deal of attention—but nothing had come of it. As if to underscore the apparent futility of the trip, terrible news arrived from Monte Carlo: Cummins enthusiast André Citroën had lost a fortune at the gaming tables, and killed himself.[53]

The Engine Company, refocused on its U.S. markets, began construction on a new building in August 1932, which it outfitted—uncharacteristically—with new machine tools. The company still was living hand to mouth, of course, but new machinery was indispensable both for achieving the finer tolerances demanded by the Model H and for incorporating lessons learned on the nonstop run. Clessie soon found himself resorting to a proven tactic, however: a coast-to-coast run to test the new 125 hp model. This time, he planned to make his run in a bus. The company was considering building engines for the fast-growing bus market, and Clessie wanted to generate publicity and gather operating data.[54]

The first step was to buy a used bus from Mack in Chicago: a ten-ton, thirty-two passenger Model BK. The bus came equipped with a five-speed transmission with overdrive; to this, the Cummins team added a double-reduction rear axle (4.96 ratio) to accommodate their high-speed (1,800 rpm) engine. The bus was painted white and blue, with ample identification on its sides. Perhaps remembering the misery he experienced on his first stunt—the frigid New York run in the Packard limo—Clessie this time planned a southern route that would take him through Maryland, Virginia, Tennessee, Arkansas, Texas, Arizona, and New Mexico.

A small band of adventurers left New York through the Holland Tunnel at noon on November 13, 1932, headed first for Harrisburg, Pennsylvania. As usual, Clessie and Dave Evans were the primary drivers. Ted Kelley from the Cummins factory was along for mechanical help. Two automotive editors—Arthur Buck, automotive writer for the *Indianapolis Star*, and Joseph Geschelin of *Automotive Industries*—came along to chronicle the journey. Once again, they used Western Union desks along the way as official checkpoints, and times were logged by a locked, on-board device called a Servis recorder.[55]

The bus and its engine performed far beyond expectations. Though the throttle was governed, Evans and Cummins found that they sometimes could hit 65 mph. (Steep ascents through the Rockies, by contrast, were made at 15 mph.) The bus was running a full day ahead of schedule when the team reached New Mexico. Temperatures climbed into the nineties, and although Cummins and Evans watched their water temperature carefully, they never saw the need to install the radiator cooling fan they had picked up in Nashville, just in case.

Still the unexpected happened. In the small town of Lordsburg, New Mexico, at the end of the third day of the run, the bus's rear axle broke as Clessie drove it across a railroad track. Aided by sympathetic locals, Clessie rousted out a deaf and elderly blacksmith to make the needed repairs, and the bus soon was back on the road to the coast. They completed this latest run to Los Angeles, a distance of 3,220 miles, in ninety-one hours and ten minutes (with an actual running time of seventy-eight hours, ten minutes). They consumed 365 gallons of fuel for a total of $21.90 (based on an average price of 6 cents per gallon). Gross weight, including the crew, fuel, and luggage, was 21,550 pounds. As Clessie was quick to point out, his bus had beaten the schedules for express railroad trains.[56]

"All in all," Joe Geschelin wrote in a detailed account of the run in *Automotive Industries*, "the Cummins Diesel gave a good account of itself." It "took everything" from mountains and desert detours, and completed the 250-mile "home stretch from Holtville to Los Angeles through a hot, dry, sandy desert at a speed of 65 mph."[57]

Reading Clessie's autobiography, one gets the sense that the nation hung on his every exploit, writing and talking of little else. The reality was different. Clessie and his colleagues worked hard to earn their ink-and-column inches. Articles produced in-house were the first to appear in the press. The drive to and from the New York auto show, for example, was recounted by

Clessie himself in an automotive trade journal. But the sympathetic press pros whom W. G. and Clessie built into the trips did their expected work. Sturm, as noted, placed a detailed account of the New York run in the prestigious, high-profile *Scientific American*. The *New York Times* devoted a paragraph to the nonstop Indianapolis truck run.

Far more valuable, however, were the arm's-length stories that began to make their way into national magazines and trade journals. In October 1932, *Science* wrote up Clessie—and *only* Clessie—in its status report on the automotive diesel. The same was true of "The Triumph of the Diesel," a feature story published in the July 1934 issue of *Popular Mechanics*. Later that year, *Scientific American* opened a diesel article with an exciting paragraph about Clessie's exploits. Though the magazine failed to mention Clessie's name in connection with these feats, it featured him first in the automotive section. In 1935, an article on Clessie (including a photo portrait) appeared in the nation's leading news magazine, *Time*.[58]

This welcome trend toward celebrity was well reflected in the influential pages of *Fortune*. In its first article on diesels, in 1930, the magazine did not even mention Clessie's name in connection with automotive developments. Four years later, in the "Automotive Diesels" section of another diesel story, *Fortune* devoted a long passage to the Engine Company and Clessie. It prominently displayed the inventor's unshaven, smiling face after the 14,600-mile truck endurance run, and called him "the man who has so far done most to [improve diesel performance] in the U.S. automotive field."[59]

Turning the corner

By the mid-1930s, the Cummins Engine Company was finding itself in an unaccustomed position: It was showing signs of doing well. The diesel was catching on in several markets, including the automotive market. Clessie Cummins, more than any other individual, fostered demand in the automotive industry. This success came at considerable personal cost to Clessie. Almost all of the so-called Barnum and Bailey stunts were "endurance runs," in the sense that they tested Clessie's own endurance. He and his family later felt that he had ruined his health for the company.[60]

The overall growth of the industry, combined with Clessie's promotions, brought about a great surge in the Engine Company's sales—and the first profits in its history. Predictably, this good fortune invited competition. This meant applying scrutiny to the product line and looking for new opportunities. The combination of increased sales and heightened competition forced the company to buttress its management, which in turn meant adding new people and inventing a new organization.

Building Locomotives

One of the reasons why the diesel industry surged in the 1930s was its invasion of the railroading field. Diesels were restricted mainly to switching and other "local" applications until 1934. At that point, they began to be installed in streamlined trains, and the stage was set for the eventual displacement of the steam engine in the postwar decade.[61]

The diesel locomotive made a slow start in the 1920s, despite its many advantages over steam. Its most important advantage, of course, was its lower per-mile fuel cost, due to greater thermal efficiency. But other advantages soon came to the fore. One was easier fuel handling: One carload of diesel fuel—pumped, rather than shoveled—equalled eight carloads of coal. Diesels did not require large volumes of demineralized water. They needed less maintenance, had a higher proportion of in-service time (a remarkable 95 percent), and caused less track wear. And although many railroad men had an enduring attachment to steam, the diesel simply performed better in many ways: quick warm-up, constant power at low speeds, reduced smoke and noise, and so on.

Despite these compelling attributes, the railroads were slow to adopt the diesel in the 1920s. Diesels required heavy capital investments (two to three times more per horsepower than steam) in an era when leading railroads were siphoning off cash to pay heavy dividends and invest in other fields. In the late 1920s, municipal safety and smoke-abatement legislation persuaded railroads such as the Pennsylvania and the New York Central to order a few dozen diesel switchers from consortiums of engine builders, car body builders, and electrical manufacturers (Ingersoll-Rand, GE and Alco, and Baldwin and Westinghouse, among others). This production reached a peak in 1929–1930, then fell off during the early Depression. Even so, word was beginning to spread. "By the mid-1930s," notes one diesel historian, "it was well understood that diesel switchers could reduce fuel costs by 75 percent."[62]

It was within this context that W. G. Irwin decided to enter the locomotive business. Oddly, his vision entailed producing not merely *engines* for locomotives—an activity for which the Engine Company increasingly was qualified—but also the locomotives themselves. "One of my big dreams is the substitution of the Diesel for the steam locomotive," he wrote in 1932.[63] He began making plans to do so in 1933. This was a daunting prospect, financially as well as technologically; locomotive manufacturing was a highly capital-intensive endeavor, and one that was subject to radical demand fluctuations. W. G. minimized the start-up costs by purchasing an abandoned box car factory (including cranes) in Indianapolis for a mere $4,000. The plant was disassembled, shipped to Columbus, and reassembled for an additional cost of $3,500. (It is present-day Building 7.)[64]

Clessie Cummins announced the company's ambitious diversification to the Depression-weary community of Columbus on July 24, 1934. For the remainder of the year, local residents watched the transformation of the property along Fifth Street, just west of the Cummins building finished the previous year. Concrete was poured for the building's 21,250-square-foot foundation; two railroad spurs were run from the nearby Big Four line to the center of the locomotive assembly building; and the three-story, 200-ton structure was set into place. Although the *Evening Republican* reported in early 1935 that "machinery is beginning to hum in the spacious new addition," it also noted that the facility was staffed principally by underemployed Cummins workers. This time, Cummins' expansion was creating no new jobs in the community.[65]

The work began on a note of optimism. Cummins held an order from the Midwest Locomotive Company to build three diesel-electric locomotives, each powered by a pair of 350 hp Model L engines. Meanwhile, in the three years since W. G. had decided to enter the business, diesel railroading had captured the popular imagination in America. The reason was the coming of streamlined, diesel-powered trains. The first of these, the Zephyr (for the god of the west wind), was put into service in April 1934 by the Burlington Railroad, which faced stiff competition from the Union Pacific's streamlined trains (both gasoline- and diesel-powered). The Burlington's exotic new train was extolled for its sleek "modern" design and its remarkable operational characteristics. Inspired by this wave of enthusiasm, General Motors announced plans to spend $6 million on a new diesel locomotive plant (Electro-Motive) at La Grange. The announcement came in the same month that Cummins opened its Columbus locomotive plant.[66]

But tiny Cummins never competed with mighty GM in the locomotive field. After completing one locomotive for Midwest in eighteen months, the company signed over the balance of the contract to General Electric. The same fate befell the 100-ton locomotive in which Cummins installed two experimental 500 hp, twelve-cylinder Model VL engines. The reasons for the company's quick exit from the business are not entirely clear. Clessie later claimed that he had tried mightily to stay out of the business in the first place; W. G., for his part, left few writings on the subject.[67]

Clearly, though, demand for diesel-powered locomotives did not materialize as quickly as W. G. and other enthusiasts had hoped. Orders for diesel units exceeded those for steam throughout the balance of the decade; but nevertheless, by 1940 only 10 percent of the nation's locomotives were diesel-powered. Economic conditions did not favor huge capital investments, and railroad leaders moved slowly toward the new technology. As one industry analyst had observed at mid-decade, "attention has been out of proportion to the volume of business." Said another in 1938: "Which the public fancied more—streamlining or diesel-electric power—is still an open question." Not until after World War II did the diesel locomotive really take hold.[68]

This was too long for a modest enterprise like Cummins to wait. To make locomotives—not just engines—required broad skills and very deep pockets. In very short order, this became a business dominated by big players such as General Electric (which had the know-how on the generator side) and General Motors. In 1934, Alco and General Motors together owned 100 percent of the domestic diesel locomotive market; five years later, though Alco had lost its commanding lead to the Detroit company, the two still held 95 percent, with Baldwin taking up the balance.[69] Clearly, this was not a game for small players.

Managers for a Growing Enterprise

The Engine Company's new focus on the automotive market in 1930 created a managerial dilemma. The revised direction rejuvenated W. G.'s confidence in the small company's future and helped convince him that it was time to begin transforming the "tinkering shop" into a well-managed and viable business. At the same time, the new strategy further removed Clessie from the day-to-day operations of the business. Throughout the 1930s, he spent much of his time on the road: setting records, testing equipment, and generating publicity. To fill the managerial vacuum thus created, W. G. and Clessie appointed the company's first "general manager."

Not surprisingly, they recruited a manager with close family connections. John Niven of Purity Stores in the San Francisco area had long-standing ties to both W. G. Irwin and the Miller family. He was born in the central Indiana city of Thorntown, descended from two generations of country bankers. (His grandfather had been friends with Hugh Thomas Miller's father.) Although Niven possessed little formal education, by the age of twenty-six he was general manager of the Van Camp Packing Company (Indianapolis), where he attracted the attention of W. G. Irwin and Albert Lasker after they acquired Van Camp in 1914. When Irwin later sold his interest in the packing company, he backed Niven (and a partner named Ivan Heddon) in launching a chain of West Coast grocery outlets called Purity Stores. The chain grew to include more than 100 stores.[70]

Niven's keen sense of obligation to the Indiana banker, combined with his confidence in Heddon's ability to run the California chain, prompted him to accept W. G. Irwin's offer early in 1930 to join Cummins.[71] Irwin held high hopes for the new manager. As he told a business associate: "Before [Niven] went to California, he had been with Mr. Cummins in the development of the engine, so that he is very familiar with everything that has been done up to this time. The organization will be built up by him."[72]

Niven met these high expectations after his arrival at Cummins in May 1930. But he was unable to remain in Columbus long enough to have a significant impact on Cummins' management, nor did he "build up" its organization as Irwin hoped. Heddon died unexpectedly in mid-1933, forcing Niven to return to San Francisco on short notice. For the remainder of the year, the Engine Company limped along under the intermittent guidance of Clessie Cummins and W. G. Irwin. But the Irwin-Sweeney-Miller family immediately began to explore ways of filling the management void at Cummins. The plan that paid off involved one of their own: Irwin's twenty-four-year-old great-nephew, J. Irwin Miller.

A family huddle led to a quick decision: Miller would drive back to the West Coast with Niven and spend the rest of the year in various positions with Purity, learning the nitty-gritty of business. This would serve as a useful training ground for management at Cummins, though Miller was hardly starting from scratch. In fact, he had been learning about business in general, and diesels in particular, for most of his life.

Joseph Irwin Miller was born in the family mansion in Columbus on May 26, 1909. From the moment of his birth, he was the heir apparent to his uncle and partial namesake, Joseph Irwin Sweeney, who had died nine years earlier in a swimming accident at the age of nineteen. Although he had a sister, Clementine, who was four years his senior, Miller was the first and only male child in his generation. "When you look back on it now," recalls a long-time friend, "they had a whole lot invested in that guy."[73]

Irwin and Clementine spent their early childhood in an intense and unusual household. Their father, Hugh Thomas Miller, was intermittently hospitalized for tuberculosis treatments; but others in the household took up the parental slack as necessary. The family's sense of mission and responsibility was strong. All in all, it was a lot for a young child to deal with, and beginning at about age ten, Irwin started hanging around Clessie Cummins' machine shop. "I lived in a family with six adults," he later recalled, "and that was a good way to get away from 'em."[74]

After attending the local elementary school, Irwin was sent by his family to the Taft School in Connecticut, which they hoped would provide Miller with a classical humanities education and college preparation. He was a shy child with a noticeable stammer, but he became close friends with several boys who remained friends for life. One was Seymour Dribben, also the scion of a wealthy family, who later would play a prominent role in the affairs of the Engine Company; and Maynard Mack, who like Miller was a member of a small Midwestern Protestant sect.

Miller, Dribben, and Mack were graduated from Taft in 1927, and the two Midwesterners went on to room together at Yale. (Dribben enrolled at Princeton.) By all accounts, including his own, Miller remained an intensely private person as an undergraduate. A competent swimmer, he never tried out for the swim team. He practiced his violin regularly, but never played in any kind of ensemble. His social life was restricted mainly to moviegoing, often with another classmate named Edward P. White. White found his new friend something of a cipher. "He was a very internal guy," he recalls. "A thorough, unorthodox thinker. He liked coming up with startling statements in a dead-pan way, and watching people's reactions."[75]

Miller also agreed that he was an academic underachiever at Yale. "I think I was kind of slow to grow up," he explains, "and in an adolescent fog." He was partial to practical jokes—the more elaborate, the better. Maynard Mack recalls receiving a snapshot from Miller one day, which depicted Miller stretched between two windowledges on the outside of a building, grimacing in imitation of a gargoyle alongside him. Eventually, Mack figured out that Miller had been photographed far up on the tower of Bingham Hall, a hundred or so feet off the ground. "God knows J. I. was no mountain climber," Mack says. "It was a hair-raising position. If he had slipped, he'd have had it."

Although Miller was a child of privilege, he never flaunted his wealth. (In fact, he was a notably shabby dresser, and family visits to New Haven were often the occasion for forced shopping trips.) Just before the start of his junior year, his family surprised him with the gift of a new LaSalle roadster, which he took back to Yale with some embarrassment. These and similar episodes reflected the family's unorthodox approach to financial affairs. As Miller recalls:

> *They didn't have me on an allowance. I don't know whether this was good or bad, but my father always said, "This is a community pot. Whenever you need something, why, you let me know, and I'll send you the money." He didn't believe in allowances. He believed the money belonged to everybody, so everybody should dip in. A communist society!*

Following his graduation from Yale in 1931, Miller spent two years studying Greek and Latin at Oxford. He had contemplated enrolling at the Harvard Business School, but his father steered him toward a master's degree in the classics, which the family considered to be a path to broader thinking. Although Miller did not excel academically at Oxford either, he was starting to emerge from his shell. "I made up for my lack of socializing at Yale," he later said of this period. He joined the crew team and enjoyed it immensely. (His Yale classmates were greatly surprised that Miller had joined a team of any sort.) At the request of his great uncle, Miller paid a visit to Thorneycroft, the British diesel maker. On one occasion, he met Gandhi. It was a fun, broadening, and exciting interlude, capped off by a tour of Europe with his Taft School friend, Seymour Dribben.

All of this only begged the question: For what was Miller being prepared? From his college days, he had talked about the high probability of his going into the family business.[76] But there was more than one family business. Miller jokes that he was steered toward Cummins in mid-1933 because his father and great-uncle "were very active in the other businesses, and they didn't want me messing around in there with new ideas."[77] There may have been some truth to this.

The apprenticeship at Purity was not oriented toward the corporate suites. Miller remembers:

> *I worked in the back room of stores, sorting potatoes. I waited on the counter. I lived in boarding houses. John Niven moved me around. I worked up in the gold country; I worked in the Valley. I worked everywhere from Eureka down to Salinas. I worked in warehouses and offices—in fact, everywhere but in management.*

Early in 1934, Miller returned to Columbus and the Engine Company. It was still operating with minimal management and producing few financial rewards. But forces were now converging to push the company into the fast lane—and into the unaccustomed state of profitability.

The Diesel Comes of Age

Some of technology's most important trends are difficult to document. The transformation of the perception of the diesel, in the minds of engineers as well as the general public, is one of these trends. At the beginning of the 1930s, diesel technology was relatively unknown. Those who were familiar with it saw it as inflexible and immobile, good only for a few limited applications. It was a product still produced by a relatively small number of experimental shops like Cummins.

By the late 1930s, in sharp contrast, the diesel was widely agreed to be the most efficient form of internal combustion motive power available, suitable for a wide and growing range of applications. It was produced by dozens of companies, including some of the nation's largest. It was being installed in cars, trucks, and buses, attracting the serious attention of Detroit's Big Three. Its appearance in locomotives signaled that General Electric and Westinghouse were committed to the newly popular technology.

What happened? Early criticisms of the diesel centered on a few key themes. In mid-1930, writers for *Fortune* magazine took a hard took at the state of the diesel art, and concluded that the technology had made some respectable gains in certain areas—most notably shipping, municipal electric power generation, and general industrial use. They labeled the diesel an inflexible "bourgeois brutus," limited to a "middle class of from 100 to 20,000 horsepower." In speaking of the aircraft diesel, said *Fortune*, "we enter on the engine's potentialities rather than its actualities." Progress in locomotives looked promising, but would require "solving transmission problems." As for the automotive diesel, one passes "from the potential to the improbable." Injection limitations, the *Fortune* writers concluded, simply made the diesel too inflexible: "Automobile engines must have a wide and instantly controllable range of speed." Diesels had a high initial cost, and would surely lose much of their economic advantage as the price of diesel fuel rose. *Fortune's* verdict on the diesel: "distinctly unpromising."[78]

These arguments were typical. At a meeting of technical experts in 1931, Colonel George A. Green, an engineering vice president at GM, derided the diesel for its "lack of acceleration or pick-up and giving off of a dense cloud of black smoke when running at full load." He faulted the technology's high initial cost, greater weight and size, and "roughness of operation and noise." Even if diesels caught on, diesel fuel costs would then rise enough to wipe out its advantage, asserted Green. Yet he saw one ground for optimism: Diesels probably would prosper in the heavy-truck field.[79]

These critics were correct in noting that the diesel was most competitive against other forms of power when it was used for constant running—that is, *not* at variable speeds. But they badly underestimated the rapidity of technical advancements in the diesel field, and therefore misjudged how quickly diesels would penetrate transportation markets.

The tone in the business press had begun to shift by 1934. *Scientific American*, for one, gave the automotive diesel more serious attention. While it was doubtful that diesel automobiles would be common "for some time to come," the magazine's writers noted significant progress with trains and trucks. And even if the automotive diesel had "yet to win its spurs," it nevertheless had "accomplished feats which have stirred the imagination." When *Fortune* revisited the industry in that same year, it found "a piece of machinery . . . as exciting as a weekend visit with your maiden aunt." Nevertheless, *Fortune* grudgingly conceded, this was one of the few expanding segments in the national economy, a "vastly encouraging industry" that was "seething and boiling with ideas." "The Diesel industry today is about where the automotive industry was in 1914," *Fortune* concluded—in other words, on the brink of a revolutionary expansion.[80]

In the pages of *Fortune* and elsewhere, the diesel industry was gaining recognition as an engine of economic growth in the languishing economy. "At least one branch of the durable goods industries has ceased to talk about the depression—the diesel power industry," noted *Business Week* in early 1935. After reaching its nadir in 1932, the industry had grown quickly ever since, spurred on by "new manufacturing methods and diversified application."[81] Industrialists designated November 30, 1936, as "Diesel Day" at the Power Show in New York, which was followed (on December 2) by a luncheon attended by business and engineering leaders. *Science* magazine called it "the first time public interest will have been focused on the progress and importance of the Diesel industry as a whole." Clessie Cummins shared membership on the Diesel Committee with Charles Kettering (General Motors), David S. Sarnoff (RCA), Eddie Rickenbacker (Eastern), Walter Teagle (Standard Oil of New Jersey), and the presidents of several leading diesel makers.[82]

By the end of the decade, diesel power had carved out its niche—and it was a rapidly growing one. Most of the technical doubts about the diesel had been put to rest. "Diesels are front page news," *Business Week* noted in a 1938 retrospective. True, they still faced considerable challenges, especially in their higher initial cost and inflexible injection systems. But their great weight disadvantage had been virtually eliminated. The diesel that weighed 50 to 250 pounds per horsepower in 1930 now weighed about 20 pounds per horsepower, versus 15 for gasoline. Revolutions per minute increased dramatically: from 250–500 in 1930 to 1,800–2,000 in 1938.[83]

With many technological hurdles overcome, the engine manufacturers' emphasis began to shift toward marketing. Now Cummins and similar companies had to sell into a skeptical market—a "show-me" market—rather than a nonexistent market. The "key problems in the diesel industry," concluded one observer, "are those of sales distribution rather than of engineering."[84]

In terms of land-based motive power, the diesel had made its greatest inroads on the farm, where its impressive power and economy attracted the interest of farmers. By 1937, tractors accounted for nearly 1 million diesel horsepower. The second largest application by horsepower was trucking, with 215,000. Buses were a distant third, with only about 100 vehicles in operation (some 10,000 horsepower); but some of these pioneers already had logged upwards of a million miles, and hundreds more diesel buses were on order. As for passenger automobiles, *Business Week*'s reporters could identify "practically none." "One or two brave experimenters have coursed about the country with diesel-equipped cars," they noted, probably with Clessie in mind, "but there is no record of any in private home garages."[85]

The Rise of Trucking

Diesels made great headway in the trucking market during the later 1930s. This happened, in part, because trucking itself boomed. Technological advances brought trucks out from behind the shadow of passenger cars. The industry began to unite and consolidate, just as the automobile industry had a decade earlier. Economies of scale transformed the trucking marketplace. Trucks surged out onto the nation's roads, and trucking took its place as a key form of transportation. "By 1932," observes one industry scholar, "the trucking industry was ready . . . to compete with the railroads for the declining transportation market."[86] Notes another: "By the middle of the depression, interstate trucking had become big business."[87]

At the turn of the century, American manufacturers produced only a few hundred trucks per year. By 1914, annual output had risen to 24,000, with a total of perhaps 100,000 on the road. But these vehicles were crude affairs—produced by the grafting of a truck bed onto the chassis of a car—which effectively guaranteed that they would perform only light duty.[88]

Farmers were the first truck customers. They bought trucks in the years just after World War I, in large part to increase the speed at which they could bring products to market. The number of farm trucks rose from 139,000 in 1920 to 900,000 a decade later, when the total of registered trucks barely exceeded 1.1 million.[89]

Gradually, though, trucks came into commercial use. Most were private carriers—in other words, purchased by companies to carry their own freight. But there was also a growing segment of for-hire trucking, which included "contract" truckers, who operated on a regular schedule over fixed routes for published rates; and common carriers, hired for specific haulage needs. In the 1920s and 1930s, commercial carriers made up about 15 percent of total trucking.

Another distinction emerged between long- and short-haul carriers. Commercial carriers tended to make longer runs. The average truck haul in the early 1930s was only 100 miles. Intercity, or long-haul, truck mileage grew by five- or sixfold between 1925 and 1940.[90]

U.S. truck registrations grew from about 3 million in 1934 to some 4.5 million by 1940—a huge increase in a time of economic depression. Much of this growth came at the expense of the railroads; and in retrospect, the reasons are clear. Trucks offered door-to-door service. On the whole, trucks carried higher-value cargo for shorter distances. In the vast short-haul market, their rates were lower than railroad rates, with the advantage being especially pronounced for partial loads.[91]

Truck driving was a grueling occupation in the interwar years. Drivers endured long hours over poor road conditions. Crude steering systems made rigs difficult to maneuver, while primitive truck suspensions ensured that drivers would feel every jolt and vibration up through their arms and shoulders. After days of virtually nonstop driving, some drivers suffered from "hypnagogic hallucination" (the then-common term for seeing objects that weren't there). Through the 1920s, truck and cargo hijackings were common.[92]

These burdens were gradually eased by improving technology. Electric headlamps, enclosed cabs, and automatic windshield wipers made driving safer and more comfortable. Truck brakes evolved from rear-wheel-only automobile-style "P and P" ("push and pray") to heavy-duty, four-wheel hydraulic pressure systems, with power-assisted air brakes for trailers. Tires also improved dramatically, from the cord pneumatic tires to balloon tires, which offered a better ride with lower pressures. The average tire cost per mile fell from 1 cent per mile in 1918 to .01 cent in 1930.[93]

Public policy had an enormous impact on the trucking industry in the 1920s and 1930s. Industry representatives regularly expressed dissatisfaction with their treatment at the hands of regulators—and with some justification. Regulation first emerged in the 1920s as a wildly inconsistent patchwork of state laws. "A glance at regulations in the Midwest and Northeast as they evolved up to 1933," explains one historian of trucking regulation, "illustrates the lack of uniformity."

> *If a trucker began a trip in Chicago, heading east, he could load a truck and trailer with a total of 39,000 pounds, 20,000 on the truck and 19,000 in the trailer. When he approached the Indiana border, he had to remove 16,000 pounds from the truck and 12,800 pounds from the trailer to meet the Hoosier state's limit of 10,200 pounds. Once in Ohio he could add a total of 8,000 pounds; Pennsylvania allowed an additional 14,000 pounds (to total 31,200).*[94]

The first federal regulation—the Motor Carrier Act of 1935—earned the scorn of truckers for its railroad-friendly provisions. Artificially raising rates and limiting competition by prohibiting smaller operators from competitive rate bidding, the legislation hurt more than it helped the industry.[95]

On balance, however, the government's impact on the nascent trucking industry was overwhelmingly positive. The reason was, in a word, highways. State governments supported highway construction, but successfully resisted federal intervention until the passage of the Federal-Aid Road Act of 1916. This law allocated $75 million over five years for postal roads. Three years later, the Post Office Appropriations Act added another $200 million. By 1930 the federal government had spent a total of $790 million for highways. Then came FDR's New Deal, characterized in part by ambitious construction projects, and the federal government in the 1930s alone invested an additional $2.2 billion in highways. (Most were in-state; the *inter*state highway movement was a post–World War II phenomenon.)[96]

This burgeoning investment in infrastructure contributed enormously to the nation's economic health—and to the trucking industry—by lowering the cost and increasing the speed of highway transportation. Though the benefits are difficult to measure, two economists who attempted to gauge the hidden trucking-industry subsidy that the highways represented concluded that this government investment was the "prime factor responsible for the industry's rapid growth," even more important than efficiency gains.[97]

These broader developments—the rise of trucking, and the role of public policy in that transportation revolution—created an extremely favorable environment for Cummins in the 1930s. Nevertheless, since diesel trucking was still a young idea, Cummins had to cultivate this emerging market aggressively and intelligently.

Going to market

In 1933, Cummins Engine Company sold 133 engines. In 1941—until America's entry into the war interrupted the normal distribution channels—Cummins sold 4,745 engines, the vast majority of them for use in trucks.

This remarkable progress reflected the stunning success of the Model H engine: the durable product of a fruitful collaboration between Clessie Cummins and H. L. Knudsen. But it also reflected the work of others—especially those who took the inventions of a small town in Indiana and marketed them to an indifferent industry, through channels that were already clogged with competitors. With the arrival of new players—some every bit as colorful and gritty as the founders back in Columbus—the Engine Company's distribution function was professionalized.

Necessity and Invention

John Niven—during his stint as Cummins' general manager and while still co-owner of the San Francisco-based Purity Stores chain—was responsible for the Engine Company's introduction to the West Coast. Through that introduction, he and another recent addition to Cummins, Paris E. "Pappy" Letsinger, finally put Cummins into the heavy-duty truck business.

Early in 1932, Niven asked the White Motor Company's branch office in San Francisco to give him a quote on a used truck for Purity, in which Niven planned to install one of Cummins' new Model H engines. (The H had been introduced the previous October.) Clessie's 1931 publicity tour in the Cummins experimental truck had sparked interest on the West Coast, and Niven saw advantages in a commercial test some 2,000 miles from Columbus. But the manager of White's San Francisco office, Paris E. Letsinger, talked Niven out of the plan. Letsinger—by all accounts a born salesman—told Niven that it would be a mistake to risk a test of this importance on a used truck: "I convinced Mr. Niven that he should get a new White chassis without engine and transmission and have the chassis delivered to Columbus, Indiana, where Cummins Engine Company would make the installation."[98]

Letsinger then called White's president, Robert Black, at company headquarters in Cleveland, and explained the situation. Black went along with the plan, although his company—which made its own gasoline truck engines—

could not have been pleased about encouraging a new entry in the engine field. Clyde Tatman, one of the Purity fleet drivers, picked up the retrofitted truck with its new engine in Columbus on April 27, 1932. The vehicle still lacked a body—which was to be installed in San Francisco—so the Columbus factorymen bolted five barrels of oil to the frame to weigh down the rough-riding truck. It took Tatman seven days to reach San Francisco, where the body was installed. On May 10, the truck went into service.

Thanks to Letsinger's prodding, Cummins already had registered a commercial "first": the first diesel engine in a commercial application in the United States. The next milestone was less auspicious. On the truck's fourth run, a woman crashed her car into the back of the truck—apparently confused by the thick plume of black smoke that poured out from under the back end of the experimental rig—and was badly injured. The state highway commissioner immediately declared the truck unfit for highway driving and impounded it.

Letsinger again demonstrated his resourcefulness. He drove the White service manager, Dave Craven, up to Sacramento where the truck was being held and instructed him to rebuild the truck's exhaust system. The new scheme seems obvious in retrospect: Craven installed an elbow just behind the cab and ran a new exhaust pipe vertically up between the cab and the body—so high, Letsinger later recalled, "that it would just get under the bridges." Then Letsinger fetched the highway commissioner and took him for a ride in his car, trailing the offending truck. The official, seeing most of the smoke being dispersed high above his head, reinstated the truck to the highways. Out of necessity, the vertical exhaust was born.[99]

Broadening the Base

It is not recorded exactly when Letsinger officially stopped working for White and began working for Cummins. For a short time, he seems to have blurred the line. (Briefly, he and three colleagues also considered asking to be named the exclusive Cummins distributors for the eleven western states.) Through the spring of 1932, however, he and Niven pushed White to accept orders for diesel-powered trucks. White refused, but agreed to sell chassis without engines through its West Coast branches. These White dealers would then buy Cummins engines (at a 20 percent discount from the list price of $1,975) from Purity. This almost certainly was another commercial first: wholesaling diesel engines through a supermarket chain.

Purity Stores placed another four diesels on the road during 1932. Within a year, the five trucks had logged 219,899 miles. They averaged 7.1 miles per gallon, as compared with 3.34 miles per gallon for comparable gasoline engines. The diesel fuel used by the five trucks (selling at six cents a gallon) cost $1,855. To move these trucks the same distance with gasoline, which was then selling at fourteen cents a gallon, would have cost $9,217.

Letsinger and Niven were excited by these numbers, but they also saw the need for a tougher test. Purity's trucks usually ran as "single bottoms"—that is, without trailers attached—with a gross weight limit of 34,000 pounds, and at elevations up to only 5,000 feet or so. Letsinger contacted a friend, Gus Savage, who owned the San Francisco-based Savage Transportation Company. (The company later evolved into Pacific Intermountain Express.) Would Savage be willing to put diesels on his San Francisco-to-Salt Lake City route? This route demanded "double bottoms," which were used to haul general freight east and perishables west. With gross weights of up to 68,000 pounds, crossing deserts and mountains, the Savage trucks would put any engine through its paces.

Savage agreed, ordering four trucks from White's "Indiana" subsidiary, in which White permitted diesel installations. This was another modest first: the country's first order for trucks with diesels as original equipment. Hard on the heels of the Savage order—and also reflecting the remarkable salesmanship of Paris Letsinger—came an order from Fresno-based Valley Freight Lines. Valley Freight wanted H engines for four trucks on its San Francisco-to-Los Angeles run. This route included the notorious "Grapevine" between Bakersfield and Los Angeles, one of the longest and most severe grades in the United States. Less than a year after the H engine was introduced, therefore, it was being subjected to some of the most grueling commercial tests available. These operations "gave the engines a terrible beating," Letsinger later recalled. Clessie assumed that he and Knudsen had overbuilt the H engine; but for this application, at least, they had not. The West Coast runs called upon every horsepower built into the engines.*

Sales and Service

The West Coast experiences also demanded a new approach to service. On one of the first Savage runs from Salt Lake City, a Cummins engine broke down, ruining a truckload of chickens. The Engine Company, now on unwelcome new ground, promptly reimbursed Savage for the full cost of the chickens. It also sought to limit any further exposure by dispatching Clessie's versatile brother, Don Cummins, to San Francisco for several months to tear down and rebuild all four of the Savage engines. "The way the company handled this transaction from a service standpoint," Letsinger later commented,

---

*Longtime marketing executive C. Raymond Boll recalls that Savage used both four- and six-cylinder Cummins engines, depending on what his engine compartments would accommodate. Although the four-cylinder engines vibrated terribly, Savage defended them: "Yes," he supposedly said at a West Coast truckers' convention, "they shake pretty bad. They shake so bad, they've shook all the red ink off my books."

"placed the reputation of the Cummins Engine Company on a very high standard, and this traveled throughout the state just like wildfire."

After rebuilding the Cummins engines in the Savage fleet and inspecting those in use at Valley Freight, Don Cummins concluded that the company's product was holding up reasonably well. The engines had logged an average of 40,000 hard miles, made harder by the Valley drivers' habit of tinkering with the engines to coax more power out of them. Don Cummins solved this problem by locking shut the engine compartments, leaving one key in Los Angeles and another in San Francisco. ("We had to take some pretty extreme measures," he noted.) More important, Cummins' troubleshooter established a company tradition by prescribing engine modifications that were based on real-world experience. He recommended, for example, that a screen be placed in the oil pan to prevent hardware that might fall into the pan from being sucked into the lubricating oil pump, a change that was incorporated into the engine design.

But Don Cummins could fight only one fire at a time. If Cummins was to grow, it would have to change its policy of performing all engine tests and repairs in Columbus. As the company entered new markets, it had to find a way to service those markets. For example, in 1933, Cummins received an order for twenty engines from Consolidated Freight Lines in Portland, Oregon. Who (besides the overcommitted Don Cummins) would service this new account, which was even farther from Columbus than Valley Freight in California?

Cummins' first step was to recruit distributors, and Letsinger—who by now was working for the Engine Company—began in the territory he knew best: San Francisco. There he persuaded an established distributor of truck transmission and drive lines, Howard S. Watson, to take on Cummins sales and service as well. Watson, busy with his existing accounts, hired Richard P. Meehan as his salesman. Within a few months, Meehan purchased a half interest in the company, which was renamed Watson and Meehan. Letsinger's next target was Portland, where Consolidated Freight Lines' growing inventory of Cummins engines needed attention. Robert H. Wills (later called the "fireball of the Northwest" in Cummins literature) became the distributor in that city.*

Next came Diesel Motor Sales and Service in Los Angeles, run by a truck fleet owner named G. M. Duntley and a partner, Joe Gutman. Their operation, like the others in the fledgling network, was forced to feel its way along. Duntley and Gutman "found that service was the heart of the entire operation," Letsinger later commented, "and that sales would be easy if we had the proper service."

---

*In the company's early days, the terms "distributor" and "dealer" were used more or less interchangeably. Today, a distributor is someone in a direct contractual relationship with Cummins to distribute (only) Cummins products in a specific geographic area. A "branch" is an extension of a distributor, and "dealer" refers to an original equipment manufacturer (OEM). Except in the case of direct quotes, the authors have used contemporary terminology throughout.

One of Letsinger's unwritten rules was that his distributors had to be actively involved in their business. No one better personified this trait than Ken W. Davis, the owner of a small chain of oil-field supply stores called Mid-Continent Supply Company, who was appointed Cummins' Texas distributor in 1933.

Davis—a flamboyant Texan—had taken Cummins by storm on an unannounced visit to Columbus in the early 1930s. First, according to company lore, he introduced himself to Abe LeBlanc (Clessie's brother-in-law, and Paris Letsinger's predecessor as sales manager), and told LeBlanc that he could commit himself to taking five engines a week for his oil-field business—but not one engine more. LeBlanc, taken aback by the Texan and his offer, finally admitted that if he gave Davis five engines, he would not have enough left for his other customers. Amazed, Davis demanded to meet the owner of this odd company. W. G. Irwin was characteristically imperturbable. As Davis later told the story, Irwin replied, "Here's a piece of paper, and there's a pencil. We'll write you a contract, and I'll make the factory big enough for you to make any number of engines you need."[100]

Davis had correctly anticipated a major shift in the Oil Patch from relatively immobile steam-driven rotary drilling rigs to moveable diesel ones. Selling the slow, powerful Model L industrial engine throughout the oil fields, Davis's company (later named Cummins Sales and Service) grew rapidly. In part to manage the unpredictable Davis, Letsinger in 1934 appointed Jay Chambers (then Cummins' service manager) as the "regional manager" for Texas. These were the origins of what would become an extensive network of factory representatives in the field.

Another important step was the creation of a network of what later came to be called "branches." The Engine Company's initial plan to perform all service itself in Columbus had proved impractical as soon as the Savage trucks started plying the deserts and mountains of the Southwest. And even the newly appointed distributors, necessarily a modest network in the 1930s, could not cover the vast territories of the West.

To address this problem, San Francisco distributor Richard Meehan finally proposed—and Cummins reluctantly agreed—to identify competent truck stops in carefully chosen population centers and stock them with selected Cummins parts at a 15 percent discount. Meehan began with mechanics he trusted in Reno and Sacramento, and gradually built a broader network of branches, or subdealers. (By the late 1950s, he had nine branches—into which he put none of his own capital—in addition to three Watson & Meehan dealerships.) "But I had terrific opposition from the factory," he recalled many years later. "Oh, boy. And even after the war, they were still saying that the distributors should keep all the repair work to themselves."[101]

Eventually, though, Cummins followed Meehan's lead by naming selected original equipment manufacturers (OEMs) as "dealers," thereby extending the company's geographic coverage at a minimal cost.

In the East, where shorter distances and lesser grades made the Cummins diesel less indispensable, the sales effort moved more slowly. (Cummins had a sly practice of skipping whole blocks of engine serial numbers in an effort to convince West Coast buyers that large numbers of Cummins engines were being sold in the East.)[102] Ralph Rogers, head of the recently established New York distributorship, one day called Letsinger with a peculiar problem. Clessie's earlier bus run notwithstanding, New York authorities were refusing to allow diesel-powered trucks into the Holland Tunnel between New York and New Jersey. As a result, Rogers could not close a deal with the Colonial Sand and Gravel Company. Could Letsinger help? "We put a diesel engine in a building downtown," Letsinger recalled, "closed it off except just enough to give it some breath, and took carbon monoxide levels. After that, Colonial was permitted to run a diesel into the tunnel."[103]

In the half-decade before the war, the issue of distributor incentives was addressed several times. Repowering existing equipment—that is, putting a $2,000 engine in a used truck barely worth $2,000—proved a tough sell, so distributors soon focused on persuading local customers to specify Cummins engines in their new equipment. Beginning in 1935, in recognition of these unpaid efforts, Cummins began to pay its distributors a "service commission" on every engine that was delivered into their territories in new equipment. Five years later, the company began paying a sales bonus on Cummins-powered equipment if the distributor had been involved in the sale. (In order to earn this commission, the distributor had to tell the Engine Company in advance of the pending sale.) These incentives, in addition to markups on engines and parts, helped build the Cummins distribution network over the next two decades.

By combining a good product, aggressive salesmanship, competent service, and innovative sales incentives, Cummins became a significant force in the heavy-duty truck market in a remarkably short period of time. Clessie had driven the first Cummins-powered truck to Los Angeles in 1931. Less than five years later, there were over 300 Cummins-powered trucks operating commercially on the West Coast. The 107 engines purchased to that point by Portland-based Consolidated already had logged some two million miles. Foreshadowing the future of American heavy-duty trucking, Pacific Freight Lines in Los Angeles replaced all of its gasoline engines with Cummins diesels.

The rise of trucking as a mode of freight transportation—and, to a large extent, Cummins' own well-publicized success in that market—was spawning competitors in the diesel industry. Between 1932 and 1934, the American truck makers who added standard diesel models to their offerings included Kleiber, Gramm, LaMoon, Marmon-Herrington, Indiana, Kenworth, Ward LaFrance, and Sterling.[104] A few years later, in the spring of 1937, General Motors joined the fray by announcing plans to manufacture light diesels "on a sizable scale" through a newly created Diesel Engine Division. "It is correct to assume," a business journalist explained, "that the corporation is girding itself for an invasion of the truck and bus field with diesels." In early 1938, the Detroit giant opened its first diesel engine plant, which soon was turning out fifty light engines (in the 20–160 hp range) per day. Two other GM plants, opened soon thereafter, made larger engines. Unlike Cummins, however, General Motors produced two-cycle engines. The technological battle lines were being drawn.[105]

Cummins had been first into the on-highway trucking market, and was aggressively touting its products in the field. For the time being, it was winning the automotive diesel race. But there was no time to look back.

Labor and management

The 1930s were a tumultuous time for industrial workers at Cummins, as across the nation. Although the company fared relatively well during the economic slump, there was belt-tightening, and Cummins soon found itself caught up in larger currents of worker discontent and union activism.

The economic downturn had an impact on employment at Cummins within a few months of the Great Crash. In the summer of 1930, W. G. Irwin, general manager John Niven, and Clessie Cummins considered a temporary shutdown of the factory, but decided instead to lay off part of the work force—initially, fifteen shop workers and two administrators—and reduce the hours of those who remained. "We are running 7 hours per day and 5 days per week now," Niven reported late in the summer.[106] Many U.S. employers were trying to preserve jobs in the same manner.

As the Depression stretched into the middle and late decade, Columbus experienced its share of hard times. Each morning, unemployed workers gathered outside the gates of Cummins and other large employers. Although few were lucky enough to make the cut, job hunters knew that the odds at Cummins were better than at most establishments. (Young men who came recommended by Linnie Sweeney—especially students in her Bible class at the Tabernacle Church—enjoyed especially good odds.) This was in part because turnover at the Cummins plant, especially among machinists in great demand within the community, was high in the 1930s. Stanley Shaw, hired as employee 165 in mid-1935, was 37th in seniority within two years. The company's periodic expansions, spurred by its newfound success in the automotive market, boosted employment in the late 1930s. Between 1929 and 1939, employment at Cummins grew from 50 to 700.[107]

Nevertheless, Cummins managers and Cummins workers, like those at thousands of other industrial firms, struggled to redefine their relationships in the context of the Depression's heightened union activism. Compared with the state of affairs at many other companies, relations between factory workers and managers at Cummins were characterized more by consensus than by conflict. The coming of unionism created new, formalized modes of interaction between the two sides. It also posed the first serious managerial challenge faced by the company's young general manager, J. Irwin Miller, who—as we have seen—took over the reins at the Engine Company in 1934.

A Federal Law Comes Home

Organized labor in America fared poorly in the 1920s and suffered even greater setbacks with the onset of the Great Depression. Union membership fell from its historical peak of five million in 1920 to a mere two million in 1933, the Depression's low point. Although President Franklin Roosevelt was no champion of the union movement, his National Industrial Recovery Act of 1933 set in place a sweeping system of industrial "codes," which governed prices, wages, output, and working hours, and offered hope to struggling workers. The NIRA's key labor provisions were contained in Section 7a, which required employers to recognize and bargain collectively with worker-endorsed unions. However, employers generally resisted the expansion of national unions. They were especially hostile to the American Federation of Labor (AFL), the leading coalition of craft unions. Many owners and managers fought the AFL by sponsoring what came to be called "company unions." Others resorted to various methods of union suppression, including violence.[108]

Encouraged by the federal government's support, and galvanized by employer resistance, workers banded together and struggled to increase their power over work and the work place. In 1934, some 1.5 million industrial workers took part in approximately 1,800 strikes, including dramatic struggles in Toledo, Minneapolis, and San Francisco. The following year, two events changed the course of American labor history. First, in the wake of the Supreme Court's ruling that the NIRA was unconstitutional, Congress passed the National Labor Relations Act (commonly known as the Wagner Act). This new law guaranteed workers the right to organize freely and required employers to bargain collectively; established mechanisms for preventing unfair employer labor practices; decreed that company-sponsored unions were not legitimate collective bargaining agents; and stipulated that duly elected unions would represent all employees in a shop. The Wagner Act also established the National Labor Relations Board, empowered to issue cease-and-desist orders against noncompliant employers.[109]

The second key development in labor history in 1935 was the rise of John L. Lewis through his formation of the CIO (Committee for Industrial Organization) within the AFL. As head of the Federation's powerful United Mine Workers, Lewis had urged the AFL's leaders to organize workers by industry, rather than craft. In that way, he argued, automobile or rubber or steel workers could gain representation in powerful, industry-wide unions (such as the United Auto Workers) rather than in a diverse group of craft unions. At the same time, the AFL could recruit members from among the vast and growing ranks of semiskilled mass-production workers. But the AFL spurned Lewis's strategy, so in 1937 he took the CIO (renamed the Congress of Industrial Organizations) independent. By forging shrewd political alliances, organizing well-funded campaigns, and launching highly effective strikes at General Motors, United States Steel, and smaller firms, Lewis quickly organized a large segment of the industrial work force.[110]

Within this context—tough new labor legislation and the rise of industrial unionism under Lewis—the CIO came to Columbus, Indiana, in the spring of 1937. For several tumultuous weeks, CIO representatives attempted to organize several leading firms in Columbus—including the Cummins Engine Company. The results were mixed. At Cummins, unionization was an unusual, complicated, often unpleasant process that ultimately took more than a year.

It began in May, when R. L. Crowmer and Gertrude Boberick from the CIO's Chicago office branch launched a recruitment drive at Cummins. Their efforts were no secret to company management. After a week or two of this activity, and with a union vote imminent, the company's twenty-eight-year-old general manager decided to express his views on the matter to rank-and-file employees. On the evening of May 21, 1937, J. Irwin Miller stood up to address a large audience of Cummins workers assembled in the high school gymnasium.[111]

Testing J. Irwin Miller

Unlike many of his peers in American business, Miller strongly endorsed the new federal labor legislation. That evening, speaking to his employees, he called the National Labor Relations Act "a good law." It was good, he explained, because it enabled workers to act in their own interest. "We can't stop you from organizing, nor can a union force you to," he continued. Given this choice, the matter at hand "boils down to this: A salesman has come to town to sell you something . . . and if it's worth the money, you buy."

Miller certainly hoped that the Cummins workers would not "buy" (though he later suggested they "make allowances" for his bias). But how to make the case? How could the young manager—new to the company and to the industry, a scion of one of Indiana's elite families—appeal to working-class factory men and their families? How could he persuade them to spurn the union's promises of higher wages, increased benefits, and improved job security—especially amid the wreckage of the Depression?

Rather than sidestep these stark disparities in experience and class, Miller confronted them head-on, and with remarkable candor. He noted early in his speech:

> *Now, in all this talk, there is one thing at least that is undeniable, and that is that I am the last fellow on earth that has any business coming here and talking to you. Because, if there has ever been a fellow who has had a soft, easygoing life it has been me, and I can't have the least idea what it is like to wonder every night when I go home whether I'll have a job when I go back in the morning or whether I will be eating this time next month.*

But he did understand, Miller went on to explain, that everyone seeks the security that comes from money in the bank and a steady job.

Miller then asked the company's workers to consider the short, troubled history of their company—how Clessie began with a vision but a poor product, how W. G. stayed with him, absorbing loss after financial loss. "Listen very carefully to this, for it is something I have wanted you to know for a long time," he said, and then explained that neither W. G. nor Clessie had collected "a penny" of returns from the business (apart from Clessie's "small salary"). "There is not one of the officers of this company, with the exception of myself," he said frankly, "who could not go to another company tomorrow and be offered a job at more money than they get here." Miller asked the men to consider "how have we treated you" throughout this period of financial hardship. And now, he asked rhetorically, were some "gentlemen from Chicago" likely to treat them better?

At noon the following day, the employees of Cummins rejected the CIO's bid. Instead, they chose to negotiate directly with the company management through an eight-man worker-appointed committee, which would cull employee suggestions from a grievance box. By most accounts, the CIO "outsiders" had not been popular among Cummins shop workers. Stanley Shaw recalls taking an informal poll of CIO support after an organizer told him that most of the workers had signed up. Shaw found only a few dozen union sympathizers, and he told the organizers to leave town. (To emphasize the point, he dumped a bucket of machinists' "soup"—a mixture of water and soluble oil used for cooling machines—on a CIO organizer's head.)[112] But Miller's remarkable speech, which steered the debate toward a moderate middle ground, surely weakened the union's position still more.

Elsewhere in town, affairs were not as calm. CIO organizers were busy canvassing at the Reeves Pulley Company and Mooney's tannery. Workers at the Morgan Packing plant joined the CIO, and then struck. When half a dozen outside supporters came to Columbus, fifteen local policemen and deputized officers ran them out of town. Soon the Department of Labor was making plans to intercede. R. L. Crowmer (who was soon replaced by William Seibel in a CIO shake-up) threatened strikes at three organized plants in Columbus. J. Irwin Miller recalls that members of the local Chamber of Commerce, hearing of the CIO's recruitment plans, called together local manufacturers to "raise some money to buy guns and deputize people and run them out of town. I had the feeling that this was disaster, and I said, 'Well, count us out. And furthermore, we'll make it known that we're not in.' So [the plan] collapsed."

Soon after the CIO's defeat at Cummins, the employees' committee presented company management with an ambitious request: to reduce the workweek from fifty to forty hours without cutting weekly wages, and to pay overtime above forty hours per week. The answer came back two days later. Management agreed to keep the current pay level (based on fifty hours) while reducing the workweek to forty-five hours, with overtime pay above fifty hours per week. The committee accepted, thus ending the first round of negotiations between the nonunion employees' group and Cummins management on a note of compromise.[113]

Less than a month later, however, the consensus broke down. The United Auto Workers branch of the CIO launched a new effort to organize Cummins. On June 21, management dismissed a dozen workers. The following day, Clessie announced that the company's plans for expansion had been canceled and that more layoffs were expected. (The total reached fifty within a few days.) Clessie stated that the company was scaling back because the industry was "befogged," its immediate future uncertain, in part because of the rising tide of "industrial disturbances." As disheartened workers filed out of the plant, CIO representatives handed them flyers announcing a union meeting outside Columbus on June 23.[114]

The motivation behind the layoffs remains puzzling, and therefore so do the events that immediately followed. The company's management may have been genuinely concerned about undertaking a large-scale expansion amid the uncertainties of the day. But the precise timing of the layoffs, combined with other evidence, suggests that the cutbacks were a deliberate escalation in the struggle, a tough response to the CIO's renewed attempt to organize the company.[115]

Cummins' workers once again rejected the CIO's entreaties. Instead, with the help of local attorney Lew G. Sharpnack, they organized a company union called the Cummins Employees Association (CEA). (Reliance workers soon followed the lead of their peers at Cummins and organized their own in-house union.) Officers were elected on June 28: Otto C. Yeley, president; Forrest

Eddleman, vice president. The following day, 322 of the company's 367 employees—plus 15 laid-off workers—disbanded their original employees' committee and joined the CEA. Cummins management immediately endorsed the CEA as the sole collective bargaining agent for its plant workers.[116]

Did the move represent a capitulation to management's pressure? Was the CIO's defeat a victory for management? Both would seem to be true; yet Cummins' management still demonstrated a willingness to compromise. The day after the CEA's creation, its representatives asked company management to resume the previous production schedule and rehire all dismissed workers. These moves were called for, said the CEA's representatives, because the new organization and its recognition by Cummins management had ended earlier "uncertainties" about maintaining high production levels. Miller, the conciliatory young general manager, agreed. "We are pleased to grant your request to return to the former level of production as rapidly as possible," he announced on July 1. "This will mean the reemployment, as needed, of many of those laid off." But the planned expansion, and the reemployment of all fired workers, would not come immediately, he added.[117]

Reversals

Both sides had yielded ground, and both had aggravated the CIO. Since the June layoffs, Ralph Riddle, a UAW organizer and a former Columbus resident, had actively protested the company's actions. Riddle discussed the matter with J. Irwin Miller, and soon filed charges against Cummins with the state labor relations board for violating the Wagner Act. The day Miller announced the partial rehirings, an agent with the labor relations board visited the Cummins plant. On July 6, Riddle presented evidence before the board's Robert H. Cowdrill. The following day, Irwin Miller and Carl Fox, Cummins' superintendent, met with Cowdrill to present their side of the case.[118]

Meanwhile, Cummins' management and the CEA, now representing nearly all of the company's workers, reached another accord. On July 16, the two parties signed a one-year contract that precluded strikes or lockouts and addressed pay increases, seniority rights, and grievance methods. Labor relations at Cummins then quieted for several months.[119]

But the spring of 1938 brought dramatic developments. On March 17, after long consideration of the Cummins case, the National Labor Relations Board ordered Cummins' management to withdraw its recognition of the Cummins Employee Association, which it declared invalid as a collective bargaining body. In addition, the board ordered the company to rehire all workers fired in June 1937 and give them (and others called back since then) back pay for their time out of work in connection with the layoffs. Although the ruling ordered Cummins to "cease and desist" from "discouraging membership" in the CIO (or any other independent union), the NLRB's attorney stated that the company's management had acted in good faith and had cooperated with its investigation. This finding did not discourage Riddle from deeming the ruling a "victory for labor in general."[120]

But Riddle's victory turned out to be incomplete. On April 21, 1938, Cummins workers voted to form an independent company union—the Diesel Workers Union (DWU)—again spurning the CIO. In part because the union's charter contained several "arm's-length" provisions—the right to call strikes, exclusions of salaried men, foremen, and "confidential" employees from membership—DWU officials secured the sanction of the NLRB. Under its first president, Clarence Everroad, the union entered into negotiations with Cummins in August, and two months later reached an accord that guaranteed a forty-hour workweek with overtime beyond forty-four hours.[121]

The DWU initially was less popular among workers and managers alike than had been the Cummins Employee Association. Only half the work force joined the DWU in its early months, although it represented all nonsalaried employees. For his part, Miller disliked the closed shop for allowing non-dues-paying "free riders" to reap the same benefits as those who paid dues. But he clearly preferred a local union over a nationally affiliated CIO branch.[122]

Miller's views on these matters evolved in subsequent decades—as times changed and unionism spread, as the company grew, and as Miller gained experience. For the time being, Cummins Engine Company remained one of the cooler spots in the impassioned wave of late 1930s unionism in Columbus. This was due in large part to J. Irwin Miller's unique position as the beneficiary of the tremendous goodwill built up by the company's founders; but it was also due to his open acknowledgment that both sides possessed legitimate interests and concerns.

Miller discussed his outlook with Stanley Shaw soon after Shaw became the DWU's third president.

"Uncle Stanley," said Miller, "we don't want any labor problems."

"Well, Brother Miller," replied Shaw, "in like manner, we don't want any management problems." Miller conceded that most labor problems were actually labor-management problems. "I only say labor problems because labor 'l' comes before 'm.' It could just as easily be management problems."

Who's in Charge Here?

Throughout the 1930s, leadership of the Engine Company was a confusing and ever-shifting terrain. Clessie Cummins surely was a central force. He was president of the company that bore his name, and he was indisputably its inventive genius. Along with a slowly declining roster of original investors, Clessie was, moreover, a principal owner of the company's common stock—although the ownership of the Engine Company and its key assets was increasingly a cause for concern. But the Irwin-Sweeney-Miller family also had a powerful voice in the affairs of the company. Mainly because of W. G. Irwin's faith in Clessie and his inventions, the family had invested nearly $2 million in Cummins by the late 1930s. W. G. Irwin, moreover, was one of the more astute businessmen of his day. He was willing, and well positioned, to help the company in a wide variety of ways.

In the company's early years, Clessie and W. G. had worked out a rough but functional division of labor. W. G. attended to the financial aspects of the business, and Clessie worried about everything else—at least to the extent that anyone did. (The fact that Clessie headed south in the winter and W. G. went north in the summer reinforced the separateness of their respective turfs.) The hiring of John Niven and Paris Letsinger in the early 1930s represented the company's first efforts to move beyond this arrangement. Clessie seems to have warmed up slowly to the presence of Niven, but then realized his importance to the organization.* "Will be glad when John gets back," he wrote to W. G. (then in Canada) in August 1932. "He is the real missing link."[123]

Niven worked out a distinctive technique for dealing with his company's mercurial president. As Irwin Miller recalls:

> John and Clessie fought a good deal on business, because it was very hard to keep Clessie on the job. If the pressures got too great, Cless would get in the boat and go down to the Ohio, and nobody would know where he was for days. John told me that he used to say, "Now, Clessie, this injector isn't working. And if it doesn't work, it's going to ruin this company. If you don't fix it, I'm going to fix it, and put it into production, and I don't think you want me to do that." And every time he backed Clessie into a corner, Clessie would come up with another good idea.

The appointment of Irwin Miller as Niven's successor in 1934 created some rich complications in the management of the company. Although he owned an inconsequential portion of company stock, Miller clearly was the current proxy and the future head of the family that controlled the Engine Company's financial fate. The job was his by birthright, but he had much to learn about the company he now ostensibly managed. To complete his education, he asked questions and listened:

> There was a lot of unrest and objection among the managerial group. You see, until I got out of Oxford, I had never held a job that paid any

---

*According to Clessie's son Lyle, John Niven and Clessie Cummins became the closest of friends, a relationship that was reinforced after both relocated to California.

money. But I had lived in a family that talked business all the time. So even though I didn't have a business school background, none of it was strange to me. My technique was to keep asking questions about the things that were brought to me until I understood them. Well, they all thought, "This guy can't make up his mind. He's asking questions about something that anybody ought to know." But I thought that was the only way to go.

Miller also made an effort to build bridges to the shop-floor workers (an effort that evidently paid off in the 1937 labor disturbances). Mary C. Bottorff worked on several volunteer committees with Miller in the mid-1930s, and dated him briefly.* She recalls a 1936 tour of the plant with Miller: "I didn't get the sense that he was completely in charge of things, but I noticed how many of the men on the line knew him. . . . He'd call these people by their first name, and explain the process they went through. He was very relaxed in there."

Today, Miller says that his father and great-uncle were not active in the Engine Company's affairs after 1934. This is certainly true of Hugh Thomas Miller, whose bouts with tuberculosis took him out of the action on a regular basis. The record suggests, though, that W. G. Irwin remained a key behind-the-scenes player at Cummins throughout the 1930s. Most important, of course, was his continued willingness to finance the operation with family resources. Miller recalls with chagrin the regular trips that he and Clessie made to W. G.'s office, where they would present big plans for Cummins. "[W. G.] wouldn't look up. He would go on signing papers or whatever he was doing, while I was making my big speech. Then he'd say, 'How much do you want?' And I'd say, 'I want to finish my speech.' And he'd say, 'How much do you want? I'm busy.'" Miller would name the amount, and leave with check in hand, frustrated by his limited authority.

But W. G. was influential in a wide range of corporate and financial circles, and the young management team at Cummins did not hesitate to call on him to exert his influence. There also were times when Cummins executives would try to enlist W. G.'s help in influencing Irwin Miller. In the fall of 1937, for example, sales vice president Paris Letsinger attempted to persuade Miller to set up a separate company to build industrial engines, and incidentally to serve as a sales organization for the entire company. "Now don't throw this report away," he admonished Miller, "but study it." He also sent a copy of the memo to W. G., directing him to "not let Irwin [Miller] know that I have sent you a copy of this memo, because he just might 'hit the ceiling.'"[124]

*Bottorff recalls a time when all but one member of the Irwin-Sweeney-Miller clan became vegetarians. "We'd go down to Wehmeier's, at Third and Jackson, where they had the best hamburgers in town. Big, thick juicy hamburgers. Irwin would inhale that hamburger, and then he'd get another one and inhale that. But he didn't want his family to know about it."

Letsinger evidently was convinced that no important financial decisions could be made by Irwin Miller alone. In the same year that he lobbied for a separate sales organization, he also pushed Miller to plan on increasing manufacturing capacity. He was anything but subtle in suggesting how Miller should handle the problem: "Here is something I think you should discuss with your uncle tonight. . . . I believe that this is a subject which should be gone into thoroughly before Mr. Irwin goes away. . . . Please, please, let's have a meeting before Mr. Irwin leaves."[125]

There is no record that W. G. ever succumbed to this kind of end-run strategy. "He never did," Irwin Miller says flatly. On the other hand, there is ample evidence to suggest that Miller had to work extremely hard to earn W. G.'s approval of major capital expenditures, such as the one Letsinger was advocating. It appears, too, that Miller's first and strongest ally at Cummins was V. E. McMullen, the experienced engine builder pirated away from Hercules at the suggestion of Clessie.

McMullen's influence on the company, and on Irwin Miller, cannot be overemphasized. For one thing, he insisted that Cummins stop buying secondhand machine tools. (The new H engine demanded closer tolerances.) He helped transform the company from a fly-by-night manufacturing entity into a much more professional operation. The need, as Miller recalled many years later, was dire: "With a certain amount of desperation, we persuaded an older man, who was at the close of his career, to join the company and take charge of its manufacturing function. From this great teacher, always addressed as 'Mr. Mac,' I learned much."[126]

Miller and McMullen were natural allies in the shifting sands of Cummins' management structure. Miller had access; McMullen knew how to manufacture engines. In the spring of 1936, for example, in a note to both Clessie and W. G. Irwin, Miller broached the subject of new buildings. "Mr. McMullen and I have talked this matter over," he wrote to his great-uncle, "and we would like to call in outside assistance."[127] The issue was deferred, in part because Clessie opposed the expansion. It was not taken up again until the fall of 1937, when Irwin again invoked McMullen in a letter to W. G.: "Mr. McMullen feels that here again twice the doubled area will be necessary for the assembly of the H engine."[128] This time, though, Miller and McMullen had made a point of enlisting Clessie Cummins as an ally. And although Clessie disapproved of the particular site that Miller had chosen for an expansion of the factory, he came down squarely on the side of General Manager Miller. "I believe," he assured W. G., "that you will come to the same conclusion that Irwin and I have reached—that the thing must be done and done quickly."[129]

One final episode from the 1930s illustrates the complexity of the challenge of running Cummins in this period. In July of 1939, evidently reacting against the multiple ambiguities of managing a company with at least three plausible leaders, the operating managers of Cummins (that is, J. Irwin Miller, Paris Letsinger, V. E. McMullen, H. L. Knudsen, and C. Hofmeister) sent a manifesto to the owners of the company (that is, W. G. Irwin and Clessie Cummins). The memo—which has the clear ring of Miller's prose—began with an unabashed indictment of the status quo:

> *It is the opinion of several of us who are engaged in the daily manage-ment of the business that the conduct of the business suffers at the pre-sent time from the absence of an announced and reasonable policy of operation. No one can do his intelligent best unless the job at which he is working makes sense to him. To a degree, many of our jobs and plans do not now make sense, and there has resulted an amount of confusion and friction that is costly and hampering the company.*[130]

The solution, according to the five signatories of the memo, was to adopt a clear statement of what the company was trying to accomplish. They pro-vided a draft of such a statement, which they encouraged the "owners" of the company (as distinct from "management") to adopt: "We believe that this company should set as its policy the manufacture of nothing but light-weight, high-speed Diesels of the highest quality possible, and that the owners should direct management to shape all policies and actions to accomplish this."

Six decades after the fact, Irwin Miller remembers nothing about this particular episode. But several inferences can be made. The five signatories clearly wanted either W. G. or Clessie (or both) out of their hair on a day-to-day basis. Equally, they wanted affirmation that the company was com-mitted to lighter and faster diesels—probably as opposed to the heavy loco-motive engines of which W. G. was still enamored. Probably most impor-tant, they wanted consistency in the directives that came down from the "owners."

The reactions provoked by this memo are revealing of how easily the landscape fractured and shifted during this period. Under normal circum-stances, W. G. and Irwin would have been natural allies, as would Clessie and H. L. Knudsen. But not this time. In response, Clessie sent back a rather stern six-page letter. "I am sure," he noted, writing as an owner,

> *"that it has never been the intention of Mr. Irwin nor Mrs. Sweeney, nor myself, to build up a gigantic industry or to become the 'Ford' of the Diesel Engine Field.*
>
> *Therefore, I am sure we are safe in setting down as No. 1 Matter of Policy the building of as nearly a perfect machine as is humanly pos-sible, regardless of the cost, and let the final cost be what it may and sell accordingly. . . .*

> *The second major point of policy is that of training and developing of the man power of the community. It has always been our aim and desire to pick out the best talent and train it to the best of our ability, not only as mechanics, but as God-fearing, useful citizens in the community. To accomplish this, a third policy automatically becomes necessary—a non-paternal but very earnest interest must be taken in the affairs of the employees. . . .[131]*

W. G. Irwin responded to Clessie's letter with a ringing endorsement. He did so, he wrote, on behalf of the entire family (of "owners"):

> *Mrs. Sweeney, Mrs. Miller, and all of us are greatly pleased with your reply to the policy statement. It covered the entire situation. We are particularly pleased that you mentioned one of our main reasons for doing our part in the development of the business. Had it not been for our desire to have a place to develop the young men around Columbus, we should not have taken the risks we did. . . .*
>
> *We are very proud that you have the ability to state the case so clearly. I think it would be well for it to be typed (the last page) so that Mrs. Sweeney can join us in signing the reply.[132]*

To the question, "Who was running Cummins in the 1930s?" there is no easy answer. "His name was on the door, and he had the biggest office," says Lyle Cummins of his father. "Or I should say, one of the *only* offices, at that point." (Lyle and other family members feel strongly that Clessie's management contributions to the company have been greatly undervalued.)[133] Irwin Miller says he was in charge from the day he walked in the door—but also gives ample testimony that he had to earn his stripes over many years. And W. G. Irwin was understandably proprietary about the company he had helped to sustain. "I am trying to build an organization of men," he wrote in 1935, more than a year into his grand-nephew's tenure as general manager, "who will be capable and at the same time, will be interesting to each other."[134] This and similar statements testify to W. G.'s ongoing involvement, especially at crucial junctures.

Old allegiances, such as that which existed between W. G. and Clessie, died hard. The introduction of new and powerful characters on the scene, sometimes without the departure of their predecessors, complicated the calculations. In some ways, the rapid growth and newfound profitability of the company made things harder. (For one thing, the once-moribund company was now worth fighting over.) But growth also made it possible for the Engine Company to sustain more than one dream, and more than one vision of the future. J. Irwin Miller did not gain full control of the company until he came into his inheritance, and until Clessie left the scene. Meanwhile, the two old friends continued to learn from, and manage, each other.

In the brief period of a decade, Cummins had grown from a "tinkering shop" into one of the city's largest and most reliable employers. The company now had most of the hallmarks of an established manufacturing firm, including a large factory, a sales and service network, a labor union, and a more competent and self-confident management team. And Cummins made national news on a regular basis—thanks mainly to the exploits of its colorful president, but also because of its pioneering position in the automotive diesel field.

Even so, Cummins had a great deal of work to do as the 1930s drew to a close. Its market position depended almost exclusively on a single engine model. A second product line—the small-bore A engine, introduced in 1935 with an eye to the automobile market—was a victim of neglect: The Engine Company was too focused on the truck market to put substantial resources behind this smaller, two-valve engine. The company and its distributors had few codified procedures to fall back on; instead they relied on their own knack for improvising and their customers' tolerance for experimentation. Of necessity, its managers lived with overlapping responsibilities. They supervised the company's operations almost like those of a family: informally and personally, with a complex set of unwritten and ever-shifting rules.

Despite this fuzziness around the edges, prospects were encouraging. The company's sharpening focus on the automotive market, after a misguided effort at locomotive making, provided a unifying and valuable mission. Customers—especially truck fleet owners—were beginning to respond. At long last, profits were beginning to flow.

Then came shattering news from overseas. In 1939, Germany ended years of speculation about its true intentions by invading Poland. Two years of intensifying hostilities finally drew the United States into full-scale war. As America mobilized to fight battles in two hemispheres, the young and newly confident diesel maker in south-central Indiana contemplated its future.

4 | Investors and Inventors, 1940–1946

By 1940, the Cummins Engine Company had in place most of the components it would need to compete successfully in the new decade. The completion of a research facility in May 1940 was a key building block. Now, new ideas could be tested more fully before their introduction to the field. This promised to improve product performance and also to reduce the in-field refittings that preoccupied the company in the past.

Cummins products were good, and the Cummins reputation for quality was growing. The 100,000-mile warranty offered by the company in 1940 signaled that it was both confident in its products and determined to endure. On a larger stage, the diesel industry was emerging from its prolonged adolescence, and the Cummins Engine Company was well positioned to benefit from the trend. In September 1940, a Cummins-powered Cotant Lines truck was pictured on the cover of *Business Week*, with a cover story titled "Diesels clinch place on highways." Out in Hollywood, a Cummins-powered Sterling truck was used for the George Raft/Humphrey Bogart movie *They Drive by Night*.

As the nation prepared for war, Cummins faced five real challenges. The first was the company's continuing dependence on the three people who had contributed the most to its creation and development: W. G. Irwin, Clessie Cummins, and Linnie Sweeney. Irwin was in his early seventies, and under treatment for high blood pressure. Clessie Cummins continued to be plagued by the aftereffects of the inner-ear virus that had afflicted him in September 1938. (For the rest of his life, he could not maintain his balance when his eyes were closed.) Clessie more and more sought to escape the Indiana winters that seemed to aggravate his condition. And finally, investor and major stockholder Linnie Sweeney was then in her eighties.

This underscored a looming threat inherent in the company's financial structure. The Engine Company was overly dependent on the patience and longsightedness of its founders, and owed a huge backlog of interest and stock dividends to the Irwins and Sweeneys. If the family ever demanded payment in full, the Engine Company would be bankrupted overnight. Equally troubling was the almost-dormant Oil Engine Development Corporation (OEDC)—the research and development entity created in 1922 by Clessie and W. G. In theory, the company had been obligated since the 1920s to pay the OEDC a per-horsepower royalty on two of the engine models it produced. It never had done so. Depending on how it was calculated, this cumulative sum also had the potential to cripple the Engine Company.

The problem of financial structure was becoming more pressing. The company was growing rapidly. The dramatic rise in profits of the late 1930s (from none to measurable) and an inadequate capitalization structure combined to put the company in the federal government's highest excess-profits tax bracket.[1] Because of a mounting backlog of defense-related orders— which required much larger inventories than the company had been carrying previously—the Engine Company needed infusions of new capital, at levels which eventually would exceed the Irwin-Sweeney-Miller family's willingness or ability to sustain the company.[2] Outside investors, if and when they arrived, almost certainly would demand an untangling of the company's assets and liabilities.

A third challenge was one that the company shared with thousands of other American manufacturing firms: the need to increase wartime production on an unprecedented scale. The U.S. government was engaged, for the first time, in fighting a fully mechanized global war. Gasoline and diesel engines played an absolutely vital part in the war effort, both at home and in campaigns around the world.

This led to a fourth and related challenge. As a result of the defense mobilization, America's engine makers—including Cummins—came under the direct supervision of the federal bureaucracy for the first time. For most, the experience was painful.

The last challenge that Cummins faced in the war and immediate postwar period was its second recapitalization of the decade. The goal this time was to simplify the elaborate four-class stock system created in 1941, and to make Cummins' preferred and common stock available (and attractive) to outside investors. Coincidentally, several of the key players in the Engine Company's formative years retired in this same period. As new money was coming into Cummins, the voices of experience—including that of Clessie Cummins—were departing.

The first recapitalization

Almost from the day Cummins became profitable, would-be underwriters began expressing an interest in the company. Late in 1938, for example, W. G. Irwin received a letter from a New York investment banking firm offering to help Cummins restructure or sell itself. There was little chance of either action, Irwin responded, because the company was "practically a family matter. Mr. Cummins has his interest because of his invention, and I have been furnishing the necessary capital for the business. My nephew has the management of the property. We, at least for the present, would not care to dispose of any part of our interests."[3]

Individuals, too, were increasingly interested in obtaining stock in Cummins; but the existing stock rarely came up for sale. Company lore has it that two of the original Cummins investors—discouraged by the company's bleak prospects in the 1920s—had traded their Cummins stock for a typewriter.[4] In any case, few shares had changed hands since then. Clessie Cummins had sold thirty-five of his shares to Miller family members in June 1936 to purchase a farm (for $3,500) in Harrison Township.[5] There had been almost no arm's-length transactions involving Cummins stock.

When one of the minority owners sought to sell her shares in November 1940, therefore, she found a somewhat reluctant buyer in W. G. Irwin. He had ample reason to establish a high price for the stock, but was not eager to own more. "I am in a peculiar position," Irwin wrote to the broker involved in the sale, "having a considerable amount of this stock and also having an indebtedness of about $2 million to us from the Company." Irwin also confessed to being concerned about the impact on Cummins of the newly revised federal tax laws, which included stiff new excess-profits provisions. Cummins' "overnight" climb into profitability looked as if it might now have severe tax implications for the company, and, by extension, its major stockholders.[6]

Irwin offered the seller $133 a share for her stock—the same price paid for several shares sold a year earlier. "There will have to be a reorganization of the Company," Irwin wrote, "and we will have to take stock, I am afraid, for much of our indebtedness. Including the arrears on Preferred stock, all the capital had been used up and there was a deficit of about $1 million at the beginning of this year. . . . If we can reorganize so that the tax situation will be different, I still have hopes for the Company, or I would not make the offer that I have. There does not seem to be a possibility for dividends, however, for several years."[7]

As Irwin noted, by 1940 the Engine Company owed the Irwin-Sweeney-Miller family more than $2 million in demand notes, on which no interest had been paid. In addition, the company had outstanding bank loans totalling $475,000, which had been made available only because the Irwins, Sweeneys, and Millers had agreed to subordinate their own claims to those of the banks. If one of those family members were to die, it was unlikely that the executor of his or her estate would continue this subordination. Moreover, new loans would be difficult to secure, and existing credit might be closed off.

The consequences of this looming liability became clear early in 1941, when W. G. Irwin approached the First National Bank of Chicago for advice about putting the Engine Company on a more sound financial footing. Several First National representatives spent three days in Columbus, examining the company's books and interviewing key Cummins officials. Their fifteen-page report to the First National's president, Ned Brown, was discouraging. Brown passed along its conclusions in a letter to Irwin. The Cummins Engine Company, he wrote, was not a proper object for bank credit until it reorganized, cleared up its backlog of demand notes, and did something about the OEDC.

"I was with W. G. when he received that letter," J. Irwin Miller later wrote. "He was irritated, and said to me, 'I *know* we have to reorganize the company, but I was expecting some concrete proposals and suggestions as to how it ought to be done. That was why I wanted them to make a study.'"[8] Instead, Cummins would have to define its own options.

Moving Toward Merger

With the help of an Indianapolis consulting firm, Irwin Miller undertook a study of Cummins' recapitalization options in the summer of 1941. (There already had been two restructurings in the 1920s, as described in Chapter 2, but they had addressed very different kinds of problems.) Among other things, Miller's new effort involved a kind of shuttle diplomacy between Clessie and W. G. Concurrently, Miller had to provide a running interpretation of the process for those family members who had a financial stake in the outcome.

Miller soon reached a number of conclusions. First, the family could not simply demand payment on its overdue notes. The sum was so large, and the company's resources so small, that such a move would bankrupt Cummins, wiping out the shareholder investment in the processs. Second, if the family took long-term notes or debentures in exchange for its notes, the company's credit picture would not improve. Cummins still was not making enough money to sustain such high levels of debt; and such a scheme would not resolve the problem of subordinating an estate's interest to that of a bank.

Third, if the company could begin paying dividends, family members stood to benefit from a conversion of their notes into common stock. This approach also would improve the company's credit picture, since an optional dividend would give the company far more flexibility than a mandatory loan payment. But it would so dilute the interest of the minority shareholders—including Clessie, who owned about 20 percent of the common stock—that they would lose much of the value of their investment. The bulk of any future dividends would flow to the Irwins, Millers, and Sweeneys.

There was, moreover, a matter of principle involved. W. G. felt strongly that the interests of the minority shareholders (who, excluding Clessie, held some 5 percent of the total stock) should be protected from excessive dilution. They were Columbus residents, friends, and longtime business associates of W. G. Irwin. They had purchased the stock in part due to his reputation for integrity. They had stuck with the company through almost two decades of losses. W. G. simply was unwilling to reshuffle the deck to their disadvantage.

Fourth, the existence of the Oil Engine Development Company (OEDC) greatly complicated the process of reorganization. The OEDC had been set up, in part, as a research and development effort. But for most of the preceding decade, the Engine Company had been involved actively in research and development, assigning patents to the OEDC. (The OEDC, by contrast, had been dormant since its inception.) By 1941, this assignment process was creating a potential legal exposure for W. G. Irwin and Clessie Cummins, who—as directors of the Engine Company—conceivably could be accused of not protecting the interests of the company's stockholders.

To move forward, Cummins Engine would have to control its own patents. This argued for a merger between Cummins and the OEDC, with the OEDC's patents being reassigned to Cummins. But to merge the OEDC at a high value would, again, effectively wipe out the minority shareholders' stake. This argued for a low valuation on the OEDC. On the other hand, Clessie's 50 percent ownership in the OEDC represented a significant but undefinable proportion of his own wealth. Because of its years of losses, the Engine Company never had paid royalties to the OEDC. (To have done so, it would have been forced to borrow more money from the Irwin-Sweeney-Miller family, thereby deepening its own financial hole.) Clessie estimated that the overdue payments in what he considered a "royalty fund" totaled millions of dollars, and that the engine and fuel-system patents held by the OEDC were extremely valuable.[9] Moreover, if the OEDC survived, it might be paid royalties in the future, especially since the Engine Company's operations had turned profitable. At least in Clessie's mind, these facts seemed to argue for a high valuation on the OEDC.

At some point in late 1941 or early 1942, as a direct result of this complex financial puzzle, the history of the Cummins Engine Company splits into two unhappy streams. The split led to recriminations and estrangement—between Clessie Cummins, on the one hand, and the Irwin-Sweeney-Miller family, on the other—that lingered for many years.

Clessie's version of the events of 1941 are summarized in his otherwise breezy and engaging autobiography, *My Days with the Diesel*, published long after the period in question.[10] In his book, he describes the 1941 recapitalization as a secretive process from which he was largely excluded, and through which he was cheated of his stake in the company that bore his name. The reorganization, according to Clessie's account from a quarter-century later, set in motion a chain of events that ultimately drove him out of the company.

Not surprisingly, the Irwins, Sweeneys, and Millers saw it differently. They recalled a process in which Clessie was a full participant, and at the end of which Clessie described himself as "perfectly satisfied."[11] What follows is an effort to reconstruct what the written record shows—and to venture some conclusions based on that record.

A Deal Goes Sour

The record shows that on November 11, 1941, Clessie chaired a special meeting of the Cummins board of directors. At that meeting, Clessie presented a plan whereby the company's financial problems would be resolved.[12] It called for the issuance of 8,515 shares of a new "Class A" preferred stock, which would pay a 3 percent dividend, while reimbursing the Irwin-Sweeney-Miller family for $851,000 of its outstanding notes. It stipulated the subordination of the existing "Class B" preferred stock and a new "Class C" preferred stock—both held entirely by the family, and both to pay a 7 percent dividend—to the new Class A preferred. It provided for an increase in the number of common shares from 4,600 to 5,000, which would allow for a merger between the OEDC and Cummins. This would be accomplished by awarding to the holders of the 200 shares of OEDC stock—at that point, Clessie (100 shares), W. G. (50 shares), and Linnie Sweeney (50 shares)—2 shares of Cummins stock for each share of OEDC stock they held.

The Cummins stockholders met on November 25 and ratified the plan unanimously—an action which they repeated at a second special meeting on December 4. And, at a special meeting of the board on December 26, Clessie reported that because no stockholders had objected to the plan, the board was now free to approve the merger. It did so, and the deal was done.

Within a year and a half of this six-week exercise in apparent unanimity, Clessie—who had presided over each step of the process—was bitterly unhappy with his lot. What went wrong?

Throughout the reorganization process, Clessie had attempted through Irwin Miller to reach a side agreement with the Irwin-Sweeney-Miller family. He wanted additional compensation from the Engine Company in recognition of the value of the patents the OEDC was transferring to Cummins. Specifically, he sought $50,000 per year for five years, in addition to his salary; after which his salary would revert to $25,000. This "should have been done at the closing of the Development Company," Clessie wrote to Irwin Miller in the fall of 1942, "and it is the idea I am suggesting [again] now."[13]

But the founding family was not responsive. One reason may have been that encumbering the Engine Company with a new quarter-million-dollar obligation would pose a threat to the ongoing refinancing effort. Another may have been the family's own continuing sacrifices on behalf of the undercapitalized company—sacrifices which made them reluctant to put even more money on the table. "You must bear in mind," W. G. Irwin wrote to Irwin Miller, in a note that effectively scuttled one of Miller's proposals, "that the money put into this has not had one cent of cash. . . . I doubt if anyone else would have been willing to risk money over 20 years with no return. I am sure the money could have been invested elsewhere and been doubled or trebled."[14]

Nevertheless, the solution finally settled upon called for additional sacrifice by the family. On the last day of 1941, the seven family members who held all 3,399 shares of Cummins' new Class C preferred stock wrote a letter to the company's board. They announced that they were waiving their rights to the anticipated 7 percent dividend on Class C. After recounting to the Cummins board their reasons for foregoing preferred dividends since the founding, they added that "even now it is evident that it will be some years before dividends of any sort can be prudently paid."[15]

Even so, in the year and a half that followed the merger between Cummins and OEDC, Clessie Cummins became increasingly upset with its outcome. He felt trapped. Unless and until the common stock began paying a dividend, his only income would be his salary as the Engine Company's president. He brooded, and knew that brooding made him less productive. "My work is of a creative nature," he wrote to John Niven in April 1943, "and such work requires a contented, happy mind to function properly and reliably. You cannot put a nickel in a slot [and] turn a lever . . . not on work such as mine."[16]

Perhaps if Clessie's pride had not been injured, the disputes over money would not have caused him such distress. But Clessie was an extremely proud man. At regular intervals, he sought reassurance that W. G. considered him to be an astute businessman, and acknowledgment that his creative contribution was at least as important to the success of the Engine Company as the Irwin-Sweeney-Miller family's financial contributions.[17]

Instead, as he came to see it, Clessie was excluded from the key decision-making processes. His fate was decided "by star chamber methods, in which only once was I allowed to hear or speak. And then was given a beating that cut me to the bottom of my heart. I was insulted in the presence of an outsider"—presumably one of the representatives of the First National Bank—"and told the decision was made and settled. My equity was ridiculed, and a token value of 200 shares of CECo common was issued for it."[18]

A half-century later, when Irwin Miller looked back on this episode, he emphasized the respect and affection that all the participants in the drama had for each other. These were ties that only made the ensuing troubles more painful. "This is one of the things I regret," he commented. "I could have played a better role there. I could have said to Clessie and Uncle, 'Look, this is past history. You guys quit complaining to me, and sending me back and forth between you. *You* work it out.' Or else I could have gotten into it with all four feet, and really done it."

Clashes between inventor-entrepreneurs and their financial angels are not so rare; and family-dominated companies often suffer through periods where passion and calculation do battle. The Cummins Engine Company's rites of passage, between December 1941 and December 1943, were only more distilled, dramatic, and personal than many.

It is not difficult to see why. Up until this juncture, Clessie and W. G. had complemented each other almost perfectly. Clessie had an intuitive feel for technology; W. G. was equally at ease in the worlds of business and banking. When one lost his faith in the company, the other took up the slack as company cheerleader. Clessie was the "people person": mercurial, outgoing, and impulsive. W. G. was reserved and formal—even shy, in Clessie's estimation—but a shrewd judge of character. These were contrasts that helped the company survive.

Other contrasts, mainly submerged until 1941, now surfaced to hurt the company. Clessie had an eighth-grade education, and had lived by his wits since adolescence. Everything he owned he had earned for himself. But after decades of hard work, and despite the fact that thousands of high-quality engines in operation around the world bore his name, he had relatively little to show for it. With few assets, and so forced by circumstance to focus on breadwinning—feeding, clothing, and educating his large family—he had had almost no experience with tax and estate planning.

The Irwins, Millers, and Sweeneys, on the other hand, had been very wealthy for two generations. (Few other families could have supplied millions of dollars in venture capital to a long-shot manufacturing operation over the course of twenty years.) They were well educated. They were intimately connected with local, state, and national power brokers. They knew how to structure deals, and how to protect their considerable interests in the process of deal making.

In the 1941 restructuring, the Irwin-Sweeney-Miller family sought a way to protect an investment, manage a family portfolio of assets and tax liabilities, and help a particular business (one of several they controlled) move forward. They were willing and able to forgo a short-term payback on their $2 million, especially if the new preferred stock soon began to yield its mandated 7 percent dividend. They were determined to defend the interests of the minority shareholders (including Clessie Cummins), who had placed their faith in the competence and integrity of the family. On all counts, the family got what it needed.

Clessie did not. He needed security, and in a form he could understand. On the day that the deal was closed, Clessie was two days away from his fifty-third birthday. He had six children. He was plagued by a baffling, sometimes frightening illness—apparently the aftereffects of a virus that had destroyed the nerve endings in his middle ear—that disabled him at unpredictable intervals. As a result, he was very concerned that soon he might be unable to work.

Belatedly, it seems, Clessie thought through all the consequences of the merger, and realized that the company would not pay a dividend on its common stock any time soon. In fact, as a direct result of the restructuring, the prospect of dividends had dimmed considerably. Now, there were *three* classes of preferred stock on which debt had to be serviced before any dividend on common stock could be declared.

In effect, Clessie had traded one ephemeral asset for another. Instead of a stake in the OEDC—which Clessie valued at several million dollars, and the family valued in the low five figures—he now had to settle for the limited prospect of gains on his common stock. True, he owned over 20 percent of a rapidly growing company, and his share of the company's common stock had been restored to its original 1922 level, largely at W. G. Irwin's insistence. But that stock still was not traded publicly, and had no established market value.

Proportionately, Clessie made the bigger sacrifice by far, and he was ill prepared to do so. He and his family felt, with ample justification, that he already had contributed his health and the best years of his life to the Engine Company.[19] But the power of his subsequent complaints against the Irwins, Sweeneys, and Millers is undercut by the inconsistency of his actions. Briefly, it seems, he adopted the long time horizons typical of the Irwin-Sweeney-Miller family. Within a year, though, he abandoned that outlook, and began focusing again on his short-term needs. And, as subsequent events unfolded, the consequences of this short time horizon were to hurt him a great deal—much more, in fact, than the dissolution of the OEDC.

On the morning of December 14, 1943, Clessie Cummins sent a letter of resignation—the first in over a decade—to W. G. Irwin's office at the Irwin Bank. It reflected his deep unhappiness with the outcome of the Cummins/OEDC merger:

> *I made this decision two years ago during the reorganization, but I have waited to be certain that I was right. It is not possible for me to work unless my whole heart and enthusiasm is in my work. This I lost, and although I have tried my best, I have not been able to tackle my work wholeheartedly. As a consequence, I have kept myself in a "stew"*

all the time. This has played havoc with my health, and the only
answer is to give up the sorrow or irritation regardless of the cost.[20]

W. G. was quite upset by the letter, according to Irwin Miller's mother, who drove W. G. to a meeting at the Indiana National Bank in Indianapolis. Arriving at the bank, he had a heart attack, and died in the lobby.[21]

"There were never any recriminations," Irwin Miller later recalled. But suddenly the ground had shifted. Clessie immediately withdrew his resignation. He recommitted himself to leading the company that carried his name. He reached out to help the Irwins, Sweeneys, and Millers. In particular, he extended his support to J. Irwin Miller, who—although at that moment overseas in the Navy—soon would inherit his family's heavy mantle of leadership.

Engines for war

While Cummins struggled through its recapitalization and transition, the world was going to war. In contrast to most previous conflicts, this was a war of mechanized vehicles. Planes, tanks, ships—and increasingly, trucks—played a deciding role in the major campaigns of World War II.

A quarter-century earlier, during World War I, the German army had made the first significant use of trucks in support of combat units. In 1914, there were some 4,000 trucks in use supporting German maneuvers. But poor roads, inept logistical management, lack of spare parts, and weak vehicle maintenance limited the impact of this truck fleet. By the Battle of the Marne, some 60 percent of Germany's trucks were out of action.[22] For these and similar reasons, there were lingering doubts in the minds of military planners about the importance of trucks to warfare. When the United States made its relatively late entry into World War I, American military officials placed orders for trucks and planes; but they also ordered 945,000 feedbags, a million horse covers, and 195,000 branding irons.[23] The machine age had not yet truly arrived.

By the outset of World War II, these doubts long since had been dispelled. Planners on both sides saw that trucks were indispensable in supplying troops across huge distances, especially along fronts that shifted and reconfigured themselves almost daily. True, railroads carried far more material, and were not dependent on the increasingly rare resources of rubber and gasoline; but trucks took supplies directly to the fast-moving action. Rommel's exploits in the deserts of Northern Africa were made possible, in large part, by trucks; and his setbacks came when he leapt out too far in front of his supply lines. Rommel disdained logistics, but he nevertheless recognized the value of trucks. At one point, he demanded an additional 8,000 trucks from Berlin—a request that astonished the German High Command, which then had only 14,000 trucks available for the massive invasion of Russia.[24]

Logisticians on both sides also were finding entirely new uses for trucks. Ever since tracked vehicles had entered battles early in the 20th century, they had been expected to propel themselves when they moved from point to point. But when the British Army battled the elusive Rommel, it began to employ tank-transporting trucks to shuttle its A9 Cruiser tanks around North Africa. "The use of tank transporters," writes one military expert, "saved track mileage and therefore increased operational endurance, particularly in a harsh environment like the desert."[25] It also got the tanks to the action much faster.

New uses for trucks only underscored their importance. In 1940, German industry was producing only 1,000 military motor vehicles per quarter—far too few to keep up with losses at the front. The German juggernaut depended in large measure on vehicles captured from the Polish, French, Dutch, and Belgians. But soon it was clear that such a patchwork fleet created problems of its own, especially when it came to spare parts. On both sides of the Atlantic, therefore, two pressing needs began to drive the industry that produced trucks: to increase output and to increase standardization. These twin imperatives applied even more stringently to the engine makers who powered those trucks.

Cummins at War

Officially, the war came to Columbus on December 7, 1941: the day of the attack on Pearl Harbor. In the late afternoon, city workers and Cummins employees worked together to throw up temporary barricades on all streets leading up to the Engine Company. Like Noblitt and Reeves—the other two major manufacturers in town—Cummins immediately announced plans for stepped-up plant security. Meanwhile, Mayor Fred C. Owens asked the citizens of Columbus to report any suspicious activity that might suggest a sabotage effort, and police chief Clarence Everroad imposed a ban on parking near any manufacturing plant, power plant, or filtering facility.[26]

But these changes only put a more warlike face on what was already going on inside the plant. Months before, the Cummins Engine Company had gone on a war footing. In the preceding eight months, production had shifted dramatically toward priority (defense-related or essential civilian) accounts. Such priority shipments accounted for 52 percent of the factory's output in May 1941; 80 percent in June; and nearly 95 percent in July.

The company's recently completed labs already were preoccupied with substituting noncritical materials for critical ones without hurting engine performance. By Pearl Harbor, the nickel and copper content of a Cummins engine had been reduced by more than 50 percent from the norm, its aluminum by even more.[27] Even so, materials remained a critical bottleneck. In addition to nickel, copper, aluminum, steel, and other common metals, Cummins engines used scarce, noncorroding steel alloys capable of withstanding high levels of heat and stress. These alloys were becoming increasingly difficult to procure.

Along with this, three-quarters of the components of Cummins engines were purchased as finished parts. Since the beginning of the national defense mobilization effort, there had been growing competition for these components—a competition that Cummins often lost. This struck some at the Engine Company as ironic. "In many cases," as one internal memo noted late in 1941, "our standards of manufacture, development, and research are responsible for the existence of such [high-quality] sources today."[28] Now those sources were in jeopardy, and the gap between the materials that the company was able to procure and the engines it was being directed to provide was widening dramatically. In January of 1941, for example, Cummins received $660,434 worth of materials needed for production, but had $2.2 million in unfilled engine orders. Seven months later, with only $520,232 in materials coming in, Cummins' unfilled orders reached $4.8 million! It was an unsustainable trajectory.

At midyear, the factory's highest monthy output—460 units—was a mere 73.5 percent of capacity. This gap, according to Cummins, arose solely due to a lack of materials. "Emphatically, we face no shortage of skilled labor," noted one observer. "The reason is a lack of material required to make this many engines."[29] Nor did the company lack for paperwork. Engine orders arrived at Cummins with a government-assigned priority rating—"A1" being the highest. Cummins, in turn, had the authority as well as the responsibility to extend this priority rating to all the materials it put into its engines. When Cummins placed an order for a crankshaft slated for an A1-rated engine, for instance, the company was required to inform its supplier that the crankshaft, too, had an A1 rating. In theory, this would help Cummins procure the needed part. But obtaining, logging, tracking, extending, and upgrading ratings was a complex and time-consuming task. By late 1941, ten Cummins employees were working full-time on procuring and extending priority certificates.

Cummins' experience in late 1941 and early 1942 was not atypical. All of the major competitors in the high-speed diesel engine field struggled with two paralyzing evils: dwindling supplies of raw materials and components, and growing mounds of paperwork. In late 1941, an official of the Hercules Motors Corporation wrote a plaintive letter to the head of the Office of Production Management's Automotive Section.[30] He pointed out that his company was extending priority ratings to 185 of its key engine-parts suppliers. Each extension involved typing a "PD-3" form in septuplicate on both sides (requiring new carbons), signing all seven originals and mailing them to a government agency, filing one of the two returned copies, and mailing the other to the vendor, with a return receipt requested. An upgrading of the order's priority rating—which could happen several times over the life of the order—started the whole process over again.

Hercules at that time had 267 rated defense orders on its books, placed by many of the same customers that Cummins served. Because each order was required to have its own rating certificate, and because 185 vendors were involved in each order, Hercules thus theoretically was responsible for issuing roughly 50,000 certificates to cover current work in its plant. In practice, of course, the company cut corners. On one occasion, Hercules tried to estimate what it would cost to extend a rating to the two tiny fiber units that it used in one of its models. When company officials discovered that the cost was approximately $3.46 per unit—for units that cost 3.2 cents apiece—Hercules simply did not extend the rating, and took its chances.

Uncle Sam and the Diesel Engine Business

Cummins, Hercules, and their half-dozen peers in the high-speed diesel engine field were struggling with the consequences of a series of deliberate decisions made by the federal government in the fast-moving months that preceded Pearl Harbor. These decisions were reached jointly by civilian authorities—particularly the Office of Production Management—and military officials. They reflected how the federal government viewed the engine industry, which included both gasoline and diesel engines of all sizes, as well as air-cooled and liquid-cooled engines.

To begin with, the government saw engine production as absolutely vital to the national defense. The lessons of Hitler's motorized advances across Europe were not lost on Washington. Whenever a new government edict with broad manufacturing implications was issued, it tended to be applied very early—sometimes first—to engines. Second, government planners concluded that the country's production capacity for internal combustion engines was "entirely inadequate to meet the tremendous requirements of the essential war effort."[31] Even the inadequate levels of production prevailing in 1941 were inflated artificially, since they were only possible due to the drawing-down of prewar inventories. Demand for engines, and the spare parts needed to maintain them, was expected to grow geometrically.

Third, the government viewed gasoline engines as more central to the war effort than diesels. In large measure, this was a case of the status quo reinforcing itself. Prewar engine production facilities and engineering know-how were, of course, predominantly gasoline-oriented. Despite the progress made in the late 1930s by Cummins and its competitors, "dieselization" still had a long way to go in the industrial and automotive fields. On the ground and in the air, therefore, World War II was to be fought preponderantly with gasoline engines. Of the 2.5 million nonaviation and marine engines ordered from the government by "claimant agencies" (military and essential civilian entities) in

1942, for example, some 2.3 million were for gasoline engines, only 237,000 for diesels.[32] By a factor of ten to one, the customer still wanted gasoline.

Why? There was constant pressure to choose a single, standardized fuel (gasoline), rather than setting up a system that required keeping open two separate lines of supply. Concurrently, there was strong need to settle upon the engine that best lent itself to standardization, in order to minimize parts-supply problems. Most armies had concluded that the gasoline engine was the most appropriate choice, at least from this vantage point. True, diesels were durable and economical to operate. But engine experts around the world had concluded—as had Clessie Cummins—that although the diesel was a flexible technology, it worked best when tailored to a specific application. With diesels, one size did not fit all.

Fourth, the government saw the independent engine companies as middlemen, as *assemblers*, rather than as manufacturers in the traditional sense. A government study of a Hercules gasoline engine revealed that 72.4 percent of its components were purchased by Hercules in a completely finished state, while 27 percent were either fully or partially processed by Hercules. This the government took to be typical of the independent engine producers.[33] (Cummins' in-house percentage was, in fact, slightly higher.) This "assembler" view—in which the engine companies were engaged in a constant juggling act between small suppliers and large end users—led the government to focus primarily on engines *shipped*, rather than engines produced.

Throughout 1941, government agencies, end users, engine companies, and components manufacturers attempted to work out their relationships under a set of relatively loose government controls administered by the Office of Production Management in Washington. But beginning in January of 1942, trial and error gave way to a much more structured set of relationships. Henceforth, these relationships were managed by the newly organized War Production Board (WPB), under the direction of Sears executive Donald M. Nelson. Nelson's agency had overall responsibility for securing supplies and increasing output in all basic industries. Among its other early actions, the WPB tacitly suspended existing antitrust rules, which enabled competitors within the same industry to collaborate on one of some 200 "Industry Advisory Committees."

The U.S. armed forces, meanwhile, kept a watchful eye on the WPB's efforts in the engine field. The Army in particular felt a growing anxiety about the state of the nation's engine program, and the pressure applied by the Army and the other armed forces led to a continual fine-tuning of the WPB system. At first, for example, responsibility for the production and distribution of engines was divided among seven separate divisions of the WPB. But within a year, responsibility for all internal combustion engines (with the exception of aircraft and slow-speed diesels) was centralized in the WPB's Automotive

Division. This division grew from fewer than 10 employees to more than 200 between 1942 and 1944.[34] It was the Automotive Division that supervised the wartime activities of Cummins, Buda, Waukesha, Hercules, and the other independent diesel engine producers.

One explicit goal of this restructuring was to cast the engine companies as the government's proxies in relationships with component suppliers. In other words, rather than attempting to manage tens of thousands of small suppliers around the country, the government's production czars made the engine companies their principal point of control in the vertically uninte-grated engine-manufacturing system. Cummins and its peers, rather than Uncle Sam, thus would ride herd on the producers of crankshafts, camshafts, piston rings, and other subcontracted engine parts. Over time, the WPB became more and more involved in the affairs of these subcontractors, but its official posture was to rely on the engine companies.

A second explicit goal was to cut off competition between end users. To have the Quartermaster Corps and White Motors, for example, competing for Cummins' products was highly counterproductive. This was a lesson learned early in the mobilization period, when, as one bureaucrat noted, this sort of competition "was developing [into] a situation that was bordering on chaos."[35] Even without active competition, noted another official, a lack of coordination among end users could impede truck production. "In order to be certain that the Reo plant used engines not in immediate demand at the White Company plant, Cummins' men have had to watch production in both places and to direct a flow of Cummins' assemblies to plants which have immediate use for them from plants which are tied up for parts not under the control of the Cummins Company."[36]

According to the new arrangement, engine manufacturers now served as the government's control point for the *distribution* of finished engines. To the degree that this reflected the long-established habit of the engine makers, it was a highly pragmatic policy. The sheer scale of the build-up, however, tended to overwhelm even the most logical of structures. And even the seemingly omnipotent War Production Board had difficulty controlling some of its pow-erful "clients," who included (for example) the Army, the Quartermaster Corps, and the Navy. Responding to a particular military crisis, for instance, one ser-vice or another simply would pull rank and *demand* engines from a given man-ufacturer. This would result in a particular order being "leapfrogged" over oth-ers, most of which had their own priority rankings.

For a variety of complex reasons, the engine industry—viewed by the mili-tary as one of the most vital to the nation's defense—was operating at only 60 per-cent of capacity. Customers of the engine companies found they no longer could get a straight answer out of their formerly reliable suppliers, including Cummins. "Manufacturers," complained a harried Cummins official to a WPB representative, in a typical exchange, "are expecting engines that they are not going to get."[37] But the WPB, lacking a better plan, was not inclined to change its approach.

By the end of 1942, friction was increasing throughout the system. Claimant agencies (again, those military and essential civilian customers placing orders for engines) routinely inflated their orders to increase their chances of getting the smaller number of engines that they really needed. Meanwhile, the WPB accused the engine companies of building engines on the sly for preferred customers, hoping to create "a better prospect for post war business."[38] The engine companies, for their part, took marching orders from a government which they saw as both intrusive and out of touch. Simultaneously, they tried to maintain relations with their frustrated customers, and kept a suspicious eye on their competitors. Even in the darkest moments of the war, "post war business" was never far from their minds.

Clessie Goes to Washington

To remedy this increasingly troublesome situation, the War Production Board called a meeting of the Industrial Liquid-Cooled Engine Advisory Committee in the second week of January 1943. At that meeting, the assembled gasoline and diesel engine manufacturers were told once again of the dire need to increase engine production. They were invited to select one of their own to serve as the WPB's diesel-engine consultant, whose job it would be to help the Board break existing production logjams. The group chose Clessie L. Cummins.

"WILL HEAD U.S. DIESEL OUTPUT," read the headline in the January 25, 1943 edition of the *Columbus Evening Republican*. The accompanying article suggested that Clessie had been chosen first because of his long experience in the diesel field, and second because the Engine Company recently had been awarded the Navy's prestigious "E" award, recognizing excellence in production. "As director of production," the article went on to say, "Mr. Cummins will have almost unlimited powers."[39]

Clessie later recalled in his autobiography that he "went to Washington to watch over an industry and to be watched, in turn, by my doctor." The latter certainly was true. By now, Clessie had experienced three serious bouts of his inner-ear ailment, which at its worst rendered him incapable of even standing up unassisted. (When Clessie suffered his second attack in San Francisco, passersby mistook him for a drunk.) But a Washington, D.C.–based doctor who had the same affliction—and also had Cummins H engines in his yacht—agreed to take the ailing inventor in his charge.

For public consumption, Clessie cited the "splendid cooperation" received from the participating companies, who helped him tremendously in his task of "scheduling production of all diesel and gasoline engines, with the exception of aircraft engines."[40] Privately, he had less kind things to say about the government. Speaking off-the-cuff to the advisory group in October 1943, nine months after his relocation to Washington, Clessie expressed frustration that had been building for many months. "For the first three months on the job as consultant I snooped around, learning all I could. I had no desk assigned to me for months. When someone in the Internal Combustion Engine branch was absent or attending conferences, I slid into their chairs. . . ."

"The facts are indisputable," Clessie stated bluntly. "Either you must cut schedules back to meet material, or get us the material to meet schedule." But the WPB, which officially was supposed to "control production and the flow of material" was failing to do so. During a September meeting with his increasingly disgruntled industry colleagues, Clessie recommended that they collectively send a telegram to "Engine Charlie" Wilson, the General Motors executive who served as executive vice chairman of the WPB, "asking him to give us a hearing."[41]

The steps Clessie had taken to circumvent the bureaucracy and help his industry were in many ways typical of his approach to business: unconventional, impulsive, and tolerant of risk. The fact that Wilson attended the October 1943 meeting and sat through Clessie's sweeping denouncement of his Board bespeaks the importance that the government assigned to engine production. And Clessie was not alone. Waukesha's president J. N. Delong complained about excessive paperwork. Hercules president Charles Balough bristled at the implication that his company might have exaggerated its capacity: "We have not oversold our own capacity, but can very definitely state that our difficulty in keeping to our schedule has been the result of the unfavorable material situation."[42]

In the week following this hearing, government bureaucrats worked overtime trying to confirm or deny the comments made by Clessie and his peers. The bureaucrats admitted the problems of material shortages and bad planning on the part of the government. But they also faulted the engine companies for doing precisely what Balough had denied they were doing. "The present practice of industry is to accept orders for deliveries considerably beyond any reasonable anticipation of capacity," said one summary report. "Evidence indicates that overloaded manufacturers are continually accepting additional business, and that, when such business is accepted for indefinite or unsatisfactory delivery dates, pressure quickly develops to expedite such orders at the expense of others."[43]

The government fact finders also put together an interesting snapshot of how the seven major players in the industry had conducted their respective businesses in the month of August 1943. At issue was the relative emphasis on new engines versus spare parts—a subject of keen interest to the government, since increased production of the one led to decreased production of the other. The analysis showed what percentage of each company's dollar volume came from parts, and how much from engines:

	Engines	*Parts*	*Parts-to-Sales*
Hercules	$4,920,000	$934,000	19%
Caterpillar	3,158,635	821,255	26
Buda	2,719,000	600,000	22
Continental	2,390,000	311,000	13
Cummins	1,548,000	626,800	41
Waukesha	1,419,870	457,210	32
LeRoi	563,254	176,655	31

Another analysis, produced six months earlier on the basis of on-site visits to five of these same six manufacturers, provides another interesting perspective. It lists the number of basic models each company produced and the approximate number of specifications that each company built into its basic models:

	Basic models	*Built-in specifications*
Waukesha	25	200
Buda	19	300
Hercules	17	300
Continental	14	200
Cummins	6	600

The Cummins manufacturing strategy starts to become clear in these charts. More than 40 percent of the company's sales in the summer of 1943 came in the highly profitable parts end of the business—twice as much as some of the company's competitors. This was made possible, in part, by the company's insistence on producing only a small number of basic and perennial models. (Cummins produced only a quarter as many models, for example, as comparably sized Waukesha.) "Sell spare parts out of current production," Clessie Cummins liked to say.[44] Tooling costs were kept down, while manufacturing profits were kept in-house. And the high number of built-in specifications—twice as many as the nearest competitor—reinforced the close ties between Cummins and its customers. Beyond the short block and heads, Cummins could customize almost any aspect of an engine's operation for a specific customer's needs.

Riding a Production Roller Coaster

For Clessie, life in Washington evidently was one of sustained frustration. Back home in Columbus, meanwhile, the war period was a strange mix of predictable routine and deep crisis, against a backdrop of steadily increasing production. The first of these crises had come on September 15, 1942, when the

Quartermaster Corps cancelled several orders totalling more than 2,500 truck engines. The result, as sales manager Robert Huthsteiner later wrote, was "pandemonium."[45] Up until that point, the Quartermaster Corps had nearly monopolized the Engine Company's production—so much so that the Navy grumbled about the fact that their old friends at Cummins were now refusing to work on Navy diesels.[46] Suddenly, in the midst of a national engine emergency, Cummins did not have enough short-term orders to consume its output.

Fortunately, the consortium of truck builders (White, Reo, and Federal Motors) that had been manufacturing the Quartermasters' fleet continued to accept Cummins engines well into the month of October.* Meanwhile, Cummins representatives scrambled to rebuild ties with the other armed services. Good news came quickly: The Signal Corps ordered 376 Model H engines almost identical to those that the Quartermasters had abruptly cancelled. Next, the Navy Department promised contracts for 1,000 generating sets, although these would require special engineering and would therefore have to come more slowly. Before long, a variety of orders large and small filled the huge hole left by the Quartermasters. And although the essential armed forces were creating the most dramatic swings in Cummins' fortunes, civilian business also was growing at a rapid pace. (By 1943, 95 percent of the heavy-duty trucking on the West Coast was Cummins-powered.)[47] The continuing challenge was to secure WPB approval for this business.

A second, less dramatic crisis came in June 1943. At that point, Cummins found hairline cracks in between 400 and 450 crankshafts supplied by Ohio Crankshaft, the Cleveland-based subcontractor that machined and heat-treated all Cummins cranks. The cracks, which forced Cummins to reject the critically needed cranks, apparently resulted from a bad load of steel. Later that summer, Cummins was forced to reject 8,500 defective bearing shells, whose flaws apparently resulted from the manufacturer's increasing dependence on untrained help. Smaller materials-related crises abounded. On a particular Saturday night in September 1943, for example, a Cummins car was dispatched to Indianapolis at midnight to pick up enough rocker levers to keep the "A" engine line running on Sunday morning.[48]

Between and around these low points, the Engine Company gradually built up production, both of engines and of spare parts for engines. (As the war progressed, the government's emphasis shifted from whole engines to engine parts.) This was accomplished by a more intensive use of existing assets, rather than by the addition of new facilities. In April 1942, for exam-

---

*Why Cummins was dropped as a supplier remains a mystery. At least some of the Cummins–powered trucks, according to Ray Boll, were supposed to be used as tank retrievers in North Africa, and were equipped with huge radiators for cooling in the tropics. After the war, Cummins regularly heard from operators in Alaska, who complained that their trucks—which somehow had been rerouted to the Alcan Highway—never seemed to warm up.

ple, a third shift went on for the first time, leaving production lines idle for only an hour and a half in any given twenty-four-hour period.[49] But staffing problems went from being a nonissue in 1941 to a pressing concern a year later. New approaches were needed, and at least one was found: On November 16, 1942, four women went to work on the Cummins line, breaking Engine Company precedent.[50] But by the summer of 1943, Cummins had lost 325 out of 1,800 workers to the armed forces; and only 58 percent of its shop employees had more than a year's production experience.[51]

Despite these problems, the push for increased production was on balance extremely successful. Net sales (after renegotiated refunds on excess profits demanded by the government) totaled $6.8 million in 1940, $17.6 million in 1942, and $26.4 million in 1944.[52] In retrospect, learning to make engines and engine parts at high volumes was a valuable lesson for Cummins, and helped complete the company's transition away from its job-shop, "cut and try" roots. But it also occasioned some soul searching, which in turn led to a clearer definition of what distinguished the Engine Company from its competitors. As general manager J. Irwin Miller wrote in 1942:

Early on, we had to decide whether we wanted to be large-volume builders of low-cost Diesels or whether we wanted to be medium-sized builders of high quality Diesels. Since the efforts of all of us had from the company's start been directed toward the perfection of our engines regardless of cost, and since we knew from experience that there was a need for the best engine that could be built, regardless of cost, we decided to become QUALITY ENGINE BUILDERS rather than QUANTITY ENGINE BUILDERS.[53]

Coming Home

J. Irwin Miller learned of the death of his great-uncle, W. G. Irwin, in December of 1943, while aboard an aircraft carrier in the South Pacific. (Within a week of Irwin's death, Miller's mother and father had managed to reach him by phone.)[54] Shortly thereafter, a letter of sympathy from Clessie Cummins caught up with Miller somewhere at sea, and Miller's response indicates how deeply he felt the loss of his relative. "Clessie," he wrote, "it is utterly impossible for me to realize Uncle won't be home when I come back. I'm afraid the shock of his death is more ahead of me than behind me."[55] Miller also noted that he had petitioned the Navy to allow him to return home for a few months to help the family cope with Irwin's passing.

Miller had been commissioned as a lieutenant in the Navy Air Corps in October 1942. Immediately after Pearl Harbor, he had applied for commissions in both the Army and Navy. The Army first offered him a post at a tank-repair facility in Burma, but Miller—"fascinated with the sea," as he later described himself—decided instead on a lower-ranking Navy commission.[56] His first stop was an air-combat intelligence school in Washington, because a Navy official had advised him that a six-month stint in Washington would help him get his desired post as an officer on an aircraft carrier.

That job came through in the spring of 1943, shortly after Miller married Columbus resident and Cummins employee Xenia R. Simons in a modest Washington ceremony. (Clessie Cummins, still in Washington as the War Production Board's diesel consultant, represented the family at the wedding, and Stella Cummins "stood for" the bride.) Miller's Navy experience left an indelible mark on the young officer; in later years, he often cited Navy-derived lessons to make a point in discussions with Cummins executives. One reason why the Navy had such an impact on the young executive officer was that, for the first time, he was judged solely on his own merits. "It was very important to me to make good [in the Navy]," he later recalled. "I always felt there was a cloud hanging over my head in Columbus—the thought that I wasn't exactly the people's choice, and that I had been inserted in the job."[57]

The Navy also gave Miller a new perspective on the strengths of his own region of the country. His ship carried young sailors from all over the United States. Miller noticed that when things on board broke down, as they often did, the sailors from urban environments tended to be at a loss. But their shipmates from Midwestern farm towns, like Miller's own hometown of Columbus, were mechanically inclined and resourceful, and usually were able to coax a machine back into operation. "It struck me," he recalls, "that they knew how to work with other people, and they knew how to fix things. People like them were a natural for what lay ahead of us at Cummins."[58]

In asking the Navy for a two-month leave, Miller emphasized the Engine Company's contributions to the war effort and argued that his presence in Columbus at that juncture might lend some stability to the company. The Navy was not immediately responsive, even though Miller's commanding officer supported his request. Meanwhile, Miller carried on as a junior officer, and one night summarized some of his experiences in a contemplative letter to Clessie:

> *I have had my tail paddled and my head shaved on crossing the line, and it is only now beginning to be combable, and I have knocked me down a coconut, and eaten of it; I have visited me some native isles to see how they live. But such things as these have been extremely rare. Mostly life is cruising, cruising, cruising. The waves become very familiar. I have seen every dawn since sometime way last year. And I can sleep anywhere at any time on a second's notice. . . .*
>
> *At the moment, there isn't a one of us who wouldn't trade for home. The sea, however, is as good a place as I had imagined it to be,*

*and, if I hadn't come out here, I would always have had the desire for
it in my system. It is a good thing to feel at home here. . . .[59]*

After a few months' delay, the Navy granted Miller a ninety-day leave,
which was later turned into a formal release from the service. Miller returned
to Columbus in time to attend the May 18th directors' meeting, and took up
the reins almost immediately.[60] His election as executive vice president of
Cummins in September 1944 only validated the new reality at the company:
Miller's authority was now approaching that of President Clessie Cummins.

A time of transition: the second recapitalization

Beginning in the spring of 1945, Irwin Miller and the Cummins Engine
Company turned once again to the issue of recapitalization for growth. With
painful memories of the 1941 recapitalization and subsequent recriminations
still fresh in the minds of the principals, reopening the subject must have been
an unappealing prospect.

Clessie Cummins was in the process of moving to California. A June
1945 newspaper account of Clessie's departure from Columbus attributed the
move to an "arthritis condition" that had bothered Clessie for a number of
years.[61] Clessie's medical problems no doubt played a role in his decision to
leave Columbus, as did his eagerness to leave behind the Indiana winters. But
perhaps most compelling was his desire to set new limits on his relationship
with the Engine Company.

Beginning in the spring of 1945, from his winter home in Florida, Clessie
began negotiations with Irwin Miller to define a new status for himself. High
on Clessie's list was the opportunity to cash out: "I desire to sell a certain portion of my stock in CECo at the highest possible price."[62] Clessie also demanded clear title to any inventions he might create after December 31, 1945
(although he indicated that he might consider a three-to-five year engineering
contract that would assign fuel-system improvements to Cummins). And
Clessie asked that, in the event that such a contract was worked out, the Engine
Company pay for any extra costs associated with company-specific projects.

Miller was unhappy with Clessie's attitude, and the tone of his subsequent letters certainly conveyed that fact. (This is a notably cool period in a
twenty-year correspondence generally characterized by good humor and
affection.) Miller strongly suggested that Clessie, who was still the president
of the company, should consider himself bound by the terms of the
Engineering Agreement that Clessie himself had required all Cummins engineering personnel to sign, and which assigned to the company the ownership
of all innovations developed by company personnel. On Clessie's other key
point, however, Miller offered more encouragement; he promised to work

with Clessie and the firm's bankers to fashion a new capital structure that would "give equal consideration to the problems and needs of your estate, of our interests, and of the Company's interests."[63]

In subsequent months, the lawyer who was serving as a go-between in the negotiations tried hard to understand the two positions, and then to capture those positions in writing. This proved difficult. As in previous negotiations between Clessie and the Irwin-Sweeney-Miller family, ties of friendship, loyalty, and tradition greatly complicated matters. "Maybe I'm not smart enough for the job," the attorney wrote in a letter to both Clessie and Irwin, "but I can't help feeling that what you are trying to work out is not an easy thing to wholly understand, or to express explicitly in writing."[64]

Within a few months, though, relations again had improved. Clessie couldn't hold a grudge, it seems; and more important, Irwin was making progress on the recapitalization front. At the June 26 board meeting, he had presented a preliminary proposal for a capital reorganization, which the board approved for further development. By November, Miller was putting the finishing touches on a plan developed jointly with the Chicago-based investment firm of A. G. Becker & Co. "During this year," he wrote to Clessie early in 1946, "we should get the recapitalization done, and you should be able to determine about how much work you feel like doing and how much not."[65]

Finally, on January 22, the board was presented with a "proposed plan of reorganization." Its goals were to simplify and stabilize the capital structure of the company, to protect its working capital, to "relieve the Corporation from part or all accumulated and unpaid preferential dividend requirements," to divide the existing common stock into a greater number of shares, and—reflecting Clessie's top priority—"to make the outstanding shares of stock more readily marketable."[66]

To accomplish these ends, the company would do away with the four existing classes of stock (common, and three classes of preferred), and create two new classes: common and preferred. The existing "A" preferred stock (held entirely by the estates of W. G. Irwin and Linnie Sweeney, who died shortly after W. G.) and the existing "B" preferred stock (held principally by Nettie S. Miller and Elsie I. Sweeney) would be exchanged for the new preferred; and—significantly—accumulated unpaid dividends would be rolled into the base of this stock. (Once again, the founding family was declining to take out money that was owed to it by the company.) The new preferred stock would be paid a cumulative dividend of 4.5 percent annually and, at the participating banks' insistence, a sinking fund would be established to retire this stock as quickly as possible. Concurrently, the existing "C" preferred (owned principally by Irwin and Clementine Miller) and the existing common stock (of which Clessie held the largest block) would be traded on a one-for-fifty basis for a new common stock, of which 500,000 shares were to be authorized. Although neither Irwin nor Clessie was present to argue on behalf of the plan, the board read a letter from Clessie, who stated his support for it.[67]

The board approved the plan, as did the company's shareholders, at a meeting on February 19, 1946. As a by-product of the reorganization, the Cummins board was increased from five to nine members (to ensure that a quorum always could be obtained, even with Clessie out of state); and at a special board meeting on April 16, V. E. McMullen and Paris Letsinger were elected to the Cummins board. In Letsinger's case, election to the board was in a sense a farewell tribute; at the same meeting, the board accepted his resignation with regret.

Clessie Cummins owned 1,692 shares of the old common stock. At a one-to-fifty exchange rate, this stock was worth 84,600 shares of the new common stock. Within a few months of the reorganization, he sold a block of his shares to A. G. Becker, which was then headed by David B. Stern, a close friend of the Irwin-Sweeney-Miller family; and a second block to the First Kentucky brokerage firm.

Clessie had been the first to sell—over 20,000 of his shares—but he was not alone in that intention. The Irwin-Sweeney-Miller family needed to diversify the family's holdings to a greater degree; moreover, they needed cash to pay the taxes that were due on the estates of W. G. Irwin and Linnie I. Sweeney.

The important difference, though, was that the family intended to sell *preferred* stock. Clessie, by contrast, was selling his common—his only stake in the Engine Company. Perhaps to help effect this transition, he first cut another symbolic tie to the company. At the April 1, 1947, shareholders' meeting, he expressed his satisfaction that Cummins had proved to be "one of the very few corporations where the original shareholders retained their holdings in the corporation, and obtained the benefit of the greatly increased value in their stock."[68] Then he announced his intention to retire as president of the company, in order to allow someone more active in the business to become its head.

That person was J. Irwin Miller, who was elected president at the board meeting later that day. (Clessie was elected chairman of the board, replacing Hugh Thomas Miller, who died less than two months later.) Almost immediately, Miller set out to register his family's preferred stock for sale—either to an institutional buyer such as an insurance company, or directly to the public.

It was a happy coincidence that the agendas of the founding family and Clessie Cummins were converging once again. In July 1947, at Clessie's request, the board voted to register both the preferred *and* common stock of the company with the Securities and Exchange Commission; and by the fall, both classes of stock—the family's preferred and Clessie's common—were on the market.

But the relative ease of "piggybacking" Clessie's common onto the same offering as the preferred in the long run proved to be a terrible disservice to Clessie. Many of his friends, including Irwin-Sweeney-Miller family members, strongly urged Clessie to resist the convenience of this public offering, and to hold on to his Cummins stock until anticipated earnings—and long overdue dividends—could drive up the price of the stock. Some, at least, were convinced that the stock was about to increase dramatically in value. "I don't like to see Clessie sell his stock," a mutual friend wrote to Irwin Miller in July. "I hope he will hold all of it."[69]

He did not. In fact, he sold 50,000 shares of common (the great majority of his remaining shares) in 1947 for approximately $1 million. It was a great misfortune. Had he been in a position to hold on to his 84,600 shares of common for another twenty years, he would have earned more than $5 million in dividends alone. In the same time period, his shares would have grown to 974,592, worth just over $33 million.[70]

"It seems clear that he sold the orchard just when the trees began to bear," as one observer later commented.[71] But Clessie already had waited more than twenty years for the orchard to bear. Financially and psychologically, he could wait no longer.

Leaving the war behind

Between 1939 and 1944, sales of the diesel industry nationwide increased from $45 million to over $1 billion—more than a twentyfold increase.[72] More diesel horsepower was produced in 1944 alone than was produced during the forty years preceding Pearl Harbor.[73] On first glance, Cummins did not win its "fair share" of this astounding growth. Sales increased from $6.8 million in 1940 to $26.4 million in 1944: less than fourfold. Unlike many other American manufacturers, Cummins did not use large sums of federal money to expand its plant and production capacity dramatically. The Cleveland Diesel Division of General Motors, for example, was the beneficiary of a $10 million dollar expansion to build 500 new engines a month for the Navy; Cummins, by contrast, received a total of only $578,000 in federal loans for expansion.[74]

There were several reasons for this relatively modest growth. The most important was the company's leadership transition. After W. G. Irwin's death, Irwin Miller's departure for the Navy, and Clessie Cummins' departure for Washington, there was no one left in Columbus with the authority and inclination to commit the company to a new path.[75] A carefully reasoned and fairly modest "Proposal for Expansion of Facilities of Cummins Engine Company," prepared in 1942, found no audience.[76] Added to this was the sheer difficulty of expanding during wartime. Materials and personnel were impossible to find on a predictable basis, and the federal government proved an erratic and inflexible overseer.

A final important brake on growth, however, was the company's explicit policy of making a smaller number of higher-quality engines. This was in part a principled stand. "The efforts of all of us," wrote Irwin Miller in 1942, "had from the company's start been directed toward the *perfection* of our engines."[77] It was also a practical hedge against the inherent cyclicality of the automotive trade. No one at Cummins Engine, in the small town of Columbus, Indiana, wanted to lay off hundreds of friends and neighbors when the next economic downturn hit.

Contrary to long-held local legend, it appears that Cummins engines did not power many (if any) of the trucks in the celebrated "Red Ball Express," which supplied General Patton's Third Army in its 1944 dash across Europe. For reasons that remain unclear, Cummins was abruptly "fired" by the Quartermaster Corps in 1942. Hercules, Cummins' larger competitor, went on to make some 26,000 engines for the quartermasters.[78] Logically, if there were any diesel engines on the Red Ball—a dubious proposition, given the difficulty the Army experienced in keeping a single fuel source (gasoline) in adequate supply—they probably were Hercules engines.

But Cummins nevertheless did extremely important war work. Its diesels were selected for airport construction, for trucks operating in the desert and on Alaskan highway construction, for construction of new locks on the Panama Canal, for power-generating sets in remote radar and Signal Corps installations, for continuous-duty generating sets on minesweepers and patrol craft, and for mine-protection "degaussing" units on Navy ships.

And Cummins did its war work well. In 1945, as in every war year, the federal government reviewed the company's work from the previous year in order to establish "renegotiated" contract prices. The government negotiators at that juncture praised Cummins for being "unusually cost-conscious" and for accomplishing its war work with the utmost conservation of materials, facilities, and manpower. "There appeared," the government concluded, "to have been no extravagant expenditures of any kind whatsoever."[79]

These were good habits, and they carried forward into 1946, the first full year of postwar operations. Cummins' volume fell off from its wartime peak less than that of any other diesel manufacturer. In 1946, only Cummins, Buda, and Waukesha made money; while Continental, Hercules, Atlas, and LeRoi lost money. In fact, in a year when the majority of the industry was losing ground, Cummins enjoyed the most profitable year in its history.[80]

5 | Becoming a Big Business, 1947–1958

The United States emerged from the ashes of World War II as the leader of the free world. The flames of war never reached American shores, and the nation's industrial might remained intact. Still, many American business leaders looked toward the postwar era with apprehension. If mobilization and production for war had pulled the nation out of the Great Depression, they wondered, what would prevent the economy from slipping back into hard times with the return of peace? Cummins was among the many industrials that moved cautiously in the late 1940s.

The uncertainty proved unfounded. By the early 1950s, the United States had entered a period of robust economic expansion that ultimately would last longer and advance faster than any in history. Cummins benefited from the general health of the economy, but it also contributed to the postwar boom by producing large numbers of powerful, reliable engines for construction, transportation, electric power generation, and other key sectors.[1]

The company's most important market since the 1930s—transportation—became even more vital to its success after the war. Between 1946 and 1958, the number of trucks registered nationally nearly doubled, from fewer than six million to more than eleven million. A major reason for this rapid rise was the ambitious interstate highway construction work carried out in the Truman-Eisenhower era. Through major postwar legislation, most notably the Federal Highway Act of 1956, the federal government each year funneled millions of dollars in fuel, vehicle, and tire taxes into the construction of thousands of miles of interstate highways. This federal money, combined with contributions from state and municipal governments, boosted total public spending on highways, roads, and streets from $398 million in 1945 to $5.5 billion in 1958.[2]

The trucking market became central to Cummins' success in the 1950s. To be sure, the company made gains in other markets, from marine to locomotives to stationary power. Sales for construction equipment were especially strong—also due, in large measure, to massive highway and road building. Still, as J. Irwin Miller told Cummins shareholders in 1950—the year the company abandoned caution for expansionism—"The industry that is giving us our volume today is the highway truck industry."[3]

But Cummins was not a passive beneficiary of the highway trucking boom. The company's decision to devote most of its resources—in research, manufacturing, and marketing alike—to the heavy automotive market was not inevitable. Moreover, as the trucking market burgeoned, competition flared. Often, Cummins confronted larger, better-financed rivals. In the end, however, Cummins' strategies and policies proved successful. The company's net sales rose from $27 million in 1947 to $108.7 million in 1958, while in the same period assets climbed from $12.5 million to $68.7 million. Cummins emerged as the leading producer of high-speed diesel engines for the heavy automotive market, and in the process became a substantial business.[4]

The main contours of the company's strategy—an approach that would serve the company for decades—took shape in the late 1940s and 1950s. As articulated by J. Irwin Miller, and eventually diffused through all layers of the organization, the strategy had several key components. First, Cummins placed a high value on research in order to constantly "obsolete" existing diesel technology, including its own. Second, the company pushed hard to lower costs and improve efficiency, but only when the quality of its products could be maintained at a high standard. Third, Cummins defined itself as a service-oriented supplier by cultivating close relations with customers through a national network of independent distributors. These distributors not only helped persuade OEMs that Cummins was a safe bet, but also carried both the company and its customers through periods of product difficulties. (Distributors made only a minimal markup on warranty service they provided.) Taken together, these policies enabled Cummins to supply the highway trucking market with what it most demanded after the war: powerful, efficient, reliable engines.

Transformations in technology and manufacturing

Cummins engineers and researchers, working in the laboratory and in the field (including the Indianapolis Speedway), devoted much of their time in the late 1940s and 1950s to enhancing the performance of the company's basic engine models. Out of this work came critical advances in air and fuel injection systems—through supercharging, turbocharging, and other enhancements—that enabled Cummins to remain technically competitive. The goal always was the same: to increase efficiency, reliability, and—especially—horsepower. As its product line evolved, Cummins put more and more power into smaller and smaller packages.

From Supercharging to Turbocharging

One way to boost the power of an internal combustion engine is to increase its ability to breathe. Getting more oxygen in permits the introduction of additional fuel, which in turn yields more power. The two leading methods for mechanically compressing intake air to emerge by the late nineteenth century were pistons and air turbines (or "blowers"). Both employed the principle of reducing the space occupied by intake air, although blowers—which emulated centuries-old rotary displacement water pumps, in a process of positive displacement—were more practical.

The most successful variety of American-made rotary displacement air compressor, later known as the supercharger, was born fifty miles northwest of Columbus, at Connersville, Indiana. There, in 1859, the brothers P. H. and F. M. Roots jury-rigged a water turbine for their textile mill. The prototype malfunctioned, but before scrapping it, the brothers flipped it over for another trial. The turbine blew the hat off a foundryman, who remarked sagely, "This will make a better blower than it will a turbine."[5]

Supercharging had a checkered history at Cummins, beginning in 1937, when the company began to install Roots units on a few engines. Over the next decade, the technology enjoyed limited application in the Cummins product line. It also engendered debate among management, as well as no small amount of customer dissatisfaction.[6]

Late in the war, for instance, Paris Letsinger looked hopefully toward markets for NHV and NHVS engines (the S suffix denoting supercharged models), and J. Irwin Miller recommended that Cummins scale up to make twelve-cylinder VH and VHS engines "as rapidly as possible." But others, including V. E. McMullen and Clessie Cummins, were less confident that supercharging was an easy path to higher horsepower. In 1945, Cummins acknowledged to the Executive Committee that a blower would likely increase the A engine's rpm considerably, but was quick to add that "the big market will be for a non-supercharged engine, and . . . we should not resort to supercharging, except as an absolute last resort." The company built two or three experimental supercharged As, but abandoned the model at the end of 1946.[7]

By that time, supercharging-related problems were beginning to multiply. Some Cummins customers complained that supercharged models were excessively noisy. A more serious drawback was the supercharged engine's tendency to guzzle fuel. The blowers not only consumed for their own motive power up to 30 percent of the additional horsepower they generated, but also produced less efficient combustion. This poor fuel economy restricted sales of Cummins supercharged models mainly to construction and other off-highway markets.[8]

Meanwhile, hoping to overcome these problems, chief engineer Hans Knudsen had been investigating the closely related technology of turbocharging. Like the supercharger, the turbocharger uses the injection of compressed air to enhance engine performance—but with a critical difference. The turbocharger is driven by "free" exhaust gases rather than mechanical power from the engine. (It does not therefore add *and* subtract horsepower like the supercharger.) As a result, turbocharged engines generally achieve greater horsepower for a given volume of piston displacement, and consume fewer gallons of fuel per horsepower hour, than supercharged models.[9]

"I feel it would be desirable for us to start our own turbo-supercharger development right now," Knudsen told the board in the spring of 1947. The directors agreed, authorizing him to buy a war surplus turbocharger for experimentation and to hire a turbocharger specialist. But the man who soon filled that position—a young Hoosier engineer named Bill Schwab—nominated himself for the job.[10]

Schwab graduated in 1941 from Rose Polytechnic Institute, a private engineering school in Indiana, and then joined General Electric. After a stint at GE's steam turbine division in Schenectady, he transferred to Lynn, Massachusetts. There, under the prominent engineer Dr. Frank Moss, Schwab worked on GE's aircraft engine turbo-supercharging program (a technology crucial to the war effort because it enabled high-altitude flight). One day in Lynn, Schwab saw a Cummins diesel on a GE test stand. Intended for a rail car that would climb Pike's Peak, the engine was being tested for high-altitude performance at Cummins' request. Schwab thought the engine could use a turbocharger. Hoping to return to his Midwestern roots, he wrote letters to Cummins and Caterpillar about the virtues of engine turbocharging. Caterpillar expressed no interest, but Cummins invited him for an interview.[11]

The bright and ambitious young GE engineer expected to find little in the way of opportunity or turbocharger expertise at the relatively tiny Columbus firm. Then he met Knudsen. "I was surprised to find out how much they really knew about turbochargers," Schwab recalled. "I think [Knudsen] had read every article that had ever been written about turbocharging." Schwab joined the company, beginning a career with Cummins that eventually took him to the top of the company's research organization. Knudsen, having launched yet another critical research program, retired later that year (on June 24, 1947), completing twenty-five years of vital service to the company.[12]

The turbocharging program moved ahead under Schwab's direction. The researchers bought an aircraft turbocharger and tore it down for analysis. Cummins also searched hard for a supplier; none seemed to make a device small enough for use with automotive engines. Finally, in 1951, the company located the Elliot Corporation in Pennsylvania, which made a sufficiently small unit (along with larger turbos for locomotive diesels and other applications). Cummins began to install and field-test the devices on a few of its engines.[13]

In one sense, the experiment was successful: turbocharging boosted horsepower. When installed on a 300 hp NHRS engine, for example, an Elliot turbocharger boosted power by about 10 percent (to 335 hp) without appreciably altering fuel consumption. Turbocharging also enabled diesels to perform well at altitudes as high as 8,000 feet, an attribute critical for inter-mountain trucking and unequaled by gasoline engines. And the devices were more compact and lighter than superchargers.[14]

But the technology soon proved to have troubling shortcomings. Far too often, bearings deteriorated and castings warped under the stress of the turbines' high-speed rotation at very high temperatures. The most serious problem with turbocharged engines, however, was their acceleration lag. The inertia of the turbine blades, plus the dependence of the turbine on the presence of exhaust gases, delayed the onset of turbocharged combustion by several moments. (Because they are mechanically driven, superchargers do not lag similarly.) For this reason, drivers of turbocharged trucks learned to expect sluggish acceleration, accompanied by bursts of exhaust smoke caused by the temporarily out-of-kilter combustion. Engineer Joe Butler, who joined Cummins in 1949, recalls efforts to prevent drivers "from blowing soot all over the neighborhood while they were getting the truck in motion."[15]

With the Elliot turbochargers "causing us a bundle of trouble" (as Schwab put it), Cummins switched suppliers. The Schwitzer Corporation of Indianapolis offered a slightly smaller turbo based on an innovative design by German engineer Kurt Beirer. The new brand eliminated some of Cummins' turbocharger-related engine problems, although the "T" engines (the suffix applied to turbocharged models) remained less reliable and more expensive to maintain and repair than engines without turbochargers. In 1954, Cummins offered turbocharged versions of its twelve-cylinder V (the VT-12) as well as six-cylinder NTs, NRTs, and JTs. Yet the great majority of engines sold by Cummins were naturally aspirated. In the laboratory and in the marketplace, Schwab recalled, "the turbocharger engine kind of limped along."[16]

Two developments helped change this state of affairs. First, as we will see in the next section, Cummins garnered valuable technical know-how about turbocharging from the experimental race car it entered in the Indianapolis 500 Memorial Day race of 1952. Second, as described later in the chapter, the company improved the quality of its turbochargers by manufacturing them in-house. Within a few years, Cummins-installed turbochargers became efficient and reliable, and they helped the company sell its products to the growing number of diesel customers who were hungry for higher horsepower.

Back to the Races

On the afternoon of May 12, 1950, the tension inside Garage #3 at the Indianapolis Motor Speedway was palpable. In the middle of the workshop stood a large green race car, the "Cummins Diesel Special," Number 61, informally dubbed the "Green Hornet." The color choice was odd. Most Indy drivers—a notoriously superstitious breed—considered green to be an unlucky color. Cummins mechanics and engineers busily tended the car: Vern Gressel and Milt Fellows worked beneath the chassis, while Don Cummins bent over the engine compartment. Even the aging Thane Houser, the company's riding mechanic in the 1931 and 1934 races, lent a hand.[17]

The chassis and body of Number 61 had been fabricated by Kurtis Kraft of Los Angeles. The engine—specially designed and tested in the Cummins research lab—was a supercharged, four-cycle Cummins Model JS-600, with six cylinders (4.125-inch bore, 5-inch stroke) displacing a total of 401 cubic inches. To reduce weight, engineers had crafted most of the engine (including the block and heads) out of aluminum. The engine ultimately was coaxed into producing 300 brake horsepower (bhp) at 3,600 rpm. A duplicate engine was kept in ready condition back in the Columbus research laboratory.[18]

Off to the side, sitting on an oil drum, Jimmy Jackson puffed on a big black cigar. Jackson, the thirty-year-old driver slated to pilot the Cummins Special in the upcoming race, had burst upon the racing scene in 1946 by placing second in his first Indianapolis 500. Every year since then he had finished "in the money." Jackson chatted with Neville Reiners, the Cummins engineer on the project. "We're hunting for four more miles an hour," Reiners told a reporter who entered the garage. "Four more precious miles per hour."[19]

Like all of the men on the Cummins race crew, Reiners was concerned about the upcoming qualifying trials. After a long absence, the Cummins Engine Company had returned to the Indianapolis Speedway to seek publicity and gather engineering knowledge. There was an important distinction between the 1950 race and the runs of the early 1930s, however. This was much closer to a real contest. True, weight, length, and piston displacement restrictions were being waived to allow the heavy Cummins Special to compete. But when it came to qualifying speed, Number 61 had to engage in head-to-head competition with entries from Gasoline Alley.

Several times earlier that day, Jackson had taken Number 61 for practice test runs. The fastest lap was clocked at 124.3 mph. The Cummins crew estimated that an official qualifying time of at least 128 mph would be needed to secure a place among the thirty-three starters on Memorial Day. Still, the men were confident they could hit the mark. They were learning more each day, making repairs and improvements that were bringing incremental advances in speed.[20]

But prospects for the Cummins Special were dimming as the race day approached. The car required, among other things, new shock absorbers, front-end "surgery," and gear-ratio adjustment. After more than 300 unsatisfactory practice laps, the crew found it necessary to replace the engine with the standby, which ultimately yielded a remarkable 345 bhp at 4,000 rpm. This added horsepower was desperately needed. Qualifying trials that season were yielding uncommonly high average speeds. The Cummins team delayed sending Jackson out to make his bid until the second-to-last qualifying day. By that time, most of the cars had qualified at more than 130 mph.[21]

Jackson brought in a time of 129.208. When the track dust settled at the end of the day, the Cummins Diesel Special ranked thirty-second. But one more day of trials remained—a day in which more than twenty drivers would compete for the thirty-three starting positions. Only two needed to better Jackson's time to force Cummins out of the running.[22]

Jackson had told reporters weeks earlier that winning a race required a good car and driver, but also "a whole lot of luck." Luck was surely with the Cummins team that day. Of all the contestants, one alone beat Jackson's time. Though barely making the cut, the Cummins Diesel Special became the first diesel race car to qualify competitively for the Indianapolis 500. And it was the fastest field in Speedway history.[23]

The hundreds of Cummins employees and fans who packed the stands that day enjoyed the thrill of competition, but not the taste of victory. The Diesel Special was steadily moving up in the pack when its luck ran out. According to the *Columbus Evening Republican*, the car was crippled roughly 400 miles into the race by a broken supercharger shaft. But a more technically detailed account in *Motor Trend* recorded later that "on the fifty-second lap the car came into the pits with the mounting flange of its torsional vibration damper broken," and the car was kept off the track because "any quick repair would have been unsafe."[24]

Cummins soon retired Number 61, but not before the big green racer enjoyed a last hurrah. On September 11, with Jackson driving, the car set six diesel speed records at the Bonneville Salt Flats in Utah, breaking standing records for one and five kilometers and one and five miles, and establishing original records for ten kilometers and ten miles.[25]

Cummins was spurred on, rather than discouraged, by its experience at the 1950 Indy 500. Over the next two years, the company marshalled its resources to make a much more ambitious bid for the trophy in 1952. Rather than modify Number 61, Don Cummins and Nev Reiners—again with the help of

Kurtis Kraft—engineered a completely new, high-performance racer dubbed Number 28. The vehicle was so innovative in design and loaded with state-of-the-art diesel technology that some called it a "laboratory on wheels."[26]

To begin with, the racer looked radically different. Whereas Number 61 stood 41 inches off the ground, the top of the 1952 racer—painted radiant yellow and bright red—sat only 23 inches above the pavement, lower than the tops of its tires. This streamlined body design was made possible by two key engineering innovations. First, as in 1950, Cummins installed a four-cycle Cummins Model JS-600. This time, though, the engine was horizontally oriented (a so-called pancake configuration). The drive shaft ran down the left side of the car, next to the driver, instead of down the center of the chassis, with the driver sitting atop the transmission housing. This not only created the car's squat, aerodynamic profile, but also shifted its center of gravity to the left, enhancing its cornering ability on the left-turn-only Speedway. One more feature distinguished Number 28 from its predecessor—and from all other Indy 500 race cars to date: It was the first "Brickyard" entry to be turbocharged.[27]

Cummins recruited a new driver for its new Diesel Special. Freddie Agabashian, a handsome and "golden voiced" Californian, had begun his career in midget car racing, and competed in his first Indianapolis 500 in 1947 at the age of thirty-four. So good was Agabashian at diagnosing mechanical troubles at the wheel that many of his racing cronies called him "Doc."[28]

Don Cummins and Nev Reiners once again headed the effort, but a new aggressiveness and confidence infused the team. They began track testing the race car in mid-April, a full month before qualifying trials were to begin. (The extra lead time proved invaluable, in part because it soon became clear that this car, too, required a higher-horsepower replacement engine.) Agabashian boasted that he would qualify at 140 mph. This year, he insisted, Cummins was entering the race not to put on "a colorful spectacle," but to win. Few took him seriously, including the hometown newspaper, which drolly concluded that "Agabashian's mount is not an outstanding contender."[29]

The qualifying trials changed everything. This time, rather than wait until late in the trials, Cummins entered its car the first day. To the amazement of spectators, Agabashian completed the first lap in 139.104, setting a new track record. (The record was toppled a few days later by "Mad Russian" Bill Vukovich.) But as Freddie pushed the car through the remaining three laps, its tires began to smoke and disintegrate. The Cummins Special not only weighed significantly more than the average racer (some 3,300 pounds versus about 2,000) but it also suffered from weight distribution problems. Although well aware of the danger, "Doc" refused to stop. He completed the run with an average speed of 138.010. "As Fred drove into the pits," one reporter wrote, "rubber from the tire littered the track." Since no one drove faster that first day of trials, the Cummins Special captured the coveted pole position.[30]

This feat sparked a new wave of "diesel fever" in Cummins' hometown. Storefronts sprouted racing emblems, souvenirs, and white-and-black checkered clothing. One cafe featured an "Agabashian" cocktail ("one drink and you go 138 miles per hour"). When race day arrived, several thousand fans from Columbus, including twelve busloads of Cummins employees, packed the Speedway stands to cheer on the new Cummins Diesel Special.[31] Police from neighboring towns volunteered to watch over the nearly deserted city of Columbus.

When the race began, Freddie got off to a slow start, in part due to turbocharger lag. But soon he moved up into fifth place, and held that position for 100 miles. On his forty-fourth lap, Agabashian stopped for new tires, then fought his way back to fourth or fifth place. Sometime around the seventy-second lap the car began to smoke. By most later accounts, the car's Elliot turbocharger had become clogged with track dust and rubber. When Freddie shut down the device, the engine became sluggish and began to overheat. He dropped out of the race, and was ultimately awarded a twenty-seventh place finish.[32]

As with the 1950 race, the reason why the Cummins Diesel Special was forced out of the 1952 contest became a matter of some debate in racing lore. Years after the fact, Joseph C. Miller, a member of the 1952 pit crew, told company historian John Rowell that "when Fred Agabashian came into the pit the car had a broken front suspension. . . . The engine had begun to smoke because of rubber in the turbo and we decided to use that as the reason for stopping." Rowell speculates that Cummins may have fabricated the turbocharger story to protect its relationship with Kurtis.[33]

Another controversy surrounds the speed of Number 28's practice runs. One racing historian has suggested that Agabashian "sandbagged" officials by deliberately slowing down at irregular intervals to avoid detection. "We knew," explained racetrack-savvy Don Cummins, "that there was a good chance that our cubic inch displacement was very likely going to be cut down for the following year, after our showing." Indeed, shortly after the 1952 race, Lou Moore, who had sponsored more winning cars than any man in Speedway history, noisily announced his permanent withdrawal from the competition, citing as one of his reasons the unfair advantage enjoyed by diesels. And in 1953, AAA officials lowered the maximum allowable displacement for diesel engines.[34]

For a combination of reasons, Cummins never reentered the Indy 500. The most important was the fact that despite Number 28's ill-fated finish, the project achieved its primary purpose. As Don Cummins explained, "We didn't *need* to return. The main reason we were there in the first place was to show the world what we thought was the potential of the diesel engine. It worked. Our truck engine sales skyrocketed after that." Speedway president Wilbur Shaw recalled that in 1952 "the car everyone was talking about . . . was the Cummins Diesel Special."[35]

Racing also yielded useful technical knowledge. This was a point that the company's directors certainly emphasized when justifying the endeavor to shareholders. Racing was expensive. The 1952 "laboratory on wheels" cost as much as $500,000, and consumed prodigious amounts of top engineering talent that might have been used on other projects. Cummins' managers decided to rechannel these resources directly into the company's research and engineering organizations.[36]

Ironically, the single most important technical trial-by-fire was barely noted by the public. For company engineers, the focal point of the 1950 and 1952 racing dramas was neither turbocharging (common on some Cummins models by 1952, though new at the Speedway), nor the use of aluminum (impractical for standard commercial engines), nor the left-side drive shaft (also impractical, and used by another competitor in a Kurtis-Kraft car that year). Rather, it was the company's new fuel system, tested in 1950 and refined in 1952, that emerged as one of the most important technical innovations in the company's history.[37]

From Double Disc to PT

"At the present time, the major difference in the cost of comparable gasoline and Diesel engines lies in the very large additional cost of the Diesel's fuel injection system." So wrote J. Irwin Miller to company president Robert Huthsteiner in the summer of 1951.[38] From the diesel industry's earliest days, in fact, fuel injection had been the key technical challenge. Compared with gasoline carburetors, diesel injection systems were large, heavy, and expensive. They also were the chief factor limiting engine performance. Cummins advanced the state of the art in the early 1950s by developing two new injection systems—one an interim and ultimately unsuccessful modification of its existing technology, the second a revolutionary breakthrough.

Cummins' continuing need for a smaller, lighter, simpler, higher-speed injection system was intensified after World War II by its release of increasingly sophisticated engine models. The new VH engine posed a special problem. Some within the company doubted that the single-disc fuel system could adequately supply these twelve-cylinder giants.[39]

Not surprisingly, Cummins engineers first tried to build upon the company's existing fuel injection technology, the single-disc pump. This effort began sometime in the early 1940s, and by the summer of 1946 several hand-built prototypes were being tested. The first patent was filed in May 1947, by which time the device—originally dubbed the TD ("two disc") fuel pump—had been named the DD (for "double disc" or "dual disc") to avoid confusion with products made by the Twin Disc Clutch Company. "Double disc" became the standard designation.[40]

It was an awkward and ungainly injection system: lighter than its single disc predecessor, but extremely complicated and potentially expensive to manufacture. As its name implies, the DD employed two rotating discs (instead of one) to distribute and inject fuel. One disc was dedicated to fuel inlet, the other to fuel discharge to the injectors. Still, the pump had many features that were attractive to Cummins and its customers. It was 65 percent lighter and 56 percent smaller than its predecessor, and was said to be easier to maintain by virtue of its design and unit-replaceable pressure pump, governor assembly, and distributor discs.[41]

In early 1949, Cummins' directors considered launching the DD into commercial production. Clessie Cummins—still chairman of the board, and still actively monitoring his company's progress from his California home— had argued against this step several months earlier. He suggested that Cummins modify existing pumps instead of bringing out an entirely new product. But pressure was mounting for a more dramatic move. Huthsteiner told the Executive Committee that the DD was "the only practical and successful pump" for at least two Cummins models, and that the company needed to offer customers "something new" to meet growing competition.[42]

Even Huthsteiner doubted that the DD could be manufactured profitably, at least in the near term. Materials costs for DD production were running 235 percent above the single-disc norm, overall manufacturing costs more than 70 percent higher. Huthsteiner saw large-scale production (roughly 750 units per month) for a robust replacement market as the most promising road to DD profitability. The directors authorized a 250-unit-per-month plant in 1949, and soon invested additional capital for expansion.[43]

By early 1950, Cummins was offering the DD as standard equipment on several models. Early reports from the field were encouraging; but the honeymoon ended quickly. As DD pumps proliferated on the market (factory output climbed from 196 in 1949 to 3,302 in 1950), so did customer complaints. The pumps were plagued with mechanical problems, including chronic leakage. The DD shared with its single-disc predecessor a fundamental mechanical limitation: Neither could operate at very high speeds under high pressure (the DD's maximum was about 200 psi). This limitation, in turn, limited engine rpm and horsepower.[44]

The financial picture was not much better. In mid-1950, Huthsteiner expressed his frustration with the fact that DD manufacturing costs were still "completely out of line with the old-style pump"—about twice as high, in fact. As late as 1951, an internal study showed that Cummins still would need to sell about 8,000 DD pumps to recoup its investment.[45]

This never happened. Fortunately for Cummins, the DD's invention and commercialization overlapped with the development of an alternate diesel fuel injection technology eventually known as the PT ("pressure-time") system.

Whereas the DD had been patterned after its predecessor, the PT was a radical departure in the state of the art. And whereas the DD was a financial flop, the PT became a resounding success. The fact that the PT's rise accelerated the DD's demise only made Cummins and its customers that much happier.

The PT's basic operating principles date back to Clessie's original work with fuel systems. The Model F, released in 1924, featured the first Cummins direct-injection system in which fuel circulated continuously and injection was timed mechanically by the plunger, which in turn was activated by the camshaft. The system was based on a patent for "a circulating fuel system for oil engines," secured by Clessie in 1921. (The system circulated the fuel both to cool the injectors and to carry away bubbles.) This new system, incorporated into the Model U in 1928, distributed fuel to all cylinders at low pressure, then mechanically injected it at high pressure in the injector heads. The great weakness of the early Cummins system was its poor performance under varying speeds. For that reason, Clessie and Knudsen developed the disc-based fuel systems (patterned after gasoline engine electrical distributors) that served the company throughout the 1930s and early 1940s.[46]

However, the dramatic increase in engine rotating speeds after the 1920s, combined with the single disc's shortcomings, spurred the company's designers to search for a faster, simpler injection method. Clessie made the critical breakthrough by the spring of 1949. On March 23, he explained his ideas to Hans Knudsen in Santa Monica, California. Based on this conversation, Knudsen drew up two sketches of what he named the "P.T.D." ("pressure-time-distributor") system, and showed them to Nev Reiners and Don Cummins. These two men took the sketches back to the Cummins Engineering Department, where Reiners led development of a modified version of the new fuel system.[47]

Clessie did not apply for patent protection of his invention until more than a year had passed, and then only at the urging of one of the patent attorneys representing the company. (Clessie first wanted to improve the technology.) The first application for a PT "fuel supply apparatus for internal combustion engines" was filed under Clessie's name on June 14, 1950. It was granted on March 2, 1954.[48]

Interestingly, this patent offered two alternative methods for regulating the pressure and time of fuel injection. In one method—the more conservative of the two—timing was determined by a rotating disc, as in existing Cummins fuel systems. But in the other, more innovative system—the true PT—the fuel pump supplied fuel at low pressure to a common rail, where it was distributed uniformly to all cylinders, then injected at high pressure by a small mechanically driven plunger within each cylinder head. "The principle of the 'PT' fuel system," explained one expert, "is . . . the fact that by changing the pressure of a liquid flowing through a pipe the amount of liquid coming out of the open end is changed."[49]

Clessie's original PT patent application assigned all rights to the Cummins Engine Company. Three weeks after it was filed, a patent application was filed in Nev Reiner's name on a PT system that was essentially the same as Clessie's but included a setting for engine torque control.* A Nev Reiners patent filed in February 1953 further improved the device; the new version increased engine responsiveness by automatically purging unwanted air from the fuel system. These and other modifications, by improving the PT's performance characteristics and simplifying its manufacture, made the technology (in the words of one Cummins engineer) more "producible, predictable, and practical."[50]

Unfortunately, the emergence of the PT opened another unhappy chapter in Clessie's late-career relations with the company. At issue were royalties from the invention. The dispute came to a head through an exchange of letters between Clessie and J. Irwin Miller in the fall of 1954. As Clessie explained to the chairman, he had assigned his PT-related patents to the company "with the expectation that, maybe sometime before my beard tripped me, you would get around to working out a Royalty Agreement." Miller, on the other hand, believed that Clessie's $20,000 annual Cummins salary compensated him for all work he did on behalf of the company, including technical contributions such as the PT. "As is the case with all other employees of the company, including myself," wrote Miller, "I consider that the salary paid is compensation in full and that, as the result of the salary, all ideas, helpful suggestions, and advice received while the salary is being paid belong morally and legally to the company." Retorted Clessie: "I never considered the $20,000 paid me [to be] payment for any inventions I might turn over to CECO."

Since moving to California, Clessie had not forged an agreement with the company addressing the royalty issue. As had been true with Clessie and W. G. Irwin a generation earlier, Clessie and J. Irwin Miller worked within the bounds and bonds of mutual interest, delicately balancing business and friendship. In most day-to-day matters, the balancing act worked. But not when royalties were involved; not in situations where the importance of financial backing seemed (at least in Clessie's eyes) to be pitted against the importance of technical genius; and not when the financial stakes were high for Clessie. All of these conditions pertained in the earlier case of the OEDC, and now arose again with the PT.

Indeed, the struggle over PT royalties refocused Clessie on the OEDC affair. He complained once again of the "high handed and unfair method

---

*Reiners had continued the precedent, established by Clessie Cummins, of having the name of the R&E head on all company patents. According to Lyle Cummins, the critical development work conducted on PT–like systems by the company in this period was actually led by engineer Bob Schmitt.

used in disbanding the Oil Engine Development Co." Miller countered, once again, that W. G. Irwin never earned a return on his investment in the Engine Company, and suggested that the main reason Clessie was not rich was because, against the advice of the bankers, he had sold his stock too early. But Miller and Clessie managed to put the OEDC matter behind them and to focus on the important issues at hand: PT rights, and a new arrangement between Clessie and the company. For Clessie, the key question was (as recorded by Miller): "Did CLC give CECO something in the PT patent for which he should be paid something."[51]

Naturally, Clessie desired that "any deal should be retroactive . . . as to cover the P. T. Fuel Pump." In the end, it did not. The agreement signed by both men on June 21, 1955, gave Clessie a lump-sum payment of $125,000 ($25,000 a year for five years).[52] It also guaranteed that Clessie could independently create and market his own inventions, while preserving for the Engine Company the right of first refusal of Clessie's diesel-related technologies.

As for Clessie's original PT patent, the company agreed to reassign it (and corresponding foreign patents) back to Clessie, but in exchange for a free license and with the stipulation that he could make no future claims against the Reiners-designed PT system then in production. With the help of patent attorney Lowell Noyes, Miller had convinced Clessie that the PT manufactured by Cummins did not rely on Clessie's original PT patent (because it did not contain his distinctive "needle valve" technology). Through this agreement, the company assumed it was indemnifying itself against future infringement actions by Clessie.[53]

Twice during these negotiations, Clessie told Miller he planned to sever all connections with the Engine Company. But his actual resignation came more than two years later, on August 28, 1957. Clessie was resigning, he said, to "be free to promote my ideas" without conflict of interest. "I would not want any stockholder or officer of CECO to have any grounds for thinking that I had inside knowledge of CECO's problems which could be used in my dealings with CECO's competitors." Clessie was especially interested in promoting his new compression brake, which Cummins had decided not to license. "This does not mean," Clessie concluded, "that my friendship and regard for CECO and its officers and stockholders is any different than in the past."[54]

But there was one more unhappy chapter yet to unfold in the PT saga. The system that the 1955 settlement had given the Engine Company clear title to—and the system that had premiered at the Indianapolis 500—was the "PTR," which was controlled by a pressure regulator. The company had declined to license a variant already patented in Clessie's name: the "PTG," a governor-regulated system. The 1955 settlement included the reassignment to Clessie of the patent for the PTG.

In the two or three years following the 1955 settlement, the Engine Company discovered that the PTR had basic flaws that limited its long-term potential. Around 1960, therefore, the company switched to a governor-regulated PT system, for which it evidently felt it held a valid patent. But Clessie disagreed, and threatened the Engine Company with a patent infringement suit. Replaying elements of the 1955 settlement, the company ultimately agreed (on August 7, 1962) to pay Clessie an additional $175,000 to buy back the patent for the PTG.

By this time, Clessie's youngest son Lyle—a recent engineering-school graduate—was involved in his father's business affairs, and had a firsthand view of this last round of negotiations. He assigns the blame for the multiple misunderstandings between Clessie and the Engine Company to engineer Nev Reiners, who had been in a competitive relationship with Clessie for the better part of two decades. "The sad part," he says, "is that the company could have had both patents for nothing. All they had to do was to bring Dad in on the proceeds, in some way."[55]

All of this was still ahead for the PT when it made its covert debut at the racetrack in the "Green Hornet." The new fuel system obviously had promise, but it needed extensive refinement before it could be put into commercial production. Miller, Huthsteiner, and Don Cummins considered halting expansion of DD manufacturing in 1951 in order to bring out the PT, but decided that a viable product was still eighteen to twenty-four months away. With demand for new fuel systems running high, the executives feared they might "seriously jeopardize our market position" by curtailing DD production.[56]

Still, Cummins moved toward commercial production of the PT at breakneck speed. In late 1951, Ray Boll, the Cleveland regional sales manager, urged the Executive Committee to "make every effort" to produce the new fuel system "at the earliest possible moment in order to have a competitive advance," even if that meant Cummins had to skip the normal "design, field testing, tooling, etc."[57] Cummins' management accepted a portion of Boll's advice. Instead of building "pilot test units" by hand, the company began to tool up for production, and turned out 444 PTs by the end of 1953. Meanwhile, beginning in July of that year, the company instituted an extensive field testing program.[58]

As reports on the PT came in from the field, some Cummins managers bubbled over with excitement. "Everybody loves a winner! We do too! And we know we have a future champion in the PT fuel system," enthused the company's field test supervisor, E. W. Wright. Vice President and General Manager E. Don Tull, for one, found such news too good to be true. "All of the reports which we are getting on the PT fuel systems are so good that they make me skeptical of the real value of these reports. Most of them are verbal reports . . . from our own people." Then, drawing a hard lesson from the recent past, Tull warned: "This is the same pattern that we had when we were field testing the DD fuel pump."[59] But there was solid evidence to support the reports. By mid-1954, a scant 54 of the 1,215 PTs in commercial operation had developed trouble.[60]

The news from the factory was equally encouraging. Whereas single-disc systems had cost an average of $268 apiece to manufacture, and DDs were then running $325, the PT pumps—even at this early stage of production— were being turned out for an astoundingly low $143 per unit. One key reason was the PT's mechanical simplicity. It contained 182 parts, compared with the single disc's 415 and the DD's 448. Cummins began to install PTs on a wide range of engine types and sizes.[61]

By that time, Ray Boll was spearheading an ambitious marketing campaign for the PT's official release, which was slated for July 1, 1954. By the time the release date arrived, Cummins PTs in the field had logged a total of 21 million miles of service. The PT became standard equipment on virtually all Cummins engine models. (Another great advantage of the PT was that it could be retrofitted on every Cummins engine manufactured since 1932.) Nine thousand PTs hit the commercial market in 1954. Unlike the DD nearly five years earlier, the PT quickly emerged as the most popular and successful engine component in decades.[62] As expected, the impact on DD production was immediate and profound. Cummins manufactured 2,930 DDs in the first half of 1954, then production "dropped sharply" in June and halted by the end of the year."[63]

The PT fuel system earned the company recognition and respect in technical circles as the developer of one of the industry's leading injection systems. In that respect, the timing of the PT's release was propitious. Both Bosch and the Hartford Machine Screw Co. (the latter selling under the brand Roosa-Master) released greatly improved fuel pump systems in the early 1950s. Cummins' reputation would have suffered severely without a comparable breakthrough. Ironically, the new Bosch pump featured a disc-type fuel distributor similar to the configuration Cummins was now abandoning.[64]

While engineers debated the relative merits of the competing systems, the PT had a profound impact in the marketplace and, correspondingly, on the company's bottom line (especially after the shift from the PTR to the PTG). As research engineer Joseph Butler observed about his early years with Cummins—the years of the PT's birth—"the PT system gave us a minimum of twenty years ahead of everyone else in the market, particularly with respect to higher engine rotating speeds." Such speeds enabled Cummins to remain at the front of the pack in the automotive diesel race.

Scaling Up Manufacturing and Research

The new technologies that Cummins introduced in the late 1940s and 1950s—from turbochargers and pioneering fuel systems to new engine lines—were no guarantors of success. Nor was the company's fast-expanding distribution system. Cummins also needed the capacity to manufacture its products in quantities large enough to satisfy demand and to preempt competitors. As business historian Alfred D. Chandler, Jr., has demonstrated, hundreds of large American firms have disappeared because they failed to adequately scale up their manufacturing and research capabilities.[65]

At Cummins, uncertainty and caution predominated in the late 1940s. Locally and nationally, business was disrupted by demobilization and economic adjustment in the immediate postwar years. (In 1948, for example, Cummins was forced to close down several times due to gas shortages and strikes against suppliers.)[66] The company girded itself for the anticipated return of hard times by feeding profits into a special reserve account and, from 1947 through 1949, curtailing borrowing for future expansion.[67]

Sales and profits declined in 1949, but there were signs of recovery, such as the engine plant operating on three shifts. Cummins began to relax its defensive posture by rolling back its "declining price" reserve fund and building a new fuel-pump factory.[68] The real turnaround came in 1950. "We are approaching the maximum capacity of the plant," J. Irwin Miller told shareholders that spring. "Competition is keener than ever," cautioned the chairman, but he added that Cummins "can compete on price and quality and make a profit with the best in the industry." Miller predicted a strong year— yet hardly the 84 percent jump in sales (to $42.8 million) and quadrupling of profits (to $6.6 million) actually posted at the end of 1950.[69]

The company's managers moved quickly to reinvest most of the new-found earnings in new manufacturing capacity. They added 9,600 square feet of new manufacturing space and erected a $1.1 million, 2.1-acre Stores Center (Building 44, south of Sixth Street) that consolidated Quality Control, Service Parts, Chemical Laboratory, and Materials Control.[70] The company then launched an expansion program of unprecedented scale. In April 1951, its directors approved a $6 million plan designed to increase overall manufacturing capacity by 50 percent within two years, with much of the capital going into new machine tools.[71]

With expansion came the rationalization of many production processes. The most dramatic evidence of this new focus on plant logistics was the making of the company's first moving assembly line. Activated on February 8, 1954, the line stretched along three hundred feet of what had been Wilson Street (between Fifth and Sixth). The first engine blocks began their electrically driven crawl at 7:05 a.m., passing through three dozen assembly points, many of which were fed by subassembly spur lines.[72]

These ambitious plant expansions of the early 1950s were dwarfed by even grander programs in the second half of the decade. Much of the new capacity was needed for—and funded by—PT fuel system technology. The centerpiece of the late 1950s growth was the acquisition of the Hamilton Manufacturing Corporation of Columbus and its conversion into Cummins "Plant 2." Planning a relocation to State Street, Hamilton offered to sell its 97,000-square-foot manufacturing building at Cottage Street (between Fourteenth and Sixteenth). Cummins bought the property for $500,000— well below the per-square-foot cost of new construction—and in early 1956 transferred eight parts-production lines and 263 machines from the Main Plant to Plant 2, making it the company's sole manufacturing site for engine parts and components.[73]

Along with acres of new manufacturing space, in the 1950s the company also undertook the first major expansion of its R & D facilities since their completion in 1940. A two-story extension was erected on the north (Sixth Street) side of the laboratory in 1954. The first floor housed test cells "equipped with the latest type of electric absorption and motoring dynamometers and electronic instrumentation" as well as a shop for machining experimental parts; the second contained design, drafting, and office space.[74]

This $600,000 investment reflected a growing commitment to fundamental research as a means of remaining competitive. The research organization, which included approximately seventy-five engineers and an equal number of support people in 1950, grew rapidly in the next decade. Moreover, the company increasingly recruited engineers with advanced degrees and outstanding professional experience. Marion Fast from Detroit Diesel, Dave Marks from Packard, and John Beck—who held a Ph.D. from the University of Wisconsin, and had served as chief power-plant engineer at Douglas Aircraft—were among those who emerged as key researchers at Cummins in the 1950s.[75]

Research had no greater advocate at Cummins than J. Irwin Miller. As more of his time became available for Engine Company matters in the late 1950s, Miller regularly visited researchers in the company's test cells, laboratories, and drafting rooms. At the same time, in speeches, boardroom discussions, and other high-level forums, the chairman spoke again and again about the strategic importance of research and development. In Miller's view, advanced research was neither a corporate luxury nor an abstract endeavor for ivory-tower academics; it was a competitive imperative. "It is the Corporation's responsibility to obsolete its own products with new developments," he told shareholders in 1956. "If it doesn't, someone else will." Through well-chosen words backed by corporate resources, Miller, more than any other individual, ensured that technological innovation became a central tenet of Cummins' postwar corporate culture and strategic direction.[76]

Each year of the late 1950s brought other major expansions. Capital expenditures in 1957 alone doubled (to $12 million), and the following summer the directors allocated another $6.5 million to build and equip a 289,000-square-foot facility that would increase its total manufacturing space by 38 percent.[77] With that investment, the company's capital expenditures since 1950—a year in which the entire company was valued at $20.6 million—totalled $42 million.[78]

Financing these and other costly fixed assets placed unprecedented demands on the company's capital structure. Retained earnings were healthy in the early 1950s, but not ample enough to fund such rapid expansion. Increasingly—although still with the company's traditional conservatism—the company's executives turned to banks and capital markets. Again and again, they learned a central lesson about the expansionary 1950s: Demand for capital consistently outpaced expectations.

In late 1950, the board forged a five-year agreement with a consortium of three banks—Chemical Bank & Trust Company, Indiana National Bank of Indianapolis, and Continental Illinois National Bank and Trust Company of Chicago—which made available up to $4 million in term loans through the end of 1954. This ceiling was reached by the end of 1951, at which time the company directors seriously contemplated establishing a $10 million credit line. Projections showed that rising taxes, dividends, and, especially, capital investments were likely to cause a severe capital shortage within a few years.[79] The heavy investments of the late 1950s exacerbated the problem. In early 1958 Cummins borrowed $15 million from a consortium of five insurance companies.[80]

Still, the rapid increases in retained earnings and borrowings do not explain fully how Cummins grew so robustly in the 1950s. The company also expanded by reducing costs, through a highly effective new program. In the fall of 1946, Clessie Cummins recommended that the board undertake a careful study of costs to help it meet future competition. J. Irwin Miller and other directors echoed this sentiment during several board meetings in 1948, when they discussed cost cutting and inventory control. Robert Huthsteiner later cited this "economy drive" as a key reason for the company's success that year.[81]

Miller provided the impetus behind cost reduction efforts in early 1949 by writing a comprehensive memo on the subject to the Executive Committee. The chairman outlined four "lines of attack." First, Cummins should strive for "price reductions" by buying materials at lower prices and reducing inventories. (This was the most promising area, argued Miller, because "better than half of our total cost of sales is found in purchased materials.") Second, the company should lower the percentage of "returned goods" by improving the quality of design and manufacture. Third, subsidiaries, which were beginning to lose money, should be made profitable "within the next thirty to sixty days." Finally, the Columbus operation should reduce expenses in four key areas: manufacturing, engineering, sales and service, and administration.[82]

In typical fashion, Miller did not spell out precisely how to achieve these aims. Rather, he asked key managers to carry out the work within each area, and provided rigorous examples of how costs could be analyzed. Most important, Miller conveyed a central message: Cost reduction was now a top priority.[83]

On March 28, 1955, purchaser K. Stanley Shaw was named the company's first "Supervisor of Cost Analysis"—a new department devoted specifically to cost reduction, and reporting directly to vice president Don Tull. Even then, Shaw later recalled, "it wasn't formalized." Each week, Shaw, along with Tull, chaired a cost reduction committee made up of representatives from manufacturing, engineering, and purchasing. Managers were instructed to quantify the savings they realized. The results were encouraging; the program saved roughly $1 million in its first six months. Enthusiasm within the group ran high, as each success in cost cutting seemed to inspire another.[84]

Within three years, cost reduction became a central part of the company's strategy. In early 1956, Shaw estimated that his committee (now called the Cost Analysis Group) would save nearly $4.5 million in that year alone. At the company's annual meeting a few weeks later, J. Irwin Miller gave tangible examples of the program's impact. In a period when labor costs had risen significantly and raw materials prices had jumped 20 percent, Miller pointed out, Cummins had reduced its prices and increased its profit margins.[85]

By this time, the cost reduction program was yielding savings in three main areas in roughly equal proportion: Research and Engineering, Purchasing, and "make or buy."[86] This last realm of cost reduction—outsourcing versus vertical integration—was of particular significance, eventually resulting in a fundamental redefinition of the company.

Make or Buy? Vertical Integration in Components

One of the key strategic choices confronting every manufacturing firm is whether to vertically integrate—that is, whether to internalize various "upstream" and "downstream" functions. Forward integration entails taking over distributive functions—usually wholesaling and retailing—that stand between the plant and the consumer. Like many producers of complex producers' goods, Cummins took steps to closely control its distribution system, building a carefully monitored network of dealers and distributors, some owned and some independent.

Manufacturers also can integrate backward. In the case of machinery makers, this involves the production of components, and in some cases can even extend to the extraction and primary processing of raw materials. While only the largest manufacturers invest in complete backward integration—as when Henry Ford bought rubber plantations—most find advantages in producing at least some of their own components. (Otherwise, they remain essentially assemblers.) There are many advantages to insourcing parts manufacturing, including lower parts prices, better quality control, and greater reliability of supply. And there are two main ways to carry out the step: acquiring established parts producers, or building up the capability from within.[87]

In the early days of the Engine Company, when capital was scarce, Cummins bought virtually all of its components from outside suppliers. But as the company grew and became profitable, it began to internalize the manufacture of certain critical parts. After World War II, the push for "upstream" integration grew strong. First, Cummins now could afford to expand into parts making, either through acquisition or internal expansion. Second, through its aggressive cost control programs, the company discovered that it was paying high margins to suppliers. Third, as a large-scale, rapidly growing enterprise with high fixed costs, Cummins was increasingly vulnerable to interruptions in its supply of parts. Fourth, Cummins increasingly was defining itself as the high-quality producer in its field. Only by taking over the manufacture of critical components could the engine maker ensure that its quality standards were met. And finally, the more engine components Cummins produced in-house, the better the company could control the pace and direction of technological innovation.[88]

In each case, the decision to make or buy a component was, as Cummins executive Dick Stoner later recalled, "based on a combination of factors: quality, shortage, price, and control." The complexities of make-or-buy decision making can be seen in two such moves made by Cummins in 1958. One was a case of building a business—the manufacture of filters, later sold under the Fleetguard name—from the ground up. First, however, we turn to the story of Atlas Crankshaft, an acquisition with important strategic consequences for Cummins—not merely because of its scale, but also due to its ultimate financial success.

From its earliest days, Cummins had grappled with the problem of obtaining a reliable source of high-quality crankshafts. The problem was acute during World War II, when crankshafts became the tail that wagged the diesel-engine dog. "It wasn't how many engines we could sell," explained the head of purchasing during that period, "it was how many cranks we could get."[89] The problem persisted in the immediate postwar years, in part because the field of suppliers was uncomfortably narrow. Cummins required crankshafts that were hardened through a special heat-treating process. Ohio Crankshaft in Cleveland met this need with a proprietary "Tocco" hardening process. In 1951, Cummins also began to order the components from Atlas Crankshaft of Fostoria, Ohio, a lower-priced supplier that employed a similar flame-hardening process. But Ohio Crankshaft put an end to competition from Atlas (and several other manufacturers) by threatening patent litigation. Cummins searched urgently for additional suppliers, at one point even encouraging a milling company to develop a flame-hardening method for Atlas.[90]

Fortunately, Atlas developed its own proprietary heat-treating process in the early 1950s. Cummins returned to its longtime supplier with heavy orders, and the two companies resumed their symbiotic relationship. By 1958, Cummins was buying 60 percent of its crankshafts from Atlas, with the remainder coming from Ohio Crankshaft. Atlas, in turn, sold more crankshafts to Cummins—some 40 percent—than to any of its other twenty or so customers.[91]

As Cummins' need for crankshafts climbed steeply in the 1950s, the company's managers began to investigate the economics of manufacturing the vital component in-house. The numbers were daunting. To install production capacity for one hundred crankshafts per day would require two years and nearly $5 million. Moreover, there was no guarantee that Cummins could meet its own exacting quality standards.[92]

Then came a fortuitous turn of events. In late 1957, Stanley Shaw received a telephone call from a machinery dealer who wanted to know whether Cummins would be interested in buying a used crankshaft assembly line from an unnamed manufacturer. Shaw knew that Cummins was extremely interested in such an acquisition, but said otherwise. The reason: Shaw suspected that he knew the identity of the client, and hoped to negotiate directly. Among the many American crankshaft manufacturers, only Ohio and Atlas manufactured to diameters suitable for Cummins engines. Shaw knew the presidents of both companies. In his estimation, Ohio's president "wouldn't sell out for love or money." But Edward A. Harper—the aging founder, president, and dominant shareholder of Atlas—just might be interested. And there was another clue. Although the machinery dealer was based in Atlanta, his call had come in from Miami, where Harper was known to vacation.[93]

Cummins' managers confirmed Harper's interest in selling his firm and immediately dispatched a negotiating team to Florida. The group included Richard B. Stoner (vice president of manufacturing), whose presence underscored his increasing importance to the Engine Company. Stoner was a native Hoosier, having grown up in a small town north of Indianapolis. After military service and graduation from Harvard Law School, Stoner moved to Columbus in 1947 to take a job in the small local law firm headed by Edwin Crouch. ("I wanted to practice law," Stoner explains, "in a community where I could put my feet up on the porch and know the people who walked down the street.") Stoner quickly became involved with the business affairs of the Miller family and the Engine Company, two of Crouch's most important accounts. When Irwin Miller invited Stoner to join Cummins in 1950 to help establish the company's first formal personnel department, the young lawyer agreed readily, and thus began a relationship that was to last half a century.[94]

Once in Florida, Stoner and his colleagues found Harper to be more than cooperative. "Over the years," Stoner recalls him saying, "you've been the ones who have made it possible for me to grow." More than that, Harper said, his managers "preferred that he sell to Cummins" rather than to any of the other active suitors. Harper stated three conditions for a sale to Cummins.

First, the diesel maker had to agree to retain "key personnel" at Atlas. Still, none of the company's three hundred nonunion workers would hold employment contracts, and all would be informed that they would ultimately retain their positions on the basis of their performance. Second, Cummins had to agree to supply Atlas's non-Cummins diesel and gasoline engine crankshaft customers. Finally, Atlas's founder insisted that Cummins receive a fair deal in the sale. Harper's concern for Cummins' welfare, recalled Stoner, seemed almost to overshadow his own self-interest.[95]

The Cummins team was happy to comply with these generous conditions, and agreed to Harper's $1.5 million asking price. (The company's insurable value was more than $2.6 million, its appraised replacement value more than $4.5 million.) On Stoner's strong recommendation, the board approved the deal quickly. Under the terms of the contract signed February 2, 1958, Cummins purchased 2,000 shares at $750 each for full ownership of Atlas and Induction Heating, including their 62,000-square-foot manufacturing facilities.[96]

In May, the three Fostoria plants were put under the charge of Cummins manager J. R. "Bob" Beesley—who was for a time the only manager sent from Columbus—and were operated as the Atlas Crankshaft division of the Cummins Diesel Sales Corporation. The crankshaft business was profitable from the beginning, and in the first year Cummins invested more than $1 million to expand and upgrade its new subsidiary's facilities. More important, the acquisition provided Cummins with an immediate, reliable, cost-effective means of meeting one of its critical component needs, while simultaneously making the company a key supplier of high-quality crankshafts to the industry.[97]

Later in 1958, Cummins took a second major step toward vertical integration by entering the filter-manufacturing business. The rationale behind this move was fundamentally the same as that which inspired the Atlas acquisition: to secure a reliable supply of high-quality components. In this case, however, price and quality were more important motivations than uninterrupted supply. And in this case, Cummins ultimately decided to build up a manufacturing operation from scratch, rather than acquire an ongoing business.

Although the idea that Cummins should produce key engine components was in the air in the late 1950s, J. Irwin Miller put the wheels irrevocably in motion one day while walking through the main plant with Huthsteiner, Stoner, and Boll. "Fellows, we tell everyone how to make a filter," Pete Fritsch later recalled Miller as saying, "Why don't we make them ourselves?" The suggestion, once taken up, was never dropped.[98]

Filters are simple devices, and therefore hold little interest for most engineers. Nevertheless they are critical to proper engine operation. Diesel fuel, oil, or intake air fouled with impurities can degrade engine performance and shorten engine life. Cummins had been receiving numerous complaints about its cloth-bag filters, then being produced by the Nugent Company in Chicago. One frustrated Cummins distributor even began to fabricate his own filter bags. Not long after Miller made his comment, Fritsch (who was responsible for purchasing all of Cummins' filters) bought a variety of brands—variously filled with horsehair, sawdust, paper, and other materials—for laboratory analysis.[99]

But what "set the house on fire" regarding filters, recalled Stanley Shaw, was the discovery through Shaw's cost reduction program that Cummins was paying a premium of some 50 percent for filters of dubious quality. As Shaw put it, "We were getting an awful roughing on filters." Moreover, the situation was about to worsen. Dick Stoner visited the Nugent factory and was told of an imminent 40 percent price increase. As of that moment, Stoner recalls, he was touring the plant with an eye toward learning the business.[100]

Cummins first explored the possibility of entering the business through acquisition. Huthsteiner sent Shaw to California to look over Luberfiner, a manufacturer of by-pass filters. But when Shaw cut open more than two dozen of Luberfiner's hand-packed filters, he found that no two were alike. This was unacceptable; Huthsteiner and Miller insisted that Cummins would enter the business only if it could make high-quality filters.[101]

The solution came through an accident of timing. As part of its aggressive late 1950s expansion, Cummins bought a former textile mill in Seymour, Indiana, eighteen miles south of Columbus. The Seymour Woolen Mills had been established during the Civil War and became best known for its "Lady Seymour" line of blankets. In 1956, Seymour was sold to Louisville Textiles of New York, which in turn sold the property to Cummins in July 1958. Even after it razed a Civil War-era structure, Cummins was left with about 75,000 square feet of manufacturing space. At $55,000, the property was a bargain.[102]

The new facilities were immediately commandeered for filter making. "We're going into a new business, and you're going to start it for us, " Dick Stoner told young Cummins engineer W. J. Hergenrader. "I want you to hire two women, buy two sewing machines, and put them up down there in that woolen mill we bought last week, and start making filters." In its first month of operation (December 1957), operators toiled with sewing machines and hand scissors to turn out 20,000 filter bags for Cummins and a growing list of outside customers. In the next month, the plant produced 100,000 units and, remarkably, turned its first profit.[103]

Manufacturing processes became more sophisticated, and the product line more diversified, as the business grew. For the Model 750 by-pass filter, Hergenrader explained, "we not only had to design the filter, we had to manufacture the processes to manufacture it, and we obtained a patent on a key process." Within a few years, the Cummins "Fleetguard" line (so named in 1963) included a variety of fuel, oil, and air filters.[104]

Not Invented Here: The Jake Brake

As the Fleetguard experience demonstrated, invention could be a profitable approach to vertical integration. But an experience in this same time period involving Clessie Cummins—by now a self-employed inventor living in California—illustrated just how complicated the field of new products could be.

Clessie Cummins learned firsthand, in the summer of 1931, about the dangers of driving a fully loaded diesel-powered truck in mountainous terrain. On a thirty-mile-long downhill grade outside of Barstow, California, the truck's red-hot brakes gave out entirely. "We had escaped certain death by inches," Clessie later wrote of the experience.[105]

The fault was not in the brakes. True, the modified Indiana truck was equipped with a fairly primitive primary braking system that was typical of trucks in that day. But what had changed the braking equation in the truck was the installation of the Cummins diesel engine. In the customary drive-train configuration of a 1931-vintage commercial truck—that is, a gasoline engine and a standard transmission—braking was accomplished largely by the creation of a vacuum within the engine, which worked against the vehicle's forward momentum. Compressed air was, and is, a powerful engine-braking device. It is the compression of air within the cylinders of a gasoline-powered car that "holds back" that vehicle as it runs down even the steepest incline.[106] Diesels, by contrast, provide no inherent engine braking. On a steep grade, they "freewheel," and a heavy load running downhill can create an awesome amount of momentum.

Clessie's diesel truck was the first to experience the problem, but as diesel trucks became increasingly prevalent in subsequent decades, "runaways" became more and more common. Highway departments in the mountainous western states responded by providing runaway-truck ramps on the most dangerous mountain passes, but everyone in the trade knew that a better solution was needed.

In 1955, a decade after he left Columbus and the Engine Company, Clessie began to apply his inventive genius to the problem. Then in his mid-sixties and working in the garage of his Sausalito home, Clessie came up with a system he called a "diesel engine brake control device," designed to sit atop the endlessly modifiable Cummins Model NH engine. Simply put, the apparatus used the motion of the injector cam to open up the engine's exhaust valve near the end of the compression stroke. Compressed air that otherwise would push the piston down in the cylinder instead would be released through the exhaust valve, causing the cylinder to "retard" the engine rather than power it. While the device was in operation, in other words, the diesel engine it acted upon was transformed from a power plant into an air compressor. Clessie likened the result to a mule, which not only worked when it was going up a steep hill but also worked when it was going down.

To be sure, Clessie's brake created heat within the engine. (The laws of physics dictate that stopping a heavily laden truck always must create heat.) But in the case of the Cummins invention, the heat no longer was generated within the brake pads (which become less and less effective as they get hotter). Instead, the heat was generated within the engine, where it would be carried off harmlessly by the engine's cooling system, which on downhill grades was underutilized anyway.

Clessie was aided in this effort by his youngest son, Lyle, an engineer trained at Stanford.[107] According to Lyle, who later became an authority on the history of diesel engine development, altering the compression cycle was far from a new idea. In fact, there were patents dating back almost thirty years which outlined the same basic principles. But Clessie's invention was a deliberate and elegant simplification:

> *There had been many attempts to do it before, but they were all greedy, in that they tried to convert a four-stroke engine into a two-stroke, and to totally change the exhaust-valve timing. Dad's concept was that, yes, it would be nice to build it into the engine. But your engine is basically a power producer, so you don't do anything to your engine that might mean you couldn't come home in a "limp-home" mode. So he superimposed, onto an existing exhaust-valve motion, a motion to open the exhaust valve at or near the end of the compression stroke. The key was to superimpose. That's the key word.[108]*

The fate of the invention was complicated by Clessie's ongoing relationship with the Engine Company. According to the terms of the agreement signed by Clessie and Irwin Miller in June 1955, Cummins had the right of first refusal on any of Clessie's engine- or fuel-system-related inventions. Less than six months after this agreement was signed, Clessie sent his brother Don a letter informing the Engine Company about his new braking device. By mutual agreement, the requisite forty-five-day time limit was extended— "in order to take the pressure off of you, and me as well," as Clessie put it[109]—and was subsequently extended several more times. In the summer of 1957, Don Cummins formally asked chief engineer Nev Reiners to make a study of Clessie's invention, "in order that we may make a decision concerning this patent."[110]

The Engine Company's decision, reached principally by Reiners, was negative. Based on their examination of Clessie's prototype, Reiners and his fellow engineers at Cummins were convinced that they could produce a better braking device.[111] When the patent for the engine brake was registered in March 1959, therefore, it was registered solely in Clessie's name. Clessie was free to market his brake to any interested party.

This he and Lyle set about to do in the spring of 1959. At first, they were frustrated. Detroit Diesel, afraid of drawing antimonopolistic fire from federal regulators, would do no more than promise to buy brakes if Clessie could get them produced elsewhere. White Motors turned them down flat, as did International Harvester. Finally, a solution came from an unlikely quarter. Clessie's nephew Don—the son of his brother, Deloss, who was the Engine Company's service manager through World War II and then took over the company's Phoenix distributorship—had married a young woman from Connecticut. Her father, by coincidence, was a vice president of the Jacobs Manufacturing Company, a small firm in West Hartford, Connecticut. Jacobs was then casting about for new products to manufacture. Through the family tie, Jacobs heard mistakenly that Clessie had invented a new type of air compressor, and company executives arranged a meeting with the inventor to secure an option. Upon learning what Clessie was really trying to sell, they regrouped, and optioned a novel device that the inventor called an "engine brake."[112]

Under the terms of the agreement, Jacobs was to manufacture a small number of the brakes for field testing. This testing began in September 1959, and produced promising results. Jacobs and Clessie struck a deal, the "Clessie L. Cummins Division" of Jacobs was formed, and Clessie and Lyle worked to refine the design of the brake. (The Cummins Engine Company was upset about the similarity between the new division's name and its own—some vendors inquired whether Jacobs had purchased the Engine Company—but took no legal action.) The first production models came off the Jacobs line in July 1961.[113]

Meanwhile, as part of its larger effort to create the "new products" that were needed for diversification, the Engine Company was hard at work trying to develop a competing device. Reiners and his colleagues were investigating a different technology: the exhaust brake. Whereas Clessie's brake used engine lube oil under high pressure to open the exhaust valves, the exhaust brake was supposed to use a minor alteration of the camshaft profile, engaged only when called upon, to achieve a braking of the engine. But it didn't work; and in October 1961, Reiners, Don Tull, and Ray Boll gave up the effort. They stopped all development work on the exhaust brake, and set out instead to develop a hydraulic retarder, which would pump fluid in through a veined flywheel to open the valves.

The market, of course, was not waiting, and Cummins distributors were growing anxious. Customers already were asking for the new "Jake Brake." Some distributors were being approached by Jacobs to serve as distributors of the brake, and most—like Los Angeles distributor Syd Cook—were very interested:

> *I wrote a letter to the factory and said, "I'm very tempted by this opportunity. We can sell them right along with our parts, and so on, because*

*they're really similar things." And they said, "Syd, we're going to have
one in a relatively few months, and it will be a superior product."*[114]

That product never came. The Engine Company's experimental
hydraulic retarder had the advantage of being quieter than the Jake Brake.
("The stored energy in the cylinder," as one trade journal wrote of the Jake
Brake, "is released to the exhaust pipe, producing the familiar 'Jake Bark,'
long the mating call of drivers to attract the attention of female pedestri-
ans.")[115] But field tests conducted by Pacific Intermountain Express and others showed that the hydraulic brake retained too much heat, among other failings. Eventually, this project too was abandoned.

"We made a big mistake in not buying and producing Clessie's brake,"
concludes Irwin Miller. "There was a certain amount of 'not invented here' in
our engineering department. 'We can do a better brake than that in six
months,' they were saying, 'so we don't have to buy that.' Ten years went by,
and we never developed our own."[116]

Throughout that long decade, Jacobs sold thousands of brakes per year.
Fleet operators had discovered that they could save at least one out of four
brake overhauls by installing the brake. And it was in life-and-death situations, such as the one Clessie faced in the Cajon Pass, where the Jake Brake
really proved its worth. Unlike competing devices of that time, it could bring
a truck to a dead stop after a complete failure of the primary braking system.[117] The higher the rpm, the more braking power the Jake produced.[118]
"With the Jake Brake," says Lyle Cummins, "you could go down a 6 percent
grade, fully loaded, at forty-five to fifty miles an hour, and not even touch
your brakes."[119] Truckers loved it.

In response to strong hints from Columbus, many distributors turned
down the opportunity to sell the Jake Brake, only to find that other kinds of
parts business soon drifted away along with the Jake. For the first time, loyal
Cummins customers had a compelling reason to go to another store across
town. There, they began purchasing not only Jake parts and service, but also
"gyppo" piston rings, filters, and other parts that were providing good margins to Cummins distributors during this era of level engine prices.

Distributors who went ahead and stocked the Jake Brake found it a risky
venture. Each time Cummins announced the imminent release of its own
brake, Jake sales plummeted. "If there is some reason, Nev, why you want to
put [us] out of business," one unhappy distributor wrote to Nev Reiners, "we
out of necessity will have to change our attitude towards Cummins diesels,
and I would dislike very much to have to do this."[120]

Cummins, too, was unhappy about the Jake Brake. The Jake could not
be installed without opening up the engine. Initially, the company took the
position that if an engine brake was installed in the aftermarket—that is, any-

where other than the Columbus factory—that act would void the warranty on the engine. But in practical terms, as Ben Bush recalls, this was an untenable position:

> *I got a call from Don Tull one day. Don told me that he'd received a call from someone at PIE, who had said, "Don, I want to clarify something. I just heard something from my shop that I know isn't true. They told me that if we put brakes on these 2,000 engines we just ordered, Cummins would void all the warranties. I told them that couldn't be true, because if Cummins did that, I wouldn't buy these 2,000 engines. So I'm going to call my good buddy at Cummins, Don Tull, to prove it's not true." The fact was, as a practical matter, we really couldn't stop them. They were our customers, and if the engine failed, it was our engine that failed.[121]*

The situation was exacerbated by hard feelings between Jacobs and the Engine Company. Jacobs refused to give Cummins a special price on the brake, treating the Engine Company exactly like it treated all of its other customers. (In fact, every sale to Cummins was made through the Cummins distributor in Cincinnati.)[122] Nor was there a high level of trust: Jacobs refused to allow Cummins representatives on the shop floor in West Hartford, for example. "We used to joke," recalls former Cummins purchaser John McGovern, "that we didn't know whether there was really a factory there or not."[123] Despite serving an estimated 25 percent of the North American heavy-duty truck market by 1981—and a much higher percentage in the West—Jacobs had only a limited production capacity.[124] The brakes often were on allocation, forcing Cummins to scour the globe for alternative sources.* "We went everywhere to get brakes," recalls John McGovern, "and paid a fortune for them. Anything to get brakes, and keep the assembly line going."[125]

In retrospect, it was simply improbable that Clessie Cummins, working in his California garage in the late 1950s, could come up with the world's best engine brake. It was so improbable, in fact, that the brightest engineers

---

*From the Engine Company's perspective, the engine-brake situation did not begin to change for the better until the early 1980s. This was when two unrelated events coincided to alter the relationship between Jacobs and Cummins.

First, Chicago Pneumatic—Jacobs' parent company—was acquired by the Danaher Corporation. Second, the original patent on the Jake Brake ran out in late 1982. Cummins was now free to make its own brake, based largely on Clessie's design; and for that reason, Danaher was determined to recast itself in Cummins' eyes as a good supplier. The effort was successful. Even though Cummins introduced its own "C–brake" in the early 1980s, it continued to buy large numbers of brakes from Jacobs, as well as components for its own brake. By the end of the decade, Cummins was competing with Jacobs in the marketplace for the brake business on one family of Cummins engines, and was sole-sourcing with Jacobs for two other engine families' brakes. "Within the last five or six years," comments John McGovern, "they have been an outstanding supplier."

at the Engine Company (and their counterparts at perhaps a half-dozen other companies) couldn't see Clessie's invention for what it really was—a "wonderful product."[126]

It was the last time, but far from the first time, that Clessie's inventive genius was underestimated.

Transformations in marketing

Postwar marketing at Cummins began with a changing of the guard. In April of 1946, Paris Letsinger resigned after a decade and a half as the company's manager of sales and distribution. "He has steadily and courageously kept the company mindful of its responsibilities to the users of its products," J. Irwin Miller told the board. He thanked Letsinger "for his great services as leader, for his thoughtful advice as counselor, and for his warm heart as friend."[127]

Letsinger, who was elected to the Cummins board at the same meeting, occupies a special place in the history of the company. He knew intimately the field of truck sales, but invented a very different approach for marketing Cummins' products. Blunt and scrappy, he was willing and able to cross swords with anyone in the company. "He drew the gun pretty often," one distributor commented.[128]

He was not easy to replace. His immediate successor, Leonard Beck, also "drew the gun" on marketing issues and soon found himself out of a job. Not until the late 1950s did another marketing head achieve a level of credibility and authority that approached Letsinger's.

A second transition occurred in October 1947, when the board noted the death of Spencer W. Curtiss. For most of Letsinger's tenure, Curtiss had written the Engine Company's advertising and promotional materials. Letsinger felt that the Engine Company's tight-fisted control over its ad copy—all of which was prepared by Curtiss in his Indianapolis office—had kept overenthusiastic distributors from making excessive claims for their engines. "His absence from our midst will be deeply felt," the board concluded, although Spencer W. Curtiss, Inc., carried on with the Cummins account.[129]

Life with the OEMs

Cummins had two distribution channels in the early postwar years: direct through original equipment manufacturers, or OEMs, and indirect through its growing distributor network. Of these two channels, the larger by far was direct sales to OEMs, which generally composed at least three-quarters of the company's engine sales. (Parts, as we will see, were a different story.)

Within the OEM channel, most of the activity centered on truck engines. Just after the war, there were still dozens of truck manufacturers in all regions of the country. Few of these companies made their own engines; instead, most installed (according to their customers' specifications) engines from Hercules, Cummins, Buda, Hall-Scott, Waukesha, and other independent engine producers. Cummins catered extensively to these smaller companies, in part by charging them exactly the same prices that it charged larger customers. "The smaller customers really were the loyal customers," recalls Ray Boll. "It wasn't International Harvester, and Ford, and White that got Cummins going. It was these little guys—Brockway, Brown Equipment, Diamond T, Kenworth, Peterbilt, Corbett, Sterling, and so forth—who were small, flexible, hungry, and met the customer's needs."[130]

As Cummins grew, it acquired more experience with applications for its engines, and shared that expertise with its smaller OEM customers. "Over time, we came to have better technical capabilities in engine applications and operations than they did," Boll adds. "So we were supplying a real service to these people. We knew that, and we worked at that awful hard."[131]

Cummins also recognized the need to approach larger OEMs—especially those with their own engine plants—more carefully. White Motor, International Harvester, Mack, and others much preferred to sell their own engines in their trucks, thereby capturing more profit and keeping their factories busy. As long as Cummins was a relatively tiny operation, its inroads in engine sales were only a minor irritant to the leading OEMs. But Cummins' explosive growth in the late 1940s and the 1950s came, to some extent, at the expense of these manufacturers. Relationships with the larger OEMs therefore became more difficult to manage. But they also became increasingly important to Cummins, as a growing number of smaller truck companies were swallowed up by aggressive competitors like White and Mack.

In other Cummins product lines, such as engines for industrial applications and generator sets, relationships with OEMs tended to be both close and complex. One case in point involved the NVH engine, introduced in the mid-1940s. General Electric wanted badly to install the new Cummins V-12 engine in several locomotives for the Transportation Corps, in hopes of generating a large government order. Cummins turned down GE repeatedly, throughout 1945 and 1946, not wanting to take the engine to market prematurely. In a testy meeting held in Columbus in November 1946, GE's representative accused Cummins of having a "pessimistic policy" about its own product, and said pointedly that his company was fully prepared to go instead with Caterpillar's new 500 hp, 1,200 rpm diesel. Cummins quickly agreed to "consign" two NVHs to GE—giving the giant what it wanted, while still reserving to itself the right to call back the experimental engines in case of trouble.[132]

Dealing with Distributors

Cummins decided early not to own more than a small part of its distribution network. Capital was too valuable to the cash-poor company to have it tied up in land, buildings, and overhead across the country. The two notable exceptions to this policy were the Cummins Diesel Export Corporation (CDEC) and the Cummins Diesel Sales Corporation (CDSC).

CDEC was set up in 1944 in New York City to stimulate exports of Cummins engines. From the beginning, relations with the nearby New York distributor were confusing, and CDEC's enthusiasm for selling and export-ing—combined with its remoteness from Columbus—soon led to difficulties with the home office. "The Export Corporation has recently been accepting an increasing number of orders," executive vice president Robert Huthsteiner wrote to Paris Letsinger in 1944, "and a fair amount of this business is not at all attractive to our company."[133] Within two years, Cummins was seeking "closer contact and liaison with the Export Corporation," and CDEC was relocated to Columbus on January 1, 1947.[134] This, combined with the com-pany's decision to place the head of CDEC on salary (rather than salary and commission), prompted that executive to resign abruptly.[135]

CDSC was established as an internal "holding company" for distributor-ships that the Engine Company either wanted to control or was forced by cir-cumstance to take over. "The company will at all times probably have to own some dealerships," Irwin Miller wrote in 1944, "for the reasons that in some ter-ritories the interest of the factory predominates, and in other territories sales or service considerations may make this necessary."[136] In the late 1940s, Cummins took over—among other distributorships—Chicago (financial difficulties), Salt Lake City and Denver (death of the owner), Boise and New York (poor perfor-mance), and Norfolk (essentially a Navy-oriented war spin-off).[137]

The company also took steps in the later 1940s to strengthen its network of regional sales managers. This small group (which in 1947 comprised rep-resentatives in New York, Washington, Cleveland, Chicago, Fort Worth, Los Angeles, Portland, and Columbus, Ohio) grew out of the prewar effort to ride herd on some of Cummins' more rambunctious distributors. Gradually, the job evolved away from watchdogging to a more managerial role, making the regional representatives "responsible for the overall development of the terri-tory without individual emphasis on engine orders as such."[138] In keeping with that trend, the regional representatives also were placed on straight salary beginning in 1947.

Of course, all hints of direct Cummins involvement in sales could be taken as threats by the company's network of independent distributors. In fact, some went as far as to accuse the Engine Company of allowing the dis-tributors—whose own money was on the line in every case—to "build up the local business, only to have it taken over eventually by the Engine Company when it is firmly established and showing a profit."[139]

Cummins' willingness to be tough with its distributors only reinforced these concerns. The Cummins "Uniform Dealer Contract" (drafted in part by Irwin Miller) was limited strictly to three years. In some cases—for example, where the distributorship was financially shaky, or where its owners insisted on continuing to carry competitive engine and parts lines—the contract was limited to one year.[140] Beginning in the mid-1950s, moreover, Cummins began to specify a uniform look for its distributorships, designed by architect Harry Weese. In effect, the company was dictating how the dealers would spend the money they themselves were putting up, with no guarantee that their contracts would be renewed past a third year.

But the Cummins-distributor relationship was far from one-sided. This was almost guaranteed by the kinds of people Cummins recruited as distributors: independent, entrepreneurial, competitive, active in their businesses, and hungry for success ("under financial pressure," as one internal memo phrased it approvingly).[141] Indeed, from the days of Paris Letsinger, Cummins had been inclined to sign dealer contracts with individuals who were ambitious but undercapitalized. The company also was inclined to underestimate how much money actually was needed to establish and sustain a distributorship. "One thing that Letsinger certainly got wrong," Syd Cook recalls, "was when he said, 'Now, you fellas have got $100,000. I think that will do you for a long time.' Well, it didn't. It 'lasted fast,' as I like to say, and we got into the bank pretty deep."[142]

J. Irwin Miller stated the problem succinctly in 1951: "One of the obstacles to getting good dealers is that the best prospects for dealers are quite often young, aggressive persons who have not yet accumulated adequate capital to buy an existing Cummins dealership."[143] He and other executives considered setting up a separate realty company within Cummins, but eventually opted to establish a Realty Division of CDSC. In March 1956, the board approved the new venture, which was then estimated to cost some $10 million over the next three to five years. About $3.3 million of this amount was to be invested by the company, the rest by participating distributors.[144]

Balance between Cummins and its distributors also was reinforced by their interdependence. As the business grew larger and more complicated, mutual trust and goodwill were indispensable. Los Angeles distributor Sydney Cook recalls an incident in which Cummins made a billing error and charged Cook and his partner, Jim Flanagan, a tenth of what a particular shipment of crankshafts should have cost: "I said, 'Jim, do we need money that bad?' He said, 'Hell, no.' I said, 'Well, that's my thinking, too.' He called Bob Huthsteiner and told him about it, and boy, Huthsteiner was a friend of ours from that day on."[145]

Cook recalls another incident that underscored the fluid nature of the relationship between Cummins and its distributors. He had been trying for months to sell engines to United Parcel Service. Finally, he got an audience with the appropriate buyer, and offered to install Cummins engines free of charge in two UPS trucks for a six-month trial period. UPS—with nothing to lose—agreed, but Columbus flatly refused to go along with the deal. "So I said to the factory, 'Look, it's okay with me,'" Cook recounts. "I told them, 'We'll spend *our* money if you don't want to do it. This is a hell of an opportunity.' Which it was. We sold hundreds and hundreds of engines to those people."

It was not the only time Columbus said no to Cook, whom at least one Cummins manager remembers, more or less affectionately, as a "pain in the fanny" who was "always pushing us for things. 'More power out of the engine, Irwin!' There was always something."[146] Cook had the added clout of serving as the first president of the Western Highway Institute, a lobbying group of carriers and suppliers founded in 1947. In that capacity, he fostered close ties among Cummins, its western dealers, and truck companies in the thirteen western states.

J. Irwin Miller made annual visits to the West Coast distributors and key western accounts from 1947 through 1952. On those trips—timed to coincide with visits to the Purity Store chain, in which the family retained a large interest—he sought and received candid opinions about Cummins and its products. In the conclusion to his report to the Executive Committee on his 1947 trip, Miller wrote, "We must accept the fact that our dealers and owners are generally competent persons, whose opinions are important to our existence, and whose ideas and suggestions must be seriously considered." In each subsequent visit, he painstakingly followed up on the distributors' complaints from the previous year.

This give-and-take was formalized with the inauguration, in 1947, of the Dealer Advisory Council.* This group of peer-elected distributors visited Columbus on an ad hoc basis to discuss issues of mutual concern. In 1947, for example, they considered the issue of engine inventories in the face of a steep decline in booked orders. Beginning in December 1953, Cummins invited the Council to participate in the introduction of the new PT fuel pump. Distributors had a major stake in the timing and strategy of this introduction. On the one hand, increased sales were likely. On the other hand, the distributors carried an inventory of single- and double-disc pumps, only a few of which would be needed if the PT was a success. Would they be credited for double-disc pumps that they returned to the factory? At what rate? (The compromise solution: current distributor net price for the outmoded parts, less a flat charge of $25 per unit.) "Most of the dealers," recalls Syd Cook, "were pleased that Cummins was willing to lay this stuff out."

---

*Again, "distributor" and "dealer" were used interchangeably in this period. Today's roughly equivalent group is called the Distribution Council and includes both distributors and Cummins factory representatives.

Tom Shenk worked in Syd Cook's and Jim Flanagan's Los Angeles distributorship—then the second largest Cummins distributorship in the world—for many years. He reflects on how Cummins and its distributors did business in those days:

> *Syd and Jim gave the rest of us underneath the opportunity to go out and do the things that we did. Without that kind of support, without that kind of integrity at the top, it plain wouldn't have happened. But Cummins was also very vitally interested in much of the same thing. And so we went together. It was family. I think that's a good way of phrasing it.*

The inevitable tensions between the powerful parent and the ambitious offspring—which by 1958 included over forty distributors and seventy branches in the United States, Canada, and Mexico—were consistently overcome by a commonality of interests, mutual respect, and even friendship.

Distributors made most of their profits through the sale of Cummins parts, which they bought at a discount and resold to their customers. Cummins parts could be obtained only through a Cummins distributor. For the distributors, it was a good business, which got better with each engine sold. "Without the parts," Syd Cook says flatly, "you were nowhere."[147]

Over time, Cummins distributors gradually were restricted to carrying only Cummins products (with the exception of such basic necessities as batteries). This limited parts competition and also mollified the OEMs. "Our distributors couldn't handle transmissions," recalls Ray Boll, "or get into the brake repair business, or those kind of things. That was just sort of an understanding between Cummins, the truck manufacturers, and the truck dealers: that all Cummins parts would go through the distributor in some way, and we would stay out of the rest of the truck business. It was live and let live out there in the field."[148]

But there was continual pressure from other suppliers to supplant Cummins in the parts trade. "Genuine Cummins parts" were sold at a premium; competitors' products—scorned by Cummins as "gyppo" parts—sold for less and were broadly available through parts chains. Gyppos often fell short of Cummins specifications and carried weaker warranties.[149] Cummins defended its turf successfully through the late 1940s and 1950s, in part by delivering on its promise of quality. "Both San Francisco and Los Angeles say that the gyppo competition on parts sales is becoming less," Irwin Miller reported after his 1949 visit to the West Coast, "and both of them give more credit to our own quality program than to any other one factor in reducing gyppo sales."

But Cummins' 100,000-mile warranty also played an important role in the parts trade. If a driver or a trucking-company owner paid the premium for Cummins engines, he generally wanted the Cummins warranty that came with those engines. This meant that, at least for the first 100,000 miles, he also wanted Cummins parts. More broadly, however, Cummins' reputation for reliability—manifested in a thousand small ways—sold lots of parts for its dealers. All Cummins marketing old-timers have anecdotes that make the point. Ray Boll's favorite concerns an incident on the Pennsylvania Turnpike:

> *There was this guy carrying kosher beef. He was going over the mountains, and the engine broke down, and the beef had to be blessed by midnight. Well, I got hold of our distributor in Pittsburgh, and by golly, he found a rabbi someplace, and they went out and blessed the beef on the back of that truck.*

Syd Cook recalls how one of his biggest customers used to put it: "When we've got trouble with a Cummins engine, Cummins doesn't run under the bed."

Governance and corporate citizenship

A critical element of the Cummins story between 1945 and 1958 is the company's redefinition of its basic functions and responsibilities. The Cummins of 1945 still very much reflected its cut-and-try, nonhierarchical, small-scale origins. Cross-functional integration—a prerequisite to significant corporate growth—was still ad hoc and event-driven. Internal communications were, in the words of one executive, "catch-as-catch-can."[150] The "softer" business functions, such as personnel administration and public relations, were given short shrift. Employee benefits were minimal, in keeping with the prevailing standards of the day. Except for competitive concerns, Cummins paid little attention to its place in the larger corporate context. And although Cummins was viewed in Columbus as an increasingly important source of jobs, and although the founding Irwin-Sweeney-Miller family involved itself in the affairs of Columbus, the company was not a particularly progressive force in the community.

These modes of governance were forced to change as the company grew from net sales of $27 million in 1947 to $147 million in 1959. This pace of growth both demanded and sustained a much more sophisticated business organization—and also allowed for a much broader definition of the company's "interests."

In 1944, the company took an important first step toward recasting its organizational structure. In that year, Irwin Miller established the aforementioned "Executive Committee," which consisted of the heads of the company's major departments. (In subsequent years, the committee comprised between six and ten managers.) Every Monday morning, the Executive

Committee met to discuss issues of cross-functional concern. These issues were labeled "problems." They were numbered in the order in which they arose, and were tracked until they were resolved.

Improving corporate governance meant fostering collaboration. President J. Irwin Miller, in a memo to the Executive Committee, made this point forcefully: "We are a *team* with the general manager as *quarterback*, not *competitors* with the general manager as *umpire*."[151]

It also meant making the corporate rules clear. Cummins did not have any written policies until August 18, 1942, when Irwin Miller composed Policy #1: on desirable behaviors and characteristics in Cummins employees, which included, among other things, regular churchgoing.[152]* But such policies were issued sparingly, in part because Cummins old-timers were uncomfortable with them. "There is such a thing as a company becoming too heavy in policy," grumbled longtime sales vice president Paris Letsinger.[153]

Better corporate governance (and increased levels of outside financing) also necessitated a more sophisticated use of outside expertise. In 1949 Cummins elected the first outside member to its corporate board: David B. Stern, the Chicago banker who played a key role in the 1947 recapitalization. Stern—although almost a family member as a result of his forty-year relationship with W. G. Irwin and Clessie Cummins—was added to the board because the company wanted access to his "knowledge of various business organizations."[154]

The company also had to clarify the role of subsidiary organizations, such as the Cummins Diesel Export Corporation and the company-owned distributorships. By the early 1950s, the subsidiaries were themselves becoming substantial organizations. They were incorporated and (at least on paper) had independent boards. "It has bothered me for some time," Irwin Miller wrote in 1951, "that although I am a director and president of the subsidiary corporations, I seldom find it possible to attend the meetings and to participate in the discussions that take place in them." The solution settled upon was local boards of directors, comprising people who knew the specific business at hand.[155]

The biggest change in governance in this period, however, was individual rather than procedural. In 1951, Miller took steps to broaden the leadership base of the ever-larger parent corporation, and also to strengthen the company's links to the outside world. He proposed, and the board agreed, to promote executive vice president Robert Huthsteiner to the presidency of Cummins. In a letter to Clessie Cummins, Miller stressed that Huthsteiner—an MIT graduate who had arrived at Cummins in 1942 to handle government relations and strengthen the sales department—had a broad-based "acceptance outside the Company" as well as strong support inside Cummins.[156]

---

*"In my mind," Miller later recalled, "a commitment to a church implied that a person was interested in things other than himself."

Miller later recalled that he implemented the shuffle in part to free himself from the day-to-day responsibilities of the chief operating officer, which was the role that Cummins' president played in that period:

> You buy a sort of freedom that way. As long as you're president, you're stuck. There's a lot of things that people think you have to do for them. If someone else is president, you're much freer to decide what you're going to work hard on.

In the same year, and for the first time, one of Cummins' own officers other than Irwin Miller was named to another company's board.[157] Gradually, the Engine Company was placing itself in a larger corporate context.

The company's spectacular rate of growth in the late 1950s overwhelmed the last vestiges of resistance to a more complex corporate structure. In 1957— the year that Cummins ranked number 330 in the Fortune 500 industrials[158]—the company doubled its public relations staff: from one to two.[159] In 1959, Cummins launched its first employee newsletter (soon named *Power Plus*). Cummins then had 4,300 employees working full shifts, and internal communications were a challenge. Like other in-house organs, *Power Plus* filled the need for the kinds of internal communication that earlier had been met by bulletin boards, word-of-mouth, and other informal networks.[160]

Governance of employee relations also changed dramatically between 1945 and 1960. One reason for the change was Irwin Miller's insistence that his company could do better. On the occasions when he chose to intervene, he pushed the Engine Company's managers to tackle difficult issues. In a characteristic memo, Miller laid down a challenge to his Executive Committee:

> We understand the fact that we must give a machine the best care and the best treatment, if we are to receive from it the best work. We have sometimes shied away from the similar fact that we must give a person the best care and the best treatment, if we are to receive from him the best work. We don't have to worry about being accused of "coddling" a turret lathe—or even a good hog which we are fattening for market— but we (I speak of business men in general) are mortally afraid of being accused of "coddling" an employee. I mention this to encourage us to have the nerve to consider treating our people as well as we would a good hog. So far, I think good hogs have received rather better treatment than good people.[161]

Cummins first considered a pension plan in 1944 but concluded that the $100,000 price tag was too steep for the cash-starved company. But by 1950, the company's finances were stronger. And, the directors noted, all of Cummins' competitors had such programs. For these reasons, they approved a $300,000 plan in 1950. In 1953, the board voted to add a group life insurance plan to the benefits package; and the following year, it voted to liberalize the retirement plan significantly.[162]

The wider community

Meanwhile, the Engine Company was scrutinizing its own position on charitable contributions, as well as the company's larger role in the community. Although some managers argued against any bureaucratization of corporate social responsibility, the tide was about to run in the other direction. External forces helped: Internal Revenue Service rulings in the late 1940s established a corporation's legal right to make philanthropic contributions. And once again, Irwin Miller's behind-the-scenes prodding of the Engine Company proved decisive.

The directors took a halfway step in 1951, when they voted to buy 7,000 shares at $10 apiece in a still-unbuilt Columbus housing development called Columbus Village. A committee headed by Mayor R. L. Stevenson had concluded that the city had a shortage of some 200 housing units. Cummins was therefore asked to underwrite about a third of the cost of the first 54 units. The board agreed, citing corporate self-interest as its motivation. "Lack of housing has been a real problem in connection with attracting qualified man power," the secretary explained in the board minutes, noting that many Cummins employees traveled fifty miles each way to work at the Engine Company.[163]

In the same year, Cummins contemplated its first major contribution to education in Columbus. Robert Huthsteiner's December 1951 memo to Irwin Miller argued strongly for a $100,000 contribution to the Columbus City School Building Program. According to city planners, Columbus needed some $400,000 to build at least two new elementary schools. (None had been built in the city since 1929.) Because Cummins had helped create the problem of overcrowding at the elementary level, Huthsteiner argued, it now shared responsibility to help solve the problem. In addition, "the future growth of the company could be limited by inadequate school facilities." And finally, he argued, since industry pays much of the cost of schooling, "any contribution which we might make in connection with the current [school] fund solicitation might be considered advance payment of probable future taxes."[164]

It seems likely that Miller elicited this memo from Huthsteiner. In any case, Cummins made the gift. (The board was assured by attorney Edwin Crouch that this $100,000 contribution to the Jefferson School building site would be tax deductible.) The Jefferson School gift initiated a flurry of contributions by Cummins to local education. In mid-1952, the company gave $20,000 to Columbus Township to help build two new elementary schools—one to the east and one to the west of Columbus. Later in the same year, the company contributed $100,000 to the Columbus schools to build a new physical education building at the high school on 25th Street.[165]

Gradually, Cummins was becoming comfortable with the idea of gifts for the general good (and its increasing profits were making such gifts feasible). Late in 1953, the company made a $45,000 contribution to the construction of a parkway along the west bank of Haw Creek, and made additional gifts totaling $74,126 for various city improvements.

In 1954, however, Cummins' contributions took a new direction. The company now was feeling some frustration with the Haw Creek project, which was not under way nearly a year after the company's donation. (We have "lost control of the contribution," a management memo concluded grumpily.)[166] Cummins also wanted to establish a strategy for philanthropy rather than responding on a "request-by-request basis." Therefore, in the fall of 1954, the board of directors established the Cummins Engine Foundation "to make contributions for the promotion and support of religious, educational, and charitable purposes." The majority of its nine directors were members of the Executive Committee, and its recommended funding was set at $100,000 per year, although this amount was subject to the availability of corporate funds.

Acting on its educational mission, the foundation announced a college scholarship program for selected sons and daughters of Cummins employees (with at least five years' seniority) in early 1956, and began participating in the National Merit Scholarship Program a year later.[167]

But the foundation was to become most celebrated for a large-scale architectural intervention. This project built on a tradition dating back to 1942, when the Irwin-Sweeney-Miller family's church commissioned architect Eliel Saarinen to design the First Christian Church in Columbus. Twelve years later, J. Irwin Miller—in his role as chairman of the board of the Irwin Union Bank—commissioned Saarinen's son, Eero, to design a new building for the bank. Both buildings would have been architectural departures in any American city. In tradition-rich Columbus, they were revolutionary.

The revolution was soon brought home to the Columbus public school system. The Engine Company's initial contribution to school architecture (the $100,000 grant for the Jefferson School) had led to disappointment. The building was prosaic, at best. "The architects just took an old institutional design off the shelf," one observer recalls, "and put it there. Their attitude seemed to be, 'And we'll put it over *there* tomorrow, and down the street the next day.'"[168]

Because Cummins had long encouraged involvement in community affairs, many of its employees held prominent positions in churches, charitable organizations, and town boards of Columbus and surrounding communities. This was the case with the Columbus Board of School Trustees, which in the mid-1950s included young attorney Dick Stoner.

Stoner was troubled by the outcome at the Jefferson School, and in the fall of 1955, he approached his boss with the problem: "I said to Irwin, 'We've *got* to get better architects on this.' And Irwin said, 'Well, we've used Harry Weese as an architect. Why don't we have him design a school, and we'll pay the architect's fees?'" Weese, later to emerge as a nationally prominent architect, recently had helped Cummins on a variety of projects, including plant expansions, the 1954 standardization of the design of the distributorships, the new Cummins "iron cross" logo, and the color scheme of the 1952 race car.[169] Without ceremony—perhaps to avoid ruffling the feathers of local architects—Irwin Miller committed the Engine Company to making a gift of $25,000 to the Board of School Trustees, to pay Harry Weese's fees on what would soon be called the Lillian C. Schmitt Elementary School.

On December 16, 1957, following the successful completion of the Schmitt School, the president of the Columbus Board of School Trustees read to his board a letter from Irwin Miller. Miller now proposed a formal program of support, whereby the Cummins Engine Foundation would pay the architectural fees for future school buildings in Columbus. There were only three conditions. First, the school board had to ask for the help.* Second, the board had to agree to employ for each building a different architect, to be selected by the board from a list of six nationally known architects. (For the time being, Miller would help to identify these six architects; later, they were prescreened by a "jury" of three nationally known senior architects.) And third, the board had to agree to let the selected architects design any additions to their buildings.

The board approved the proposal unanimously. And although three more years were to pass before the city built its next school, the Cummins Engine Foundation's program was firmly in place. The face of Columbus soon would change dramatically.

A multinational enterprise

In limited ways, Cummins became a "multinational" corporation within two decades of its founding. Its durable engines made their way into unlikely corners of the world—powering ancient buses on moonlight runs across Middle Eastern deserts, providing primary power to isolated Signal Corps installations during World War II, and a thousand other colorful applications—and made

---

*"We never pushed it after the first time," Miller later recalled. "In fact, we tried desperately not to make it paternalistic. And I'm not a nut for architecture. I was concerned about our students working in crummy conditions."

a good and growing reputation for the company. By 1955, Cummins diesels were being sold in 110 countries, and the company had 140 officially sanctioned sales or service organizations outside the United States and Canada.[170]

But despite these overseas experiences, making the jump to a manufacturing facility in a foreign country was a major stretch for Cummins. Clessie Cummins, for one, opposed the move strenuously, and others in Columbus had their doubts as well. Cummins chose one of the friendliest contexts imaginable—a town in Scotland—to explore the realities of multinational business. Nevertheless, there were many surprises, and many lessons to be learned.

Precursors to Multinationalism

The first Cummins engine ever manufactured overseas rolled off the line in the small town of Shotts, Lanarkshire, Scotland, on May 9, 1957. It was a 335 hp Model H. Before the engine was fully crated, the small staff of Scottish and American workers posed for pictures. Then the crating was completed, and the Model H was shipped to Euclid (Great Britain) Ltd., for use in a piece of earth-moving equipment.

By the time the Shotts plant produced this first engine, the idea of Cummins going overseas already was a quarter-century old. The European tour made by W. G. Irwin and Clessie Cummins in 1932 was, in part, a search for an appropriate European partner, who presumably would have manufactured under license to Cummins.

The idea of manufacturing in the United Kingdom arose later in the same decade. At that point, J. Irwin Miller and the Chemical Bank's Seymour Dribben were thinking and talking internationally. Dribben—Miller's American classmate at the Taft School and at Oxford, and his 1931 European travel companion—had worked in Chemical correspondent banks in London, Paris, Amsterdam, Berlin, and Tokyo before taking his New York post.[171] In August 1938, Miller wrote to W. G. Irwin about "some friends of Seymour in New York, who . . . have become enthusiastic about the possibilities of forming a company to operate within the British Empire and to manufacture and distribute Cummins Engines there, exactly as our company is now doing in the U.S." Miller explained that the New York group was prepared to raise up to $3 million in British capital. In spite of some risks, Miller considered the scheme plausible. "I would like to know what you think of it," Miller concluded. "There has been no talk yet of what sort of a deal would be worked out with the Engine Company."[172]

Apparently the European war, and later the death of W. G. Irwin, forced a suspension of these investigations, but the issue of a European venture remained on Miller's mind. Late in 1944, he again corresponded on the subject with the Chemical Bank, which had just forwarded an inquiry from a would-be Chinese manufacturer. Miller wrote that he looked forward to discussing the possibility of selling Cummins engines in China after the war: "We are also much interested in making a connection somewhere in the British empire, and quite possibly in England itself. If you ever run across any group in which you think we might be interested, I will appreciate your letting us know."[173]

In addition to Miller's, other voices within Cummins were calling for the creation of an international manufacturing presence. One of these was Paris Letsinger, the energetic vice president of sales who regularly found an excuse to reach into areas beyond his own functional niche. In the spring of 1943, Letsinger was holding informal meetings with his industry contacts about various postwar prospects. One of these contacts—the executive vice president of General Electric's international subsidiary—asked if Cummins would be interested in a joint venture for manufacturing and assembling Cummins engines in South and Central America. Mexico, in particular, seemed like a promising prospect.[174]

But a definitive voice weighed in against this proposal. Clessie Cummins, once the champion of licensing overseas, now flatly opposed the idea. "History shows that, outside of one or two of the largest corporations, any export arrangement, particularly such as branches or branch manufacturing, or licensing, has been very disastrous and costly," he wrote. "This is so universally the case that it would seem that a small company like ourselves has no business getting tangled up in anything of this sort." Until the company proved itself in the domestic market, Clessie declared flatly, it had "no business in wasting time or effort in trying to solve the problem of sales in foreign countries."[175]

Not until the end of the decade did the Engine Company again begin thinking internationally, and this time, the motivation was quite different. Due to material restrictions during the mobilization period that preceded the Korean War, Cummins (like other domestic manufacturers) was forced to apply to the government for permission to procure raw materials. In 1949, Cummins requested enough steel, aluminum, and alloys to make 1,500 engines per month; the government allocated only enough for 750 engines. To compound the problem, Cummins had made a mistake in its requisition, forgetting that its new supercharged engines required an extra 500 pounds of materials. Instead of having 50 percent of what it needed, the company had only 45 percent. "At that point," recalls former purchasing head Stanley Shaw, "[executive vice president] Bob Huthsteiner called me in and said, 'You got any ideas that we might investigate for getting more material?'"

In fact, Shaw did. The previous day, he had read an article in the *Wall Street Journal* about U.S. companies importing European steel. With Huthsteiner's encouragement—and with a letter of introduction from Chemical's Seymour Dribben in his pocket—Shaw and Cummins' chief metallurgist H. H. Lurie headed for Europe.[176] "The steel industry in Belgium and Germany welcomed us with open arms," Shaw remembers. The Chemical Bank connection was a critical contributor to this warm welcome. "The steel industry over there is run by the money—the bankers. I could have spent months over there and never gotten to the top guys without that letter. But when you got in to the top guys, they would send you up to the plant, and tell the plant what to do."[177]

For the next three years, Cummins bought 55 percent of its steel in Europe. (One purchasing team visited Belgium, Germany, Luxembourg, Norway, and England in mid-1951, making purchases of both steel and aluminum.)[178] Seymour Dribben, who advanced letters of credit for all of these purchases, followed the developments with interest and continued to work on other overseas opportunities for Cummins.[179]

In the late 1940s and early 1950s, Cummins' principal focus was on the domestic U.S. truck market, where it was scoring remarkable successes. But gains in that all-important market actually worked against an overseas initiative. European trucks, for example, did not need to climb steep grades and travel long distances, as did carriers in the western United States. Cummins engines—which were growing more powerful year by year—already were over-powered for most European over-the-highway applications.

Shotts, Scotland

Of course, Cummins and its New York bank were not alone in their interest in overseas expansion during the 1940s and 1950s. In the years following World War II, according to a leading authority on multinational enterprise, American business adopted a new "international orientation," shifting away from its prewar focus on controlling raw materials and taming foreign monopolies and instead moving toward large-scale direct foreign investment.[180]

The foundation for this transformation was laid in the immediate postwar era, when the international business environment became more open and stable, and when U.S. trade policy (at least toward noncommunist nations) became freer. In 1948 alone, the United States launched the Marshall Plan, became a founding member of GATT (the General Agreement on Trade and Tariffs), and passed the Economic Cooperation Act, which provided government guarantees for investment in Western Europe. President Truman's Act for International Development was passed in 1950.

U.S. policy did not support foreign business expansion on a uniform basis. Nation by nation, local economic and political conditions played the major role in determining the scale and nature of American investment. But the robust expansion of the U.S. economy, the near-miraculous economic recovery of most of war-torn Europe, and the political stabilization of the West under the discipline of the Cold War—all combined to encourage an unprecedented level of international economic cooperation, much of which was orchestrated by the United States.

By 1957, the year in which the Shotts plant made its first engine, some 2,800 U.S. companies owned more than 10,000 foreign facilities. Foreign investment by the U.S. manufacturing sector grew 108 percent between 1946 and 1954—a rate surpassed only by the petroleum and mining sectors. Most of these facilities, including Shotts, were established to provide American companies with better access to foreign markets for their leading products. And despite the U.S. federal government's efforts to encourage investment in less developed nations during this period, American multinationals tended to favor advanced economies. In particular, beginning in the early 1950s, American firms were attracted to opportunities in Western Europe. There, they often found that their production simply could not keep pace with exploding demand.

There were also disincentives to investing overseas. European governments occasionally moved to address huge trade imbalances with the United States by restricting imports. In 1950, for example, the United Kingdom cut back on imports. At that time, British trade regulations applied in all countries that traded in British currency (pounds sterling). A U.K. trade restriction therefore created serious difficulties for Cummins, which marketed its Columbus-made engines worldwide. For Cummins, being frozen out of the "sterling market" meant sharply reduced sales around the world. The curtailing of the engine parts business, in particular, was a serious threat.[181] Sales and profits dwindled, and the company's reputation for service was imperiled.

No one understood the rules of this game better than British entrepreneur Bernard Sunley. Sunley (along with colleague William Shapland) headed John Blackwood Hodge and Company, which served as the British dealer for Cummins, Euclid Road Machinery Company, and various other American manufacturers. Blackwood Hodge began importing Cummins diesels in 1946. (Its first orders were for 250 Model Hs destined for use in Euclid 15-ton mining trucks, and ninety Model Ls to be installed in strip-mining equipment.)[182] It had built a major international business selling Cummins engines and parts.

In 1950, Euclid built a new plant in Glasgow, Scotland. Reacting to the import restrictions imposed that year, Euclid announced that henceforth it would power its British equipment with Rolls-Royce engines. Sunley—a colorful figure, big and brash, who looked like John Bull and often brought along his own box of Havana cigars to meetings—made his preferences known: He wanted to keep selling *Cummins* engines to Euclid. He therefore began a long process of pushing Cummins to establish a manufacturing presence in the United Kingdom. Meanwhile, because the importation of Cummins parts also was restricted, he sought and received permission to begin manufacturing some of the parts needed to repair the Cummins engines already in his country.

Not much progress was made until the spring of 1955. At that point, Irwin Miller informed Chemical Bank's Seymour Dribben that he would be going to England during the last two weeks of May. (The trip had been demanded by an increasingly impatient Sunley.) Miller planned to investigate "what the chances are of getting someone to manufacture our engines for sale to our dealers and others within the Sterling area, [and] failing that, [to] see what I can do to get someone to make some parts for our engines within the Sterling area." Miller was particularly interested in any "red hot bankers" known to Dribben who might "assist in this effort."[183]

In 1955, the Engine Company never had manufactured an engine or even a major component outside of its main plant in Columbus, Indiana. On the other hand, when Miller left for England in that spring, he benefited both from his personal experience of the island nation and his knowledge of the company's far-flung international sales. Moreover, Cummins' steel and aluminum purchases of the early 1950s had initiated other executives into the realities of international business. Research director Don Cummins, who would play a key role in the company's first foreign subsidiary, made his own seven-week tour of England, Switzerland, Italy, Germany, Spain, and France early in 1955, and came back confident. "I did not see anything in the engine line that we'd take our hats off to," he told a Rotary meeting back home in Columbus. "In fact, industry abroad wonders how we do it."[184]

Miller was much encouraged by his reconnaissance, and company president Robert Huthsteiner soon headed for Europe to continue the search for a feasible manufacturing and exporting facility. Huthsteiner met with government officials, Cummins dealers, and customers, both in England and on the Continent. While in England, he also met with officials from the all-powerful Board of Trade, who learned for the first time about Cummins' interest in manufacturing in the United Kingdom. These government officials were receptive, but made it clear that they would attempt to steer any Cummins facility away from the prosperous Midlands, and toward one of the country's more depressed regions, euphemistically known as "development areas."

Many of these development areas, Huthsteiner learned, were in Scotland. The collapse of both the textile and mining industries in the United Kingdom's northernmost region had created widespread unemployment there. Factories were standing idle, and young people were leaving Scotland in search of opportunity.

The hard work for Cummins began in July 1956, when a company task force went to the United Kingdom to locate a possible factory site and begin lining up potential suppliers. According to team leader Don Cummins, the work was difficult in part because it was so speculative. "We had no legal authority to commit for a single thing," he later recalled. "We were just tourists." Cummins and his team would show a blueprint, and ask if a plant could produce this particular part. Yes, would come the answer; how many do you want?

Meanwhile, Cummins contacted Allen Young, an official with the national Board of Trade and Ministry of Supply. Among many other activities, Young's boards financed the Scottish Industrial Estates, Ltd. (SIE), a non-profit company dedicated to settling industries on "industrial estates" in Scotland. By 1955, SIE already had leased new or refurbished factory buildings to twenty-five American firms, including Johnson & Johnson, Coca-Cola, IBM, Massey-Ferguson, and National Cash Register.[185] SIE officials, eager to add Cummins to their roster, toured Don Cummins and his colleagues around site after site. They also made a variety of proposals to the Cummins team, including the building of a new factory for lease or purchase. But Cummins felt some urgency and was inclined to find a factory for quick conversion and operation.

Finally, they found one: a vacant former textile mill in Shotts, Scotland, eighteen miles southeast of Glasgow. The facility, vintage 1948, comprised some 150,000 square feet of floor space. Formerly a spinning mill, it was full of obsolete machinery, most of it driven by an antiquated overhead belt-and-shaft system. The Shotts plant, which formerly had employed 600 women and a handful of men, was the subject of much local interest. Margaret Herbison, the local Member of Parliament, was deeply interested in the fate of the plant. She personally had vetoed an American textile company's plan to take over the mill, in part because she felt the region needed an enterprise that would employ men as well as women.

On the morning of October 3, 1956, the small delegation of Cummins representatives presented the company's proposal for Shotts to the Board of Trade in London. One trade official was openly hostile to Cummins' proposal, apparently because it included plans to import some used machine tools from Columbus. The Cummins group was taken aback: This was the first negative voice they had encountered in the United Kingdom. Allen Young, embarrassed, suspended the meeting abruptly. When it resumed in the afternoon, the hostile official had vanished.

The following day, the Cummins plan was approved. Among other important features, it allowed for the repatriation of all Cummins capital invested in the Shotts facility. It permitted the company to import certain machinery that was not readily available in the United Kingdom, and to ship in complete engine "kits" for assembly at Shotts—but only until the facility could produce its own components. In return, Cummins agreed to meet a two-year deadline for making engines at Shotts with 100-percent British content. Shotts was established explicitly as an export-oriented concern: 75 percent of its production (of Model N and H engines of between 200 and 335 hp, and of related parts) was intended for sale outside the United Kingdom.[186]

The Cummins Engine Company Limited was incorporated as a British company on November 7, with Don Cummins named managing director of the Shotts plant. His first task was to oversee a major rehabilitation of the facility (which Cummins had leased from SIE). "We didn't have proper loading docks or other facilities," recalls Robert Barr, a former steelworker from the Shotts area who signed on early with Cummins. "There was very little head room, mainly because low ceilings maintained the humidity and kept the yarn from breaking. There was insufficient light, which was pretty typical. So we had a tremendous amount of work to do."

Cummins knew some of the inherent advantages of the Shotts location. For one thing, the Euclid plant—the initial target market—was only three miles down the road. As anticipated, Euclid quickly abandoned Rolls-Royce engines in favor of Cummins engines. This was significant, because deep-shaft coal mining was giving way to strip mining, and Euclid dominated the strip-mining equipment market.

But there were surprises. One was the quality of the local work force. Shotts turned out to have two kinds of workers who were well suited to Cummins' manufacturing techniques. The first were the trained engineers and apprentices who had worked for local manufacturing companies. "We took an awful lot of Americans by surprise," recalls Barr. "They really didn't have to teach us much. They had to teach us the product, but they didn't have to teach us any basic concepts at all about engineering practices, because we really knew it. In fact, in many instances, we knew quite a lot more than they did."

The second group was unemployed miners, forced out of work by the closure of the local deep-shaft mines. (By the time Cummins arrived in Shotts, only a half-dozen of the area's twenty-two coal mines were still active.) "The miners were very easy to train," says Barr. "People used to say, 'Hey, here you are letting these miners loose on precision parts like injector bodies, turbo chargers, and all the things you have to work with!' But the miners learned very easily, very quickly, and they had a tremendous thirst for knowledge. Plus, I think because they were so used to working with their own devices down below, they could use their own initiative to great effect. That was very helpful to us."

In the early years at Shotts, the managing directors—all of whom were Americans—lived like the British gentry. The company obtained not only a chauffeured Austin Princess for Don Cummins' use, but also acquired "Ravenscourt," a drafty and rambling turn-of-the-century manor house with more than a dozen large rooms. The dining room table sat twenty-four. "We paid about as much to renovate it as we did to buy it," recalls Dick Stoner, who as Cummins' head of manufacturing had authority over Shotts in its early days, "and I think it cost more to heat Ravenscourt than it did to heat the plant." But a second tier of American managers lived in a more typically American style, in eight company-built houses south of Glasgow.

Both Americans and Scots had things to learn from each other. Americans called their bosses by their first names, operated on the assumption that employees of all ranks would use the same cafeterias and washrooms, were addicted to transistor radios, and (from the Scottish perspective) put strange combinations of food on their plates. Scots were blunt, preferred traditional management-labor hierarchies, rode bicycles in all kinds of weather, and—as the Americans saw it—reveled in dampness and unnaturally cold temperatures. "We had problems in the plant," recalls Stoner, "because the British and the Scots felt that we were heating the buildings too much."[187]

The difficulties inherent in setting up Cummins' first overseas manufacturing facility should not be minimized. Distances were effectively greater then. (A brief transatlantic phone call cost $50 in 1957 dollars.) In the start-up phase, factory output was necessarily low: Only one engine was assembled per day for much of 1957, and only around three per day through 1958. Capital investments were unexpectedly heavy.[188] Some participants in Shotts's early days recall an "air of uncertainty" about the enterprise—a sense of "not getting things right."[189] Columbus was seen as overly critical of Shotts's product; and meanwhile, the American-supplied management was erratic. "We sent the wrong people on some occasions from here," a veteran Cummins employee confesses. "And that was our fault."[190]

Another issue was quality control. "Major components of Cummins engines produced at Shotts or Columbus will be completely interchangeable," a Cummins promotional brochure predicted hopefully just before the Scottish plant opened.[191] But many British subcontractors were unaccustomed to Cummins' high quality standards. And despite a regular exchange of engineers, managers, and machinists between Shotts and Columbus, the transfer of technology was difficult and frustrating. Back home in Columbus, Cummins continued (as it always had) to make countless small modifications to its engine designs. The company's engineers did not always remember to incorporate these changes into engine blueprints. In many cases, when Shotts made a "mistake," it was simply the result of following outdated American blueprints sent over on microfilm from Columbus.

But Shotts almost immediately provided some of the hoped-for advantages to the parent company. For example, the first Cummins-powered Euclid equipment shipped from Glasgow went to Canada, a traditional Cummins market that had been closed to Columbus by sterling-market tariff barriers.[192] From the day the first engine rolled off the line, Shotts engines employed both the PT fuel system and the Cummins turbocharger, both of which had been proven out by 1957. OEMs finally began to specify Shotts-built diesels for their on-highway vehicles in 1959, and trade publications soon were giving high marks to the distinctive Cummins product.[193]

Even the hitherto standoffish European truck market began to show interest in the Cummins diesel, which on the Continent had a reputation for being "thirsty but powerful."[194] In the late 1950s, the British government began to raise the vehicle gross weight limits, and to contemplate plans for a national motorways network. As both trends intensified, they tipped the balance away from economy and toward more power in engine operation.

The Scottish facility became profitable in March 1959. At that point, several positive factors converged. First, operating costs had been cut to more reasonable levels. (Ravenscourt was not sold until 1961, but Don Cummins' successor at least drove *himself* to work in the big black Austin.)[195] Second, and far more important, the plant's rising production yielded economies of scale. As more parts were made locally, and as local inventories were built up, fewer and fewer Columbus-made parts had to be air-freighted in. By the spring of 1959, Shotts was the largest-volume producer of diesels within the sterling market.[196]

It was many years before Shotts felt it was on an equal footing with Columbus. When the parent spoke—or visited—the subsidiary paid heed. "There's a Scottish comedian who reckons that the Queen of England must think the world smells of fresh paint," Bob Barr says. "So Irwin Miller must have thought the world of Shotts smelled of fresh paint, because every time he appeared, we seemed to be painting things up."

Miller, in retrospect, draws a lesson about flexibility in the face of change from the Shotts experience:

> *We just about got the plant built when the strip-mining industry stopped growing. All of a sudden, the markets that our business plan called for weren't there. But then the motorways picked up, and trucking in Britain moved into our horsepower range, and the higher weight laws came into effect, and Shotts became a profitable outfit.*
>
> *The lesson I take from that is that Shotts was a success not because the original business plan was good at all, but because we were flexible enough to shift into the automotive business. That applies so many times in business. Your original reason turns out to be no good, but if you are flexible and have a good product and can move quickly, you can shift to profitable markets.*[197]

Ambition and achievement

"The first boom in diesels," noted *Business Week* in 1957, "didn't come until General Motors and Caterpillar entered the field shortly before World War II." After the war, three out of four diesels installed in American trucks were produced—in equal shares—by Detroit Diesel (GM's diesel subsidiary) and the

Cummins Engine Company. But by 1952, the article continued, Cummins alone supplied more than half the diesel truck engines sold in America. And over the next five years, although Caterpillar still produced the greatest number of diesel engines by virtue of its tractor sales, Cummins held a commanding lead in truck engines. The Columbus-based company now supplied 55 percent of the market, versus the 37 percent sold by Mack, its closest challenger. GM, meanwhile, had slipped badly, now accounting for a mere 8 percent of truck diesel sales.

To explain Cummins' remarkable success, *Business Week* focused mainly on the company's aggressive marketing: its "first class promotion," its "personal touch," its attention to the "ultimate user." J. Irwin Miller was interviewed for the story. In typical fashion, he used the opportunity neither to celebrate his company's progress nor to gloat over its victories in the marketplace. Rather, the chairman and majority shareholder of Cummins spoke of failure. "We have proceeded from one failure to another," he said. "Every engine at some stage has been a turkey. We try to salvage what we can." But those familiar with the inner workings of Cummins understood the greater positive message behind the self-deprecating words. For Miller, failure was instructive.

Miller also looked to the future. His vision encompassed two basic tenets: Cummins would remain independent; and Cummins would stay loyal to its core business. To some, these commitments may have seemed innocuous, almost mundane. To others, they may have appeared quaint. In the late 1950s, Miller's philosophy already was beginning to seem out of vogue. Each year, a growing number of engine makers were merging with their suppliers, rivals, or customers. At the same time, the conglomerate movement, fundamentally premised on unrelated diversification, already was stirring to life.

Under Miller's direction, Cummins was driven by a less glamorous mission. Despite the enormous growth of diesel trucking since the war, the vast majority of heavy trucks produced in America—an estimated 80 to 85 percent—still had gasoline engines under their hoods.[198] Therein rested an opportunity.

6 | The Go-Go Decade, 1959–1969

FOR THE NATIONAL ECONOMY, THE 1960s were exciting and expansionary times—a "go-go decade," in the parlance of the day. For Cummins, too, this was a remarkably successful decade. Sales increased dramatically, from $135 million in 1960 to $410 million in 1969. In the middle of the decade—April 1966—the company reached a milestone: the production of its 500,000th diesel engine. The frail creation of W. G. Irwin and Clessie Cummins now was a robust competitor, climbing into the middle reaches of the Fortune 500 industrials.

Still, the 1960s did not bring Cummins unmixed success. The competitive context grew tougher in these years. On the public side, Cummins faced newly aggressive government efforts to tax away the price advantage (or differential) that diesel fuel enjoyed over gasoline. Industry competition grew more formidable, as a result of a wave of consolidations among engine makers and OEMs. Cummins' responses to these challenges were not always successful. And while its lobbying efforts in the regulatory arena were fruitful, there was some troubling news on the technology front—especially the introduction of the ill-fated "V" engine line.

The key strategic move of the decade was the Engine Company's attempt to consolidate with its largest customer, the White Motor Company. When this initiative failed, Cummins' leaders regrouped and reformulated their plans in ways that would have significant long-term consequences. Two key Cummins initiatives in the 1960s were prompted by the collapse of the White merger. First, the company redoubled its efforts to diversify beyond heavy-duty automotive diesels—plans that went largely unfulfilled. Second, the Engine Company increased its commitment to technological innovation by building a $22 million state-of-the-art Technical Center. The benefits of this move were not apparent immediately, but were enormous in the long run.

Meanwhile, as Cummins continued to expand overseas manufacturing—establishing important new operations in India, Mexico, England, and elsewhere—it became a much larger and more international company. And this growth, in turn, fostered a major expansion of the company's philanthropic activities. Programs that began as highly personal, "back-pocket" kinds of operations in the 1950s now blossomed and—when combined with new initiatives—helped transform the physical fabric and civic culture of the city of Columbus.

In spite of these achievements, however, Cummins' strategic position did not evolve in hoped-for ways during the "go-go decade." Growth still came mainly from the explosion of the domestic diesel market, particularly in trucking. It is therefore not surprising that, on the occasion of the company's 50th anniversary in 1969, J. Irwin Miller sounded a cautionary note, advising Cummins to look forward, toward a future whose outlines were only dimly apparent.

In spite of the company's growing size, managing Cummins continued to be an intensely personal endeavor. In some key operational positions, the company enjoyed the continuing and maturing guidance of stalwarts such as Dick Stoner (in manufacturing) and Ray Boll (marketing). In others—such as finance and research and engineering—leadership shifted. At the highest level of the corporation, Cummins continued to derive its strategic direction from the interactions among a small and close-knit cohort of top executives and the firm's chairman (and prominent shareholder), J. Irwin Miller. Between 1961 and 1963, Miller devoted substantial amounts of time to the National Council of Churches, of which he served as the first lay president; but post-1963, he was again actively involved in charting Cummins' future.

Gradually, and inevitably, the cast of characters in Cummins' executive offices changed in the 1960s. Many of these leadership transitions reflected a new pattern: older, homegrown managers were succeeded by young professional managers from outside the community. By mid-decade, several professionally trained managers had been recruited to Cummins, including two recent graduates of the Harvard Business School—Henry B. Schacht and James A. Henderson—each of whom would later head the company. By the end of the decade, the company was aggressively recruiting managers "whose average age is under 40" (noted the 1969 annual report) to lead Cummins into its second half-century.

The decade opened, however, with a key leadership transition of a different sort. On February 29, 1960, Cummins announced that Robert E. Huthsteiner—then in his eleventh year as the third president of Cummins—would be replaced by the homegrown E. Don Tull. Publicly, Huthsteiner's departure was described as a resignation, prompted (according to Irwin

Miller) by an "honest difference of opinion between two people"—Miller and Huthsteiner—who had "the greatest respect for each other."[1]

Privately, the departure was a termination, and a painful one. Miller loathed firing people, but by early 1960 he knew that Huthsteiner had to go. Cummins had outgrown Huthsteiner; and as a result, Huthsteiner's long-tolerated idiosyncrasies were increasingly unacceptable. A bachelor who lived with his two sisters in the faded St. Denis Hotel, Huthsteiner had almost no personal life outside of the company. He worked seven days a week, explicitly disapproved of colleagues who did not, and often spent Sunday afternoons writing brusque memos that he deposited on the desks of his absent subordinates. One reason why the company's international sales and service arm was sited in the Bahamas was that the parent company had a president who refused to fly.* But what finally sealed Huthsteiner's fate, in Miller's eyes, was his inability to work collaboratively with his colleagues—including the one who was to replace him as president.

E. Don Tull was born and raised in Columbus. He first went to work for Cummins in 1922 at the age of fourteen, but was caught by the local truant officer and sent back to school. Tull soon quit school again and spent four years at Reeves Pulley. He returned to Cummins in August 1928, running a horizontal boring machine in the machine shop for thirty-seven-and-a-half cents an hour. He rose quickly through the ranks. In 1935, Tull was named a line foreman on the cylinder block and rod lines, supervising some 35 employees; and five years later he became superintendent of the machine shop, in charge of 700 people. In 1945, he was selected by Cummins for training in the Harvard Business School's Advanced Management Program.[2] By 1955, Tull had risen to executive vice president, and on March 7, 1960, he was elected Cummins' fourth president.

Tull was a rare combination: extremely popular with the rank and file, skilled at identifying and meeting the needs of customers, and thoroughly comfortable in his dealings with Irwin Miller—whether in the boardroom or on the golf course. Three decades later, colleagues emphasize both the incongruity and the ease of the fit. As John Hackett puts it:

> *Don Tull and Irwin Miller represented the extreme ends of the spectrum. Don had come up from the shop floor. Irwin Miller was a much more worldly, erudite, and sophisticated person. And yet those two people were the closest of friends. In my lifetime, I've never seen two people with such different life experiences who had such a great respect for each other.[3]*

---

*Huthsteiner's aversion to airplanes led to the remarkable corporate policy of *sailing* in one direction whenever a Cummins executive visited Shotts, in Scotland. "The president went that way," recalls Dick Stoner, "so you had to go that way, at least once."

Tull is recalled by his coworkers as a flexible manager, very much open to new ideas. At the same time, recalls current Cummins chief executive officer Jim Henderson, he didn't hesitate to hold his young executives' feet to the fire:

> *Don could be a pretty tough guy. There was definitely some intimida-*
> *tion there, and you had to win your spurs with Don by being strong*
> *with him. I remember one time when he was holding one of these great*
> *big staff meetings. My relationship with Don was not working too well*
> *at that time—I had been head of both personnel and facilities, and he*
> *had taken facilities away from me, telling me he didn't think I could*
> *do both. So there we were in this staff meeting. He was at one end of*
> *the table, and I was at the other. He said, "Jim, I understand you laid*
> *off so-and-so up in Canada. He's a friend of mine. In fact, it looks to*
> *me like you're laying off a lot of my friends." I don't know what pos-*
> *sessed me, but I looked at him and said, "Don, I'd like a list of your*
> *friends, because I'd like to get 'em all." He looked at me with just total*
> *shock on his face—and then he started laughing. And from that day*
> *on, it was clear that I had passed some sort of test with Don.*

Tull had his limitations, some of which would impede Cummins' growth during his nine-year administration. He had heart problems that flared up at both the beginning and end of his tenure.[4] Perhaps more significant, Tull was—like his predecessor—a leader from the old school. He expected to issue orders and have them obeyed. "Don Tull was a very directive manager," Henderson says. "Management all sat around the table. Don basically heard everybody's report, and then told them what to do." It was a management style that the Engine Company eventually would need to leave behind. But for the moment, the fact that Tull had the complete confidence of the Cummins work force, the unqualified support of Irwin Miller, and a fierce loyalty among the customer base and the distributor network made possible many of the changes that soon followed.

In August 1960, a few months after Huthsteiner stepped down, Don Cummins resigned his post as vice president of engineering. Don Cummins— brother of the founder, a creative designer in his own right, director of the rac- ing programs of the early 1950s, and prime implementer of the Shotts initia- tive—was truly a bridge between generations. Three months later, longtime board member and financial advisor David B. Stern died. In close succession, therefore, Cummins' president for more than a decade, a "family member" of a quarter-century's standing, and a board member from the founding era left the stage. As new leaders entered the scene in the new decade, they often con- fronted challenges different from those faced by their predecessors. Nowhere was this more apparent than in the shifting terrain of the trucking industry.

A new competitive context

For diesel makers, two of the overwhelming realities of the 1950s and 1960s were the continued growth in trucking and the accelerating dieselization of the heavy-duty truck market. In 1940, trucks carried about 62 billion ton miles of freight, or 10 percent of the total freight movement. By 1961, this had grown to 305 billion ton miles, or 23 percent of the total movement. Meanwhile, the percentage of heavy-duty trucks (over 26,000 pounds of gross vehicle weight, or GVW) powered by diesel engines also increased dramatically—from 36 percent in 1950 to 50 percent in 1962.[5]

For Cummins in particular, there was even more good news. The Engine Company's share of this expanding market was growing. In 1950, Cummins sold roughly half of the heavy-duty truck engines in the United States. By 1962, the company commanded more than 60 percent of this market. This growth derived in part from the demise of key competitors. Buda dropped out of the heavy-duty engine business, while Waukesha refocused its efforts on industrial diesels. Hall-Scott, the leading producer of high-quality heavy-duty gasoline engines, succumbed in the wake of a disastrous explosion of a test-stand engine. Even once-dominant Hercules was slipping into an also-ran status, with its sales declining by about 30 percent between 1953 and 1960.[6] Cummins—although dueling with the integrated Mack, and ever wary of the mighty General Motors—was emerging as the leading independent engine producer in the most important commercial transportation sector.

Fighting the Diesel Differential

Of course, the triumph of the diesel (and by extension, Cummins) had not gone unchallenged. As far back as 1955, when the details of the proposed federal interstate highway system were being hammered out, lobbyists for the railroads were arguing strenuously that higher taxes should be imposed on automotive fuels to offset the huge, indirect federal subsidy that the highways would create for the trucking industry. In particular, they argued for a dramatically higher tax on diesel fuel: five cents a gallon rather than two cents. This so-called diesel differential became a battleground between railroad and diesel advocates for the next decade and a half.

In the summer of 1955, Cummins had assembled an ad hoc coalition—of truck manufacturers, truck sales and service organizations, fleet operators, and independents—to urge Congress to find alternative ways to fund the Highway Trust Fund. The effort (led by Cummins' executive vice president for marketing, Ray Boll, and executive vice president for operations, Dick Stoner) was successful. "That was our first effort at lobbying for anything on a national scale," recalls Stoner. "And we were lucky on that one, as much as anything."[7]

As it turned out, though, the victory was only temporary. Shortly after President John F. Kennedy was inaugurated in 1961, he announced plans to increase the tax on diesel fuel from four cents to seven cents a gallon—a 75 percent increase. Kennedy's motives evidently were mixed. As subsequent events made clear, he was eager to help the nation's ailing railroads, some of which were then verging on bankruptcy. But more to the point, he faced a huge and mounting deficit in the Highway Trust Fund. The 1956 projection of the total cost of the 41,000-mile interstate highway system—$27 billion— had been increased to $41 billion by the lame-duck Eisenhower administration, and insiders suspected that even this startling new total was significantly understated. Kennedy needed to find at least $900 million in new revenues annually to keep the Highway Trust Fund solvent. Increasing the diesel fuel taxes seemed promising.[8]

But there were effective counterarguments. Chief among them was the fact that according to the government's own studies, diesel fuel yielded 50 percent more miles than gasoline under comparable circumstances. And diesel fuel wholesaled for between two and three cents a gallon less than gasoline. Advocates for the diesel industry were certain to raise the obvious questions: Why penalize vehicles that were designed to use a cheaper and more efficient fuel?

Once again, Cummins mobilized its highly effective coalition, which brought pressure to bear not only in Washington, but also on the district level. State by state, district by district, senators and representatives heard from angry and well-prepared constituents about the inequities of the diesel differential. The case they made was summarized in Ray Boll's testimony before the House Ways and Means Committee on March 21, 1961. First, Boll argued, the diesel tax unfairly penalized the diesel segment of the heavy-duty truck market. Second, diesel operators already paid higher taxes, in the form of higher excise taxes on their more expensive equipment. Third, a diesel tax was a tax on the "efficiency and ingenuity" of the diesel manufacturers. "Increasing the federal diesel fuel tax from 4 cents to 7 cents a gallon without a corresponding increase in the gasoline tax," Boll told the committee, "has exactly the same effect as decreasing the efficiency of the diesel engine by 14 percent."

Finally, the proposed diesel differential would hurt Cummins—which had invested disproportionately in technological advances. "Since 1933," Boll explained, "this company has specialized in the development of the heavy-duty diesel truck engine, and has been instrumental in developing this type of engine to its present state of dependability and efficiency. . . . It is not proper to deny this company a portion of the market that it has struggled to create over the past thirty years."[9]

Earl Wilson, Indiana's influential representative from the Ninth District, also joined the fight against the diesel differential, arguing before the Ways and Means Committee that the proposed tax would "serve notice that the future success of private enterprise will always be in danger of tax penalties."[10] By June, Kennedy knew he had lost the battle, and the highway refinancing package passed by Congress in that month left the gasoline and diesel taxes unchanged—and equal.

Struggling with V Engines

The diesel-differential controversy taught Cummins at least two lessons. One was very specific: This was a fight that threatened to recur each time the government needed additional funds. In fact, it did recur—first on the national level in 1965, and again (to the company's astonishment) at the Indiana state-house in 1969. "The passage of a differential tax on diesel fuel in this, our home state," Ray Boll told the Indiana House Roads Committee in January, "would be a most unfortunate precedent."[11] Again and again, the differential was defeated.

The second lesson was a reiteration of an old theme at Cummins. The diesel's competitive edge over the gasoline engine still was small and fragile, an edge that could be wiped out by even a modest tax differential. Of course, the Engine Company would fight tooth and nail against such tax penalties; but equally important, it had to keep pushing its own technology—first to create an ever-broader gap between the diesel and all its competitors, and second to make the diesel appropriate for multiple classes of vehicles. Politics were important. Gasoline was virtually immune to targeted taxation in part because huge numbers of drivers depended on gasoline. If diesel had a similarly broad base, it would be much safer from attack.

These were among the many reasons why, as far back as the early 1950s, Cummins became intensely interested in a new kind of engine: a foreshortened diesel with its cylinders offset in a "V" configuration that made it shorter, lighter, and lower than any existing automotive diesels.

Cummins' interest in the small V engines grew in large part out of the basic economics of diesel power in this period. In the case of heavy-duty trucks, the diesel engine (whether in an in-line or V configuration) was simply more efficient than its gasoline counterpart. Given the large loads and long hauls involved in the intercity operation of heavy-duty trucks, the operating savings of diesel engines were significant, and more than justified the higher initial cost of such engines. In fact, heavy-duty truck operators could save enough in two or three years of diesel operation to eliminate this initial cost differential. After that, the diesel's lower operating costs translated directly into increased earnings.[12]

But the economics for light-duty (16,000 to 19,000 pounds of "gross vehicle weight," or GVW) and medium-duty (19,000 GVW to 26,000

GVW) were different. For operators of vehicles in these weight ranges, the potential operating savings of diesel engines were largely offset by the engine's larger size and weight, as compared with gasoline engines. Due to state and local overall GVW limitations, each pound of increased engine weight meant that the maximum useful payload of the truck was correspondingly reduced. Since diesel engines in this power category (130–250 hp) weighed between 800 and 1,200 pounds more than their gasoline counterparts, diesel-powered trucks had to give up an average of about a half-ton of maximum payload. Over the period of a year, this loss of payload capability would reduce the truck operator's revenue by one to two dollars per pound of excess weight. In some cases, the loss of earnings due to decreased payloads eliminated the potential savings of diesel operations. In other cases, the margin of potential savings over reduced revenues was so small that the higher initial cost of the diesel engine took too many years to pay off.

One reason why these pre-1960s diesel engines were heavier than their gasoline counterparts was the diesel's higher compression ratio. Because diesel engines use the heat of compression to ignite the fuel injected into the cylinder, the compression ratio must be relatively high, usually 16:1 or greater. The diesel's higher cylinder pressures mean that its principal parts, including the cylinder block, cylinder head, pistons, connecting rods, crankshaft, and associated bearings, must be stronger and heavier than their counterparts in gasoline engines.

Finally, 1950s-era diesels were larger and heavier than comparable gasoline engines because diesel manufacturers at the time were convinced that the diesel's piston strokes had to be longer than the diameter, or bore, of its cylinders. An engine is said to be "undersquare" when the bore is less than the stroke, and "oversquare" when the bore is greater than the stroke. Diesels in the 1950s, whether in-line or V-configured, all were undersquare, necessitating the use of long connecting rods and tall cylinder blocks. An increase of one inch in the stroke of a diesel engine usually resulted in approximately a three-inch increase in the overall height of the engine.

In other words, because they were too tall, long, and heavy, diesel engines were inappropriate for use in light- and medium-duty trucks. But for the company that could develop a lighter, short-stroke, V-configured diesel, vast new markets would open up. (The existing market alone was huge. In 1959, Cummins estimated that some 550,000 of the 1 million gasoline-powered trucks on the road between 12,000 and 16,000 pounds of GVW were suitable for diesel repowering.)[13] And, as a bonus, heavy-duty tractor operators would buy the Vs if their smaller profile and reduced weight would allow for increased cargo space and a larger percentage of GVW being preserved for the payload.

Cummins first began designing a compact V-engine line in 1953—the same year General Motors launched a program to develop a short-stroke four-cycle diesel engine. Both companies encountered serious difficulties. Over the next decade, GM launched at least five more initiatives to design an oversquare diesel, all of them unsuccessful. For its part, Cummins had little to show after six years of intermittent work. By 1959, Irwin Miller had run out of patience. Earlier in the year, Detroit Diesel had announced the introduction of eight new V-type engines, including models aimed at the light- and medium-duty truck markets. In a confidential memo to his top subordinates, he asserted that the "sales and profits lost by this delay and failure to have a commanding product edge are astronomical." Things were so desperate, as Miller saw it, that Cummins could afford to spend "*any sum of money* required to get this *family* of [smaller V] engines selected and in existence before the end of 1960, and in *full production, commercially proven*, by the end of 1961." Miller added that money was "*absolutely no object*" in accomplishing this vital goal.[14]

Miller was not given to the indiscriminate use of italics—nor to asserting that money was no object—and those who saw this memo got the message. Two days later, a series of weekly "New Engine Meetings" was inaugurated. "This Company has never given proper attention to the weight of its products," Miller noted after the first of these meetings. "Every time I ask what an engine weighs, no one in the Research Laboratory can tell me right away. . . ."[15] Weight, Miller knew, was the all-important factor in the light- and medium-duty markets.

Layouts of the new engines from "clean paper" began on January 2, 1960. Efforts to design a V-6 (six-cylinder, codenamed Vim), a V-8 (eight-cylinder, codenamed Vine), and a V-12 (twelve-cylinder, codenamed Voom) were launched simultaneously and progressed rapidly. On May 24, Cummins' principal officers and directors assembled in the research lab to watch engineer Nev Reiners start the new Vine engine for the first time. (The first six-cylinder Vim engine was built on August 1, and ran for the first time two days later.) In July 1960, a Vine engine was installed in a truck and operated in and around Columbus; and in December, the research department released for production all 238 of the original Vim and Vine drawings.[16]

Not until July 1961, however, did the first Vines go into commercial field testing, when Oakland-based Pacific Intermountain Express (PIE) put thirty-six Vine-powered Peterbilt tractors into service on the West Coast. It was a gamble on PIE's part, since up to that point the oversquare engines had gone through only minimal road tests. "Obviously," PIE's assistant vice president J. W. Riesing wrote in a report, "we had confidence in both Cummins laboratory procedures and in the factory's willingness to rectify anything found to be fundamentally wrong."[17] The experiment was judged a success—the compact V-8s allowed increases of 1,000 cubic feet of cargo space and 700 pounds of payload, with acceptable fuel mileage—and PIE ordered an additional thirty-five Peterbilts powered by Vines.

Even more significant, PIE also ordered six V-6 "Vims" for city pickup and delivery service. This was a promising indication that Cummins' customers might be willing to dieselize the vast "stop and go" market. But the Vines (at 265 hp) and even the Vims (at 200 hp) were still too large and too heavy for much of this market. What was needed was still smaller and lighter engines. Irwin Miller spoke optimistically in September 1961 to a *Time* magazine reporter about the imminent introduction of two more engines: the "Val" (V-6, 140 hp) and the "Vit" (a V-6 turbocharged engine). These engines would tap a market "so large that volume production would make a diesel as cheap to purchase as a gasoline engine."[18]

But once again, Miller and his company encountered frustration. One problem was mileage: the Vs simply were not as fuel-efficient as their in-line counterparts, and fuel efficiency was supposed to be the main selling point of the diesel engine. A much more troubling problem was performance. The Vims and Vines, which hit the market in volume in 1962, were generating major warranty costs by 1963. They were then averaging almost five failures per warranty period—more than six times as many as the non-V Cummins engines. The average warranty cost on an NH engine (in May 1963) was $61; on the Vine the equivalent figure was $1,285.[19]

Irwin Miller was aghast. As more and more Vs were sold, Cummins' warranty liabilities could only grow. Vim/Vine warranty costs in 1963 totaled $3.4 million, and were projected to cost (if hoped-for improvements went *well*) another $3.1 million in 1964, for a projected two-year total of $6.5 million. Miller bluntly interpreted the significance of this figure in a memo to Don Tull and Nev Reiners: "This is more than the total dividends paid the Cummins shareholders in these two years. I wonder if the Research Division of the Company understands this? . . . A lesson to be learned from this is that in the development, testing, and introduction of new engine models, there is every reason to go twice as far as one thinks necessary in product design to minimize failures, for you cannot possibly spend in this area as much as we will now have to spend to correct our errors."[20]

Even more ominously, as Miller was well aware, contracts recently had been signed with two overseas manufacturers—DINA in Mexico and Chrysler in the United Kingdom—to manufacture the relatively untested Vals and Vales (eight-cylinder models of the Val), even before they were introduced in the domestic marketplace. Were they about to create the same huge liabilities for Cummins?

Cummins had rushed its first two oversquare Vs to market; it would now go slower with the smaller Vs. Another six months of fine-tuning passed before a Val was installed in a White 1500 van for road-testing in the Columbus area—in June 1964—and fully two more years elapsed before (in September 1966) Cummins formally put the small Vs on the market in the United States.[21]

Initially, responses from the domestic market were positive. But continuing bad news about the Vims and Vines soon was reinforced by reports of customer problems with the Vals and Vales. Then, in 1967, International Harvester announced that it would introduce its own small-V engine, code-named the DV550. All of this forced a rethinking of corporate strategy at Cummins. Peter W. Schutz, director of engine division planning, laid out the options for management in late 1967. The Vals and Vales, he concluded, were "an outclassed product that does not represent the 'state of the art.'" Cummins either could improve the Vals and Vales, and then fight to establish them in the marketplace, or tacitly redirect development efforts into an improved (and heavier) engine.[22]

Ultimately, the company took the latter route. For public consumption, Cummins still proclaimed that it fully intended to conquer the stop-and-go market. (Irwin Miller told the New York Society of Security Analysts in June 1967 that this market represented potential annual sales of $150 million, or slightly less than half of Cummins' entire sales volume.)[23] But development efforts focused instead on the new V-903 model—which, at 320 hp, was exclusively a heavy-duty engine. For the time being, Cummins was forced to retreat from the light- and medium-duty markets.

Henry Schacht, a relatively new Cummins executive who was called upon to solve some of the problems created in the European market by the over-square V engines, summarizes the overall experience:

> We said, "We're going to obsolete our own product." And nobody talked us out of it, or said "let's go slowly," or "let's make sure it works." So we brought out the engines and put them in the field, and they didn't work—they weren't anywhere near developed. We had decided to leapfrog to a new technology, which was very unusual, and very risky. And it cost us a bloody fortune. Those engines were a bloody catastrophe.

It was a painful lesson, and one that was very much in the minds of Cummins' managers, years later, when they next ventured into the stop-and-go marketplace.

Industry Consolidation

In this period of rapid expansion along two crucial vectors (trucking and dieselization), an engine company could reasonably expect to sell every diesel it could produce. But concealed within this overall growth was a major threat to the independent engine producer: consolidation within the trucking industry. Cummins' initial postwar strategy presumed the continued existence of a large number of small, independent truck manufacturers, all of which would be predisposed to buy engines from Cummins rather than from a fully integrated competitor. But by the mid-1950s, the small producers—unable to achieve economies of scale—were either going out of business or selling out to larger competitors. The prosperous White Motor Company, based in Cleveland, acquired numerous small competitors, including Sterling, Diamond T, Reo, and Autocar. Mack bought Brockway in 1957. Pacific Car and Foundry purchased Kenworth in 1945 and Peterbilt in 1958. Corbett went out of business. Hendricks stopped building trucks to specialize in axles.

Of Cummins' ten biggest customers in 1950 (in descending order, Mack, Autocar, Euclid, Kenworth, International Harvester, Peterbilt, Diamond T, White, General Electric, and Sterling), five either had been bought or had gone out of business by 1960 (Autocar, Euclid, Peterbilt, Diamond T, and Sterling). Three of the remaining five (Mack, International Harvester, and White) either had gone into direct competition with Cummins or had announced plans to develop diesel engines of their own.[24]

The Cleveland-based Euclid Road Machinery Company was a case in point. Euclid was Cummins' biggest customer immediately after World War II, in part because of the postwar boom in construction equipment. In 1953, as Cummins vice president Ray Boll testified at a November 1955 Senate hearing, Cummins sold $4.5 million in engines to Euclid. But in the first nine months of 1955, the first full year after Euclid's purchase by General Motors, Cummins sold only $1 million worth of engines to Euclid. Raymond Q. Armington, the member of Euclid's founding family who negotiated the sale of the company to GM, told the senators that his industry was "too big for a small family company."[25]

Back in Columbus, the trend toward consolidation was viewed with increasing alarm. As marketing head Ray Boll recalled:

> As these little guys went out of business, we began to wonder about our disappearing base. It's nice to have a business where you sell to twenty-five people. It's another thing to have a business where you sell to three, four, or five. If you lose one of the twenty-five, you're not dead. But if you lose one of the five, you've got a different kind of problem. And what was happening was that these small guys just plain couldn't make it. The bigger players began to throw their weight around as they got bigger and bigger, and the little ones began to drop out, or get eaten up.

Deliberations in Columbus about how to respond to this trend continued throughout the first half of the 1960s. (To some extent, they continue today.) Ultimately, the company settled on two responses, each of which required a major corporate commitment. First, as foreshadowed in the 1961 annual report, the company would "enter new fields and manufacture new products." Second—and more surprising, given the company's deep senti-mental and strategic commitment to its own independence—Cummins itself would try to join the consolidation trend.[26]

How to Diversify?

To answer this question, the company in 1961 began working with the management consulting firm of McKinsey & Co.; and out of these conversations came the decision to create a "Special Sales Division." The division's new vice president and head was Marion C. Dietrich, a former sales manager at both Ford Motor Company and the Kiekhaefer Corporation, who had arrived at Cummins in 1961 to head up the parts department.[27] By Cummins' standards, Dietrich was outgoing, ebullient, and energetic. (As one colleague later commented, "Cummins didn't hire those kinds of people.")[28] Dietrich's initial posting had led him naturally to a focus on the filter and crankshaft businesses, in which Cummins was already increasingly involved, and made him an obvious choice as the new vice president.

One morning in late January 1962, Dietrich sat down for breakfast with Miller, Tull, Reiners, and Stoner. "At that time," recalls Dietrich, "the division had about three people in it. And at the breakfast meeting, they turned to me and said, 'Your job is to find $200 million in outside sales. You figure out how to do it—whether it's through buying companies, or associations with other companies, or whatever.'" There were no capital limits placed on Dietrich, except that the return on investment from any proposed undertaking had to be sufficiently attractive. Dietrich was instructed to seek out opportunities that would "capitalize on the quality name and reputation of Cummins and its distributor organization." Finally, he was cautioned not to divert attention away from the current priority of making and selling as many heavy-duty diesels as possible.[29]

It was a tall order. Cummins' net sales for 1961 were under $130 million (down 4.8 percent from the previous year). And—as Dietrich noted in a summary memo—he had been told that it was "particularly important that our first undertakings be successful."[30]

Perhaps for that reason, Dietrich first looked for opportunities very close to home. Filters and crankshafts already were proven successes, and it made sense to broaden these product lines and to find new outside customers for them. Dietrich invented a new name—"Fleetguard"—for the existing Cummins filter line, in large part to make it more palatable for Cummins' competitors to buy the products. By the end of 1963, Fleetguard had a new, distinctive identity of its own, and 132 new products to go with it.[31] Cummins also won a contract with Magnavox to engineer and manufacture aluminum frames for military radios—a short-lived experiment in subcontracting that was not repeated. "We couldn't *make* the damn things," Jim Henderson recalls ruefully. "We tried to take on this contract machining, and found out that we weren't any good at it."

But these conservative efforts didn't come close to hitting Dietrich's targets. To have a real impact on Cummins' "outside" sales, Dietrich needed to make some major acquisitions. Again working with McKinsey, Dietrich developed a list of "screening criteria" for acquisition targets, including minimum annual sales of $10 million, technological self-sufficiency, a good fit with Cummins skills, and the capacity to "enhance Cummins' image as a quality supplier of industrial goods."[32]

By December 1962, Dietrich had a list of six targets that met the criteria. These included Dallas-based Frigikar, a manufacturer of automotive air-conditioning systems; Perfect Circle, a longtime supplier of piston rings, based in Hagerstown, Indiana; an oil-tool manufacturer; and three other companies in more or less related fields.

In this period, Dietrich seems to have come closest to purchasing Perfect Circle.* The company was then going through a management transition, and was being courted by several would-be buyers. Cummins executives were sure it would be a good fit, but (according to a Cummins insider) the president of Perfect Circle, who evidently knew Cummins well, disapproved of some of what he knew: "He is not sure our two companies would be compatible, for he believes we are more aggressive than is necessary to secure a larger percentage of the market. We cut our prices, in his opinion, when we would not need to do so; we push harder than we should for cost reductions with suppliers and with our own organization." Although there had been plenty of hints that the deal would not be consummated, Cummins nevertheless was disappointed to learn (in May 1963) that Perfect Circle was going to another suitor: the Toledo-based Dana Corporation, a manufacturer of automotive parts.[33]

For a short time, Dietrich went back to his list. But his mission—to grow Cummins and diversify its base—soon was shoved aside by another initiative, which commanded not only Dietrich's attention, but also that of every other high-ranking Cummins executive.

The White courtship and its aftermath

In mid-January 1962, the president of the Cleveland-based White Motor Company, J. N. "Nev" Bauman, made an upbeat presentation about his company to the New York Society of Securities Analysts. One reason for his opti-

*Perfect Circle once had been dominated by the Teetor family. The company's longtime president, Ralph Teetor, was a close friend of Clessie Cummins, and was by all accounts a remarkable individual. Although blind, he was an inventive genius and a skilled manager.

mism, Bauman explained, was the fact that his company—long a manufacturer of gasoline engines—was soon to begin manufacturing its own heavy-duty diesel truck engines.[34] One of the analysts in attendance then asked a fairly obvious question. Wouldn't it make more sense for White to merge with the Cummins Engine Company, which already knew how to make diesels, and in any case already supplied almost all of White's heavy-duty diesels?

Bauman agreed that, at least on paper, such a merger would be "logical and complementary." But he also saw obstacles to White and Cummins ever coming to terms, mainly arising from disparities in how the market valued the two companies. As the assembled analysts well knew, White was traded at roughly book value, whereas Cummins traded at about twice its book value. Bauman hinted broadly that, as long as Cummins was "overvalued," negotiations would be fruitless. What Bauman did not say was that negotiations along these lines had been taking place for several years. They were soon to intensify.

White was an old and prosperous enterprise. By 1950, it was Cummins' eighth largest customer, with some $334,000 in engine purchases. During the following decade, White not only grew its own business, but also purchased Autocar (Cummins' second largest customer in 1950), Diamond T (Cummins' seventh largest customer in 1950), Reo, and Sterling, and acquired distribution rights for Freightliner. By 1960, as a result of these acquisitions and of Mack's transformation from a Cummins customer to a competitor, White was Cummins' single biggest account. Including all subsidiaries, White was producing about fifty Cummins-powered vehicles per day.[35]

The relationship was not always mutually satisfactory. For one thing, White (like other OEMs) resented giving up the profitable heart of its truck business to Cummins. In addition, White sometimes made difficult demands on Cummins. In 1957, for example, White asked Cummins to begin putting a small bag of bolts and nuts in each trailer that delivered a load of Cummins engines to the White factories. This would allow White to declare a "mixed shipment" and save on interstate freight rates. (After nine months, an uncomfortable Cummins gave up the practice.)[36] But White was an increasingly important account; and when a White truck was stolen in San Francisco, Cummins alerted its dealers to keep an eye out for Engine #NH 241751.

Meanwhile, Irwin Miller was thinking about opportunities in the truck field. In a memo to his top lieutenants, Miller described the evolution and prospects of the truck industry. Truck manufacturers, he wrote, were still following practices that had arisen during "the impoverished times of the 1930s." They spent little on research, invested little in their plants, and didn't demand adequate returns on their invested capital. "There lies at hand an opportunity," Miller concluded, "for a truck company which is aggressive in research and design, cost reductions and capital improvements, the use of capital and credit, and distribution to capture a very large place in a new and growing market, and possibly make surprisingly improved profits."[37]

The problem was that those profits were most likely to accrue to a company like Mack, which as an integrated manufacturer was in a position to devise end-to-end design improvements. An engine company alone, or a truck maker alone, was far less likely to make such advances. In fact, the chairman of White Motors, Robert F. Black, who had reached the same conclusions on his own, several times had discussed with Irwin Miller the possibility of a merger.[38]

So Cummins initiated serious conversations with White in April 1960 out of two key motivations: concern about a shrinking customer base, and a conviction that a merger between the two companies might eventually lead to a single, stronger, integrated competitor in the trucking field. But Cummins made it clear to White, in these early discussions, that Cummins did not "fear the future." Furthermore, Miller (who with other family members remained by far Cummins' biggest stockholder) told the White representatives that he was "only interested in making a deal if it made sense from the point of view of the Cummins stockholders, and would enable [those] stockholders to do better than if no deal were made."[39] White, for its part, opened negotiations by announcing that it had no particular interest in Cummins' research and development efforts, distribution network, crankshaft business, or international operations. It wanted the Columbus engine plant—and more specifically, according to one Cummins insider, it wanted the tried-and-true NH engine:

> We were all fired up about the V engines. And [White's] Nev Bauman kept saying, "Oh, that NH engine, that's a peach!" And finally, down toward the end of the thing, Nev said, "Well, now, Irwin, I know you're really sold on those V's. Why don't you keep the V's, and put them in another company, and we'll merge with the NH."[40]

Outside-world developments complicated matters greatly. These Cummins-White merger discussions began in the final year of the Eisenhower administration, which was relatively laissez-faire on the subject of antitrust. When Robert Kennedy took over as his brother's Attorney General in 1961, however, the atmosphere toward mergers chilled noticeably. "Kennedy Administration (FTC and Justice Dept.) is new and believes it must be tough," one Cummins manager wrote. "Approvals which were more or less routine a year ago are most difficult to obtain today."[41]

And as both Cummins and White knew, getting Washington's approval for a merger of the two companies would constitute only a partial success. A second phase of the plan, already tentatively agreed to by all parties, would be a subsequent merger between White-Cummins and the Pacific Car and Foundry Company (PACCAR). PACCAR, which had absorbed both the Kenworth and Peterbilt companies, was an important Cummins West Coast customer, then purchasing about 2,000 Cummins engines per year.[42] The company was headed by Paul Pigott, who—in an informal conversation with Irwin Miller one day at an Indiana airport—had agreed in principle to the two-step merger.[43] Unfortunately, nothing was committed to writing, an omission that led later to unhappy consequences.

Yet another complication arose in the summer of 1961, when Mack—a major Cummins customer and competitor—made a surprise overture to Cummins about a possible merger between the two companies. By this time, Mack was buying only a quarter as many Cummins engines as White (2,200 versus 8,000 in 1960), but was an increasingly formidable force in trucking in the East. Cummins quietly examined the pros and cons of a Mack deal, and concluded that, among other drawbacks, such a combination would have even less chance of Justice Department approval than the White merger. After huddling with his advisors, Irwin Miller decided to make himself unavailable to his counterpart at Mack. "Date for meeting," as one note put it, "is most indefinite."[44] It never took place.

On a regular basis, White president Nev Bauman turned up the heat on Cummins. In a January 1962 interview with a hometown Cleveland reporter, Bauman disclosed that White was well along in developing its own diesel engine. "We will not build all our own diesels," he said. "We expect our output to grow, but Cummins still makes a fine diesel." He later told the New York Society of Securities Analysts roughly the same thing. And in the spring of 1963, he told a reporter from *Metalworking News* that White was determined to improve its mediocre 3.75 percent profit-to-sales ratio—and that this meant building its own diesel engines.[45] The message to Cummins was clear: The Engine Company's biggest customer was determined either to get married or end the relationship.

Negotiations between the two companies came to a head at a meeting on May 27, 1963, at the Union Club in Cleveland. Representing White were Nev Bauman and executive vice president J. P. "Pete" Dragin. Irwin Miller, Don Tull, and George Newlin represented Cummins. The basic problem faced by the five negotiators was that while White's earnings were significantly higher than those of Cummins, the Engine Company's market value was much greater than White's. The challenge was to strike a deal in which the dilution in earnings suffered by White's shareholders would roughly equal the dilution in value of shares of Cummins stock. At one point, Bauman observed pointedly that both sides were trying to look good, and that perhaps to make a deal, both were going to have to look bad.[46] In retrospect, it was a prophetic comment.

The deal, as outlined that day in Cleveland and refined throughout the summer of 1963, would give Cummins a tiny but sufficient margin of control over the consolidated company (50.9 percent of the equity for Cummins versus 49.1 percent for White). The Miller family agreed to take two kinds of stock in return for each of their 2.3 million shares of Cummins—0.795 shares of common stock, and 0.795 shares of "Class A" common stock. The latter class was to be a limited-dividend stock for two years before automatically converting to common stock. (The two-class stock scheme was devised by Irwin Miller and his advisors to limit the family's initial dividend stream to what other shareholders would consider a reasonable level.)[47] Both companies agreed to set up a new headquarters in Chicago (considered neutral ground) and designated executives for the new head office. But there was no doubt that Cummins would be the senior partner in the new company—a remarkable outcome, in light of the fact that Cummins was significantly smaller than White ($167 million in 1962 sales, versus White's $447 million). "To some observers," as *Business Week* later observed, "the terms of the consolidation were startling."[48]

On September 25, 1963, the Cummins Engine Company and the White Motor Company announced their intention to consolidate, thereby creating a new company: the White-Cummins Corporation. The boards of both companies already had approved the consolidation agreement. All that was needed to complete the deal was the approval of the stockholders of the two companies, a favorable ruling from the IRS on the tax implications of the merger, and the blessing of the Justice Department regarding antitrust.[49] But almost immediately, stockholders began registering their disapproval. A letter from one Chicago-based stockholder summarizes the opinions of many:

> *In no way can I figure how the merger with the White Motor Company can be of any benefit to the Cummins stockholders. We are asked to trade our stock of one of the best "growth" companies on either board for an ordinary, "run of the mine" company. . . .*
>
> *I am clinging to the hope that this merger may not be as bad as it looks on the surface—and that is my faith in Mr. Irwin Miller. In my opinion, he is one of the outstanding men of the country. I have read a lot about him, and I have heard him speak. My faith in Cummins has always been tied in with Mr. Miller. I realize he and his family have more to lose or gain by this merger than anyone.*
>
> *To surrender my Cummins stock is like losing a favorite relative.*[50]

Miller and the other dealmakers at Cummins were confident that they could ride out this kind of stockholder disgruntlement. (The Miller family owned 63 percent of Cummins, in any case.) But they were less confident about securing favorable rulings from the government. It was welcome news, therefore, when the IRS ruled in December 1963 that it would recognize no gain or loss to the shareholders of either company if the consolidation went forward. The two companies had argued that the reorganization represented a "continuity of interest," and therefore should be a tax-free transaction; and the federal government had agreed.[51]

Still to come were opinions from the Justice Department and the Federal Trade Commission. Both were considered by Cummins to be "anti-merger minded." But Cummins had reason to be guardedly optimistic about getting at least a fair hearing from Justice. For the previous two years, the National Council of Churches, under the leadership of Irwin Miller, had played a critical role in the registration of black voters in southern states. The Kennedys appreciated Miller's willingness to take the lead on this issue, thereby sparing them a politically thankless task.[52]

By 1963, therefore, Robert Kennedy and Irwin Miller were on a first-name basis and in regular telephone contact. But Cummins had no illusions that this relationship would lead directly to a favorable opinion from the Justice Department. In fact, a study commissioned in the spring of 1963 from legal consultant S. Chesterfield Oppenheim had reached several sobering conclusions. "Investigation by government is virtually certain," Oppenheim warned. It was probable, he suggested, that either Justice or the FTC would bring an antitrust suit against the merger under Section 7 of the Clayton Act, and there was only a 50-50 chance that a litigated suit would end with a judgment in favor of the merger.[53]

On September 25, 1963, attorneys Jerrold G. Van Cise (representing Cummins) and Gerhard A. Gesell (representing White) submitted a letter to Assistant Attorney General William H. Orrick, Jr., informing Justice of the impending consolidation. The lengthy letter presented the case for the merger in vivid terms. ("Cummins is now approaching a dead end. The long-range prospects for its diesel truck engines are very poor. . . . For some years, White's position has been precarious. It desperately needs engine manufacturing know-how and assistance. . . .") It stressed that the merger would be good for competition against the "entrenched vertically integrated truck manufacturers," and reassured Orrick that neither company intended to move forward until Justice had all the answers it wanted. Finally, the letter posed the key question: Would Justice support or oppose the proposed merger?[54]

Thus began a long and uncomfortable period of waiting, negotiating, and more waiting. Meanwhile, the beehive had been kicked soundly. Cummins distributors, besieged by complaints and canceled orders from White's competitors, were themselves angry and upset. PACCAR's new president, Chuck Pigott—whose father Paul had died suddenly from a brain tumor without telling his son about PACCAR's anticipated participation in a second phase of merger—reduced Cummins' share of his company's engine purchases from 82 percent to 40 percent in two months. A letter from Cummins chairman Miller to all company shareholders, formally announcing the merger, generated a second wave of complaints.[55]

Meanwhile, Assistant Attorney General Orrick and the workings of his Antitrust Division remained mostly a mystery. Orrick (who supervised some 300 lawyers) was in only his third month on the job. At a chance meeting in Europe, Orrick told Jerry Van Cise, Cummins' outside counsel on the deal, that he used Van Cise's latest book—*Understanding the Antitrust Laws*—as a desk reference.[56] And in an interview published in October 1963, Orrick said that he wanted his division to be "more selective with respect to the types of cases we will bring," and that he was "certainly not against bigness per se."[57] To the would-be consolidators in Columbus and Cleveland—who were now reduced to reading the tea leaves—these seemed like hopeful signs.

Their strategy was simple. If Justice announced that it would not oppose or was neutral toward the merger, the deal would go forward. If Orrick said that he intended to fight the merger, Cummins and White would "appeal up the line" by taking their case to Robert Kennedy.

On February 27, 1964, bad news arrived from Orrick. In his letter to Gerhard Gesell, the assistant attorney general stated that he saw "serious competitive problems" in the proposed consolidation, and therefore could not guarantee that Justice would not sue to block it. And in a case of unavoidable bad timing, White on the same day made public its 1963 operating results, which included all-time record sales and earnings. Cummins' own sales were up only 16 percent, but profits had increased by 27 percent.[58] On the face of it, these did not look like two desperate companies.

Nevertheless, Cummins' and White's lawyers scrambled to try to get Orrick to change his mind. Apparently there was some doubt at the Justice Department about whether vertical integration actually saved money. Cummins quickly pulled together excerpts from Alfred P. Sloan, Jr.'s autobiography and his 1955 Senate testimony on the advantages of vertical integration and forwarded them to Justice. A hurriedly drafted memo, aimed at Treasury Secretary Douglas Dillon but apparently not sent, stressed how beneficial the merger would be to the U.S. balance of payments.[59]

Soon it became clear that there were paralyzing disagreements within the Justice Department. Orrick's immediate supervisor, Nicholas Katzenbach (himself later named Attorney General), was personally inclined to let the merger go through. On the other hand, he was *not* inclined to overrule Orrick, nor to bump the matter up the ladder to Robert Kennedy. And at a crucial juncture, Katzenbach left for a two-week vacation.[60]

On April 6, Irwin Miller wrote directly to Kennedy, indicating that he and Nev Bauman would "appreciate an opportunity to present our views of the business and competitive reasons for this consolidation." One week went by, and then another, and still there was no response from Kennedy. Indirectly, Miller got the message: There would be no "fair hearing" from the Attorney General. In fact, there would be no hearing at all. On April 25, Cummins and White announced jointly that in the face of Justice Department opposition, the two companies were abandoning their efforts to merge.[61]

In Columbus, there was great disappointment in the outcome. And there was a profound bitterness about the behavior of Robert Kennedy. George Newlin, Irwin Miller's longtime financial advisor, felt personally stung:

> *He really was something, I'll tell you. . . . We didn't hear. We didn't hear. We didn't hear. We finally concluded that that was their way of telling us it was off. And then, about three days after Irwin announced that the deal was off, we got one of those slick little political letters from Bobby Kennedy. It said something to the effect of, "Dear Irwin, I know you've been trying to see me, but I gather from the recent news that the subject that you wanted to talk to me about is moot."*

Briefly, Cummins considered other ways of accomplishing its hoped-for vertical integration into trucking, even including a hostile takeover of White. But in the words of one participant, the company's leaders were tired of "manufacturing hay to feed a dead horse."[62] The Engine Company now had nothing to show for nearly three years of hard work—except, of course, a group of confused stockholders, an agitated distributor network, and a reservoir of suspicion among most of the company's key customers.

Regrouping: Two Responses to Frustration

As the White merger was collapsing, Cummins' management was casting about for new ways to do business. The competitive threat that originally inspired the merger still loomed. In fact, the surprise announcement of a proposed merger between Mack and Chrysler, which became public during the interval in which Robert Kennedy was proving so elusive, rekindled Cummins' competitive anxiety.

One response to the White merger's derailment was a stepped-up effort to recruit outstanding management talent from outside the company. The company's own top lieutenants—Ray Boll, Nev Reiners, and Dick Stoner—had made this recommendation in a memo about corporate reorganization issued to Miller and Tull just two days before the White merger failed. Miller himself had been pushing his vice presidents in the same direction and had begun to recruit outside talent at the board level. In rapid succession, beginning just before the public announcement of the merger's failure, he recruited three new directors: Eugene R. Black, the former president of the World Bank; Henry

Hillman, president of Pittsburgh Coke & Chemical; and Henry H. Helm, chairman of Chemical Bank. Within the 1964 calendar year, the nine-man board went from one truly "outside" director to three; and First Boston's president Paul L. Miller joined in the following year. (This shift also was inspired by the need to conform to the requirements for listing the company on the New York Stock Exchange, which occurred in September 1964.)[63] "Insiders" still held sway—five to four—but new voices were being heard.*

Meanwhile, the effort to identify and promote "outstanding individuals" intensified. One of the first to be hired was Henry B. Schacht. Schacht, who spent his boyhood in Erie, Pennsylvania, was the son of a broker at New York City's Fulton Fish Market. The father abandoned the family while Schacht was still young, and Schacht helped his mother make ends meet by selling eggs from the family henhouse. His academic prowess and determination earned him a full scholarship to Yale, from which he graduated in 1956. After Yale, Schacht spent a year selling railroad supplies for the Buffalo-based American Brake Shoe Company, and then signed on for a four-year stint in the Navy. (He was an early American advisor in Vietnam, where—among other tasks—he helped determine that elephants were more appropriate for moving goods than Jeeps.) Returning to the United States, he met and married his wife, and enrolled at the Harvard Business School. Again, he excelled academically, graduating second in his class.[64]

Thus, by the time Schacht received his MBA from Harvard in 1962, he already had worked in a large manufacturing firm and served in the Navy. Both were contexts that he had found stultifying. His resulting inclination to find a "more nimble, more open" environment, combined with an interest in finance sparked at business school, led Schacht to accept an offer from Irwin Management Company—the small, Columbus-based investment firm run by George Newlin, which managed the Irwin and Miller assets. "The approach of the Management Company at that time was to recruit vigorously," Schacht recalls. "I was impressed by the fact that there were relatively young people doing its investing. It was by far the best opportunity that I could see, of any that I had in front of me. They split some capital off, and I was given the job of running it."

Despite having a staff of only about a dozen, the Management Company captured Schacht and two of his HBS classmates in the same "net." "But," Schacht points out, "Irwin Management Company was not viewed by those of us who went there as some sort of back-door way into Cummins. I never saw Cummins. I didn't walk through the Cummins plant. The myth is that Irwin Miller inspired all these people to go to Columbus, but I didn't meet

---

*Longtime research head William Schwab commented in 1996 that Cummins' outside board members had an enormous impact on the company's fortunes. "They were outstanding," he says, "and only Irwin Miller's stature enabled us to recruit talent like that."

Irwin until I had been here for months. I wasn't the least bit interested in Cummins."

But two things soon began to trouble the young manager. First, the venture capital schemes that arrived in south-central Indiana were mostly picked-over ideas. Irwin Management either had to generate its own ideas—much as W. G. Irwin had done in the early decades of the century—or it had to accept high-risk, low-return propositions on which professionals elsewhere already had passed. And, as Schacht was discovering, these tended to be propositions in which the Millers would not be wise to invest.

Second, Schacht began to realize that in the case of small companies, capital was never the real constraint. In fact, there almost always was more capital around than either good ideas or good managers. Schacht found himself wanting to be more involved in the operations of a company, rather than simply providing capital. He had a series of discussions with George Newlin, and wondered aloud if he should be looking for a new opportunity—a question he never got to answer.

> *One day, George Newlin called me into his office, and there was Don Tull, whom I had met two or three times in the two years that I had been there. Don said, "Our merger with White Motor Company is off. We're going to make some major changes at Cummins, and we would like you to be the Vice President of Finance."*
>
> *Well, you could have knocked me over with a feather. Nobody had prepared me for it. Nobody had said "boo." I asked, "Can I think about it? Can I talk to my family about it? When do you need to know?" He said, "Tomorrow." And that's how it happened.*

Schacht was brought in as vice president of finance, replacing longtime finance head Waldo M. Harrison. Harrison (who remained treasurer until 1965 and corporate secretary until his retirement in 1969) was a holdover from the Huthsteiner era. By all accounts, he was better at implementing than inventing. His skills had been honed in an era when Cummins historically had tried very hard to avoid borrowing money.[65] Through most of Harrison's tenure, Cummins reinvested its earnings to finance its operations. It paid relatively low dividends, and engaged in what one insider labels relatively unsophisticated "stock jiggling"—five-for-four stock splits in three different years, for example—to retain investor loyalty.[66]

At the board level, there was considerable debate about whether Harrison (then in his mid-fifties) should be asked to work for Schacht (then in his early thirties). Irwin Miller argued that if Schacht was to have any impact, he would need full control over Cummins' tiny financial operation, including Harrison. Miller, as usual, carried the day.[67]

One of Schacht's first efforts was to reinvigorate the company's moribund Finance Committee, as part of a larger effort to professionalize and modernize Cummins' finance function. He persuaded his superiors that Cummins should retain First Boston Corporation to advise the company on long-term borrowings and other financial issues. Within a month of their retention, Schacht was using the outsiders to help draw up pro forma income statements, balance sheets, and cash flows in multiple currencies through 1970 in three different scenarios ("very optimistic, very pessimistic, and most realistic").[68]

Another hire of long-term significance in this same time period was James A. Henderson. An Indiana native and the son of a faculty member at Culver Military Academy, Henderson was a graduate of Princeton who served five years in the Navy (achieving the rank of lieutenant) and then enrolled in the Harvard Business School. Graduating in 1963 with high distinction, Henderson spent a year as a research assistant to the legendary HBS professor Georges Doriot. The following year, he was hired as personal assistant to Irwin Miller.

Early in his tenure, Henderson used his recent ties with Harvard to help recruit additional Business School graduates, now one of Irwin Miller's priorities.[69] But Henderson soon evolved into Miller's general sounding board on the affairs of the Engine Company. A typical task early in his tenure was to explain to Miller (in December 1964) why the 1964 profit plan was coming up almost $2 million short—an analysis that had particular significance in the wake of the blocked White merger. Henderson reported that the V-series engines were performing badly, domestic and foreign subsidiaries were failing to meet their sales goals, the expenses of domestic operations were running high, and parts sales were down sharply. Each of these failures elicited a pointed question from Henderson—for example, "What does the experience with V engines in 1964 tell us about introducing new engines? Is closer coordination among all areas of the company needed?"[70]

In part by providing this sort of blunt and impartial analysis, Henderson emerged as a valuable resource to Miller. He also created opportunities for himself within a job that previously had been self-limiting. "We had a lot of communication," recalls Henderson of this period, "to the point where I think he trusted my judgment." Within a year, Henderson was named vice president of management development, with sole responsibility for hiring the "outstanding individuals" that Cummins felt it needed.

A second response to the failed White merger was an intensification of Marion Dietrich's efforts to diversify the company's products, which had been put on hold during the later stages of the merger effort. For the first time, Cummins' management (and especially Irwin Miller) began to talk about what soon became known as the "15/15" goals: 15 percent return on equity, and a 15 percent annual rate of growth. These were the measures of a good company. (IBM, as an internal memo noted, was then growing at 23 percent a year.) Anything less than 15/15 created what came to be known as "the gap." The challenge, which fell squarely on Dietrich, was to fill the gap between the returns that the core business could generate and the ambitious 15/15 goals.[71] According to Henry Schacht, this became an enduring mind-set: "'Filling the gap' became an important concept that drove Cummins. It drives Cummins today. . . . That is the underlying drive of much of what's gone on in the thirty years I've been here."

In May 1964, Irwin Miller made a speech to the Cummins distributors. In it, he explained that much of his family's fortune was invested in Cummins only because he was convinced that the company could compete with the world's best corporations. This was neither an emotional attachment nor a necessity:

> *I am not in it just to survive. I could survive much more easily and effectively by selling out, diversifying, and taking life a good deal easier; and I have offers to purchase at prices well above today's market value. But I am not selling, because I think there exists a first-class opportunity for Cummins to become the number one producer in every market it serves—world wide—and I should like to see us achieve this together. . . .*
>
> *You see, I have a choice: I could sell Cummins and reinvest in those companies which appear to me in each industry to have the best chances of growth and leadership. If I did so, I would personally be relieved of a big management load. I could switch any time it appeared I had made a wrong guess, and, in addition, I would have the security of more diversification than can be achieved by keeping my eggs in one basket.[72]*

A middle road, of course, was to diversify Cummins itself, and this was what Dietrich was now trying to do. In the spring of 1964, Cummins announced the purchase of the former Studebaker foundry in South Bend, Indiana, a move toward vertical integration that Don Tull described as "in line with Cummins' diversification program." A more significant departure came in September, when Cummins paid $8.4 million for the Dallas-based Frigikar Corporation, a Dietrich target long before the distractions of the White merger. Frigikar, with 1963 sales of just over $14 million, had introduced the first low-cost, under-the-dash automotive air conditioning unit in 1955. While much smaller than the industry-leading Transicold—which already had declined to be purchased by Cummins—Frigikar looked to be the most promising point of entry into the allied business of car and truck air-conditioning units. "Frigikar was doing pretty well," recalls Dietrich, "and they had a product line that would fit with our distributors. So the fit was pretty good." Cummins sold off a desk company that Frigikar owned, changed the unit's name to "Frigiking," and then began a multi-year effort to (in Dietrich's words) "clean up the company."[73]

Another step toward enhanced financial sophistication came in May 1965, when Cummins announced the hiring of Dr. John T. Hackett, the Irwin Management Company's resident economist since late 1964. Hackett, who held a Ph.D. in economics from Ohio State, had spent several years with the Federal Reserve system in Chicago.[74]

When Hackett switched over to Cummins full time, he recalls, "there was a lot of concern about what Cummins was going to do. Marion was really struggling with it. He and I spent a lot of time trying to put together a strategy for Cummins Engine. It was a period in which the company was really looking at itself. It was an exciting time, because it was kind of an honest, open, democratic process."

Hackett succeeded Schacht in March 1966 as vice president of finance. This signaled the beginning of a real change in the Engine Company's approach to financing its operations.* The company began to augment its standard financing arrangements—term loans and revolving lines of credit—with more exotic instruments. This, in turn, made possible massive increases in the base business, expansion of foreign operations, and new kinds of acquisitions. The change became apparent in 1965, when Hackett helped secure $4.5 million to finance the company's overseas activities. Hackett continued to steer the company into uncharted financial waters. In 1968, for example, Cummins used First Boston to go to Europe and sell a $20 million Eurodollar convertible debenture issue—not a large sum nor a particularly exotic device by today's standards, but unusual enough (as Hackett recalls) to cause a lot of "stomach churning" in Columbus:[75]

> *The funny part of it was, two days before we were supposed to price the close-up deal, we got a terrible write-up in* Fortune *magazine. I'll never forget it. It was called, "The Cough In Cummins Engine." And Irwin Miller began saying that we had to call off the issue. I kept saying, "No, no; we can't do that. We've got to raise this money. We've got to go forward!"*
>
> *We had an advisor in New York, Robert Neumann, an old sage who had lived his whole life in the world capital markets. I was sitting in my hotel on the day that we were supposed to close this thing. To say that I was tense is an understatement. Neumann walked in and said,*

---

*Jim Henderson asserts that it was no accident that many key leaders in the company's future, including Schacht and Hackett, came by way of Irwin Management. "The management company had George Newlin and Harold Higgins out there recruiting aggressively at the top graduate schools," Henderson recalls. "The Engine Company focused on undergraduate schools and was less welcoming to MBAs in those days."

> *"Well, John, I tell you what let's do. Let's take the elevator to the top of the hotel, go out onto the roof, and jump."*
>
> *But it was a successful issue, and as a result, Cummins' first real voyage into the capital markets was not in the U.S., but in Europe. I think it was a very smart thing to do, because it established us in the U.S., as well. The U.S. capital markets said, "Well, if these guys can go over and sell $20 million worth of convertible Eurodollar bonds, they can be a player in the U.S. capital markets, too." It really changed the capital markets' perception of Cummins Engine.*

Meanwhile, Cummins continued to try to fill the gap between the returns generated by the base business and the "15/15" goals. The ReCon Division, created in 1966, was a pilot effort to capture some of the lucrative engine- and parts-rebuilding business. Reconditioning activities that had been scattered across several distributorships were now concentrated in Memphis, with promising initial results.

Some of the diversification opportunities explored during this period ranged far from the core business. (One colorful example was the Harvey Harvester Company, a Grand Haven, Michigan-based manufacturer of blueberry pickers and other mechanized fruit-harvesting equipment.) But as the effort to stimulate growth and earnings gradually merged with an increasingly sophisticated long-range planning effort, the company considered fewer odd acquisitions. John Hackett inherited the planning mantle from Marion Dietrich in 1966 and used the opportunity to launch a much more systematic initiative. Planning documents from the later 1960s emphasize the benefits of a "structured" approach to diversification, in contrast to the "unstructured" strategies of conglomerates like ITT and LTV.

The dramatic growth of the core engine business during the later 1960s somewhat concealed the profit-after-tax gap, but it did not make that troubling gap go away. Looking forward from 1968, Cummins' planners were concerned. Their 15 percent return on equity goal called for a $91 million profit after tax by 1980, which would translate into earnings of $18.20 per share. Along the trend lines of 1968—when Cummins was again enjoying record sales—the company by 1980 would show only a $38 million profit after tax, or $7.66 per share.[76]

By Irwin Miller's exacting standards, this wasn't good enough. After almost a decade of experimenting, Cummins still hadn't found ways to "fill the gap."

The Tech Center

The proposed White merger, and the collapse of that plan in the spring of 1964, sent reverberations throughout the Cummins organization. While the merger plan was still alive, the fate of Cummins' research and development group was somewhat uncertain. White's president, Nev Bauman, made it clear that he wanted to get control of Cummins' *current* engine designs. Explicitly, he was not interested in investing in the kind of research and development that would be necessary for future designs.[77]

When the consolidation plan fell apart, Cummins once again was on its own; and once again, the company had to look at innovation from the perspective of an independent engine producer in a highly competitive field. What skills were needed? Which facilities and equipment were required to support those skills? As a result of this forced scrutiny, plans that were already afoot shifted dramatically. The process of reassessment continued throughout the decade, with major implications for the Cummins of the 1970s.

As Cummins' leaders assessed the company's R&D capabilities in the late 1950s and early 1960s, there were both strengths to take comfort from and weaknesses to give them pause. Cummins' biggest technical strength probably was its determination to stay ahead of the competition technologically. As Irwin Miller regularly reminded his engineers, the goal was to obsolete the company's products before the competition did. This way, Cummins not only would be the first to market with a new technology, it also would discourage OEMs from investing large sums in competing with existing Cummins technologies, which were always at risk of being made obsolete by Cummins itself.

The drive to be first necessitated significant capital investments at regular intervals. But in spite of the expansion of R&D space in the early 1950s (described in the previous chapter), by the early 1960s Cummins again saw an acute need to upgrade its research and test facilities. "We are planning at one move," Irwin Miller told the assembled Cummins distributors in March 1960, "to double our research facilities."[78]

In March 1963, Cummins announced plans to build a new research and engineering building on an eighteen-acre tract of land in Columbus, across a small stream—the Hawcreek—from the Main Engine Plant. Newspaper reports noted that the new facility, at an estimated 188,000 square feet, would increase the overall Cummins plant only by about 15 percent.[79] What they missed was that the new building, as then contemplated, would represent a five-fold increase in space allocated by the Engine Company to the R&D function.

Preliminary estimates placed the cost of the new facility at $8.2 million. But in the wake of the White merger collapse, Irwin Miller began to worry that even this was too small an investment. One key measure of an engine development facility is the number of "test cells" available for use. These are small, sealed rooms in which engines are run under various load and speed conditions to test performance, reliability, and durability. In the early 1960s, Cummins had 50 test cells available for research use, of which only 15 were reasonably well equipped. In the same time period, General Motors had nearly 100 cells available for testing diesel engines alone. As of the early months of 1964, the Cummins plan called for a building with 64 engine test cells, which even an in-house memo described as "inadequate from the start."[80]

Miller agreed. In his public statements, he hammered away at the need for Cummins to lead through research. He also upped the ante for the new facility:

> We are building the most important diesel research center in the world, and when we finish, I think we shall have invested in this in excess of $10 million. We mean business. We mean never again to have to respond to a competitor's development. We mean to beat him on each move, and be out first with a product so clearly superior in economy, bulk, weight, and long life that our excellence does not have to be argued.[81]

By March 1964, the project had grown dramatically—from 188,000 square feet to 280,000 square feet—and needed twenty-four acres of land (up from eighteen). Harry Weese, longtime architectural advisor to Cummins and most recently the designer of the expanded Atlas Crankshaft plant in Fostoria, Ohio, was selected to design the building. Plans kept enlarging. By the time construction began in December 1964, the facility consisted of two buildings—a six-story office building and a separate engine test center—for a grand total of 350,000 square feet. According to the Columbus building inspector, this was the single largest project ever undertaken in the city—even larger than any single year's total of construction projects in Columbus.[82]

Less than a year later, in October 1965, the project cost was being estimated at $15.5 million. One reason for this latest increase (over 50 percent) in the estimate was a large increase in the number of test cells planned for the facility. These were now to be eighty-eight instead of sixty-four, and little expense was being spared to make them represent the state of the art. Individually controlled but also monitored from a central console, the cells were to sit on massive concrete "inertia pads," designed to soak up vibration and isolate the pads from the building around them. Extensive soundproofing also helped seal off the test cells from other work spaces.[83]

Costs continued to climb. In the spring of 1966, the facility was projected to cost $16 million, with half of that total allocated for equipment. By the fall of 1967, the newly named "Technical Center" was projected to be finished in 1968—at a dramatically higher cost of $22 million, with a total of 360,000 square feet. About a quarter of the budget, according to an internal newsletter, was allocated for mechanical and electrical services. The test cells alone required over 40,000 feet of capillary copper tubing to draw out heat for transfer to cooling towers.[84]

Cummins personnel began to occupy the Tech Center in the fall of 1967. Sixteen of the eighty-eight test cells had yet to be completed, but all testing related to new products was moved into the new facility. (For the time being, production-oriented testing continued in existing facilities in the Main Engine Plant.) Within a year, some 600 engineers and support personnel moved into the building, which Cummins justifiably described as "one of the most modern and extensive facilities in the world available for engine development and investigation of new forms of power."[85]

Despite its high aspirations (and associated high costs), the Tech Center was far from perfect. The company's preoccupation with test cells had led, inadvertently, to a shortage of laboratory space. For the first few years, the building had several empty floors, contributing to a general sense that the facility was a "white elephant."[86] And, according to Jim Henderson, who worked closely with Irwin Miller in the 1960s, Miller was dissatisfied with the design of the building, a sentiment that became contagious: "Irwin's never been happy with the building. . . . He wasn't involved day-to-day. He didn't have the person to lead the effort. . . . He said to me several times, 'That building just got away.' And I guess I inherited that feeling from him."

Another limitation on the building's immediate usefulness was the fact that it was completed and occupied before computer-aided design was available in a broadly useful form. In a sense, the Tech Center had to wait for technology to catch up with it. But even in 1968, Cummins had an inkling of how important the building would become in the near future. "One of our major research efforts," the company reported to its shareholders in that year, "is concerned with solving a major environmental problem. Throughout 1968, Cummins concentrated on programs to improve air quality through better pollution control."[87] This was a focus that was about to leap to a dramatically higher place on the corporate—and the national—agenda.

The drive to be *first*—the first to develop a technology, and the first to bring that technology to market—created high expectations of the R&D staff. Unfortunately, these expectations were not often met. Irwin Miller constantly pushed his senior managers to recruit better technical people. In a 1962 memo to Don Tull, Miller complained that "we do not have enough qualified personnel or adequate facilities to accomplish such a [research] program as fast as I think it ought to be done." Little more than a month later, in a memo to Dick Stoner, Miller demanded to know why no progress had been made toward the hiring of a new vice president of research. "Until we get him, we cannot attack the problem of a basic research group. . . . I don't think it is unreasonable of me to be disturbed at our not having found and hired [him]. How much longer do you think I should have to wait?"[88]

Two vice presidents of research came and went between 1962 and 1965.[89] One problem that recurred on the technical side of the shop was that most researchers and engineers found it difficult to work with research head Nev Reiners. According to his colleagues, Reiners—although a talented engineer—was uncomfortable with independent thinkers, and also was far too inclined to take credit for the work of others. By most accounts, Irwin Miller retained his faith in Reiners long after others in the organization had begun looking elsewhere for technical leadership.[90]

Henderson, named the head of executive recruiting in 1965, took responsibility for finding that technical leadership. (The perceived need for more depth on the research side was underscored when, late in 1964, Nev Reiners was involved in a serious car accident.) The candidate Henderson came up with was Vaughn L. Beals, director of research and technology for North American Aviation's Columbus, Ohio, division, where for ten years he had directed the work of some 400 scientists and technicians.[91] "He was a research manager who thought like a businessman," Henderson recalls, "and that was terrific."

Taking over as vice president of research and engineering in the fall of 1965, Beals soon established himself as a quick thinker and a strong leader. Drawing on his training at North American Aviation, he gave the Cummins "R&E" (research and engineering) group a far more structured form of management style than it had had before—or perhaps needed. His colleague and successor as head of research, Bill Schwab, later recalled: "He was a tough guy to work with—very demanding. He brought some more structure to the company. But in some ways, I think it was overdone. We ended up with tons of black books, a lot of reports, and controls over projects, and so on."

Beals also established himself, in the eyes of Irwin Miller and others, as a highly competent and aggressive manager, in part by helping to move forward the Tech Center project. Cummins was then looking actively for the young managers who might lead the company into the next decade, and Beals had emerged as one of them. In 1967, he was promoted to the vice presidency of the engine division. This initiated another several years of rapid turnover in R&E—which mirrored major changes of leadership going on elsewhere in the corporation.

Growing the international business

The failed White merger had relatively little impact on Cummins' international business. Throughout the negotiations with White, Cummins was regularly surprised to find out how little interest the Cleveland-based truck manufacturer had in overseas expansion.[92] At Cummins, by contrast, growth of the international side of the business was viewed as an absolute necessity for long-term success.

Shotts—Cummins' first overseas venture, in Scotland—was only minimally profitable by the early 1960s, but it provided much-needed flexibility to the parent company. Many of the Cummins products sold in Canada, for example, were produced in Shotts and imported to North America under the British Commonwealth's trade umbrella. But the perception of opportunity overseas, compounded by the ever-present imperative to "fill the gap," led Cummins to launch multiple international efforts during the 1960s.

Just as the problems of the core business called forth a colorful personality (in the person of Marion Dietrich) to lead the search for domestic growth opportunities, the international business produced its own idiosyncratic champion: Reece Hatchitt. Hatchitt was a product of the Oil Patch—the oil- and gas-producing regions of Texas and Oklahoma—and had worked for the international division of Dresser Industries, a major U.S. manufacturer and exporter.[93] "He had lived overseas," recalls Henry Schacht, "and had all the understanding of international markets that our very insular southern Indiana company did not."

Hatchitt's first major task for Cummins was to set up the Bahamian sales subsidiary in 1958. Beginning in 1959, with Irwin Miller's blessing, Hatchitt became the designated advocate for international activities. Certain existing Cummins territories—for example, Mexico and the United Kingdom—were ruled off-limits to Hatchitt. But the rest of the world was his.[94]

Almost from the beginning, Hatchitt argued in favor of the "beachhead" approach—that is, in favor of Cummins' establishing a presence in a key market, regardless of the short-term profitability of that position. Making the case for establishing a Brazilian subsidiary in the spring of 1959, for example, Hatchitt noted that "the prime reason for entering the market is to maintain our reputation and establish a beachhead for future expansion." In 1960, Hatchitt (along with treasurer Waldo Harrison) made a 40,000-mile trip around the world, visiting Cummins' international distributors and exploring manufacturing opportunities in Japan, Australia, India, and the European Common Market.[95] Not surprisingly, these scattershot and highly personal forays produced some duds and nonstarters. This category included unpromising Cummins operations in Brazil and Australia (at least in their original incarnations), and a small but enduring venture in Japan (see Chapter 10). But Hatchitt's travels also helped create some of Cummins' most successful international operations.

Manufacturing in India and Germany

Of all of Hatchitt's brainchildren, the most interesting and durable was born in India. The story of Cummins in India illustrates the great value of patience and hard work—in combination with very good luck.

The first piece of luck grew out of the fact that Robert Huthsteiner, Cummins' president in the 1950s, had a friend and classmate named S. L. Kirloskar, an Indian national, in his 1924 class at the Massachusetts Institute of Technology. The two men had kept in touch over the ensuing decades, and Kirloskar later visited the Cummins plant in Columbus, partly for professional reasons. He was then head of Kirloskar Oil Engines, Ltd., a manufacturer of slow-speed, 2 to 40 hp industrial diesel engines; and of Kirloskar Pneumatic, Ltd., a licensed manufacturer of air compressors.[96]

Both of these companies (which were only two of the Kirloskar family's many holdings) were based in Poona, India. Poona, a city of two million people about 100 miles east of Bombay, sat on a high plateau and enjoyed relatively temperate weather. For this reason, the British had situated their military headquarters there, and the old city still had many of the trappings of the colonial era: a racetrack, cricket fields, and so on.

On at least one occasion in the late 1950s, Huthsteiner and Kirloskar had a preliminary discussion about a joint diesel-making venture.[97] This led Hatchitt to put India on his itinerary; and in January 1960, Hatchitt and Kirloskar met with the Indian Minister of Finance, Manubhai Shah, about the possibility of Cummins and Kirloskar setting up a jointly owned manufacturing facility. The deal that they proposed, informally, was a corporation with 45 percent ownership by Cummins, 45 percent by Kirloskar Oil Engines, and 10 percent by Indian banks.

Shah was receptive, in part because the timing was right. India was preparing to launch the third of three ambitious "Five Year Plans." The first of these plans had stressed reconstruction after India's war of independence. The second plan, then in its fourth year, had aimed at expanding heavy industry. The third plan was scheduled to begin in April 1962 and would again emphasize heavy industry, with the government committed to supplying up to 45 percent of the additional needed investment. The Cummins-Kirloskar proposal would coincide neatly with this schedule. A subsequent proposal, in which Cummins would own 60 percent and Kirloskar 40 percent, also met with informal approval from the ministry.[98]

Hatchitt was the rainmaker, but more deliberate minds helped execute the plan. Two months after Hatchitt's meeting with Shah, two Cummins manufacturing experts surveyed the entire Indian manufacturing landscape. They estimated total start-up costs at $6 million, and made a series of recommendations (including that Cummins be prepared to import all the machinery needed to be "self reliant").[99]

The Indian government also laid down some preconditions. Cummins, said the government representatives, should think of its entry into India as being in three "periods." (A period generally lasted a year, but could be extended to eighteen months or more.) In the first period, Cummins should plan to import no more than 50 percent of the engine. Local content would increase gradually, so that by the end of the third period, no more than 15 percent of the engine would be imported. Even this would not be onerous (noted one Cummins manager), since it would still allow the import of blocks, cylinder heads, and crankshafts.[100]

From the beginning, Hatchitt (according to his traveling companion, Waldo Harrison) was impressed by S. L. Kirloskar:

> *He was convinced that Mr. Kirloskar was the person to become associ-*
> *ated with Cummins in an Indian company. Mr. Kirloskar's reputation*
> *and ability are of the highest type, and apparently Reece believes that*
> *an association with him would be far better than an association with*
> *any other individual or group.*[101]

Harrison soon came to share Hatchitt's opinion. In a memo to Irwin Miller, Harrison emphasized that Kirloskar was ambitious, well connected, and knew how to run a manufacturing operation in India. "Many Indians who have money to invest," Harrison wrote, "are not interested in working hard. In this respect, Kirloskar is quite different." In addition, Harrison noted, Kirloskar was committed to improving his home town of Poona, enjoyed a happy family life, and appeared to possess high "moral standards." On the negative side, Harrison concluded, Kirloskar's "aggressive spirit might cause him to become over extended"—an outcome that Cummins could set up mechanisms to avoid.[102]

The Indian government tossed a monkey wrench into the works in November 1961, when Finance Minister Shah informed Kirloskar that the proposed ownership structure (60 percent Cummins, 40 percent Kirloskar) was unacceptable. As an alternative, Shah proposed that Cummins own 40 percent, Kirloskar 30.5 percent, and the Indian public 29.5 percent. Privately, Shah apologized to the Cummins and Kirloskar representatives for failing to keep them fully informed about the government's position; but now, he reported, that position was nonnegotiable.[103]

Negotiations ensued, nevertheless, and the final ownership structure settled upon was Cummins, 50 percent; Kirloskar, 25.5 percent; and the Indian public, 24.5 percent. On this basis, Kirloskar-Cummins Ltd. was formally incorporated on February 17, 1962, and its board met for the first time in March. It included four representatives from Cummins and three from Kirloskar (including S. L. Kirloskar and his son Chandrakant).[104]

From the government's point of view, a public stock offering was of critical importance. Local control was, of course, attractive. But in addition, the Indian government was convinced that there was a pent-up public demand for opportunities to invest in manufacturing operations, and finance officials therefore were determined to create such opportunities.

Their hypothesis was put to the test in the second week of May 1962, when 36,750 shares in Kirloskar-Cummins Ltd. were offered through the Bombay Stock Exchange. "So enormous was the response," a Cummins newsletter later noted, "that by the end of the second day the supply of application forms had been exhausted." More than 70,000 individuals and institutions subscribed for over 2 million shares—fifty-five times the number of shares available![105]

Cummins was only beginning its Indian education. The formal groundbreaking at the ninety-acre site of the planned 133,000-square-foot Kirloskar-Cummins facility in Poona (which took place on September 24, 1962) was preceded by *bhumi poojan*, a ceremony of ground-worship traditionally observed by Hindus before the commencement of construction.[106] Construction itself was unlike anything Cummins had experienced. Dick Stoner, deputized to set up the Indian manufacturing operation, recalls his impressions of that phase:

> *I took with me a couple of manufacturing engineers, and S. L. Kirloskar wanted to know why I brought them along. I said, "Well, we want to make sure we lay out the plant as efficiently as we can and install the right machinery." He said, "Dick, let me tell you something. The reason I entered into this was that India needs employment. People we've got. Machinery we don't need. We're only going to sell in India, and the last thing we need are your manufacturing engineers. I want labor designed into the place, not out of the place."*
>
> *We were still clearing the land, at that point, and the women were working on making the bricks out there on the ground. They had their little tent there where they would eat, and their family was right there with them, you know, and you would pay all these people just a couple of rupees a day. And S. L. said, "We've got to employ this kind of labor."*

The deliberate use of unskilled labor and minimal construction equipment delayed the opening of the Poona plant until the beginning of 1964.[107] Within a few months of the plant's start-up, four- and six-cylinder H engines, ranging from 135 to 335 hp, were coming off the line at the rate of five engines a day.

Kirloskar-Cummins experienced a variety of difficulties in its early years. These included an erratic local utility (which tended to shut down power to the plant in the late afternoon when people were cooking), an inadequate network of Indian subcontractors, very limited foreign exchange, and the 1965 Chinese invasion of India. But the joint venture also had strengths, which helped it achieve profitability in the later months of 1965.[108] These strengths included, first, Cummins' absolute insistence on the right to manage the company. (This was done mainly through Indian managers, who had the benefit of regular guidance from Cummins people at all levels. Dick Stoner, for example, estimates that he made fifty trips to India over a twenty-five-year period.) Another strong point included the nurturing of an indigenous research and development activity, which allowed customization of the product to local needs (for example, the installation of a V-903 into an Indian bus). And perhaps the most important strength of the venture was the Kirloskars themselves.

"My impression," concluded Waldo Harrison, three years into his relationship with his Indian counterparts, "is that the Kirloskars are more widely known today for their business ability and achievements than they were when we entered into the collaboration agreement with them. . . . We have an excellent partner, and one which is gaining stature in India."[109]

Gradually, the realization dawned in Columbus that the Kirloskars and their countrymen were the best at running their own business. "That business turned around almost on the day we got all the expats and mercenaries out of there," Jim Henderson recalls. The fact that Irwin Miller had a high level of trust in S. L. Kirloskar helped hasten the transfer of decision making from Columbus to Poona.

Another stop on Reece Hatchitt's and Waldo Harrison's world tour, in the spring of 1960, was Europe. The pair made stops in Frankfurt, Paris, London, Brussels, and Shotts, looking for opportunities for Cummins to establish a beachhead in the new European Common Market.[110]

Apparently their report was positive, for in July the Cummins board authorized "Project ECM," which had two stated objectives: to establish a source for Cummins engines and parts in the European Common Market, and to make Cummins a major factor in the European diesel market.[111] Cummins assumed that the soon-to-be-released V-series engines—smaller than previous Cummins models—would be well received in Europe, and hoped that European demand for the Vs would warrant the creation of a new subsidiary. Cummins hoped to retain 50 percent ownership in this subsidiary and distribute the remaining 50 percent across several participating OEMs. Specifically, the project anticipated a new manufacturing plant in Europe for high-volume production of the entire family of V engines.

But as Hatchitt soon discovered, few European truck manufacturers had any interest in allying themselves with Cummins. In many ways, the European truck business in 1960 resembled the prewar American truck industry. There were numerous small companies and a small number of large ones. Almost all were integrated manufacturers, producing their own engines. Negotiations for a deal with the German manufacturer Rheinstahl-Hanomag went nowhere, as did talks with Berliet, a French truckmaker. In fact, the only

European OEM interested in dealing with Cummins was the German firm of Fried. Krupp Motoren und Kraftwagenfabriken.

Krupp and Cummins began negotiating in the fall of 1961, and it soon became clear that Project ECM would have to be entirely rethought. Krupp had no need for the lighter Val and Vale engines, and only was interested in the Vim (200 hp) and Vine (265 hp) models. And for the time being, at least, volumes would be relatively small. Even if a deal were struck, no new factory would be needed, since all of the necessary manufacturing could go on in Krupp's existing plants.

Those plants were not impressive, reflecting the fact that Krupp-Krawa (the site of the Krupp truck factories) was a relatively marginal player in the European truck business. Daimler-Benz, maker of Mercedes, controlled some 20 percent of that business, while Krupp was one of a number of companies with about a 5 percent market share.[112] Cummins therefore went into the Krupp negotiations with some reluctance: The only European truckmaker that wanted to strike a deal was in some ways one of the weakest ones. (Although Krupp did not issue separate financial statements for its various divisions, Cummins suspected that Krawa had not had a profitable year since 1945.)[113] Nevertheless, Cummins needed a toehold in Europe, Krupp had fourteen service centers that were reputed to be the best on the Continent— and most important, Krupp needed an engine.

The deal was struck in the spring of 1962, licensing Krupp to manufacture Vim and Vine engines in Germany for a term of fifteen years, both for its own use and for other Cummins accounts. The agreement also called for joint engineering and research activities aimed at "combining the latest in both American and European engine design and manufacturing techniques." A little more than a year later—in June 1963—the first Vim-powered truck came off the assembly line at the Krupp factory in Krawa.[114]

For about a year, the relationship worked mostly as anticipated, with Cummins shipping engine components to Germany until the Krawa plant was able to produce them on its own. Krupp sold the Cummins-powered trucks through its existing distribution network. But beginning in the early months of 1964, reports of failures of the V engines began coming into Krawa—first in a trickle, then in a flood.[115] As the reputation of the engine plummeted on the Continent, Krawa sales also plunged. Krupp-Krawa's projected sales for 1964 were 2,074; the actual total was 1,420.

At the same time when Cummins was trying mightily to solve its V-related problems at home, therefore, the company found itself compelled to provide extensive technical assistance to Krupp. Between late 1962 and mid-1965, several of Cummins' top engineers and researchers spent many months in Germany.[116] And Cummins took further steps in the spring of 1964. First, it authorized Krupp to spend up to $400,000 annually to conduct research at Cummins' expense—on paper, to solve noise problems and examine multifuel engines, but in reality to solve V-related design problems. "Task Force K," an ad hoc technical problem-solving team, was created to provide technical support and improve the product. A Cummins office was set up in Essen to provide technical assistance. Finally, a co-owned distributorship was organized in Gross-Gerau to help provide service on Cummins engines and fuel systems.

But from Krupp's point of view, this was not enough. In August 1964, Krupp's managing director, Berthold Beitz, dispatched a stinging letter to Irwin Miller. He was "dismayed," he wrote, at the results of the collaboration between Cummins and Krupp-Krawa. Krupp was unable to find new customers for the Cummins engine, and longtime Krupp customers were going over to Krupp's competitors. In the preceding months, some 25 percent of Krupp's truck salesmen had quit, apparently due to their inability to sell the product. "To sum up," he wrote, "the V 6 engine does not have the promised characteristics in regard to performance, economy and service life, and the reputation of both Cummins and Krupp has thereby suffered alarmingly."[117]

The disaster was real enough. While the total German domestic truck market in the over-fifteen-ton category was increasing from 13,700 (in 1961) to 17,700 (in 1965), Krupp's sales fell from 3,000 to 1,800, a market-share decline from 22.2 percent to 10.3 percent. In May 1965, Krupp formally notified Cummins that it intended to reopen negotiations between the two companies in order to seek reimbursement of "excess losses" totalling some $7.9 million.

Cummins, for its part, was not eager to bail out Krupp. In its estimation, Krupp had made representations to the public about the warranty on the V engine that were excessive. According to an internal estimate, Cummins' total Krupp-related expenses had exceeded $10 million.[118] And Cummins still was fundamentally committed to making the V engine succeed, both at home and abroad. If Krupp insisted on getting tough, Cummins was prepared to follow suit.

The stalemate dragged on until the summer of 1966. At that point, Cummins' Henry Schacht—recently named vice president of international operations—negotiated a deal that, in effect, transferred all R&D-related expense from Krupp to Cummins, and implicitly committed Cummins to the development of an "undersquare" V engine. Then came another twist in the story. In the spring of 1967, the Krupp empire got into such deep financial trouble that the German federal government, the provincial government, and twenty-eight banks were forced to step in to save the company.[119] The new outside board of directors that was imposed on Krupp was a major unknown to Cummins. Would that new group look to the Engine Company to solve Krupp's financial woes?

Ultimately, it did not. Krupp briefly considered designing and producing its own engine, but it soon gave up the plan. In the spring of 1968, Daimler-Benz bought out Krupp's fourteen dealerships—thereby positioning itself to become an industry leader—and in September of that year, after some fifty years in the business, Krupp stopped manufacturing trucks. Cummins, released from its contractual obligations to Krupp, announced that it would shut down its Essen office effective January 1, 1969.[120]

In retrospect, the Krupp-Cummins partnership, founded as it was on the unsuccessful V-engine technology, was doomed from the start. But both companies further complicated the relationship. For its part, Cummins did not commit itself fully to the Krupp partnership, being wary of putting all of its European eggs in what it considered to be a fragile basket. (A severe money crunch in 1967 also forced Cummins to retrench in many areas, including international.) And in Krupp's estimation, Cummins was far too inclined to observe the letter, rather than the spirit, of its engine warranties. On the other side of the table, the workings of the Krupp empire—at least up until the spring of 1967—were baffling to Cummins and most other observers. "It was found amazing," as one German employee of Cummins wrote, just as Krupp was collapsing, "that in this stage, Mr. Alfried Krupp has left Essen for South America, and Mr. Beitz is visiting the Leipzig fair."

A flawed technology, lack of commitment, and some measure of mutual incomprehension: These were not the foundations of a strong partnership.

Manufacturing in Mexico and England

During the period when Cummins was struggling to establish its "beachheads" in Europe and on the Indian subcontinent, the Shotts facility in Scotland finally began to make a significant contribution to the company's profits. This improvement continued throughout the decade. Sales increased from just over $5 million in 1960 to more than $22 million in 1970, and profits before tax increased from a negative $889,000 in 1960 to almost $3.5 million in 1970.[121]

But Shotts was conceived (and by mid-decade was prospering) as a small-volume producer of in-line H engines for the Commonwealth countries. The arrival of the new V engines signaled, at least to the decision makers back in Columbus, that the venerable H was soon to be obsolete. Soon, the superior V technology—in light-, medium-, and heavy-duty ranges—would overwhelm its competitors around the world as it was produced in volumes that no diesel maker previously had contemplated.

This was the spirit in which Cummins began negotiations with Krupp. It was also the conviction that led the company in 1963 to establish additional manufacturing operations in both Mexico and England.

The Mexican connection was made with Diesel Nacional, S.A. (DINA), based in Mexico City. In the spring of 1963, DINA was licensed to build the relatively untested Val (V-6, 140 hp) and Vale (V-8, 185 hp) engines. The company was one of three huge government firms with plants in Sahagun, sixty miles northeast of Mexico City, a city built in the desert by the Mexican government as part of a huge industrial development scheme. Under its agreement with Cummins, DINA—an established producer of trucks, buses, and cars—would at first assemble engines from parts supplied by Columbus, and then gradually increase the Mexican content of its output. The target markets of Central and South America were familiar territory to Cummins. What was new was the V engine—sold to Mexico by Ray Boll and Reece Hatchitt on the basis of a wooden mock-up.[122]

Only a few months later, Cummins unveiled another surprise when it announced a partnership with the international division of Chrysler Motors. This story was somewhat more complicated than the DINA deal.[123] When Krupp showed no interest in the smaller Vs (the Val and Vale models), Cummins began to look for another partner to help introduce those engines into the European market. Ideally, the Engine Company would find a partner that would promise to take a major part of a large volume—the same strategy originally envisioned in Project ECM. This time, in contrast to the Krupp deal, a partner was identified fairly quickly: Chrysler Motors International Limited. Contract talks in Detroit went relatively smoothly, and the two companies agreed to build a new plant at Darlington, England, 250 miles northeast of London. (Cummins also agreed to build a second plant in the same area to manufacture fuel systems and other necessary components.) The deal was announced to the press in December 1963.[124]

There was one sticking point in the negotiations, as well as a turn of phrase in the final contract that, in retrospect, *should* have been a sticking point. The former, recalls Cummins attorney Ben Bush, had to do with the allocation of overhead costs at the new plant:

> *Their attorney had in mind that Chrysler was going to have the biggest volume. So his idea was that we'd split the overhead 50-50, and that Cummins would therefore be subsidizing Chrysler's volume. After thinking that one through, I told him that would be a mistake, because whenever you divorce the cost from the volume, you get into all kinds of problems. It's divisive in the organization, and it's hard enough to make these things work without the contracts building in divisiveness. But they were determined to do that, and so we did it. And the way we drew up the agreement, they would get a benefit—that is, unless their volumes dropped, in which case we would get the benefit.*
>
> *What happened, of course, right off the bat, is that their volumes went down and we signed a big contract with Ford. And one day, our counterpart at Chrysler realized that Ford was getting their engines cheaper than he was, and he went ballistic. Now, we could have gone in*

at that point and said, "Okay, we'll rewrite the agreement and split the overhead proportionately." That received a lot of discussion here, but we never did it. It sort of got pushed to the back—"Oh, we'll decide that one next week." As a result, it never got decided, and the thing festered.

The second problem grew out of a technicality in the joint venture agreement, signed in August 1963. The agreement stated that engine transfer prices between Chrysler and Cummins would be calculated in dollars rather than pounds. This meant that in the event that the pound was significantly devalued in relation to the dollar, Chrysler would be at a significant disadvantage.

The problem for the partnership was that both of these potential problems became real, and both of them broke in a direction that favored Cummins. The plant opened in July 1966, and the pound sterling was devalued in the fall of 1967 (from $2.75 to $2.39).[125] Meanwhile, the small V engines (according to an internal Cummins assessment) were "relatively sophisticated and costly for the U.K./European market" and did "not offer significant competitive advantages in the critical areas of horsepower and performance." As a result, Chrysler could not achieve the necessary volumes to make the plant pay.* Although export sales between 1964 and 1967 were at 82.5 percent of their targets, sales in the United Kingdom were dismal; only 7,980 engines out of a projected 28,500 units were sold. And the cost of designing and producing the small Vs was almost 50 percent higher than originally estimated.[126]

In January 1968, Henry Schacht opened intensive negotiations with Chrysler. From the start, the negotiations were designed to give Chrysler what it wanted—a way out of the Darlington co-venture—at a price that was fair to Cummins. Liquidating both Chrysler-Cummins Ltd. and the Cummins Darlington plant (CUMDAR) was out of the question, since the book cost of such a move would have been $11.8 million—far more than any conceivable purchase price Chrysler might demand. And purchase by Cummins was what Chrysler had in mind. "The logical course," wrote Schacht in a strategy memo, quoting the head of Chrysler's European operations, "would be for Cummins, which has product control and is selling the engine, to buy out Chrysler."[127]

Two weeks later, Schacht put a fundamental question to his senior colleagues at Cummins:

Neither getting out [of Darlington] nor going forward is going to be financially attractive when considered in isolation. Further probing of the numbers is not going to change the status dramatically. It will probably come down to this: Is our future in the independent diesel engine busi-

---

*Somewhere in this same time period, recalls Ray Boll, Chrysler also concluded the purchase of Roots, a British truck manufacturer with a diesel engine line. This purchase made a partnership with Cummins less interesting to Chrysler.

ness? If so, do we have the option of not competing in this horsepower range? Is leaving this range open to Caterpillar and/or self-sourcing consistent with this strategy? If not, and we elect to exit, what are we exiting in favor of—what is our alternate plan for the use of the funds? . . .

Take some time . . . to think about the problem in the strategic sense, i.e., "Do we really have to be in this business to compete successfully as an independent diesel engine manufacturer?"[128]

After the due deliberation that Schacht encouraged, Cummins' senior management concluded that the Engine Company had to stay in the medium-duty engine range—this despite the troubled Chrysler partnership, and despite all of the other mounting problems associated with the V engines. After two more months of negotiations, Cummins agreed to pay Chrysler just over $2 million (Chrysler's book value), in installments through 1976, for Chrysler's share in the joint venture. The deal was completed in April 1968. "We now carry this modern engine plant at a very favorable cost figure," Cummins later reported to its shareholders, "substantially below today's cost of reproduction."[129]

Ben Bush, general counsel, recalls writing a letter to Chrysler which served as a cover to the final sale agreement. In that letter, he strongly advised Chrysler to remain a partner in the venture, because Cummins was convinced that the plant could be made profitable. But Chrysler had made up its mind: It was going to focus on the automobile business, and it wanted out of Darlington. Once again, Bush recalls, events broke in Cummins' favor shortly after Chrysler's exit:

Mexico was going to build the small V in Mexico. But the Mexicans at that point had a lot of enthusiasm for negotiating and signing agreements, and very little enthusiasm for implementing *the plans. So we signed a three-year deal with them to bring engines in from the Darlington plant in England, and ten years later, we were still providing over 80 percent of the internal content of that engine. So the plant grew and grew in England, and exported engine kits to Mexico—which was wonderful, because the British government was subsidizing exports at that point.*

Darlington lost $183,000 in 1968, the year that Chrysler bailed out. In the following year, due mainly to the increased Mexican volume, it made a profit of $1.6 million, and thus began a decade of profitable operations.

On balance, Cummins' overseas forays in the 1960s were a hugely expensive venture—a "hole in the dike," as Henry Schacht puts it. Schacht was the company's "fresh-caught" vice president of finance in 1964, and one of his first tasks was to figure out where all the cash generated by the company's domestic business was going. This did not take long. "We were losing between $10 million and $20 million a year over there," Schacht recalls ruefully. "The international operations were sucking cash out of this place at an enormous rate."

So why did Cummins persist in a losing enterprise? One answer is that Cummins' products—for use in earth-moving equipment, trucks, and generator sets—had (or seemed to have) broad application. Countries that were rebuilding in the wake of war, or were industrializing for the first time, were (or seemed to be) obvious fields of opportunity.

And, as Ben Bush recalls, being overseas was exciting:

> *That was a very glorious time for Cummins. What you did were the things that were the most exciting. Frankly, I think that had more of an impact than any critical analysis of economic structures or long-term strategies. And I think that was one of the charming aspects of Cummins, and maybe even one of the reasons it survived when a lot of the independent engine companies didn't.*

And finally, Irwin Miller was determined to position Cummins as a world-class company. "I think you had to attribute the push to Irwin," concludes Ben Bush. Except for the Shotts contingent, as the 1960s opened, only three Cummins-affiliated individuals—Irwin Miller, Miller's friend and fellow board member Seymour Dribben, and Miller's protégé Reece Hatchitt—had any significant overseas experience. Especially in the early days of the decade, it was Miller who continually looked for ways to make his company a credible international player, for what he saw as compelling competitive reasons. "We are engaged in setting up a business overseas," he wrote in 1964, "which will in not too many years be as big as or bigger than our present U.S.A. operation, and will have a broader base."[130] Gradually, with the addition of executives such as Henry Schacht to the international team, Miller won allies, and Cummins gained momentum internationally.

But the company still had a lot to learn about striking deals that would benefit both itself and its partners. It also needed a broader range of potential partners—which meant, in turn, that it had to get to a position of greater strength and credibility in the world marketplace. By the end of the decade, the company was leaving behind the "rug merchant" approach to global trade—but had yet to invent a more rewarding strategy.[131]

The broader community

One of the first jobs undertaken in the new Tech Center was a study of ways to improve air quality through pollution control. Ever since the unhappy day in 1932 when a smoke-related tragedy caused the only diesel-powered truck in America to be banned from the California highways, the Engine Company had remained acutely aware that smoke was bad business. In 1945, Paris Letsinger reported on the seriousness of the "smoke situation" on the West Coast, and H. L. Knudsen proposed a summit meeting of all truck OEMs in Columbus to discuss ways to reduce smoke caused by poor truck design, manufacture, and maintenance. (The OEMs let it be known that they preferred to deal with Cummins one-on-one.)[132]

In some ways, diesel exhaust was (and is) less unhealthful than gasoline exhaust; and due to their much greater numbers, automobiles created far more pollution than trucks. But trucks were highly visible, and the black, sooty smoke belching out of their stacks was a looming liability. The company's effort to break into the stop-and-go market in the early 1960s only compounded the problem.[133]

During the 1960s, Cummins' practical reasons for controlling pollution gradually converged with the company's interest in being a "good corporate citizen."[134] In its 1967 report to shareholders, for example, Cummins noted that it was maintaining its "orientation toward the solution of societal problems," including "the reduction of air pollution in the automotive market. Community involvement was stressed in all of Cummins communities."[135]

But this was a decade in which the definition of "involvement" broadened dramatically. Commitments that began as the personal convictions of a few individuals (especially Irwin Miller) developed into corporatewide programs. And Cummins' increasing profitability over the decade meant that the company's financial support of the Cummins Engine Foundation (5 percent of its taxable income) became a more and more meaningful sum of money. Continuing programs, such as support for architecture in Columbus, received greatly increased funding in the early years of the decade. And new programs, reflecting the pressing issues of the 1960s, also began to receive significant financial support.

In the fall of 1963, the Cummins Engine Foundation renewed its offer to pay architectural fees related to new school buildings.* (Four buildings already had been designed and constructed under the program. The designers of each of these buildings, mostly young and relatively unknown when they were hired, all later emerged as major American architects.) Two years later, the offer was extended to all of the towns in the newly consolidated Bartholomew Consolidated school district. Irwin Miller remained the prime mover in this effort, both in public and behind the scenes. "I am happy to learn that steps are being taken to replace the old Lincoln school," Irwin Miller wrote to the superintendent of schools. "I have been in this building many times, and am sure that it is impossible to conduct elementary education according to the standards which you set for our city in these ancient surroundings."[136]

---

*"But we never pushed it," Miller insists. "We waited to be asked."

Gradually, the foundation (and in some cases, its corporate parent) broadened the architectural and building program to include other kinds of public buildings. In 1963, for example, the foundation made a $125,000 grant to help pay for a youth and community center in Columbus. In the same year, the Engine Company donated 218 acres of land to Columbus for a municipal golf course designed by Robert Trent Jones and a clubhouse designed by longtime Cummins architectural consultant Harry Weese. Three years later, the foundation paid architect Robert Venturi's fees to design a new city fire station, and contributed $800,000 in support of a county library designed by New York–based architect I. M. Pei.[137]

Meanwhile, the Irwin-Sweeney-Miller family was pursuing its own vision. After retaining architect Alexander Girard to renovate the drab Victorian storefronts on Columbus's main drag—Girard used "daring" paint schemes to liven up the building facades—the family engaged Los Angeles-based architect Cesar Pelli and a Chicago shopping-mall developer to draw up plans for a new "superblock" in the heart of the downtown.[138] As it turned out, this effort would take several years, extending into the early 1970s. But through these and related initiatives, mostly concentrated in the downtown area, the Cummins Engine Foundation, the company, and its founding family played a central role in defending Columbus against the disinvestment and decay that increasingly were afflicting American cities in the 1960s. Indeed, the small southern Indiana city emerged as a showcase for contemporary American architecture.

In this same period, the Engine Company was attempting to come to grips with other troubling issues of the day. "The Company stands in favor of Civil Rights," stockholders were informed in 1963. "It has long been the policy and practice of the Company to employ non-whites." With goading from Irwin Miller—most often in the form of memos to personnel heads—the company was striving to bring its policy and practice together. "In order to extend leadership in this community," Miller urged, "I should like for each of you gentlemen to make a vigorous effort to hire qualified Negroes in the next few months. To be meaningful, such employment will have to be in positions outside the menial services for which Negroes are usually employed."[139]

Both Miller and T. Randall Tucker (secretary of the foundation and community relations manager for the company) were named to the "Human Relations Honor Roll" in 1963 by the *Indianapolis Recorder*, a black-owned newspaper.[140] But Miller continued to badger his subordinates on the subject of "meaningful" black employment. Upon being told that black employment was up at Cummins' Atlas and Seymour plants, Miller asked pointedly, "Are they *janitors only*?"[141]

In March 1964, Miller asked his personnel head to look around the country for models of municipal antidiscrimination ordinances. "Maybe we can urge it on the city administration," he speculated.[142] But this was southern Indiana, which in 1964 was still receptive to the message of the Ku Klux Klan and other racist organizations. Several years passed with no progress toward open housing in Columbus. For the nation, these were tumultuous years, during which dozens of cities around the country erupted in deadly and destructive riots. In a speech to shareholders of the Irwin Bank and Trust Company in early 1968, Miller called publicly for action:

> *We have examples on every side of communities who didn't solve their problems while they could, and now their cost will be staggering—civil disturbance dangerous in its proportions, and the possibility of imminent collapse.*
>
> *Will we have the foresight to learn from the experience of others? I think the next year or two will tell. And the real test will come in our community response to discrimination, and specifically, to the proposal for an open housing ordinance.*[143]

And Miller put his company's money where its mouth was. Upon learning that black Cummins employees still were being prevented from buying houses in white neighborhoods, he wrote a pointed letter to the mayor. "No company," he warned, "can commit itself to further growth in a community that does not, in turn, commit itself to the elimination of discriminatory practices."[144]

Miller—intolerant of intolerance—did not endear himself to some in the community with his interventionism and his principled stances. He relished the opportunity to root out bigotry. He seemed not to worry about the possible negative consequences for his company. The highway authority in one southern state allegedly threatened to stop specifying Cummins engines if Miller did not throttle back on his voter-registration efforts, conducted mainly through the National Council of Churches. Miller told him, in so many words, to go to hell.[145] In 1964, a Connecticut-based architect warned Miller not to go through with the White merger, because (in his estimation, at least) White was dominated by Jews. "I read your letter of March 9 with great interest," Miller responded icily:

> *It is not clear to me whether you are now a shareholder of Cummins, or were formerly a shareholder. In either case, I am sure you would never want any shares in a company with our philosophy of management.*
>
> *We select, hire, and promote persons on the basis of individual ability and capacity as we are able to judge them, and on no other basis. Race or color of skin are not factors in this process. We have in*

important positions in our company Jews, Negroes, and persons from many nations, and this is part of our strength. Not a one of these should be barred by color or race from rising as high as he is able, and this policy will not be changed as long as I am chief executive officer of the company.[146]

Courageous and outspoken, largely immune to "conventional wisdom," Miller was far from the bland mainstream of American business. Gradually, in part through their activist stances, Miller, Cummins, and the Cummins Engine Foundation began to develop distinctive profiles. The national press took note, especially after First Lady "Lady Bird" Johnson took an architectural tour of the city in September 1967.[147] What most of the reporters eventually wound up focusing on was the enigmatic and highly quotable character at the center of the story: Irwin Miller himself. *Life* magazine was intrigued by Miller's far-ranging interests, including his Greek studies and his Stradivarius violin.[148] *Business Week* credited Miller with making Columbus an "architectural showcase," and quoted him extensively. And *Esquire*—no doubt looking to have the final say—put Miller on its cover, along with a large headline proclaiming that "this man should be the next president of the United States."[149]*

New leadership

The 1960s were a period of almost uninterrupted growth for the Cummins Engine Company. Between 1960 and 1966, earnings increased every year, and sales rose every year but one: from earnings of $6 million on sales of $136 million in 1960 to earnings of $16 million on sales of $331 million in 1966. Even more remarkable, Cummins nearly tripled its sales and more than doubled its earnings without raising the base price of its engines. Between 1953 and 1966, although prices of Cummins parts and components rose significantly, the company held the line on base engine prices.[150] This was possible, in large measure, through the unrelenting application of the cost-reduction program implemented in the early 1950s (see Chapter 5), which by the early 1960s was saving the company an estimated $4 million a year—roughly equal to half its capital expenditures.[151]

Then came 1967. Reflecting the broader national economy, Cummins sales contracted (from $331 million to $306 million). But profits almost fell off the table, shrinking from $16 million to $3.5 million.

---

*Miller's wife, Xenia Simons Miller, recalls her husband's acute embarrassment when this article appeared. "This, too, shall pass," he said when the *Esquire* surprise was revealed. "But not soon enough."

What happened? Several external factors converged. Nationally, heavy-duty truck purchases fell from 131,000 units in 1966 to 112,000 in 1967. And as trucks were driven fewer miles, fewer Cummins parts were sold. In other words, the overall drop in Cummins' sales in 1967 was exacerbated by the decline of its profitable parts business. Meanwhile, strikes at suppliers' plants made Cummins' production less efficient.[152]

But internal factors, planned and unplanned, also contributed to the earnings crunch. As noted above, the company's reluctance to break its thirteen-year record of no engine-price increases—even in the face of an increasingly inflationary national economy—cut profits to the bone. The V-engine program was still a drain. The Tech Center was requiring huge investments. (Cummins' research and development budget increased from $9.6 million in 1966 to just under $13 million in 1967, and its investment in buildings, machinery, and equipment increased from $126 million in 1966 to $143 million in 1967.)[153] And although international operations were marginally profitable in 1967, they did not begin to make a contribution commensurate with the corporate investment they represented.

Cummins' management was to blame as well. A trend toward decentralization that had begun in 1964 led to a lack of coordination and a duplication of effort among the company's operating units. The crunch of 1967 prompted the first of two corporate reorganizations in two years. In November 1967, the company took steps to "recentralize" some of the activities that had been decentralized in 1964. Vaughn Beals, who had demonstrated his management skills as vice president of research, was named head of the domestic engine division, encompassing all of Cummins' Columbus-based activities. Henry B. Schacht, the former vice president of finance who had stanched the flow of cash into the company's international division, was assigned the rest of the world: international operations and domestic subsidiaries.[154] (This allowed Cummins to eliminate the London international office and promised to give domestic subsidiaries more potential for "independent growth.")[155] And although both Beals and Schacht reported to executive vice president and chief operating officer Dick Stoner, the two men were implicitly anointed through these promotions as potential successors to president Don Tull.

That decision came in June 1969, when Tull was promoted to chairman of the executive committee, and Schacht—then only thirty-four years old, and looking not a day older—was named president. Jim Henderson, Irwin Miller's former assistant, who was by then vice president of management development (and was himself only in his early thirties), was involved in some of the discussions that led to Schacht's selection. Henderson speculates that it was Don Tull, in poor health and failing noticeably, who persuaded Irwin Miller to place his bet on a younger generation: "Irwin intellectually knew that Henry was the guy. But I suspect that Don was the guy who said, 'Let's do it now, Irwin. You know you're not going to be happy until Henry is calling the shots. So let's try it.'"

Although Schacht professes to have been surprised when the call to the presidency came ("my jaw hit the floor"), he had clearly established himself as a potential leader of the Engine Company. Schacht was a "person of character," according to Irwin Miller, "who cared about the time he was living in." On a more practical level, he was "one hell of a salesman," in the recollection of Marion Dietrich, who worked with him in trying to persuade European OEMs to buy Cummins engines. Although Schacht had had almost no contact with the company's main business—making heavy-duty engines in Columbus, Indiana—he was fully versed in the company's international and subsidiary operations, which Miller and others understood to be the future of the company. He was well educated and had a formidable intellect. When necessary—according to Irwin Miller—he could go toe-to-toe with Miller:

> *When Henry was in Europe, I always had him out to the house to dinner whenever he returned—say, every three or four months. He just never hesitated to give me hell, and dump on me about the lousy relations between Columbus and London. I always knew it had the potential to be an unpleasant visit, because I was going to get the truth with the bark off. And that just instinctively made Don and me turn to him for management.*

Schacht's promotion was not received with universal acclaim. The ongoing competitiveness between Schacht and Vaughn Beals was only exacerbated by the new arrangement, and within four months of the announcement, Beals left Cummins.[156] (He went on to a distinguished career at Harley-Davidson and was responsible for snatching that company back from the brink of extinction.) And by no means had Irwin Miller forfeited his right to disagree with his new president. In one planning memo from the period, Schacht made an assertion about the economics of a certain business. *"Not necessarily at all,"* wrote Miller in the margin. "Argue."[157]

Success in business derives in part from luck and good timing; Schacht had both. Cummins was enjoying a dramatic rebound from the depths of 1967: sales were up 20 percent in 1968, and earnings 262 percent, from the abysmal 1967 baseline. Now, as Schacht was taking the reins, the Engine Company was turning in another stellar performance. Schacht told a *Wall Street Journal* reporter in the fall of 1969 that Cummins had had a "whopping" third quarter (traditionally a weak selling period); that engine output was expected to reach an unprecedented 60,000 units; and that Cummins had the highest backlog of orders in its history.[158]

No event better exemplified the coming of professional management to Cummins than Schacht's promotion to the presidency. And no event better embodied the eclipse of the founding era than the passing of the company's founder and namesake, Clessie L. Cummins. The indefatigable inventor and diesel promoter died in California on August 19, 1968—twelve days after he received his final payment from Cummins for work on the PT fuel system, and fourteen months before Schacht's promotion.

At a special memorial service in Columbus, J. Irwin Miller delivered a moving eulogy for the inventive genius who had such an enduring impact on his own life:

> *Clessie Cummins was my best friend. He taught me how to shoot a gun. He taught me how to navigate the Ohio River after dark. And he taught me about business.*
>
> *We began all this before I was ten years old. Although there was twenty years' difference in our ages, I cannot remember a time when we did not deal with each other as contemporaries.*
>
> *We had furious arguments—over guns, boats, business, whether a car got better gas mileage in level or hilly country, and whether the New Deal was wholly evil or was there some small word of good to be said about it. In all these arguments we carefully avoided reference to the facts, because they might have settled the argument, and that would have been somehow like the death of an old friend.*
>
> *I always understood that if I were ever to be in real trouble, Clessie was not only willing to stand by and help, but was also the kind of person who would go down with you if you went down.*[159]

Clessie's death closed a chapter at the Cummins Engine Company. What is most remarkable is how long a chapter it was, and how productive its central character proved to be over that span of time. Clessie Cummins began his career as the age of the heroic inventor was ending. The model of corporate invention established by Edison—and later refined by General Electric, Bell Labs, and others—was the dominant approach to innovation as early as the 1920s. Clessie was the antithesis of that model: small-scale, self-taught, intuitive. And with his late career successes—from the PT fuel system to the Jake Brake—he continued to defy the age of institutionalized invention.

In Cummins' 1961 report to its shareholders, the company asserted that it planned to "enter new fields and manufacture new products" in the new decade. Nearly ten years later, it made almost the same promise: "to enter new lines of business either by internal development or acquisition."[160]

Clearly, Cummins did not achieve all its hopes for the decade. By the end of 1969, after several efforts at merger and diversification, the Engine Company still was largely dependent on the overall health of the heavy-duty truck market, and specifically on the willingness of truck OEMs to buy Cummins engines. Those OEMS had been angered by the failed White merger, and—a half-decade later—were still suspicious of Cummins. The distributor network, too, had been shaken by the failed merger. One of Cummins' traditional strengths badly needed shoring up.

At Irwin Miller's insistence, Cummins set ambitious goals for annual return and growth—15 percent return on equity (ROE), and 15 percent growth in earnings per share (EPS)—but had only mixed success in hitting these goals. ROE came in over 15 percent as often as it came in under, but growth in EPS never reached 15 percent, and tailed off significantly toward the end of the decade.[161] Could growth rates be turned around, either through adjusting the existing Cummins mix or by adding new ingredients?

International operations began to be profitable at mid-decade, and a few overseas plants became very profitable by the end of the decade; but the return from the international division was disappointing in light of the huge sums that had been invested. It was a large and open question at the end of the decade: Were international operations the wave of the future, or just a wild goose chase?

The research and development effort was another significant question mark. The attempt to "leapfrog" to a new technology for light- and medium-duty trucks had proven unsuccessful (although not everyone within Cummins had given up on the V series). Attempts to invent breakthrough products were equally unsuccessful. But Irwin Miller's commitment to R&D was unshakable. R&D expenses were at 1.7 percent of sales at the beginning of the decade, and inched their way up to an average of 3.4 percent in the last five years of the decade. Significantly, research expenditures were highest (4.2 percent) in the grim year of 1967, illustrating a remarkable steadfastness.[162] But the jury was still out. Could Cummins innovate? Was the new Tech Center the white elephant that some suspected? Or would increased regulatory and competitive pressures help justify the $22 million (up from the original estimate of $6 million) that had been spent on the facility?

These were the questions that Henry Schacht and his colleagues knew they had to answer, as they looked forward into the 1970s. But other questions, equally insistent and perplexing, soon presented themselves for attention.

Joseph Ireland Irwin and great-grandson
Joseph Irwin Miller. J. I. Irwin began his
business career in 1846 with a bankroll
of thirty cents. His investments in land,
retailing, toll roads, and, particularly,
banking laid the foundation for the
Irwin-Sweeney-Miller family fortune.

Clessie L. Cummins' first patent in the field of compression injection oil engines, better known as diesels. By using mechanical timing in the injection cycle, Clessie improved upon existing diesel technology and also escaped from an oppressive licensing agreement.

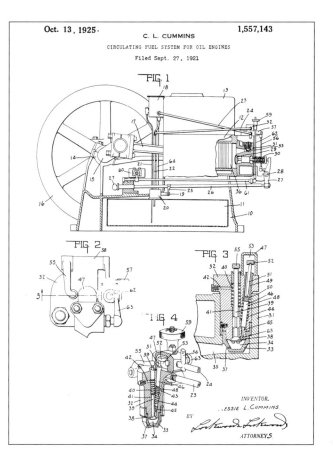

The "Cummins Machine Works," in the former stable of the Irwin mansion on Fifth Street in Columbus, Indiana. Here Clessie repaired cars, produced a propeller-driven bobsled, and did contract machining during World War I.

CUMMINS OIL ENGINES

STOP USING GASOLINE!

IT COSTS TOO MUCH, AND IS DANGEROUS

The Cummins Oil Engine will not operate on gasoline, but will start and operate on practically any other free flowing oil without priming.

When a gasoline engine fails to start and run properly, it is usually very hard to tell just where the trouble lies, as electricity is an invisible force, and any weakness in insulation of wiring or any connection that is not tight and clean will break the circuit.

On the Cummins Oil Engine, however, you are dealing with no unseen, mystifying force, but with only two things, fuel and air. It is an easy matter to hear and correct any air leaks that would be serious enough to interfere with proper running. It is still easier, of course, to check up on any trouble from the fuel stoppage, as the piping is simple and anyone, no matter how unfamiliar with engines, can tell when the fuel is flowing to the engine.

INSTALL A CUMMINS OIL ENGINE IN YOUR BOAT AND START SAVING MONEY

Remember that the extra money you pay to oil companies for gasoline will put one of these fine engines in your boat, as the saving in fuel cost will usually pay the entire first cost in less than one year.

ONE CYLINDER 8 H. P. ENGINE

Diesels were a product looking for a market in the 1920s. In early advertisements aimed at boat owners, Cummins played on the dangers of gasoline and the "mystifying" nature of the electricity used to create the spark in gasoline engines.

The "Cummins Oil Engine." Clessie Cummins' first big sales contract for diesel engines ended disastrously when giant retailer Sears, Roebuck & Company cut its ties with the newly formed Cummins Engine Company.

Clessie Cummins (rear, framed in cockpit of the record-setting Number 8) and the Cummins workforce in the early 1930s. Future president Don Tull is second from left in back row.

Clessie at the wheel of the Cummins marine engine-driven 1925 Packard limousine that saved the day in late 1929, when co-founder and financial backer W. G. Irwin was ready to shutter the Engine Company.

This "Indiana"-brand truck made a celebrated cross-country run in late 1931, traveling 3,214 miles on $11.22 worth of fuel. Depression-weary truckers took note.

Clyde Tatman (left) of San Francisco–based Purity Stores picking up America's first diesel-powered commercial truck in April 1932. Troubleshooter Jay Chambers (right) kept an eye on Cummins' more rambunctious distributors.

Clessie Cummins posing with driver "Stubby" Stubblefield and mechanic Bert Lustig at the Speedway in 1934. After this race, the Engine Company retired Number 5—and the troublesome two-cycle technology it embodied.

Clessie waving New York City good-bye on the eve of his grueling transcontinental bus run in November 1932.

Several companies claim the "first" diesel-powered passenger car. Clessie drove this Cummins-powered Auburn from New York to San Francisco in 1935 on $7.62 worth of fuel.

*Clessie Lyle Cummins,
inventive genius
and tireless promoter
of the engines that
bore his name.*

*William Glanton "W. G."
Irwin, son of Joseph Ireland
Irwin, whose faith in and
financial backing of Clessie
Cummins allowed the Engine
Company to survive nearly
two decades of losses.*

The Texas Cummins distributorship, owned and operated by the flamboyant K. W. Davis beginning in 1933. Davis correctly anticipated the displacement of steam-driven oil-drilling rigs by diesel-powered ones.

Cummins workers flanked by the mighty 500 hp VL-12 and the modest 85 hp AA-6. Future president Don Tull is third from left in the second row.

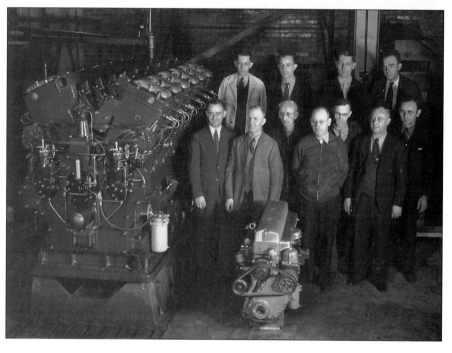

For a brief period in the 1930s, Cummins made engines for locomotives—and even completed a locomotive. The vision was too ambitious, and expensive, for the then-small engine maker.

Lieutenant J. Irwin Miller (center, rear) served aboard an aircraft carrier in the South Pacific during World War II, where he gained confidence in his leadership abilities.

Cummins receives the government's "E" award for wartime production excellence in 1943. W. G. Irwin is second from left; Clessie Cummins is to Irwin's left.

	SINGLE DISC PUMP	DOUBLE DISC PUMP	PT PUMP
Weight	104 Pounds	33 pounds	11 pounds
Number of Parts	415	448	182
Bulk	100%	40%	12.5%

Lighter, simpler, smaller: the evolution of the Cummins fuel-injection system.

The October 1956 press conference in Glasgow announcing Cummins' first overseas venture. Bernard Sunley (left) and Don Cummins (center) played the key role in setting up the Shotts plant, supported by Irwin Miller (to Cummins' left) and Cummins president Bob Huthsteiner (right).

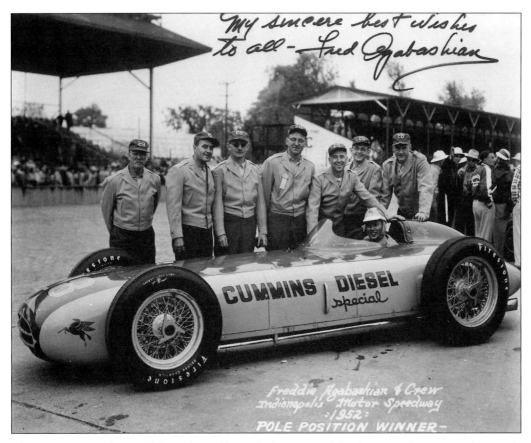

The "Cummins Diesel Special," driven by Freddie Agabashian, astounded Indy in 1952 by capturing the coveted pole position. Don Cummins (center, both arms on car) and Nev Reiners (to Cummins' right) engineered the coup.

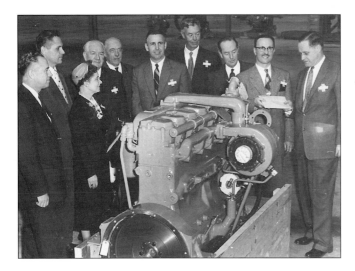

The first engine comes off the Shotts line on May 9, 1957. Member of Parliament Margaret Herbison (third from left) was determined to bring manufacturing jobs to her economically depressed home district.

Starting the new V-8 engine assembly line in Columbus. Left to right: Dick Stoner (vice president and general manager), Carl Fox (vice president, manufacturing), Waldo Harrison (treasurer), Joe Butler (research engineer), Don Cummins (vice president, engineering), Dave Marks (research engineer), H. E. Bollwinkle (service manager), Nev Reiners (director of research), V. E. McMullen (former vice president and general manager), and Bob Huthsteiner

The Oklahoma distributorship in the 1950s. "Selling engines to engine-makers" was a tough business.

Outside (left) and inside (below) the Hibbing branch distributorship in Hibbing, Minnesota, circa 1955. Cummins emphasized the importance of "genuine Cummins parts"—and the profits on the sale of those parts were the distributors' bread and butter well into the 1980s.

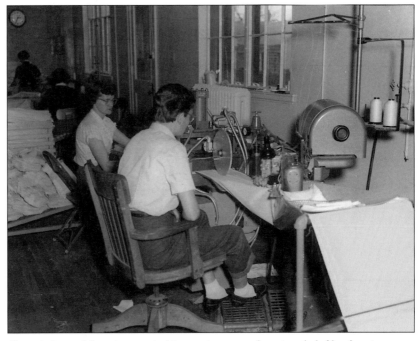

Cummins' second foray into vertical integration: manufacturing cloth filter bags in Seymour, Indiana, circa 1960.

Engine testing in the 1950s.

The Cummins Technical Center, built between 1964 and 1968 at a cost of $22 million, was intended to help Cummins "obsolete its own products."

New assembly line, Building 61, June 1962. By 1962, Cummins commanded more than 60 percent of the nation's heavy-duty truck market.

Chairman J. Irwin Miller and
President E. Don Tull: formidable
allies and unlikely friends.
Between 1960 and 1969, they
built Cummins from a $100
million to a $400 million
enterprise.

S. L. Kirloskar, head of Kirloskar-
Cummins, with Irwin Miller in 1961.
The Indian joint venture was a success,
and a continuing education for
Cummins.

Henry B. Schacht huddling with Don Tull and Irwin Miller. Tull encouraged Miller to name the thirty-four-year-old Schacht president of Cummins in 1969. Miller later commented that he could count on Schacht to give him "the truth with the bark off."

Cummins is listed on the New York Stock Exchange, September 10, 1964. In this period, following a failed merger with a key customer, Irwin Miller was urgently seeking ways to strengthen the Engine Company.

Henry Schacht (right) consciously patterned himself after J. Irwin Miller (below), who insisted that his young managers "think like owners." Schacht eventually inherited Miller's mantle as business-statesman, providing leadership to much of the American manufacturing sector in a trying era.

Cummins' short-lived foray into unrelated diversification in the 1970s was terminated by a chronic shortage of capital. Here, shareholders at the 1971 annual meeting inspect skis—produced by the colorful K2 subsidiary—and diesels.

Finance vice president John T. Hackett, Irwin Miller, and Henry Schacht: charting Cummins' course in the challenging early 1970s.

James A. Henderson (holding pen, facing camera) was named Cummins' vice president of operations in February of 1970 and was immediately plunged into a "desperate search for floor space." To Henderson's left are treasurer Eriberto R. Scocimara, vice president of operations Robert E. Sexton, and John Hackett.

DWU members Robert Dunham (left) and Morris Bradley on strike in 1972. The fifty-seven-day strike prompted Cummins' leaders to rethink the company's entire approach to manufacturing.

Henry Schacht and Komatsu's chairman Ryoichi Kawai (to Schacht's left) celebrating the signing of a key-supplier agreement in the early 1970s. A decade later, relations between the two companies were less harmonious.

The Columbus engine plant in 1932 (above) and 1976 (below). As Cummins grew over the decades, its leaders periodically worried that their company was becoming too potent an economic force in its small host city.

Bigger, better: A 1983 contest turned up the longest-running Cummins engine in a forty-three-year-old Diamond T truck (foreground) and provided a striking contrast with a Cummins-powered 1983 Marmon.

The Engine Company's first home was in a shed adjacent to the former Cerealine factory in Columbus. When Cummins built its new headquarters building in the early 1980s (below), it incorporated the old brick warehouse—an object of local affection—into the heart of the new facility.

Interior of the Komatsu facility in Oyama, Japan. Jim Henderson's trip to Japan in 1983 left him deeply impressed and concerned: Could Cummins compete in a changed world?

Labor relations head Ted Marston (left, rear), operations head Pat Snyder (center, rear), Jim Henderson (right, rear), and Cummins secretary Chieko Kawanishi (right) strike an impromptu pose with a group of Komatsu office workers.

Phil Jones, Irwin Miller, and Henry Schacht examine a midrange engine prototype mounted in a van, circa 1980. The decision to launch multiple new engine families concurrently was a risky gamble—a "bet the company" proposition, in Henry Schacht's words.

The L10 "COMMAND" engine, originally designed for European use, became an immediate favorite among cost-conscious domestic truckers.

Production workers at the Columbus Midrange Engine Plant posing with the B engine. Left to right: Kapila M. Patel, Rick A. Stepp, Ann C. Branom, James E. Johnson, Terry L. Grider, David Womersley, and Frank S. Westbrook. The company's successful effort to diversify its product line into smaller engine sizes—including the B, offered in Chrysler Ram pickups and numerous other applications—has helped inoculate it from the cyclicality of the heavy-duty truck market.

*Chief operating officer Tim Solso (left) with board members Will Miller and
Hanna Gray. Miller, who played an important role in the Hanson drama of
1988–1989, is the fourth generation of his family to be involved with Cummins.*

Henry Schacht of Cummins and Ratan Tata of Tata Engineering and Locomotive Co., Ltd., formally inaugurate their companies' joint venture in July 1993.

Jim Henderson and Henry Schacht were the team that guided Cummins for more than two decades. Their collaborative relationship—and successful division of labor—helped Cummins survive and prosper in the tumultuous 1970s and 1980s. In 1994, Henderson succeeded Schacht as the company's chief executive officer.

7 | The World Changes, 1969–1975

WHEN HENRY SCHACHT TOOK OVER as president of Cummins in 1969, he stepped into what looked like an enviable position. Cummins was doubling in size every five years. The company's share of the domestic heavy-duty truck market, although down from its historic peaks of the early 1960s, was holding steady at around 43 percent.[1] Its stock, meanwhile, was trading at an all-time high, and was appreciating steadily. The company's international investments were beginning to pay off. The domestic economy, still making up for time lost during the recession of 1967, was white-hot. In some ways, business had never been so good.

But Schacht, perhaps inheriting some of Irwin Miller's perennial skepticism, saw trouble on the horizon. The domestic economy not only was hot, it was overheated. The incoming Nixon administration had declared its determination to slow down economic growth in an effort to control inflation. If that effort went too far, it could drag the economy back into recession and once again choke the domestic truck market. On the other hand, if the effort didn't go far enough, money would become increasingly expensive—and the Engine Company's voracious appetite for cash might be impossible to satisfy.

Growth was why Cummins was so hungry for cash, and the company was explicit about its intent to grow. But *profitable* growth was the key, and this sometimes proved hard to come by, even in the best of times. In fact, the Engine Company's operations during the entire 1964–1969 period had been characterized by gradually falling margins.[2] Straight-line projections from numbers like these were sobering indeed.

Under internal and external pressure to increase corporate profitability as well as overall growth rates, Schacht and financial vice president John T. Hackett hatched an ambitious plan for diversification along several fronts. Even if the plan succeeded only modestly, it would demand major investments of time and money. If it succeeded beyond expectations, it would demand even more of these limited resources.

Growth had a human aspect as well, and this was another cause for concern. Contract negotiations with the Diesel Workers Union in 1969 culminated in a brief strike and left an unaccustomed aftertaste of mutual suspicion between management and labor. Union members felt they had been bested by the company in the 1969 negotiations and looked forward to righting the balance when their three-year contract came up for renewal in 1972. And as the company continued to grow, working conditions worsened steadily in the sprawling plant at 1000 Fifth Street. The time had passed when Don Tull could run the Engine Company out of his back pocket. But the company's new management had yet to devise an alternative approach to handling day-to-day operations.

One reason for this lag was the incomplete transition from one generation of managers to the next. Titles not withstanding, Irwin Miller (chairman of the board) and Don Tull (chairman of the executive committee) still were very much in charge of the Cummins Engine Company.[3] The new team of Schacht, Hackett, and the increasingly prominent Jim Henderson—an MBA, an economist, and an MBA, respectively—knew relatively little about the core business. They brought new strengths, but they also lacked experience and balance. As Henderson puts it:

> *The old guard was conditioned to figuring out what Don and Irwin wanted, and then carrying it out. I think the direction of the new management was much more, "What's good for the business?" But we were terribly inexperienced. We really were. And as a consequence, I think we were a little theoretical, and there was a bit of a financial bias there.*

The new managers spent the next half-decade, and more, learning their business. They did so in a period that included some of the most tumultuous episodes that the company had yet experienced. Meanwhile, the pace of change was accelerating, and Cummins' young managers had to scramble to find ways to respond. Unlike the glory days of the 1950s and 1960s, nothing was straightforward. "We are better able to plan," Henry Schacht told a meeting of his Research and Engineering personnel in the early months of 1970, "but we're less able to foresee what to plan *for*."[4]

It was, in a sense, a theme for a new decade. The economy was beginning to swing more quickly and more dramatically than was comfortable for most

American managers. Inflation was raging—so much so that Richard Nixon (the conservative who had vanquished the liberal wing of his party) felt compelled to put the national economy under wage and price controls. The ground rules weren't changing so much as they were disappearing. The confident young managers who were taking the reins at Cummins certainly possessed new tools and new skills—but figuring out how to apply them was more and more confusing.

Planning and diversification

By 1969, the Cummins Engine Company was running out of manufacturing capacity. The heavy-duty truck market was growing too fast for Cummins to supply. Despite increasing its output of heavy-duty truck engines by some 7,300 units, Cummins' undercapacity cost the company two points of diesel market share.[5]

One reason for this lack of manufacturing capacity was the conservatism of Don Tull, president of Cummins during most of the 1960s. Day to day, Tull either was absorbed in the workings of the plant or was cultivating his famously strong relationships with both customers and distributors. This left little time for issues that he found less interesting, including capacity planning. "Capital budgets for him," said one colleague, "were individual machine purchases."[6] But equally important, Tull (like his friend and superior Irwin Miller) was determined to protect Cummins and the Columbus community from the dramatic cyclical swings that long had plagued the automobile business and its host communities. Tull's personal inclination, greatly reinforced by a series of relatively small but still traumatic layoffs during the 1967 recession, was to control corporate growth in order to limit the damage when the next down cycle struck.[7] Jim Henderson recalls a typical Tull exercise:

> *I watched him, at budget sessions, sit in the conference room with [operations head] Bob Sexton, take out his pen, and draw a line through individual machines on the capital budget. He loved it, and Sexton just about died. It was based on a personal knowledge—but it was an old knowledge.*

More generally, at least since the boom times began in the 1950s, Cummins had lived beyond its managerial means. Its governance structure was ad hoc, informal, and even shaky. "Cummins has always been a company that has struggled," Henry Schacht once commented. "Its growth has always exceeded its formal governance system."

Schacht, assisted principally by John Hackett, undertook to create a new planning capability at Cummins. He began this effort early in 1969, even before taking over as president. Explicitly cast as a "planning foundation"— and constructed under very real time pressures—the new initiative was essentially a top-down planning process, with division managers being asked to react to the emerging plan rather than shaping it themselves.[8] Reflecting the professional training of its two principal authors, the plan was a strategy- and finance-oriented document. It focused primarily on potential sources of growth and income, rather than on operations.

The new plan embraced ambitious goals. The most dramatic of these was the doubling within five years of Cummins' heavy-duty engine capacity: to 90,000 units a year. The plan allotted Schacht ninety days to steep himself in the engine business—with which he was still largely unfamiliar—and then called for him to spend up to 40 percent of his time in subsequent months on efforts to diversify the company. The corporate organization chart was revised to provide for "a very strong man [other than Schacht] to supervise the day-to-day operations and to some extent the planning *within the agreed upon boundary conditions*."[9] This qualification was part of an effort to define a circumscribed role for the dynamic general manager of the Engine Division, Vaughn L. Beals, with whom Schacht had crossed swords more than once. But Beals simplified the process by resigning. For the time being, Schacht was left without his "strong man."

The plan that emerged from the basement conference rooms of 301 Washington Street—the original home of the Irwin Bank, where Irwin Miller still maintained his office—had at its core what became known as the "three-legged strategy." As noted, the first of these three legs, the engine business, was slated for unprecedented expansion. Ambitious financial goals also were set for the allied businesses—the second leg—such as Atlas Crankshaft, Fleetguard, and Frigiking. The company would seek out additional growth opportunities in this area, either through internal development or acquisition.

Finally, based in part on the expectation of a substantial cash flow from a still healthy core business, the plan called for diversification into entirely new businesses. Schacht and Hackett were convinced that the potential for growth in the core business was finite. Cummins would look first to its allied businesses (described in a subsequent section) and then to "exotics." It was growth in these new industries, completely unrelated to the engine business, that would enable the company to hit its established financial goals of 15 percent return on equity and 15 percent annual growth. These steps into unrelated diversification, although small, would be held to an even higher standard of performance: 20 percent return on equity and annual growth.[10]

Much about the plan was not new, not only because most changes at Cummins were evolutionary, but also because John Hackett's first boss at Cummins was Marion Dietrich, who early in the 1960s had come up with a somewhat similar strategy for growing the company. What *was* different from the Dietrich plan, in addition to the rapid expansion of the core business, was the proposed plunge into *unrelated* businesses. In John Hackett's recollection, it was a decision made on the basis of a sober assessment of the company's real prospects in 1969:

> *It was very clear to us at this point that the new V-series engines weren't working, and we were still very, very dependent on the NH engine. That engine was what would today be called a "cash cow"—it was producing everything for us, in terms of cash and profitability. And we were tied to an extremely cyclical industry. We decided that we ought to take some small steps out onto the ice of diversification.*

The goal was twofold. First, Cummins sought to find businesses that were just embarking on the "S-curve" of growth and help them prosper. Second, Cummins hoped to acquire companies in industries that had not yet gone through consolidation, and which might emerge as "core companies" in a consolidated industry a half-decade or a decade later. "That was always in the plan," Jim Henderson recalls. "We intended to leverage good managers across a broader base of companies."

Looking back from today's vantage point, Cummins' managers of the day say that they had no illusions that the "Cummins style of management" had universal applicability. Universality was a claim commonly made by managers in that period, especially graduates of leading business schools that focused on general management and strategy issues. Conglomerates—assemblages of diverse businesses with little in common except an overarching financial and control structure—still were very much in vogue in the late 1960s. The Textrons, ITTs, and Gulf + Westerns were the darlings of Wall Street as well as the envy of some managers in more prosaic, single-product settings.

But in fact, Cummins' leaders *did* feel that they had something special to offer rapidly growing businesses. "We are looking," Henry Schacht told a group of analysts in 1970, "for industries where our expertise in management and technology can be used to its fullest."

For public consumption, these would be businesses with at least one basic thing in common with Cummins: "manufacturing processes based on proprietary assembly and test."[11] In truth, though, Cummins was trying to spot industries where growth would come the fastest, return would be the highest, and consolidation was imminent. The first two industries that it settled upon—recreation and financial services—underscored how far afield the company was willing to look. Unrelated diversification was proving an irresistible temptation to much of corporate America, and even the level-headed engine company out in Columbus was hearing the siren song.

Unrelated Ventures

What do diesels and skis have in common? Except for a relatively brief interlude in the 1970s, the answer is nothing. Two decades after the fact, many Cummins employees still are bemused by the company's six-year foray into the ski business, which began with the acquisition of the K2 Company in October 1970. But skiing was a growth industry, and Cummins saw it as an interesting opportunity to take one of John Hackett's "small steps out onto the ice."

Hackett, who masterminded the acquisition, recalls the origins of the deal:

> *There were three sports we were interested in that we thought were going to develop rather quickly: skiing, tennis, and sailing. We found a little [ski manufacturing] company out on Vashon Island, in Puget Sound, called K2. When we first went out to talk to them, they were doing about a million dollars in sales, and they were running out of money.*

K2 was the creation of a former mining engineer named H. William Kirschner.[12] A lifelong skiing enthusiast, Kirschner became interested in fiberglass technology while designing cages for research animals. In 1962, he made himself a pair of fiberglass skis. The following year, Kirschner (in partnership with his father and brother) produced and sold twenty-five pairs of skis. They also secured a patent on their unique ski design, which eventually combined wood, steel, fiberglass, and plastic. By 1969, when Cummins came into contact with K2, the Kirschners were netting $66,000 on sales of $1.7 million.[13] Their skis were being used by more racers than any other American brand, and the resulting free publicity—reinforced both by the skis' distinctive red, white, and blue design and by a series of irreverent ad campaigns—was catapulting K2 toward the top of its field.

Cummins liked the look of the ski business. There already were some five million skiers in the United States, and that number was growing by 15 percent a year. American skiers spent more than $1 billion a year on their sport, second only to the total spent on golf. In the early 1970s, skiing surpassed golf as the nation's most expensive sport.[14] Cummins also liked the look and feel of the cash-starved little company out on Vashon Island, a setting that combined a rustic, down-home atmosphere with easy access to downtown Seattle. Kirschner himself set a special tone: He rarely wore a tie, shared a secretary with three other executives, asked his employees to call him "Bill"— and went to the altar with Cummins only reluctantly:

> *I never wanted to sell in 1970. But we grew too fast, and I was tired of hanging by my thumbs at the bank every two weeks. I sold when Cummins promised me autonomy. They knew nothing about skis—not even why they turn up at the tip.[15]*

The sale was concluded in the summer of 1970, when Cummins acquired K2 for 143,498 shares of common stock.[16] In a letter written shortly after the sale, Irwin Miller assured Kirschner that Cummins appreciated his "remarkable" accomplishments. And in his idiosyncratic way, Miller also made the point that Cummins would welcome a process of mutual education:

> *I am not very confident that we will have much good advice for the ski business (except that Mrs. Miller and I are the parents of a very critical consumer panel of five skiers), but I am sure that a perceptive person with an uncontaminated point of view can ask a lot of embarrassing questions about the diesel business.[17]*

K2 lived up to Cummins' expectations, becoming the biggest domestic producer of skis in the 1971–1972 season (up from number five in 1970–1971). Manufacturing floor space was doubled in 1972, and plans for further expansion were developed almost immediately. Cummins and Kirschner sought ways to accelerate even this startling rate of growth. Early in 1972, K2 announced the purchase of JanSport, a backpacking equipment manufacturer north of Seattle. The acquisition was aimed in part at offsetting some of the inherent cyclicality of the ski business, and also at positioning K2 to become a "core company" in the recreational equipment business. JanSport sold some 50,000 backpacks in the first year that K2 owned it. Under pressure from the parent company, it also began importing hiking boots and launched a highly successful line of tents.

The business of making and selling skis held lots of surprises for Cummins, including some unpleasant ones. It was a highly seasonal activity, and one frequently at the mercy of external factors. (Cummins' senior management never before had to worry about snowfall in the East, for example.) Inventory was a special challenge, in part because it was so perishable. K2 built up inventory in the off-season, shipped it to dealers, and shifted it into accounts receivable. "And then," says John Hackett wryly, "you hoped like hell it snowed, because if it didn't snow, you were going to get all that inventory back." A retailer in a Colorado outlet might call in March, looking for immediate authorization to put his entire stock on sale to capitalize on the last snowstorm of the season. The Cummins decision-making process—although relatively nimble by the standards of a traditional capital-goods company—nevertheless was hard-pressed to respond fast enough. And when it *didn't* respond fast enough, the skis came back.

Somewhat closer to the heart of the Cummins operation was a different kind of diversification: into the rarified world of international banking. Financial services was one of the first growth industries that Henry Schacht and John Hackett examined as a candidate for unrelated diversification. Initially, the company considered acquiring the Merchants National Bank and Trust Company of Indianapolis (MNB), not only to benefit from the potential for rapid near-term growth, but also to use the bank as a "vehicle to enter other financial markets." Banks required relatively minor capital investments, and the cash flow generated by a Cummins-owned commercial bank might finance entry into other industries. Talks between Cummins and MNB were far along in early 1969, at which point U.S. banking laws were changed to prohibit industrial companies from owning commercial banks. The MNB deal was abandoned.[18]

Frozen out of the U.S. banking market, Cummins decided to look for a different point of entry into the financial-services field. Within a year, John Hackett came up with an interesting overseas alternative: a small Geneva-based commercial bank called the Banque Des Transactions Internationales S.A., or "Transinterbank." Cummins purchased the bank in December 1970 for $1.7 million through the Cummins International Finance Corporation (CIFC), which had been established in 1968 for the issuance of Cummins' Eurodollar debentures. In 1970, CIFC was reorganized as an operating company to enable it to play a more aggressive role in Cummins' overseas growth; and Transinterbank was its first acquisition.[19]

Cummins was not the first American company to take over a Swiss bank (but it became the last, thanks to changes in Swiss law designed to protect this important local industry). Dow Chemical ran the largest of these American-dominated Swiss banks (established in 1965), and Firestone Tire and Rubber also operated a major bank in Geneva. Another Swiss competitor, the Bank for Investment and Credit, was owned by a consortium of eleven U.S. corporations, including Boeing and Coca-Cola.[20]

Transinterbank was smaller than these competitors. Nevertheless, the Geneva "newcomer" signaled its intention to begin competing more aggressively. Cummins received permission from Swiss banking authorities in July 1971 to begin managing the bank actively.[21] Among the bank's first transactions under its new owners were loans to rapidly growing small-to-medium-sized firms in Sweden, France, Ireland, and Switzerland. As John Hackett explained the bank's new strategy:

> *Our primary purpose in acquiring the bank was to take advantage of opportunities to provide intermediate credit for small and medium-sized businesses that are not being adequately serviced by traditional European banks. Such loans carry higher interest rates, and also provide opportunities to generate additional deposits and sell additional banking services to such firms.*[22]

It was Transinterbank's loan in Ireland, in fact, that led Cummins into its most unlikely field of diversification: beef cattle. For years, Cummins had been selling engines to the Monfort Company, a cattle business based in

Greeley, Colorado.[23] Monfort was a forced-feeding operation, which fattened cattle in pens rather than on the range, an approach that shortened cycle times. Sometime early in 1971, three Cummins employees—Brendan McDonald, Tony Kelly, and Thomas Casten—began wondering about the feasibility of transporting this feed-lot method to Ireland. McDonald and Kelly, Irish nationals, were well aware that the grass in their native country was high in protein content.* This fact, as well as centuries of tradition, had oriented Irish beef farmers toward range feeding. But if an Irish feed-lot operation could be established, incorporating the local grass into the feed mixture and capturing other efficiencies of the Monfort approach, it might revolutionize Irish (and perhaps European) meat production.[24]

Using Transinterbank as an intermediary, Cummins, Montfort, and other partners invested approximately $1 million to set up the Irish Agricultural Development Company, Ltd., in 1971. (Cummins' stake was $500,000.) By the end of the year, McDonald and Casten (picked to run the IADC) had nearly 2,000 head of cattle in their charge on a farm in Castlebellingham, County Louth. McDonald sent occasional progress reports to Irwin Miller, who first visited the farm in the fall of 1971. In one of those reports, McDonald expressed his astonishment at how much manure (or "slurry," to use the Irish term) the animals generated:

> *Would you believe nine gallons per animal per day. We've just installed an enormous chopper pump to condition and mix the stuff before spreading it back on the land as manure. This thing handles 1,000 gallons per minute, and we're thinking of charging 10p admission to see it at work. Can you imagine a Niagara Falls of slurry?*[25]

When IADC sent its first "crop" to market, in mid-January 1972, initial reactions were very encouraging: The IADC beef commanded a 2 percent premium over the previous market high, and local cutters and inspectors expressed enthusiasm for the product.[26] In the ensuing twelve months, the operation grew rapidly, reaching some 4,500 head by early 1973. Every aspect of the business was designed to keep costs down and feed-conversion rates up. IDAC's purchasers monitored livestock prices daily, and bought cattle at the auction markets where the best prices could be obtained. IDAC's nutritionists mixed feed according to a computer program, which factored in the cost of various components (wheat, barley, maize, and grass) as well as the changing

---

*It is worth noting that both Casten and McDonald arrived at Cummins through the "back door" of the Irwin Management Company, which continued to play a critical role throughout the 1960s in supplying Cummins with managerial talent.

dietary needs of the cattle as they matured. Noise was kept to a minimum so that the animals would not be distracted from their primary task: getting fat.

By late 1973, Cummins had driven a credible stake into the ground of unrelated diversification. The company now owned the fastest-growing ski manufacturer in the United States. In 1971, K2 earned approximately $500,000 on $6 million in sales, and that winter it became the leading U.S. ski maker. And although Transinterbank's relatively small asset base limited its ability to participate in underwritings, it was a reasonably venturesome enterprise. In 1971, the bank participated in twenty-one European security sales, and successfully sold some $1.3 million in new issues, while its profits nearly doubled.[27] As for the cattle business—a colorful diversion, where slurry met computers—early returns were promising.

Growing Allied Businesses

Fleetguard—Cummins' very successful homegrown filter company—left Indiana in 1967 for a new plant in Cookeville, Tennessee. (The vacated facility in Seymour, Indiana, then became available for additional Cummins turbocharger machining space.) Cookeville, eighty miles west of Nashville, wooed Fleetguard with $2 million in municipal development bonds, which provided Cummins with a brand-new facility for its ten-year-old filter business. The 135,000-square-foot Cookeville plant soon reached its anticipated payroll of 450 people.[28]

The decision to grow the filter business became the source of significant friction between Cummins and its distributors. Already, a considerable percentage of Fleetguard's output went directly to OEMs such as International Harvester, White, Ford, and Mack. In April 1970, Cummins told its distributors that effective July 1 of that year, independent parts distributors also would be authorized to sell Fleetguard parts. The news was not welcomed by the existing distributors, who correctly anticipated that a percentage of their profitable parts business now would be diverted to competitors.[29]

But Cummins was convinced that there was a vast market for its filters, which could not be tapped through the existing Cummins distributor network. It also seemed possible that existing distributors' sales might actually grow as overall demand for Fleetguard products increased, even though the percentage of Fleetguard's total output sold by Cummins distributors almost certainly would decline dramatically.[30]

Events soon bore out these predictions. Fleetguard's sales increased from $9.1 million in 1970 to $21.2 million in 1973, while before-tax profits increased from $979,000 to $2.4 million. The percentage of Fleetguard's output consumed "internally"—that is, for use on new engines from the Columbus Engine Plant—shrank to less than 10 percent. The overall dollar value of service parts sold by the distributors did slip between 1971 and 1972, for the first time in decades; but then resumed its steady march upward in 1973.[31] This success led to a major expansion of the Cookeville facility, as well as an expansion of Fleetguard sales to Europe, in 1973. Within five years, European sales constituted 15 percent of Fleetguard's total dollar volume.

A less successful holdover from the 1960s diversification effort was Dallas-based Frigiking. Marion Dietrich's initial effort to "clean up the company" had paid off in dramatic increases in sales (from $2.5 million in 1964 to $23.1 million in 1970). But the division's profits were modest at best—and more often nonexistent.[32]

Throughout the 1960s, Frigiking's basic problem was that it was unable to come up with a truck refrigeration system (cab or trailer) that could compete effectively with that of the market-leading Thermoking. Cummins abandoned that effort in the late 1960s, and experimented with a variety of new strategies for the subsidiary: selling automobile air conditioners in the aftermarket; equipping foreign cars sold in the United States; and offering a private-label product to giant retailers (including Penney and Ward). These efforts met with mixed success. Frigiking finally turned a full-year profit in 1968, after it began selling an air-conditioning unit (the "Chiller") for car trailers, recreational vehicles, and mobile homes.[33]

By the first quarter of 1972, Frigiking was operating at a before-tax profit margin of 12.25 percent, which—while well below its 20 percent target— still represented a significant turnaround from the flat years of the 1960s. John Hackett was encouraged: "I feel that Frigiking and K2 have demonstrated the most progress among the various companies . . . in developing and implementing a logical and reasonable business strategy."[34]

On first look, computer software might seem as far removed from the diesel engine business as skis and beef. But Cummins' acquisition of a small software firm in Princeton, New Jersey, was consciously an "allied businesses" venture, rather than an unrelated diversification.

Management Information Systems, Inc., was founded in 1965. Its product was a package of hardware, software, and forms that could be tailored to create an industry-specific computer-based system for tracking a variety of operating costs. When Cummins acquired MIS in the spring of 1970 (in a stock swap involving eighteen Cummins shares for each of the 532,000 MIS shares outstanding), the Princeton-based company already had developed computer software systems for hospitals, jewelry companies, and the paperboard industry.[35] A unique feature of the MIS system was its industrywide time-sharing approach, which provided inexpensive computer access and comparative data to a range of businesses that otherwise could not afford them.

Of particular interest to Cummins was MIS's wholly owned subsidiary, Mainstem, developer of a cost-control system called "Fleet Maintenance

Management" aimed specifically at the trucking industry. In part due to timely endorsements from both the American Trucking Association and the American Public Works Association, Mainstem had a growing stable of clients in both the private sector (including REA Express, Consolidated Edison, and Safeway Stores) and the public sector (including Jacksonville, Florida; Richmond, Virginia; and Pueblo, Colorado). By the time Cummins acquired Mainstem, the software firm was tracking some 20,000 vehicles.[36]

For Cummins, the Mainstem acquisition was part of a larger corporate strategy. The Engine Company was then trying out a concept it called "lowest total cost," whereby it would provide customers with a "total system of performing work," rather than just engines. This package would include not only the optimal power plant—with guaranteed availability to participating clients—but also maintenance of that power plant and its accessories for a predetermined useful life. In response to narrowing margins, Cummins was anticipating a possible industrywide shift to something like a leasing model.

The company already had taken an interesting step in response to this changing environment by setting up a marketing tool called "Vehicle Mission Simulation" (VMS), which combined data on the characteristics of certain equipment (engines, transmissions, axles, cab-and-trailer combinations, etc.) with data on the characteristics of a given route (grades, road surfaces, speed limits, etc.).[37] By 1970, Cummins had programmed profiles of 43,000 miles of North American highways for the VMS program.

In other words, the front end of a full-service, leaselike arrangement was in place. The acquisition of Mainstem added the record-keeping function needed to carry through on VMS. In a speech at the Cummins annual meeting in April 1970, Henry Schacht made what must have been—in the minds of longtime shareholders, at least—a startling prediction:

> *We are moving from a marketer of hardware to a marketer of software systems, in which the hardwares play a vital role, but where the specification of the hardware is derived explicitly from the needs of the customer through very careful analysis of records and simulation of mission.*[38]

The "lowest total cost" strategy also had implications for the far end of an engine's or a major component's original life cycle. In some cases, of course, fleet owners insisted on a new Cummins diesel (or new parts and accessories) every time they needed to upgrade their equipment. But in other cases, Cummins customers preferred a less expensive option—such as a "reconditioned" (rebuilt) part or engine. Because Cummins' major components were heavy-duty to begin with, many lent themselves to retooling and reuse. In fact, fleet owners had been doing so for years. But in the mid-1960s, entrepreneurs around the country (including several of the larger Cummins distributors) began entering the rebuilding business in a significant way.

Typically, a customer turned in a worn-out fuel pump and purchased a rebuilt one, and was happy to get an almost-like-new pump for a fraction of the cost of a new one. The distributor then would replace the pump's rings and other consumable parts—rebuilding around the more or less indestructible castings—and sell the pump to the next "recon" customer. The distributor, too, was pleased, since this was a highly profitable business—by some accounts, even more profitable than selling new parts.[39]

The "Recon Division" was organized in Memphis in 1966 as part of a corporate effort to capture some of the substantial profits that were already being reaped in this trade—and also as a way of ensuring quality work. But the early years of the Recon Division were characterized by recurrent quality problems. In 1968, for example, the division experienced major difficulties in the remanufacturing of fuel injectors, and many potential clients went elsewhere for these vital parts. The division, moreover, operated at a loss. Sales increased tenfold between 1966 and 1970—but as sales climbed, so did losses.[40]

Cummins estimated that the total market for reconditioned products was roughly $50 million. But given the mounting losses, how much of this business did the company really want? A study conducted by John Hackett's planning staff in late 1970 supplied a clear answer: as much as possible. "It was imperative for Cummins to implement a recon program as a defensive move," John Hackett wrote.[41] Margins never would be high enough, in and of themselves, to justify Cummins' full-fledged entry into this field. But if Cummins did not jump in with both feet, competitors most likely would, and would "gain a lowest total cost advantage."

The planners also recognized that part of Recon's problems grew out of a misguided effort to scale up the distributors' small-scale, job-shop operations. As it turned out, centralizing the rebuild activity without changing its nature was counterproductive. What was needed was a high-volume assembly line operation, like those used to build the engines and other major components in the first place.

That new operation took shape in the spring of 1971. Cummins announced that it was forming Diesel ReCon, Inc. (DRI), a cooperative parts-and-engines remanufacturing operation owned jointly by Cummins and its thirty-seven distributorships in the United States and Canada. Each distributor would be required to contribute $25,000 to the venture (with an additional $25,000 callable by the cooperative on six months' notice). Collectively, they would own 70 percent of the new company; and Cummins, which was contributing its Memphis-based Recon assets to the venture, would own the remaining 30 percent. Four plants—in Memphis, Chicago, Los Angeles, and an unnamed east coast city—would cover geographical "zones" and have functional specializations. (The coastal plants, for example, would be engine oriented, and cater to their respective half-continents.) For the time being, at least, Cummins would supply parts to DRI at subsidized prices.[42]

The first Recon plant (in Los Angeles) went into operation at the end of 1971, and others across the United States became active within a few months. By that time, Diesel ReCon was earning its keep (although a planned phaseout of subsidized parts from Columbus loomed ominously on the horizon.) Distributors steered more and more business to DRI facilities—in part because of their enforced sense of ownership in the operation, but also because DRI began to offer good value to the distributors. DRI did some things better, and more cheaply, than many distributors. Customers, too, were reassured by the phrase "factory rebuilt." And finally, as noted by DRI's president, V. Von Boll, DRI's activities were increasingly relevant in light of the nation's growing environmental consciousness. Rebuilding was, in a sense, recycling: "Diesel parts, components, and engines will need to be recycled just like any other resource. Diesel ReCon, Inc., is one answer to good conservation principles coupled with sound business practices."[43]

Pushing the core business

By 1973, toward the end of Cummins' first five-year plan, the company had ventured well out onto the ice of diversification. It had tested two legs of the three-legged strategy—unrelated diversifications and allied businesses—with relative boldness. But Schacht and Hackett, godfathers of the plan, already were discovering that their vision was either flawed, or at least obscured, in fundamental ways. The first problem was the steadily increasing cost of money during this period. With double-digit inflation, ever-larger amounts of fixed and working capital were required.[44] To the extent that diversification depended on increasingly expensive borrowed money, it would be an unsustainable strategy.

A second and related problem was that these two legs of the three-legged strategy were not turning out to be especially profitable. On the combined 1973 sales of $81.5 million at Frigiking, K2, Fleetguard, and CIFC, Cummins made only $2.4 million, or less than 3 percent. From ventures that were expected to earn returns of at least 20 percent, these numbers were extremely disappointing. To be sure, bad luck and bad timing were responsible for some of the problems. The 1973 Arab oil embargo smothered sales of recreational vehicles—Frigiking's growth business—and three years of meager snowfalls in the eastern United States depressed K2's sales.[45]

But bad management hurt as well. "We tried to do too much too fast, without building the proper management base," Schacht wrote of Frigiking, which again lost money in 1973. And the grand visions that had looked plausible to Schacht and Hackett in the basement room on Washington Street were not panning out in the real world. "We must make a sober assessment of the lowest-total-cost strategy as part of the U.S. automotive strategy," John Hackett concluded in one internal memo. "The lowest-total-cost thesis seems quite rational on paper, but it has not met with the success that we originally anticipated."[46]

Management challenges inherent in taking on new businesses, such as the cyclicality of the ski business, were becoming obvious. But there were cultural problems as well. Reflecting its many decades under the leadership of J. Irwin Miller and his family, Cummins was fundamentally a sober, principled, even straight-laced company. The Engine Company was indisputably a voice for progressive change in Columbus—most notably in the open-housing debate of the 1960s and 1970s—but its core values placed it in the conservative mainstream of its host community, and of southern Indiana in general.

It was against this backdrop that the swashbuckling K2 subsidiary got into trouble. In the early months of 1971, it came to John Hackett's attention that strange things were going on out in Colorado:

> *We had a lot of professional skiers out on the slopes who were representing K2 as part of a marketing program. And at night, when they weren't skiing, they'd go into the local taverns and they'd have the "K2 wet T-shirt contest," in which young women in the community would come out with wet T-shirts on. And ultimately the winner was always the one that came out carrying her T-shirt in her hand. Well, this made* Sports Illustrated, *and there was a big splash about K2. We were all mortified.*

Hackett sent out the word in no uncertain terms: This was *not* the way Cummins did business. ("I don't want to debate," he wrote to a colleague. "I don't want to be told that I don't understand how to market skis. I DON'T WANT TO HEAR ANYTHING ABOUT THIS PARTICULAR PROGRAM OTHER THAN IT HAS BEEN STOPPED.")[47] But a year later, over Cummins' strenuous objections, pictures from the defunct competition showed up in *Playboy* magazine.[48] An out-of-town friend called up Hackett to congratulate him on all the free publicity K2 was getting. "All we could think of," Hackett recalls ruefully, "was the *embarrassment* of one of our companies being associated with something like that."

Misadventures like these may have been one reason why Irwin Miller and Don Tull remained fundamentally uncommitted to unrelated diversifications like K2. But what ultimately doomed the three-legged strategy was the overwhelming growth of the domestic heavy-duty engine business in this period. In 1969—when the Cummins strategists were laying their plans—128,000 heavy-duty trucks were sold in the United States. In 1973, this number had surged to 203,000: a 60 percent increase in four years. And the "dieselization" of this growing fleet increased in the same period from 70 to 80 percent.[49]

The upshot was that while the number of new Cummins-powered trucks rose from 45,000 in 1969 to 62,000 in 1973, the company's share of the heavy-duty market declined from 44 percent to 38 percent. Cummins simply could not keep up with the staggering growth of the diesel engine business, and every point of market share it surrendered to its competitors was a hugely expensive lost opportunity. In this context, it made no sense to divert scarce capital to ventures that did not support the core business. "The engine business just went like a house afire," recalls Henry Schacht. "So in the middle '70s, we decided to fold up Leg Three, because those businesses were also expanding rapidly, and were screaming for capital, and we didn't have it. These things never made the diversification impact we hoped they would, because no matter how fast they grew, the engine business was growing faster."

A revised strategy statement drawn up in 1974 declared that Cummins would henceforth concentrate all of its assets on the diesel engine business. The following year, Schacht told attenders at the annual planning meetings that Cummins would become a "one-product company," although that product would come in many varieties and would evolve over time.[50]

The ax fell in 1975. Frigiking was sold for a loss totaling some $12 million. (By finding a last-minute buyer, Cummins narrowly avoided the distasteful process of liquidating the company.) Mainstem was sold for $1.9 million to a Baltimore-based company.* Cummins sold two-thirds of Transinterbank to an Indianapolis bank for $3 million (the purchasing bank insisted on a gradual transition) and began negotiations to dispose of its stake in the Irish Agricultural Development Company. Profitable (and colorful) K2 stayed in the fold until the following year, when it was sold to a group of investors who included the ski company's founder, Bill Kirschner. "I didn't want K2 to end up in the hands of a faceless conglomerate," Kirschner told the *New York Times*. Although company lore has it that the divestitures were unprofitable, the sale of the five businesses netted Cummins some $39 million, at a juncture when the company was desperate for cash.[51]

In retrospect, John Hackett—principal architect of the unrelated diversification effort—regrets only that Cummins was forced by external circumstances to sell off the small stable of businesses:

> *I look at the growth of those companies since that time, and it's too bad in a way that we couldn't retain them. K2 is the leading U.S. ski manufacturer today. JanSport is the leading day-pack producer.*

---

*Jim Henderson, for one, thinks that Mainstem was Hackett's most visionary acquisition and that its sale was a significant miscalculation in light of the subsequent evolution of technology.

> *Transinterbank was sold to Merrill Lynch, and someone at Merrill
> Lynch told me that it's one of their most successful European operations.
> Frigiking never made it, but the last I heard, the little [software] com-
> pany down in Princeton is doing well. And the Irish Agricultural
> Development Corporation was sold to an Irishman who managed it so
> successfully that he became the richest man in the Republic of Ireland.*
>
> > *But the capital requirements for the engine business were so overwhelm-
> ing that there was no way that we could support these growth companies.*

Hackett's comments accurately characterize the rise and fall of unrelated
diversification at Cummins. Hackett and Schacht—like Marion Dietrich before
them in the 1960s—had no illusions about remaking their conservative diesel
company into a Midwestern Textron or ITT. (Even if the core business had been
standing still, it would have taken decades to effect a substantial transformation
of the Cummins product mix through unrelated diversification.) Despite occasional lapses, Cummins' management mostly understood what they did not
know, and refrained from meddling excessively in the affairs of their exotic subsidiaries. Meanwhile, they kept their eyes on the real targets: growth and profitability. When it became clear that growth and profitability were easiest to find
in the core business, Hackett and Schacht coolly unloaded the exotics.

Cummins never seriously contemplated getting out of its allied businesses. Atlas Crankshaft and Fleetguard, although occasionally capital consump-
tive, were both strategically important and consistently profitable. (Atlas's
profits increased from $4.4 million in 1969 to $10 million in 1974, and
Fleetguard's profits increased from $744,000 to $2.4 million during the same
five-year span.)[52] And a fortuitous 1973 acquisition—a British turbocharger
manufacturer called Holset—already was proving its value as an allied business (see Chapter 8). But the company's attention was now explicitly refocused on the engine business. This involved a number of parallel efforts,
including expanding capacity and changing the distributor mix.

Expansion and Allocation

Even before the end of the 1960s, Cummins' shortage of engine manufacturing
capacity was pressing. The heavy-duty truck market had rebounded from its
disastrous year of 1967, and by 1969 was 13 percent larger than in 1966.[53] But
in part because of Don Tull's and Irwin Miller's reluctance to expose the company to traumatic contractions during the next (inevitable) economic downturn, and in part because of the huge cash drain imposed by international operations, Cummins had refrained from expanding along with its market.

Shortly after Henry Schacht was named president in mid 1969,
Cummins announced what it called a "major expansion." In fact, the expansion entailed some fairly modest measures, such as additions to the Columbus

parts distribution center and to the Atlas Fostoria plant. These were stopgap measures, reflecting Cummins' uncertainty about the growth of the heavy-duty business. The engine shortfall worsened, with predictable consequences. By the end of the year, Cummins had to plead with its employees to make a "big push" to meet the soaring demand for engines. "In the next two months," Dietrich told one group of workers, "Detroit Diesel will make every effort to 'fill the demand gap' and supply the customer with engines we can't meet at our current rate of production."[54]

In other words, rather than commit itself to adding significant new manufacturing capacity, Cummins was trying to put its existing assets (including its people) to more intensive use. The company was, as Irwin Miller saw it, "shoehorning an extra machine tool every week or two" in the Main Engine Plant, rendering working conditions "dreadful."[55]

As a first step toward change, Cummins deepened its management team. In February 1970, James Henderson was named the new vice president of operations.[56] Again, Irwin Miller had made the call. Henderson, most recently in charge of executive recruitment and before that Miller's personal assistant, had no operating experience. On the other hand, he enjoyed Miller's complete confidence. And in a period when Schacht often was preoccupied with diversification efforts, both Schacht and Miller wanted someone they could trust in the factory. As Henderson recalls: "What Irwin said to me, very early on, was, 'Jim, those guys can go and do all that stuff. But *this* [diesel engine making] is our business, and this is what you've got to help us straighten out.' And then Henry Schacht came in one day and said, 'How would you like to head manufacturing?'"

Schacht now had the kind of "strong man" called for in the 1969 five-year plan. But what "operations" meant was shifting rapidly. Plans already were afoot to open a new components plant in Oklahoma—a reaction to the testy 1969 negotiations with the Diesel Workers Union—and one of Henderson's first tasks in his new job was to meet with the governor of Oklahoma to settle on a final site. Unexpectedly, Henderson pulled the plug on Oklahoma, lobbying against the scheme because a large-scale move to Oklahoma would have meant major layoffs in southern Indiana.[57]

Instead, Cummins decided to build a 400,000-square-foot manufacturing facility for parts-machining and subassembly in the rural town of Walesboro, ten miles southwest of the Main Engine Plant. Cummins was enjoying record sales and earnings, Schacht told shareholders at the 1970 annual meeting, and "the order backlog is at an all-time high for this time of year."[58] Even to the traditionally cautious Engine Company, this boom market seemed to be more than just a bubble.

Schacht and Henderson pushed hard to make the new plant a reality. As the first major Cummins facility outside of Columbus, Walesboro was the "new guard's" first attempt to change significantly the company's core operations. (Some younger Cummins managers bet Henderson that he would never get it built.) The Walesboro ground-breaking took place on October 5, 1970, with Irwin Miller wielding the ceremonial shovel. By this time, the scope of the project had grown significantly; floor space was up from 400,000 to 563,000 square feet. In part because of these expanded plans, it took almost two years to complete the huge building, which put more than thirteen acres under one roof. In the third week of July 1972, the new plant produced its first vibration dampers.[59]

Meanwhile, Cummins was transforming the Main Engine Plant as well: adding 60,000 square feet of manufacturing space and renovating another 100,000 square feet. Included in this package was a new $6.5 million automated engine-block transfer line—at 1,400 feet, perhaps the longest single assembly line in the world, and certainly the first complete line for an engine block the size of Cummins'. All told, the domestic expansion of 1970–1972 comprised nearly 1 million square feet of new or rehabilitated manufacturing space.[60] Whereas Cummins had averaged $15 million per year in capital expenditures between 1967 and 1969, it invested three times as much in both 1971 and 1972.[61]

One compelling reason why Schacht and Henderson had to commit the company to these large outlays, and the many that were to follow, was the highly uncomfortable situation in which Cummins had found itself in August 1971. This was the first time since the glory days of the 1960s that the company was required to start allocating engines among its customers.[62]

Cummins spent nearly eight years in the 1970s on allocation, using one formula or another to dole out its products among its customers. To be sure, there often had been backlogs in Cummins' production, but (except in wartime) Cummins never had been forced to turn away would-be customers. Having a guaranteed customer—or two, or three—for every engine might seem to be cause for celebration. But the reality of identifying winners and losers among the customer base was grim. "It was terrible," recalls Jim Henderson. "Every week we sat down and said, 'How many engines does PACCAR get? How many engines does IH get?' It was an awful period. The OEMs hated us."

Because the formulas for allocating engines were based on history, the previous year's big customers tended to get relatively large allocations. But this ran the risk of penalizing the company's fastest-growing accounts. "We are hurting ourselves," Henry Schacht noted ruefully, "with the very people on whom we will be most dependent in the future." He knew firsthand what he was talking about. PACCAR, International Harvester, and Ford—all growing rapidly in this period—had complained to him personally in the previous two months.[63]

A second customer category hurt most by allocation formulas included OEMs that Cummins recently had won over from competitors. One such customer—the Crane Carrier Company, manufacturers of material-hauling vehicles—illustrated the dilemma in dramatic terms.[64] Cummins had wooed Crane away from Detroit Diesel through a concerted marketing effort that promised good service and an adequate supply of engines on a timely basis; and in 1972, Crane began offering Cummins engines as standard equipment in its material-hauling vehicles. Crane needed at least seventy-five engines per month, and was under the impression that it had been promised that number. But in 1973, Cummins allocated only twenty-five engines per month to Crane—except for July and August, when the monthly allocation was cut back to sixteen. "This places us in an impossible situation," complained Crane's president, "which not only inhibits growth, but will cause a severe decline in Crane's present level of business, which could be disastrous at this time."[65]

Many factors contributed to the production shortfalls at Cummins in the 1970s. The company had put most of its capital into building capacity for the ill-fated V-series engines, rather than the stalwart NH. In addition, acute materials shortages were common in the early years of the decade. Strikes shut down key factories (including, as we shall see, one Cummins factory). By taking up all the available slack with its vendors, Cummins had made itself more dependent on them. "We will need *all* our vendors if we are to increase our build rates as scheduled," Schacht observed early in 1974, in the wake of a wildcat strike at Cummins' rod and cam forging supplier.[66]

But the most important factor, by far, was undercapacity. Cummins simply had miscalculated the potential for growth in the heavy-duty engine business. "And as a result," Henderson explains, "we found ourselves in a desperate search for floor space in this period, and making big decisions in a hurry. Before buying our Jamestown [New York] plant, we looked at 119 sites. We bought Daventry [England] in a week. I basically spent the 1970s looking for floor space around the world. It was a wild, wild time."

Changing the Distributor Mix

As the 1970s opened, both Cummins and its distributors were suffering from the persistent evils of the national economy: historically high interest rates and a shortage of investment capital. For Cummins, the problem came home in 1969, when traditional means of financing new or expanded distributor facilities suddenly dried up. The Chemical Bank announced that after the completion of the Boston and Charlotte distributorships, no more money would be available for this purpose. In the wake of this unpleasant surprise, Cummins informed its distributors that each of them, "as an independent businessman, should be responsible for financing the assets he needs in pursuing his business." At the same time, however, the company acknowledged the importance of a "strong independent distributor system" and offered to guarantee local loans to distributors within specific guidelines.[67]

At the same time, Cummins wrestled with another problem of even greater concern to its distributors. Increasingly, OEMs were demanding the right to distribute Cummins parts to their end users through their own distributors. International Harvester and White Motor, in particular, were pressuring Cummins to liberalize its parts policy to increase their role in wholesale parts sales; and Cummins felt that such a liberalization was inevitable. In fact, this transition had been going on throughout the 1960s. In 1961, only 23 percent of automotive parts went through the automotive dealer channel (that is, Ford dealers, International Harvester dealers, and so on). Seven years later, fully 43 percent were going through that channel, with the increase coming at the expense of the Cummins distributor network. But the OEMs wanted more. Concurrently, the sale of competitive parts through independent distributors— another kind of competition for Cummins distributors—was increasing.

After considerable internal debate, Cummins decided that a new approach was needed. Its distributors had become overly dependent on their wholesale parts margins. This dependence was increasingly untenable, not only because powerful OEMs demanded an ever-larger piece of this business, but also because the lure of the business distracted Cummins distributors from the all-important focus on the end user. "Once a distribution system fails to maintain its contact with the end user," Henry Schacht argued, "it atrophies quite quickly."[68]

Of course, the margin on wholesale parts had long been a mainstay of the Cummins distributor network, and would remain so for the foreseeable future. What was needed to complement that bread-and-butter business was a shift in emphasis toward retail and service activities—in other words, the distributors' contribution to the corporation's overall "lowest total cost" approach. "The greatest concern about the change in distributor orientation," John Hackett wrote in this period, "is distributor reaction and profitability. . . . I believe this [profitability] problem can be overcome with a properly designed and timed compensation system, and much closer distributor-factory cooperation on asset management."[69]

In part to reinforce this closer cooperation, Jim Henderson in the early 1970s revived a dormant strategy of "seeding" the network with former Cummins executives.[70] The company saw multiple advantages in the strategy, says Henderson. "In addition to reinforcing the traditionally close ties across the network, it also provided a ladder and an outlet for some of our most talented marketing people."

The first example of this reinvigorated policy came in the spring of 1970, when C. L. "Chuck" Grace, former vice president of field sales based in Columbus, took over the Charlotte distributorship.[71] (He was joined there by T. C. "Tom" Lockwood, former controller of Fleetguard.) Grace, then in his fourteenth year with Cummins, had an entrepreneurial streak and a long-standing desire to run his own Cummins distributorship. When Cummins offered him Charlotte—strategically located within a ninety-minute drive of eleven of the top one hundred U.S. common carriers—Grace, thirty-four years old, jumped at the opportunity:

> *I called my father down in Florida and said, "Hey, I've got a chance to get into business for myself." He said, "How much does the god-damned thing cost?" I said, "Oh, about $2 million." He said, "Well, then, you'd better get the hell down here and talk to me about it." After he looked at all the forecasts and projections, he put up some dough, and I put up some dough, and I borrowed a little bit from my uncle, and Cummins guaranteed a portion of the term loan on the deed, and that's how we got into it.*

With his broad corporate experience, his energy and ambition, and his more-than-total financial commitment, Grace was Cummins' notion of the ideal distributor. Given his personal financial exposure, there was no chance that Charlotte would suffer from lackadaisical ownership.

The next "seeding" came in lower Michigan, where the former president of Diesel ReCon, V. Von Boll, took over a new distributorship in the fall of 1971. In rapid succession, the "franchises" in Toronto, Montreal, Memphis, and Columbus (Ohio) were sold to Cummins officers. In 1979, former corporate controller Thomas A. Lyon became vice president of San Francisco-based Watson & Meehan, Cummins' oldest distributorship; two years later, he took over the newly renamed "Cummins West."[72]

The hoped-for shift toward a retail- and service-oriented perspective among the distributors was accelerated by the arrival of individuals like Grace and Boll. But progress in this direction remained limited. This was in part because the corporation's "lowest total cost" strategy was proving unworkable, but also because the company still lacked the products needed to make real change possible. As long as the bulk of the distributors' business was heavy-duty truck engines (and parts and service for those engines), change would come slowly. Isolated voices were being heard in favor of a broader line of engines that might help create new categories of customers; but these voices were far from the company's mainstream.

Meanwhile, some of the more ambitious distributors took Cummins' new message to heart. One example was Cummins-Wisconsin, which in the mid-1970s aggressively began selling generator sets overseas. Drawing on its own assembly capacity, this distributor assembled and delivered to customers in Britain more than one hundred gensets in a six-week period in 1975. This business otherwise would have been lost to Cummins, because the company was running flat out making truck engines and lacked assembly space for the job. Cummins-Wisconsin soon was earning a third of its annual sales of $5 million from overseas clients, mostly in the genset trade.[73]

Most Cummins executives today see the company's distributor network—built on a base of former Cummins marketeers—as one of the company's key strengths.* The Engine Company occupies a very unusual niche in the American business scene: selling almost exclusively to OEMs, while attempting at the same time to understand and appeal to its own end-users. Whereas the typical OEM prefers to view the engine in its equipment as a commodity, Cummins (through its distributors) trains end-users to demand a *Cummins* engine.

Strikes and teamwork

During a chance encounter with Henry Schacht in 1973, a General Motors executive commented: "You guys play that small town 'Mr. Clean' bit so successfully you can probably get away with exporting back to the U.S. We just can't do the things you can."[74]

There was more than a little truth in the GM manager's depiction of Cummins. However, the "small town 'Mr. Clean' bit" that he derided worked strongly *against* Cummins' sending jobs offshore in the early 1970s. The Engine Company had been founded in large part to provide employment to the young men of Columbus, Indiana, and a half-century later, the founding family (in the person of J. Irwin Miller) was still very much in control of the company's affairs. At the same time, there were practical bounds on this core value. The most important of these was Miller's unwavering insistence that Cummins had to perform according to the standards of a world-class company. Despite its highly visible "good deeds," Cummins was not a charity. It competed in the marketplace with giants such as GM—for customers, raw materials, and components alike. As Cummins had learned, this meant adopting a national (and in some cases an international) perspective.

Engine building itself, though, was somehow different. With the exception of the modest output of the various overseas ventures, every single Cummins engine built since the company's founding came out of the Main Engine Plant in Columbus. This was a powerful tradition. As noted earlier, it made even the construction of a parts-machining and subassembly plant only ten miles outside of Columbus seem unlikely to many.

Tradition, along with capital constraints, had kept Cummins a one-plant company. But events in the early 1970s began to undermine that tradition, and forced the company to rethink completely not only where, but also *how*, it made its products.

---

*By the mid-1990s, almost all of the thirty-three North American distributors were Cummins "alumni" with significant Engine Company experience.

How to Set Up a Strike

Except for the tumultuous days of the 1930s, the relationship between Cummins and the Diesel Workers Union (DWU) was a harmonious one. Cummins, which usually saw its business grow from year to year, could afford to concede competitive pay increases and fringe benefits. At the same time, rigorous cost-cutting allowed the company to avoid price increases for most of the 1950s and 1960s. Over the decades, the terms of the contracts with the DWU got longer, which gave the company an ever-increasing measure of predictability. During World War II, contracts were written for one year; in the 1950s, they were extended to two years; and beginning in the 1960s, three-year pacts became the norm.[75]

Dick Stoner, longtime executive vice president and operations head during the 1960s, did much of the bargaining for the company during that period. "What's important is the approach you take," he recalls. "I've seen some people go into negotiations with the idea that they're not going to change their position, and that's *that*! But eventually you've got to come together, so you have to put yourself in a position where you *can* come together. Unless, of course, you want to have a strike. You can always have a strike if you want a strike."

Stoner did not take part in the negotiations that began in the early months of 1969. These were conducted by Vaughn L. Beals, then head of the Engine Division, and personnel director Melvin Darrow. This bargaining team was, by most accounts, far tougher and more legalistic than those that had preceded it.[76] Randy Tucker, then a relative newcomer in the public relations area, recalls an assignment he received during this period:

> My supervisor said to me, "We're going to break this union, and the way we're going to do it is to use [the in-house newsletter] Power-Plus *to show all the bad things that unions do. I want you to go to New York and get a bunch of pictures of strike-related violence in the 1930s." So I dutifully got on the airplane, went to the UPI photo morgue, went through their stuff, and came back and told him they wouldn't let us have them. Of course, that wasn't true. But this wasn't the Cummins Engine Company I knew, so I wasn't going to be a part of it.*

Union-busting may not have been the tradition at Cummins, but more confrontational union-management relationships were becoming the norm nationwide. Younger labor leaders across the nation increasingly were antagonistic toward management, in part because their own membership was losing faith in them. To regain credibility, these young labor leaders felt they had to demand more and more on behalf of their membership.[77]

This new, tougher atmosphere was triply damaging to the company in 1969. First, Cummins endured an eighteen-day strike (only the second authorized work stoppage in four decades, and far longer than the fifty-six-hour strike in 1966). Cummins also agreed to the biggest single percentage pay increase in the company's history. And finally, despite this major concession, the DWU wound up feeling as if the company had "slid one by" them.[78] The rank-and-file were determined to right the balance next time out.

Union politics also played a role in this outcome. In January 1969, the DWU retained Truman Davis, president of the Congress of Independent Unions out of Alton, Illinois, to assist with its upcoming negotiations. Davis and the other members of the union team, including DWU president Lawrence Mosier, did extremely well by their membership, extracting a substantial pay increase from the company. But in the wake of the settlement, representatives of the United Auto Workers apparently spread the word that Davis and the DWU had been "beaten" by Cummins, and that the UAW—a sophisticated and powerful international union—would have represented the interests of the Columbus diesel workers much more effectively.[79] As usual, the independent-minded DWU membership rebuffed the UAW's overtures, but the implication of amateurism on the part of the local union seems to have stuck.

Another factor that contributed to the worsening relations between Cummins and its workers in the early 1970s was the steadily intensifying pace of production. This, explains Henry Schacht, gradually undid the "social contract" that had been built up over the decades between management and labor: "We had been working so much overtime, and running so fast to expand, that we had gotten sloppy in our day-to-day relationships. We were pushing people very hard. We weren't managing the place very well. We were just trying to get production up, somehow."

While this kind of push would have caused problems at any company, it was particularly corrosive at Cummins. Many new hourly workers arrived with the happy expectation that Cummins would be a humane and satisfying place to work—only to be placed under managers newly recruited from companies with long histories of hostile labor relations. Mixed messages bubbled up through the system, confusing management and muddying the signals that management sent back. On May 11, 1971, for example, the company experienced its first major wildcat strike since 1959. (It lasted only a few hours.) Two days later, nearly 1,000 people stood in line for hours to apply for eighty-three jobs the company had advertised.[80] Which was the "real" message from the work force?

Summer often was the season when Irwin Miller found time to think deeply about the state of the Engine Company. In the summer of 1971, he crafted a thoughtful memo to Jim Henderson, pushing his young manufacturing head to think harder about how Cummins managed its people:

Are we talking one way and acting another? It is our custom to subscribe to Peter Drucker's phrase "age of discontinuity," and to advocate fresh thinking in the society. However, when it comes to the problem of productivity of our workers (shop and office), and solutions to worker satisfaction, we seem to be much more refining and improving the past than making a break with the past and taking the risk of fresh new approaches.

    What are to be the new forms of business organization? Why not experiment with them at Cummins—NOW? How do we involve the people themselves in working these out—NOW? . . .

    The purpose of this memo is simply to give expression to a fear that we will wish that we had been bolder—sooner. We will wish that we had involved the people in the thinking. . . .

    Don't let this frustrate you. Give me hell if I'm wrong.[81]

Miller was not wrong. Cummins managers and workers (unlike their counterparts in Detroit, for example) were relatively isolated, which meant that their work practices sometimes fell behind the times. The Cummins assembly line, for example, was highly fragmented; it afforded little opportunity for line workers to learn from and help each other. As longtime employee (and later DWU president) Larry Niehart recalls:

For years, when I worked on the assembly line, I rode in a car pool with people who worked in test block. I thought we were doing one heck of a job on the assembly line. And then one day, these guys who worked in test block started talking about us putting parts on, in the assembly line, that they had to take back off again in test. And here we're working a hundred feet apart! We just didn't have a system to communicate. I mean, we communicated more in the car pool than we did at work.

Among the inevitable results—in addition to reduced quality and increased inefficiency—was frustration. In both 1966 and 1969, worker dissatisfaction with Cummins had led to strikes. The company was getting a reputation for being a supplier that could not be counted on at contract time.[82] Looking ahead to the 1972 negotiations, some customers began to hedge their bets, adding a second engine maker to their vendor list. Others simply dropped Cummins.

The 1972 negotiations began on January 10. Heading up the union team were DWU president Chet Fleetwood, secretary-treasurer Evan Bridgewater, and outside advisor Truman Davis. Briefly leading the management team was Theodore L. "Ted" Marston, who had taken over as head of personnel little more than a year earlier. Marston was a former teacher in the Columbus public schools who in 1963 organized a job action against the board of education. (Irwin Miller asked him to lunch one day to try to get him to end the protest, but Marston wound up winning Miller over to his side.) When the school board prevailed in the dispute, Marston decided to pursue his doctorate at the University of Illinois. Cummins recruited him back to Columbus in 1964, when he joined the company's personnel department.[83]

After three weeks of fruitless negotiations with the DWU, Marston called in reinforcements: Henderson and Stoner. "I knew Irwin well enough to know that when things really started to crumble," he recalls, "if we didn't have everybody at the table that Irwin trusted and respected, we would be in real trouble. So Jim and Dick came in, and Jim became the spokesman."

By the third week of February, after twenty-eight meetings and some two hundred hours of negotiations, all parties were willing to admit that they were in trouble.[84] Ten of the most difficult articles in the contract, including all of the economic issues, remained unresolved. (According to participants, at least two of the key negotiators were alcoholics, which put practical limits on the length of bargaining sessions.) At the request of both parties, Cleveland-based federal mediator Leon E. Groves began sitting in on the sessions on February 22, but it already was too late. Cummins aggravated a deteriorating situation by distributing a proposed "total package" to the entire work force three days before the existing contract was set to expire. Jim Henderson recalls the tactic as an "act of desperation," reflecting the company's sense of urgency about resolving the impasse.

This did not sit well with the leadership of the DWU. "We had no time to negotiate the package," complained Evan Bridgewater, "and we had never seen the package prior to Sunday night." On Tuesday, February 29, the DWU voted 4,265 to 548 to strike at midnight. The next morning, picket lines went up around the Main Engine Plant at 1000 Fifth Street.[85]

Management initially saw the strike as an inconvenience. It began doling out a reserve of engines and parts, hoarded in anticipation of a strike, on the assumption that the strike would end in a week or two. Nor were the workers particularly concerned about the strike. "Based on previous experience," recalls Jim Henderson, "they figured we'd give up in a week or two, and give them more money to get people back to work. But we felt we simply had to break that pattern." Many had been working extra overtime hours and had enough money in the bank to ride out a short strike. In fact, some Cummins employees—having months earlier correctly anticipated a strike—took off in the first week of March on prebooked trips to Disneyworld.[86]

But this was not to be a short strike. One week passed, then another, then two more, with very little progress toward a settlement. During the first month of the strike, the negotiators focused almost entirely on language

issues rather than economic concerns.[87] This was an ominous sign, since settling on wages and benefits was almost always more difficult than resolving
language-related disputes.

As for the language issues, the thorniest was whether Cummins would continue to exercise complete control over subcontracting, especially the machining of parts outside of Columbus. The company insisted on retaining "sole and
exclusive decision-making authority with respect to the letting of all future sub-
contracts for specific components," and was unwilling to budge from that position.[88] The DWU feared the loss of local jobs to foreign workers, and its representatives cited as an example a series of layoffs on the block line in 1967 which
they claimed resulted directly from the importation of short engine blocks from
Komatsu in Japan.[89] Management disputed the specifics of that example, but
went on to argue (and reargue, in subsequent weeks) that buying and selling
parts, both domestically and overseas, was an absolutely vital aspect of
Cummins' business, and one that on balance created jobs in Columbus. Pressed
by the union to provide new language to move the negotiations along, the management team declined, declaring that on this particular point, it could only
produce language that was strongly pro-management.

These were the kinds of circumstances—as Truman Davis warned at the
March 21 session—that led to "long strikes." Jim Henderson attempted to
adopt a conciliatory stance, but Davis was having none of it. "Let us know
when you change your mind," he said. "I'm going home."[90]

Learning (from both sides) of this impasse, the local paper published an
editorial entitled "$3,750,000 Pinch," which blamed the $3.75 million in
payroll lost since the beginning of the strike on the DWU's alleged intransi-
gence. This editorial came hard on the heels of news reports about striking
Cummins workers applying for food stamps, which didn't sit well in conservative Columbus. The balance of public sentiment, already tipping against
the workers, tilted further in favor of management. In a long letter to the
paper, DWU secretary-treasurer Evan Bridgewater apologized to the community for the strike's negative impacts. At the same time, he defended his
union's right to strike. "We are only trying to acquire some things that are
very important to us," he wrote. "Things like job security, health insurance,
retirement, and security, not only for ourselves, but most important of all, for
our families."[91]

As the strike dragged on, and as economic distress began to spread outward to Cummins' suppliers and other local businesses, J. Irwin Miller
became increasingly agitated. Just as breaking unions was not what Cummins
was about, neither were strikes that dragged on indefinitely, hurting
bystanders as well as participants. At least one open letter appeared in the
local paper chiding the Cummins chairman for his inaction.[92] "Irwin Miller
was beside himself," recalls Ted Marston. "He told me so. And he told Jim.

In fact, he told anybody who would listen." At one point, with his anxiety boiling over, Miller ordered the management team in no uncertain terms to get people back to work. Henderson recalls what happened next:

> *So I went to the next meeting and they handed me the most ridiculous proposal I had ever seen. I threw it back across the table and said, "Call me when you get serious." I walked out of there thinking I was a dead duck. I went right to Henry and I said, "Henry, I've gotta tell you what I just did." And then the two of us went down to see Irwin. Irwin didn't like it, but he supported us.*

For some, the financial hardship imposed by the strike was fast turning into desperation. At the beginning of the strike, Larry Neihart was buying cheese, crackers, and bologna for picketers on the line; six weeks into the strike, he barely had enough money to put gas in his car. Ted Marston recalls desperate phone calls from wives of Cummins employees, begging him to end the strike before their family savings were completely wiped out.[93] Even Tim Solso—later the company's president, but then a junior member of the labor relations department—received threatening calls at home. "I got a couple of ugly anonymous calls," he remembers, "and that's very unusual for this community."

Some cause for hope came at the end of March, when the two sides agreed on tentative subcontracting language. (In fact, the new language was little more than a fig leaf for the union, leaving subcontracting firmly in the control of the company.)[94] Meanwhile, settlement of a month-long strike at nearby Reliance Electric also seemed like a good omen.[95] On April 6, after fifty-five bargaining sessions, a tentative settlement was reached on all language and money issues. In accordance with a union bylaw, the package was sent first to the DWU shop stewards for a preliminary vote.

As it turned out, though, it was the financial part of the package—deferred until the difficult issue of subcontracting had been hammered out—that sent this proposed settlement off the rails. Cummins was in a "Category I" industry, as defined by President Nixon's wage-and-price-control system, and therefore was prohibited from awarding more than an average 5.5 percent annual pay raise over the ensuing three years, excluding life, health, and retirement benefits. But elsewhere in the country, dock workers and aerospace employees—not under the jurisdiction of the federal Pay Board—were winning substantially higher settlements.[96] This angered the DWU shop stewards, who on April 7 voted down the proposed settlement.

Now the stakes were escalating dramatically. In a public statement, Henry Schacht reported that several of Cummins' most important truck-manufacturing customers had announced their intention to restart their lines with Caterpillar or Detroit Diesel engines. "Cummins' reputation as a dependable supplier continues to suffer," he wrote.[97] Schacht took the highly unusual step of delaying the company's annual meeting on April 14, hoping that by May 16 (the date of the rescheduled meeting) there would be happier news to report to the shareholders.

After another ten days of stalemate, the two parties were summoned to Washington, D.C., where the U.S. Mediation and Conciliation Service took over the mediation effort. Four days of intensive negotiations, led personally by National Director of Mediation Gilbert J. Seldon, finally extracted a new proposed settlement from the two sides. The deal included a substantial pay increase—seventy cents per hour over three years, in contrast to the sixty-one cents per hour that Cummins had offered before the strike—and a number of small improvements in various insurance and retirement benefits. But management had protected all of its key prerogatives, especially regarding the thorny subcontracting issue.[98]

The shop stewards quickly approved the deal. On April 27, the full union membership voted on the proposed new contract, and the vote was almost three to one in favor. After fifty-seven days, Cummins' longest strike was over. Management had demonstrated its resolve to break the pattern of large wage increases to get people back to work—although this resolve was undercut by the mediation process. The DWU had demonstrated how seriously it took the issue of job security, but was unable to effect changes in the contract on this score. And although management had lost less, on balance, the strike had raised more questions than it had answered.

Satisfiers and Dissatisfiers

Anxiety and bitterness lingered long after the strike ended. Many of the workers were in serious financial trouble, having gone without paychecks for almost two months. And in the immediate aftermath of the strike, sympathy for the workers among Cummins' management was limited. "Perhaps in the future," one company officer wrote to a friend, "they will be less willing to strike."[99]

But the company, too, had suffered, and would continue to pay strike-related costs for months and years. Lost production and profitability were only the most obvious of these costs. Also very costly were the many hours of overtime incurred in the wake of the strike as the company attempted to catch up with backlogged orders. Pretax profits plunged from $37 million in 1971 to $13 million in 1972, while return on equity dropped from 12.9 percent to 5.2 percent. And when the federal Office of the Oil and Gas Agency allocated oil and natural gas to Cummins for 1973, it did so based on the unnaturally small amounts of fuel that the company had consumed during strike-bound 1972.[100]

Many OEMs stuck with Cummins throughout the strike, in part by scheduling their non-Cummins production to take place during the work stoppage. "Several truckers and OEMs took me aside quietly and said they agreed with our stand," Henry Schacht reported a month after the strike was settled. But the growth of the heavy-duty truck market punished Cummins anyway. For the first time ever, Cummins' share of that market (36 percent) dipped below Detroit Diesel's (37 percent).[101]

Neither the union's leaders nor the company's gained many plaudits for their role in the strike. The financial community made its concerns known. One institutional investor informed Irwin Miller that his fund was now "bearish" on Cummins. "His first statement was that the management appeared young," Miller told Schacht, "and [appeared] to have botched the labor situation. . . . He felt there was a strong probability of other strikes."[102]

Cummins' young management team was well aware of this perception, which they felt was unfair. They were convinced that the DWU had entered the negotiations determined to force a strike—mostly to stave off the perennial incursions of the UAW—and that it was a largely unnecessary strike that had cost the company dearly.[103] In June, two months after the settlement, the federal Pay Board underscored the futility of the strike when it rolled back the negotiated pay increases from 6.5 percent to the prescribed 5.5 percent.[104]

Emotions ran high in the wake of the strike. Still, the consensual processes whereby Cummins usually makes its most important decisions prevented any precipitous actions. Shortly after the strike, Irwin Miller wrote a confidential memo to the company's top managers. Yes, some three thousand DWU members had ratified the contract, and the strike had ended. But Miller was thinking about the one thousand or so workers who had voted *against* the contract: "I know that the 1000-plus negative votes puzzled and disturbed us. I doubt whether we understand a) how they feel about the strike, b) how they feel about the union, c) how they feel about the company . . . . We need to understand our people in depth—or we are flying blind. What is your reaction?"[105]

Questions like these prompted Cummins' senior managers to think more deeply about the events of February, March, and April 1972. What if battles over subcontracting and fringe benefits were only symptoms, rather than causes? What if working conditions, broadly defined, were really at the heart of the workers' discontent?

If this was true, then the bearish analysts probably were right: There *would* be more strikes at Cummins, because nothing fundamental had changed. Almost from the day the strike ended, the Main Engine Plant once again was running flat out, seven days a week. And the company again was pressuring its workers to accept significant numbers of overtime hours, under the same "dreadful" conditions—Miller's description—that had prevailed before the strike. Extrapolating from the number of backlogged orders, this circumstance was likely to continue for months, or even years.[106]

At least three things had to happen before any fundamental changes could occur. First, the company needed to add still more capacity. The soon-to-be-completed Walesboro components plant would provide some relief, but more space was needed. Most likely—in light of the company's recent union troubles, but also in light of Cummins' desire to "reduce [its] dominance in the community, and allow other industry to grow and prosper in [the] area"—some of these plants would be outside Columbus.[107] Jim Henderson's search for floor space would have to intensify.

Second, as Cummins planned for these new plants, it would need to pay much more attention to the kind of work that would go on within them. Was there a way to structure work, for example, so that people were not simply extensions of their machines, and so that one group of workers—as in Larry Neihart's example—was not paid to undo the work of another? And finally, as more plants came on line, there would be a need for a much more effective planning mechanism—one focused largely on *operations*—so that Cummins' managers could plan, manage, and assess the affairs of an increasingly complex organization.

Within two weeks of the end of the strike, the team that had negotiated on behalf of management—Jim Henderson, Ted Marston, and Dick Stoner—reassembled for a strategic postmortem and a look forward. As Marston recalls that meeting:

> *I think what came out of that was a feeling that we had lost touch with what happened on the shop floor—that we really didn't under-stand what was going on with our employees, and that we clearly couldn't let that happen again. So the initial thrust was, "Hey, how do we get back in touch? What can we do to ensure that we're listening, rather than just reacting?" I think we all got the order to go out and think about those kinds of things.*

Marston reflected on the various publications he had read over the years on the subject of industrial relations. Well before the strike, he had come across a book that he found intriguing: *The Motivation to Work*, by Dr. Frederick Herzberg, a professor at Western Reserve University.[108] Jim Henderson, too, was aware of Herzberg, having read his work at Harvard and met with him following a 1966 strike at Atlas Crankshaft. Impressed at the apparent overlap between what Herzberg had written about and what Cummins was now experiencing, Henderson and Marston began a dialogue with Herzberg.

As a clinical psychologist, Herzberg was more interested in individual motivation than social structures. His fundamental premise was that challenge is essential to motivation. An employee who was challenged to learn, grow, and develop (wrote Herzberg) was likely to be far more productive than an employee who felt stuck in a job where effort was disconnected from achievement. The traditional predictors of job satisfaction, such as compensation, were what Herzberg called "hygiene factors"—considerations that became paramount only *after* the work proved dreary and unchallenging. Far more important to long-term satisfaction, according to Herzberg's research, were factors such as achievement, recognition, and responsibility. Although hygiene was important, hygiene alone was not enough. A six-year study of Herzberg's hypotheses conducted at Texas Instruments Incorporated in the 1960s seemed to bear out many of his conclusions, especially the counterintuitive notion of compensation as a "dissatisfier."[109]

Ideas like these were not entirely new to Cummins. The Chicago-based management consulting firm of Cresap, McCormick and Paget, Inc., was retained by Cummins in 1970 to propose job-enrichment possibilities for the planned Walesboro facility.[110] But the resulting ideas never were tested on a large scale, because tradition and union work rules proved insurmountable. As new facilities came on line, it seemed that existing problems were destined to be duplicated. Early returns from Walesboro, which opened in 1972, were discouraging. According to an internal memo, the new components plant suffered from low productivity, vandalism, and a "negative climate" almost as soon as it opened.[111]

It was time for a change; and the hypotheses that Herzberg floated in his conversations with Marston and Henderson soon were put to some very real tests—first in the antebellum city of Charleston, South Carolina, and subsequently in the semirural environment of Jamestown, New York.

Charleston and Jamestown

In 1972, Cummins briefly considered purchasing the huge White Motors diesel- and gasoline-engine plant in Canton, Ohio (to serve as its new assembly and test facility), but decided that the plant was too elaborate and expensive.[112] Instead, Cummins selected a vacant Avco Lycoming plant eight miles northwest of downtown Charleston, South Carolina.[113] The 800,000-square-foot facility previously was used for the production of Lycoming helicopter engines, and it lent itself well to traditional large-scale assembly techniques.

But Henderson, Marston, and other Cummins managers were looking to make a departure from old techniques. Irwin Miller had been encouraging his senior managers to examine the experience of the Saab automobile company in Sweden, which used teams of workers to assemble a whole engine. (Miller had seen a television news clip about a nineteen-year-old Saab worker who was able to assemble a complete engine by herself after three months on the job, and "seemed to get quite a bang out of being able to do so.")[114] The Cummins managers looked not only at Saab, but also at Volvo and other companies that were pioneers in team-based manufacturing. Cummins recruited Leo H. Everitt, Jr.—a Columbus plant manager who had served on the 1972 negotiating team and had grown bored with his routine—to head the new plant. A small manufacturing force was held over from Avco, and some twenty employees were transferred from Columbus to Charleston. In the spring of 1973, the "Pilot Operating Team" set out to invent a new approach to manufacturing.

From the beginning, recalls Marston, the Charleston plant was thought of as a laboratory for Herzberg's principles:

> *Jim and I talked about it, and we said, "Well, as long as we're starting with a clean piece of paper, why don't we bring Fred Herzberg in and apply his principles on the shop floor?" So we basically used Fred Herzberg to get the Charleston plant started. And that's when the team concept came up. When we started talking through how we would actually do this, we came up with the idea of a team.*

Herzberg conducted a series of off-site meetings that eventually came to be known as "Theory Days." These sessions led to the so-called Charleston Concept, which incorporated a focus on hourly job design, job enrichment, forced job rotation, flexible time, elected team leaders, few (or no) supervisors, and a single hourly compensation level.[115] Participants later recalled the "fervor" and the "gung-ho" attitudes that characterized these discussions. *Create motivating jobs*, the group was asserting, *and everything else will take care of itself.*

This rarified atmosphere produced a vision of the workplace that was dramatically different from the Columbus model. One early discovery at Charleston was that the Columbus manufacturing system—a highly fragmented system, in which individuals tended to do only one task, over and over—had a great deal of overhead structured into it. Logically, it *seemed* efficient to have the line worker do only one thing. As it turned out, however, this was a highly inefficient approach—not only because workers were unhappy and therefore less productive, but also because the system demanded extensive support services. If one worker could not leave the line to get needed parts, another was required. If a line worker could not set up his or her own machine, that created the need for a specialized set-up person.

These were intensely practical problems, which did not lend themselves to solution through Fred Herzberg's highly theoretical approach. In part to answer these kinds of pressing, practical questions, Leo Everitt mandated sixty-hour weeks for his managers. Even so, the new K engine (described in the next chapter), scheduled to begin production at Charleston in the fall of 1973, fell behind schedule, in large part due to design problems originating in Columbus. Working literally around the clock, the 142-person Charleston team managed to start up a K engine in October. When the K engine design fell further behind schedule and demand for NH engines became overwhelming, Charleston stepped sideways and began assembling NH engines. In December, against great odds, the new plant shipped fifty-six NHs; and in the spring of 1974, the plant shipped its first K engines.[116]

Predictably, tensions arose between Columbus and Charleston. The Charleston cadre felt it had one-third of the resources that it needed to do the job right, and complained to Columbus of a "quadruple whammy": a new product (the K engine), a new plant and location, new employees, and new organizational concepts. Columbus, for its part, asked pointedly if Charleston really had to reinvent *everything*—the accounting system, credit union, personnel policy book, and so on.

At the end of 1974, two years into the experiment, the jury was still very much out on Charleston. Plant manager Leo Everitt was coming under fire for his obstinacy in sticking to the original vision for the plant. (He refused, for example, to build a cage around the plant's inventory, asserting that this would be "against the concept.") And in Columbus, Henderson faced mounting pressure to abandon the Charleston organizational concept. "It's not going to get there," he was told.[117]

But Henderson dug in his heels—not only in South Carolina, but also at a second plant in upstate New York. Located in the small city of Jamestown in the southwesternmost corner of New York, roughly halfway between New York City and Chicago, this second facility was a sprawling, 930,000-square-foot plant built in 1968 by the Art Metal Furniture Company for the manufacture of office furniture. (When the plant was constructed, it was the largest ever built for that purpose, measuring nearly a quarter of a mile in length.)[118] Cummins leased the building in April 1974 with the goal of supplying K and NH engine parts to the Charleston plant. "It was a beautiful plant," recalls Jim Henderson, "and it was *big* enough."

Jamestown, in the heart of union country, was credible evidence that Cummins was not decentralizing its manufacturing operations to escape from union influence. The city of 40,000, located on the southern edge of Lake Chatauqua, had a long tradition of skilled woodworkers and metal-benders, many of whom were union members. Art Metal had failed not because of aggressive unions but as the result of an ill-considered marketing strategy, and other local businesses had run into similar troubles. By the early 1970s, unemployment in Jamestown was running at 10 percent, and union-management discord was on the rise.

At that point, Jamestown Mayor Stanley N. Lundine took an unusual step. He established a joint "Labor-Management Committee" consisting of the heads of local businesses and labor organizations. Although the committee never involved itself in specific negotiations, it did help dispel the kinds of rumors that inevitably arose during labor disputes. Lundine and his committee aggressively wooed Cummins, and—according to Ted Marston—made a very strong and positive impression:

> We spent three days in Jamestown talking with town leaders, and decided that it was a highly organized community, and that its leadership was really there to help us. And Stan Lundine was one of the keys. When he came in as mayor, he said, "This stuff has got to stop. We've got to find a way." And he started talking about some of the same things that we were thinking about when we were working with Fred Herzberg in the Charleston plant.

In some ways, the tranquility and scenic beauty of the Jamestown area, its small-town qualities, and its homogeneous population (mostly of Italian and Swedish descent) worked against the city as Cummins debated its plant-location decision. "How can the company begin to achieve corporate-wide affirmative action goals if it locates in overwhelmingly white areas?" worried one manager. If the company really wanted to make a difference in society, "should it seek to locate our facilities in communities which are sheltered from many of today's problems?" And if Cummins took over the Art Metal plant, it would become, almost overnight, one of the major employers in the area. "Significant responsibilities accompany such dominance and power," the memo writer pointed out. "Is the company willing to make a similar commitment in Jamestown (money, time, people) to that it has made in Columbus?"[119]

As it turned out, the answer to the last question was yes. In both Charleston and Jamestown, Cummins saw advantage in being one of the largest employers in the area—in part because it enabled the company to exert a progressive influence on its host community.

Shortly after Labor Day in 1974, twenty Cummins managers arrived in Jamestown to begin the cavernous plant's transformation.[120] This group had the benefit of a year and a half of lessons from Charleston, and those lessons were built into Jamestown from the start. They hired a large number of talented workers with union backgrounds—some of them former union leaders—because they were confident that the company's team-based approach would appeal to these individuals. Cummins bet that it could go at least five years without a union in Jamestown, which would be long enough to give the team-based system a chance to take root, after which unionization would be less of a concern. The team-based system made its own friends. "The union people we hired in those early days," recalls Ted Marston, "were our biggest supporters later on when the unions tried to organize us."[121]

Charleston and Jamestown in the 1970s were the crucible for the system of team-based production that emerged as one of the true distinguishing characteristics of the Engine Company in subsequent decades. The labor-related challenges that Cummins faced in those decades—described in later chapters—were twofold. First, the company had to channel the general enthusiasm for teams into specific procedures that would increase quality, reduce costs, and enhance customer satisfaction. And second, Cummins had to find ways to bring home to Columbus the benefits of teamwork—an approach of which the Diesel Workers Union was justifiably suspicious.

Planning Across the Company

As noted above, three things were needed for Cummins to make a significant change in its operations: additional manufacturing capacity, a better approach to manufacturing, and a new way of planning. The third ingredient, which was largely an outgrowth of the first two, was critical to a company that soon would have major manufacturing facilities in three states, as well as numerous other operations in the United States and abroad. The 1969 approach to planning had to be amended to focus more specifically on operational issues.

The prime mover behind this expanded planning effort was Jim Henderson. He was motivated by the 1972 strike to get a better handle on the operations for which he was directly responsible. But he also cites a second inspiration. Even before taking over as vice president of operations in 1970, Henderson had ambivalent feelings about Cummins' approach to its day-to-day business. As he saw it, the company was adept at "pulling rabbits out of hats."[122] When a crisis arose, Cummins scrambled, depending on its proven skills at implementation to improvise its way out of this week's dilemma.

But was this the way it *should* be? Shortly after taking over company operations, Henderson made a series of visits to the United Kingdom that suggested otherwise. Darlington and Shotts struck Henderson (on his semimonthly visits there) as "among our most disciplined and effective operations." He decided to bring some of this discipline back home, and invented a new tool to do so: the annual planning conference. The first of these conferences was held at nearby Nashville, Indiana, in May 1973. The conference topics were not remarkable: marketing, products, manufacturing capacity and delivery, internal "emphasis programs" (that is, specific problems that the company would address in the coming months), and future planning efforts. What was remarkable—at least for Cummins—was that dozens of senior managers were meeting to talk about these subjects.

The pattern established at this first conference was repeated in subsequent years. Henderson welcomed the group and introduced the themes of the conference. Henry Schacht then made remarks on a "visionary" level:

Where was the company going? How was its competitive context changing? Especially in the mid-1970s, when the national economy was in a volatile state, John Hackett made presentations on the company's financial condition in a broader economic context. Henderson, following up, pushed into the specifics of implementation. As financial officer John McLachlan remembers:

> *I can recall Henry having no overheads, just chalking at the boards, saying, "This is what we'll be doing, and this is why we'll do it." But in Jim's response, he'd have forty or fifty slides on each of the various facets, which meant that they had integrated their thinking as they had developed the themes. And gradually, as Jim broke his pick on the nitty-gritty of* how *we would do it, people in the audience would start to understand where their respective tasks lay.*

Functional area heads, such as the vice presidents of marketing and manufacturing, also made presentations, most often working within specific time horizons: two years for operations, five years for capacity planning, ten years for technology. But much of the real work of the planning conferences went on in break-out sessions, consisting of small groups whose composition changed over the years. Initially, these groups either were functionally oriented or had a shared business focus (e.g., international). By the 1980s, these groups reflected a larger trend at Cummins toward cross-functional, product-oriented groups.

The planning conferences were not a panacea. Cummins continued to react to events and improvise to a degree that still troubled its senior management. But in an era of rapid growth, these conferences, sometimes held twice a year, provided a way for the organization to understand itself. The conferences made the president and vice presidents of the company directly accessible to the line managers and greatly clarified their respective roles. They also gave Jim Henderson a structured way to drum a particular message into the ears of management.

By this time, Henderson and Schacht were settling into complementary roles that re-created the dynamic between Don Tull and Irwin Miller in earlier decades. Miller and Tull had been close friends first, superior and subordinate second. Miller was a hands-off, cerebral, and shy strategist, who spent a great deal of his time on corporate boards and philanthropic activities that had little or no immediate connection to Cummins (although Miller often came across new ideas in these outside-world contexts and brought them home to Columbus). Tull was content to mind the store—not a simple task, even in the relatively tranquil 1960s. The key was that both men were completely confident and comfortable in their respective roles, and that those roles were big enough for each of them.

Against considerable odds, Schacht and Henderson recreated the fundamental aspects of this relationship. Schacht demonstrated the self-confidence and long time horizons of an owner, even though he was not and would not become a major Cummins shareholder. He tackled operational issues rarely, and then only when invited to do so by Henderson. Groomed by Miller to play the business-statesman role, Schacht participated energetically in outside activities, eventually serving on some of the same boards Miller had served on. Henderson, for his part, readily ceded the chief executive officer's turf to Schacht, playing Mr. Inside to Schacht's Mr. Outside and serving as the resident realist.

Separated by only one year at the Harvard Business School, both bright and ambitious, Schacht and Henderson easily could have been intense competitors. Instead, they became close friends. They lived on the same street and helped raise each other's children. And as early as the 1970s, Cummins was the clear beneficiary.

Falling Out of Bed

In October 1974, Henry Schacht attended the annual meeting of the American Trucking Association (ATA) and found the mood "very gloomy." The mild recession that had begun earlier in the year was deepening, and the trucking business was hypersensitive to swings in the economy. The tonnage of the typical trucking fleet already was down by around 10 percent. Truck prices were soaring, as was the cost of financing a new truck, with interest rates bouncing between 12 and 14 percent. "Most are not going to buy at all in 1975 but will rebuild and run another 250,000 miles," Schacht noted in a memo to himself. "A sampling of nineteen large fleets showed all have dramatically reduced their buy plans for 1975."[123]

Part of the problem was the traditional business cycle, which was then clearly on the downslide. But a complicating factor was FMVSS 121, a federal braking standard announced in 1974 for implementation on March 1, 1975. Designed to improve tractor-trailer braking systems in ways that would reduce the risk of jack-knifing, the new law would add between $2,000 and $5,000 to the cost of a new truck.[124] Truck purchasers rushed to buy new equipment before the new standard took effect, pushing scheduled 1975 purchases into the 1974 calendar year.

Cummins anticipated this dangerous convergence of a weakening economy and an artificially propped-up market, and took steps to blunt its impact. A companywide cost-cutting program was implemented in the fall, and Schacht ordered his senior managers to "overreact," as he put it: "Let's really get tough on ourselves so that we can set the example for the Corporation." Meanwhile, the company intensively courted the Department of Defense in hopes of winning a large recession-proof order.

But no one anticipated the severity of this recession. As it turned out, Cummins was perched on the side of a high cliff—the worst economic downturn since World War II. "We had a pretty good shock," Schacht recalls of the late 1974–early 1975 period. "The thing just fell out of bed." Cummins found itself in a strange netherworld: Even as the company was reporting record sales and earnings for 1974, its market was collapsing. Heavy-duty truck sales dropped 40 percent between 1974 and 1975. At first, Cummins thought it could ride out the storm by cutting back on overtime and reassigning employees. As late as the third week of January 1975, Irwin Miller assured a radio audience that Cummins saw no immediate need for layoffs. But so many orders were canceled in the following week that the company called for emergency discussions with the Diesel Workers Union and the Office Committee to plan the layoff of nearly 10 percent of the work force, effective February 1.[125]

These were Cummins' first layoffs in eight years. They affected nearly 1,000 shop, office, and management personnel. Salaries, too, were cut on a graduated scale, increasing to 12 percent in the upper ranges. Internal training programs were halted, and optional capital expenditures were deferred. In April came a piece of good news: the U.S. Army's Tank Automotive Command (TACOM) had renewed its contract with Cummins for engines to power its five-ton trucks, which meant guaranteed sales of almost 5,800 units, and possible sales of another 6,000 units.[126] But 30 to 40 military engines a day couldn't stanch the bleeding. The company soon announced a second round of layoffs, this time affecting some 800 people.

From management's perspective, the only bright side to the recession surfaced during the contract negotiations of spring 1975. The layoff of nearly 20 percent of the Columbus-area work force helped keep union demands extremely modest, and Cummins and the DWU signed their first contract in nine years without a work stoppage. But by every other measure, the recession was a disaster. Even as the hard-won Charleston and Jamestown capacity was coming on line, demand for the products made in those plants was dropping through the floor. (Charleston alone lost $21.8 million in 1975.) Cummins made only $491,000 after taxes in 1975—its worst showing (even in non-inflation-adjusted dollars) since 1940. Return on equity, targeted at 15 percent, fell to 0.02 percent.[127]

Along with these external conditions, Cummins struggled with an unwelcome internal problem: the "inventory crisis" of the mid-1970s. Even in favorable capital markets, working capital—including inventory—was (as Irwin Miller aptly reminded his managers in 1970) the "most expensive money" Cummins owned. "The probable annual cost of owning a dollar of inventory for twelve months is between 25 percent and 30 percent. This is because of a) high cost of money, b) loss of parts, c) obsolescence and write-offs, d) scrap."[128]

But there were strong forces at the operational level that worked against a lean inventory. Inflation, of course, was one: It made some sense to buy extra parts today if there was certain to be a price increase tomorrow. But more important was the relentless pressure Cummins faced from its OEMs to meet production levels that were beyond its capacity throughout much of the 1970s. Over the decades, Cummins had worked its way into the heart of its customers' businesses. Now it could not afford to send out signals of unreliability. It could not afford to have the production of a much-needed engine delayed by the lack of a component part.

It was this kind of pressure that led to the "high-bay" design of the Walesboro components plant. Parts and components could be—and very quickly were—stockpiled from the floor up to the facility's very high ceilings. Along with the high bays at Walesboro came a high-bay mentality: More is better. Better to buy a few extra crankshafts when they are available and tuck them away somewhere.

By the early 1970s, Cummins was not exactly sure what it had in inventory, or where it was. The company had signed on to the then-popular "controlled stores" movement, which simply meant that Cummins was committed to establishing good computer-based inventory records. But Cummins' information systems were still rudimentary, especially in light of the company's explosive growth. As late as mid-1972, some 10 percent of the company's inventories were still entirely uncontrolled, and even the controlled stores were suspect.[129]

The scope of the resulting problem faced by Jim Henderson and his colleagues in operations turned out to be staggering. By the fall of 1974, the company had more than 75,000 active part numbers, and in that year alone engine business inventory grew by some $65 million.[130] There was an eighty-day supply of parts on hand—far more than normal—worth some $100 million, of which only $88 million could be accounted for. The "missing" $12 million in inventory was almost enough to supply a seventh assembly plant. Not surprisingly, Henderson and his colleagues began to refer ruefully to their "phantom" plant.

Inventories reached a record 34.3 percent (versus the 20 percent average in the 1960s) when stated as a cost of sales. The collapse of the truck market in 1974 lent this problem a new urgency. Suddenly, Cummins went from having all of its engines spoken for to having 2,000 completed engines without customers. (Some of these had been stockpiled in expectation of a 1975 strike that never came, but the bulk of the problem was external.) Now, the "phantom plant" no longer was a source of irritation and wry amusement, but part of a larger threat to the health of the company.[131]

In response, Henderson's team mounted an intensive study of how the company was managing its inventories, and how Cummins' overall commitment of cash to that part of the operation could be minimized. Ambitious goals were set to increase inventory "turns" at each inventory-holding facility. (If it takes a given plant a year to go through its inventory, that plant accomplishes one "turn" a year. The higher the number of turns, the more efficient the facility.) In 1974, the companywide average was only 5.1 turns, down from the historical average of 6.0 turns. The Henderson team set ambitious goals of 7.5 turns for all engine-producing plants, 10 for components plants, and 9 for warehouses.

The biggest exposure, of course, was in Columbus, where the company had to shed some $19 million in unwanted inventory. As the managers assigned to the problem reported, "There is a special problem in Columbus, because we are still learning where the inventory is and how to account for it."[132] Thus, Henderson still had to go hunting for his phantom plant. His technique was direct, and typical: He simply roamed from site to site, asking people at all levels of the organization if they knew of any squirreled-away inventory. One day, he recalls, he struck pay dirt:

> One guy says, "Oh, yeah, go to the Mater Mill." Well, I knew that "mater" was Hoosier talk for "tomato." After a little more investigation, I found out that we had rented an old warehouse on 17th Street from the Morgan Packing Company, a tomato canning company. So I find this place, and walk in, and it's a huge warehouse, absolutely full of stuff. There were flywheels with dust this thick on them, as I ran my hand over them. Not a soul around, except for one guy alone in this office with the shade half pulled down, with a naked lightbulb hanging down. And the guy looks up and says, "Oh, hi, Jim. I thought I'd see you in here one of these days."

Henderson asked the materials attendant if there were records that detailed the inventory under his control, and the attendant produced a thick computer printout. One column in the printout was entitled "days' supply," meaning how many days of average production could be supplied by the parts on hand. "In some cases," Henderson recalls, "there were numbers like '11,382.'"[133]

The "Mater Mill" was only the most dramatic discovery on Henderson's tours. Over the course of 1975, Henderson and his colleagues reduced the company's inventories by $52.5 million (from $196.4 million to $143.9 million).[134] Obsolete inventories were written off and sold for scrap. This was progress, but the very occurrence of such a problem revealed a larger weakness in the company: In the scramble to crank out more engines, Cummins' manufacturing practices were getting sloppy. It was a subject to which the company would return, under duress, in subsequent years.

At the midpoint of the decade, things looked grim for the Cummins Engine Company and its still youthful (although now painfully experienced) management team. Cummins had failed to anticipate the explosion of the heavy-duty truck market in the early 1970s. The company's long-standing reluctance to expand capacity not only ensured that Cummins would miss much of the engine boom, but also that extra burdens would be placed on both OEMs and the labor force. Allocations cost customers, and poor working conditions (as well as an uncharacteristically militant union leadership) brought about the strike of 1972. The rush to expand capacity was terribly timed, given the disastrous collapse of the truck market in late 1974. The "three-legged strategy," with its colorful diversifications, was abruptly abandoned to shore up the core engine business.

But it would be unfair to lay the blame for all of Cummins' problems at the feet of Schacht, Henderson, Hackett, and their colleagues. Never before had there been a 60 percent increase in the heavy-duty truck business in a four-year interval (1969–1973); never before had there been a 40 percent drop in that business in one twelve-month period (1974–1975). And no one in Cummins' management—or elsewhere in American business, for that matter—had experienced the pernicious combination of a severe economic recession (with six million Americans out of work) and double-digit inflation.[135] Indeed, Cummins' managers deserve credit for their willingness and ability to improvise when things failed to go according to plan. They were appropriately bloody-minded when it came to disposing of their unrelated subsidiaries, and tenacious in holding on to their allied businesses.

Moreover, it would be a mistake to overlook the progress that the company made in the first half of the 1970s. Cummins was growing, and the *pace* of growth was accelerating dramatically. It took the company forty-seven years to build its first 500,000 engines (a milestone recorded in 1966). It took only eight years for the company to build another 500,000 engines. (The millionth engine was shipped in May 1974 to Kenworth Truck Company in Seattle, one of Cummins' oldest customers.)[136] Sales increased from $392 million in 1969 to $802 million in 1974, and return on equity averaged 12 percent for this five-year period. And when strike-torn 1972 is removed from the calculation, Cummins' average ROE was close to 13.5 percent—not much below the corporate target of 15 percent.

Meanwhile, Cummins was investing for the future. Between 1969 and 1975, its consolidated fixed assets increased from $176 million to $416 million.[137] For the foreseeable future, there would be no return to the capacity shortfalls that had plagued the company for years.

Other kinds of investments were going on as well. A few visionaries within the company, working with outside consultants and newly hired hourly employees, were struggling to invent a new approach to manufacturing—an approach based on teamwork, flexibility, and common sense. The system was far from sophisticated, and it took some body blows during the layoffs and related hardships of 1975. But it was an essential foundation for changes that were to follow in the 1980s.

8 | Playing by the New Rules, 1973–1978

IN THE MID-1970S, CUMMINS STRUGGLED to find its way in a changed world. Increasingly important to the success (and perhaps the survival) of the company was the management and conservation of its capital. This was true even before the financial community began to express alarm about Cummins' debt-to-capital ratio in 1974; but as the crippling recession of 1975 cut ever deeper, the pressure from Wall Street intensified. In response, Cummins took emergency steps, and retrenched on various corporate initiatives. As recounted in Chapter 7, the company abandoned one leg of its "three-legged strategy," selling off its more exotic subsidiaries and using the freed-up cash to reduce debt. As soon as the recession began to ease in late 1976, however, the Engine Company found itself back in the uncomfortable position of allocating its products among customers. Once again, more manufacturing capacity was needed, which once again meant finding more capital.

But debt-derived capital was terribly expensive in the later 1970s. The backdrop for all of the dramatic changes of this period was a baffling and persistent inflation, coupled with historically low rates of economic growth—a conundrum plaguing economies worldwide that became known as "stagflation."

Committed as it was to growth within a capital-intensive business, Cummins changed the ways it controlled its inventory and adopted new inflation-sensitive accounting procedures. But these housekeeping measures only bought time. Eventually, despite Irwin Miller's strong philosophical disinclination to dilute the shareholders' stake in the company, Cummins was forced to turn to the equity markets.

Other external forces also were at work, reshaping Cummins' competitive environment both directly and indirectly. The Clean Air Act of 1970, for example, at first seemed a distant threat. It was strongly opposed by the automobile companies, and did not single out diesel trucks for specific attention. Meanwhile, the "energy crisis"—whether real or perceived—pushed concerns about the environment to the back burner, as Americans for the first time worried about whether their energy-intensive style of life was sustainable. Then, just as Cummins and many other companies readjusted their sights to accommodate demands for increased efficiency, the environmental movement reasserted itself. With good intentions but very little relevant experience, Cummins found itself involved in helping the government draft suitable amendments to the Clean Air Act, and leading a reluctant industry in a search for new mechanisms for government-industry cooperation.

These rapid shifts put a new kind of pressure on Cummins' research and engineering group. Product lead times shortened dramatically. A brand-new engine was rendered largely unsalable in its intended market. Suddenly, the horsepower race that Cummins had promoted for decades was suspended—or perhaps even over. In its place came a drive for engines that worked better along every dimension: power, fuel efficiency, dependability, and versatility.

In the course of the 1970s, Cummins also went through an evolution in its conception of corporate citizenship. J. Irwin Miller's role as the conscience of Cummins—and to some extent a conscience of American industry—was undiminished. But over time, the personal and idiosyncratic nature of the Engine Company's corporate ethic was complemented by a more formal, systematic approach.

This was in part the inevitable result of enormous corporate growth. But it also was a conscious response on the part of Cummins' leaders to a rash of scandals that beset American multinational corporations in the 1970s—scandals that in turn led to the passage by Congress of the Foreign Corrupt Practices Act in 1978 and to a generally heightened public awareness of corporate misbehavior. Cummins actively sought to avoid the traps that snared Lockheed, ITT, and others. It promulgated new policies and procedures, and also hired new kinds of people, in a purposeful effort to keep its ethical house in order.

Managing capital

Throughout the dramatic boom of the early 1970s, the Cummins Engine Company was chronically short on cash. Rather than waiting for bad times in order to undertake piecemeal expansion, Henry Schacht and operations head Jim Henderson made huge plant investments in Columbus, Walesboro, Charleston, and Jamestown and increased the company's research and engineering budget by 70 percent. Concurrently, Schacht and John Hackett also made a series of cash-hungry acquisitions and encouraged a limited number of overseas investments.[1] (See Chapter 9.) As a result, Cummins needed capital, and tried almost every conceivable means between 1969 and 1974 to (in the words of chief financial officer John Hackett) "keep the animal fed." By force of circumstance, Hackett blazed trails that other institutions later followed. As Henry Schacht recalls: "We were trying to finance this growth from 1 million to 10 million square feet. We used everything. John wound up in the Middle East, at one point, and we became one of the first companies to borrow from the Saudis."

Cummins already had surprised financial analysts by issuing Euro-dollar convertible debentures in the late 1960s. In October 1970, the company brought a modified version of this financial instrument home, offering twenty-five-year sinking fund debentures through the First Boston Corporation. Two years later, Cummins provided a cash infusion to its international operations with another $20 million in convertible debentures sold in the European money market. The novel Saudi bank loan—for $4.9 million—was made in this same time period. At the 1974 shareholders' meeting, Schacht won approval for the issuance of $25 million (or 236,000 shares) of convertible preferred stock. Internally, Schacht described this as a tactic to "get a bit more margin for error into our system."[2]

By the fall of 1974, therefore, Cummins had three convertible debentures outstanding, as well as a significant new block of preferred stock with a 6 percent cumulative dividend. In 1974, Cummins' debt-to-capital ratio reached an alarming 58.6 percent (up from 34.4 percent three years earlier). And although John Hackett advocated the preferred-stock deal as the best available method for raising needed capital, he cautioned his colleagues that the associated dividend would constitute a "burden" if the company failed to achieve its earning goals.[3]

Then came the crash of 1974–1975. Between the end of 1974 and late 1975, with its cash stream essentially shut down except for receivables, Cummins struggled under a $20 million debt burden. Much of 1975 was devoted to paying off the most expensive short-term debt. Fortunately, the strong revival of the truck market in 1976 generated an internal cash flow of almost $100 million and permitted Cummins to reduce its long-term debt significantly (from $211 million in 1975 to $143.7 million in 1976). In July 1977, the company called in all 236,000 shares of preferred stock issued in 1974, converting those shares to common and thereby significantly reducing its dividend obligations.[4] For the time being, Cummins was out of the woods.

But the cyclical nature of the engine business remained a constant and worrisome backdrop to the company's operations, and largely determined its financial strategies. When times were good, they could be spectacular; when they were bad, they could be terrible.

A second and related backdrop was the financial philosophy of J. Irwin Miller, who was a strenuous opponent of diluting shareholder value through the issuing of additional equity in the company. Certainly, Miller—whose family in the late 1970s still owned 29.4 percent of the company's common stock, valued at over $125 million—had a vested interest in resisting such a dilution.[5] But Miller's stance also seems to have been based on principle; and this was a key reason why, in the heady days of the early 1970s, Cummins had stayed out of the equity markets, and had resorted instead to a variety of more or less exotic forms of debt. "Irwin was just pathologically opposed to selling equity," recalls Henry Schacht.

Another good reason to refrain from selling stock was the depressed price of Cummins' stock at key junctures. In the spring of 1974, for example, Schacht and Hackett considered advocating the sale of common stock rather than preferred, but Cummins' stock had dropped from a high of 69 in the second quarter of 1972 to a low of 29 5/8 in the second quarter of 1974. And it got worse: At one point in the dismal fourth quarter of 1974, the stock plunged to a low of 11 5/8.[6]

But by late 1976, Cummins was again hungry for capital. Heavy investments were needed to bring the Jamestown facility on line. The Atlas facility in Fostoria, Ohio, needed capacity expansion. Inventories were creeping back up to their 1974, pre-recession levels, in support of a roaring engine business. Once again, as Hackett recalls, the subject of selling common stock came up—but this time it was a dramatically different circumstance:

> I'll never forget it. I had lunch with Irwin Miller at a local restaurant one day. His objective was to convince me not to sell an equity issue. I remember sitting at the table, with him giving me all the arguments. And I finally had to look at him and say, "Irwin, I've heard everything you've said. But this isn't a question of 'should we?' We don't have a choice." And that was one of the most uncomfortable things I ever had to say, to a man for whom I really have incredible admiration. I was ashamed that we had gotten into that situation. But we were just not in control.

For his part, Henry Schacht attempted to persuade Miller not only that the company had exhausted all of its other options, but also that Cummins would again "miss its market"—as it had as a result of the strike of 1972—if it didn't get an infusion of cash for much-needed expansion. Miller, under combined pressure from his two top financial experts, finally relented. In April 1977, Cummins issued 700,000 additional shares of common stock, in a highly successful sale that generated $35.3 million.[7]

The company's cash crunches, both immediate and longer-term, were far from resolved. Hackett recollects that the proceeds from this sale were swallowed up into inventory within ninety days. (If this is an exaggeration, it is only a slight one, given the fact that inventories increased from $192.9 million to $233.7 million in 1977.)[8] But in a year when capital expenditures alone totaled $67.4 million, the stock sale probably had a greater impact on the hearts and minds of the company (and its biggest shareholders) than on its wallet. The long-standing psychological barrier against diluting the shareholders' base—personified in Irwin Miller, but shared by others in the company—was broken down conclusively. For better or worse, Cummins was to return to the equity well many times in subsequent years.

Regulation comes home

Regulation was a subject of great interest to Cummins almost from the company's first ventures into automotive diesels. Because most of the Cummins engines manufactured between the 1930s and the 1960s went into trucks, and because trucks were intensively regulated on both the state and federal levels, Cummins kept a watchful eye on legislative bodies and administrative agencies with authority over transportation. As noted in Chapter 6, legislators made periodic efforts to impose a surtax on diesel fuel, which Cummins opposed vigorously. Other federal laws and regulations—affecting truck lengths and widths, braking standards, and gross vehicle weights—had more or less impact on Cummins, and were revisited often over the decades.

But beginning at a modest level in the late 1960s and intensifying in the 1970s, federal regulators intervened much more aggressively in the American home, workplace, and natural environment. Air-quality legislation began to have an indirect impact on Cummins' operations in 1970. And as that impact became stronger and more direct in subsequent years, Cummins was compelled to develop both corporate policies and technological strategies to respond to the ever-tougher iterations of the Clean Air Act.

Among the new products introduced in the Christmas shopping season of 1969 was a toy that annoyed some managers at the Cummins Engine Company. The offending toy was a realistic-looking battery-powered dump truck, complete with a vertical exhaust stack that emitted "smoke." An in-house Cummins newsletter complained: "The dump truck is supposed to smoke 'like a real diesel.' Or so it is advertised. The ad doesn't say it smokes like a poorly built diesel, or an improperly maintained diesel. Only like a 'real' diesel."[9]

As far back as the 1930s, when marketing vice president Paris Letsinger improvised the vertical stack in order to keep his company's relatively primitive and smoky engines on the roads of California, Cummins was well aware that the exhaust from diesel-powered trucks posed a regulatory risk. Over time, the billowing, sooty smoke clouds emitted by the early Cummins diesels were greatly reduced—although poor maintenance could always re-create the problem.

The burning of hydrocarbons produces a veritable witch's brew of complex chemical by-products, about which relatively little was known back in the 1960s, when the federal government first became involved in the regulation of diesel-related pollutants. (A principal reason for this lack of information was that most research up to that point had focused on gasoline-burning engines, rather than diesels.) Two encouraging things *were* known, however. First, diesels emitted very little carbon monoxide, a toxic component found in high quantities in gasoline-engine exhaust. Second, unlike the gasoline engines of the day, a well-maintained diesel produced relatively few unburned hydrocarbons, which by the late 1960s had been identified as a chief culprit in the "smog alerts" that were becoming regular summertime events in the nation's largest cities.

As a result, most of the company's pollution-control efforts through 1970 focused mainly on amelioration of the visible-smoke problem. (In 1970, for example, Cummins licensed a new filtering system from a Dallas-based manufacturer which was "aimed at eliminating visible smoke from diesel exhaust.") Seen in this context, the smoky toy dump truck mainly was a public-relations problem, reinforcing in the public's mind an exaggerated correlation between diesels and pollution. As the in-house newsletter phrased it:

> *Diesel smoke is primarily a nuisance, and is not a significant contributor to the dangerous elements in air pollution which, incidentally, for the most part cannot be seen or smelled. Nevertheless, John Q. Public, quite understandably, does not like to see an over-fueled truck pass him on the highway laying down a cloud of black smoke and being told it is not polluting the air. He cannot see or smell the air pollutants from his own automobile, but is now forced to pay $50 to $100 for emission control equipment on a new car. It is understandable, therefore, that he will not be willing to see what he believes to be the "obvious" air pollution from diesels go uncontrolled.[10]*

In the late 1960s, the federal government began responding to John Q. Public's intolerance of diesel exhaust. The original basis for the government's actions was the Clean Air Act of 1963, which gave Washington (through the Department of Health, Education, and Welfare, or HEW) authority to conduct research and training on the subject of air pollution.[11] The Air Quality Act of 1967 raised the stakes significantly, giving the federal government limited authority to control automotive emissions, and also made Washington responsible for coordinating federal and state air-pollution regulations. This was the first piece of federal legislation to set limits on the amounts of smoke that could be emitted by diesel engines. Beginning January 1, 1970, the Secretary of HEW had to certify that any engine manufactured and sold in the United States fell within these specified limits.

At the 1969 Cummins shareholders' meeting, chairman J. Irwin Miller announced that the company foresaw no difficulties in living within these prescribed limits, and even saw the possibility of "additional profitable business for the Company" in the new regulations. A month after the new regulations went into effect, vice chairman Dick Stoner told the Transportation Institute in New York that the company's goal was to produce engines that were "socially acceptable." Cummins would do so, Stoner said, "not waiting for an adjustment in federal requirements or incentives, but in an attempt to fulfill our responsibility to improve the quality of our environment." Of course, Stoner continued, it would make good sense for the government to implement a program of "pollution penalties," whereby a manufacturer of high-polluting engines would be assessed a pollution tax at the time of licensing. But Cummins was committed, in any case, to increasing dramatically the "sociability" of its engines.[12]

Stoner's New York speech was an early public articulation of what eventually became the cornerstone of the Cummins corporate policy regarding pollution: that the *cost* of pollution should be fully internalized by the companies (including Cummins) that *caused* the pollution. President Henry Schacht elaborated on the policy in a speech to local Harvard Business School graduates a month later, attributing its central notion to board chairman Irwin Miller:

> *Our chairman's thesis has been for several years now that the day and age is coming when industry is going to be asked to pay for the full cost of what it uses and the full cost of what it creates. . . .*
>
> *We ought to put that full cost into the product, and then let people decide if they want to buy the product, rather than to understate the cost by putting out a product which does pollute and then asking the taxpayers to fund a massive cleaning-up process.[13]*

In retrospect, it was a sensible stance. (It also was a safe stance, since Cummins had not yet seen any standards that it couldn't meet with ease.) But it turned out to be a policy that would sharply distinguish Cummins from other engine manufacturers. In particular, it came to irritate the "Big Three" automakers, who—bearing most of the burden of the government's increasingly tough air-quality regulations—felt put upon, even betrayed, by what they saw as grandstanding by the engine company in Columbus.

Collaboration and Industry Leadership

The federal government raised the environmental stakes dramatically in 1970 through two key actions: the passage of the Clean Air Amendments of 1970 and the creation of the Environmental Protection Agency.[14]

Title II of the Clean Air Amendments of 1970 was of particular interest to engine makers, particularly manufacturers of light-duty (principally automobile) engines. It specified that carbon monoxide and hydrocarbon emissions from new motor vehicles in the 1975 model year had to be reduced by at least 90 percent from those emitted by 1970 model-year vehicles. It also mandated a similar 90 percent reduction in oxides of nitrogen (NO_x) by 1976. The newly created EPA was ordered to test engines for their conformity with air-pollution regulations and to issue certificates of compliance.

Beginning in the early 1970s, therefore, Cummins and all other engine manufacturers entered into an increasingly rigorous program of testing and certification defined by the EPA. The program had the potential to degenerate into a bureaucratic morass. But the government and the engine manufacturers found ways to make the program work. For example, the EPA soon abandoned any notion of performing all the tests itself, and instead assigned this task to the manufacturers.

In Cummins' case, two engines from each new family served as proxies for the rest. These were taken off the assembly line and delivered to the in-plant "Certification Department," where up to an hour of preliminary fine-tuning was allowed. After that hour elapsed, the engines were put through two different tests. One was a straight 125-hour emission test. The other was a 1,000-hour durability test, with emission data gathered every 125 hours. The results of these two tests were combined, and the combined rating was used by the EPA to determine whether the engine family under scrutiny conformed to the relevant standard.

Once a given engine family was certified, it did not have to be tested again unless that family went through a significant design change—or unless a standard tightened and it was not apparent that an existing engine could meet the new standard. Testing was expensive: The 1,000-hour test, for example, took four months, and certifying an engine family could cost in excess of $60,000. In any given year, Cummins might submit 2,000 pages of test results to the federal government, and another 1,800 pages to the California Air Resources Board (CARB), which consistently promulgated standards even tougher than the EPA's.[15]

It was the actions of CARB, in fact, that tended to derail the tacit agreements that emerged between Washington and the engine manufacturers. In November 1970, for instance, CARB announced that all new vehicles sold in California after January 1, 1975, could emit no more than five grams of unburned hydrocarbon plus NO_x—a standard roughly twice as tough as the EPA's equivalent. "This has turned the industry upside down," Henry Schacht told his distributors at their annual meeting in January 1971. "Nobody, including ourselves, was thinking of this dramatic a reduction in the requirements, and we have been scrambling ever since to try to assess what it means to us."[16]

First, Cummins had to decide whether it was going to stick with its policy of "internalizing" pollution costs. The answer came quickly: The company would stick. Credit for this decision belongs to Irwin Miller. "Never fight the inevitable," he reminded his managers throughout this period.[17] The trick, as Miller saw it, was to identify with the public interest, acknowledge the inevitable—and then be the first to take profitable advantage of it. Testifying before the EPA in 1971, Miller chided his own industry: "Manufacturers, ourselves included, sometimes tend to sell themselves a bit short. The answer is for the government to set tight standards to cause everyone to run hard at them, ease up only if *nobody* makes them, but always remember why the standards were set."[18]

The first significant breach between Cummins and the Big Three was opened by the proposed federal standards for 1975 (issued as part of the Clean Air Amendments of 1970). In the spring of 1972—Miller's advice notwithstanding—U.S. automakers formally requested the EPA to delay implementation of these 1975 standards by one year. (This they were entitled to do under the provisions of a 1970 law sponsored by Edmund S. Muskie, Democratic senator from Maine.) The public response to this request from Detroit, as expressed at hearings on Capitol Hill, was hostile. "If they kill us all," complained the corporate counsel for New York City, "there won't be anybody to buy cars."[19]

Cummins' approach was more subtle. Building on existing ties between Miller and policy makers in Washington, the company successfully positioned itself as an honest broker between Washington and the engine industry. Cummins built additional bridges in many directions. In 1973, for example, Cummins vice president Tom Head was elected president of the Engine Manufacturers Association, a trade group that lobbied legislators both on the national and state levels.[20] When former EPA administrator William D. Ruckelshaus was fired from his post in the Justice Department during President Nixon's celebrated "Saturday Night Massacre" and returned to private practice, he was promptly invited to join Cummins' board of directors. (He did so in 1974.) Cummins also served as an invisible intermediary between the pollution czars at the EPA and their counterparts in Sacramento, who were still learning to deal with the Washington "newcomers" to the pollution field. As Henry Schacht explained in a 1972 strategy memo, Cummins was sustaining a delicate position:

> *Cummins has an excellent relationship with EPA and CARB. We have worked hard to be helpful and have scrupulously avoided public rhetoric. We have built a tenuous bond of trust; we are the only ones who really have. We probably move more quickly than anyone else. We want to maintain the "help" attitude. It is the right posture, regardless of Cummins' gain.*[21]

Cummins wanted EPA and CARB to agree to uniform and reasonable standards that, once established, would be held to consistently. From industry's point of view, it made no sense for California to establish tough standards unilaterally. (This would only promote increased truck registrations in neighboring states.) But it would be disastrous if one or more companies tooled up to meet a tough standard, only to discover that the standard had been relaxed by a vacillating regulator. Such a sequence of events, Cummins argued, would penalize the nonpolluters rather than the polluters. It made much more sense for the regulators to set, and then hold all manufacturers to, a fair standard.

Two dramatic changes occurred in 1975, as Congress once again set out to amend the Clean Air Act.[22] The first was a change in status for heavy-duty diesels. In the original act of 1970, heavy diesel-powered vehicles such as trucks and buses were classified in an "other vehicles" category along with motorcycles.[23] Through 1975, therefore, the brunt of the regulatory pressure had been borne by the light-duty manufacturers, especially the Big Three. Now, for the first time, heavy-duty diesels were singled out for attention, and Cummins found itself in the same boat as the carmakers.

The second big change was far more ominous. Largely at the insistence of Representative Andrew Maguire, a New Jersey Democrat, the House Subcommittee on Health and the Environment adopted a set of extremely tough emissions standards that required a further 90 percent reduction in gaseous emissions (including hydrocarbons, carbon monoxide, nitrous oxides—NO_x—and smoke) by 1983.[24] This was a major departure. Previously, it had been solely the EPA's responsibility to set standards at the federal level. Now, Congress was injecting itself directly into the standard-setting process. Cummins and the rest of the industry reacted with genuine alarm.

Even some members of the relevant congressional staffs thought the proposed standards were uninformed and arbitrary. (In fact, in its final form, the bill significantly relaxed the standard for NO_x and extended the time frame for its implementation.)[25] At Cummins, however, the real concern lay less in the specifics of the proposed standards than in the process by which they were established. Was it fair and realistic, Cummins asked, to have an entire industry's fate hinge on the seemingly arbitrary processes of a single congressional subcommittee, or on the opinions of a single legislator?

Acting unilaterally, Cummins undertook a large-scale "crash" study of every major aspect of air-pollution control. Through this focused research, Cummins developed a four-part process for standard setting—the "criteria for good legislation," as Cummins saw it.[26] The first part restored the EPA as the setter of standards (while still leaving Congress considerable authority to raise or lower these standards). The second called for periodic review of the standards to make sure that they were still in line with the latest data about health effects and reflected the latest technologies. The third refined the certification procedure; and the fourth specified financial penalties to be levied by the EPA for noncompliance.

Cummins presented this package of reforms—contained in what came to be known informally as "the Cummins book"—to the industry, Congress, and the EPA in October 1975 for consideration as part of the 1976 amendments to the Clean Air Act. Although the package was passed by the House, it failed to come to a vote in the Senate that year. In 1977, however, both houses of Congress approved the Cummins proposals without substantial modification, and they were incorporated into Section 202 of the Clean Air Act Amendments of 1977.

Cummins—and in particular, Irwin Miller, Henry Schacht, and vice president of public policy Charles W. Powers—took justifiable pride in their work.[27] Almost singlehandedly, and with no effective precedents to draw upon, Cummins' leaders succeeded in persuading the government to take a number of innovative steps in the control of air pollution. They managed a complex political process with great skill. (Not a single member of Congress voted against Section 202 when it was put to a separate vote in both houses.)[28] More important, they helped bring into being a much more sophisticated kind of legislation. Among other things, the Clean Air Act henceforth would provide incentives for radical technology innovations, rather than just incremental change. At the same time, it would be governed by an increased sensitivity to the "rhythms" of research and development; it would allow nonconforming manufacturers to stay in business—but at a significant financial penalty; and it would provide for a continuous monitoring of health effects, and for a quantification of those effects as part of a larger cost-benefit analysis. All in all, it was a remarkable achievement for Cummins.

The Health Effects Institute

Authorities in the field of public dispute-resolution cite four prerequisites for credible standard setting in the public arena: fairness, efficiency, wisdom, and stability.[29] The procedures outlined in the Cummins-sponsored amendments to the 1977 Clean Air Act spoke, to some extent, to the issues of fairness, efficiency, and stability. But "wisdom"—that is, the existence of a mutually agreed-upon body of knowledge concerning the public-policy issues under debate—was still lacking in the Clean Air Act process even after the 1977 amendments.

One problem was that the Cummins-inspired plan reinstated the EPA (rather than Congress) as the standard setter, and stipulated that emissions standards should grow out of health-effects studies directed by the Agency. But this and similar mandates presupposed the EPA's ability to direct appropriate research into health effects, and then to establish rational standards based on that research. Despite the existence of the EPA's extensive laboratories in Research Triangle Park, North Carolina, the government's research into air pollution had not been notably successful.[30]

Other problems arose out of the 1977 Clean Air Act amendments. One section required engine manufacturers to certify that no "unregulated" emissions from engines and vehicles certified for use on U.S. roads would pose "an unreasonable risk to public health." In other words, the burden of proof was shifting to the manufacturers to guarantee that none of the thousands of components contained in diesel emissions—beyond the half-dozen that were already under scrutiny—was dangerous. Another section (206a3) stipulated that the EPA administrator could "conduct such tests and require the manufacturers to conduct such tests" as might be needed to back up the manufacturers' claims for their engines. Still another relatively obscure clause in the 1977 act required the EPA for the first time to set standards for airborne "particulates" of various kinds, including diesel particulates. In the case of diesel exhaust, the particulates were mainly carbon-based molecules, about which little was known, except that they seemed to attach themselves readily to the linings of human lungs.[31]

There were several ways to attack the problem of diesel particulates— if, indeed, there *was* a problem. One was to tinker with fuels. (The EPA already had used this tactic to ban lead, which was the primary source of gasoline-derived particulates.)[32] Another was to tinker with engines and engine components, which history suggested might be the path of least resistance. Still another was to minimize the number of diesel-powered vehicles on the road—obviously not the first choice of Cummins and other diesel makers.

This last possible "solution" begged another, related question. Fuel economy never had gone away as a critical public-policy issue, and different groups advocated various ways of promoting it. According to at least one observer of the regulatory process, top EPA administrators were determined to push fuel economy by a "downsizing" of the American automobile fleet. Detroit, meanwhile, wanted to save the large car—whether to preserve the historically larger profit margins on big cars, to serve the customers' established tastes, or both—and therefore wanted instead to "dieselize" the U.S. fleet. But diesel automobiles generated between thirty and ninety times more particulates than their deleaded gasoline counterparts.[33]

In November 1977, the EPA's Research Triangle Park lab revealed preliminary findings of a study of bacterial responses to diesel particulates, which suggested that diesel exhaust might cause genetic mutations. Oddly enough, the EPA's "announcement" of this seemingly dramatic result came in the form of a warning to scientists working with diesel extracts—a warning that also was circulated among diesel manufacturers, ostensibly so that they could take steps to protect their workers.[34] The EPA, it seemed, was sending a very deliberate shot across the diesel makers' bows.

At Cummins, the reaction was shock and dismay. The company took pride in providing a safe working environment. More than that, Cummins assumed it was putting out a product that, although far from environmentally blameless, at least was better than the known alternatives—and was improving steadily. Stunned company officials briefly considered suspending operations until more was known.[35]

The EPA's next step was to ask engine manufacturers to sign a revised engine certification form. The new form assigned personal liability to its signer, in the event that the certified engine was found to produce unregulated emissions that were a risk to public health. Even aside from the personal legal exposure, the implications of this order were staggering. In order for manufacturers to sign such a document with confidence, they would need to conduct animal studies and similar tests that were completely out of their background and expertise. (Even if they chose not to, they could be *ordered* to, based on Section 206a3 of the 1977 act.) The nation's engine manufacturers were in an extraordinary and unprecedented bind.

Fires seemed to be breaking out on all sides. Responding to a 1978 government commissioned study of airborne contaminants (including diesel) in underground mining, a Cummins environmental specialist reminded his colleagues that there were bigger issues at stake:

> *Cummins' concerns relating to the health effects of diesel exhaust emissions are obviously not limited to underground mining. There is a strong possibility that exposure limits adopted in underground mining will also be adopted at some future date in aboveground mining operations. Also, EPA is looking at the toxicological aspects of automotive diesel emissions. DOT [the Department of Transportation] has similar health effects interests because of the predicted widespread future use of diesel cars to improve fuel economy.*[36]

But Detroit had not backed down. General Motors introduced a diesel-powered Oldsmobile in 1978, and announced plans to triple its production of diesels in 1979. The public was clamoring for diesels, in part because of the continuing gap between diesel and gasoline prices. Foreign manufacturers, including Mercedes, Volkswagen, and Peugeot, were planning increased diesel exports to the United States, while Fiat, Volvo, and Mazda also were considering exporting diesel cars to the U.S.[37]

The EPA and the auto industry were on a collision course. And although the EPA held the regulatory trump cards—required testing, personal liability, and so on—Detroit had powerful allies, including some within the federal government. The Council on Wage and Price Stability, for example, dropped hints that the EPA was being unduly hard on the diesel industry. And an assistant secretary in the Department of Energy told a reporter that the EPA's animal tests had been "rather quick," and that there was "a lack of conclusive evidence with animals and human beings."[38]

Into this volatile situation stepped Cummins CEO Henry Schacht. Schacht arranged a series of meetings in the late winter and spring of 1978 with EPA administrator Douglas Costle. Together, Schacht, Costle, and their respective staffs came up with the idea of a "consortium" of industry and government representatives to commission the necessary tests on emissions from "mobile" sources. All engine manufacturers, as well as the EPA, would join the consortium. Both "sides" would provide financial backing. The goal would be to support unbiased research, which in turn would establish the best possible basis both for future regulations and corporate decision-making.

It proved incredibly difficult to sell all the concerned parties on the idea. Schacht and Costle had hoped to have their invention launched within six months; it actually took two years and nine months. One reason was a time-consuming evolution in the concept of the organization: from a dependent to an independent entity; from a research body to a research-commissioning organization; and from an entity focused solely on unregulated emissions to a center for the study of all mobile source emissions.

There were many other reasons for the delay, including the search for an appropriate funding mechanism. The EPA did not want to pay less than half of the costs of the new entity, fearing that a smaller percentage might make that entity appear captive to the engine industry. For its part, industry did not want to make its financial contributions directly to the EPA, since that would ensure that consultants hired by the new organization could only be paid the unrealistically low per-diem consultant rates established by the federal government. This, in the opinion of the engine makers, would virtually guarantee scientific mediocrity. In this and other areas of contention, compromises emerged only after months or years of negotiation.

The "Health Effects Institute" was formally launched on December 12, 1980. The ceremony was attended by EPA administrator Costle and by high-ranking officials from all nine U.S. manufacturers and three foreign manufacturers. (Both the outgoing chairman of General Motors, Thomas A. Murphy, and his successor, Roger Smith, were present.) Costle outlined his high expectations for the Institute:

> *EPA fully supports the charter and the leadership of the emerging institute. We have created, I believe, a new kind of institution, whose orga-*

*nization will give it both the competence and independence so essential
for disciplined and credible scientific inquiry. . . .*

*We anticipate that the Institute will become, if all goes well, the
major source of studies on the health effects of motor vehicles in the
country, and key to improving EPA's capacity to tie its regulatory action
to sound health effects findings.[39]*

In short order, HEI's Research Committee was set up, chaired by physicist and former MIT provost Walter Rosenblith. This board reviewed studies that already were under way, established a specific research agenda for HEI, and issued requests for research proposals based on that agenda. This, too, took time. It was not until 1982 that the first animal studies—the original impetus for HEI—were begun, and not until 1985 that the results of those studies were reported (although not published). Rats and mice exposed to high levels of diesel exhaust throughout their lifetimes did indeed develop lung tumors more frequently than unexposed animals, although not at a rate that prompted the EPA to take any steps toward tightening the already promulgated 1991 standards.[40]

The launching of HEI was only the beginning of an experiment that continues to this day. In the years since its founding, the Institute's fortunes have waxed and waned. In some political climates, HEI has been held up as a model resource and has even been nudged into playing a role in new fields of controversy. (The most notable of these to date has been the thorny field of asbestos regulation.) But in other political contexts—for example, when the EPA itself has fallen from grace—HEI has been viewed less favorably. And throughout the early 1980s, the EPA proved unable to set durable standards for NO$_x$, particulates, and other diesel-exhaust-related substances. While this did not necessarily reflect poorly on HEI, neither did it suggest that HEI was a miracle worker.[41]

Perhaps the biggest miracle associated with HEI was that it ever came into being. The EPA and its administrator, Douglas Costle, took a huge risk, going against the expressed wishes of some of its most powerful backers—including, for example, Maine senator Edmund Muskie, the most powerful environmentalist in Washington, who categorically opposed the notion of cooperating with industry. Cummins also took risks, beginning with the decision to ally itself with larger, sometimes recalcitrant, often unpredictable companies, some of whom were key customers. (For their part, the big automakers found Cummins—a relatively small player in the industry—a bit hard to take as the lead negotiator in this process, but chose not to interfere with what seemed to be an increasingly successful formula.)[42] Cummins' chairman, Henry Schacht, gambled not only that he could assume Irwin

Miller's mantle of industrial statesmanship, but that he could wear it even in a particularly vexed regulatory context. He won the bet.

"The Health Effects Institute was an inspired idea which you originated," wrote former GM chairman Thomas Murphy to Henry Schacht in December 1980, "and it would have remained no more than that were it not for your determination and dedication."[43] From his own experience of jousting with Washington and his industry colleagues, Murphy knew just how improbable Schacht's achievement was.

Technological excursions

Diesels emerged as a competitive technology in the 1930s thanks to their inherent fuel economy (at least in specific operating conditions) over gasoline engines. In subsequent decades, as the heavy-duty gasoline engine was driven from the marketplace, Cummins focused its technical expertise on further improvements in diesel efficiency. "We poured our technology," explains Henry Schacht, "into incremental differences in fuel consumption." With the gradual vanquishing of the heavy-duty gasoline engine, the new race was between Cummins and other diesel producers. Which company could produce the most *efficient* diesel?

Then came the Clean Air Act, which changed the rules in a fundamental way. This was because reducing emissions and achieving high fuel economy are contradictory ends. Sir William Hawthorne—a Cambridge-educated turbine expert who joined the Cummins board in 1974—explains the paradox:

> *To control emissions, you have to retard the timing, which means that you have to reduce the temperature in the cylinder. Reducing the temperature is bad for the thermodynamic cycle, which damages the fuel economy. And then, of course, when you retard the timing, you get more black smoke, and you have more particulates, so you have a new problem then. The whole thing tends to end up with an engine of poor fuel economy.*

In fact, in the case of each of the EPA-targeted culprits—hydrocarbons, carbon monoxide, and especially NO_x —there was a clear trade-off between fuel economy and emissions control. And, as Hawthorne points out, reducing one kind of emission risked increasing another.

There was a third variable in this equation of contradictory ends and means. Throughout the 1960s and the early 1970s, operators continued to demand higher horsepower from their engines. Federal and state weight limits on truck loads were being relaxed, inviting larger loads.[44] Operators were well aware that they could run their trucks more efficiently (and safely) if they could maintain constant highway speed, rather than losing speed on upgrades and trying to build momentum on straightaways and downgrades. These pressures—as well as the greater profitability of the higher-horsepower engines—led Cummins to push toward ever-higher horsepower ratings, first across existing product lines, and subsequently in new products, including the K engine (see below).

Then came the energy crises of 1973 and 1974. The Arab oil embargo had its most dramatic impact at the retail level, with drivers competing at the nation's filling stations for limited supplies of gasoline. (Fuel oil and natural-gas shortages also ensued, with very real consequences for American industry, but these shortages didn't produce compelling imagery for the evening news.) And to further complicate the situation, Congress passed a 55-mile-per-hour speed limit in the fall of 1973. Almost overnight, this law transformed Cummins' vaunted K engine from the company's best bet for the future into an also-ran. It also forced the company to revisit established technologies, such as turbochargers, and to begin the difficult search for new kinds of engines.

As noted in Chapter 6, Cummins' massive investment in its new Tech Center in the 1960s was a major gamble that did not enjoy universal support within the company. It was not until the end of the 1970s, and beyond, that the Tech Center's most skeptical detractors finally were won over. But evidence of the new facility's real importance to the future of the company began to mount much earlier.

One of the Tech Center's first benefits was the rejoining of the engineering and the research-and-development functions. But more important was the improvement in communications that took place almost immediately. In the former Research and Engineering (R&E) set-up, the Research group would pass an engine along to Engineering, which was then housed in a separate facility. Engineering would prepare the engine for production; while a third group, housed in yet another facility, conducted the necessary product testing. "So the engineering people would have to write messages to the test people," recalls one former head of research. "And there was always this problem of not believing the other people's data, and so on."[45]

These barriers to communication broke down almost immediately with the opening of the Tech Center. Bill Schwab—the turbocharging expert hired away from GE in 1947—credits the Tech Center with prompting a "rapid and almost spectacular advancement in technology." One reason, as noted earlier, was that the new facility allowed Cummins to begin using computer simulations to test design variations. Another was that Cummins now could draw upon the latest work then being conducted at the nation's top research laboratories, bring those innovations in-house, and adapt them to Cummins' own needs.[46] Gary Nelson, later vice president of research and development and chief technical officer, sees this as "the point in our history when we went ahead of our competitors in developing a fundamental understanding of thermodynamics, structural analysis, stress vibration, and so on."

Still another piece of the puzzle that fell into place during this period was new leadership for the Cummins research effort. The Tech Center had experienced problems with Vaughn Beals' highly centralized approach to running the technical effort; but it had suffered from a revolving-door leadership after his departure. The first person to head R&E after Beals was Thomas W. Head, a longtime Caterpillar engineer who had led that company's Gas Turbine Division and had joined Cummins in 1964. His successor in R&E was a twenty-two-year Chrysler veteran, Jack E. Charipar, who signed on as vice president of R&E in October 1970. But Charipar died of a brain aneurysm the following year, and Bill Schwab was asked by Henry Schacht and Jim Henderson to fill in temporarily while Cummins looked for a permanent replacement. By the fall of 1972, Schacht and Henderson had decided that Schwab—who had established himself as a level-headed consensus-builder, as well as a talented engineer—deserved the full-time appointment.[47] "He was a very quiet individual," recalls one colleague, "but he was very quietly an innovator, and a leader of people."[48]

Schwab's steadying hand came just in time, in light of the technical problems Cummins now faced. In emission control, for instance, Cummins began the decade of the 1970s lagging behind Caterpillar. Cat's lead was an "accidental" one, as Cummins saw it.[49] (The Peoria-based company traditionally had produced heavier, bulkier, in-line engines for use in construction equipment; and as it turned out, these engines were environmentally friendly.) But in the worst-case scenario, Caterpillar (like overseas rival Daimler-Benz) might be able to survive a set of regulations that Cummins could not. As early as 1970, therefore, some 40 percent of the annual Cummins R&D budget was devoted to "sociability" issues.[50]

There also were a number of exotic developments in the engine environment that needed hard-nosed review. Great claims were being advanced for the new rotary engines, for example; and—at least according to accounts in the industry press—the long-standing promise of the gas turbine seemed about to be realized. Should Cummins plunge into one or more of these exotics? And finally, Cummins knew it was about to face an unprecedented situation: the need to develop multiple families of engines at once. These challenges would tax fully all the technical resources at Cummins' disposal.

There had been voices within Cummins calling for technological diversification as early as the 1960s. Such diversification promised to achieve what company engineers called "high power density"—that is, greater power output from a smaller package. This goal was embodied by the unhappy V-series engines, but there were other, more exotic technologies that looked like they might fit the bill as well.

Some of the earliest experiments were entirely in-house ventures. Nev Reiners, father of the V engines, worked for two years on a novel "swash plate" (or "barrel") engine. Vaughn Beals and engineer Dave Marks tried to develop a two-cycle "rocker beam" engine. Neither of these engines survived into the 1970s. A slightly more durable experiment came in the natural-gas turbine field, also championed by Beals. Turbines—which used hot combustion gases to drive a turbine wheel inside a housing, rather than relying on pistons, connecting rods, and a crankshaft—had some clear advantages over diesels, including their relatively low weight and high "sociability." Cummins contemplated purchasing an idle Boeing facility in Seattle for the manufacture of turbines, and at one point even announced publicly that it was about to manufacture its first prototype turbines.[51]

But the fact that Boeing was trying hard to get *out* of this allegedly promising business—as had both Ford and General Motors—gave Cummins pause. Bill Schwab predicted that some "tough technical breakthroughs" would be needed for the turbine to become commercially practical, including much higher operating temperatures. Financial vice president John Hackett also saw the turbine business as a "horrendous capital requirement that would just eat us alive."

An investigation of the Wankel rotary-engine technology led to some similar conclusions. The Wankel—which in the early 1970s was being introduced in some automobiles—had a compression ratio too low to properly serve as a high-horsepower diesel, at least without extensive modification. Cummins became interested in the possibility of "pairing" two rotary devices to create a new kind of diesel, the first of which would compress air and channel it into the second, or power, stage. This was, in essence, a turbocharging technology. But experiments revealed that high friction in the compression stage made the rotary-based diesel too inefficient to be competitive.

Once again, an intensive investigation by Tech Center staffers concluded that the traditional diesel would remain the basic power plant for at least the 1970s, and probably beyond. To their credit, senior managers at Cummins worried whether this was a case of the company only being able to see what it wanted to see; and this anxiety kept the "exotics" pot simmering throughout the 1970s.[52] But both investigations had underscored the increasing importance of a tried-and-true technology: turbocharging.

Holset Turbochargers

On October 1, 1970, the first production model of the new N-927 engine came off the assembly line in Columbus. This was a more powerful (although somewhat less efficient) version of the old standby NH line, with ratings of 250 hp at 1,950 rpm and 270 hp at 2,100 rpm. The N-927 was naturally aspirated—that is, it was not turbocharged. The following day, the first VT-903 production engine came off a second line in Columbus, destined for on-highway use by Freightliner. Available *only* in a turbocharged model (using the standard Cummins T-50 turbo), the VT-903 was conservatively rated at 320 hp.

In retrospect, the first week of October 1970 can be seen as a turning point for Cummins. It included the release of what turned out to be the company's last major nonturbocharged engine for on-highway use, as well as the release of a new turbocharged engine that was "expected to set new standards for low-smoke, on-highway diesel engines."[53] Partly due to the increasing pressure from the regulators in Washington, all the momentum now was in the direction of turbos. As Bill Schwab recalls:

> *Around 1970 we went almost overnight from around 50 percent naturally aspirated engines to almost 100 percent turbocharged engines, in the N-engine family. We knew the performance was great, and the reduction of smoke was important, but the durability of the turbochargers was the question. We had not had enough long years of experience in the field to determine whether our warranty costs would go out of sight. So there was a lot of fingernail chewing at that time. But we finally said, "Let's do it," and from then on, they were practically all turbocharged engines. But we did our homework well enough, I think, that we sort of bet the company on that.*

Through a combination of circumstances, Cummins' fate now was strongly tied to the effectiveness and durability of its turbochargers. But all of Cummins' turbos were being produced in an aging facility in Seymour, Indiana, which clearly was not adequate to support a "bet the company" strategy. In 1972, therefore, Cummins launched $1.2 million in capital improvements at the Seymour plant.[54]

Still more depth was needed, however, which made the results of a 1973 overseas prospecting trip by financial vice president John Hackett all the more important. Hackett—then looking for new business opportunities for Cummins and exploring the possibility of creating a freestanding turbocharger business—was in Sweden trying to pitch Cummins turbochargers to Volvo. Volvo rejected the offer, saying that it already had the best turbocharger supplier in the world: a company called Holset in the gritty English industrial city of Huddersfield, Yorkshire.[55] "I walked out of that place," says Hackett, "and I said, 'By God, we're going to see those guys before I go home.'"

Hackett arranged a meeting with Paul Croset, founder of a group of engineering companies that included Holset. By a curious coincidence, Croset's father, Louis, had met Clessie Cummins in 1932 when Cummins and W. G. Irwin were touring Europe looking for diesel licensees.[56] Several years later, his son Paul became interested in the problem of torsional vibration (which increased with engine speed, and tended to break crankshafts) and had explored the possibility of silicone-filled "dampers" to minimize this vibration. In 1947, he formed the Holset Engineering Company, Ltd. (The Holset name combines half of Croset's name with half of Holmes, another company in the larger group of engineering companies.)

By the time Hackett stumbled onto the company, Holset had annual sales of $21 million. In addition to turbos, the company produced rubber vibration dampers, viscous dampers, flexible couplings, and fan drives. It had a reputation for first-class engineering and manufacturing skills, and counted among its customers Perkins, Ford, Rolls Royce, Scania, and numerous other international manufacturers.

Hackett, already interested in buying Holset, found to his chagrin that he was four months too late. Holset had been bought by Hanson Trust, a British conglomerate run by James Hanson and best known for its low-tech building-materials businesses, such as brick making. It seemed an unlikely fit, but (as Hackett soon discovered) James Hanson had acquired Holset for the express purpose of "getting at" Paul Croset. Hanson was then plotting to take over the Rolls Royce Motor Car Company, and wanted Croset— whom he had known all his life—to run Rolls for him. Hackett approached Hanson directly, and was told that Holset was not for sale—that is, until the Rolls Royce situation was straightened out. But, as Hackett recalls, "Hanson never got Rolls, as it turned out. So he called me and said, 'Do you want to talk some more about Holset?' So I went over, and I learned more about negotiating from Jim Hanson in one month than I learned in ten years previously."

Cummins paid a steep price for Holset—only slightly less than the full $27 million that Hanson demanded. It was the largest acquisition in Cummins' history. But Cummins was betting that the worldwide turbocharger business would grow from 600,000 units to more than 1 million units annually within five years, with more than 80 percent of all U.S. diesels turbocharged by 1978.[57] The company also was betting that turbocharging would prove absolutely vital in the emerging trade-off between increased efficiency and reduced emissions. These bets, notes Bill Schwab, paid off handsomely:

> *As far as I know, Cummins was and is the only engine manufacturer that makes both the fuel system and the turbocharger, and therefore controls the turbocharger interfaces. And the turbocharger and the fuel system ended up being the two most critical things in meeting the emissions standards and lowering fuel consumption. We were able to have that technology right in front of us, and we could play the interfaces between the two.*

Cummins spent the balance of the 1970s trying to transform the turbocharger from a lightweight, add-on component to an integral part of a high-performance system, designed in ways that would use all available exhaust energy and reduce all types of emissions.[58] It was a tough assignment, made tougher because relations with Holset were not always smooth. The fact that the Holset model "H" turbo—technologically superior to the Cummins model "T"—was slowly emerging as the company standard did not endear the English turbo makers to their counterparts in Seymour.[59] And the inclination of one senior manager at Cummins to run Holset as an independent operation led, at one point, to the issuance of an unusual edict: "We were told that no Cummins people could visit Holset," recalls Jim Henderson wryly, "because we were screwing everything up."*

The high valuation of the pound in the late 1970s also hurt Holset, which by then was exporting some 80 percent of its output. In 1978, Cummins briefly considered selling Holset, but the move was strongly opposed by Irwin Miller and director William Hawthorne and soon was abandoned. By 1980, Holset was producing 160,000 units annually, or slightly more than its Seymour counterpart. It had total sales of some $73 million—more than three times its sales volume at the time of its acquisition by Cummins, although far below the optimistic projections of 1973—and held a commanding 50 percent of the European turbo market.[60]

Big Engines in an Era of Conservation

Shifts in the regulatory environment, as well as in the larger-world context of energy supplies and prices, had profound effects on the Engine Company in the 1970s. An engine that seemed destined for great success ran into a stone wall in the marketplace, and less visible products assumed unexpected importance for the company.

Feasibility studies for a brand-new engine, dubbed the "K," began in Columbus in 1968.[61] It was not unprecedented for Cummins to start an engine design "from a clean sheet of paper"—that is, without any tooling constraints or other similar limits. But experience had shown that the most successful Cummins products tended to be those that evolved over many years, incorporating incremental refinements developed from experience in the field. Conversely, the company's least successful product in recent decades—the small V series introduced in the 1960s—had sprung from a clean sheet of paper.[62]

The K came at a unique juncture in the company's technological evolution. The workhorse of the Cummins product line, the venerable NH engine,

---

*Eventually, Henderson further recalls, the Seymour operation was folded into Holset. By the mid-1990s, the combined operation had annual sales of more than $200 million.

still dominated the 200 to 300 hp market. But as Cummins looked forward, it foresaw the need for a substantially more powerful engine—one that could perform in the 400 to 600 hp range. There was a move afoot in Congress (and also in many state legislatures) to raise the weight limits on heavy-duty diesels. (For example, Warren Magnusen, a senator from Washington, was promoting a bill that would have legalized "triple bottoms"—that is, a cab pulling three trailers.) Other pending legislation, aimed at keeping traffic flowing on the highways, proposed to mandate minimum speeds on uphill grades. If any of these efforts was successful, it would render even the relatively mighty NH underpowered. Meanwhile, none of Cummins' competitors had an engine that could be pushed up to a 600 hp rating. If Cummins could get there first, it might well enjoy a significant competitive advantage.[63]

The lead designer on the K project was Phillip E. Jones, a research engineer whom Vaughn Beals had recruited away from Perkins, the British engine maker, in 1967, as part of an ill-starred effort to create a new engine for the European market. When that engine (codenamed the "E70") was abandoned in favor of a short-lived "V555" engine (a restroked member of the small-V family), Jones became available for work on a much heavier engine, aimed at the domestic market.

Jones already had an excellent reputation within the organization. "Phil was a superb designer," recalls Bill Schwab, "and also very strong analytically, with lots of research experience." He was British—an outsider—who never considered himself part of the company's "establishment."[64] He was known for his strong convictions, even prejudices, about certain engine designs. "When I was at Perkins and I had heard there was a Cummins oversquare engine," he says, "I laughed all the way home. It was to me such an obviously wrong thing to do." After arriving at Cummins, he continued to make his strong opinions known on a wide variety of engine-design parameters. For example, he concluded that V-configured engines were inferior to in-line configurations. "I was determined to make it into an in-line six," he later recalled of the new engine. "Why? Because an in-line six is the perfect engine. It's simpler and less costly. Everything is balanced."

Three years of study, design, and testing ensued. The first six-cylinder in-line K prototypes, developed in 1972, were subjected to some sixty thousand hours of laboratory testing at rated speeds and loads, and held up well.[65] All told, Cummins spent some $13.3 million developing the K engine; and at the end of the four-year development phase, Jones and his team could point to some remarkable engineering accomplishments. Perhaps the most impressive of these was the creation of an engine that was not substantially larger than the NH engine, but had a displacement that was approximately one-third greater. This was accomplished through a number of design tricks, ranging from the simple (such as removing what Jones refers to as "that whole pile of garbage" on the front and back of the engine) to the sophisticated (such as reducing the width of the bearings at the ends of the engines, which did not need to be as wide as those in the center, but—for uniformity's sake—always had been). In marked contrast to earlier Cummins engines, key accessories (including the fan, water pump, lube pump, air compressor, and steering pump) were powered by hardened helical gears, leaving only the alternator and optional freon compressor to be belt-driven.[66]

In September 1973, Cummins announced that the first commercial models of the K engine would be available in December. These working prototypes were tested in the field by selected Cummins customers. But external forces quickly converged on the K engine and undercut its incipient success. In October, war broke out between Israel and its Middle Eastern neighbors. The Arab nations—deeply offended by American support of Israel—cut off oil supplies to the United States. Suddenly, energy conservation became the national priority. President Richard Nixon introduced and Congress passed a nationwide truck speed limit of 55 miles per hour. Now, an engine that enabled a heavy-duty truck to barrel uphill at 65 miles per hour was a much less valuable commodity.[67] John Hackett recalls the dark days of 1974, when the truck market was collapsing and the K's potential market was vanishing. "We were facing the prospect of five-dollar-a-gallon gasoline, and all of that hysteria," recalls Hackett, "and nobody wanted an engine like [the K]. What people wanted was an engine that put fuel efficiency as Number One."

Cummins' first response (in 1975) was to begin revamping several existing engine lines to achieve greater fuel efficiency. This program—known as the "FORMULA" concept—lowered an engine's operating speed, increased its torque, and applied a low-rpm drive train. A second fuel-saving step, introduced in 1976, was the "Big Cam" program. Increasing the camshaft diameter from two inches to two-and-a-half inches permitted a shorter injection period and more efficient combustion. Together, these and other fuel economy programs increased the efficiency of Cummins engines by some 15 percent overall between 1976 and 1979.[68]

"Big Cam II was a huge winner," Jim Henderson recalls. As a direct result of the Big Cam series (I through IV)—especially Big Cam II, which engineer Gary Nelson describes as a "wonderful product" from a technical standpoint—Cummins' heavy-duty market share went from 29.6 percent of the heavy-duty market in 1975 to 63.2 percent in 1983. So high was that percentage, in fact, that Cummins wondered whether its success might draw antitrust fire from Washington.[69]

But Cummins still had to decide what to do about the K engine—a good power plant that had lost its market. Even after a FORMULA retrofitting, the K was a fuel guzzler; and Cummins' marketers had to make the best of a bad situation. In 1976, therefore, they launched the "Reserve Power" campaign, premised on the notion that higher horsepower engines (such as the K) provided enough power to maintain constant speed on grades, thereby assuring "optimum vehicle productivity."[70] The company premiered a slick fifteen-minute film on Reserve Power at the November meeting of the American Trucking Association, along with a commissioned country-and-western song—*Hummin' Cummins*—performed by United Artists' recording artist Ed Bruce. The song (which to Cummins' astonishment soon was being played on truck-stop jukeboxes across the country) was a cheerful, Nashville-soaked bit of propaganda:

> *Re-serve Power*
> *For constant speed*
> *Re-serve power*
> *That's what a trucker needs*
> *Hour after hour*
> *The trip don't take as long*
> *When you got a Hummin' Cummins*
> *With Re-serve Power comin' on!*

Henry Schacht joined the chorus—figuratively—in a 1977 *Forbes* interview, when he argued that high-horsepower engines always would have their advocates. "Higher power," he told the interviewer, "pays for itself, because drivers spend more time in high gear."[71]

The Reserve Power campaign pushed unit sales above 3,000 in 1977; but in that same year, by contrast, the NH sold more than 100,000 units in the United States alone. Almost from the start, the on-highway six-cylinder K sold mainly in places like Western Canada and Australia, where local topography made power more important than fuel efficiency. Unexpectedly, the six-cylinder K also emerged as an ideal engine for some industrial applications, including marine power generation and front-end loaders.[72]

Meanwhile, the huge twelve- and sixteen-cylinder Ks, which were built (in the company's Daventry, England, plant) to produce horsepowers in excess of 1,600, became a favorite of the mining industry and helped open the door to the burgeoning Chinese market. Capacity constraints initially impeded the development of these huge industrial engines, but once manufacturing space was secured, these high-end Ks won Cummins a 60 percent market share of the mining industry, which had long pushed the company to produce an engine better suited to its purposes.[73]

On the highways, though, the K was destined to be a niche player. It represented at least a plateau—and perhaps even the peak—in the big-engine, high-horsepower competition that Cummins had promoted since the 1950s. Now, thanks to the abrupt changes wrought by the energy crisis, Cummins had to cast about for alternatives.

The Rainbow Experiments

Throughout the 1970s, the overwhelming majority of the Tech Center's non-pollution-control-related resources was devoted to the progressive improvement of existing engine lines and components—especially the NH engine, in all its many variations.[74] Projects like the K engine were expensive, but they placed a distant second in terms of the percentage of the overall R&E budget they consumed. Lowest of all in the allocated-resources rankings were experimental, "blue-sky" sorts of R&E projects, in which champions of an offbeat idea pursued their own vision. Cummins usually had one or more such projects under way, tucked away in the corners of buildings and budgets.

Very few of these projects ever got beyond the earliest stages of development. Occasionally, though, one of these quixotic investigations *would* prove out, and alter the course of the company's history in dramatic ways. One such series of experiments—which came to be known collectively as the "Rainbow engine project"—began in deep obscurity in the mid-1970s.[75] But within a decade, the Rainbows and their spin-offs had prompted a fundamental shift in the company's product mix.

Once again, the protagonist in the story was Liverpool-born Phil Jones. Jones had been hired away from Perkins in part because of his familiarity with small engines—the field in which Perkins specialized, and which Cummins knew it had to investigate in order to break into the European market. But more broadly, Jones was hired because Cummins had made a conscious decision to recruit engineers with a different perspective: more international, more iconoclastic, less dogmatic. "We were concerned," recalls Jim Henderson, who was involved in hiring technical staff during this period, "that we were getting too inbred."

After his four-year detour through the K engine project, Jones was given the freedom once again to think about new kinds of engines. A group of engineers at the Tech Center staff had begun to talk among themselves about what they called an "integration project"—something that could pull together their various new skills and areas of expertise. Ideally, it would be an exploratory activity with no deadlines. As Jones, the leader and spokesman of the group, recalls:

> I started campaigning for an engine with no market. Most engines are done as a result of a market need. I was saying, "There are all these things we've been wanting to do on an engine, and we're always prevented—because production can't make it, the machinery is wrong, it won't fit in a truck, or whatever. Let's do something different."
>
> So the company gave us a million, or a million and a half, to do this engine with absolutely zero interference. It didn't matter if there

*was no market. There was no production date. It was an exercise to see
how crazy people would get if they had the freedom to make an engine.*

Of course, the new product—developed on the fourth floor of the Tech
Center—had some basic parameters, mainly established by the engineering
team. First, it would be aimed at the heavy-duty market. Reflecting Jones'
strong prejudices, it would be an in-line six. It would be limited to twelve
liters of displacement—two liters smaller than the NH—because the engineers were determined to make their product smaller and lighter as a package, and a smaller displacement would allow that. Their initial power-rating
target was a fairly conservative 400 hp.

But the real goal was to demonstrate what was possible. Accordingly, the
project employed new project-management tools, such as PERT (the
Program Evaluation and Review Technique, a new version of the critical-path
method), to place the design process on a timeline and hold it to that timeline. It also called on the Tech Center's new computer-aided design tools. For
example, cycle simulations—which involved plugging in variables such as
cylinder pressure, degree of turbocharging, rpm, and others—were used to
predict and refine the engine's performance in the "paper" stage, well before
any metal was cut. This new application of computer technology dramatically reduced the amount of "cut and try" in the development phase. "You could
optimize the engine for whatever you wanted to optimize it for," recalls Bill
Schwab. "And that was a first for the diesel industry."[76]

Another factor that came into play was the substantial upgrading of
Cummins' expertise in technology development that had occurred over the
previous half-dozen years. Beginning with Vaughn Beals, and continuing
through the tenures of Tom Head, Jack Charipar, and Bill Schwab as heads
of R&E, Cummins had spent significant sums to assemble teams of experts
in key areas: materials, chemistry, emissions, combustion, structural design,
applied mechanics, and so on.

The first rough sketch of the engine was put down on paper in January
1974.[77] As it developed, the new engine began to display some novel characteristics. It was smaller, lighter, and more compact than the NH. It had an
oversized cam, reflecting the "Big Cam" work that was going on elsewhere in
the building. Its valves were rotated 90 degrees from the standard position. It
acquired an aluminum crankcase and a linerless cylinder block. Taking the
no-belts philosophy of the K engine one step further, the new engine had a
gear-driven alternator.

In the summer of 1975, some eighteen months after the first sketches of
the twelve-liter engine were made, and only four months behind schedule, a
prototype of the engine was fabricated, assembled, and started up. "It produced phenomenally low fuel consumptions," recalls Jones, "the likes of

which hadn't been seen in our regular products." In the summer of 1975—in the wake of widespread layoffs at Cummins, in the midst of a severe recession, and with the energy crisis slowly throttling the overpowered K engine—the company was thirsty for this kind of good news.

Only one prototype of the engine was ever built. This was in part because the twelve-liter was never intended for production, and certain of its elements could not be mass-produced economically.* But it also was because there was a more pressing demand from the market. "After the twelve-liter engine was going well," Jones recalls, "Hank [Schacht] came in to have lunch with me. He said, 'I just got back from Europe, and we can't sell these NHs in Europe because they're just too darned big. Can't we do something smaller?' I said, 'Yeah, I've always wanted to do a 10-liter engine.' So they shelled out the money again."

Once again, Jones' fourth-floor team took on the assignment, which was a natural outgrowth of the twelve-liter engine project. And again, part of the assignment was to show what could be accomplished when the Tech Center was pushed. This time, however, the company also had in mind a specific market (Europe), a specific partner (Ford, with whom Schacht was conducting a series of preliminary discussions), and a specific time frame (six months from clean sheet of paper to starting up in the test cell). The ten-liter project therefore was similar to its predecessor, except that its designers had to pay strict attention to the "buildability" of the engine. They also had to build relationships early on with selected suppliers. This time, PERT and similar critical-path tools also were used to manage suppliers, who—working with incomplete prints—had to place preliminary orders and begin rough fabrication work.

It was at this point, sometime in late 1975 or early 1976, that the "Rainbow" label emerged. It was a child of confusion, more than anything else. Somewhere in the development phase of the twelve-liter engine, Jones had conducted a conference with senior management during which he had superimposed a green transparency—showing the proposed profile of the twelve-liter engine—on a similarly scaled profile of an NH engine. His point was simply to underscore the new engine's smaller size, but it turned out to be an enduring image. As Jones recalls:

> So during the twelve-liter presentations, I had been showing the engine in green. Then two or three months later, I was showing the ten-liter, and I used a blue outline. Then somebody in the meeting got the two engines confused, and I said, "No, you mean the green engine, not the blue one." And those names stuck.

---

*Henry Schacht emphasizes that features of this experimental engine were incorporated successfully into the mainstay NH engine.

The "Blue" engine, as it came to be called, was targeted to be very light (in the range of 1,700 pounds) and very compact (perhaps a foot less in both length and height than the NH). This time out, Jones' team scrutinized possible innovations for their manufacturability, cost, and possible impact on the engine's durability and serviceability. For example, the Blue engine had fewer parts. "We had a little rule," explains Jones, "that the cheapest part is no part." Components were made more accessible. Cooling surfaces were limited to the upper couple of inches of the cylinder liners, an innovation that computer analysis had suggested was possible. Perhaps the Blue's biggest departure was its camshaft, positioned at the top of the block, and its separate aluminum crankcases.

The Blue engine was completed on time, and—remarkably—achieved its performance targets within two weeks of first being started up. "Again," says Gary Nelson, "this proved the value of using these tools, rather than spending months cutting and trying after you got the hardware."

The Blue engine combined some of the hard-won lessons of the struggling K engine, the Big Cam and FORMULA initiatives, and the Green engine. But unlike the Green engine, the Blue engine was not intended as an end in itself. It had been called forth by a pressing need to break into the European truck market, a need that in the late 1970s continued to grow. The Tech Center had produced what appeared to be an exciting new engine, but Cummins—perennially strapped for cash—was not in a position to capitalize on that technological leap forward.

Once the Blue thread was dropped, would it be picked up again? If so, would Cummins go it alone, or with a deep-pocketed partner? When these questions were answered in the 1980s, they more than justified Cummins' bet on Phil Jones and the Rainbows. But well before the fate of the Blue engine was known, Jones' team started in on yet another phase of their Rainbow efforts. This second phase—which included engines dubbed the Red and Pink—was a reversion to the philosophy of the Green engine. Once again, some of Cummins' most talented designers were asked to imagine that they were free of the restraints normally imposed by manufacturing, sales, and the marketplace. From the beginning, the Red engine (and its Pink spin-off) were conceived of as "paper" engines, never intended to be manufactured. But this time, rather than looking at the heavy-duty end of the market, Jones and his team were asked to look at even smaller engines—smaller, in fact, than anything Cummins ever had produced.

Small engines were not entirely new to Cummins. The relatively small A engine was introduced just before World War II, and its unsuccessful successor (the J) struggled on into the 1950s. And by the 1970s, the ill-fated small-V engines were entering their second decade of production. Ironically, although the Vs had acquired a terrible reputation in much of the world, after a decade of refinement many of their original problems had been ironed out.* They were still extremely popular in the Mexican market, for example, where their simplicity and durability more than made up for their noisiness, smokiness, and tendency toward excess vibration. But most of the world market would talk to Cummins about small engines only if the company could come up with a new product.[78]

There were formidable obstacles to such a development, not the least of which was Irwin Miller's skepticism. In response to a 1973 proposed study of producing a low-cost diesel in the 160 to 200 hp range, Miller told Jim Henderson bluntly that there was "not any such animal," at least that could be manufactured and sold at a profit:

> In my opinion, I could pretty well predict now where you will come out on the so-called low-cost diesel, and I think that you should tell us pretty soon why this is going to be different from Val/Vale before you divert a lot of time from other issues to it and a lot of money. I am not necessarily negative, but I see no reason why we should go through this drill all over again without carefully learning the experience of the Val/Vale history.[79]

On the other hand, Miller expressed his willingness to approach Henry Ford II at an upcoming meeting on the subject of a small diesel for a novel application. "Do you want me to mention at all the fact," he wrote to Jim Henderson, "that we would like to come up and talk to him about a possible diesel development for passenger car engines?" Although the passenger-car diesel project soon stalled—evidently because Henry Ford II was scared off by the massive cost of retooling for diesel—the wooing of Ford continued. By 1975, Cummins was again talking with Ford, this time about supplying a small engine for use by Ford's tractor division in Egypt.[80]

But as noted earlier, for such a courtship to be successful, Cummins needed a new product. The Red engine project, undertaken sometime in 1975, was a first step toward that goal. By this time, Jones and his eight-person team had been relocated to a separate facility. This move occurred in part because the Tech Center was filling up, and in part because Jones and his strongest internal ally, Thomas W. Head—then formally in charge of management systems, but increasingly a player in the small-engine field—wanted to create a buffer zone between the new project and the rest of the company. As Henry Schacht recalls:

---

*"The 903," says Jim Henderson of the final iteration of the V engines, "was in the end a terrific engine, but it had too much iron in it. We couldn't make money on it, especially at our volume levels."

> *Both Phil and Tom, the two leading advocates within our technical community of small engines, had serious reservations as to whether Cummins could ever get committed to doing something different—or if it did, it inevitably would be polluted by our heavy-duty thinking, and we would not be cost-effective. And Jim [Henderson], John [Hackett], and I were worried enormously about that, because we didn't have the surge capacity to write off the Vs another time.*

The initial design work focused on an eight-liter, six-cylinder in-line engine, with indirect injection, to run at 3,600 rpm. While this Red engine was in the sketching phase, Cummins also entered into conversations with a European automaker who wanted an even smaller engine. "So in a few months flat," recalls Jones, "we made a smaller one, which we obviously called Pink, because it was only a shade different from the Red one."

At first, the Red and Pink engines, like their Green cousin, were only productive exercises in new-engine design. Then circumstances changed, and the Red engine was badly needed in the marketplace. At this point, the Reds—like the Blues—were stalled by the immense practical problems inherent in tooling up to launch a new engine line. Jones states the problem succinctly:

> *So you come up with a new engine design. You build a factory, make the engine, and then you say, "OK, now, who wants to buy my engine? And by the way, I need to sell five hundred or a thousand a day or I won't make a dime." Well, that's a tough way to go.*

Henry Schacht recalls that even Irwin Miller—who not long before had expressed deep pessimism about a new small-engine project—was "ecstatic" about the Rainbow engine projects. "But when it came to investing in small engines," Schacht continues, "we didn't, because we couldn't figure out for the life of us how to get into the business."

The Red engine (like the Blue engine just ahead of it) was pointing in a profitable direction for Cummins. But it was clear by 1978 that Cummins would require both vast amounts of new capital and a very different distribution system to make the leap into the small-engine business.

One approach, of course, would be to try to develop these resources in-house: not a very good bet, according to almost everyone in the company. A second approach would be to find a small-engine partner that could share in the tooling costs, guarantee at least a minimum volume, and perhaps provide a strong distribution network. There certainly were models of such partnerships in Cummins' past, including Krupp in Germany and Chrysler at Darlington. But were there new partners out there for this kind of venture? At Cummins, no one knew.

Cummins in the community

The dimensions of Cummins' role as a "corporate citizen" changed markedly in the 1970s. Along with Dayton Hudson, Cummins was one of only two companies in the Fortune 500 to allocate as much as 5 percent of its pretax profits to charitable donations. (The Fortune 500 average was then 1.3 percent.)[81] This unusual degree of generosity began to earn public notice. At the same time, investments that the company and its foundation had made in the 1960s—especially in the architectural and physical landscape of Columbus—were receiving international recognition. With regular nudges from Cummins, the city had earned the nickname "the Athens of the prairie," and was becoming an unlikely venue for prepackaged architectural tours. Even Irwin Miller must have been surprised at the return on the investment that the Cummins Engine Foundation had made in a handful of up-and-coming architects.

Miller himself remained the personification of both the foundation's and the corporation's good deeds, winning acclaim, awards, and appointments to influential national boards. His letters and public statements from this period are a compelling combination of modesty and intellectual rigor, all pointing toward one consistent (and to many, surprising) conclusion: *We should be doing more.*

Ironically, even as the plaudits were rolling in from around the world, the foundation that was being praised was also experiencing setbacks. To the surprise of Miller and others, local officials for the first time rejected the services of a foundation-sponsored architect. Farther afield, other well-intentioned programs supported by the foundation were having unexpected consequences. Cummins' miserable economic performance in the mid-1970s cut back the foundation's programs across the board, and by 1978, the foundation was engaged in some fundamental soul-searching about its mission and relevance.

Meanwhile, Cummins was taking careful steps to institutionalize codes of corporate and individual behavior across its employee population. These codes were inextricably bound up with the things that the company "stood for"—and therefore, were again inseparable from what Irwin Miller stood for. (One corporate measure applied in the late 1970s, and described below, was affectionately dubbed the "Irwin Miller Transparency Test.") This highly personal influence helped ensure that the company's bureaucratic structure retained an essential humanity.

The Man in the Middle

At the beginning of the 1970s, J. Irwin Miller and his family continued to play a highly visible role in the improvement of Columbus. For example, the family in the 1960s retained Los Angeles-based architect Cesar Pelli (along with a shopping mall developer) to design a major new mall to "anchor" the downtown area of Columbus. In December 1971, Miller, his wife Xenia, and his sister Clementine Tangeman transferred 13,550 shares of Cummins common stock to the mall's board of directors. This represented about one-third of their final investment of some $2 million in the project. The board then hired Irwin Management Company—the family's investment managers—to serve without pay as "construction agent" for the new development.[82]

Irwin Miller, the man in the middle of these highly visible transactions, continued to be an individual who treasured privacy more than praise. Nevertheless, praise was abundant. In June 1970, Miller received the American Jewish Committee's annual Civic Leadership Award.* Keynote speaker Charles Goodell, a liberal Republican senator from New York, described Miller as "a man of power who has understood his commitment to his fellow man."[83]

In his public statements and his personal correspondence, Miller was reluctant to accept these laurels. Aware of what he saw as the gap between his ideals and his performance—and also his company's performance, with which he identified so personally—he exhorted his audiences to set higher standards, and to demand more from him. "Don't let Cummins' plants smoke any more," he told a meeting of the Bartholomew County Taxpayers' Association. "Pass an ordinance. Don't let *any* plant smoke."[84]

A senior at Sarah Lawrence College wrote to Miller after reading an article in *Saturday Review* that described Miller's approach to corporate social responsibility. "I am not trying to be threatening by asking," she wrote, "but do you practice what you preach?" In his response, Miller acknowledged a series of what he considered to be progressive efforts—in minority hiring, open housing, architecture, and the like—but concluded with this: "We are at least aware of a broader range of responsibilities than the traditional responsibility to shareholders. We try to discharge these as we understand them today. . . . In all this, we may deserve some marks for effort, but I wouldn't claim any at all for results. We ought to be doing better."[85]

Miller's internal communications display many of the same characteristics: honesty, bluntness, and an underlying tone of dissatisfaction, even anxiety: *We ought to be doing better.* In some cases, this meant thinking about an issue more broadly than did most corporations—as, for example, in the spring of 1971, when Miller suggested strongly that Jim Henderson develop a policy aimed at employing the Vietnam veterans who were then returning to the States in large numbers. Miller asked that the policy cover not only veterans with honorable discharges, but also conscientious objectors, young peo-

---

*Closer to home, however, Miller acquired a small band of persistent detractors, several of whom wrote letters to the local paper decrying his power and alleged leftist political leanings. One Miller critic dubbed the new mall "Red Square."

ple "who for reasons of conscience served jail terms," and "persons who for conscientious acts received dishonorable discharges."[86]

Similarly, Miller in this same time period worried about the company's treatment of women. "We should formulate and implement a policy for hiring of women at all levels," he chided Henry Schacht. "We have as yet really done nothing here."[87] Think broadly, penetrate a little deeper, try to stay an issue or two ahead of breaking events: These were the precepts that Miller tried to instill in the younger managers who would succeed him as the conscience of the corporation.

Rethinking the Foundation

Over the years, Cummins continually reexamined the philosophy, rationale, and mechanics of the Cummins Engine Foundation (CEF). No single approach proved to be satisfactory after the early architectural focus of the late 1950s, and all subsequent configurations of the CEF were the subject of spirited debates.

The CEF began the 1970s in the midst of one such debate.[88] In 1968, then executive director Philip Sorenson proposed to focus the foundation's activities on three issues: race, poverty, and the physical environment. The board's approval of this agenda led to the hiring in 1969 of five "field officers," who would represent the black community in major U.S. metropolitan areas: Walter Bremond (Los Angeles), Ivanhoe Donaldson (Washington), Richard Lawrence (Chicago), Walter Lively (Detroit), and Stanley Wise (New York and Atlanta).* Approximately $750,000 was allocated to this new field-officer-based approach, a sum that was intended to cover both grants and operating costs. Each of the five field officers controlled approximately $25,000 in discretionary funds for small local grants; larger grants would be controlled from Columbus with inputs from the field.

Trouble arose in late 1970, when Sorenson—following a heated philosophical disagreement with Irwin Miller over the appropriateness of supporting a Ralph Nader-sponsored shareholders' rights initiative—resigned abruptly. At the next foundation meeting in Columbus, Miller explained his side of the story and reassured program directors that nothing had changed as a result of Sorenson's departure. Edwin Booth, then acting executive director of the CEF, recalls what happened next:

> *Stanley Wise, who is a great orator, starts rocking back and forth in his chair. Now, you know Stanley is going to say something, and you know*

---

*Cummins credits James A. Joseph, described subsequently, with principal authorship of this unique program.

you better put your seat belt on. They had already heard Phil Sorenson's side, and now they had heard Irwin Miller's side. So Stanley rocks back and forth, and finally says, "I do not know which of two great African proverbs holds true. One is that when two elephants dance, only the grass gets hurt. And the other is that when the old man can no longer dance, he refuses to listen to the beat of the drums."

Being scolded by strong-willed and articulate black activists was new for Cummins. In fact, the field-officer program was an uncomfortable eye-opener on a regular basis. Walter Bremond's Los Angeles house was bombed when a radical black group took exception to his local mediation activities. The president of a key OEM lodged a strong protest with Henry Schacht when he heard a rumor that he had been placed on a "hit list" by an activist organization partly funded by one of the field officers. (The rumor turned out to be unfounded.) In 1975, a Chicago grand jury investigation revealed that Irwin Miller's finances and personal life had been covertly investigated by "Chicago police spies" because of a 1971 $20,000 CEF grant to the Afro-American Patrolman's League, an organization comprising some 3,000 black Chicago police officers.[89]

On the other hand, the field-officer program succeeded in steeping the white managers who ran Cummins in the realities of the black urban experience. This, it seems, was part of Irwin Miller's design from the start. "It had a huge influence on me," recalls Jim Henderson. "I'll never forget those guys. It was a fantastic experience—having those guys come in and tell us what was really going *on* out there, and challenging us."

The more traditional activities of the CEF also continued, under the rubric of the physical environment. For example, the foundation regularly renewed its offer to pay the architectural fees for public buildings in Columbus. By 1973, this program had been dormant for several years, mainly because the city temporarily had caught up with its school building needs. But in the fall of 1973, local officials began planning for a new school in Taylorsville. To the surprise and disappointment of the CEF, when the foundation's offer of financial support came to a vote in February 1974, the Bartholomew Consolidated School board—which had asked for that support—voted not to accept it, and instead hired an Indianapolis-based architect. Board member Alvin Burbrink explained that many people in his district, which included Taylorsville, wanted to "just once try a building on our own and see what happens."[90]

The CEF did not retreat from either its activist agenda or its architectural program as a result of these unhappy surprises. But the economic crunch of 1975 severely limited the funds that were available for the foundation's work. (The CEF had no endowment, and was almost entirely dependent on annual contributions from the Engine Company.) Spending fell from $1.3 million in 1974 to $700,000 in the difficult year of 1975.[91]

Although the CEF's resource stream was replenished when the economy recovered in 1976, its leaders—particularly Irwin Miller—continued to puzzle over the appropriate role of a large company and its "captive" foundation in a small city, especially in light of hints of local resentment. "My guess," wrote longtime confidante George Newlin to Miller in 1978, "is that we've done better than *most* big companies in small communities."* The Engine Company, Newlin argued, could not deny that it was a "dominant force" in Columbus, and had to acknowledge that it had an "enormous stake in the quality of this community."

But the company and the foundation tended to get into trouble when they attempted to dictate terms to the community. Newlin chided Cummins and the CEF for taking umbrage when the community did not admit to the "obligations and responsibilities that we've projected on it." The best that Cummins and the CEF could do, Newlin advised, was to make explicit their agenda and then act on it, without expecting that others would follow their well-intentioned lead. "Above all," Newlin concluded, "let us expect neither appreciation nor applause for doing what is in our best interest."[92]

The Corporate Action Division

By the 1970s, Cummins employed some twenty thousand people, only half of whom worked in the Columbus area. These numbers and this degree of geographic dispersion presented many challenges to the company's managers, including making sure these twenty thousand people were all pulling in the same direction. But on a more subtle level, the corporation had to ensure that its agents represented the company's *values* accurately and consistently, no matter where they were in the world.

Toward that end, Cummins established in the spring of 1972 a "Corporate Action Division," headed by James A. Joseph. Joseph, an ordained minister in the United Church of Christ, had a distinguished career in the civil rights movement before first joining the Cummins Engine Foundation as its associate director in 1967. After serving for two years under foundation head Phil Sorenson, Joseph left Columbus to serve as chaplain of the Claremont Colleges in California. Following Sorenson's abrupt departure in 1970, Joseph was recruited back to Columbus to serve as the head of the "Association of Foundations," a loose umbrella organization comprising the Cummins Engine Foundation, the Irwin-Sweeney-Miller Foundation, and the Irwin-Union Foundation. When he joined Cummins in 1972, he was appointed at the vice-presidential level, reporting directly to Henry Schacht—a signal intended to give the new post visibility and clout.[93]

*Miller, digging deeper, circled this comment on his copy of Newlin's memo and scribbled in the margin, "Who has done better? Is there a model?"

Joseph was assigned broad responsibility for corporate philanthropy, governmental relations and public affairs, community relations, human resources development, and affirmative action programs. "It is clearly in the self-interest of business," he told an Indiana audience shortly after assuming his new post, "that we recognize and accept our responsibilities to the society which gives us our charter."[94] Joseph's challenge was to figure out concrete ways for the corporation to *act* on those lofty but vague responsibilities—and thereby to avoid having his group perceived as a corporate backwater.

The Corporate Action Division first developed an aggressive charter for its activities, assigning to itself the following tasks, among others:

> *Serve as an in-house resource for understanding the social and political context in which the company does business. Interpret political and social issues, propose corporate policies, and coordinate public affairs programs. . . .*
>
> *Work with management at all levels to ensure that all business analyses—new plant sites, new ventures, market penetration, product development, functional planning, etc.—include corporate responsibility considerations.*[95]

The latter goal was acted upon in the spring of 1973, when Cummins "decentralized" its Corporate Action staff. From then on, at least two members of the group were deployed in specific functional areas around the corporation, where they became involved in a broad range of issues. Corporate Action staffer Ron Hoge, for example, was assigned to John Hackett's finance group, and attended all of that group's staff meetings. He worked with financial analysts, raising issues of corporate responsibility where appropriate, and served as "a catalyst for the discussion and analysis of social responsibility issues" as they arose during financial decision making. He also helped plan an affirmative-action strategy for the finance group, and—working with colleagues in the various Cummins subsidiaries, including K2, Frigiking, and Fleetguard—was involved in "overall strategic business planning." In subsequent years, a complementary "rotation" system was implemented, whereby functional managers were brought into the central Corporation Action division for twelve to eighteen months of training.[96]

The Corporate Action division at Cummins began its life with some clear advantages. One lay in the nature of Cummins' markets: The Engine Company tended to deal with OEMs on a worldwide basis, and its agents therefore were somewhat buffered from the temptations and corrupting opportunities that afflicted companies doing more direct business in local markets. In other words, Cummins was more likely to be dealing with Ford on a proposed Middle Eastern deal than with any Middle Eastern governments involved.

But a more important strength derived from the fact that key Cummins executives—especially Schacht, Hackett, and Henderson—put their weight behind Corporate Action. John Hackett, in particular, pushed the company and its subsidiaries to take seriously the social responsibilities of business. In February 1974, for example, Hackett arranged a two-day meeting in Dallas between top Cummins executives and Frigiking's management. The session was to be led by Charles W. Powers, a Yale University faculty member who was then working with Cummins on issues of corporate responsibility. "I would like to deal with some of the broader social aspects of business management," Hackett explained, "as they affect both the company and the communities in which we are involved."[97]

Powers, co-author of a book (_The Ethical Investor_) that later served as the basis for the investment policies of numerous universities around the country, later took a leave from Yale and joined the Cummins Corporate Action staff. He recalls the indispensable influence of Irwin Miller and Henry Schacht:

> _Irwin and Hank really understood that if you said you wanted ethical practices in the corporation, then you really had to guarantee that someone wouldn't suffer a career disadvantage for raising questions about something that he or she thought was wrong. That was something that Hank really saw first, and that Irwin understood the importance of—figuring out how to administer that._

Through the Corporate Action group, Jim Joseph and his colleagues set out to create a "loose-tight" set of ethical norms. In other words, they first focused on creating clear, broad-brush policies at the corporate level, which were then subject to interpretation and specific application in all corporate functional areas. Beginning in 1976, however—in part because of the highly publicized misdeeds of once-admired corporations like 3M, Gulf, and Lockheed—these rules began to be collected, codified, and formally adopted by the company. As Henry Schacht explained in a memo to all of the corporation's officers:

> _It is not fair for the Company to promulgate general principles but leave the specifics to the "field personnel." By being vague, we place all the responsibility for marginal decisions on the person in the worst place to make the reasoned decision. . . . It is imperative, therefore, that the Company remove this burden from individuals by being very clear about what it expects._[98]

The risk in all of this was increased bureaucracy, and Cummins eventually proved that it was not immune to overkill.* Current managers recall with discomfort the "corporate social responsibility balance sheets" that they—and in some cases, their suppliers—were required to fill out. But even this cumbersome exercise had value. For example, Cummins learned to its chagrin that in many cases it was treating its suppliers shabbily. "That ended up moving Cummins more toward long-term partner relationships," recalls Jack Edwards, "that we later learned were the right way to do it anyway."

But the Corporate Action group understood that ethical behavior was a moving target, and it therefore tried to maintain a fundamental flexibility. For instance, the Cummins policy manual originally prohibited the payment of "expediting" fees—that is, small payments to the kinds of middle men who made things happen in underdeveloped countries. (A 10 percent payment to a middle man, for example, could ensure that one's household goods were delivered to the right place, on time.) After lengthy debate, the policy was changed to permit such payments. As Jack Edwards explains:

> We adopted what came to be called the "Irwin Miller Transparency Test." Mr. Miller said that if you were willing to explain to the local minister what you were doing, then it passed the transparency test. It's a matter of judging whether something could stand the light of day. And that phrase—the Irwin Miller Transparency Test—was very powerful for a lot of the international expatriates that I met when I first came to Cummins. It helped guide them through tough times.

One example was the case of a South American official from whom the Cummins representatives in that country badly needed an approval for the year's import quota. This key approval had been delayed again and again. Finally, the official invited the Cummins reps to his daughter's wedding—and made it clear that an appropriate wedding gift would be a new refrigerator. Such a gift far exceeded the twenty-five-dollar limit established by corporate policy, and the Cummins group puzzled over a response that would pass the Irwin Miller Transparency Test. Finally, they decided to make the gift—but only if it would be displayed at the wedding reception wrapped in bright blue Cummins gift-wrapping paper. The official agreed, and the gift was made.[99]

In the last third of the decade, Cummins ran one more unusual experiment in corporate social responsibility. Conducted by the Corporate Action division's "public policy group," this effort attempted to help the company decide where to invest its limited resources overseas. The group produced a series of "country reports," which tried to look ten years into the future and

---

*"The real risk," comments Irwin Miller, lies in creating a Department of Self-Righteousness. The most bureaucratic person in the world is someone who knows he's right."

answer key questions about the country's prospects. (The ten-year time frame was selected because experience had shown that it took at least a decade for an investment in a diesel-manufacturing plant to make a return.) The questions were:

- In that ten-year period, would Cummins be able to "treat the stakeholders for whom it is responsible (particularly its employees) in accordance with minimal Cummins' standards"?
- Would Cummins "have the opportunity to conduct a profitable business without engaging in activities which violated Cummins' ethical practices policy"?
- Would Cummins "make a contribution to the host country's development process"?[100]

The effort was headed by Powers, who succeeded Joseph in 1977 when the latter left to become Undersecretary of the Interior. In its first five years, the group studied nineteen separate countries or regions. Of course, others within the company, most notably the international group, had strong opinions about these same topics, and the "country reports" did not always carry the day. Nevertheless, they played a key role in the company's decision to invest in South Korea, rather than the Philippines; and in dissuading Cummins from pursuing a potentially lucrative manufacturing opportunity in apartheid-divided South Africa in the late 1970s.[101]

"We compete on a straight commercial basis," Henry Schacht told attenders of the 1975 Cummins planning conference. "If something more is required, we're not interested."[102] This statement was true, as far as it went. But Cummins, during this critical period of rule setting and self-definition, ranged far beyond a "straight commercial basis" in its dealings at home and abroad. It asked broad questions, and set extremely high standards for itself and its employees. It legitimized the finding of problems, rather than their concealment. By example, it encouraged other corporations to behave similarly, and thereby had a disproportionate impact on the landscape of corporate behavior in the United States. ("Cummins has really plowed the first ground in this field," one admiring CEO wrote to Henry Schacht, as he asked for permission to "borrow" Jim Joseph to set up a similar program at his own company.)[103] By bringing new kinds of people into the dialogue about corporate citizenship, Cummins learned to speak and act in new ways.

Escaping a decade

How to do business: This was the key question that Cummins struggled to answer in the 1970s. The company enjoyed some spectacularly profitable years toward the end of the decade, racking up a record $58.6 million in net earnings in 1976, more than twice as much as the previous record, set in 1973. It then set another record in 1977 ($67 million), and came close again in 1978 ($64.4 million).[104]

But the managers at Cummins were not sanguine. Their diversification strategy for the 1970s had failed. It was a victim of the booming heavy-duty truck market in the first half of the decade, which had sent operations head Jim Henderson scrambling around the globe in search of new capacity. The Walesboro, Charleston, Daventry, Jamestown, and Seymour plants, all built or acquired between 1972 and 1975, collectively comprised more than 2.9 million square feet.

As a result of booming demand and a market-leading product—the fuel-efficient Big Cam II—Cummins arrived at the end of the 1970s still overdependent on its heavy-duty engine sales. The domestic heavy-duty market had rebounded after the 1975 rout: to 119,568 units in 1976, to 169,134 units in 1977, to 202,640 in 1978, and to more than 215,000 in 1979. But by 1979, hints of impending recession again were evident, and Cummins was worried. On the one hand, it was satisfying to command more than 40 percent of the domestic heavy-duty market.[105] On the other hand, it was scary to be so dependent on that highly cyclical market.

Of the 160,000 engines that Cummins sold worldwide in 1979, 124,000 were NHs.[106] Most of the remainder consisted of small V engines and kits produced at Darlington. But both the NH and the small V, Cummins knew, were aging technologies. Someday—probably sooner rather than later—Cummins would have to step away from these engines. Developments at the national level, with the government making ominous noises about the alleged carcinogenicity of diesel particulates, suggested that entirely new technologies might be needed soon. Although Cummins had greatly improved its technological skills in the 1970s and made significant progress toward medium-duty and small ("Rainbow") engines, it still had no viable replacement technologies.

"How to do business" also involved increasingly complex issues of corporate citizenship, as Cummins became a significant force in more and more communities around the world. Cummins in the 1970s invented a series of policies and public postures that effectively protected it from the kinds of embarrassments that beset other U.S. multinationals in this period—and, almost inadvertently, showed other companies how they might "do well by doing good."

One of the most important transitions of the 1970s went almost unheralded. On February 8, 1977, the Cummins board of directors picked the company's CEO, Henry B. Schacht, to be its new chairman; and it elected James A. Henderson as the new president of the company. J. Irwin Miller—who had served as chairman of the Cummins board since 1951—was named chairman of the executive and finance committees.[107]

Of course, Miller remained intimately involved in the affairs of the company. He still exercised his time-tested means of gathering information and influencing events: inviting people to his Washington Street office for chats, having lunch with senior managers, and sending carefully worded memos to selected individuals around the company. But the tone of these communications began to change. They were still insightful, articulate, challenging, sometimes funny and sometimes barbed; but they were increasingly benedictory. The opening and closing paragraphs from one long memo—written to Schacht and Henderson in October 1977—make the point:

> *Here comes another one of my "view with alarm" memos. It is written, not feeling that you are unaware, but maybe a) to make me feel better, and b) to encourage you to think about doing sooner what you will probably do later. . . .*
>
> *Here endeth the memo. Bear this in mind: 1) You know more about current business than I do. 2) You are running the company and will make the decisions. 3) This memo reflects my own regret that I almost always over-thought and took too long to do the obvious. As a result I cost Cummins millions of unnecessary profit dollars.*[108]

In the decade to come, Schacht and Henderson would not have the luxury of overthinking, or taking too long to do the obvious.

9 | Betting the Company, 1979–1985

BY THE END OF THE 1970S, it was clear to the managers and workers of the Cummins Engine Company that a new era had dawned—for the U.S. economy, as well as for the company. The glory days of robust postwar economic expansion were over, supplanted by instability, uncertainty, and stagflation. For Cummins, as for many other U.S.-based manufacturers, the happy combination of stability and rapid growth had given way to uncertain markets and new constraints.

As the new decade approached, Cummins' managers focused their attention on a sweeping plan to restructure and reposition the corporation for long-term competitiveness. This drama, played out over several years, would be the crowning achievement of the administration of chairman/CEO Henry Schacht and president/COO Jim Henderson, whose symbiotic working partnership now had to perform under new kinds of pressure. But because the restructuring demanded huge infusions of new capital and a formidable reorientation of manufacturing and marketing, it would leave the company vulnerable until its completion several years hence. Even so, Schacht and Henderson were convinced that Cummins required no less. The company's long-standing dilemma—how to grow beyond the nearly saturated U.S. market for heavy automotive diesels—had become acute.

Cummins became a multibillion-dollar corporation in the 1980s, six decades removed and a world apart from the crude machine shop crammed into a shed alongside the Cerealine Building in the 1920s. But in some ways, the U.S. economy in the rough-and-tumble 1980s was reminiscent of the pro-business "Roaring Twenties"—including the stock market crashes that punctuated the latter half of both decades. For Cummins, remaining independent seemed no less precarious, and staying competitive no less daunting, than in its founding decade.

The plan and the products

"It tells neater than it was. We sort of packaged it in a way that makes the telling useful." Henry Schacht, reflecting on events that occurred more than a decade earlier, tried to convey the complexities of a defining era—in the history of the Cummins Engine Company and in his own career—events that still live vividly in his mind. The subject in question was the massive new corporate strategy and structure that Schacht engineered and launched with President Jim Henderson and other key executives. ("You've got to understand, it was 'we,' not 'me,'" he insisted.) So monumental was this new strategic direction that it remains the crucial moment in the company's modern history. But as Schacht cautioned in his remark about neatness, the story of the restructuring (as it was *later* termed)—its genesis, its execution, and its consequences—took on linearity and clarity only in retrospect.

The passage of time accomplished much of this, condensing events and washing out details and subtleties. But some of the logic and clarity also was infused along the way: by Schacht, who became a vocal spokesman for the plan in the business press; by Jim Henderson and others responsible for operations, who had to explain the company to itself; by the company's financial experts, who tried to convince the investment community that it should support such a drastic set of moves; by labor negotiators, who had to broker massive layoffs with the least possible pain and damage; and by public-relations staffers, who tried to reassure one group of stakeholders after another that Cummins would survive the decade.

Even when the role of chance and the complexity of the truth are acknowledged, it remains clear that *something* happened at Cummins— beginning in 1979 and gaining momentum thereafter—that was tangible, premeditated, broad-minded, risky, and enormously important. Its genesis lay far in the past, when postwar managers began to envision the eventual saturation of the heavy automotive diesel market; but also in the recent past, when market shifts and trucking deregulation overturned short-term expectations. Thus, the restructuring was animated by contemporary concerns, yet was fundamentally a long-term answer to a long-standing dilemma.

In spite of Cummins' rapid growth in the late 1970s, the view from 1979 was murky. The central dilemma of the period was the future of the company's core business. Cummins had embarked on a gigantic expansion of its heavy-duty engine manufacturing capacity in the 1970s, but nevertheless had seen its market share steadily decline, due mainly to its inability to meet demand. From its 49.3 percent of the Class 7 and Class 8 market in 1976, Cummins slid to 39.3 percent—about the same as depression-worn 1975—in 1979.[1] "We were back on allocation," Jim Henderson recalls, "and we simply couldn't keep up. As a result, we were bringing other competitors on, and we were really concerned."

Meanwhile, the dieselization of the heavy-duty market had increased from 81.2 percent in 1970 to 94.9 percent in 1979. This suggested that future growth in Cummins' traditional markets might have to come at the expense of competitors—a far more difficult task than scooping up new entrants into a growing market.[2]

Inflation, the most virulent economic virus of the 1970s, still raged. Henry Schacht recently had called inflation "the nation's most serious problem" in a letter to a Washington official.[3] But in the previous decade, almost every conceivable anti-inflation tool had been tried, to no avail. Wage and price controls implemented on the national level in June 1973 merely created pent-up demand that put upward pressure on prices. In 1974, after the price controls were relaxed, Cummins raised its engine prices four times—in April, June, October, and December—for an average cumulative price increase of 25.5 percent in one year. Double-digit price increases were the rule, rather than the exception, for the remainder of the decade.[4]

Meanwhile, Cummins was contemplating a grim scenario at the other end of the inflation spectrum. As Henry Schacht recalls:

> *As we looked at the world in front of us, we saw that this wild inflation had to stop. In order for it to stop, we would probably have to go through a period of deflation. There was a big debate in the industry as to whether this market was going to rocket right on through to 250,000 units. We were almost alone in the industry in saying, "No, no; this thing is going to plateau."*

At the end of the 1970s, Cummins' return on investment again was declining (from a high of 22 percent in 1976, the post-recession year, down to 12.8 percent in 1979). Material costs were a key factor, as were ever-higher wage rates. In 1978, for example, Cummins agreed to a one-year, 10 percent raise (plus cost-of-living adjustments) for its two largest unions.[5] Engine prices, although rising steadily, were not keeping pace with rising costs.

Regulation was another complicating factor. Despite Cummins' effective cultivation of regulators in Washington, California, and elsewhere, things could and did go wrong. An emission-control device attached to one Cummins engine in 1978 caused that engine to leak fuel, which contributed to a 16 percent increase in warranty costs in that year.[6] More ominous was the EPA's new and mostly unanticipated focus on the alleged cancer-causing nature of diesel particulates. "The whole question of carcinogenicity," Henry Schacht told a group of analysts and investors in April 1979, "takes our attention hourly."[7]

Along with the uncertainties of regulation were those wrought by the coming of trucking industry deregulation. Stagflation was inspiring some surprising macroeconomic policies. Conservative Republican Richard Nixon had imposed wage and price controls in the early 1970s; and now liberal Democratic president Jimmy Carter was presiding over a wave of industry deregulation, hoping the relaxation of controls would spur investment, promote efficiency, and break the stagflation stranglehold. Much of the earliest and most important federal legislation was aimed at industries in the transportation sector: airlines (the Airline Deregulation Act of 1978); railroads (the Staggers Act of 1980); and trucking (the Motor Carrier Act of 1980).

It was easy to predict that deregulation would reshape these industries, but tough to know exactly how. In the case of trucking, Cummins and other industry interests could only speculate. The consensus on the Cummins board in 1979 was that deregulation would create "short-term dislocations" and alter the company's customer mix, yet probably not bring "any drastic long-term change in primary demand for our trucks." But once enacted after the election of 1980, trucking deregulation became a source of considerable uncertainty, more than Cummins' managers anticipated.[8]

None of these challenges arose in a vacuum. Any costs—whether government-induced or otherwise—that hit Cummins harder than its competitors could result in a loss of market share; and the field of Cummins competitors was growing larger and stronger. Between 1972 and 1979, Caterpillar Tractor Co. (Peoria, Illinois) invested more than $1 billion to design new diesels and to quadruple its diesel-manufacturing capacity. An alliance with Ford in the early 1970s had given Caterpillar a 50 percent share of the medium-duty truck market; and in 1978 Cat completed a plant capable of producing 70,000 medium-duty engines per year. Meanwhile, Cat was pitching aggressively to the major heavy-duty OEMs. PACCAR, one of Cummins' key customers, let Cummins know that it considered Cat to be a "coming force" in the diesel industry, and that it was reducing Cummins' share of the PACCAR heavy-duty business to increase Cat's.[9]

International Harvester—then Cummins' single biggest customer—also was making competitive noises. It planned to experiment with selling "loose" mid-range engines to Detroit, and if that effort succeeded, to undertake a major plant expansion. "We are going to be marketing diesel engines to people we have never marketed to before," an IH vice president told *Business Week*. Longtime Cummins rival Detroit Diesel Allison recently had abandoned its outmoded two-cycle technology and invested $200 million in a new plant to produce an 8.2-liter, 200 hp engine. And overseas, the British-

based Perkins had announced plans to double its worldwide diesel manufacturing capacity by the year 1985, thereby tightening its grip on the lower end
of the market.[10]

These factors—especially the near-saturation of the heavy diesel market
and stagflation—were forcing Cummins to fight harder and harder to keep
growing. In many ways the situation was the opposite of the expansionary
days after World War II, when Cummins rode the crest of a multiplier, whereby each percentage increase in GNP yielded two points of industrial production and, in turn, three points of diesel engine growth. Now, recalls Henry
Schacht, "it took three units of GNP to get one and a half of industrial production, and one unit of diesel engine growth."

Making matters worse, Cummins managers had discovered a parallel—
and equally scary—internal multiplier effect that also moved in the wrong
direction. In the late 1970s, managers looked hard at costs and expenses to
understand why the company's financial performance seemed so sensitive to
changes in volume. The conclusion, presented at the spring 1978 Planning
Conference, was that Cummins was overburdened by fixed costs. (A key finding: "Only half of our total costs and expense are truly variable.") As a result,
changes in sales volume were amplified at the bottom line: A 5 percent swing
in revenues, for instance, could knock down profits by 20 percent.[11]

As Schacht recalls the grim outlook, "In the equation, nothing worked as
we looked forward. The slower growth, increased competition, more costs,
more international competition, overcapacity pricing for the first time, and
this huge new EPA demand that was going to generate much larger requirements—so we had no growth available to us."

And so the company set out to transform itself. The plan originated from
within. By the 1970s, executives at large U.S. industrial firms regularly relied
on outside management consultants—McKinsey & Company, the Boston
Consulting Group, and others—for strategic planning.[12] Cummins turned to
McKinsey for limited kinds of advice, in this instance. But for the most part,
Schacht, Henderson, and Hackett took on the task themselves, spending
"enormous amounts of time [recalls Hackett] just thinking about strategy and
outlining things on the blackboard."

It was a time to reconsider fundamental issues. The path of least resistance—to continue on course—was rejected outright. True, Cummins' market share was large enough, and its reputation strong enough, to allow shareholders to "harvest" the benefits of previous investments for years, perhaps
decades. But the company's top managers were convinced that the constrict-
ing forces of the 1970s and 1980s eventually would strangle the company if
it stayed on its present course.

A second possibility was for Cummins to diversify into unrelated businesses in pursuit of greater growth and higher profits. Such a conglomerate strate-

gy would harken back to the company's early 1970s "three-legged strategy," although it would require much larger investments. This alternative was considered seriously, but ultimately was rejected. It was a critical juncture in the company's history. Scores of American companies pursued unrelated diversification in the 1970s and 1980s, in spite of the conglomerate era's tainted reputation. But Cummins was determined to capitalize on its long-cultivated know-how in research, production, and marketing—a process Hackett called "leveraging our knowledge and experience."

According to the eminent business historian Alfred Chandler, the most successful strategy for large industrial corporations throughout history has been "building organizational capabilities" in key functional areas.[13] The central tenet can be summarized simply: Learn your business, stay in it (or in closely related fields), and compete fiercely. To enable Cummins to compete fiercely, Schacht and his collaborators were prepared to invest aggressively. But their estimation of the new capital investment needed to make the new strategy succeed was unprecedented, almost staggering: more than $1 billion. At the time, the company had a total book value of $1.1 billion, and a total market value of only $240 million!

The central strategic dilemma facing Schacht and his colleagues—the maturation of the company's core business, heavy-duty automotive diesels—inspired a two-part response. Each part depended on new technology, and reflected the strong conviction among the company's executives that the 1980s would be "an era of scarce, high-priced petroleum."[14]

More than any other single factor, the expectation that high energy prices would climb even higher was central to the new strategy. Schacht thought diesel-fuel prices might climb from $1.10 to $5.00 a gallon during the 1980s.[15] This kind of assumption was widespread at the end of the 1970s. The "energy crisis" of 1973 had driven up the price of oil fourfold, with OPEC pegging the crude barrel price at $11.65. Now, in the latter months of 1979, a second oil panic swept the globe, driving crude prices up to $26 per barrel, and convincing millions of Americans that the age of cheap energy was gone forever.[16]

For Cummins, steeper prices at the pump promised to open new markets by augmenting the diesel engine's operating cost advantage, and by pushing the technology into applications previously served by gasoline engines and older diesels. Even the more efficient diesel, however, would feel the pinch of expensive petroleum, and over the long run—reasoned Cummins' managers—this pressure would transform the industry. The marketplace increasingly would favor makers of lighter, more compact, fuel-efficient models over producers of fuel-guzzling behemoths. Europe seemed to prove the case. The birthplace of the internal combustion engine also was burdened by some of the world's highest petroleum prices, and as a result its makers of cars, trucks, and engines turned out models that were smaller and more efficient than those produced in America.

Yet like the rest of the world, Europeans needed to haul heavy loads over great distances by truck. All of this led Cummins' strategic planners to envision a family of European-style ten-liter engines. These were aimed initially at markets in Europe—especially England, where Cummins enjoyed commercial success and goodwill. But the company had much longer-term aspirations for the new engine family: as a global product for an energy-scarce world.

The second prong of the new strategy rested on the same assumptions as the first, plus more. The company laid plans to launch two new families of medium and small engines, serving Classes 3 through 6. Compact and efficient like their ten-liter cousins, these products anticipated the same future energy scenario. With its new Class 6 models, Cummins finally would be able to compete in the vast market for medium-range automotive engines. There, OEMs were snapping up 400,000 diesels a year, twice the number sold in Class 7 and Class 8 *combined*. None of these midrange engines—used in delivery and other trucks but also a wide variety of nonautomotive applications—currently were made by Cummins.[17]

Meanwhile, in the lower-horsepower ranges (Classes 3–5), Cummins would move into markets still overwhelmingly dominated by nondiesel power sources. Again, the potent combination of high energy prices and more efficient diesel technologies presumably would open vast new markets. Although only a few tens of thousands of diesel engines were sold per year in each of these classes, Cummins expected those numbers to increase dramatically in the next decade or so.

Two other important strategic considerations molded the company's plans: a strong desire to expand international manufacturing and sales and a push to cultivate nonautomotive markets. These goals were fundamentally intertwined with, and dependent upon, the new engine programs. If the new engine families proved successful, Cummins would increase its presence outside U.S. borders both as a supplier and—a key component of the long-range plan—as a manufacturer. And since the variety of diesel applications was greater in the lower horsepower ranges, the company's sales to nonautomotive customers would grow hand-in-hand with sales of smaller engines. This greater market diversity and balance would help to alleviate the cyclicality that had plagued the company for so long.

So it all came back to technology—and, of course, money. On the financial side, the timing might have been better. In fact, one of the more daring aspects of the restructuring was that it was deliberately launched at a time when the company's analysts predicted—correctly, as it turned out—the onset of a national economic depression. Such conditions might be helpful to a degree; in hard times, manufacturing facilities often can be had cheaply, and capital markets can loosen. But on balance, Cummins surely would have preferred to launch the most ambitious capital investment program in its history during flush times, when plants were humming at capacity, order sheets were backed up, and inventories lean. It moved ahead at this less-than-propitious moment because there simply seemed to be no time to delay.

As for the necessary new technology, the company hardly was starting from scratch. Experimental engineering efforts in the 1970s had yielded some promising designs, most notably the clean-sheet Rainbow series. Some of these technologies had reached the prototype stage, but none was advanced to anywhere near the production stage. The restructuring would provide the occasion. Even with this running start, however, Cummins was reluctant—and probably unprepared—to assume technological and financial burdens of this scale on its own.

Therefore, as talk and speculation increasingly turned to action in the late 1970s, Cummins scrambled to find resources to draw upon. Assuming it could raise the capital (a hefty $1 billion assumption), the next question was: What was the best way to launch the new engine families, to diversify markets, and to grow in foreign markets? Internally? Or through acquisitions? Or perhaps joint ventures? Would joint efforts be aimed at raising capital, developing technology, sharing markets, or some combination of these? And how much independence was Cummins prepared to bargain away in its quest for a more secure long-term future?

In seeking answers to this complex nexus of questions in the late 1970s and early 1980s, Schacht, Henderson, Hackett, and other key executives were drawn into a dizzying array of decisions and negotiations. The quickest and surest path to advanced products and broader markets was far from obvious. But by 1980, most of the possibilities had fallen away, leaving Cummins to launch its ten-liter engines alone, and its lower-horsepower engine families with a sole partner.

The European-style L10

The new engine families commercialized by Cummins in the early 1980s spanned the horsepower range from 50 to 290. The largest was the ten-liter—designated the "L10" before its introduction—which traced its origins back to the experimental Blue engine (from the mid-1970s Rainbow series). With the Rainbows, recalls Schacht, Cummins was "starting with ten-liter and moving south," that is, down the horsepower scale toward smaller models. In this spectrum, the L10 family (230–290 hp) was created to fill an important market niche. With the K relegated mainly to heavy-duty industrial use, and with the top end of the heavy-duty automotive business served by the NH, there was need for a lighter, more compact engine to power the kind of cargo trucks common throughout Europe.*

---

*According to Irwin Miller, many at Cummins thought the L10 might prove to be the successor to the NH engine. But slowing down the NH for emissions purposes once again rescued the old stalwart from oblivion.

The L10's main commercial target was the United Kingdom, where Cummins was competing well. Shotts' sales there had grown fourfold between 1970 and 1977, while before-tax profits surged from $3.4 million to $7.8 million. Competition on the Continent—where more OEMs were vertically integrated—was tougher. Indeed, with its new European-style heavy engine, Cummins would go head-to-head with such industry stalwarts as Daimler-Benz, Volvo, DAF, and Renault.[18]

Nor did the company propose to neglect the U.S. market. At the lower end of the L10 family's range—below 270 hp—it would compete with Mack and Detroit Diesel, which each commanded larger domestic market shares. But even within Cummins, some doubted that the L10 would find a home stateside. Henry Schacht remembers the woeful prediction of one company manager: "U.S. volumes for the ten-liter will be zero. We're going to use fourteen-liter engines forever." To most, however, the ten-liter seemed a reasonable gambit for an age of scarce energy.

The L10 family shared some fundamental principles with the smaller engine families that were born in the same historical circumstances. To begin with, Cummins engineers steered away from V-engine configurations and returned to in-line designs. By this time, they better understood some of the technical weaknesses that had hobbled the V-engine family. V engines were more difficult to turbocharge than in-lines, for instance, because in the V engine each crank pin was shared by two connecting rods. In-lines also offered more room to accommodate bearings.[19]

These and similar design decisions had enormous implications not only for engine performance and reliability but also for production and rebuild costs—the second key consideration in the new engine launches of the early 1980s. Phil Jones continued to hammer away on this issue, just as he had done at the earlier experimental stage. The burden of proof now fell to those advocating more parts and more complex designs when fewer and simpler might do.[20]

One of the chief accomplishments of the L10's design was to pack more power into a much smaller space. With not much less displacement than the NT, the L10 weighed only two-thirds as much. This was accomplished by reducing the number of parts, but also redesigning and reconfiguring many of those that remained.[21] Thanks to new methods and technologies, the engine design and development process was far less hit-or-miss than it had been in early eras. Many of these (structural design and simulation, finite element methods, and combustion simulation) were techniques for pre-design and modeling that allowed engineers to simulate the performance characteristics of pre-prototype designs. "[We did] a lot of paper studies and analysis like that before going into hardware," recalls Nelson. And by accelerating the pace of development, such methods helped in the battle to hold down costs.

As R&E head Bill Schwab recalls: "We were able to take the L10 from a clean sheet of paper, design it, get the prototypes made, and get the first one on test in less than a year. Within thirty days, we had met our performance goals—thanks to diesel cycle simulation" and other new analytical methods.

Early working models of the L10 were tested, fittingly enough, in Europe beginning in 1978. In Dublin, one of the city's public transport buses was outfitted with an L10 for its daily rounds. Meanwhile, Cummins representatives began to canvass European OEMs. By the middle of 1979, development work had progressed far enough—with the regular machining of parts and twenty or so prototypes—for a public announcement of the L10.[22]

Back at home, the focus shifted to manufacturing. The former office furniture plant at Jamestown, New York, which Cummins took over in 1974, was selected to become the first L10 factory. Technical refinements to the L10 continued throughout the next three years, as the plant was equipped for production. It gradually became clear to Cummins' marketers that the L10 had a much larger domestic market than originally anticipated—for example, in areas where vehicle weight limits made the NH engine uncompetitive.

Compared with the simultaneous launching of the company's other two engine families—the new, lower-horsepower models—the L10 project seemed relatively straightforward. For one thing, although the L10 was technically innovative for Cummins, it was less of a departure than the high-volume smaller engines launched at the same time. More significantly, the design, production, and marketing of the L10—launched commercially in 1982—were carried out solely under Cummins' control.

The Case-Cummins Joint Venture

As it turned out, however, Cummins could not retain complete control of its smaller engine projects. Finance was the compelling reason. As Jim Henderson recalls, "When we did the numbers, we couldn't afford it. There just wasn't any way we could afford that kind of investment"—that is, the investment needed to simultaneously launch L10s *and* new smaller engine lines. "So we had pretty well concluded that we were going to need some sort of alliance."[23]

Cummins executives were looking hard for such an alliance in 1978, by which time the L10 had reached the road-testing stage. This second major component of the new corporate strategy was both riskier—since Cummins was a neophyte in the mid-range diesel business—and, if expectations about the future proved to be true, more essential to the company's long-term health. So there was considerable pressure to find a way to break into the market *quickly*, yet without bankrupting the company or bringing out inferior products.

In the mid-1960s, Henderson had speculated that Cummins eventually would enter the small diesel business. "And I remember thinking," recalls Schacht, "'That makes a lot of sense.'"[24] By the mid-1970s, the idea gained currency—and increasingly was linked with the notion of some kind of partnership. In particular, Cummins hoped to buy or join with a company that possessed a healthy internal market for mid-range engines, such as a vertically integrated manufacturer of agricultural or industrial equipment.

One candidate was Perkins, now owned by Massey-Ferguson. The chief strategist at Massey-Ferguson was Vic Rice, whom Henry Schacht had hired away from Ford when Schacht was posted in London. In an effort to raise capital for Massey-Ferguson's equipment business, Rice offered to sell Perkins to Cummins. Schacht was intrigued with the notion of using cash flow from Perkins to fund a small-engine program. But before the talk turned to action, the guard changed at Perkins, and so did the options. In mid-1978, Conrad Black, a Canadian investor who also controlled Argus, became chairman of Massey-Ferguson. Black made Rice the head of Perkins, but once in power Rice reversed his position on selling to Cummins. Even so, Schacht would continue to pursue other options with Black related to small engines.[25]

Cummins looked to many of its key customers as potential partners. As Hackett later recorded, "Ford was twice offered an opportunity to invest in the Small Engine Project," but declined the first time for "a better deal" from Detroit Diesel, the second because of "inadequate capital." GMC was "offered the same deal as Ford," but declined. International Harvester was planning its own foray into the small engine business. Mack and Freightliner were not seen as large enough customers for the new line. Only PACCAR was under consideration for some kind of financial collaboration. There was, at least, a secondary advantage in speaking with all of the major domestic OEMs; as Hackett pointed out: "No one can claim mistreatment or lack of opportunity."[26]

Ford came through with a license agreement in the summer of 1979. Cummins signed an interim agreement with the Detroit giant in May to develop an extremely lightweight, turbocharged diesel for automobiles. Ford agreed to pay development fees and—if the engines were incorporated into some if its heavier passenger cars—licensing fees. The potential for Cummins, of course, was enormous, but only if Ford or other leading automakers moved ahead with plans to dieselize some of their heaviest models. That decision, in turn, depended on environmental regulators. As Schacht put it succinctly, massive investment by the Big Three in dieselization "hangs solely on the thread of legislation."[27]

The project never moved forward. The relationship began on a rocky note, at least from Cummins' perspective. "We have had some confusion on the Ford engine project," Schacht reported after the first month. "Ford has run a lot of people down here [and] seems to be thinking at middle management levels that they control the design." And the draft contract presented by Ford seemed far from Cummins' own vision of the future relationship. But the erupting controversy over diesel emissions at this time, and the auto industry's ultimate retreat from plans to dieselize big cars, spelled the death knell for this and similar agreements. Cummins never finalized its 1979 development pact with Ford.

Meanwhile, Schacht was negotiating with European OEMs—especially Daimler-Benz (DB) and Fiat—for another means of moving forward Cummins' strategy. A deal with one of these powerful world competitors might accomplish several ends, at minimum softening the blow if and when DB or Fiat followed through with plans to expand in the U.S. market. During a meeting in the fall of 1979, Schacht and Gerhard Prinz (chairman of DB) spoke of a technology and market-sharing arrangement that would open Europe more to Cummins and the United States to the German diesel maker. But the two executives also talked about a possible Daimler-Benz takeover of Cummins. To this notion, Schacht responded with the oblique remark that "we were looking for both volume and financing."

In the midst of this confusion came a bolt from the blue. One day—probably in mid to late 1977—a small group of Cummins marketers were meeting in the Tech Center's "Blue Room" with representatives from J. I. Case of Racine, Wisconsin. Case, a leading world producer of agricultural and light construction equipment, long had made its own engines. The goal of the Cummins marketers was to persuade Case to start taking a Cummins product—any Cummins product—into their line of offerings.

Jim Farrar, who headed the Cummins team, remembers making a very general pitch to the Case representatives, who included the company's new chairman and CEO, Thomas J. Guendel. The pitch was necessarily general, Farrar recalls, because Cummins did not have an engine that was small enough for most of Case's applications. One possibility was that Case would take the nearly obsolete Cummins V engine—the smallest engine then made by the Engine Company. But that was a remote possibility, at best. "So we presented this story about how good we were," says Farrar, "and about how we were an independent manufacturer, and about how we could do all these great things."[28]

At one point, Guendel turned to Jim Henderson—who was in the room because the ranking marketing executive, Marion Dietrich, was recovering from a recent heart attack—and asked if he could speak privately with him. In the hall, Guendel sketched out a dilemma. His company, he explained, needed new engine lines that it did not want to develop itself, given the growing competitiveness and technological sophistication of the diesel engine business. Would Cummins be interested in jointly developing new engine models that Case could install in its equipment, and that Cummins could market to OEMs?

Henderson agreed immediately, and soon rejoined his colleagues in the Blue Room. "Jim came back in the room," says Farrar, "and told us what had happened. We said, 'Well, that was absolutely the right thing to say, Jim.'"

The scale and scope of Case's operations made it an attractive potential partner for Cummins. Case was a well-established company with a venerable history. Founded in 1844 (as the Racine Threshing Machine Works), it diversified into a broader range of mechanized agricultural equipment in the late nineteenth century. In 1880, the firm was incorporated for $1 million and renamed J. I. Case Threshing Machine Company—capitalized at $1 million. With a budding market for its gasoline tractors, Case moved into construction equipment in 1912 and bought a leading maker of harvesting, tillage, and haying equipment (Emerson-Brantingham of Rockville, Illinois) in 1928. It emerged as the world's leading producer of steam tractor engines and grain threshers. In 1967, Case was acquired (along with automotive partsmaker Walker Manufacturing, also of Racine) by Houston-based Tenneco. But its mammoth tractor-making operations were vertically integrated, and Cummins had been unable to displace Case engines in Case tractors with its own.[29]

From Cummins' perspective, the Case proposal promised to bring two key assets to the table: capital and a large internal (captive) market for engines. The latter was crucial, for as Cummins understood the small engine business, the only way to make money was to boost production to high levels—and quickly. For its part, Cummins would supply the other half of the capital requirements, and take primary responsibility for technological development.

Case and Cummins signed a preliminary "study and design" agreement on March 12, 1979. This provided an umbrella for beginning joint research. The research and engineering needed to create the new product lines were carried out by a new "Case/Cummins Engineering Group," staffed primarily with Cummins engineers. Although ostensibly independent from Cummins, the organization was housed in the Cummins Small Engine Development Center at 14th and Hutchins in Columbus, and relied on Cummins for certain kinds of technological support, such as computer programming, modal analysis, materials development, noise testing, and fuels and lubricants.[30] Still, the group's relative isolation from the Tech Center carried forward the Rainbow engine approach to innovation. On matters of basic design and engineering, Cummins and Case wanted the engineering team unhindered by convention.

The group worked quickly. The first team of about twenty engineers set to work in April 1979, apparently beginning with the fundamentals of the Red engine (described in Chapter 8) and building new elements into that foundation. Certain criteria were non-negotiable: The engine had to be a low-cost product, in order to compete with existing Perkins products. This meant that the number of options on the engine (flywheel housings, turbocharger position, and so on) had to be strictly limited. For obvious reasons, Case wanted the engine to be small enough along all dimensions to fit into existing Case products, including at least some of the equipment already in the field that might return for repowering.

Other design issues were the subject of intense debate. For decades, Cummins had maintained that the fuel system was the heart of its product, and a key differentiator between Cummins products and those of competitors. Now, due to cost constraints and technical risks—and over the strong objections of Jim Henderson, among others—Cummins decided to purchase an off-the-shelf Bosch fuel system. The decision to design cylinder liners out of at least one engine was equally controversial: Could it really be a "Cummins" engine without cylinder liners?

A prototype "Family I" engine—which became the B engine—ran for the first time in early 1983, and was the first production engine to come off the line on July 1.[31] Debate about "Family II"—later named the C engine—continued throughout this period. While engineers at both Case and Cummins debated technical matters, the Cummins marketing group lobbied for the needs of a larger market. Out of these discussions, Jim Farrar recalls, two engine families were born:

> *We in the various line marketing organizations, as well as our distributors, were out there trying to figure out the kinds of products that were going to be needed, because there was a debate about whether the C series should be a V-8 version of the in-line B series. And the work that was done both in the planning and line marketing organizations at Cummins concluded that it should not. Around 200 horsepower, the whole character of the engine is changing, and you need to put in replaceable liners, and make it much more heavy-duty than the B. So that's what caused there to be two separate products, as opposed to a B with a V-8 derivative.*

By the time the C prototype was cranked to life two years later, the midrange-engine engineering team had grown from 20 to more than 180. It occupied four refurbished buildings at the site, and used five test cells relocated from Cummins' pre-1968 research center (later augmented by eleven more from the same source).

Meanwhile, Cummins and Case continued to work toward a broader arrangement. ("I spent an awful lot of my life from 1978 to 1980 negotiating the joint venture with Case," John Hackett recalls.) On October 16, 1980, Cummins and Case signed an agreement that created the Consolidated Diesel Corporation (CDC), a jointly financed venture that would design and manufacture two new families of engines ranging from 40 to 250 hp.

For Cummins, the joint venture met two essential needs. It secured half the investment capital for an operation that was estimated to cost approximately $350 million—this at a time when the L10 and N14 were consuming even larger sums. And it provided a built-in outlet for roughly half the total planned output of the venture. Both sides knew there were significant economies of scale to be captured in the business of manufacturing smaller, simpler, lower-cost-per-horsepower engines—but also high penalties for falling below the higher break-even point. Even by assiduously cultivating new markets, Cummins could not reasonably hope to sell 150,000 or so medium and medium-heavy engines per year by the late 1980s on its own.

Case faced a similar set of constraints. Its internal appetite for tractor engines in this horsepower range was not ample enough to warrant profitable production levels; and under such conditions Case, too, was reluctant to make the necessary investment on its own. Added to this, Case predicted a trend toward engine outsourcing by OEMs as products became more sophisticated, and accordingly saw a need for design and manufacturing help from a technical leader such as Cummins.

The general terms of the deal spoke to these overlapping and complementary aims. Case and Cummins each held an option to purchase up to half the engines produced by CDC, the former for its large tractors and construction equipment, the latter for a range of possible applications, including light and medium trucks, off-highway and industrial equipment, gensets, and marine applications. To protect Cummins' turf—and identity—as an independent producer, Case agreed not to market loose engines; its portion of CDC output had to be used internally. Finally, if either parent company consumed less than its half portion, the other partner could buy the unused inventory at transfer cost.

Seemingly straightforward in its key provisions, this arrangement produced some complexities and points of conflict in operation. But these were minor compared with the challenges involved in developing, producing, and selling the new engine families. To begin with, the project needed a home. Work toward that end had been ongoing from the time Case and Cummins signed their preliminary agreement. By the summer of 1979 the search for a manufacturing site had narrowed to three: Madison, Indiana; Quincy, Illinois; and Whitakers, North Carolina. The Quincy site, an 850,000-square-foot former Motorola plant, was selected, then rejected (although the site was purchased in mid-1980 for $4.8 million). By this time the project's lack of a permanent home, according to one insider, was creating "a serious morale problem."[32]

An intensive search in early 1980 encompassed locales in a dozen states. Case looked to the upper plains states, while Cummins preferred locales east of the Mississippi, a region recommended by the Department of Energy for its long-term energy outlook.[33] Cummins also scrutinized factors such as the cooperativeness of state and local governments, the quality of school systems, and demographic conditions. "One of the things that we were interested in," Dick Stoner recalls telling the governors of Tennessee and North Carolina, "was finding a community where we could work to improve the situation of the blacks. We expected blacks and whites to work together—on the floor, in the office, and all the way through. We wanted an educational system that would accept them both."

Cummins chose North Carolina, drawing on its existing stock of real estate for a facility that could be converted and expanded. A few years earlier, while looking for additional space to manufacture turbochargers, Jim Henderson's scouts had purchased a textile plant in Whitakers, near Rocky Mount. Still idle, the 400,000-square-foot facility now would be expanded to 1.1 million-square-feet and transformed to an ultramodern medium-range engine plant.[34]

Simplified production, automation, and high volume—these central tenets of the project shaped both the design of its products and the nature of its manufacturing processes. Rocky Mount (as the plant became known) was equipped to produce ten models within the two engine families. The B series included medium-duty (54–190 hp) three-, four-, and six-cylinder engines that would run 100,000 miles before rebuilding. The more powerful C series engines were medium-heavy duty (160–254 hp) in-line six-cylinders. With replaceable cylinder liners, valve guides, and valve-seat inserts, these more durable models were designed to last 150,000 miles between overhauls. (They were also slightly larger in terms of displacement than was originally planned, in order to keep them out of competition with an existing Case engine.) Rocky Mount was equipped to turn out 100,000 units annually of the lighter, simpler engines and 50,000 Series C models, all of them turbocharged.[35]

Compared with the company's heavy-duty models, the new engines were lighter (per hp) and had fewer parts, and those parts were much more interchangeable. Cummins had decided to impose strict limitations on the numbers of "allowable" engine specifications—a departure for the Engine Company, which had always encouraged customer-specific modifications to its engines—but such a limitation was needed to permit higher levels of automation and keep costs down. (Rocky Mount required one-eighth as many factory workers per engine as the big-engine plants.) Those who worked in the state-of-the-art plant received seven months of training at a nearby school that was built with $3 million of state funding and managed jointly by Cummins and the Nash Technical Institute.[36] "We spent an enormous amount of time at Rocky Mount," Jim Henderson recalls, "training people in the team concept."

At Rocky Mount, Cummins moved closer to a mass production ideal than ever before. The problem was that it was an old-fashioned concept of "mass production," which (as is described in Chapter 12) Cummins was eventually to leave behind. As Jim Henderson recalls:

> *At that time, we didn't understand flexible manufacturing. We invested heavily in major component lines that turned out to be surprisingly inflexible. We were adhering to the old Detroit model in which you'd set up a rigid transfer line—for example, for blocks or heads—and then hope like heck you'd get high enough volumes to warrant that investment. In fact, that's part of the reason why we were looking for such large volumes out of Rocky Mount.*

In 1980 and 1981, Cummins spent more than $77 million for Case-Cummins research and engineering—more than half its total R&E budget (not including cost reimbursements for research contracts) for the two years.[37] The real trials lay ahead: whether CDC would meet its commercial startup deadline in mid-1983; and, more important, how the new products would be received in the marketplace. In the meantime, the joint venture helped Cummins considerably in the near term by reducing many of the risks associated with the new market thrust, and by shortening development time. At the same time, CDC promised to change the way Cummins did business in some crucial and enduring ways. As one manager noted, "Many, or most, aspects of the Case/Cummins project are *different* from the way Cummins normally operates."[38] This was true of the venture's research and design process, its manufacturing methods, its financial arrangements, and the marketing and distribution innovations it called forth.

Most important of all, it *happened*. Amid the mounting pressures and complex negotiations of 1979–1980, this tangible step had a huge psychological impact. More than any other single factor, the Case-Cummins venture served as the catalyst for the new strategy that, by the fall of 1980, was coming clearly into focus.

From recession to recovery

Inflation, deflation, slow growth, high unemployment, a large budget shortfall, a significant trade deficit—one or more of these macroeconomic problems has plagued the U.S. economy consistently in recent decades. And as the economy has lurched from one era to the next, the composition and order of the problems on this list has changed. One or two rise to the top to become the chief economic issues of the day, with political consequences and policy implications.

By the late 1970s, most Americans had little doubt about which two items topped the list: inflation and slow growth (which together defined the insidious malady "stagflation"). In 1980, Ronald Reagan won the White House in part because Democrats were seen as chiefly responsible for the post-1965 "great inflation"—Lyndon Johnson for scaling up the Vietnam war and launching the Great Society without raising taxes; the Democratic Congress for perpetuating FDR's and LBJ's "bloated" social welfare state; and then President Jimmy Carter, who failed to fulfill Gerald Ford's call to "Whip Inflation Now."

The 1980s version of the war against inflation began even before Reagan's election. Paul Volcker, appointed Chairman of the Board of Governors of the Federal Reserve in November 1979, immediately set about to rein in the money supply. Once Reagan took office, he joined the battle against double-digit inflation. And it worked: Inflation plunged from 12.4 percent to 7 percent in the first two years of Reagan's presidency. But the nation paid for its victory over inflation with a severe recession. By 1982, economic growth had slowed to a crawl, unemployment hit a six-year high, and the number of officially poor Americans was up 60 percent. By the time the Fed reversed its policy, which sparked a late-year recovery, America had endured one of its most severe postwar recessions.

The recession of 1980–1982 reverberated through Cummins with unexpected ferocity, despite the fact that company management had anticipated a downturn. The managers at the Fall 1980 planning conference, for example, acknowledged that they were about to embark on an ambitious expansion program "in a recession." But no one foresaw the severity of the slump. After earning net profits of $64.4 million in 1978 and $57.9 million in 1979, Cummins posted a loss of nearly $11 million in 1980, and would generate only tiny net profits of $7.7 million and $5.2 million in 1982 and 1983.

The fall in demand for its products was not the only broad economic trend battering Cummins in the new decade. The value of the dollar began a precipitous fall against the British pound, as well as against the currencies of other economies in which Cummins had a large stake. The problem in the United Kingdom became acute as early as 1980, compounded by the fact that Cummins had used up its accumulated tax credit and was now absorbing enormous exchange-rate losses as direct after-tax liabilities. The dollar would weaken dramatically throughout the first half of the decade, falling by 1984 more than 50 percent against the British pound and French franc, 37 percent against the German mark, and 19 percent against the Japanese yen. The recession's timing could hardly have been worse.

As it unfolded, the recession exceeded all of the company's grim projections. For Henry Schacht, adapting to the slump became a matter of replacing grim scenarios with grimmer ones.

We had three cases. One case was the worst recession we had ever seen before. The second case was fifty percent worse than that. And the third case was worse than that. . . . We went [down] through the third case in the first nine or ten months, just like a rock.

Well, I learned three things. Never say, "It can't happen." Don't say, "It can't happen again." And don't say, "You can't fall out of the bottom of the well." Because, yes, it can happen; and, yes, it can happen again; and, yes, you can fall out of the bottom of the well. We learned all of that the hard way all during the '81–'82 period.

As the recession ground on, Cummins joined the growing ranks of American manufacturing firms that suffered large-scale lay-offs. In early 1980, the company laid off 500 workers at its Seymour (Indiana) and Columbus plants, and announced 1,500 more cuts to come. Many of these workers were rehired during a 1981 uptick when Mexican orders increased and employment returned to within 1,000 of its 1979 level. But in 1982, bleak announcements of massive Cummins layoffs punctuated the news every few months: 3,000 in February, hundreds more in April, 1,750 in August, 300 in September. Jobs were lost on both sides of the Atlantic, but Columbus was especially hard hit. The total number of Cummins employees worldwide fell from over 23,000 in the late 1970s to 21,200 in 1980, recovered to 22,800 the following year, then plunged below 19,000 in 1982 and 1983, the lowest level since the recession of 1975.[39]

Although the bulk of the job cuts were seen as a necessary response to the downturn, the downsizing had an efficiency dimension as well. John Hackett's hard look at costs suggested that the company's payrolls had become somewhat bloated in the 1970s. "We had an incredibly inefficient cost structure. We were trying hard to cut back without taking jobs away from people. And that was a very human thing to do. But . . . it was not a good situation. We had too many people for the amount of work that was being done. We had inefficiencies all over the manufacturing operation."

Another manager recalls that the expansionary postwar years had bred laxity among some managers and rank-and-file workers. But mostly, notes the same executive, the process of handing out pink slips on this scale was "extraordinarily excruciating" for Cummins, especially in its hometown. Even during the Great Depression, the company had avoided massive layoffs. And in the decades since, Cummins' progressive labor policies and crucial presence in Columbus had forged an unusual covenant between management and labor. Now many began to wonder whether the layoffs would break that covenant.

To their credit, the company's executives continued to demand greater sacrifices of themselves, and to make greater efforts to assist laid-off wage earners, than did the vast majority of their peers in heavy industry. Business analysts looking back on the 1980s would criticize a prevailing ethic of greed among U.S. executives—sweetheart deals with lavish benefits, golden parachutes, and vast earnings disparities (between the highest- and lowest-paid employees within a firm)—especially in comparison with Japanese and European competitors. In contrast to this increasingly common pattern, Cummins "sliced the side of the pyramid," as Schacht put it—meaning, it demanded job and income cuts proportionately at all levels of the organization, with the highest-paid remaining executives taking the highest-percentage pay cuts. True, the company's executives hardly were enduring the kind of on-the-ground hardship suffered by hourly-wage shop and clerical workers. But the pyramid-slicing approach sent a clear message about equity and obligation.

This was the result, in part, of long-standing traditions in the company. But the small-town setting of Columbus also contributed. Unlike their counterparts in big-city corporations, Cummins managers found it impossible to escape the human dimensions of their actions. "I walked by the unemployment office every day on the way to work," recalls Schacht. "I knew a lot of those folks. When I went to the United Way meeting the next noon, or when I went to church on Sunday, I would wind up sitting next to the guy who just got laid off, and who wanted to know, 'How come?'"

To soften the blow for newly unemployed workers, Cummins offered a range of temporary measures, from the extension of benefits and counseling to outplacement support. Even so, this first round of large-scale layoffs in the company's history marked the beginning of a new era in labor relations within Cummins. Negotiations would become tougher, and job security would emerge as an increasingly crucial issue. Larry Neihart recalls that when he was elected president of the Diesel Workers Union in 1985, "the people wanted us to tell the company, loud and clear, 'Don't ask us to help you, if the result is going to be that we're going to get laid off.'" Unfortunately, the 1982 layoffs were only the decade's opening round.

Building Amid Austerity

The construction of the company's new Columbus corporate headquarters in this time period solved one set of problems, but posed a new set of challenges. Since the mid-1960s, when the company's top managers finally moved out of the Main Engine Plant, Cummins' executive offices had been located in catch-as-catch-can downtown facilities: in the upper floors in the St. Denis Hotel, in extra space in the old Irwin's Bank, and in offices across from the county courthouse. Clearly, the company needed better, and planning for a new corporate headquarters had begun in the early 1970s, when Cummins' growth went from robust to geometric.

Several different schemes were considered, ranging from building an office complex alongside the Main Engine Plant to a self-contained headquarters "campus" on the outskirts of town. But throughout the early planning phase, recalls former facilities manager Tom Harrison, "there was no discussion about taking it completely out of Columbus." Cummins was committed to its birthplace.[40]

To no one's surprise, J. Irwin Miller had a large hand in the design of the project. Miller nudged first Henry Schacht, and then Jim Henderson, to take a more active role in the programming phase of the building (that is, determining the appropriate uses and space allocations of the facility). "I encourage you to get over to New Haven as quickly as possible," he wrote to Henderson. "We will need a long period of planning before we build anything in the way of a new office, and I hate to see so many weeks go by without you, in particular, having a thorough idea of what's being presented."[41]

"New Haven" was Miller's shorthand for architect Kevin Roche, of the Connecticut-based firm of Kevin Roche, John Dinkeloo and Associates. Roche had trained with Eero Saarinen, and therefore had Irwin Miller's confidence. Roche-Dinkeloo had designed the Walesboro plant in 1970, as well as the company-subsidized design for the new post office in Columbus. Roche was retained in 1976 to begin design work on the new building, and Cummins invited him to Columbus in the summer of 1977. For three days, he and the newly appointed Cummins facilities-planning team conferred with local developers, planners, financiers, government officials, merchants, and community activists, working to win their support.[42]

Given the proposed location of the building, such support was absolutely vital. The emerging plan called for a massive new structure—between Jackson, Brown, Fifth, and Eighth Streets, and just one block from the downtown's main commercial thoroughfare—that somehow would not appear to be massive.

"I share your concern about monstrously large buildings," Roche assured Irwin Miller in late 1977. Accordingly, his plan called for a low-slung, story-and-a-half structure that heeded the unwritten local tradition that no building should stand taller than the city's distinctive Victorian-era county courthouse. The plan also fit neatly with other municipal needs. For example, city officials wanted to relocate the Amtrak (formerly Penn Central) rail line so that it would no longer slice through the heart of the downtown. And although the city already had torn down the time-worn railroad station on the proposed Cummins site, there was considerable public sentiment to preserve another building on the same site. This was the Cerealine Building, the old brick cereal mill alongside of which Clessie Cummins had set up his second machine shop many years earlier. The Cerealine Building sat nearly in the center of the site for the proposed "Corporate Office Building" (COB), so incorporating it into any new master plan represented a major design challenge.[43]

But Roche and his colleagues succeeded. The COB was designed to fill three sides of its long rectangular plot, with pieces of the fourth side—the side facing downtown—being carved away at asymmetrical angles, to underscore that the site was open to the community. From above, the design looked like the right half of an hourglass sliced along the vertical axis. Where the "waist" of the building was pinched to create a large open space, it would provide a home for the Cerealine Building, surrounded by greenery and a reflecting pool. The narrow-waisted footprint of the building also would ensure that few desks would be far from a window. "Surrounded by trees," Roche noted, "the occupants will have a good awareness of the outdoors."[44]

The project had been regularly slowed by outside crises and opportunities. Now, after more than a decade of false starts, it was moving toward completion—but it was gobbling up precious capital. Even though Cummins had delayed portions of the project in an effort to save some $14 million, in late 1982 the total cost of the project was revised upward to $43 million. Halting construction of its new home in the midst of the recession might make Cummins seem to be a faltering giant. On the other hand, continuing the project might appear to some to be extravagant. It was an uncomfortable moment in the company's history. "We were well on our way," recalls Schacht, "in sight of the building, and then the recession hit. So we had this giant thing going up right in the middle of the time we were laying people off."

The company's leadership decided to move forward. One reason was that stopping would have been expensive—$9 million for materials and another $3 million for contract penalties and to secure the site. Even so, this was far less than the tens of millions needed to see the project through. The solution to the conundrum came through a creative "sale-leaseback" arrangement. By selling the building to a New York City financial services firm (Integrated Resources, Inc.), then leasing it back and paying operating costs such as maintenance, taxes, and insurance, Cummins preserved a block of capital for other uses, and reduced the present value of its cash outflow by $5.5 million.[45]

There was much to applaud when the building was introduced to the community with an open house on November 10, 1985. The Cummins headquarters is an intriguing symbol of American industrial capitalism. The thin horizonal lines of the building's windows reinforce its low-to-the-ground profile, but the jagged outline of the inner court interrupts the giant rectangle's predictable right angles. Entranceway overhangs and the long concrete trellises that frame the property are supported by octagonal concrete pillars, which stand like giant Allen wrenches, a mechanical leitmotif befitting the engine maker. Deep green vines of ivy have engulfed many of the off-white concrete walls, tying them to the surrounding lawns and foliage.*

---

*"Oh, yeah," said one Columbus cabdriver in belated recognition, taking an out-of-town visitor to headquarters in the summer of 1994. "The building with the weeds all over it."

The understated exterior of geometry and asymmetry gives way inside the building to a different kind of geometry, and an other-world of light and color. Interior space is open and intriguing to the eye, thanks to the diagonal pattern of walkways and mezzanines, but mainly due to the architects' lavish use of glass and mirrors in the walls. The building's nonhierarchical design promotes an egalitarian atmosphere; executive offices are unpretentious and accessible, and the U-shaped cafeteria on the ground floor of the old Cerealine Building is open to all. The COB's striking interior aesthetic has a practical side as well; skylights, vertical walls of glass on all northern exposures, and other features make it extremely energy efficient.

It was many months before the new headquarters was filled with Cummins workers. Its opening in the depths of the early 1980s recession was a bright spot in an otherwise cloudy era. And in the dozen years since its ill-timed completion, the new corporate headquarters has helped "anchor" a large number of white-collar jobs in Columbus.

Seeing Daylight

There were many high-wire aspects to the Case/Cummins joint venture. Its high fixed costs, its novel production processes, its need to quickly reach and sustain high production levels, its new, highly competitive market—all made for a suspenseful multiproduct launching. "The project is large and fast-paced," noted Tom Head. And with notable understatement he added: "Significant delay will hurt in many ways."

Troubled times at Case in 1980 added to the air of uncertainty about CDC. With Case plants running at 55 percent capacity and returns dropping nearly 10 percent (to 4.4 percent), Tenneco chairman James Ketelsen—a former Case executive—instituted "radical cost-cutting measures," including the elimination of 4,000 jobs. Henry Schacht, understandably concerned, phoned Ketelsen for reassurance that Tenneco would continue to back Case, and that Case would back CDC.

From Irwin Miller's vantage point, the stakes indeed were monumental. "We risk here not only CECo. name, reputation, and money, but also CASE name, reputation, and money. . . . We need *now* to devise a strategy of development and introduction (including manufacturing) which will launch these engines TROUBLE-FREE." A visit to the 14th Street R&E group in 1981 gave Miller scant reassurance. "I dropped in unannounced . . .," he reported to the company's president, "and was really shocked at the dirty conditions . . . and at the appearance of no work whatsoever going on. There were groups of people standing around; there was little or no activity in test cells. . . . This is one of the saddest outfits I have ever seen. . . . Unless I am wrong, this could mean that we are in real trouble."

Miller's anxieties about the new product lines were animated in part by his vivid memories of the V engine's troubled introduction. "We can *never again* afford to introduce or make a flawed product. The quantities are too great, the cost prohibitive, market share too hard to regain," he wrote to Jim Henderson. And on another occasion: "If this project is in any way flawed, our warranty costs, product problems, factory recalls will make any problems of the past insignificant indeed."

But on this occasion, the best-laid plans worked. One reason was that Jim Henderson and other operations heads held monthly reviews on each product line. A system of "program managers" was established to monitor the progress of the new engines, under the overall direction of Tom Head. Each of these program managers was an experienced engineering or manufacturing leader with substantial clout within the larger organization. A "rolling seven" test plan was set up, whereby seven engines operated at all times so that they could be measured against expected performance at the high end of the duty cycle—some for 500 hours, others for 1,000 hours. Engineers responded quickly to failures in the test cycles. "We were all over those B, C, and L10 introductions, in terms of reliability," Henderson recalls. "We weren't gonna let those get away from us."

The first engine (a four-cylinder B) rolled off the line at Rocky Mount—on schedule—on July 1, 1983. The engines quickly gained an initial toehold in the marketplace. The Continental Baking Company placed a large order, and, as anticipated, B engines found homes in a wide range of applications (cranes and log skidders, graders and four-wheel-drive tractors, forage harvesters and street sweepers). In 1984, Cummins shipped 4,400 B engines, 3 percent of its overall total. With the slump in agriculture, Case was unable to use its half of the output, and Cummins found itself in the enviable position of buying most of Case's 50 percent at low marginal cost.

The following year, when the C Series went into commercial production, midrange engine shipments nearly doubled (to 8,400). By 1986, 16 percent of the Cummins engines shipped were Bs and Cs. Combining these numbers with L10 figures reveals a dramatic shift. Together, the three new families surged to 20 percent of total company shipments in 1985, and fully one-third of shipments in 1986. And these gains came at a time when every other product line (except engine kits) was either flat or declining.

Cummins moved quickly to build B and C capacity beyond U.S. borders. Early in the life of CDC, Cummins managers envisioned opening a midrange engine plant in Europe. But Case and Cummins held "incompatible" positions on the issue, especially when it came to building a plant in the United Kingdom. Cummins resisted this notion largely because of the "small V issue." Although some managers had offered assurances that Bs and Cs would not affect the V engine plant at Darlington, others predicted that "the family II engine would tend to displace the small V." In 1982, Cummins licensed Leyland Vehicles Ltd. to build B series engines in West Lothian, Scotland. (The plan was never carried out.) Three years later, it signed license agreements in Turkey (with BMC Sanayi, a leading truck maker) to make B engines; and in Indonesia (with Boma Bisma Indra, a government agency) to make NH and B engines. The small Vs lived awkwardly alongside the B and C engines through the mid-1980s, but soon were eclipsed by these newer, technically superior products.

The introduction of the B and C engines differed in a crucial way from the launching of the L10, however: Only the L10 was profitable. This was in part because the L10 was built in a factory that was also producing the profitable NH—Jamestown—and in part because it was being sold successfully to an existing customer base. The midrange engines would not turn a profit until volume and prices reached high-enough levels. Building volume meant finding new customers.

Breaking the cycle

The mid-1980s were a time of contradiction, upheaval, and irony for Cummins Engine. On the one hand, the company's intense efforts to expand its range in diesel engines in the midst of a major recession, combined with its hard-nosed struggle against Japanese competitors, impressed a growing number of business writers. Some painted the company in glowing colors, depicting it as a great American company fighting valiantly to protect a basic industry. The central actor in this passion play was Henry Schacht, whom the media singled out as the brilliant Cummins strategist in the struggles of the early 1980s. (Few observers then understood the critical role played by Jim Henderson as operations head and Schacht's alter ego.) Most press coverage of Cummins focused on the boldness of the restructuring plan, and the nimbleness of the company's response to foreign competition.[46]

The irony was that even as these accolades began to pile up, the company's top managers, especially Schacht and Henderson, were increasingly anxious about Cummins' future. The company was losing huge amounts of money, and was sure to lose much more before its fortunes turned. The viability of the enormously expensive new product launches was far from proven, and the company's budding truce with its Japanese rivals was still in its infancy. Far from feeling heroic, Henderson recalls, he and his colleagues at Cummins suspected in this period that they "looked like a bunch of fools to people." It was clear, for example, that the Case-Cummins venture could not survive unless additional high-volume customers were found for the B and C engines. But where would those customers come from?

A behind-the-scenes episode from the mid-1980s demonstrates the seriousness of this search for strategic options and alternatives. It involved the Aluminum Company of America (Alcoa), the world's leading producer of aluminum products. This Pittsburgh-based giant (with three times Cummins' sales volume) shared the diesel maker's concern about a mature core business, but did not take decisive steps to cultivate non-aluminum business until Charles W. Parry became CEO in 1983. Parry's vision—to garner fully half of Alcoa's revenues from new alloys and space-age materials by 1995—proved to be too dramatic for several of the company's directors. Two years into Parry's watch, W. H. Krome George (Parry's predecessor as CEO) and several other board members launched an effort to replace him.

Henry Schacht became the object of their affection in the summer of 1985. According to the *Business Week* reporter who later broke the story, Alcoa's board was seeking

> *a corporate-statesman . . . someone with senior management experience as well as the right connections in public-policy circles. George envisioned a CEO in the image of his aristocratic predecessor, John D. Harper, a co-founder of the prestigious Business Roundtable. For that cosmopolitan leader, the board went looking in an unlikely place: Cummins Engine Co.*

The two companies had more than a passing acquaintance; they shared two board members: Franklin A. Thomas (president of the Ford Foundation) and Paul L. Miller (former president of First Boston Corp.).[47]

A series of talks produced a tentative plan for a combined company, with Schacht as chairman and Parry as vice chairman. Henderson might remain in Columbus to head the (former) diesel company, or perhaps join Schacht in Pittsburgh, leaving others in charge of the Columbus-based operations. Schacht saw some strategic logic to the consolidation. Both companies were considering moves into new processes and exotic materials. "We would combine our technical efforts in advanced materials and advanced processing, not the applied efforts," he explains.[48]

The Alcoa board initially kept its plan secret from Parry, then eased him into the process. He "protested strongly" against the notion of a merger with Cummins, Henderson recalls. But the main reason why the plan faltered seems to have been the widespread sense that Alcoa and Cummins would have made an awkward couple. Alcoa wanted Schacht, but the potential organizational disharmony seemed too steep a price to pay. "There is no way," Henderson reflects, "that there was a natural fit between Alcoa and Cummins." (The Alcoa board eventually elected one of its own directors as chairman—Paul H. O'Neill, former president of International Paper Co.— who promptly reversed Parry's diversification strategy.)[49]

The almost-consummated marriage with Alcoa underscored the continual narrowing of Cummins' options, which in turn heightened concerns about the company's future. But rather than counting on another merger opportunity that might offer a dramatic resolution, the company's strategists returned to the more systematic approach they had pursued since the genesis of the 1980s strategy.

At the very earliest strategy sessions where Cummins management contemplated a major cost-cutting push (described in the next chapter), they also revisited the issue of broadening the company's base—both to permit continued growth, and to break out of the cyclicality of the heavy-duty engine business. This meant two things: going down (and perhaps up) the horsepower ladder, and looking beyond the engine business.

Management had learned important lessons from its three-legged diversification approach of 1970s; this time, they would stay away from skis, beef, and similar exotics. The new expansion plan would target businesses and opportunities closely allied with the Engine Company's product and customer base. As planning conference documents put it: "We are becoming increasingly interested in areas outside our currently defined strategy which may allow us to capitalize on our engine business expertise," including, specifically, smaller engines, components, and end products to complement the engine line.[50]

During the earlier 1980s, management focused primarily on the move to smaller engines, mainly because the B- and C-series engines demanded a great deal of attention and investment. Secondarily, Cummins cultivated new international ventures (as we will see later in this chapter), and built and strengthened the company's established components businesses. For example, in February 1980, Cummins expanded Fleetguard's manufacturing capacity by purchasing a large portion of the Delux Products Division of Walker Manufacturing from its owner, Tenneco. The next year, Fleetguard opened a new plant and warehouse in Quimper, France.[51] Meanwhile, Diesel ReCon was expanding to meet burgeoning demand, earning profits on record sales; and Holset grew as well, opening a U.S. sales and application engineering facility in Farmington Hills, Michigan.[52]

With the launch of the B-series engine in 1983, Cummins took a huge step toward liberating itself from total dependence on heavy-duty engine markets. But the Case-Cummins venture was only a highly speculative stake in the ground. Without one or more high-volume customers, presumably in the intensely competitive automotive field, the huge B- and C-engine gamble would fail—and fail spectacularly.

Further diversification was needed. Expansion into new activities (the Cummins managers hoped) would make the company more responsive to its customers, would create new jobs to accommodate the skilled work force that was being idled by the ongoing downsizing effort, and would generate much-needed revenues to offset the cost cutting attached to the smaller engine lines.[53] In 1984, the company entered a number of areas deemed to "hold promise," including electronics, materials and manufacturing technology, service products, and financial services.[54]

The focus on growth markets expanded substantially and acquired strong momentum, under the guiding hand of executive vice president and CFO John Hackett. But the dispersed, fragmented nature of these businesses—so different from the highly concentrated engine business—presented a whole host of new management challenges. They required strong controls, and would benefit from a champion who could reinforce their importance internally. In 1984, Jim Henderson and Henry Schacht recalled Tim Solso from his position as managing director at Holset in England and designated him vice president for "Special Engine Markets." Under Solso, who had help from Hackett, Special Engine Markets offered new services and acquired new manufacturing and machining capabilities.

Hackett's new ventures moved Cummins into several untested areas—radiator, generator set, and driveline component manufacture; electronics; computer software and hardware development; credit and finance services—that helped broaden the company's definition of its business and customers. But it soon became clear that this redefinition was poorly understood and poorly communicated, both inside and outside the company. In 1986, therefore, Cummins adjusted the company's structure to integrate these outside ventures into the larger corporate strategy. To the two existing business groups—diesel engines and components—Cummins added two more: Power Systems, and Information and Services. The 1986 annual report explained that "these [four] businesses have the shared objectives of growth, profit and employment for our people through an integrated family of businesses which bring value to our customers."[55]

This was the beginning of what turned out to be a three-year experiment. Because it put all four "tubs" on their own bottoms, the four-business structure turned out to be a useful way of understanding the relative profitability of the four groups. On the other hand, the structure proved to be an ineffective way to deal with key customers. Ford, for example, found itself entertaining sales pitches from a host of Cummins representatives—selling engines, radiators, electronics, and so on—whose efforts were purposefully uncoordinated.

Only one of the two new business groups survived to the end of the decade. In one sense, it was an old story: Expansion of the base business, as well as new technological demands tied to emissions, claimed most of the available funds. As a result, most of the companies under Information and Services that were not meeting target profit levels fell victim to a capital crunch in 1988.*

---

*"It's perfectly clear now," says Jim Henderson, "that John Hackett was way ahead of the curve in the information-and-services area. We've been scrambling to get back into those businesses that John first pushed us into, more than a decade ago."

But the Power Systems group (renamed Power Generation) encompassed a number of ventures—including, in particular, a generator set manufacturer named Onan—that earned immediate profits, and in time helped Cummins achieve the diversification it had long been seeking.

A Just-in-Time Account: Chrysler and the B Engine

The first B engine was started up at the Small Engine Development Center on May 1, 1979. This represented the culmination of years of effort at Cummins, both on the engineering and marketing sides of the shop. But at the same time it was the starting gun for a new race. Assuming that Case and Cummins could come to terms on financing and ownership—an agreement that was reached in October 1980—Cummins now had to find enough customers to take its half of the output of the new venture.

This was no small challenge, either in terms of distribution or marketing. In a very real sense, by introducing the small-to-midrange engines, the Engine Company was throwing an unprecedented curveball at its distributor network. Margins on parts, traditionally the distributors' "cash cow," were much slimmer in the 50–250 hp range. There was reason to fear that the lighter-duty B engines would go out into the marketplace and simply "disappear," unlike the more expensive engines that almost always returned to the distributors for repairs. Distributors feared—unjustifiably, as it turned out—that the entire output of Rocky Mount would be swallowed up by Case and other OEMs, and that no product would flow through to them. And the much greater variety of potential B- and C-engine customers, especially in nonautomotive fields, would make sales efforts more complex and distribution channels more diverse. There were fewer models to work with, and those that were available would arrive at dealerships with far fewer special features and enhancements, demanding more in-field upgrades. Thus, distributors would be working with "but a fraction of the options Cummins normally uses to attract customers."[56]

Finally, there were the intangibles of tradition. Could Cummins distributors get behind products that wore out much faster? Could they learn to put price ahead of power, durability, and quality?

Cummins took a number of concrete steps to win over its distributors. For example: The company signed an agreement with a leading generator-set manufacturer, Kohler, in October 1982 to jointly provide genset kits to Cummins distributors. The distributors would assemble the kits on site for retail sale. At the same time that parts volume might be declining, in other words, new opportunities for profit at the distributor level were being created. (And, of course, factory costs were being kept to a minimum.) At the annual distributor meetings throughout the early 1980s, Cummins stressed the exciting possibilities presented by the Bs and Cs: entirely new product lines, entirely new markets. After being restricted for decades to the top of the product pyramid, Cummins distributors finally could move down toward its vast foundation. Meanwhile, by means of the new L10 and older engine models, Cummins and its distributors would fight to hold their traditional markets.

Over the course of the 1980s, the critical role of the distributors in making the B and C engines a success became increasingly apparent to Cummins. By 1987, it was obvious that both Caterpillar and Deere intended to enter the small-engine business within two years. "The main differentiating asset in this regard," as one internal memo noted in January, "is our distributor network."[57] And by the end of the decade, it was clear that the distributor end of the B and C strategy was working—especially for those distributors who were talented and energetic enough to seize opportunity. Chuck Grace was one such distributor, who at first cast a skeptical eye on the Bs and Cs, but wound up having nothing but praise for them:

> *Cummins was moving fast, at that point in time. They'd come out and say, "This is the greatest engine in the world! This is the greatest program in the world!" And what they tended to hear back [from us] was, "It ain't going to work." The distributors had to make sure Cummins got the message, without being negative all the time.*
>
> *The fact is, before the B and C engines, we as distributors really didn't have a way to sell engines. That sounds odd, but it's true. The big engines sold themselves. When the smaller engines came out, then we were able to sell smaller manufacturers in our local areas that were too small for Cummins to call on on a regular basis, but are big opportunities for us. And that's put us in both the power-generation business and the engine business in a big way. Where 12 percent of our distributorship sales used to be engines, now it's 35 percent.*
>
> *As it turned out, those B and C engines were the two most successful engines that ever, ever came out of this place. I mean, you can't believe how good. They wind up in god-awful places. They're in wood chippers. They're in logging equipment. They're in the bayous of Louisiana, and in a million places overseas. And you just don't have any problems with them.*

But the task of harnessing the distributors—independent-minded though they were—was a relatively easy challenge. Far more difficult was the task of persuading existing customers to think differently about the Engine Company. Worldwide, the midrange diesel market was plagued with overcapacity. The market was vast—but it was already well populated with experienced rivals. In lower-horsepower ranges, quality and durability, the traditional Cummins selling points, were relatively less important. Price reigned supreme. This creep in the direction of commodification would be new to Cummins' and its traditional customers. After all, Cummins had built its reputation over decades as the industry's high-quality producer. As one manager observed clinically: "Since product superiority is not so critical in this area as in our classic markets, there is an exposure."

Cummins managers believed that Rocky Mount's products would be superior in their class. At the same time, they had to recognize that prices for the new models would not be lower than prices for comparable engines from competitors, and that OEMs might well balk at paying more for a Cummins engine—especially when those OEMs felt that a "generic" engine was best suited to their needs.[58]

What marketing stance should Cummins adopt? Initially, recalls Jim Henderson, the company decided to avoid the "generic" trap—which would guarantee low margins indefinitely—and push its new midrange engines on two strong selling points: fuel economy, and power-to-weight ratio. Later, as the new engines proved themselves in the field, durability was added as a selling point.

But the most important challenge was to find brand-new OEMs to take the new Cummins engines. Without new customers to take Cummins' half of the CDC output, the entire small-engine project surely would go under—perhaps taking the parent company with it.

At the top of the list of Cummins' targets were the pickup truck businesses of the Big Three. GM listened politely to the Cummins pitch at regular intervals in the 1980–1984 time frame, but consistently expressed its satisfaction with its own Detroit Diesel 6.2L and with the Caterpillar 3208 diesel engine that it was using. Ford was intermittently interested, asking (early in 1982) if Cummins could design a special five-cylinder diesel. (The existing six-cylinder B was too long to fit in the Ford pickup's engine compartment, and Ford feared that a four-cylinder would not be powerful enough.) Cummins, although reluctant to drift from the standard B configuration, was well aware of Ford's clout in the market, and quickly agreed to the experiment. In short order, Engineering produced two working five-cylinder engines. Ford, although interested, still declined to sign on. It continued working on its own in-house diesel program, and eventually chose a Navistar diesel for its pickups.[59]

Starting in the fall of 1981, the Cummins new-business development group, headed by Jim Farrar, began pitching the B engine to Chrysler. In some ways, Chrysler was the least likely candidate to take the new Cummins engine. The company—which had narrowly escaped bankruptcy at the beginning of the decade—was then a distant third in the pickup trade, with a market share consistently under 10 percent. Unlike GM and Ford, Chrysler had no diesel pickup at the time and no plans to offer one.

But this, Cummins suspected, was a field of opportunity. The pitch continued for almost four years. Finally, in April 1985, Chrysler agreed to offer the turbocharged six-cylinder B engine in its Ram pickup. Significantly, the automaker also expressed its eagerness to market the diesel as a *Cummins* engine. Both decisions reflected the fact that Chrysler had little to lose in the pickup field, and saw the Cummins relationship as a potentially strong selling point.

As a final clincher for Cummins, the Chrysler organization was proving extremely easy to work with. This, says Farrar, may have been a result of Chrysler's recent brush with extinction:

> *In this period of time, Chrysler was looking for help in every way possible. Anybody that could help them had a good relationship with them. So we developed a fantastic rapport with them. They saw us as helping them everywhere they turned around. We had a product that worked, and the thing took off, and it started adding volume. Not only that, it drew so much showroom traffic that their gasoline penetration started going up, too.*

But there was one hitch, early on: Chrysler had no in-house engineering resources available to take on the challenge of "up-fitting" the Cummins engine into the Ram pickup. The struggling Detroit giant told Cummins that unless Cummins was willing to take on the task of engineering the B into the Ram, the deal was off.* This was a highly unusual role for Cummins—whose heavy-duty customers rarely asked for similar services—but the timing was right (new-business development was at the top of the agenda), and the need was urgent. A separate contract was drawn up, eventually totalling some $1.2 million, and signed in May 1985. "We set up an engineering facility in what used to be called Plant 10," Jim Farrar recalls, "brought in about twenty or thirty vehicles, and went to work on the engineering." Detroit-based specialists relocated temporarily to Columbus, and Cummins engineers moved to Detroit for the duration. In December 1986, final drawings were released into the Chrysler system.

Within months, Chrysler was back with another request. The automaker's plants were operating at capacity, and for this and other reasons, the pickup program was once again in jeopardy. Could Cummins figure out a way to deliver an engine-transmission combination ready to be installed onto the Ram chassis?

Between August 1987 and the summer of 1988, Cummins organized a new Detroit-based subsidiary called Cummins On-Time Assemblies. COA received engines from Rocky Mount, configured them to meet the eight standard Chrysler specifications, married the engines with Chrysler transmissions, attached the necessary belts and wiring, and dropped off the complet-

---

*According to Jim Henderson, Chrysler also felt that diesel-powered pickup sales would be too low (perhaps 5,000 to 6,000 per year) to justify a substantial engineering investment on Chrysler's part.

ed assemblies at the nearby Chrysler plant. The first completed assembly was delivered by COA to Chrysler on August 3, 1988.[60]

This was yet another service born of opportunity and necessity. As Jim Farrar explains:

> *Again, this was a service we charged for, and was one of those things that would not have happened had Cummins not been out searching for new businesses. We saw this as another opportunity to do more than just make money off the engine. In fact, at one point in time, we were making more money off the engineering and the On-Time Assembly operation than we were making off the engines that we were selling to Chrysler.*

But the Chrysler volume—which went from zero engines in 1986 to almost 20,000 engines in 1989—was a crucial step in making the midrange engine venture, one of Cummins' most daring rolls of the dice, a success.* It provided a critical bridge to the day in the early 1990s (as described in Chapter 11) when yet another Big Three truck manufacturer agreed to sign up with the B engine.

Into Power Generation with Onan

The acquisitions that eventually made up the Power Systems group in 1986 were opportunistic: Cummins hunted for companies whose product or service fit into the engine business (as they broadly defined it for diversification purposes), and which might be amenable to a joint venture or purchase. They pursued the ones that showed promise.

For example, in late 1983 they purchased McCord Heat Transfer Corporation, a leading manufacturer of sophisticated cooling systems for trucks, as well as agricultural and defense equipment. Cummins established a wholly owned subsidiary to take advantage of McCord's capability in heat-transfer technology. Similarly, the Engine Company established another subsidiary, Combustion Technologies, Inc., when it acquired the high-speed piston-ring division from Koppers Company, Inc. But the 1986 purchase of 63 percent of Onan Corporation put Cummins in a completely different situation from the other Power Systems purchases. It was one that could enable the company finally to achieve the all-important goal of true product diversification.

The other Power Systems purchases (much like the acquisitions by the Components Group) constituted only a marginal sort of diversification. They

———————————————————

*According to a Chrysler press release from 1989, Chrysler guessed that it would receive orders for 10,000 Cummins-equipped trucks for the 1989 model year. It actually received 19,000, of which Cummins was able to supply 17,000.

increased the Engine Company's control over "the engine" in a very broad sense. And with increased control, Cummins could achieve a better-quality product, and could demand a premium for that differentiation. The move to smaller engines mitigated, but did not eliminate, the cyclical nature of engine demand. All told, then, none of those purchases substantially reduced the Engine Company's dependence on the trucking industry. But Onan commanded a substantial portion of a completely *new* market: generator sets.

Cummins management first heard that Onan might be up for sale in the summer of 1985, but they already knew a great deal about the company. Onan had produced generator sets since the early 1930s, and had produced its first opposed-piston engine in 1936 for low-vibration genset applications. Over half the generator sets required by the Allied forces during World War II, along with the gasoline engines that powered them, were Onan-produced. In 1948, Onan had moved into diesel design and production to broaden their line. They expanded their generator-set and engine lines throughout the 1960s and 1970s, in the lower-horsepower (16–24 hp) range.[61] (Cummins engines had long powered Onan generator sets in very-high-horsepower ranges.) In 1982, Onan had submitted a less-than-satisfactory bid on the genset kits that Cummins wanted to provide (along with B engines) to its distributors, and the contract had gone to rival Kohler.

Hackett recalls that Onan had a "very mixed lineage." It had been owned first by the Onan family, then by McGraw-Edison in Chicago, then by Houston-based Cooper Industries. Cooper purchased McGraw-Edison in 1985, and immediately began to look for ways to recapitalize this highly leveraged (54 percent debt-to-capital) acquisition.

One of the options Cooper entertained was to sell off Onan. Cummins, then well into its acquisition-for-diversification mode, was an obvious potential suitor. In fact, purchasing a power-generation interest already had been discussed at Cummins well before Onan came up for sale. Onan had been a steady Cummins customer up until just a year earlier—when it was persuaded to switch to lower-priced Komatsu. According to Tim Solso, "If you looked at it strategically, it really said that if we wanted critical mass and really wanted to be a player in the power-generation market, we had to buy either Kohler or Onan."

And so Cummins was receptive when Cooper made an overture. Tim Solso, then vice president of Special Engine markets, recalls, "Cooper called on a Monday, and said to John Hackett, 'If you give us a bid for our shares in Onan by Friday, we won't shop it.'" In response, Hackett and Solso drew up a proposal on a crash schedule. They met with Cooper's senior vice president of finance to discuss the offer, and soon learned that their terms did not meet Cooper's expectations. Cooper announced that it therefore would be entertaining other offers.[62] Hackett and Solso would have to do due-diligence, and bid again. Meanwhile, through the grapevine, Hackett and Solso heard that

Kohler—a longtime Cummins customer, and Onan's largest rival in the generator-set business—was also in the hunt.

Cooper next gathered a group of analysts to examine and evaluate McGraw-Edison's operations. Eventually, during the question-answer session, discussion turned to McGraw's two "trouble spots": Onan and Power Systems. A copy of the First Boston Research report from that meeting landed on John Hackett's desk, and when it did he noted the observation on Onan:

> *The sales breakdown is roughly 60 percent gensets and 40 percent engines. In gensets, over half of Onan's sales typically go to the RV market, where the company dominates. The problem in the diesel engine business: Onan evidently spent millions creating a product in an area where overcapacity and Japanese competition make profits unattainable.*[63]

Hackett forwarded the report to Schacht and Henderson, stating in his cover memo: "Apparently, Cooper Industries does not place a very high value on Onan. It seems inconceivable that a management would talk so candidly about a division they are attempting to sell."[64] Cummins completed its internal research, and made another bid in December 1985, which Cooper accepted.

The purchase still faced difficulties. Negotiations between Cooper and Cummins went far down the road before Cooper revealed that they had sold a 37 percent share in Onan to a U.K. concern, Hawker Siddeley. The negotiations were therefore necessarily protracted, as Hackett travelled to England to gain approval of the arrangements from Cummins' potential partner. Finally, in February 1986, Cummins and Cooper struck an agreement, and Cummins purchased a 67 percent interest in the power-generation company.

After negotiations were completed, Jim Henderson had to face a very dismayed customer—Kohler, which as noted was a valued Cummins customer and Onan's chief competitor in power generation. Henderson tried his best to clarify Cummins' position for that company's president: "I had a very close relationship with Herb Kohler, and I had to go and try to explain what was going on. It cost us that relationship." But Onan, Henderson explains, was simply too good an opportunity to pass up:

> *Boy, we jumped, because it was a way to catapult our business into power generation. Now, did we know power generation at that moment was going to be as big in our future as it turned out to be? No. But we knew power generation was growing rapidly, and that Onan had a major position.*

Ultimately, Henderson says, the acquisition advanced two very important corporate objectives at the time. First, it gained Cummins a substantial presence in a very important market for its diversification strategy; and second, it served to reinforce in the minds of potential Japanese competitors the extent of Cummins' determination to keep them out of American markets.

Onan produced more than 80 percent of the generator sets for the motor home industry, and was a major supplier of generator sets to the pleasure-boat industry. It also supplied standby power systems to hospitals, computer centers, retail stores, office buildings, and hotels. Those markets were growing, and Onan's order backlog was strong.[65] Onan's product line fit very well with the new smaller B and C series engines, as well as with the larger capabilities of Cummins. The existing Onan "L" engine, for example, continued to be produced at Onan's Huntsville, Alabama, manufacturing plant.[66]

Onan yielded positive returns for Cummins almost immediately following its purchase in 1986. As that year's annual report noted: "We added sales in new markets; Onan, the largest of our new activities, had sales of $259.9 million in our 10 months of ownership."[67] And in the longer term, it has made the Engine Company a major player in the expanding power-generation industry, significantly reducing its vulnerability to the peaks and valleys of truck market cycles. By 1990, Power Systems generated 15 percent of Cummins' $3.4 billion sales; by 1994, that percentage increased to 22 percent, on sales of $4.7 billion.[68] Jim Henderson sums up the impact of the purchase simply: "Onan turned out to be a huge success."

Reaping and sowing: international in the 1980s

Consistently, the Cummins Engine Company was an opportunistic enterprise when it came to setting up manufacturing and assembly operations overseas. The company also demonstrated a remarkable degree of patience with international ventures that were slow to achieve profitability—which most of them were—or whose host countries didn't allow a quick or easy repatriation of profits to the United States. This patience was possible in part because Cummins commonly managed its overseas operations on a case-by-case basis. In some of these businesses, success was measured in terms of exports to other countries. In others, success was defined as growth in domestic market share. Flexibility was the watchword. "We have been willing to use any sound technique," Henry Schacht wrote in 1974, "which suited both the need of the host country and ourselves."[69]

Company wisdom held that it took roughly a decade to transform an initial "beachhead" overseas into a profitable enterprise. Within the bounds of opportunism, therefore, Cummins tried to stagger its international investments. Profits earned in Shotts, Scotland, for example—which was making good money a decade or so after its establishment in the late 1950s—offset losses at newer operations begun in the late 1960s and early 1970s.

For Cummins' international operations, the 1980s were a period of both reaping and sowing. During most of this decade, the company's once-faltering Brazilian subsidiary repaid Cummins handsomely for its patience throughout the troubled 1970s. On the other side of the world, meanwhile, Cummins made investments in China (building on initial forays in the previous decade) that positioned the company for dramatic growth in subsequent years.

Adventures in Brazil

Cummins rarely was a pioneer in the international arena. Bigger competitors like Mercedes and Cat almost always entered markets well before the medium-sized diesel manufacturer from Indiana. But to give Cummins its due, the company aggressively pursued overseas opportunities—even some that seemed improbable—and it showed great patience with overseas ventures that did not pay off as planned. Perhaps the most extreme example of Cummins' willingness to enter a market "ahead of demand," hunker down, and improvise—waiting stoically for events to break in its favor—came in Brazil.*

Since the early 1960s, Cummins had divided the world into six zones— the United States and Canada, Latin and South America, the Far East, Europe, Communist countries, and "export territories" (a catch-all category denoting regions where intermediaries tended to dominate commercial transactions). According to a 1974 memo by Henry Schacht, Cummins approached each of these zones with a similar overall strategy, but also a willingness to improvise:

> *Our basic strategy has been to establish preemptive positions in each of the areas slightly ahead of demand, and dominate the market as it develops, networking our plants where possible to reduce capital requirements.*[70]

As far back as the late 1950s, Cummins was eyeing Brazil, which although bigger than the continental United States had a population only half as large.[71] But the fit between Cummins and Latin America's largest country was imperfect. There were very few heavy-duty trucks in service on the country's modest road system. Mercedes and Scania (strong competitors with more appropriate product lines) and Perkins (which made smaller-horsepower "loose" engines) were firmly entrenched in the Brazilian market. Nevertheless, Brazil's future looked bright to Cummins' managers in the early 1960s, so the

---

*The authors want to make clear that the Cummins-in-Brazil story is only one of many similar country-based stories that could have been included. We have chosen to present the Brazilian story in depth, rather than treating several countries more superficially.

company purchased a factory site some fifty miles from São Paulo in anticipation of the successful conclusion of negotiations then under way with International Harvester to launch a joint venture. But IH unexpectedly withdrew from the venture—which would have manufactured engines, trucks, and construction equipment—and Cummins was forced to rethink its position. Soaring inflation, exceeding 120 percent annually, was ravaging the local economy; and a military coup in 1964 gave further jitters to would-be U.S. corporate investors.

A half-decade of relative calm—reinforced by strong economic medicine and the discovery of additional vast reserves of natural resources—refocused the attention of Cummins and other U.S. corporations on Brazil. But the Brazilian government, now operating from a position of relative strength, took steps to shelter its nascent industries, including high-horsepower diesel engines and other products intended for automotive use. Steep tariffs imposed by the government effectively prohibited the importation of finished engines, while related legislation required that locally manufactured engines possess at least 70 percent local content.

In 1971, Cummins bought a plant in Guarulhos (near São Paulo) from the German manufacturing firm Klockner-Humboldt-Deutz. Along with the $2.5 million it paid for this nine-year-old plant, Cummins planned to invest another $7.2 million to manufacture ten NH industrial engines per day. Through its licensing process, the Brazilian government made its expectations clear: Cummins was to be no more than a replacement for the departing Deutz. The American company was welcome to manufacture a relatively small number of industrial engines, but it would not be permitted to enter the automotive trade.[72]

Seeking to spread some of the costs of the operation, Cummins next went looking for a local partner. Its first choice was Dr. Augusto Antunes, with whom informal discussions began in October 1971, even before the Deutz deal was concluded. Antunes was the majority shareholder in the Rio de Janeiro-based Companhia Auxiliar de Empresas de Mineracao (CAEMI), a large Brazilian holding company with extensive interests in mining, wood and paper production, and meatpacking.[73] The discussions were friendly, but ultimately unproductive. Antunes—who played a "senior advisor" role in his company similar to Irwin Miller's role at Cummins—told Cummins that while the project looked interesting, it was too small for a company like CAEMI to consider seriously. For the time being, therefore, Cummins operated its São Paulo facility as a wholly owned subsidiary called "Cummins Industrias, S.A."

But larger events began to transform the sleepy Cummins operation in Brazil. In 1972, the Brazilian government strong-armed Cummins into becoming a partner in a reconfigured version of a bus-manufacturing business formerly operated by Deutz.[74] The pet project of a particular government official, the new joint venture—called "Cummins Nordeste, S.A.," because it was located in the northeastern city of Salvador—involved three equal partners: Cummins, a Belgian bus company called Van Hool & Zonen, and a local bus manufacturer called Marco Polo. Van Hool and Marco Polo were the chassis-and-body specialists. Cummins, of course, was to be the engine provider, first importing its V-8 models from Darlington, then building automotive NH engines in Brazil as soon as the consortium developed a suitable chassis.

Through this unwieldy arrangement, the Brazilian government had granted Cummins entry into the domestic automotive trade—an unexpected opportunity to begin making inroads into Brazil's fleet of some 100,000 buses, the largest such fleet in the world.[75] And because the NH was now sanctioned as an automotive engine, this was a foot in the door to the Brazilian truck market.

Throughout the early 1970s, Cummins negotiated with the Ford Motor Company about the possibility of scaling up to produce V engines in Brazil as standard equipment in a new line of Brazilian-made Ford trucks. But a combination of obstacles—staggering capital demands, rampant inflation, and poor supplies of components—scuttled these plans.[76]

Still on the table, though, was a contract to sell fifteen to twenty NH engines per day to Ford; and largely on the basis of this commitment, Cummins and CAEMI established a new company—CAEMI-CUMMINS Motores, S.A.—at the end of 1974. Cummins sold a 51 percent share of its existing São Paulo operation to CAEMI, giving the Brazilian company control over the voting stock of the new company. (When the nonvoting preferred stock was factored into the calculation, however, Cummins retained a 63.3 percent interest in the new company.)[77] With one solid customer in hand, CAEMI-CUMMINS mapped out a small-scale assault on the Brazilian truck market.

That assault never came. As the worldwide recession of 1975 pummeled the Brazilian economy, domestic engine sales dropped through the floor, and the Brazilian government reimposed severe import restrictions.[78] Cummins had to scramble to find contract machining work to keep the São Paulo plant busy.

Negotiations with the Brazilian government to relax restrictions on imports were unsuccessful, and in 1976 the three partners in Cummins Nordeste (the bus manufacturing concern) agreed to shut it down.[79] Meanwhile, CAEMI-CUMMINS struggled to stay afloat long enough for the Brazilian economy—based in large part on natural-resource extraction and export, and therefore lagging behind the developed world—to make its slow recovery. But the Brazilian partners in CAEMI-CUMMINS increasingly were inclined to give up on the enterprise. Cummins' Brazilian strategy was dealt another mortal blow in 1978, when Lee Iacocca was dismissed by Ford.

Within a month, all Iacocca-inspired initiatives, including the Brazilian truck venture, were summarily canceled.

Throughout the late 1970s, regular feelers went out to Cummins' local competitors in Brazil, including Mercedes and U.K.-based Perkins, but these established players wanted nothing to do with Cummins. "I told him I thought a Cummins-powered Mercedes 40-ton truck would be a successful product in Brazil," John Hackett wrote back to Columbus, reporting on his pitch to a local Mercedes executive. "He smiled and said, 'That would be difficult.'"

This particular overture to Mercedes, although unfruitful, turned up some startling facts. The Mercedes operation in Brazil was much, much bigger than Cummins had previously understood. "Nearly all Mercedes trucks sold in the U.S. are manufactured in Brazil," a surprised Hackett reported. By the end of 1978, Mercedes was selling medium-duty trucks in thirty-four of the fifty United States, through at least 100 dealers—and all of these trucks were made in Brazil.[80]

By the late 1970s, the question remained: Should Cummins revamp its Brazilian operation to aim at exporting engines or components—perhaps to the United States? For Cummins, the situation was baffling. After all, *some* companies manufactured at a profit in Brazil, and (at least in certain phases of the economic moon) exported successfully from the country as well. Along with Mercedes, for example, Perkins used Brazil's inexpensive labor to build engines for profitable export.

In contrast, Cummins and CAEMI were losing as much as $7 million dollars a year in Brazil by this time. Buffeted by the worldwide economic recession of 1975, having been unable to close the small-V deal with Ford, and then having lost a huge contract to manufacture Ford truck engines in 1978 as a result of a management shuffle in Detroit, CAEMI-CUMMINS now had precious few customers. In 1975, before the collapse of the Ford deals, there were twenty-one foreign nationals working for the Cummins Brazilian operation. By 1978, there was only one. Not surprisingly, in the spring of 1978 CAEMI announced that it wanted out of the operation, preferably within two years.[81]

During those two years, the downsized company managed to limp along fitfully. CAEMI-CUMMINS broke even in 1979—largely by selling a dozen or so industrial engines a day, half to stray Brazilian customers, the other half to Komatsu for off-road vehicle production in Brazil—but it looked as if the death knell of the subsidiary was about to sound.[82] Even a long-awaited uptick in export orders toward the end of 1979 was bad news for CAEMI-CUMMINS, because it necessitated a new infusion of capital. Credit markets in Brazil were then extremely tight, and Brazilian *cruzerios* were not available to be borrowed. This meant that Cummins had to export additional dollars to Brazil, incurring large losses in the exchange.[83]

Cummins' Brazilian partner, meanwhile, became more insistent about its need to bail out. "CAEMI is fed up with Cummins," wrote one Cummins executive to his colleagues in Columbus early in 1980, quoting a Brazilian lawyer who had just endured an uncomfortable meeting with CAEMI. "The association [as the Cummins executive paraphrased it] must be ended immediately. They would prefer a friendly way to solve the matter."[84]

At this point, a five-person team from Cummins, headed by financial officer John McLachlan, visited Brazil and made an intensive investigation of the Brazilian operation. Their assignment (from vice president of international operations Tom Lyon and planning vice president Hal Davis) was straightforward: Figure out whether Cummins should stay in Brazil or not. After a five-week study, McLachlan and his colleagues reached several sobering conclusions. The first was that it made no sense to think of the Brazilian plant as playing the role in Brazil that the Columbus plant played in the United States. Volumes were simply too small; the expenditures needed to create a truly autonomous operation could not be justified. Without those expenditures, imports were necessary, which in turn made the operation uncompetitive. And finally, it was almost impossible for Cummins to operate as a "good citizen" in Brazil—doing things the "Cummins way"—by producing a tiny volume of completed engines for the domestic Brazilian market.

So if the operation in Brazil was going to prosper, McLachlan concluded, it had to export. This, he recalls, was also the Brazilian government's attitude at the time: "The real problem was that we were running the Brazil plant in a way that was contrary to what the Brazilian government was trying to get done. They were trying to build manufactured exports, rather than just commodities like iron, steel, cobalt, and coffee. And we weren't operating in sympathy with those goals."

McLachlan recommended that Cummins stay in Brazil, but only on one condition: that it begin exporting ten H engines per day. This would take some pressure off the Columbus plant, which was then stretched to capacity. It would qualify the Brazilian operation for special preferred rates for borrowing capital, and—most important—it would enable the plant to participate in "Befiex": the Brazilian Export and Financial Incentive, an export-stimulation program being launched by the Brazilian government in the early 1980s. Brazil owed some $90 billion to foreign banks, and was desperate to earn hard currency through exports.[85] The new Befiex program allowed a company to import into Brazil one dollar's worth of goods duty-free for every three dollars' worth it exported.[86] In other words, shipping out finished engines would allow for the import of fuel systems, which in turn would allow more engines to be shipped more profitably, leading to more fuel systems, and so on.

Irwin Miller and Henry Schacht paid a visit to CAEMI's head, Dr. Antunes, in 1979, and laid out this optimistic vision of the future. Antunes agreed that the enterprise could succeed—but only if it was managed solely by Cummins. As Irwin Miller recalls:

> He said, "Look—we've never been good at manufacturing. Chemical processing, yes—but not manufacturing. This is a mistake. I think you guys have a bonanza here, if you guys come down and run it. As things stand, we're just going to limp along, so we want to sell it to you. But I'm telling you openly that I think it's going to be a great deal for you, when you take it over."

In 1981, therefore, Cummins completed a 100 percent buy-out of the company. This was permitted by the Brazilian government in part because the relevant local-control laws had been loosened, but also because in 1980 the company again had lost money, and the alternative to complete Cummins ownership appeared to be liquidation. After seven years in partnership with Cummins, CAEMI made its exit from the diesel-making business.

The optimistic projections about the venture's potential almost immediately proved correct. Cummins Brazil, S.A. (as the new subsidiary was called) began making money in 1981, in part due to a surge in demand for industrial engines within Brazil. But exports—principally to Colombia and Venezuela—also were increasing by some 50 percent per year (although this increase came on the admittedly small base of 1,517 engines exported in 1981). By the end of 1981, Cummins was supplying industrial engines to six worldwide OEMs, and the company had begun discussions with Fiat and Volvo to supply truck engines to those companies.

As McLachlan and others had anticipated, Befiex was proving to be a boon. In part, this was because Cummins was playing by the rules. Although hundreds of multinational companies signed up to participate in the program, Cummins was one of a handful that actually exported enough to meet its obligations, and therefore was able to import fuel systems into Brazil's otherwise closed markets. But a second aspect of the Befiex program soon became even more valuable to Cummins. Brazil announced that it would provide a 15 percent rebate to companies on all their exported goods. Since Cummins already was exporting two-thirds of its Brazilian output, this was a windfall, and one that increased every time exports rose.

Between 1982 and 1985, Cummins Brazil sales increased from $52 million to more than $85 million. The subsidiary's profitability declined somewhat as sales increased, but this was a minor sour note in an otherwise cheerful chorus. "Brazil is an excellent low cost source of supply for achieving lower cost worldwide," noted one Columbus-based manager. "We have been able to repatriate earnings adequately ($8.2 million dividend in 1984)."[87] In the 1970s, Brazil had lost a total of $7 million for its two owners. Now it was returning more than that almost every year to its sole owner.[88]

To the surprise of many in Columbus, Brazil emerged in this period as one of the highest-quality low-cost producers of engine parts, including blocks. Although hard numbers are elusive, Cummins Brazil (later abbreviated as "CUMBRASA") exported in the neighborhood of $500 million worth of goods between 1981 and 1988.[89] As a result, over a seven-year period, Brazil paid Cummins upwards of $70 million to export engines and components from Brazil.[90] Cummins reinvested this money—plus another $9 million—in two expansion programs: the first to expand NH production, the second (in 1986) to set up B and C production lines in Brazil. Volkswagen was preparing to produce a midrange truck for PACCAR to sell stateside, and Cummins bid successfully on the engine contract.[91] By this roundabout route, Cummins continued to serve the needs of one of its oldest and most important customers in the United States. It also added much-needed capacity to its small-engine lines on foreign soil. The C engine went into production in Brazil in 1987, and the B in 1989.

Investing in China

Cummins lore has it that company representatives were on the first plane to China after President Richard Nixon's historic 1973 visit to the world's most populous nation.[92] In fact, contacts between Cummins and China began in June 1975, when board chairman J. Irwin Miller, his wife Xenia, engineer Joe Butler, and others visited the country. They were there as part of a larger group that recently had sold some heavy construction equipment to China for use in an open-pit iron mine some 700 miles northeast of Beijing. Fourteen Cummins KV12 engines were included in the package, and the Cummins contingent went to China to set up arrangements for proper service of the engines as well as to establish direct commercial relations with the government-controlled Machinery Import and Export Corporation. As a follow-up to this sale, China sent two teams of technicians to Columbus in the fall of 1975 for instruction in diesel engine maintenance.[93]

Cummins pursued the budding relationship aggressively. In this effort, it was greatly aided by Dr. Alyn Lyn. Lyn was a native-born Chinese who—through his work at the University of London—had emerged as one of the world's foremost authorities on combustion. He also had access: Several of his Chinese acquaintances from school days were now high-ranking officials in key government ministries, where they opened doors that remained closed to others. A second member of the Cummins engineering group, Andy Chu, had left China in his childhood, and he too was called upon to assist in relationship building. Along with the help of Lyn and Chu, Cummins had another important ace up its sleeve: a good product. The company's Chinese customers were very happy with their K (and increasingly, their NH) engines, which were proving themselves in a variety of off-highway applications well beyond mining.[94]

These were promising beginnings, but Cummins' courtship of the Chinese relationship proved to be neither brief nor straightforward. "It was a long, hard battle," John Hackett later recalled. Starting in mid-1978, Chinese officials and Cummins representatives (principally Dick Stoner, John Hackett, and Andy Chu) began what turned out to be two and a half years of negotiations aimed at setting up a licensing agreement for the manufacture of Cummins engines in China. As Stoner recalls: "I made fourteen trips to China, of which eleven were strictly for the negotiations. In that period, you had to go for one or two weeks at a time, because it would take nearly a week to get there."

Negotiations were slowed in part by Cummins' own reluctance to over-commit itself, especially in the untested waters of business relationships with the Peoples' Republic of China. (An internal Cummins document later described this initial phase as one of "keeping commitment and risk in balance.") Another impediment to success was the amazingly Byzantine bureaucracy of the Chinese government. "Our negotiations are temporarily stalled," as John Hackett informed the Cummins board in 1980, "while the Chinese decide which of the bureaus . . . will be responsible for the manufacture of Cummins diesel engines."[95]

Cummins signed a license agreement with China's National Technical Import Corporation on January 25, 1981. The accord was to last ten years, and included the NH, K, and KV engine families. In the first phase of the relationship, China would assemble engines from kits made at existing Cummins plants—an operation that was scheduled to begin in August 1982 at an existing diesel plant in Chong Qing, a city in south-central China. In the second phase, the Chinese licensee would manufacture and assemble Cummins engines and components in China.[96]

Engine assembly—by the China National Automotive Industry Corporation—began in 1983, after an extensive rehabilitation of a factory that one Cummins executive later referred to as "godforsaken."[97] In that same year, Cummins and the Chinese government also agreed to create a new technical and distribution center in China, thereby improving the availability of Cummins parts and service to Chinese end users.*

The next phase in the evolution of the China-Cummins relationship began in the spring of 1985, when Cummins started looking for a partner to whom it could license the rights to manufacture the B- and C-engine series

---

*"In fact," Jim Henderson recalls, "that plant was godforsaken in exactly the same ways that Shotts was, a quarter century earlier. It felt like we had been there before."

in China. Although the Chong Qing relationship was progressing satisfactorily, the factory's volume was small—about 400 units in 1984—and restricted almost entirely to off-highway applications, especially construction, mining, power generation, and marine markets.[98] For obvious reasons, Cummins wanted a toehold, or more, in the already vast Chinese truck market; and, as in Brazil, it had to manufacture its B and C engines locally if it wanted to be a player in that domestic market.

In surprisingly short order, a promising candidate stepped forward: the Second Auto Works (SAW), China's largest producer of on-highway trucks. (One measure of the difficulty of doing business in China at that time was the fact that the government agents in charge of the Chong Qing operation and those in charge of SAW had no contact with each other, and knew almost nothing about each other's operations.)[99] By the end of 1985, the outline of a new licensing agreement was taking shape, and it was an exciting prospect for Cummins. SAW was interested in a ten-year license, and expected to build approximately 60,000 engines annually. The final agreement, signed in 1986, called for SAW to use the B engine in its highest-volume truck line. SAW also signaled its intention to begin converting many of its gasoline-powered trucks to diesel—again implying the potential for huge growth in Cummins' Chinese markets.[100]

Cummins' flexible approach to its international relationships once again proved its value. In Brazil, after more than a decade of trying, Cummins finally hit upon the right combination—a favorable economic climate, strong government incentives, and a subsidiary ownership structure—which made the venture not only profitable, but also supportive of a larger corporate strategy. Almost overnight, many years of losses turned into a span of good profits, and a formerly marginal operation began to make a significant contribution both to NH parts and engine production worldwide and to the B- and C-engine introduction.

In China, Cummins was so determined to crack the closed domestic market that it resorted once again to a license agreement—a structure that it had more or less sworn off in the wake of unhappy experiences elsewhere.* This turned out to be a wise and a lucky decision. By the mid-1980s, many foreign corporations were experiencing great difficulties with their pioneering Chinese joint ventures, ranging from an inability to repatriate profits to sharp disagreements with their Chinese counterparts on their joint boards.[101] In clear contrast, Cummins in the 1980s earned an income stream from its two licenses (first modest, and later significant), and laid a solid foundation for successful joint-venture arrangements a decade later. In a period when many

---

*And, adds Henry Schacht, this license agreement—designed to avoid start-up losses—also included the right to convert to a joint venture: a step that was taken in 1995.

disillusioned multinationals were departing from China, Cummins was expanding its Chinese presence.[102]

In other words, the Engine Company figured out what was comfortably possible for both parties at each phase of the relationship, and made that particular structure work, most often through trial and error. "We were the first Western diesel engine manufacturer in China," explains Tim Solso, "and I think we were respected for how we went about doing it." A concern for not only what, but *how*, characterized the relationship, and local authorities took note.

Intermission

Cummins began the 1980s as a mature and successful American industrial corporation. It was dominant and seemingly confident in its domestic markets, and expanding rapidly overseas. Yet beneath the facade there was uncertainty and growing anxiety—as domestic sales began to plateau, due to near-saturated markets and stagflation; as government regulations limited options and imposed new costs; and, especially, as competitors merged into powerful, vertically integrated international combines. But rather than asset-milking or tinkering on the tactical margins, the company's new management team fashioned a bold program to "bet the company" on a new line of products—engines that might save the company from a slow death, but also would bring it into head-to-head competition with much larger rivals.

By the middle of the decade, the story of the restructuring launched in 1979 was moving toward resolution. J. I. Case seemed to be an ideal partner for Cummins' first expedition into the hotly competitive midrange engine market. And this time, in contrast to the ill-fated V adventure, Cummins had reformulated its manufacturing process in an effort to minimize flaws and maximize efficiency. As the new engine families gained a foothold in the market, there were strong signs that Cummins finally was escaping its perennial overdependence on the heavy-duty automotive market.

The severe recession of the early 1980s underscored the fact that this was a time of great unpredictability. National economic policy had greater and greater influence on the fortunes of Cummins and its counterparts. At the same time, the Engine Company's growing involvements overseas added still more uncertainty, as the company was buffeted by fluctuating international exchange rates, shifting policies and actions of foreign governments, and other forces mostly beyond its control.

In the late 1980s, Cummins would confront two new major challenges growing out of economic globalization and national economic conditions. But these were dramatically different variations on the theme. In the first case (described in the next chapter), Japanese diesel manufacturers made a run on the American market. In the second case (the subject of Chapter 11), two foreign corporations took major investment positions in Cummins, with the possible motive of gaining control. In these ways, the Midwestern manufacturer was drawn into trends that would define American business during the rough-and-tumble 1980s. Unfortunately, little that Cummins' managers had learned in the early 1980s prepared them for these fierce contests.

10 | Cummins versus Japan, 1984–1987

"It started quietly, in 1984, on a California dock landing with some crated truck engines stamped 'Komatsu' and 'Nissan,'" wrote a reporter for *Forbes* magazine. "Then came telephone calls from old friends—good customers—at Navistar and Freightliner, who said they were testing Japanese medium-truck engines." Thus emerged, according to this account, one of the greatest challenges Cummins faced in the 1980s: the direct threat of a Japanese diesel engine invasion.[1]

Cummins' actions in the wake of these and related events were far-reaching and decisive. Learning that Japanese firms were offering engines as much as 40 percent below its own U.S. prices, Cummins fell back, regrouped, and decided to slash the prices of many of its new engine lines. The move had enormous implications—for Cummins and, ultimately, for the U.S. diesel industry. But these price cuts—coming hard on the heels of Cummins' major recapitalization and huge capital investments—created a flood of red ink that would not be stanched for years to come. "We lowered prices," Henry Schacht frankly noted to his fellow executives in 1985, "and that has cost us $100 million pre-tax per year."[2]

Those losses precipitated other fundamental changes. To survive in the globally competitive environment that was being defined by Japanese standards in the mid-1980s, Cummins had to transform the way it conducted business, especially in production management and cost control. Moreover, as we shall see in Chapter 11, the losses sustained in the wake of Japanese-inspired price cuts eventually made the company more vulnerable to outside control.

From partners to competitors

Not surprisingly, the story of the Japanese challenge to Cummins and Cummins' response is far more complex than was suggested by the *Forbes* story. Japanese diesels landed on American shores only *after* a quarter-century of Cummins involvement, of one sort or another, in the Japanese diesel industry. Nor was the nature of the Japanese "threat" as unambiguous as some business reporters (and Cummins itself) were inclined to believe. But there is no doubt about the scope or import of Cummins' response to the perceived threat, and for that reason, Japanese diesel makers came to occupy center stage in the Engine Company's evolution during much of the 1980s.

The Heritage: Cummins and Komatsu in the 1960s and 1970s

The ties binding Cummins and Japan date back to 1960. That spring, Reece Hatchitt (Cummins' indefatigable head of international operations) and Waldo Harrison (then vice president and treasurer) departed on a 40,000-mile excursion to develop business in Europe, Australia, and Asia. Their first destination was Tokyo, then largely unknown territory for Cummins. Upon their return, the two men spoke of promising opportunities in the small but formidable island economy across the Pacific.

Initial deals followed quickly. On May 11, 1961, Cummins signed a fifteen-year license agreement with Komatsu Manufacturing Company, Ltd., Japan's leading maker of construction vehicles. Komatsu would produce four- and six-cylinder H and NH engines (the 743 series) for its crawler tractors and construction equipment. In September of that year, the two companies formed a joint venture, Komatsu-Cummins Sales Co., Ltd. (51 percent Cummins-owned), to sell and service within Japan Cummins engines and parts that were produced worldwide.[3] This pair of agreements enabled Cummins to import its products into Japan at a time when the island nation was still protecting its war-devastated industries.

At first Cummins' Japanese operations were run out of a tiny Tokyo office staffed by Wim Mulder (a Dutch-American on loan from the Columbus plant), a secretary, and a Japanese national named Art Tajima. (The two men had met a year or so earlier when Tajima, then representing a Japanese railroad equipment manufacturer, toured Cummins' Columbus facilities.)[4] Tajima served an immediately valuable role as an interpreter of Japanese language, culture, and business ways; but his value to Cummins in Japan grew quickly and inestimably. A loyal and highly responsible manager, Tajima also proved to be a judicious diplomat. Over the next three-and-a-half decades, he participated in virtually every high-level negotiation between Cummins and Komatsu—including, as we will see, some turbulent encounters.

Even from the outset, recalls Tajima, relations between the two companies "had ups and downs." Although attracted by Cummins' first-rate technology, Komatsu had to struggle to meet the U.S. company's exacting manufacturing specifications, many of which exceeded Japanese Industrial Standard (JIS) requirements or called for the use of special metals and other materials. But the Japanese company overcame these obstacles, and after a few years its build rates climbed sharply. Most of the engines thus produced went into Komatsu's own equipment (mainly tractors, in those days). Significantly, after signing on with Cummins, the Japanese company stopped producing its own diesel engines in sizes that would have been competitive with Cummins.[5]

As it turned out, potent seeds of discontent were being sown in the 1960s, a decade of radical change for Komatsu (and, as we have seen, an era of prosperity and confidence for Cummins). In 1964, Komatsu was shaken by the announcement of a joint venture between Mitsubishi, the Japanese industrial and automotive behemoth, and Caterpillar, the world's leading producer of construction equipment. In response, Komatsu sought alliances with technology leaders such as Cummins to expand its know-how and market reach.[6]

But most of the improvements at Komatsu came from within—and they were dramatic. In fact, Komatsu made such rapid progress on its own that it increasingly felt constrained by Cummins' manufacturing standards and specifications. To meet its growing array of nonautomotive applications (traditionally not Cummins' forte), Komatsu sought to modify aspects of the H and NH designs; but Cummins insisted that the Japanese stick to the terms of the somewhat confining license agreement.

Even a technology as basic as turbocharging was regarded quite differently in each of the two countries. In the United States, where the quest for power was paramount, turbochargers were sweeping across the on-road transportation industry, and Cummins was leading the charge. In Japan, by contrast, a legacy of ill-conceived introductions had tainted the technology, spooking customers and engine manufacturers alike. Compounding the problem was the fact that turbocharged versions of Cummins' most powerful NHC engines often failed when installed in Komatsu crawler tractors, evidently because this particular application—with high heat build-up, higher cylinder pressures, and significant "lugging" time—was an extremely demanding one. Clearly, the market for Cummins' big engines differed on the two sides of the Pacific.[7]

Cummins, too, felt hobbled by aspects of the relationship, particularly when it came to Komatsu's acting as local purchasing agent for Cummins in Japan. Cummins bought materials in Japan for several of its operations (including Darlington, Atlas, Frigiking, and Fleetguard). But as Jim Henderson reported in 1971: "Komatsu has not quoted attractive prices from their sources of supply. . . . [O]n only three parts out of forty have they been competitive."

Henderson concluded: "We must retain the right to negotiate directly with all potential suppliers."[8] Through careful negotiations with Komatsu Chairman Ryoichi Kawai, John Hackett sorted out the issue a year later. Komatsu was not attempting to act as Cummins' agent in Japan or "intervene with suppliers," he explained to Henry Schacht; it was merely trying to protect its own sources of supply, some of which it shared with Cummins and which had come up short when Cummins increased demand "abruptly."

The tone of Hackett's 1972 report is revealing. "I admit that I think Cummins management is paranoid on this issue," he wrote to his Cummins colleagues of the Komatsu-as-supplier question. He then concluded more generally: "I believe they are actively seeking a closer relationship. . . . We need to make a concerted effort to eliminate the negative reactions that frequently surface at Cummins middle management level in dealing with Komatsu." Such temperature taking—an effort to gauge the mood at Komatsu toward its American partner—became a common feature at Cummins over the next decade, especially as new disagreements were layered upon these early points of contention. At the same time, the first signs of "paranoid" and "negative reactions" within Cummins reflected a growing mood in industrial America, which in some circles eventually erupted into full-blown "Japan bashing."

This emerging view was nourished by economic conditions in the 1970s. Although Japan had become a net exporter to the United States in a few key areas such as consumer textiles, steel, and household appliances back in the late 1950s and 1960s, the United States had not racked up large trade deficits with Japan until fairly recently. And Japanese imports had not exceeded imports in that quintessentially American industry—automobile products—until 1968. By the early 1970s, the story of Japan's rapid eclipse of Motor City's sluggish and overconfident auto giants was reiterated with the solemn certainty of a morality play. But along with the admission of culpability came a backlash, as a growing chorus of U.S. economists and politicians began calling for Japan to eliminate import restrictions and revalue the yen. The workers and managers at Cummins hardly were immune to these powerful currents of public opinion.

Despite the continuing frictions in its relations with Komatsu, Cummins' overall impulse was to view the partnership as mutually beneficial; to build rather than sever ties; to rely on sound business practices more than on government policy; and to adhere to a long-term view of U.S.-Japanese economic relations. As John Hackett concluded in "Japanese-American Trade Relations," a sophisticated analysis of exchange rates, quotas, tax policies, and international licensing agreements: *The only lasting solution to correcting the imbalance in Japanese-American trade is to rapidly improve productivity in the U.S., control costs and maintain significant lead in research and development* [his italics]. This is what Cummins more or less consistently tried to do.

A new Cummins-Komatsu accord signed in 1972—which made Komatsu a producer of engine components for Cummins' new K engine—hinted at better relations between the two companies. Komatsu would produce eight major components (blocks, heads, cams, and crankshafts, among others) to be shipped stateside for assembly. Cummins' bullishness about its new high-horsepower line was matched by Komatsu's eagerness to scale up its Oyama plant, fifty miles north of Tokyo, to make Cummins engine components.

But the ink on the agreement scarcely was dry when the world rushed in. President Nixon's decoupling of the dollar from the Japanese yen (and other currencies) led to an immediate spike in the price of the yen against the dollar, which in turn made the K component contract much less financially appealing to Cummins. The deal was restructured in 1973. The number of components was scaled back to three—blocks, heads, and rods—but Cummins agreed to purchase minimum volumes or pay penalties in order to protect Komatsu's investment in new capacity. The two companies also agreed to set prices annually, and to share exchange-rate losses.

Then came the Middle East War, the OPEC oil embargo, and an age of energy conservation that killed demand for the high-horsepower K engine (see Chapter 8). But it took Cummins several years to scale back its expectations for the K, and in this painful period of readjustment, the company continued to submit overly optimistic sales projections to Komatsu. How many K components should Komatsu produce? How should it be compensated when actual demand fell far short of projections? These questions emerged and remained as the main points of contention between the two companies for the balance of the decade.

Cummins struggled to escape the bind. In 1975, Komatsu sought price increases of some 60 percent to support its low-volume operations. It ultimately accepted half that amount, yielding to Cummins' complaints that it was losing $4,000 on every K engine it sold, mainly because of Komatsu parts price hikes. In 1976, as shortfall penalties owed to Komatsu reached $6.4 million, the two companies agreed that in place of this obligation Komatsu would not pay royalties to Cummins on Komatsu-made NH engines for several years. It was not until the early 1980s that a fundamentally new contract was put into place, one in synch with normal sales levels and stipulating softer downside penalties for Cummins. All of this wrangling cost Cummins more than money; the American diesel maker paid dearly in trust.[9] "The Japanese began to lose more and more confidence," recalls John Hackett.

By 1980, relations between Komatsu and Cummins were a strained and tangled web. Whereas Hackett noted "three points of dissatisfaction" during his 1972 meeting with Kawai, eight years later to the day he counted eleven. The K-engine contract topped the list, but that perennial issue had been joined by concerns about the marketing and service of Cummins engines outside of Japan, especially in China (would Komatsu-Cummins Sales handle this attractive opportunity, or would each company go it alone?); questions about technical cooperation and product development (how much would be shared, and which products developed?); and other pressing issues.[10]

At the same time, powerful forces continued to draw the two companies together. By mutual agreement, Cummins was the overall technical leader, but by now Komatsu was making impressive strides in electronic controls, a frontier hitherto neglected by the Columbus company. On the manufacturing side, as we will see, Komatsu had surged ahead of the Americans on costs, quality, and automation. Yet each side remained eager to learn from the other. Komatsu readily acknowledged Cummins' better-developed distribution system, while Cummins saw Komatsu as its main gateway to the vast and untapped markets of the Eastern hemisphere. Finally, the two enterprises were locked into a common rivalry with Caterpillar. In the construction equipment business, Komatsu was second only to Cat. In diesel engines, Cummins felt the squeeze imposed by Cat, as the vertically integrated, multinational OEM internalized many loose-engine sales once commanded by Cummins.

In spite of their differences over two decades, Cummins and Komatsu had sustained a nexus of relations that were mutually beneficial. As a licensee, distributor, parts producer—and especially as a customer—Komatsu was one of Cummins' most valuable partners worldwide. But soon the Japanese firm would take on a new role with Cummins: that of competitor. By 1980, a few of the Cummins managers most familiar with Komatsu had begun to envision a day when that company (and perhaps other big Japanese diesel makers) would try to compete in U.S. markets. But none expected that day to arrive so quickly.

Japanese Ambitions

Cummins management took its first hard look at Japanese diesel making in 1978. That fall, S. H. Jenkins, who headed Advanced Product Planning for the company, toured the four giant OEMs that produced nearly all of the diesels made in Japan. Hino, Mitsubishi Motors, Isuzu, and Nissan Diesel all were vertically integrated giants based near Tokyo, each utilizing its own engines exclusively. The four divided the 260–305 hp market almost equally, but in the more popular light-duty market (150–195 hp) Mitsubishi and Hino dominated. As Cummins would come to understand, this precisely balanced oligopoly honed the competitive skills of the Japanese OEMs.

"Japanese workers seem to display an intense loyalty not only to their employers but also to their fellow workers," Jenkins observed, echoing a theme gaining currency in the American business press. As for manufacturing, Jenkins noted that facilities were "quite modern," with some automation, but added that the firms suffered from gross overcapacity. He characterized their R&D as "good, but not generally outstanding," although he was impressed by their success at meeting emissions standards with naturally aspirated engines—a feat that many American technicians considered impossible. On that score, said Jenkins, "the Japanese achievements have revised our thinking." All in all, Jenkins gave the Japanese OEMs mixed reviews. The comparisons he made with U.S. conditions probably were accurate enough, but he lacked the historical perspective needed to appreciate the great strides made by the Tokyo automakers in the previous decade.[11]

A report on Komatsu's R&D and manufacturing operations filed by two Cummins engineers two years later was more cautionary. "While it is true today that overall their products are not as advanced as ours," said the two technicians, "their current status of development is closing that gap." One example was Komatsu's SA6D110 engine, a new model of particular interest because it was comparable to the small Pink engine then under design at Cummins. The Japanese model, according to the engineers, was "very competitive," especially on fuel consumption. Had Komatsu utilized Cummins technology in this design? Apparently not, although the two men suggested that "long-time, overall exposure of the Cummins total technology could [make] an indirect contribution." Still, in their view, the best way to head off a rivalry was full technical cooperation. "Half-measure cooperation, we are afraid, will lead to a potential competitor."[12]

But there were larger forces at work pushing toward that outcome. Most had to do with Komatsu's perception of its tenuous place in the world. The first energy crisis in 1973 caused renewed interest in fuel efficiency among the world's internal-combustion-engine makers, but nowhere was this interest stronger than in Japan, which lacked petroleum resources. (And Japanese engine makers were still selling mainly to Japanese customers at this point.) To push harder into diesel, Komatsu employed the kind of "campaign" approach that it had applied successfully in the 1960s. In 1972, the company launched Project B, an ambitious effort to improve the quality of its large bulldozers. Later in the decade, with the support of an expanded research base, the Japanese company increased its product lines (in five basic categories) from forty-six to seventy-seven. These products were produced with increasing efficiency and quality year after year. With its "V-10" campaign, Komatsu had managed to cut costs 10 percent, improve product quality, reduce product parts nearly 20 percent, and rationalize its manufacturing systems. Within its own walls, Komatsu had executed a manufacturing revolution. And it was a revolution designed to support a drive for international dominance—for now Komatsu looked outward, toward the global marketplace and its arch-rival, Caterpillar.[13]

These two trends—the growing prowess of Komatsu, and the increasing tensions between Komatsu and Cummins—were converging toward a flashpoint.

As Komatsu braced itself to go head-to-head against Cat in the early 1980s, the Japanese firm came to view Cummins more as a liability than an asset. For one thing, Komatsu's managers were worried about the ability of Cummins' worldwide distributor network to provide adequate parts support. Moreover, Komatsu's technicians were more eager than ever to modify Cummins technology. They were especially interested in using their newly developed electronic-control system to govern Cummins fuel-pump technology. In mid 1980, Hackett sought and received acknowledgment from a Komatsu executive that this modification was prohibited under the terms of the license. So it was especially disconcerting to the Americans when they learned a few months later of Komatsu's plans to exhibit an electronic fuel-control system at an upcoming major industrial exposition. Hackett's telex to Art Tajima told him to insure that Komatsu portray electronic controls as purely experimental, and not to substitute for Cummins components without full permission.[14]

There was another, even more fundamental disparity between the two companies that was widening the rift, though it was seldom discussed openly. This was the growing divergence in the manufacturing practices of the two companies. Komatsu had made dramatic gains in lowering its manufacturing costs and improving the quality and reliability of the engines that rolled off its assembly lines. Cummins technology was still generally superior (although Komatsu was making progress on this front). But the Japanese were convinced that, to compete effectively in world markets, they would need products that were competitively priced, reliable, *and* technologically advanced— the last alone was not enough.

All of this drove Komatsu's managers ineluctably to wonder: Do we need Cummins? Why not make and sell our own diesel engines? And they began to act accordingly.

None of this was particularly clear—or worrisome—to the management of Cummins prior to 1983. Will Miller (the son of Irwin Miller, who gradually was becoming more involved in the Engine Company's affairs) toured several Japanese diesel plants in the summer of 1981 and wrote an encouraging report to Schacht and Stoner. He noted the "respect" with which workers were treated in Japanese factories and commended the Japanese emphasis on defining problems and encouraging communication at all levels of the organization. Miller found these parallels with the Engine Company's values and goals to affirm "the overall direction Cummins is heading with respect to methods of managing people." More than this, while Japanese managers were uniformly critical of their American counterparts for taking a "short-run view," many praised Cummins as a breed apart. Hino executives spoke of their high regard for Henderson, Schacht, and Cummins, while an executive at Komatsu (reported Miller) "believes that Cummins is philosophically much closer to Japanese management than other American companies."[15]

In the long run, these commonalities proved to be crucial. As Komatsu moved to become a full-line producer, it quickly shed its formal relations with all of its American partners except Cummins.[16] But this relationship, too, was severely strained in the early 1980s. For along with the Engine Company's discovery that Japanese diesel makers were making inroads into its home market came the disturbing news that its longtime Japanese partner was leading the charge.

Realizations about Japanese manufacturing prowess and Japanese marketing challenges came to Cummins management in a rush in the early 1980s. In a harbinger of things to come, Komatsu Chairman Ryoichi Kawai pulled away from closer involvement with Cummins during a 1981 visit to Columbus. When Cummins proposed that Komatsu become the sole manufacturer and supplier of Cummins engines for all of Asia, Kawai declined, suggesting guardedly that the two companies consider Asian opportunities on a "case by case" basis. Komatsu made its strategic intentions clearer the following year, when president Shoji Nogawa accompanied other Komatsu executives to Columbus and described their plans to manufacture diesel engines. These would be installed in Komatsu equipment, they explained, except when customers demanded Cummins engines.[17]

This was distressing news for the Engine Company, to be sure, but mainly because it represented the potential loss of large sales to a large customer. Cummins was not yet focused on the possibility that Komatsu or other Japanese firms might emerge as strong competitors. And there was still plenty of pressure from other quarters to occupy the firm's attention. When Henderson spoke of the "new competitive environment" in 1982, in his first videotaped address to employees, he emphasized competition from European diesel makers. Squeezed by excess world capacity and aided by government supports, he explained, a growing number of European producers were cutting prices and plunging into new markets—including the United States. "Eventually," Henderson added, the American market "will look promising to Japanese producers."[18]

In March 1983, Henderson and three other Cummins managers went to Japan, where they toured Japanese diesel plants operated by Yanmar, Hino, and Komatsu. Henderson had gone to Japan several times before, and would return many more times. But this particular trip affected him deeply—more so than perhaps any other episode in his professional career. "I couldn't believe what I saw," he later recalled. "Simply stated, they were doing things that we all said we couldn't do in terms of higher quality standards, lower costs, and involvement of people." The detailed report he filed soon after returning to Columbus conveyed the same sense of gravity and urgency.

To produce the same number of engines, reported Henderson (writing with the other members of the small team), Japanese diesel makers required less fixed and working capital, one-third the number of workers, and one-half the hours that Cummins required. Improvements in costs and productivity over the previous five years had been "dramatic." Of all the enterprises they toured, Komatsu was the "most impressive." With manufacturing costs 20 to 30 percent below those at Cummins, with 70 test cells to Cummins' 160, and with a product development cycle recently reduced from 50 to 30 months, Komatsu was turning out engines of comparable quality to Cummins'. Many new projects were now under way: natural-gas engines, electronic fuel-system controls, cast-iron crankshafts, and a turbocharged eleven-liter engine.

For Henderson, all of this amounted to a call for immediate action. "I was really impressed and deeply concerned by these _facts_. We clearly have a more urgent problem than I previously thought," he admitted. "We must make major progress in three years—not five years. Five years is too long."

Henderson also garnered insights from his visit about Japanese competitive strategy. He was told at Komatsu that Japanese truck manufacturers would first approach the United States by attempting to sell loose engines at very low prices. Once established in that way, they then would begin to design trucks for the American market.[19] Henderson was well aware that this approach echoed how Japanese automobile makers recently had captured a quarter of the U.S. market within four years; he had retold this story to company employees a few months earlier, with the admonition: "There's a lesson here in automobiles. . . . The same thing could happen to us."[20]

Throughout the remainder of 1983, evidence began to appear that Japanese engine makers were nibbling at the American market. Some of the OEMs they approached were Cummins customers. The evidence is sketchy, but it appears that Japanese engine makers managed to sell only a few hundred loose diesels in the United States in 1983 (although the number installed by Japanese OEMs in their own equipment was much greater).

Early 1984 was different. "We are suddenly seeing Japanese activity in our marketplace very aggressively," Henderson told the rank-and-file. He did so in a special videotaped address titled "Report on Japanese Engine Competition." Henderson began his report gravely. Some are tired of hearing about the Japanese, he acknowledged, but ignoring it would be a "grave mistake" because "there are signs that it is already our most severe competition." Since his rude awakening in Japan several months earlier, Henderson had embarked on a kind of crusade—to alert the company to the threat, and to formulate a response—_quickly_.[21]

Not everyone was persuaded. "It got so I was known as 'Hender-_san_' around here," he recalls. But Irwin Miller stresses how influential this and subsequent video presentations were in transforming the company:

They were very important. Jim was teased, and even ridiculed: "There goes Henderson on the VCR again!" But how else could he do what he was trying to do—that is, change the outlook of everybody at Cummins? People thought he was overdoing it. But I don't know any way he could have done it except by overdoing it.

The 1984 videotape was an effective opening salvo in Henderson's campaign. In it, he spoke of the tightly knit diesel-engine oligopoly in Japan, and described in detail the major players and their likely beachhead strategy. But the most powerful portion of the address came when Henderson gave the details of Japanese approaches to Cummins customers.

For example, said Henderson: Hino Motors, Ltd., Japan's oldest truck maker, had arranged to sell some of its Class 6 and 7 trucks in five southeastern states, thanks to a Florida car dealer who agreed to assemble the units from kits. Hino's older EK100 diesel engine was heavy and wasteful compared with Cummins' L10, but its new EP100 had smaller displacement, weighed less, used less fuel, featured electronic timing and two-stage turbocharging, and cost 30 percent less to manufacture. Isuzu (with fewer employees but greater sales than Cummins) already was selling diesels to U.S.-based generator-set maker Sullair, and soon would market its engines through General Motors under the GM label. And Nissan Diesel Motor Co., Ltd. was working actively with Ford and was also planning to bring Class 6 and 7 truck engines into the United States in 1984.

Then there were Mitsubishi Motors and Mitsubishi Industries, with combined sales of $13 billion and combined employment of 82,000. Traditionally strong in high- and low-horsepower ranges (including the ranges covered by the B and C families), Mitsubishi recently had introduced an eleven-liter engine that would compete directly with the new Cummins L10. And Mitsubishi sales reps were pounding the American pavement, with their prototypes currently being tested by some eighty U.S. OEMs. Said Henderson: "Ford Motor Company says they see more of the Mitsubishi people than they see of the Cummins, Caterpillar, and Detroit Diesel people combined."

Japanese diesel makers had approached Cummins customers across the product spectrum, and many were signing deals. In heavy-duty trucking, stalwart International Harvester had agreed to buy from Komatsu, GM from Mitsubishi, Ford from Isuzu. In agriculture, Allis Chalmers, Case, Versatile, IHC-Ag, and Steiger were talking with the Japanese. In construction, Champion, Koehring, Clark Industrial Truck, Clark Michigan, International Hough, and FMC had been approached, while P&H, Grove, Hyster, and Sullair had made purchases. And among Cummins generator-set customers, Kohler had been courted, and Generac and Onan already were buying Japanese.

In virtually every case, whether they succeeded or not, Japanese producers offered their engines at prices below normal market levels—sometimes as much as 40 percent below. Henderson supplied the figures. Nissan offered models competitive with the Cummins L10 and KT that were 33 percent and 41 percent cheaper, respectively. A Mitsubishi engine that did the work of the Cummins KTA sold for 18 percent less. And Komatsu's match for the NT was 22 percent cheaper to buy. Nor did Japan seem to be "dumping" these products on American shores at below cost to gain a toehold. Isuzu models that undersold Cummins Bs by 3 percent and Cs by 14 percent were (respectively) 34 percent and 27 percent cheaper in Japan.[22]

Henderson made another video presentation a few weeks later (March 1984) about the Engine Company's longtime licensee and customer—in fact, its biggest construction and KV customer in the world—Komatsu Ltd. With a single plant at Oyama (roughly the size of Cummins' Main Engine Plant), Komatsu was turning out with 1,100 manufacturing workers what Cummins would need 3,500 to 4,000 to accomplish, and with 25–30 percent lower costs. "If they choose to," concluded Henderson, "Komatsu . . . may become our toughest competitor of all from Japan."

Komatsu was wooing Cummins loyalists such as International Harvester, which already was operating a Komatsu engine in a test truck. As further evidence that Komatsu was serious about selling loose engines in America, Henderson described how the Japanese firm recently transformed the spartan conference room used by foreigners at its home office into a "very plush" welcome center, and produced a slick promotional film narrated in impeccable English. Henderson played the film for his Cummins audience so they too could see, in the Oyama plant, the dearth of assembly-line workers, the state-of-the-art machine tools—some operated by tapeless numerical control, many designed and built by Komatsu itself—the flexible manufacturing lines capable of turning out three different engine blocks, the indefatigable robots cutting gears.

It had been Komatsu that recently won over Onan, a leading producer of generator sets. This defection, perhaps more than any other, stung the Engine Company. In 1983, Onan bought 700 engines worth some $10 million from Cummins. But when Onan was offered engines comparable to Cummins models in a range of classes at 20 percent lower prices, plus the opportunity to handle their own parts business, it signed on for seven years. Henderson underscored the point: when it came to this valued customer, "Cummins is out; Komatsu is in."[23]

In 1984, Komatsu further removed doubt about its intentions to expand in diesel engines on its own terms by terminating its license to manufacture Cummins N743 engines. Only the N855 license remained intact, and it was slated to expire in early 1987. With the end of this portion of the twenty-three-year-old Cummins-Komatsu relationship, the competitive ground rules were significantly different.[24]

Relations between Cummins and Komatsu fell to a new low point. Cummins executive Mike Walsh—whose assignment as a key liaison between Cummins and Komatsu was praised by Ryoichi Kawai in mid-1984—reported a year later that "the relationship continues to go down hill." That same day, another Cummins manager reported that "the relationship with Komatsu has been steadily declining" since 1982, and that by 1984 the mood within Cummins at the grass-roots level had decisively "turned to resentment and anger."[25]

An incident involving engine sales to Turkey fanned the flames of resentment, and seemed to support the view that Komatsu was shifting from partner to competitor. During a 1984 visit to Komatsu, Henderson and Walsh learned that Komatsu would be making bids to the Turkish Coal Ministry, which typically placed hefty equipment orders. According to Cummins insiders, when it came to bidding the engines, Komatsu submitted original Cummins prices, and stonewalled efforts by the Americans to submit lower bids. Komatsu won the engine order. "In the last analysis," lamented Walsh, "Komatsu virtually 'forced' their engines on the customer (Turkey) and would not give us any opportunity to make good on our offer to reduce our prices." Henderson expressed his "surprise" at the Turkey order directly to Nogawa in a telex. The response was, according to engineer Carl Ahlers, "exactly what we expected—a polite 'no' with an explanation, and a soft hope for future business."[26]

The time had come for Cummins to respond forcefully to the Japanese incursions, at home and around the world. And more broadly, the time had come for Cummins to improve its competitive posture—an effort that would take place on multiple fronts, and significantly change the Engine Company.

The counterattack

Cummins employed three basic strategies in responding to the Japanese challenge, as well as to competitive challenges elsewhere around the world. First, simply to stay in the game, the Engine Company had to cut (or hold the line on) its prices. This is what the Big Three automakers in Detroit had declined to do, leading directly to their rapidly declining market share. Cummins elected to cut prices on its new products as quickly as it could, even if it meant selling some of those products at a loss.

The second step, dictated by the first, was to cut costs. This effort was ongoing, in light of the severe recession of the early 1980s. But now something new was called for, beyond the familiar cyclical retrenching. Having had his eyes opened by the contrasts between manufacturing practices at Cummins and several Japanese companies, Jim Henderson saw no alternative to effecting a fundamental change in the way Cummins made engines and components.

Cost cutting was inseparable from the third priority: to improve quality on every front. This effort eventually drew on the wisdom of Cummins' Japanese competitors, as well as on the experience of an American consulting firm that had been training Japanese companies in quality systems for more than thirty years.

Cutting Prices

As a first order of business in meeting the Japanese challenge, Cummins began to roll back its prices. "We needed to find a way to prevent European and Japanese competition from taking a free ride on Cummins to introduce their own engines," Schacht explained to PACCAR's Chuck Piggot in late 1983. "We didn't want to stand still for this." Ever since the company's strategists had perceived a challenge from Japan, they were consistent on this point: *Don't let them enter under a price umbrella.*

The price reductions were scaled up in proportion to the perceived threat. "We have been quietly decreasing prices for several months," Henderson reported in early 1984. According to one internal source, Cummins increased overall engine prices by a mere 6.6 percent in 1982, and held that level with no change into 1983. According to Henderson, in 1983 Cummins reduced the price of B and C engines by 5 percent; L10s by 8 percent; and all engines sold directly by 8.5 percent, with deeper discounts for key customers (such as International Hough, which received a 17.6 percent reduction). More importantly, deeper discounts were slated for 1984: an additional 10–15 percent for the B and C families, and another 6–19 percent for the L10, among others.[27]

The Cummins price reductions of 1983–1984 were not solely a response to Japanese competition, but should be viewed in a longer perspective. In large measure, they represented the rolling back of a pricing strategy initiated in the late 1970s and now considered to have run its course. As it emerged from the recession of 1975, Cummins found itself struggling against eroding profit margins. The double-digit inflation that gripped the economy in 1973–1974 surprised many manufacturers with its severity and duration. Often producers failed to recoup rising labor and materials costs because they delayed too long in raising prices after spikes in those variable costs.

Following its long engine-price freeze (1953–1966), Cummins tended to restrict price hikes to periods of high demand, rather than risk driving away customers with high prices during economic downturns. But beginning in the late 1970s, Cummins adopted a new approach. As costs climbed relentlessly, and as the perplexing new macroeconomics of stagflation began to appear intractable, the company started to tie its product prices more closely—and quickly—to the inflation rate and to its own costs. In 1979, Cummins raised engine prices an average of 7.8 percent. Encouragingly, sales continued to climb. Engine prices were boosted another 15.7 percent in 1980 and 12.3 percent in 1981, while parts prices were increased 12.8 percent and 12.5 percent, respectively.

Beginning in 1982—as the economic recession deepened, worldwide diesel engine overcapacity worsened, foreign competitors slashed prices, and Cummins posted healthy rates of return—the company reined in its prices. Thus, Cummins had begun to compete more aggressively on price *before* Japanese diesel makers posed a real threat. More to the point, the price leveling of 1983 and the price cutting that began in earnest in 1984 came on the heels of several years of hikes. Between 1978 and 1982, the average gross price of NH engines was increased by 37 percent; the V903 by 85 percent; the KT6 by 60 percent; the V1710 by 46 percent; the small V by 15 percent; and the KV by 56 percent. In contrast, Komatsu had not raised prices since 1973. In large measure, therefore, the Cummins price adjustments of 1983–1984 had the effect of rolling back prices to their late 1970s levels.

This was only the beginning, however. Soon Cummins became much more aggressive about cutting its prices to keep the Japanese out of American markets, especially to protect its new product lines. But it was clear that Cummins' relatively high prices were a symptom of a deeper cause: higher manufacturing costs. At prices this low—and soon to be lower—Cummins lost money. So this course of treatment (cutting prices) could only go on for so long before the patient died, starved of the life-giving flow of revenues. No real cure was possible unless the Engine Company could learn how to live and grow while consuming far fewer resources.

Cummins' aggressive price-cutting strategy drew inspiration from the less-than-happy experience of other U.S. industrials. By this time, the Japanese conquest of a large part of the American car market was legendary, as Henderson noted often in his speeches. Another example, which Cummins watched with great interest, hit even closer to home. In what *Business Week* called "one of the great corporate battles of the decade," Komatsu snatched an astounding 17 percent of the worldwide construction equipment market away from Caterpillar between 1983 and 1985. The main reason: The Japanese company enjoyed a 40 percent price advantage, partly due to favorable exchange rates, partly to its own pricing strategy.[28] Cummins, to its credit, did more than simply await the return of the strong Japanese yen.

Cutting Costs

It was at the September 1982 planning conference that Cummins first articulated a goal of a companywide 30 percent cost reduction to match the ongoing price rollbacks on its engines. "The competitive threat is real," Henderson told the assembled Cummins managers, citing among other developments the almost certain entry into the domestic diesel engine business by Hino (in California-based Class 6 trucks) by the late 1980s. "It is upon us. It is not so imminent, however, that we can't do anything about it. We have some time, *if* we get started now on implementation."

Henderson told his executives that the company's goals were not tough enough, that it was too internally oriented, and that it had to be prepared to learn everything it could, wherever it could, in order to do its job better. Nevertheless, Cummins was determined to stay in the diesel engine business as a low-cost producer. "If any company has a chance to make the kind of turnaround American industry must make," Henderson concluded, "it is Cummins."[29]

In the following spring, however, the Engine Company's confidence was shaken. Henderson and his colleagues returned from their eye-opening tour of Japan in March. In subsequent discussions with Henry Schacht, Henderson came up with an idea that he soon began to call the "30 Month Sprint"—a concerted effort to reduce the company's costs by 1 percent a month for thirty months. It was a combination of tough goals, high stakes, and motivational "theater." As Henry Schacht recalls:

> *Getting our people to pay attention, and getting our people to first admit that we weren't the world leaders that we thought we were, was absolutely critical. We were leaders by Western standards, but we weren't by world standards—and therefore had to do something about it!*
>
> *We finally drove enough people over to Japan and said, "Your eyes are as good as mine. What do you see?" We took just droves of people. Jim just kept pushing their nose back into it and saying, "Okay, what are we going to do?"*
>
> *And from that came the "30 Month Sprint," the point of which was that we were going to reduce our costs one percent a month for thirty months. As Jim said, "Well, we might as well start someplace."*

The 30 Month Sprint was, according to Jim Henderson, an "all-hands-to-the-pump, top-down, take-costs-out-of-this-company activity." It was fundamentally based on a cost-per-piece approach developed by Henderson and his colleagues in operations: pull the engine apart, look at how each piece was produced, and ask the key question: How can we take costs out of this piece?

The first iteration of the plan reached the Cummins work force in a Henderson videotape in the spring of 1983. It was in part a set of concrete goals—for example, reducing costs by between 25 and 40 percent (for an average of 30 percent), and achieving 31.5 percent gross margin or the equivalent.

It was also exhortation. We have to move—Henderson said—from turf to teamwork, from skepticism to openness, from "hit the standard" to continuous improvement, from fear to confidence, and from vulnerable to formidable.[30]

Tough measures associated with the 30 Month Sprint underscored the seriousness of the message. In May, Cummins announced that it was closing its plant in Quincy, Illinois (with 45 workers), and Peterlee, England (with 190 workers). An early retirement program, designed to thin out the ranks of higher-paid employees, was implemented at the same time.[31] Nevertheless, skepticism abounded. As financial officer John McLachlan recalls:

> *Henry [Schacht], with his 30 percent price cuts, was bad enough. Then comes Jim with this idea: "We're going to reduce costs by 30 percent in thirty months!" I knew he was nuts! Henry might have been hallucinating, but Jim had lost a piece. I had been pursuing cost reduction for about seven years before the 30 Month Sprint, and we had gotten between 15 and 20 percent—better than a couple of percentage points a year. But the whole idea that you could get a 1 percent cost reduction every month for the next thirty months! Well, you knew he had just flipped his lid.*
>
> *More seriously, though: If he'd said "15 percent in thirty months," people might have worried and fretted about how they were going to do it. But when he said 30 percent, people first said, "Oh, well; he's flipped." But they also said, "I've got to think differently. I can't just do what I've been doing all along." And it's when you have hopeless causes like this that people tend to rally and pull together.*

The rank-and-file, like some managers, were unconvinced. At an April 1983 meeting with the DWU executive board and shop stewards, Henderson engaged in a candid Q&A with a skeptical work force. One union member asserted flatly that a 30 percent cost reduction would not solve all of Cummins' problems. In fact, he pointed out, even reducing the work force to *zero* would not reduce the company's cost structure by 30 percent. Henderson agreed, and also agreed with the assertion that the 30 Month Sprint was not only a union responsibility. The 30 percent cost target had to be met by every person and every activity of the company, he said. There were "loafers," both in management and the rank-and-file, who no longer could be tolerated. "We need a 100 percent effort from everyone," he asserted.[32]

In fact, Henderson's visits to Japan had convinced him that wages were *not* the primary problem. True, Komatsu paid its workers lower salaries, but it provided much more in terms of benefits: housing, medical, education, and so on. "And that drove us back," he recalls, "into thinking about all the ways you could take cost out short of cutting people's wages."

So unlike similar efforts at other corporations in this time period, the Cummins campaign was aimed at getting all 20,000 company employees—not just the engineers or the purchasing department—focused on cost reduction, from plant managers to the newest hire on the shop floor. Plants that ran on the team system, for example, soon had a member of every team who was responsible for tracking cost reduction and sharing that information with his or her team. As financial officer John McLachlan recalls of one of his visits to Jamestown in this period:

> You could go to the piston line, and the ladies who worked at the end of the line could tell you what the daily cost of a piston was. They were gathering up the through-put data, the scrapper wastage, and the percent-completed numbers, and giving all that data to the cost member of the team, and he or she was updating that information. So you could go to her and she could say, "Yeah, it cost us $2.25 per piston yesterday, and we've got to get that down to $2.05 to achieve our 30 percent cost-reduction target." That's when I realized how far down into the plants this idea had taken root.

Neither Schacht nor Henderson thought that Cummins could hit the 30 percent target in two and a half years—and in fact, the company did not. But costs *were* cut approximately 17 percent in the first thirty months of the campaign, and (depending on one's calculations) the 30 percent target was achieved within five years.* Within five years of the start of the campaign, overall floor space was reduced by 30 percent, the R&E payroll by 10 percent, the manufacturing payroll by 40 percent, and the marketing and staff payrolls by 50 percent.[33]

These dramatic cuts led, in turn, to new kinds of problems. But they bought time for the company in a particularly dangerous period, and kept options open for the future.

Strategic Sourcing

A second element in the cost-cutting plan (and a vital piece of the 30 Month Sprint) was a new approach to "sourcing"—that is, purchasing materials and components for use in engine manufacture and assembly.

Throughout the 1960s, Cummins had looked for opportunities to bring more engine parts and other components under its own production umbrella. This served multiple purposes: creating employment in Columbus, stabilizing the supply and quality levels of critical components, and in many cases

---

*"We got about 23 percent through our cost-cutting efforts," recalls Jim Henderson, "and another 7 percent as a result of the yen-dollar shift."

saving money. By the end of the decade, Cummins manufactured not only the core components of its engines (blocks and heads), but also a whole host of other parts of greater or lesser criticality: pistons, liners, gears, gear-case covers, and so on. In fact, the list of parts that Cummins would *not* consider fabricating was remarkably short. It included standard hardware, such as cap screws; highly specialized parts, such as piston rings; and—mostly for historical reasons—grey-metal castings.*

In the 1970s, the related evils of undersupply and allocation kept the attention of Cummins' managers focused on capacity expansion. The pertinent question was rarely, "Which vendor can supply the best product at the lowest cost?" Far more often, it was, "How much can we get—from whom, and how soon?" The strike of 1972 occurred in large part because Cummins and the DWU disagreed fundamentally on whether the company had the right to outsource the fabrication of engine and fuel-system parts. (The company prevailed.) Gradually, the "repatriation" of manufacturing to Columbus was reversed; now, things were made wherever they could be made reliably and at a reasonable cost.

Multiple trends in the 1980s reinforced this trend toward outsourcing. The recession of the early 1980s, the corporatewide restructuring associated with that crisis, and the 30 Month Sprint were only the most obvious contributors. Meanwhile, labor forces around the world were becoming increasingly skilled at certain kinds of manufacturing. At a time when automakers increasingly were outsourcing the manufacture of key components, new domestic-content laws (both in the United States and abroad) greatly complicated the issue of sourcing. Currency swings of unprecedented speed and scale necessitated a constant revisiting of the issue of where engines and engine components should be produced.

Rapidly accelerating changes in technology—such as the advent of numerically controlled machine tools—also forced the company to look at alternative ways of manufacturing. Through the early 1970s, machine tools necessarily were operated by highly skilled people. The depth and straightness of a hole created by a drill press, for example, was determined in large part by the skill of the operator. But as numerically controlled and computer-controlled devices entered the workplace, an experienced work force was less critical to some manufacturing operations.

As new engines and engine families came on line at Cummins in the late 1970s and early 1980s, they reflected these larger trends. The Jamestown plant manufactured the block, head, rod, crank, and cam of the new L10 engine, and the L10's fuel system also was made in-house. When the B and

---

*The unhappy sale of the Great Lakes Foundry in 1969 had helped sour Schacht and Henderson on vertical integration into metal castings. "My general feeling," says financial officer John McLachlan, "was that they'd consider buying anything that didn't have the word 'foundry' in its name."

C engines were introduced, as noted above, Cummins made only the block, head, and rod, and "bought out" the fuel system. Cummins' special competence, therefore, lay in the *design* of a long list of components, in the *fabrication* of a much shorter list of components (blocks, heads, rods, and—in most cases—fuel systems), the *assembly* of the final product, and the *distribution* of that product.

When Cummins made its successful pitch to J. I. Case, it did so in part by invoking the notion of strategic sourcing. It made no sense (Cummins argued) for Case to attempt to specialize in diesel engine design and manufacture at the same time that it was engaged in the highly competitive tractor and construction-equipment businesses. You worry about hydraulics, cab comfort, accessories—said Cummins to Case—and *we'll* worry about the diesel power plant. Case agreed (although the company reserved the right to call the engine in which it was investing a "Case" engine, as well as the right to make B engines of its own, which it eventually did in Germany).

Beginning in the early 1980s, Cummins began to apply this logic to itself. Sourcing decisions most often were made at the point when a set of patterns—that is, the wooden or metal forms from which stamped or poured products are made—came due for replacement. (Patterns have a finite useful life.) Increasingly, when it came time to duplicate or replace patterns, Cummins considered a range of parameters (quality, delivery, absolute price, and currency movement, among others) to decide where to make what was usually a significant investment. As Jim Henderson explains:

> We reviewed our total supply base, considered all our options, and moved a lot of it offshore in this period, both new and existing patterns. Take the example of sourcing block castings—all of which we used to buy next door—from Brazil. Well, patterns are costly, and it takes a long time to make them. Then you've got to move them. Then you've got to get new castings, and you've got to go through the whole process of qualifying their processes, and then checking the castings. This was a huge task, and a tough task, which we repeated for many component parts.

The cost-per-piece attitude generated by the 30 Month Sprint carried through into all sourcing decisions—not just domestic versus international, but also at all international manufacturing and assembly facilities. The huge currency swings of the early 1980s greatly complicated these decisions. Germany and Japan began the 1980s as high-quality and relatively inexpensive suppliers to the United States, but largely because of fluctuations in the value of the dollar, first Germany and then Japan became uncompetitive on a price basis. Meanwhile, as discussed below, countries like Brazil were becoming increasingly competitive not only on price, but also on delivery and quality. "We had to pack the whole thing up and move it not once, but twice," recalls Jim Henderson.

The long-term implications of strategic sourcing—both in terms of domestic employment and cost structure—were profound. Many were still emerging a decade and a half after the initiative was launched.

Back to Quality

Jim Henderson and his colleagues, in the wake of their visits to Japan in 1983, struggled to unlock the "mystery" of Japanese manufacturing prowess. One thing that they discovered was a close integration between design and manufacturing. Komatsu integrated design work all the way back to machine tooling. As for manufacturing processes, the contrast between Komatsu and Cummins was striking. "I saw no 'traditional' transfer lines," observed Henderson. Komatsu's manufacturing was fashioned to achieve a triad of essential goals: higher quality, lower cost, and faster delivery, expressed as the acronym QCD (Quality, Cost, Delivery). To achieve these goals, Komatsu relied on its long-standing methods of Total Quality Control (TQC), which Henderson and his fellow observers understood to be:

> *a comprehensive process for managing the company to achieve continu-*
> *ous improvement in QCD. It includes goal setting; planning; commu-*
> *nication; allocation of goals throughout the organization; a universally*
> *shared approach to problem-solving, data gathering and data analysis;*
> *feedback; reinforcement; training; quality circles; and support activities.*
> *TQC is blocking and tackling—disciplined, detailed, comprehensive,*
> *involves all employees—and it works!*

Komatsu placed much greater emphasis on flow analysis and work-force training than did Cummins. At Komatsu's Oyama plant, each employee received forty hours of training per year. And corporate goals were literally tracked through the manufacturing process with an ingenious flag system developed by President Shoji Nogawa himself. Henderson saw the importance of such systems for making abstract goals tangible and specific actions accountable. "It is our most serious missing piece," he concluded. Without such systems, the pursuit of TQC was "probably worthless."

Of course, "quality" was far from a new concern at the Engine Company. For decades, the company had prided itself on the reliability of its engines. But this tradition included a substantial reliance on multiple inspections throughout and after the manufacturing process—"our quality system was to inspect the hell out of things," as one engineer recalls—and also on extensive testing in the field. It was a "failure-driven" approach to quality. "We were real good at fixing things," says one plant manager, "but we were lousy at stopping them from being broken."[34]

Jim Henderson had begun to worry about quality issues as the economy soured in the early 1980s, and as the risks associated with the huge joint venture with Case became more clear. "BIG volume means potential for BIG warranty," Irwin Miller noted in a memo to Henderson, Schacht, and others in 1980.[35] This and similar stimuli—including Henderson's own reflections on Cummins' strengths and weaknesses—led to a flurry of top-down initiatives in a relatively short span of time. As Henderson later explained this period:

> *My perspective was that my job was to extract the best from what might be called "Old Cummins" and bring it forward. There was a lot of good in Old Cummins. I mean, they cared about people, they worked their butts off, and by god, they shipped engines. There was great esprit de corps, and there was go, go, go, and we didn't want to lose that. But the start-up of the B and C lines meant we had to do things differently. And the launching of the L10 in Jamestown also created a new situation: For the first time, we had another domestic heavy-duty plant. The rivalry between Jamestown and Columbus was fierce—really fierce. What were we going to do with that?*

The first of these initiatives launched by Henderson eventually became known as the "Achieving Paper." This was a thirty-page document authored by Henderson in the fall of 1982, in which he attempted to capture several years of thinking about Cummins.[36] It was probably the first official Cummins document to incorporate the new—and, by Henderson's own account, somewhat baffling—concept of "continuous improvement." The building blocks for a productive organization, wrote Henderson, were trust, good information flow, and a shared set of values. But this was only the necessary organizational staging for what had to follow. What had to come next, Henderson wrote, was a structure in which work flowed flexibly through a sequence of work groups, and a participatory process in which the needs of two sets of "customers"—inside and outside of the organization—were taken into account.

The status quo was not satisfactory, Henderson concluded. Conversely, the potential inherent in a new way of operating was almost incalculable:

> *We have adopted many management techniques/tools that do not support the concept of continuous improvement—for example, production standards, learning curves, five-year plans done annually, one-way staff meetings, etc. These must be questioned and eventually changed if we*

believe people can learn and develop continuously, and therefore improve continuously.

Continuous improvement requires learning, innovation, risk-taking, and change. It also requires frequent discussion/assessment of excellence and the pursuit of new and more demanding short-term goals. It can be a difficult and sometimes painful process. However, while such change may seem risky, it is far less risky in a changing environment than standing still. And, if this process is done right, it can be tremendously rewarding to the manager and the people, and most important, to our customers.[37]

The Achieving Paper was distributed widely to senior- and middle-level managers at Cummins, who—after working their way through several drafts of the paper—were expected to disseminate its central ideas through the organization. Henderson had no illusions that the Achieving Paper alone would transform the organization; and in fact, it did not. "The Achieving Paper was a terrific piece of work," says current industrial business unit head Joe Loughrey, "but it never really got ingrained in the business." Its principal value lay in getting a small cadre of top managers to hammer out and agree on a world view—no small task, but not the stuff of organizational transformation.

The next Henderson initiative was "New Standards of Excellence" (NSE). This began as little more than a slogan, intended to hammer home a central theme of the Achieving Paper. When it became clear that more was needed, a three-day training program was launched in the fall of 1983. The program primarily was intended to help Cummins managers begin to think about managing work in *flows*—that is, a more or less seamless sequence of events across the company—in order to enhance quality and reduce costs. Secondarily, it was designed to encourage these managers to place an increased emphasis on the needs of the customer. With the almost concurrent launching of the 30 Month Sprint, the boundaries between these two efforts became somewhat blurred; and by mid-1983, NSE—then being championed by operations head Dick Allison—called for reducing the company's operating and distribution costs by one-third.[38]

The champions of NSE struggled for several years to make an impact on the Cummins organization, but they faced major obstacles. Thanks in part to the success of the Big Cam II engine, Cummins' heavy-duty market share was over 60 percent at the time, which suggested to many in the organization that there was no need to become more "customer-focused." Second, and more important, no one had figured out how to inject the principles of NSE into the operational heart of the organization. The NSE effort finally went into suspended animation in the summer of 1985, when a significant layoff of Columbus-based production workers at that time (see Chapter 12) prompted the Diesel Workers Union to break off all cooperative efforts with management.

But even as the Achieving Paper and NSE were being debated and tested within the organization, Henderson was launching yet another related initiative. This time, he was looking for a more hands-on, focused, cost-and-quality effort. In the summer of 1983, therefore, Henderson approached H. Karl Kuehner, then vice president of technology, with the urgent request that Kuehner take responsibility for developing a new Cummins approach to quality.

Kuehner was a naturalized American who had served an apprenticeship at Daimler-Benz and had joined Cummins in 1966 after receiving his engineering degree from the University of Kentucky. He had risen through the engineering ranks, serving as a project engineer on a variety of initiatives, and had become vice president of technology in 1979. Kuehner was one of the many Cummins employees who made the pilgrimage to Japan—in his case, in 1982—with the specific assignment of figuring out what the Japanese had to offer in terms of process control on the engineering side of the shop. The answer, Kuehner concluded, was not much, with two notable exceptions. The first was the "talking diagram," a technique whereby Japanese workers collectively put words and pictures on a single sheet of paper, which seemed (through multiple iterations) to build a remarkable degree of consensus. The second was a mysterious tool called the "design book." Kuehner recalls the moment of discovery this way:

> *Because of language barriers, we couldn't figure out what they meant, so they finally had to show it to us. It turns out that the "design book" was a book of mistakes. Whenever an engineer had to design a new component, he or she had to go back and search through all the mistakes that had ever been made on this particular component. The worst thing that could happen in the Japanese environment was to make a mistake that somebody else had made before, so they felt an obligation to document their mistakes. This was really strange to me. In the environment of the Tech Center, documentation was not the glorious part of the work. You'd get another project, and the previous work didn't get documented.*

Kuehner's initial reaction to Henderson's request—"Why *me?*" as he recalls it—soon gave way to curiosity and absorption in the topic of quality. He immersed himself in the published works of the leading "quality gurus" of the day, including W. Edwards Deming, Juran, and Philip Crosby, and attended their respective seminars. Deming was perhaps the most celebrated of these experts, but Kuehner soon concluded that he was not a good fit with Cummins. For one thing, the octogenarian Deming no longer made "house calls." For another, Deming had acquired a reputation for being abrasive and difficult to work with. "He was like Chinese water torture," Kuehner recalls, "and I knew that wasn't going to work at Cummins."

One day, Kuehner came across a thick book called *Total Quality Control* by an engineer named Armand V. "Val" Feigenbaum. The book—dense with specific "technologies" for achieving manufacturing quality control—was a far cry from some of the slim inspirational tracts that characterized the quality field in that period. Intrigued, Kuehner set out to learn more about its author. He soon discovered that Val Feigenbaum and his brother Donald—former General Electric engineers who had established General Systems, Inc., a systems-engineering consulting firm—were celebrated in their field. In fact, the Feigenbaums, like the better-known Deming and Juran, were among the small elite of American experts who had helped the Japanese transform their manufacturing base during the previous three decades.

Kuehner arranged a meeting with Val Feigenbaum at General Systems' headquarters in Pittsfield, Massachusetts. At the end of a day of talks, Kuehner was further intrigued by the Feigenbaums' approach:

> *The way they articulated their technology was to compare it to a physical exam on the company: the blood test, the chest x-ray, and so on. They had some proprietary software that they used to pull together all this information in a quantitative way, to figure out a company's strengths and weaknesses. Then they developed a set of specific procedures for getting the company's work done. And most important, they brought people to the task. They wouldn't do it for you, but they'd help you do it.*

After several rounds of back and forth with the Feigenbaums, Kuehner made an informal presentation to his Cummins colleagues in both manufacturing and engineering, and recommended that the company retain General Systems. The response was anything but enthusiastic: "I almost got laughed out of the room," Kuehner recalls. The Cummins managers in attendance felt the process unnecessary and expensive—to put it politely—especially in light of the ongoing budget crunch.

Frustrated at having been rebuffed and lacking any sense of where to go next with his mandate from Henderson, Kuehner huddled with his boss, Bill Schwab, then vice president of research and engineering (R&E). Schwab listened to Kuehner's story, and proposed a halfway measure: Why not ask the Feigenbaums if they would be willing to consult exclusively with the engineering group?

Kuehner suspected—and the Feigenbaums soon confirmed—that General Systems would argue that it was all or nothing. Fixing only part of a company was a less than desirable approach to total quality control. "Almost by definition," Val Feigenbaum confirms, "that approach demonstrates a lack of commitment, and almost guarantees that you're not going to get there." But several factors combined to persuade General Systems to take Cummins on. The first was accidental: Val Feigenbaum and Bill Schwab had been contemporaries at General Electric in the 1950s, and there was good personal chemistry between them. A second was the Feigenbaums' respect for what they saw as the integrity and traditions of Cummins. "It was a tinkerer's company," Feigenbaum recalls, "and that can be a great strength." Another was the 30 Month Sprint, which struck Feigenbaum as convincing evidence that Cummins was determined to achieve manufacturing excellence.

Feigenbaum also was impressed by the subtle but effective interactions among the members of the company's executive team, including Irwin Miller, Henry Schacht, Jim Henderson, and Mike Walsh. Feigenbaum recalls being impressed in these early meetings with the role of Irwin Miller as a "counselor"—a senior and respected voice of wisdom. "They were more Japanese than they realized," Feigenbaum says.[39]

Perhaps most important, Val Feigenbaum became convinced that R&E was actually the upstream point of entry into the larger Cummins organization. As he explains:

> The "functional silo" of R&E was a very effective penetration point. The marketing side was very, very heavily dependent on engineers going out and explaining things to the customers. And R&E had a good deal of the "improvement resources" of the company, without their necessarily being identified as such. So while this area was called "R&E," it turned out that a good deal of the operating guts of the company could be found there. It was thought to be something different from what it actually was. Through our eyes, we could see that very clearly.

The Feigenbaums went to work at Cummins in the summer of 1983, and by September, Kuehner was asked to make a presentation regarding their work to the fall planning conference. The response, according to Kuehner, was mixed. Several manufacturing people commented acidly that they were pleased that the inhabitants of the Tech Center finally had seen the error of their ways and henceforth would take more responsibility for quality. But Mike Walsh, the newly installed head of operations, liked what he was hearing about the Feigenbaums' work. After making the trek to Pittsfield, he decided to expand their mandate to cover the whole company.

This larger initiative began early in 1984, and became known as the "Total Quality System," or TQS, effort. It was a far-ranging intervention, covering almost every aspect of the Cummins design and manufacturing process. As Kuehner recalls:

It had a very broad reach. How do you install effective controls in a manufacturing environment? How do you do process implementation? How do you do failure mode and effects analysis? How do you conduct design reviews? In the old days, before TQS, I'd complete a design, get a bunch of people in the room who I knew weren't going to bitch about anything, take input only from the people I wanted to listen to, and move on. It was very undisciplined. Well, you don't do that with TQS. TQS says, "Here are the people that have to be in the design review. Here's how you must document what was discussed. Here are the responsibilities that flow out of that."

TQS focused on process *flows*, across the Cummins system. Whereas functional "silos" traditionally had dominated, now Cummins managers were being asked to think of a continuous flow (of ideas and products) through the company. Whereas managers previously had seen their role as handing off a finished product to the next functional area, they were now expected to regard that next station as their *customers*. How could they serve this internal customer more effectively?

This led to the development of the first and most important TQS policy, which governed new product introduction. Codenamed "New Product Planning, Development, and Introduction" (NPPD&I), the policy described a continuous flow that began with customer requirements and ended with customer satisfaction. Marketing helped engineering, which helped purchasing, which helped manufacturing, which helped service. Specific subpolicies built feedback loops into this larger process, and clear checkpoints were established, beyond which products could not move unless key quality criteria had been met.

A key focus of TQS was subsumed under the title of "classification of characteristics." Simply put, this meant collectively arriving at a definition of what was vitally important on a drawing, what was of secondary importance, and what was of minor importance—and then respecting that definition. "Before TQS," explains Kuehner, "we were saying in effect that *everything* was important." But the practical result was that manufacturing people "down the line" from engineering, having no indication of a spec's relative criticality, felt equally at liberty to change *any* spec on a drawing. The result, in many cases, was diminished product performance or reliability.

Plant by plant, practice by practice, General Systems worked its way through the far-flung Cummins empire, developing numerous procedures and subprocedures, which eventually were codified into the TQS system. (Cummins designated an in-house TQS person at each plant to work directly with General Systems.) Again, the point was to capture good "flow" and fix bad flow. Perhaps 85 percent of efficiency, Val Feigenbaum told Cummins on many occasions, is determined by how the flows are set up; only 15 percent is the content of the work.[40] When Jim Henderson argued for empowering teams, Feigenbaum reiterated his point: no team could overcome the disadvantages of a badly designed work flow. "That was a very important insight for me," Henderson admits. "It wasn't enough to turn the people loose and let them sort it out. They needed help."[41]

The Feigenbaums got a mixed reception in the plants and offices of the Engine Company. (One officer later referred to them as "the Brothers Grim.") On the one hand, many plant managers eventually came to understand that there were advantages to a systemic approach to design and production. "They were being nickel-and-dimed to death because of the lack of procedural integration," Feigenbaum explains. A coherent and consistent book of procedures, focusing on rational flows of work, would eliminate most of these problems. On the other hand, recalls one manufacturing manager, the Feigenbaum/TQS approach was simply too alien for some at Cummins to embrace:

> *The manufacturing side of the organization was not systemic in its thinking. We were—and to some extent still are—a reactive organization, in which cowboys and rescuers were rewarded, and in which systemic thinking was simply not part of what we did. Many of us wouldn't have known a root cause from the root of a tree.*[42]

In its 1984 annual report, Cummins asserted that the central focus of its manufacturing efforts was now "quality, cost, and delivery." (At other times, "cost" got the highest emphasis, resulting in a Cummins-coined acronym of "CQD.") But insiders knew that Cummins had a long way to go in terms of quality, as a series of unwelcome developments in the late 1980s soon would demonstrate.

At the same time, the company had latent strengths, which—with the help of the Feigenbaums—it was beginning to call upon in an organized way. In the spring of 1986, at Mike Walsh's request, Val Feigenbaum addressed the annual distributors' meeting. He used the occasion to reflect upon three competitive advantages possessed by Cummins.

The first, he said, was the nonadversarial relationship between the company and its distributor network. This gave the company a reasonably undiluted shot at its ultimate customers—and vice versa. Even at that early point in time, many American manufacturers were beginning to feel insulated from their customers—a circumstance that was magnified by hostility between parent company and dealers. Cummins, by contrast, had clear and effective communications up and down the line. A second key strength was a managerial willingness to adopt a "burn-your-bridges" approach. The example that

Feigenbaum cited was the 30 Month Sprint—a campaign that he later referred to as gutsy and pioneering.

And finally, said Feigenbaum, Cummins had demonstrated its willingness to face and embrace change. It had recognized that the status quo was no longer the company's friend, but its enemy. By cutting prices, by embarking on the 30 Month Sprint, and—not least—by bringing in outsiders to lead an organized upheaval of the company, Schacht, Henderson, and their colleagues had invented ways to remain the masters of their fates. Unlike their counterparts in Detroit, some of whom were already infected by an attitude of defeatism and who were calling for the erection of ever-higher tariff walls, Cummins was on its way to being positioned to compete globally.

Cummins and Komatsu: back from the cliff's edge

It had been the Japanese approach to design and manufacturing—as encountered by Jim Henderson and others from Cummins in the early to mid-1980s—that had first intensified the search for a systemic approach to quality. And it was in design and manufacturing that the unusual competitive-collaborative relationship between Cummins and Komatsu was thrown into sharp relief.

The manufacturing prowess of Komatsu, Hino, and other Japanese companies was threatening Cummins' position in the United States and abroad. At the same time, these Japanese companies, and in particular Komatsu, remained willing to share their expertise, including the process-control systems that lay at the heart of Japanese manufacturing success. Throughout the early 1980s, even as collaboration was replaced by mutual suspicion, Komatsu went to great lengths to train Cummins personnel in quality, cost, and delivery-related methods. In 1983 and 1984, some one hundred Cummins technicians were invited to attend sessions on these methods in Japan, where they received intensive instruction from a Komatsu expert as well as from the internationally renowned quality expert Dr. Kaoru Ishikawa.[43]

Jim Henderson recalls a particularly striking episode from this period:

> *One day, early in this process, Mr. Kawai did a very uncharacteristic thing. He came into the room where I was, took off his coat—which the Japanese never do—sat down next to me, and said something to the effect of, "Young man, you have to learn about total quality." He called his friend and schoolmate Dr. Ishikawa, who agreed to meet with me.*

Thus began a long and productive exchange. Ishikawa and other Japanese experts, including Komatsu engineers, visited Cummins plants stateside. Cummins engineers and operations heads visited Komatsu. As Kim Singleton of Cummins summarized the exchange: "Komatsu truly held their doors wide open for us to learn from them."[44] Of course, Komatsu continued to wield the stick, as well as the carrot. In 1983, for example, Komatsu suggested that it would curtail its efforts to help Cummins, and go ahead with plans to push its own engine program, if Cummins canceled the K engine contract.[45] On balance, though, Komatsu was a generous partner—even while it became a determined competitor.

Why? There are several answers. The first is self-interest: In the struggle for global market share, the Japanese firm was reluctant to work in tandem with an inefficient producer. As long as there were contractual ties between the two companies, Komatsu had an incentive to help improve Cummins' quality.

But on a more fundamental level, Komatsu placed a special value on its relationship with Cummins. The agreements it had forged with other U.S. firms in the early 1960s had long since lapsed. With that in mind, recalls Art Tajima, Komatsu "wanted to maintain some relationship with an American company. And Cummins was the last one. That's why they did not want to cut off relations with Cummins." Similarly, Mike Walsh reported hearing that Komatsu considered its relationship with Cummins to have been "better than any of their others, e.g. International Harvester and Bucyrus-Erie."[46]

There was a deeper, less instrumental, sense of obligation as well. Because the Cummins partnership had been forged by the venerable Ryoichi Kawai himself, and because it had endured for so long, with obvious benefits for Komatsu, the Japanese company's managers were reluctant to make an abrupt about-face.* For Mike Walsh, the central reason why Komatsu continued to cooperate with Cummins in the early 1980s plainly was "historical tradition." And as another Cummins manager observed in 1982: "Deep in the mind of Komatsu's organization there exists still a strong feeling . . . that what they learned from Cummins in the last twenty years was essential for them to achieve today's level of expertise; and association with Cummins made Komatsu known in the world."[47]

Art Tajima emphasizes a cultural dimension. Motivated perhaps by an Oriental sense of duty and responsibility, he suggests, the managers at Komatsu "wanted to repay the obligations" they had incurred with Cummins over two decades. "They were telling us, 'Look, we are not going to use your engines anymore. But on the other hand, we cannot forget the past twenty years, when we were able to learn so much from you. How can we help you? What can we teach you?"

This delicate—and sometimes awkward—balance of cooperation and competition effectively ended in 1985 and 1986, when the convergence of

---

*Irwin Miller suggests, though, that the senior Kawai's tendency to remind his juniors at Komatsu of their debt to Cummins amounted to "pouring gasoline on the fire," and contributed to ill will toward Cummins within Komatsu.

several trends persuaded the Japanese company to pull back and regroup. Cummins' aggressive pricing policy surely played a role. The Cummins price cuts severely undermined one of Komatsu's key competitive advantages in North America, where it offered good products at low prices through a relatively weak distribution system. As Henry Schacht explained in a confidential memo to Henderson and Walsh: "Komatsu has been at the task of selling loose engines in the U.S. long enough now to understand exactly how tough we are prepared to make it and how marginal their success, if any, is likely to be."[48] Moreover, Cummins' 1986 purchase of a controlling share of Onan— one of the earliest of Cummins' key customers to begin buying Japanese— must have sent another strong competitive signal to Komatsu.

Protectionist rumblings in the United States also may have made the Japanese manufacturer jittery about its North American investments and aspirations. But the body blow came in late 1985 and 1986, when the value of the dollar began to fall in relation to the yen. In the first half of 1986 alone, the dollar lost 20 percent of its value against the Japanese yen. This reversal in international exchange rates, highly favorable to U.S. manufacturers, made competition on the basis of price much more difficult for Japanese diesel makers. In early 1986, Komatsu announced a 10 percent price hike—"as if," noted a *Forbes* analyst, "the Japanese were running up a flag of truce."[49] By mid-1986, Cummins managers were feeling confident that with reliable and durable products they could compete successfully against Japanese imports as long as the yen/dollar ratio remained in the 1:160–180 range.[50]

Month by month, Cummins managers began to detect a shift in strategic direction within Komatsu, and to some extent among Japanese producers more generally. Schacht saw the reversal in competitive fortunes as an opportunity for new strategic thinking. "I believe we should think as broadly as possible, and not exclude anything in our thinking," he told Henderson and Walsh.[51] He carefully dissected the Maekewa Report, an influential analysis of U.S.-Japanese economic relations issued in April 1986, for clues about the future. The report anticipated the continuation of a strong yen, and predicted that Japanese manufacturers increasingly would seek to forge bilateral trade agreements and to establish plants in non-industrialized nations (to overcome tariffs and vast wage differentials). These changes would present opportunities.[52] Yet Schacht was not prepared to let down his guard. "The Japanese will continue to be formidable both in country-to-country competition and in our markets," he reported after a 1986 trip to Japan, Australia, Hong Kong, and China. "I think they will absorb the impact of the strong yen internally, keep market share, fight to reduce costs even further, and increase the technical sophistication of their products."[53]

Jim Henderson credits Henry Schacht with both realism and a certain dogged determination vis-à-vis Komatsu. "He simply wasn't going to let that relationship die," he recalls with amusement, "no matter how eager some individuals in Japan were to get free of us."

A leadership change within Komatsu itself added momentum to the new era of good feelings. Back in 1982, Shoji Nogawa had succeeded Ryoichi Kawai as president of Komatsu. Nogawa had spearheaded Komatsu's effort to build a large-scale diesel engine business, and he was open about his determination to compete aggressively with Cummins. Nogawa was an iron-fisted leader whose advocacy of Total Quality Control bordered on obsession.[54]

Several Cummins executives recall vividly the dramatic circumstances surrounding Nogawa's departure from the Komatsu presidency in the spring of 1987. A small delegation of Cummins executives—Henderson, Tajima, Robert Campbell (vice president of Cummins' international division), and Mark Levett—traveled to Chattanooga, Tennessee, to attend the dedication ceremony of Komatsu's new plant. Nogawa was "in his triumphancy" as he presided over the ceremonies, giving speeches and meeting delegations. At one point, Jim Henderson tried to keep the door open with Komatsu by saying, in effect, that the two companies had a common enemy: Caterpillar.

"Nogawa looks at me," Henderson recalls, "and says, 'No. *You* are the enemy!'"

A week later, Art Tajima learned in a call to his Japanese office that Nogawa had just been dismissed (on June 8, 1987).[55] Officially, the Komatsu board had done the deed, replacing Nogawa with Masao Tanaka, an executive from the marketing side of the business.[56] Campbell reported bluntly a few days later what many suspected: "Nogawa was sacked by Kawai." Later that month, in fact, Levett learned from a Komatsu insider that Kawai had been unhappy with Nogawa's stance toward Cummins, and had "given a clear instruction to Mr. Tanaka to restore the relation with Cummins."[57]

There were other management shifts as well, and Campbell saw the management shake-up as positive news for Cummins.[58] He was right. By late summer, Levett was reporting that "activity with Komatsu has picked up significantly in the last month. All of it appears to be a direct result of the change in presidency in June."[59] Tanaka soon sought an audience with Henderson, and made it clear that Komatsu wanted to do business with Cummins again.

By 1987, Cummins was feeling more confident about Komatsu and other potential competitors from Japan. Campbell happily reported, for instance, that two Japanese experts concluded a visit to Columbus by stating that Cummins "is much further along in engine manufacturing and Komatsu has a long way to go to catch up."[60] And by this time, American academics and business writers were displaying a much more circumspect and cautionary tone toward Japanese manufacturing methods and economic prowess.[61]

In the final months of 1987, high-ranking Komatsu officials visited Cummins several times. One delegation included Ryoichi Kawai, whose recent interventions had done much to restore relations between the two firms.[62] "Kawai was the Irwin Miller of Komatsu," Jim Henderson explains. "Never the operations head, but always the senior voice of wisdom, and that was key."

These were encouraging signs, but the need for careful diplomacy remained as compelling as ever. Schacht would continue to explore new partnership configurations—a U.S.-based joint venture, a technology-sharing arrangement at Oyama, a sole-supplier relationship—and would approach Komatsu with an ownership-sharing proposal later in the decade.[63] For the time being, worldwide diesel engine overcapacity, the exchange-rate roller coaster, and a common struggle against Caterpillar were drawing the battle-weary opponents together again.[64]

Second intermission

The Cummins story of the 1980s is a twisting tale. Chapter 9 described how the Engine Company launched an ambitious plan to remake itself into a global producer of large- and medium-horsepower engines; how a severe economic recession struck just as those plans were coming to fruition; and how the company forged ahead—trimming its ranks, completing its new headquarters, and, most important, sustaining its commitment to capital-intensive new technologies. The story that began with the restructuring plans of 1979 now seemed to be ending on a happy note—as the economy recovered and Cummins' new B and C engine lines were gaining ready acceptance in the marketplace.

This chapter introduced an unexpected turn. Just as Cummins prepares to settle back into profitability, a new competitor crashes onto the scene. Behind the Japanese mask—a former ally! Amid the struggle, the two companies reflect upon their former friendship. Finally, the foreigner retreats, deciding to save its strength for a true enemy. Once again, Cummins eagerly looks forward to its long-awaited profits.

But as will become clear in the next chapter, this is only the second intermission.

It would be a mistake to trivialize or oversimplify the seriousness and complexities of these events. Every group of stakeholders shared the company's struggle on one level or another—the employees who lost wages and work; the investors who placed enormous capital at risk; the customers, distributors, suppliers, and local residents whose fates were interwoven with a company with often dubious prospects; and the managers who had to make large and sure decisions with incomplete information and uncertain outcomes.

Still, the company's response to the threat of Japanese competition was a potent and telling mix: compete fiercely on price in the immediate term, learn and adapt for the intermediate term, and offer cooperation and respect for the long term. The Japanese diesel episode is more about industrial states-manship than raw competition. And when faced with need for layoffs, Cummins struggled to do right within the bounds of that harsh reality. Its work force emerged scarred; but Cummins did not suffer the kinds of strikes and intense animosities that descended upon Caterpillar and many other American industrials during this period.

11 | Circling the Wagons

As Cummins struggled to recast itself in a more competitive mold, numerous external constituencies watched with interest. Wall Street remained generally respectful of the long-term perspective advocated and embodied by Henry Schacht. Schacht himself was celebrated in the business press as the hero of Midwestern manufacturing—"Mr. Rust Belt," *Business Week* dubbed him.[1] But by 1988, the patience of the investment community, like that of Cummins' long-suffering stockholders, was beginning to fray around the edges. When would the massive reinvestments and cost cutting begin to pay off? Specifically, when would the expensive B and C engine lines turn a profit?

Cummins' longtime customers and competitors in the heavy-duty truck market also were paying close attention. The company's preoccupation with Japanese competition had left it wide open to an attack from domestic competitors, and the always opportunistic Caterpillar had plunged into the breach. Between 1978 and 1988, the Peoria-based diesel maker scooped up an additional 20 percent of the heavy-duty truck market, at the expense of both Cummins and the rapidly fading Detroit Diesel.[2]

And at least one more outside-world audience was eyeing the Engine Company. This group consisted of cash-rich corporations looking for promising acquisition targets. Earlier in the decade, the huge conglomerate Gulf + Western had swallowed a healthy portion of Cummins stock. And on its own initiative, as described in Chapter 9, Cummins had contemplated a merger with Alcoa. Now, in the space of two short years, the company was to undergo a strange sequence of events that represented a serious threat to its survival as an independent entity. First, a British-based industrial holding company, Hanson PLC, acquired a significant block of Cummins stock. But even as this first "foray" was being repulsed, a second company, Industrial Equity

Pacific (IEP), was making a run at the diesel citadel.* The result, at the far end of this process, was a much-changed Engine Company.

Reencountering Hanson

In Columbus, Indiana, it was no one's idea of a good Christmas present. On December 23, 1988, a filing with the Securities and Exchange Commission revealed publicly that Hanson PLC, a London-based conglomerate, had acquired an 8.3 percent stake in Cummins (around 886,000 shares) for approximately $45 million.[3] (Such a filing is required within ten days after a buyer exceeds 5 percent of a target company's common stock.) Over the course of the following week, Cummins stock rose dramatically—from around $50 to nearly $64 per share—and almost 11 percent of the stock changed hands.[4] In its initial filing with the SEC, Hanson announced that its stake (soon to be increased to 9.8 percent) was for investment purposes only, but investors knew that this declaration could be amended at any time. In the parlance of Wall Street in the overheated 1980s, the Engine Company was now "in play."[5] In a great many cases, a company once put in play was destined to lose its independence.

Cummins already knew a good deal about the Hanson conglomerate and about its celebrated chairman, James Hanson. In 1973, as described in Chapter 8, Hanson had driven a hard bargain in the sale of his Holset turbocharger and vibration-damper division to Cummins. Now the $13.3 billion industrial giant was coming back to Cummins in a new role—that of a significant investor.

The December announcement of Hanson's purchase of the Cummins shares cleared up one mystery. Cummins in the 1980s employed a "stock-watch" company, Morrow & Co., to keep an eye on the Engine Company's shareholder base. (Such companies specialize in getting behind the so-called "street names" of stock purchasers to determine who is actually buying a given stock.) Morrow had detected some unusual activity in Cummins' stock in the fall of 1988, and in November 1988 informed Cummins that its latest unwanted suitor was, in all likelihood, Hanson.

Now Hanson was out in the open. But this only raised another question: What did a company like Hanson want with a company like Cummins?

*The authors need to clarify the ground rules under which this section of the text was written. Our write-up of the Hanson episode, like almost all others in the book, draws in part on interviews with Cummins employees and internal documents. The IEP story, by contrast, has been gleaned entirely from documents in the public domain. This is because the settlement between Cummins and IEP included an agreement by the two parties not to discuss publicly any aspect of their dispute—an agreement that Cummins has honored by denying us access to IEP-related materials.

Hanson had been founded a quarter-century earlier by two Yorkshiremen who had been friends since boyhood. James Hanson and Gordon L. White grafted a fertilizer maker and a truck distributor onto White's family printing business, and thereby laid the foundation for what became, by 1988, Britain's fifth-highest-capitalized company. Over its twenty-five years of operations, Hanson PLC (eventually including its American subsidiary, Hanson Trust, run by White) had developed a unique formula for growth. It purchased mature, marginally profitable, nonunionized industrial corporations. Most of these acquisitions had minimal requirements for technology or other capital investments, and few were in cyclical or highly competitive industries.

When a company was "raided" by Hanson, one of three scenarios normally ensued. In some cases, Hanson held its stake only long enough for those holdings to increase in value, then sold out. (Often, this scenario was self-fulfilling, since the initial investment by Hanson in a target company tended to drive up that company's value.) This was an approach Hanson had taken many times in the past, as when it had purchased more than 5 percent of Milton Bradley, Gulf Resources, and Avon Mills, among others. In fact, at any given time, Hanson had large minority positions in a dozen or more companies. In other cases, Hanson purchased the entire company and resold it, largely unchanged, at a point when it could command a higher price. The third route was the most dramatic. In these cases, the acquired company was subjected to a rigorous—even merciless—shake-up designed to restore the enterprise to profitability. This shake-up formula was so well known in the business community that it had acquired its own name: "Hansonization."

Observers in the United States, in and out of industry, were well aware of these Hanson patterns. But no one was quite sure which road Hanson was planning to take with its new investment in the Cummins Engine Company. Did Hanson see Cummins simply as a good short-term play—an undervalued company whose shares could only increase in value? Or did Hanson plan a lock, stock, and barrel takeover of the Engine Company? This would not have been much of a stretch for the London-based firm, which was then afloat on a sea of cash. (Hanson had a $2 billion war chest, and was in the process of seeking shareholder approval to raise its borrowing ceiling from $11.7 billion to $19.8 billion. This approval was soon forthcoming.) So at least one thing was clear: If Hanson wanted Cummins, it could get it—easily. But if it intended to acquire Cummins, why didn't it say so? "In the past, when they did a hostile bid," one analyst told the *New York Times*, "they did it right from the start. There's no reason not to believe Cummins is just an investment, if that's what they say."[6]

The problem was that Hanson was sending mixed signals. Throughout the month of January 1989, for example, Hanson representatives told European stock analysts that the Cummins purchase was an investment and nothing more.[7] But in an interview with London reporters in mid-January, vice chairman Martin Taylor said his company was "keeping its options open" vis-à-vis Cummins. He noted that Hanson long had held a 5 percent share in Britain's third largest bank, Midland, and had no intention of taking over that enterprise. On the other hand, he said pointedly, Hanson was always on the lookout for companies that had "failed to perform suitably for institutional shareholders."[8] There was reason to suspect that Hanson considered Cummins—four-fifths of whose stock was now held by institutional investors—to be squarely in that category.

The View from Columbus

Almost from the company's founding, Cummins' management had been sensitive to issues of corporate takeovers and stock ownership. This sensitivity was fueled by the company's own unhappy recapitalizations in the 1940s, by the rise and fall of major Cummins customers over the years, and especially by the failure of the White merger in 1964.

But another factor kept Cummins keenly focused on the ownership of its stock. This was the declining but still large block of shares owned by the extended Miller family. As Irwin Miller, his wife Xenia, and his sister Clementine grew older, their holdings gradually were being sold, most often to institutional investors. This reduced the chances of a huge block of Cummins shares being thrown on the market at once, but it also put more and more Cummins stock in the hands of institutional investors.* Cummins' vulnerability to a tender offer was increasing. For the same reasons, the company's ability to take the long-term view (and not necessarily deliver short-term profits) was eroding. It was the Millers, and the managers they had chosen and groomed, who believed in investing for the long term. As their influence diminished, this and other corporate values became harder to defend.[9]

The plausibility of a takeover scenario increased greatly in 1980 when Gulf + Western bought into Cummins quickly and aggressively. Next, an apparently unfriendly overture from a bank that held a relatively large block of Cummins stock was turned away when Schacht, Henderson, and other Cummins managers made it clear that they would leave the company immediately in the event of a successful takeover. "You'd better be prepared to run it the next day," Schacht told them—and the overture ended abruptly. But the Millers' sale of a large block of stock in 1983 moved Cummins further down the road of vulnerability to new, less friendly kinds of investors, including—possibly—Hanson.

---

*"The family worked closely with Henry and Jim," Irwin Miller recalls, "both to create a market for the stock and to limit the company's exposure."

When Hanson surfaced in December 1988, therefore, Schacht and his colleagues reacted on two fronts simultaneously. First, they assembled a team of outside experts to help them understand and respond to the Hanson actions. This team first included financial advisor James Wolfensohn of James D. Wolfensohn Incorporated; Sam Butler and Rob Kindler of the New York law firm of Cravath, Swaine & Moore; and later—when expertise in securities was needed—Michael Schmertzler and other representatives from Morgan Stanley. What Schacht heard in his initial meetings with these experts was discouraging, at best. At one early meeting, several advisors expressed the opinion that Cummins might not be able to survive as an independent entity.[10] In other words, even if Hanson itself did not intend to acquire Cummins, the takeover ball was now rolling and the company was in play.

Meanwhile, a second team was being assembled back in Columbus. Headed by Schacht, the Cummins team included newly arrived treasurer Peter Hamilton, vice president for corporate strategy "Chip" Gulden, vice president and general counsel Steve Zeller, corporate strategy director Martha Brooks, and others. This task force went to work in a windowless room in the basement of the Fifth Street headquarters building. Its first task was to better understand Hanson. What was the British company saying, and how did that square with what it was actually doing?

The more they learned about the object of their study, the more puzzled they became about why the industrial giant was interested in Cummins. Hanson usually avoided cyclical industries, yet diesel making (at least in the Class 8, heavy-duty truck market) almost defined cyclicality. Hanson liked nonunionized, low-technology businesses. Conversely, it shied away from enterprises that required large capital outlays and continuing investments in research and development. Cummins' R&D efforts—while not directed at the highest of high technologies—were anything but cheap, and would need to be intensified to meet strict new emissions standards scheduled to go into effect in 1991 and 1994.

Perhaps even less appealing, from Hanson's presumed point of view, was the fact that Cummins would have to spend upwards of $200 million per year in each of the next five years upgrading its plants to incorporate this new technology.[11] As noted before, Hanson often looked for acquisitions with "strippable" assets, which could be sold to recoup some or all of the acquiring company's original investment. But with the possible exception of the filter maker Fleetguard, Cummins had very few operations that could be spun off without undermining its core business. Even Fleetguard was arguably too close to the heart of the business to be considered disposable.

And finally, the state of Indiana was an increasingly uncongenial context in which to attempt a takeover. When Columbus-based Arvin Industries was subjected to a raid in 1986, Arvin's CEO James Baker succeeded in getting an extremely tough antitakeover statute passed by the state legislature in Indianapolis in 1986. This law—considered by most observers to be the nation's toughest antitakeover law—was upheld by the U.S. Supreme Court in 1987.[12] And more support was on the way: In February 1989, a measure designed to tighten the original statute was passed by the Indiana General Assembly.[13]

Gradually, the team of basement dwellers at headquarters reached two conclusions. The first was that Hanson had decided Cummins was substantially undervalued. Most at Cummins agreed with this assessment, feeling that a decade of hard work and sacrifice was not yet reflected in Cummins' stock price. Hanson, among the most astute investors in the world, probably had reached the same conclusion as many at Cummins: that the Engine Company's stock was undervalued by as much as 50 percent.[14] That much about the Hanson move made sense.[15]

But their second conclusion was that despite getting the existing undervaluation right, Hanson had fundamentally misunderstood the nature of Cummins' business. If Hanson had ideas about acquiring the Engine Company, and if it intended to pay the cost of acquisition by shutting down the company's R&D and capital-investment stream (in hopes of subsequently selling a family of increasingly obsolescent engines and parts into a stable and docile trucking market), then Hanson was in for a rude awakening. Even if the truckers would stand still—Cummins thought they would not—the regulators from EPA were scheduled to come knocking in 1991 and 1994.

The etiquette of hostile takeovers calls for little or no direct contact between the principals. Schacht and Henderson decided to ignore this convention. After all, wasn't Hanson one of Cummins' larger shareholders, and didn't Schacht and Henderson regularly call on major shareholders? And shouldn't Cummins' top two executives know what was on Hanson's mind? Sometime in February 1989, therefore, they sought an initial audience with Sir Gordon White at his Park Avenue office.

"If you think you can buy the company, impose your operating standards on it, and get your money out, you're wrong," Schacht recalls explaining to White. "You will be like the person who is in the middle of a big circus tent, pulls the center pole out, and tries to get to the exit before the roof falls on him. You won't make it. You can't get there fast enough." White's response never varied, Schacht recalls: "This is a great American company, and it's enormously undervalued. We take lots of positions."

Although White himself was both courteous and consistent, there were contradictory signals coming from other Hanson representatives. One Hanson executive, for example, suggested casually that if Schacht and Henderson were interested, Hanson could acquire not only Cummins but also General Motors, and then put the two companies together—with the broad implication that Schacht and Henderson would play a major role in running the resulting giant.[16] Schacht suspected that "they were quietly seeing if they could convince the Cummins executives that they ought to be part of the Hanson family." "Absolutely not," was the answer. "We can't operate your way, and you can't operate our way."

Within a month, Schacht and Henderson again visited Sir Gordon in New York. Hanson's story remained the same: Cummins was an investment. But now the Cummins delegation had a different story to tell. Whatever Hanson's intentions, they said, the mere existence of the Hanson factor was beginning to complicate the business of running Cummins. Executive recruitment was grinding to a halt. Customers and potential joint-venture partners were getting increasingly nervous. Before Hanson entered the scene, for example, Cummins was bidding to supply a small engine for Daimler-Benz's new light vehicle. All signs looked encouraging. Then one day in March 1989, a Daimler-Benz executive called Schacht in for a meeting and told the Cummins CEO that the German company was well aware of what Hansonization would mean for Cummins. "I know these guys," Schacht remembers him saying, "and I can't start a chassis platform that's dependent on your new engine, and run the risk that Hanson will cancel the program." Daimler-Benz told Cummins that they were going with another engine maker—and then did so.[17]

Schacht and Henderson informed White that U.S. manufacturers were expressing their concern about Cummins' long-term viability, and some even were taking steps to diversify their supplier base. These included some of Cummins' most important customers. For his part, White told his visitors that he was impressed that they had made the effort to come and talk with him. "He told us," Schacht recalls, "that we were the first people that they ever made an investment in who had actually come to see him."[18] He also expressed his surprise that Hanson's investment in Cummins could be so disruptive, and told Schacht to tell these customers to call him directly for reassurances of Hanson's good intentions. (Schacht subsequently did so, apparently to little effect.) And for the first time, White indicated that Hanson might be willing to sell its Cummins shares.

This did not come as a total surprise. Prior to this meeting, the Cummins distributor in Saudi Arabia, Sulleiman Olyan, reported to Cummins on a recent conversation he had had with Hanson representatives. The Saudi businessman said that while he himself had been unable to strike a deal with Hanson to buy that company's stake in Cummins, Hanson at least had demonstrated a willingness to talk about unloading its Cummins stock.

Now Sir Gordon was confirming that willingness. The trouble was, cooperation would come only at a price. That price turned out to be a 20 percent premium above market.

Looking for Buyers

This was a tall order for a stock that had been languishing until Hanson had made its run at the company—and which was likely to fade again if and when Hanson left the scene. Of course, there was no legal obstacle to Cummins' buying back the Hanson shares itself at whatever price the two companies agreed upon. This tactic of repurchasing shares to get rid of an unwelcome suitor was known as "greenmail," and it was not uncommon in the high-flying decade of the 1980s. Technically, the process was simple enough: The purchasing company simply paid the agreed-upon greenmail, took back the stock, and incurred an accounting charge in that fiscal year. But the press tended to savage companies that paid greenmail, on the grounds that this was a device whereby inept managers entrenched themselves at the expense of shareholders. Schacht, Henderson, and the Cummins board debated the pros and cons of greenmail, and finally decided to rule it out. "That would have been too big an inconsistency with what the company had always stood for," recalls one observer, "and you can't save a company by destroying its soul."[19]

Somewhere in the world, Schacht had to find a buyer or group of buyers for Hanson's block of Cummins stock, which probably was still undervalued in real terms, but now was selling for substantially more than before Hanson made its move. On one track, he began talking seriously with domestic financial houses and OEMs about taking a position in Cummins. This was a delicate balancing act. Schacht had to make the opportunity sound interesting, compelling, and even urgent—but not desperate. These OEMs were the same companies, after all, that were entertaining offers from a resurgent Detroit Diesel to abandon Cummins altogether. And there was still sensitivity, left over from the failed White merger and other episodes, about Cummins becoming too close to any particular OEM.

On a second front, Schacht began an intensive round of globe-trotting in search of potential foreign purchasers of the Hanson stake, with a particular focus on Asia and South America. In this aspect of the search he was assisted by an increasingly important ally: William I. Miller, the thirty-three-year-old son of J. Irwin Miller.

Will Miller, like his father, was a graduate of the Taft School and Yale University, where he majored in English. Eventually, he pursued a graduate degree in business at Stanford University. Miller's only experience on the Cummins payroll came in the year and a half after his graduation from Yale. Miller let it be known that he was looking for a job that would give him experience managing people, and Cummins responded by offering him a foremanship at the Charleston, South Carolina, engine plant.

After graduating from Stanford, Miller secured an entry-level job with E. M. Warburg, Pincus & Company, then the largest venture capital firm in the country. But after two years in New York, Miller decided that he wanted to focus less on the investment-banking side of the business—the natural focus of a large firm like Warburg, Pincus—and more on small-scale, technology-oriented venture capital. When J. Irwin Miller offered his son the chance to run Irwin Management Company, the family's investment management firm, the younger Miller decided to take the job. On paper, the position—which included an unusual mix of investment management, philanthropic work, and venture capital activities—seemed particularly suited to Will Miller. Still, the transition was difficult at first. Miller's principal clients, after all, were his father, mother, and aunt, and he recognized belatedly that his role called for him to subordinate his own priorities to theirs. Eventually, reflecting the interests of those clients, Miller found himself spending as much as half of his time on community-oriented activities in and around Columbus.[20]

As president of Irwin Management Company, Miller clearly had a professional interest in the outcome of the Hanson-Cummins encounter. The family's holdings in Cummins, although much reduced from previous decades, still constituted the largest single asset under Irwin Management's umbrella. Viewed from the other end of the telescope, the family still owned more than 5 percent of the company, and continued to feel a measure of personal responsibility for its fortunes.

For its part, Cummins—especially in the person of Henry Schacht—saw several compelling reasons to involve Will Miller more closely with the company as soon as Hanson was perceived as a threat. (Schacht had known the younger Miller for years, and had gotten to know him better through Focus 2000, a Columbus study group organized by longtime Mayor Robert Stewart.) One was Miller's acumen in financial affairs. Although still a young man, Miller knew more about the rough-and-tumble world of raiders, takeovers, white knights, poison pills, and greenmail than anyone else in the immediate Cummins orbit. And although he had declined to take an active role in the management of Cummins, Miller knew the company intimately. Grounded in both worlds, Miller was an effective interpreter between Cummins and the financial community. ("I was a translator," Miller recalls. "Investment bankerese to English, English to investment bankerese.")[21]

Schacht and Henderson also saw the symbolic value of having Will Miller join the Cummins board, which Miller did in February 1989. Notes Schacht: "[Will] represented a continuation of the Miller traditions and values that have driven Cummins for so long. . . . It was important for the larger Cummins family to see that the Millers had that kind of confidence." In addition, the younger Miller opened doors both domestically (including those at his former employer, Warburg, Pincus) and overseas. Miller recalls that a great deal of his time during this period was spent on overseas trips with Schacht:

> *When it involved potential overseas investors, Henry wanted to take me*
> *along as a representative of the family, because he felt that in other cul-*
> *tures, more importance would be attributed to the* family *view of*
> *Cummins, and of Cummins' management, and of whatever transaction*
> *might take place, than was the case in the U.S. And my father's age*
> *prohibited him from globe-trotting, although he did go to Brazil with*
> *us. So I went along in the somewhat uncomfortable role of representing*
> *my father and the family.*

One consequence of these extended overseas trips was ironic: Miller, locked in an uphill battle to keep Cummins a vital force in Columbus, was drummed out of the local Rotary for missing too many of their Monday luncheon meetings.[22] But far more serious, from Miller's and Schacht's point of view, was the fact that none of these international junkets produced even a serious nibble.

After drilling dry holes in countries around the world, Schacht eventually found himself forced to fall back on a long-shot plan. This involved an offer from PACCAR—the Washington-based truck manufacturer that was then Cummins' single biggest customer—to buy the Hanson block of Cummins shares at market price. At a London meeting during the Fourth of July weekend, 1989, Gordon White dismissed the proposed deal out of hand. "He just laughed us out of the room," Schacht recalls ruefully. "Turned it down flat."

On the Monday of that long holiday weekend, therefore, Schacht and his colleagues found themselves back in Columbus without any real options for dislodging Hanson. Reluctantly, the Cummins executives called an impromptu meeting at headquarters with the Millers—father and son—to inform them that the company's future was still in limbo. This was when events took a dramatic turn.

Buying Back In

As the Millers made their way out to the parking lot after the meeting, Will Miller began thinking out loud. Hanson was still looking, he observed, for something like a 15 percent premium on their holdings, which translated into roughly $10 million. It struck Miller as bizarre that the fate of a $3 billion company hinged on such a relatively small sum.

And think of the consequences, Miller continued, if Hanson acquired Cummins and "Hansonized" it. First of all, the shareholding members of the Miller family (principally J. I. Miller, his wife Xenia, and his sister Clementine Tangeman) would be cashed out and highly liquid. Assuming that Hanson was paying the right price to buy control, and assuming that the tax implications of such a windfall could be managed in a satisfactory way, the Millers would find themselves in relatively good shape.

On the other hand (Miller said to his father), Columbus would not. The city surely would bear the brunt of the economic changes inflicted by Hansonization. Columbus had Cummins' highest concentration of employment, and was home to some of its oldest product lines, from which a company like Hanson would be most likely to strip out cash-flow expenditures. Most of Cummins' research and engineering, moreover, took place in Columbus. If R&E was the first activity to be curtailed under a Hanson regime, the Tech Center would become a much quieter place almost overnight.

"I suspect that as a family," Will Miller recalls saying to his father, "we won't feel very good about that." The younger Miller then introduced a novel idea:

> I said, "In that event, I'm sure we'll feel we have to step up to the plate philanthropically on a lot—maybe even more than ten million bucks' worth. So what would you think about what I would call 'preventive philanthropy'? What if the family stepped forward and just ate the Hanson premium, and viewed it as a less expensive way of doing the philanthropy? Is that something that would make any sense to you at all?"

Irwin Miller, for one, was receptive. And for the balance of that evening, the three Millers—J. Irwin, Xenia, and Will—talked through the implications of the plan, and tentatively agreed to commit themselves to it. "The basic concept of preventive philanthropy was one that resonated with all of them," Will Miller recalls. The following morning, Will and Irwin visited the fiscally conservative Clementine Tangeman (Cummins' largest individual shareholder) and introduced the idea to her. For his part, Irwin Miller enjoyed watching his son steer Clementine toward a positive conclusion, reminding him as it did of some difficult conversations in which he himself had participated, many decades earlier. "Will took a long time with Clementine, because he wasn't sure she got it the first time. But she did. It was a little bit like dealing with my uncle. . . . She bought it right away—but he still wanted to tell her the whole story."

With the three key family members firmly committed to the plan, the next step was for the Millers to present it to Cummins. On short notice, Will and Irwin Miller arranged another meeting with Schacht, Henderson, and Hamilton. "We were flat out of ideas," Schacht recalls vividly. "And then Will walked in with Irwin and said, 'We have a proposition for you. . . .' We didn't have any prior warning. It didn't even occur to us that the Miller family would releverage themselves at their ages, and take that kind of risk. But they did." Although Will Miller clearly was the architect of the deal, he declines to take much credit for it: "I had an idea to run by my parents and aunt, but at all times, this was *their* decision, and their money, and their commitment."

Schacht presented the proposal to the Cummins board, which gave its preliminary approval. Between July 4 and July 11, the two "sides" (company and family) worked out the specifics of the deal. Both sides agreed that for legal and ethical reasons, this would have to be an arm's-length transaction. Morgan Stanley's Michael Schmertzler negotiated on behalf of Cummins, and Will Miller and the family's lawyers from Simpson Thatcher represented the Millers.

At the core of the transaction was a potential sticking point: Even given their substantial resources, the family did not have the cash flow to finance the spread between the dividend on Cummins common shares and the borrowing cost to purchase the Hanson block. In order to close that gap, the family proposed that Cummins convert both the existing family shares and the new Hanson shares into convertible preferred stock, which someday would come back to Cummins. The interest rate on the preferred stock would be high enough to finance most of the cost of acquiring the Hanson shares at a premium.

If accepted by Hanson, the deal as structured would certainly entail some sacrifices for the Millers. As Will Miller explains: "The inclusion of the original family stake in the preferred is what allowed us to finance the deal, which we couldn't have done otherwise from a cash flow point of view. It was clear that by trading in common for preferred, we were giving up upside." At the same time, the deal would present the family with some clear benefits. Even though the upside potential of the Millers' common stock would be sacrificed, so would the downside. This was a stock, after all, which had hit an all-time low of $11 per share in the not-too-remote 1970s.

When viewed as "preventive philanthropy," this probably was the cheapest principled alternative available to the family. "We really did view it as an alternative to the subsequent philanthropy that we would have done otherwise," says Will Miller. "And on the rest of it, we expected to make a rate of return, and we structured the deal to do that."

The Cummins board (with the exception of J. Irwin and Will Miller, who recused themselves from the deliberations) approved the deal at a special meeting in New York.[23] All that remained was the task of negotiating with Hanson, which began in Los Angeles on July 12. Henry Schacht personally introduced Will Miller to Hanson's Sir Gordon White as a potential buyer of Hanson's shares, and the two principals began their talks at once. During these weighty negotiations, Schacht—the influential CEO of Cummins, accustomed to directing traffic in the center of the storm—for once was a bystander. But he enjoyed the vantage point: "I went and sat over in the corner and the two of them had at it. It was great fun watching Will. He didn't back off. He knew what he was after, and negotiated White into that range, and that was that."

It took two days. The bargaining was both hard-nosed and amicable. "Gordon White is an absolutely charming person," Will Miller later told reporters, "and conducted the whole negotiation in a businesslike manner. I'm sorry, but there wasn't a whole lot of drama."[24] Will Miller succeeded in bargaining the Hanson premium down to 7.5 percent, which meant that the Miller family paid about $72 million (or about $5 million above the then-market price) for the approximately one million shares then held by Hanson. The deal assured Hanson of a $17 million return on its initial investment, while effectively tripling the Millers' investment in Cummins.[25] The family also extracted a so-called standstill agreement, whereby Hanson agreed not to purchase any Cummins shares for a period of ten years without the family's permission.[26]

The Millers then exchanged the acquired Hanson shares for $67 million in newly issued Cummins notes, yielding 10 percent per year and convertible into common stock at a conversion fee of $.83 per share. At the same time, the Millers exchanged their existing 580,000 shares of Cummins common for $37 million worth of newly issued convertible notes, also pegged at a 10 percent return.* If shareholders subsequently agreed to award voting rights to this preferred block, the interest rate would be reduced to 9.75 percent—and the family agreed in advance to vote with the Cummins board any of its shares that acquired voting rights.

At 10 a.m. on July 17, the deal was announced to the public. At the morning press conference, the Millers stressed their interest in the long-term needs of Cummins and Columbus. Henry Schacht lauded the "wise and far-sighted stewardship that this family has provided to the company over the past seventy years."[27]

Among the investment community, response was mixed. Standard & Poor's concluded that the agreement had negative implications for the company's existing $400 million in long-term securities. It was likely to result in increased debt leverage, higher fixed charges, and reduced cash-flow protection. "On the other hand," S&P noted, "the deal removes any near-term threat of an unfriendly takeover of the firm."[28]

Other analysts were not so sure of this last point. "Now the company is more vulnerable to a takeover," said a representative of Nomura Securities. "I think this arrangement makes the [common] shares more valuable."[29] Predictably, in the wake of Hanson's departure, the price of Cummins common sagged. Meanwhile, the price of Akron-based B. F. Goodrich Co.—touted by the rumor mills as Hanson's next target—soared.

———————————————————

*This is a necessarily simplified version of the deal. In fact, within a year, Cummins sought and the Millers agreed to convert the convertible notes to convertible preferred stock, in an effort to enhance equity on the corporate balance sheet.

In the popular press, early reaction to the Miller family's action was highly positive. "Officials overjoyed by Miller plan," read the headline in the Columbus newspaper. "A modern tale of old-fashioned business values," opined the *Los Angeles Times*.[30] The *New York Times* produced a long and generally laudatory piece on the Millers—"Family pays $72 million to defend a company"—which asserted, among other things, that "making a grand and unusual gesture is nothing new for Mr. Miller." Will Miller, for his part, was quoted as saying that the family's action was "not a very '80s thing to do."[31]

In fact, the Millers, who had worked hard to structure a deal in which both the costs and benefits would be shared by the family and the company, were made uncomfortable by the extent to which the press was lionizing them in July of 1989. "I knew we would lose money in the short haul," Irwin Miller explains in retrospect, "but I had no idea that we would lose money in the long haul. And I said that publicly—that we weren't just throwing money around. We just thought that if you took a long view, this was a good thing to do."

At least a few of Cummins shareholders disagreed. One of them filed suit in the Shelby County (Indiana) Circuit Court, alleging breaches of fiduciary duties by the Cummins directors and top executives. (The suit was dismissed in March 1990.) Another demanded that the board pay shareholders compensatory damages resulting from Cummins' alleged "self-dealing" transactions and practices of executive "entrenchment." In response, the board established (in September 1989) a special committee of outside directors to investigate the allegations.[32] Again, the Cummins management was found blameless, although lawsuits originating in this period dragged on for years.

But these were sideshows. They did not prevent the charming legend of the self-sacrificing Midwestern Millers from taking root in America's consciousness. The fact that the Millers, father and son, were so colorfully articulate didn't hurt, either. "In much of the country," Will Miller told the *Wall Street Journal*, "the '80s were the decade of the grasshopper. . . . But we are a town of somewhat nerdy, hard-working ants, taking pride in our labors." At the end of the greed-soaked 1980s, it seems, the nation appreciated what appeared to be a model of selflessness and long-term thinking. The peril posed, of course, was that the next wave of reporters—if there was one—might be motivated to debunk the legend.

Hanson: The Last Word?

The better part of a decade after the fact, it is still unclear exactly what Hanson had in mind when it took its initial position in Cummins. Some at Cummins remain convinced that Hanson fully intended to buy and "Hansonize" the company, while others firmly believe the opposite. Will Miller offers one clue that he unearthed in a conversation with a Hanson employee, several years after the buyout was completed:

> *This person told me that they were running their computer programs on possible targets, and the computer screen coughed up the "Cummins Engine Company." And they had never seen a company as fundamentally undervalued as this one—in any market, worldwide. And on that basis they said, "There's no way we can lose. We'll take a big position, and we'll make it public that we have. If we're right, and our formula applies to this thing, we can take it out at a good price, and man, we can make the thing* sing*. If we're wrong, well, something else will happen." I mean, again, this was the Eighties. If you put a company in play, you were either going to buy it out, or get bought out.*

No one at Cummins doubts that Hanson had the willingness and ability to take over and even *run* Cummins, if it had come down to that. Unlike the company's previous encounters with "raiders"—and in the case of Hanson, the word still has to remain in quotes—the acquisitive company was not primarily interested in buying the services of Schacht, Henderson, and other executives. Nor was Hanson a raider, in the classic sense of the word. It was a company with a clear business strategy, which it had applied successfully to many companies that were much more complicated than Cummins.

And, according to the Cummins participants in the process, the Hanson representatives were consistently honorable people, who were true to their word—although their word was sometimes maddeningly inconclusive. Hanson didn't always say what it was doing, and if Will Miller's source is reliable, the company didn't always *know* exactly what it was doing. But when Hanson did declare itself, it did so honestly. "It was simply an investment that we held, and that we disposed of," said a Hanson spokeswoman after the fact.[33] And as it turned out, this was absolutely true.

Encountering IEP

As the Hanson episode was nearing its conclusion, Cummins already was formulating a defensive strategy to reduce the chances of a similar struggle in the future. In the second week of July 1989, the Cummins board approved the establishment of a $75 million employee stock ownership plan (ESOP) designed to put approximately 1.2 million shares of Cummins common stock in the hands of its employees.[34] Cummins announced that the plan—which had been under discussion for almost a decade—was being set up at that point because of rumors of impending changes in the U.S. tax code that would affect ESOPs.

Another event in the same week underscored the necessity to rethink Cummins' ownership structure. At a Washington, D.C., press conference, a spokesman for the United Shareholders Association (USA)—a shareholders' advocacy group founded by Texas financier and sometime-raider T. Boone Pickens—announced that the group had identified Cummins as one of fifty large U.S. corporations that needed major reforms. Specifically, USA argued that actions taken by the Cummins board had entrenched the company's management. One example, presumably, was Cummins' so-called "poison pill" defense, adopted in 1986, which allowed selected shareholders to purchase additional stock for 50 percent of market value when the company was perceived to be under attack.[35] Cummins declined to respond to USA's allegations, but took note of the fact that Pickens' group intended to attend Cummins' next annual meeting and to propose major changes.[36]

During the press conference at which the Miller family reinvestment was announced, Henry Schacht stated that he was redoubling his efforts to obtain additional equity capital from other long-term investors, both to increase corporate flexibility and to replenish Cummins' equity accounts.[37] This hinted at Schacht's larger strategy. If the Miller investment could be reconverted to common stock and combined with the existing common already owned by Cummins employees, something like 20 percent of Cummins common would be in friendly hands. An ESOP—if approved by the Diesel Workers Union through the collective-bargaining process—would gradually push that percentage still higher. But Schacht felt he needed to hit somewhere between 35 and 40 percent of Cummins common in order to vaccinate his company against raids in the future.

He got precious little time. Nine days after the Hanson buyback was completed, Cummins learned through SEC filings that a Hong Kong-based company, Industrial Equity (Pacific) Ltd. (IEP), had purchased a 9.9 percent share of Cummins. Someone new was on the doorstep, and once again, the first challenge was to figure out who it was.

IEP had been a significant Cummins stockholder for some time. (In fact, IEP was identified by stock-watching Morrow & Co. in November 1988 as the second most likely acquirer of Cummins stock, after Hanson.) As of May 1989, the Hong Kong conglomerate owned approximately 4.1 percent of Cummins. The Engine Company's management knew this, yet paid scant attention.[38] Between June and late July, however, IEP more than doubled its holdings, buying nearly 600,000 shares of Cummins common on the open market. On the day of the Miller press conference alone, IEP bought 156,900 shares.[39] According to the requisite documents filed in Washington, IEP (like Hanson before it) described its purchase solely as an investment—as opposed to the first step toward a takeover—a posture reiterated in IEP's first public comments. "We like them in terms of their earnings," said IEP's top American executive, Robert Sutherland, "in terms of their assets and in terms of their future projections. . . . I don't think [Henry Schacht] sees us as a hostile bidder in any way. . . . That's the way we like it to be." But a second required filing revealed IEP's willingness to buy up to 25 percent of Cummins' common stock, suggesting that IEP might have more than a simple investment on its mind.[40]

Friendly or otherwise, the IEP action put Cummins once again "in play." Within three days of when financial columnist Dan Dorfman broke the story publicly, Cummins common had run up by almost 8 percent.[41]

Who was this ever-more-important owner? The public record was fairly clear: IEP was 70 percent controlled by Brierley Investments Ltd., an investment firm located in Wellington, New Zealand. Brierley was the creation of Sir Ronald Alfred Brierley, a bachelor in his fifties who had parlayed his background as a publisher of an obscure investment newsletter into a worldwide financial empire. His chief deputy at Brierley Investments was thirty-nine-year-old fellow New Zealander Bruce Hancox; and his top lieutenant in the United States was Robert Sutherland, president of IEP's North American office in La Jolla, California.

By 1989, Brierley—New Zealand's second-largest holding company—employed about 20,000 people worldwide. It had investments in Britain worth more than $1 billion, and U.S. investments totaling some $700 million. IEP, Brierley's principal subsidiary for U.S. investments, owned a Chicago-based foundry and forgings company outright, and held a majority stake in a British automobile importer and retailer.[42] It had tried and failed to take control of a California firm in 1988, a play that ultimately led to a restructuring of the target company.[43] IEP also had assembled a grab bag of minority positions by the late 1980s, ranging from a Texas drill-bit manufacturer, to a casino-oriented real estate developer, to Playboy Enterprises (of which IEP owned 7 percent).

"Far cry from diesel engines," Henry Schacht observed wryly to a local reporter. But Schacht adopted a wait-and-see attitude in this opening round. His initial review of Sir Ronald's record, he noted, indicated that on a regular basis IEP bought blocks of stock solely for investment purposes. IEP was much smaller than Hanson, less aggressive, and apparently less likely to transform Cummins or scare away its customers. (There was no IEP equivalent of "Hansonization.") "If Brierley turns out to be the kind of person who wants to make a long-term investment in the company," Schacht said further, "that's just fine with us."[44]

Some independent observers were less sanguine. One market player told the reporter from the Columbus paper that IEP "creeps up on companies, gets on their boards, and makes a pest of itself."[45] A Prudential-Bache analyst observed that Cummins had long been looking for an equity partner. "But," he concluded, "I don't think this is what they wanted."[46]

Chess and Recession

For whatever reason—and, as explained earlier, IEP's and Cummins' executives are still enjoined from discussing the case—an initially cordial encounter quickly evolved into an ugly wrestling match. IEP's Robert Sutherland took an amicable tour of a number of Cummins facilities in August 1989. But in that same month, and only two weeks after IEP's major new ownership position came to light, Cummins announced that it was strengthening its existing poison-pill defense to discourage would-be raiders.[47] (Cummins avoided Wall Street's colorful terminology, preferring instead to use the term "shareholder rights plan.") Henceforth, as soon as any single shareholder acquired 15 percent of the company (down from 25 percent), existing shareholders would be permitted to buy an additional share of Cummins stock for each one they already owned at a dollar apiece (down from half of market price).

In the same week, Cummins' corporate counsel sent a letter to the Federal Trade Commission and the Justice Department. The letter complained that IEP and its parent, Brierley, had violated the terms of the 1976 Hart-Scott-Rodino Act, and suggested that IEP either had made "false and misleading statements" in its SEC filing, or had submitted a defective filing to the Justice Department. Cummins further stated its conviction that IEP intended to merge with Cummins, and had concealed that intent in order to avoid paying a "control premium"—that is, the premium that would be required to gain control of the company—on its stock purchases.[48]

But IEP continued its buying ways. In mid-September, the company informed the SEC that it had acquired another 164,000 shares of Cummins in September, which meant it now held 11.5 percent of the Engine Company.[49] Three days later, IEP announced that its share of Cummins had grown to 1.38 million shares, or 13.5 percent of the outstanding common stock. And the very next day, IEP acknowledged that it now owned 14.9 percent of Cummins—or as much as it could acquire without triggering the poison-pill defense.[50]

With IEP stuck at just under 15 percent, an unrelated set of circumstances began to change the context of the ownership struggle in significant ways. Just as IEP's enlarged stake was being made public, Cummins reluctantly announced that it now anticipated a substantial loss in its third-quarter operations—largely due to a steep decline in heavy-duty truck sales—and that it was laying off some 200 workers in southern Indiana.

Again, opinion was sharply divided about the significance of this new round of economic woes for Cummins. On the one hand, it threatened to drive the price of Cummins stock down again, which might make Cummins a more attractive proposition to an investor like IEP. (Indeed, some disaffected analysts said that only the threat of a takeover was preventing a free-fall by Cummins' stock.)[51] On the other hand, as the truck market went into its worst tailspin since 1983, owning or controlling Cummins looked like a much less interesting opportunity. "I find it rather difficult to comprehend what these [IEP] guys are trying to do," commented one analyst. "It's an environment where things are going south before they get better."[52]

And things went south in a dramatic way. It soon became clear that two hundred layoffs would not come close to relieving Cummins' rapidly mounting financial pressures, as heavy-duty truck-engine orders plunged by 40 percent and Onan genset sales declined by 30 percent. In late September, the company announced that 100 more workers would be laid off, salaried workers' pay would be cut by 5 percent, and company officers would take pay cuts ranging from 7.5 percent to 10 percent.[53] Even as these cuts were being announced, Mother Nature engaged in some vicious "piling on." Hurricane Hugo blasted its way across South Carolina with winds of 135 mph, ripping the roof and ventilating systems off a large section of the Charleston plant.[54]

By late October, the bad news was in: Cummins had lost almost $40 million in the three months ending October 1, 1989, wiping out almost all the profits earned in the two previous quarters. Wall Street signaled its strong displeasure. If Cummins could not make money *before* the truck market's collapse, what would happen in the wake of that collapse?[55]

Going to Court

Much of what happened between IEP's arrival at the 14.9 percent ownership plateau in late September 1989 and the events of late January 1990 is not in the public record. But newspaper accounts in January and a *Business Week* article published in March—as well as a complaint filed by Cummins in January—provide some details.[56]

The *Business Week* article began by posing the question, "Was Brierley's move on Cummins dumb or dangerous?" If IEP had purchased Cummins shares as a savvy investment, *Business Week* argued, it had proven to be a bad move: Cummins' stock had plummeted by 33 percent since September 1989. But if (as Cummins alleged) IEP had threatened a proxy battle in September and had threatened in January to be "disruptive" of Cummins' activities unless awarded a seat on the Cummins board, then the move was potentially dangerous.

Representatives of the two companies met at least half a dozen times during this period. All available evidence suggests that relations got worse each time the two parties met. Henry Schacht gave *Business Week* details of a tense meeting on January 15:

> He [IEP's newly installed chairman Bruce Hancox] said, "We have never been engaged in disruption before where we haven't benefited— we always get ours." I've got it etched in my mind. I didn't have any doubt that any chance we had to get them to reconsider was gone. Bullies were going to be bullies.

For his part, Hancox dismissed all of Schacht's and Cummins' charges. "You said," Hancox wrote to Schacht following this meeting, "[that your] view is that IEP acquires shares for the purpose of selling them at a future date and that we are not real long-term owners of companies, at least in the U.S. . . . I strongly disagree with this view and conclusion."[57] On the other hand, talking to a *Business Week* reporter, Hancox freely admitted that IEP had demanded a seat on the Cummins board:

> *We're the largest shareholder, and the only forum we have to work through is the boardroom. . . . [The charge of threats of disruption is] nonsense. For me to put $90 million into the company and then try to disrupt it defies all commercial common sense. . . . What are they so fearful of that they don't want me to get my foot in the door?*

On January 25, 1990, Cummins filed a complaint in the U.S. District Court of Southern Indiana against IEP, Brierley, and the two companies' top officers, and set in motion a comprehensive legal discovery process to recreate IEP's actions and motives over the previous year.[58] The complaint alleged, among other things, that IEP had violated federal and Indiana securities laws by failing to make legally required disclosures—in particular, that IEP had actively been seeking board representation for the previous four months, and had explicitly threatened to disrupt Cummins' activities if its demands were not met. "Defendants are not—and never have been—passive investors in Cummins," the brief asserted.[59] Second, the complaint alleged that IEP had violated the Hart-Scott-Rodino Antitrust Improvements Act of 1976 by acquiring more than $15 million of Cummins common in unlawful reliance on the FTC's "solely for investment purposes" exception.

Finally, and most damningly, Cummins alleged that IEP had violated the federal Racketeer Influenced and Corrupt Organizations Act (known as RICO), and a similar law in Indiana, through its actions in three previous episodes in IEP's history. In each of these three cases, Cummins alleged, IEP's target company had wound up paying greenmail to IEP to avoid disruption of its activities.[60]

Meanwhile, Cummins and its powerful legislative allies were stepping up pressure on IEP in other venues. In the wake of the filing of the Cummins suit, Michigan Representative John D. Dingell asked the SEC and the FTC to investigate IEP's activities.[61] On the same day, Indiana Governor Evan Bayh asked state officials to determine whether IEP had broken any applicable state laws.[62] A day later, North Carolina Senator Terry Sanford— a member of the Senate Securities Subcommittee, in whose home state the Rocky Mount small-engine plant was located—seconded Dingell's call for an investigation.[63]

Briefly, IEP's resolve wavered.[64] But in mid-February, the company countered with a suit of its own against Cummins and six of its directors (including Schacht, Henderson, and the two Millers). IEP denied all of the allegations in the Cummins suit, while counterclaiming that Cummins had broken the law. Specifically, IEP alleged that Cummins had violated federal securities laws by not disclosing an expected loss in the third quarter of 1989, which led IEP and other investors to purchase Cummins stock without full knowledge of material information. As restitution for Cummins' alleged misdeeds, IEP sought an undoing of the recently implemented ESOP along with some $2 million in damages. IEP also objected to Cummins' alleged "entrenchment" of its top executives. The lawsuit conveyed IEP's particular disdain for Henry Schacht:

> *His public statements are part of a carefully crafted, duplicitous public relations campaign—carried on at Cummins' expense—to portray Schacht as "Mr. Rust Belt," a hands-on manager committed to revitalizing America's industrial manufacturing base. . . . That image is at odds with reality. . . .*
>
> *Schacht and other inside directors have imposed upon Cummins a management structure designed to free Schacht from spending the time on Cummins affairs that would ordinarily be required of a chief executive officer and enable him to do what Schacht likes to do best—hobnob with individuals of national power and influence in industry and government on matters having little, if anything, to do with Cummins.[65]*

If there was ever any goodwill between the two companies, surely it was gone. "It's downright nasty," one analyst said of IEP's lawsuit.[66]

Two weeks later, on February 27, Cummins filed amendments to its original suit, in part in an attempt to enjoin IEP from buying or voting any Cummins shares in the future. In effect, Cummins and IEP had snared each other in a legal standoff. Cummins had no obvious way to dislodge IEP, and it was increasingly clear that IEP (unlike Hanson) lacked the resources to take over Cummins. *Business Week* noted the ironies of the situation as it stood in mid-March 1990:

> *Barring some decisive act in the courts or Washington, Schacht and Hancox appear to be stuck with each other. Schacht's loud denouncement of greenmail and the debt the Miller family took on to swing the Hanson deal make a buyout by a Cummins insider unlikely anytime soon. Similarly, Hancox is so far underwater on his Cummins investment that he's unlikely to swallow the loss now. So whether he likes it or not, Hancox may get a first-hand lesson in Cummins' vaunted long-term investing strategy.[67]*

But this situation was unstable and untenable. IEP was effectively blocked from exerting any influence on Cummins, was watching its large investment shrink in value, and had no prospect of unloading that investment without a huge loss. For its part, Cummins was finding itself in court far too often, and was devoting too much management time to reassuring its key accounts. "I spend a lot of time with customers," Schacht told a reporter in mid-March, "trying to convince them that IEP is not going to cause us to change our patterns of investment and returns."[68]

The second-to-last act in the drama came in the first week of April 1990, when Brierley chairman Bruce Hancox attended Cummins' annual meeting in Columbus. A local reporter likened the event to a two-ring circus. Under the "big top"—the local high-school auditorium—were gathered Cummins and its attending stockholders. Meanwhile, in a nearby motel room, Hancox (the company's single largest shareholder) addressed a group of about twenty analysts and reporters.[69] But Hancox also addressed the larger gathering, taking Schacht and his strategy to task. "This company, Mr. Chairman," he said, "has slowly but surely been taken over by lieners [i.e., lien-holders, presumably the Miller family] who have a guaranteed rate of return."[70] But the audience, which included many Columbus residents, expressed itself by giving Cummins a standing ovation for its positive impact on their community.[71]

Finally, in an out-of-court settlement reached in May 1990, the two companies agreed to a hostile truce. Each side would drop its legal actions against the other. IEP agreed to a ten-year "standstill" agreement, whereby it would refrain from purchasing any additional Cummins stock, and further agreed not to interfere with the management of Cummins. For its part, Cummins assented to meet with IEP officials twice a year to keep them informed about significant changes in Cummins' activities. And both sides agreed not to talk about each other—a sensible restriction, given the degree of ill will and suspicion that had been generated between them.[72]

For IEP, the final chapter came in February 1991, when the company began disposing of its large holdings in Cummins. Forced to sell its stock into a depressed market, IEP wound up losing between $20 million and $25 million.

A Partnership of Common Interests

Throughout this period, Henry Schacht continued his very public search for investors who might take a large position in Cummins and hold it over the long term. As Schacht saw it, only an investor whose fortunes were tied to those of Cummins would have the patience to ride out the dramatic cyclical swings that regularly buffeted the Engine Company. But founding families were hard to come by, and institutional investors hardly were known for their patience with companies that failed to regularly reward stockholders.

On one visit to now-legendary investor Warren Buffett, Schacht made his well-rehearsed pitch, and got an interesting response. As Schacht recalls the conversation:

> *"Henry," he told me, "your answer doesn't lie in financial circles, because we are people who have appetites far larger than you can satisfy. You're just not large enough for people like me. I think your customer base is where you're going to find your answer: People who really have a stake in your business, who really want you to be successful, and who have some amount of reason in their economics."*

"And as it turned out," Schacht later concluded, "he was absolutely right."

With the encouragement of Buffett and others, therefore, Schacht looked closely at his customer base. Among them he found a not-so-obvious potential partner: Tokyo-based Komatsu Ltd., Cummins' oldest joint-venture partner, and more recently—as described in the previous chapter—one of Cummins' toughest international competitors.

Discussions about a possible investment in Cummins by Komatsu began at Cummins in the late 1980s. At that time, senior Cummins executives contemplated a wide variety of devices to link the two companies more closely—ranging from a return to a simple joint-venture relationship, to a stock swap, to the purchase by Cummins of Komatsu's huge Oyama plant.[73] From Cummins' perspective, the logic was compelling. Both Cummins and Komatsu were locked in intense battles with Caterpillar for worldwide market share, and both felt pressure to diversify, which would be easier to accomplish jointly. The question, in fact, could be turned around: What good reason was there for Cummins and Komatsu *not* to join forces?

At regular intervals, Henry Schacht attempted to persuade Komatsu's top officials that a return to their formerly cooperative relationship would be mutually beneficial. Cummins, he argued, would bring important strengths to such a relationship, including labor-relations skills, protection from "Japan bashing," and a sophisticated knowledge of how Washington worked. For its part—Schacht went on—Komatsu had strong operating skills and access to Japanese financing.[74] Given Japan's astronomical land values, Schacht noted pointedly, Komatsu's office building *alone* was worth more than all of Cummins.

An October 1989 letter from Schacht to Komatsu's chairman, R. Kawai, made a formal request for a 15 percent investment in Cummins. The goal, Schacht emphasized, was to stabilize Cummins' equity base. "Our desire," he wrote, "is to find equity investors whose objectives are long term, and who are familiar with the longer-term nature of Cummins' investment and return patterns." In other words, Cummins sought partners who were willing and able to ride out the ups and downs of the company's highly cyclical industry.[75] In a six-page appendix to the letter, Schacht made a forceful "case for closer cooperation between Komatsu and Cummins," minimizing the two companies' recent differences and emphasizing the similarity of their world views.

Schacht's arguments were strong, but they did not carry the day. At a meeting in the last week of October, Komatsu's senior executives declared themselves to be "pro Cummins" and strongly in favor of closer cooperation between the two companies—but not willing to make a long-term investment in Cummins at that time.[76] At regular intervals thereafter, Cummins restated its invitation to Komatsu to invest in Cummins, in part to avoid any ill feelings that might arise if and when it found other partners—perhaps even a Japanese partner.

This was a prudent precaution. Even as discussions continued with Komatsu, Cummins was talking seriously with a second Japanese company about a possible investment in Cummins. That company was Osaka-based Kubota Ltd., a $5.2 billion farm-equipment manufacturer that was eagerly looking for a way to break into the European market.

Discussions with Kubota began in a very roundabout way in the summer of 1989, with intermediaries talking to intermediaries. This was in part because Kubota was known to be a conservative company, which—unlike many other Japanese companies—had refrained from making significant investments in heavy manufacturing outside of its borders.[77] (Kubota's semiconductor and computer arms, by contrast, had engaged in extensive acquisitions in the United States during the 1980s.)[78] As in the case of Komatsu, Cummins was looking for far more than a joint-venture relationship, and had reached the conclusion that Kubota also might be interested in diversification through alliance with Cummins.

Significantly, the engine product lines of the two companies were highly complementary, which augured well for some sort of partnership. Although Kubota had sold $10 million worth of "loose" engines in the United States in 1987, they were exclusively in the 10 to 90 hp range. Most of the company's U.S. dollar volume came from small tractors for turf maintenance and general uses.[79] And, by coincidence, Kubota had been selling engines to Onan, the genset manufacturer, before Onan's purchase by Cummins in 1986. Kubota also was closely tied to Cummins' partner in Consolidated Diesel, J. I. Case.[80]

Kubota representatives visited Cummins in the summer and fall of 1989, and the discussions between the two companies gradually worked their way up the hierarchy, and into more concrete terms.[81] A trip to Japan by Henry Schacht and Will Miller in November brought Kubota into sharper focus. Although Kubota seemed to be underinvesting in emissions control and other technical areas, it impressed the Americans as a highly competent operation with excellent manufacturing facilities. And Kubota's senior managers were receptive to Schacht's pitch for a significant investment in Cummins by Kubota. "He delivered the 'we will invest' message with some feeling," Schacht noted of Kubota's second-in-command, Kohsaku Uda.[82]

That investment took a long step toward becoming a reality in April 1990, when the Kubota board authorized an expenditure of up to $48 million to buy Cummins stock. The purchase was linked to the establishment of a successful Kubota-Cummins joint venture to make Kubota light-duty diesel engines at Darlington, England, as well as to the sharing of emission-control technology.[83] Kubota's leaders agreed with Cummins' argument that the American company could be very helpful to Kubota's efforts to break into the farm and construction equipment fields. The size of the Kubota investment—about 7.5 percent of Cummins—was roughly the same as (and determined by) the capitalization of Kubota's own engine division. Cummins well understood how important and difficult a decision this was for its new Japanese partner. "The action taken by Kubota's board," wrote one Cummins participant, "was a very significant 'first time' for this sort of investment by Kubota."[84]

The Kubota deal was an important step toward a more stable and independent ownership structure. But more was needed, so Schacht spent much of 1988 and 1989 touring the world in search of an appropriate long-term partner. Ironically, the company that turned out to be the most important partner of all—the Ford Motor Company—was neither considered nor approached until scores of other options were exhausted.

The Cummins relationship with Ford dates back to the day in the spring of 1930 when Clessie Cummins demonstrated his diesel-powered Packard limousine to an enthusiastic (if acerbic) Henry Ford. In ensuing decades, Cummins had tried mightily to expand its business with the automotive giant, but never closed a large deal. The prospect of selling huge quantities of small engines to Ford, for example, had been a principal motivator for Cummins to dive into the "Rainbow" engine development program in the 1970s. But Henry Ford II personally scotched the notion of putting Cummins diesels in Ford automobiles, evidently scared off by the massive costs of retooling for diesels. And the automaker decided against offering the B engine as an option in its popular pickup truck, as described in Chapter 9. But since then Ford remained a steady Cummins truck customer, particularly in the heavy-duty truck field. In 1989, for example, Ford purchased about two-thirds of its 12,000 heavy-duty engines from Cummins, with the remainder coming from Caterpillar.

In these and other ways, the relationship already was well established. The two companies were so different in size and culture, however, that Schacht never seriously considered making an overture to Ford. But by March 1990, despite landing Kubota, Schacht was getting desperate. Once again, he recalls, he was running out of ideas:

We had been to almost all the U.S. guys, with the exception of Ford. And finally I said one day, "We might as well talk to Ford." So I called up Red Poling, whom I had known for a while, and I said, "Look, I have an idea I want to try on you. We want to talk about worldwide partnership, and about Ford taking a position in Cummins."

So I went up there on a Tuesday, and the deal came together almost immediately. And the funny thing was that one of their guys later told me that they had just finished a review of their commercial options, and had decided that the key was in forming some sort of relationship with Cummins. And I walked in the door four days later. The two companies arrived at virtually the same set of conclusions at virtually the same time. All I did was make the call.

This momentous meeting (on April 9, 1990) and those that followed filled in the few missing pieces in Cummins' understanding of Ford's "commercial options."[85] One of Ford's principal reasons for seeking a partnership with Cummins was a mounting concern about emissions controls. Ford saw itself as behind the curve in developing technologies to meet the EPA's 1994 emission standards, and was then contemplating a $300 million expenditure to catch up.[86] Ford also faced the daunting prospect of replacing its outdated (and high-volume) Brazilian 7.8-liter engine, installed in some 28,000 trucks in 1988. Even further down the power spectrum was the Ford light-duty truck series, powered by 7.3-liter Navistar engines. Ford sold some 100,000 of these vehicles annually, and was on the lookout for a newer and better engine.[87] As part of the buy-in, Ford made a commitment to purchase as many as 27,000 C engines—a contract that would take the Rocky Mount midrange engine plant out of the red and well into the black.

"It's a minority equity investment, but it's of great strategic importance to us," a Ford spokesman said when the deal was announced publicly. "It ensures the availability of mid-range engines for our medium- and heavy-duty trucks and makes us partners in our long-term product lines."[88]

The third of three partners that Henry Schacht succeeded in signing up was Tenneco Inc., the huge Houston-based conglomerate. Tenneco, with interests ranging from gas production to table grapes, was perhaps the least obvious candidate for partnership of the three companies who ultimately signed up with Cummins. But Tenneco's subsidiary, J. I. Case, was losing large amounts of money in the Consolidated Diesel joint venture with Cummins. Since much of the new business that Ford would help generate for Cummins would be run through the Rocky Mount plant and would significantly improve the economics of that plant, Tenneco was amply motivated to invest in Cummins.[89]

The deal heated up shortly after the Ford negotiations got underway. On May 1, 1990—after detailed discussions with Tenneco head Jim Keteleson—Schacht sent a letter to Tenneco formally asking the company to respect the privacy of the materials Cummins was providing "in connection with your consideration of a possible equity investment in Cummins."[90] Tenneco's decision came in the same month; and in comments made later, the company was explicit about wanting to exert some influence on Cummins. "With this investment," said a Tenneco spokesman, "we get a seat on the board and a say in the strategy and direction of Cummins over the long term. And with that, we'll be able to keep in sharp focus the research and development of diesel technology."[91]

In other words, Tenneco wanted what Schacht wanted. But these kinds of comments created some degree of anxiety at Kubota, since both Tenneco (a 10 percent owner) and Ford (up to 20 percent) would have seats on the Cummins board, and might be tempted to arrange events to their own advantage and to the disadvantage of Kubota. Attempting to assuage Kubota's fears, Cummins pointed out that it had limited Ford's position to 20 percent, and that there was very little overlap among the product lines of the three partner companies in any case. Added Cummins: "Both Ford and Tenneco understand that Cummins' value comes from its ability to remain an independent engine supplier that does not favor any customer to the disadvantage of another."[92]

A final important piece of reassurance came in June, when Will Miller accompanied Henry Schacht on a visit to Kubota in Japan. "Will made a very helpful statement as an outside director representing all the shareholders," Schacht wrote in a note to himself. "Mr. Uda responded very favorably to this, remarking that this was very comforting since they would be without board representation."[93]

Closing the Deals

On July 16, Cummins proudly announced the agreements with Ford, Tenneco, and Kubota. The deal, as finally struck, had Kubota purchasing preferred stock equivalent to 799,760 shares of common (or 5.4 percent) for $50 million; Tenneco purchasing preferred equivalent to 10.8 percent; and Ford purchasing preferred equivalent to 10.8 percent of common, with an option to go to 20 percent.[94] (Ford and Tenneco, therefore, were in for $100 million apiece.) All three partners had paid $62.50 per share, or almost 20 percent over market price, and each agreed not to sell its shares for at least six years. The premium paid by the partners effectively inoculated Schacht against charges of dilution of equity, since the company's asset base increased proportionately with the newly issued equity.

Henry Schacht told the business press that the three deals together constituted "a clear vote of confidence" in Cummins. He also announced his intention to reduce Cummins' long-term debt to just over $300 million (down from $473 million in the previous year), thereby shrinking interest payments and freeing up resources for new investment.

Industry analysts were quick to point out how increased business from the three new partners would benefit Cummins. Assuming the light-duty joint venture with Kubota went through, and also assuming that Ford delivered on its commitment to use Cummins' B and C engines in its midrange trucks, Cummins might realize an additional $27 million per year in profits. "The ability to bring three new partners into the organization at the same time under similar conditions," wrote one industry insider, "while providing substantial advantage to Cummins is most impressive."[95]

Among the planned debt reductions was a corporate buyback of the Miller family's $67 million in high-yielding convertible preferred stock—an outcome that prompted *Business Week* to identify the Millers as the "only immediate losers" as a result of the deal. And indeed, by taking back $67 million in cash and $37 million in common stock (at a price of $64.50), the family was accepting as final the $5 million loss it had incurred by buying out Hanson. Will Miller, in response, once again expressed the family's equanimity: "We think Cummins will pay off for us down the road."[96]

The Millers' action vis-à-vis Hanson had come under closer scrutiny in the year since its denouement. As noted above, the press at the time had been largely laudatory of the family's willingness to buy out Hanson. But in the intervening months, a new interpretation had emerged. According to this view, the Millers had not taken a noble $5 million loss on the transaction. In fact, went the argument, they had *gained* on the deal, by bailing out of Cummins common just before that stock declined 20 percent in the last quarter of 1989. This assumed, of course, that the Millers originally had intended to hold on to the common that they had purchased from Hanson, and that Cummins executives had conspired with them to invent a device—the convertible note—to help the family avoid this much larger paper loss.

Henry Schacht, for one, was driven to fury by this allegation. The Millers, he asserted vehemently, never intended to hold on to the Hanson stock, but, according to the agreed-upon plan, had signed it over to Cummins in an instant. More important, as he told a reporter: "The Miller buyout of Hanson provided us the time and stability to work our way into the position we find ourselves [in today, with three new equity partners]. . . . It was a great act of industrial statesmanship. These people cared. They cared more than money."[97]

Many around Cummins, including the Millers, felt that the media had been successfully manipulated by outside forces. In particular, the members of the Miller family objected to several "revisionist" articles by reporter Alison Leigh Cowan in the *New York Times*, which—while reporting on both the IEP-Cummins battle and the Ford-Tenneco-Kubota deal—largely contradicted the very positive conclusions reached in an earlier *Times* article about the Hanson deal.[98] Irwin Miller recalls his and his son's reaction to the second (and most negative) of the articles:

> *She [the reporter] couldn't have done that calculation on her own, because she didn't know enough. That's why Will could never sell her, because when he talked to her, she was so blank, she didn't know what he was talking about. I think it's always bugged him that he couldn't go back to her and say, "Look, now the whole deal has been wound up, and we lost the amount of money that we said we were going to lose, and the IRS has acknowledged it." I think that Will will not go to his grave happily until he can go to Alison at the* Times *and say, 'Told you so!'"*

In retrospect, it seems clear that the Millers should be taken at their word. When the deal was struck in July 1989, neither the family nor the Engine Company foresaw the coming crash in the heavy-duty truck market, and therefore no one had a plausible reason to rush away from Cummins common. (In fact, Cummins had just come off two strong quarters, which is a principal reason why IEP was buying Cummins stock so heavily in this same period.) The written agreements between the Millers and Cummins make it clear that a two-step process—a family purchase of Hanson's shares, and an immediate "swap" of those shares for convertible notes—was contemplated from the outset. In fact, this was the only way the family could afford the deal. Finally, as suggested by Irwin Miller, an IRS investigation of the family's tax obligations in the wake of the Hanson deal concluded that the Millers had, indeed, lost the money they claimed they had.

At the other end of the story, moreover, the Millers made a second sacrifice which went largely unnoticed, perhaps because of its complexity. The terms of the convertible preferred stock given by the company to the family in exchange for the Hanson common stock mandated a 6 percent premium to the family in the event of an early redemption to common. When Cummins used the newly infused Ford-Tenneco-Kubota money to convert the Millers' stake, the family waived that premium, declining to take a large gain at the expense of the company they had worked for many years to build.

The drama of larger events mostly outweighed these local concerns. Financial analysts understood the motives and mechanism of the Hanson buyback, and almost all applauded the Ford-Tenneco-Kubota deal as one that would strengthen the company considerably—providing badly needed cash, ensuring management stability, increasing engine volume, and taking Cummins "out of play." To be sure, some outside observers expressed concern about the company's always-voracious appetite for cash. "The market is still nervous about the outlook and the way Cummins is spending cash," said one.

"The market is questioning just how quickly Cummins might go through the cash."[99]

But against formidable odds, Henry Schacht had achieved his odd and powerful vision: of a "private company with public ownership," as he later described it.[100] Cummins now had the clear benefit of a substantial plurality of owners (counting the Millers and employee shareholders, as well as Ford, Tenneco, and Kubota) who were likely to be tolerant of short-term economic swings because they perceived their real advantage to lie in long-term developments. In effect, Schacht had leveraged the Miller family's tradition of "patient capital" across much of the shareholder base.

As more than one observer pointed out, Schacht's triumph signaled the end of Cummins' decade-long obsession with the Japanese threat. Ironically, though, the transformation that Schacht achieved—making the interests of the company and several of its key customers congruent—rendered the Cummins Engine Company more "Japanese" in a fundamental way. And much work remained. Although the new financial structure provided Cummins with a welcome degree of stability, the company still had to prove it could compete in its chosen markets, against newly resurgent competitors, in many cases using largely unproven technologies.

12 | Pressures and Profits, 1988–1994

THE FORD, TENNECO, AND KUBOTA INVESTMENTS in 1990 gave Cummins a much-needed stable base of capital. These new investors not only understood the cyclical nature of the engine industry; they also understood, supported, and even depended on the Engine Company's commitment to improving technology, particularly emissions control. Cummins viewed these new relationships with strong partners, as well as brisk sales of B and C engines and productivity gains throughout its worldwide manufacturing operations, as the building blocks for profitability when the economy recovered.

Instead, the early 1990s proved to be the most trying time since the company's earliest decades. Following a short honeymoon in early 1989, Cummins fell into a protracted slump. Precipitated in part by war in the Persian Gulf, a severe recession beset the international economy through 1990 and 1991. Cummins' share of the heavy-duty market plummeted as a result of major problems with the 1988 engine line. To compound this misfortune, a tough "new" competitor arrived on the scene, in the form of a revitalized Detroit Diesel. In 1990, the company posted the largest losses in its history, and the cost-cutting measures that ensued required layoffs at all levels within the firm. Meanwhile, tantalizing opportunities for improvements in technology and expansion of the customer base threw the company's near-term choices into sharp relief. Could Cummins think and act opportunistically in a period of bitter retrenchments? Could it afford *not* to?

A great deal therefore was riding on the next heavy-duty introduction in 1991. The launch was a success, and the tide turned. Major competitive challenges remained, however. Like the rest of the industrial world, Cummins found itself coming to terms with sophisticated and unfamiliar technologies. Almost inevitably, technology—particularly electronic controls on the engine and fuel system—became a crucial concern. Cummins first had to build a new base of expertise, and then integrate that expertise with its other key functions.

An even bigger challenge was the extension of team-based and quality-oriented manufacturing processes across the organization, and the establishment of a competitive wage base for the domestic manufacture of the lower-margin midrange engines. Working more or less collaboratively, the Engine Company and the Diesel Workers Union tried to strike a deal that could meet the needs of both parties.

Learning from adversity

Observers inside and outside the company agreed that by the late 1980s, a foundation was in place that might allow Cummins not only to recover, but to flourish. (This was the principal reason why companies like Hanson and IEP were interested in Cummins in the first place.) The quality-improvement and cost-reduction programs described in Chapter 10 had begun to pay dividends. The B and C engines were enjoying increasing success: Units shipped in 1989 surpassed those of heavy-duty and high-horsepower engines combined. Just two years later, Cummins sold twice as many midrange engines as heavy duty.[1]

This shift in the product mix was the brightest silver lining in the cloud that hung over Cummins in this period. "In 1990," the company announced at the close of that year, "39 percent of our total corporate sales dollars were from products the company did not have when we began our new product development and diversification effort in 1980." And with the painful exception of the heavy-duty truck market, Cummins was holding its own during the recession. It held its place as the world's fifth largest manufacturer of engines 50 hp and larger, and the largest manufacturer by a wide margin of engines over 200 hp.[2]

As it turned out, Cummins soon would surpass even its own most optimistic performance projections. But fortune was not yet ready to smile on the Engine Company. It was simply a case of very bad timing: Cummins announced the agreements with Ford, Tenneco, and Kubota on July 16, 1990. Just two weeks later (on August 2), Saddam Hussein's Iraq invaded the neighboring state of Kuwait. Saudi Arabia, source of much of the world's oil, appeared to be Iraq's next target. The business community ducked for cover. "On August 2," Henry Schacht recalled, "it was like someone turned off the spigot." Demand for new engines died. PACCAR, which led the U.S. heavy-duty market, saw its new truck sales drop from 39,600 in 1989 to 29,000 in 1990, while other truck makers endured similar declines.[3]

As a result, Cummins' domestic heavy-duty engine order rate for first quarter 1990 fell 42 percent from first quarter 1989 levels, and dropped another 20 percent by fourth quarter 1990. And this was far more than a domestic crisis. Order rates in the same two periods in the United Kingdom, for example, fell 39 percent and 33 percent, respectively. Other negative forces converged in the international arena. In 1990, the company suffered substantial losses ($26.5 million) in Brazil because of hyperinflation, followed by a brutal recession; and because the crucial 14 percent Befiex export credit (described in Chapter 9) was eliminated.[4]

As usual, the company took a number of painful steps in response. First, it reduced its salaried work force worldwide by about 350 people. It laid off 175 Southern Indiana production workers, with another 35 taking voluntary unpaid leave, and eliminated a production line on the third shift at the Columbus engine plant.[5]

Financial maneuvering mitigated some of the pain. For example, Cummins retired $200 million worth of Liquid Yield Options Notes (LYONs) from Merrill Lynch for $54 million in September 1990—but the $22 million gain in the asset column from that debt retirement did not come close to offsetting the company's staggering loss of $55.8 million in that quarter. At year end 1990, Cummins posted a loss of $137.7 million on the year—far and away the largest loss in the company's history.

There were a few bright spots in this landscape of gloom. During the Gulf conflict and throughout the redeployment phase that followed, Cummins won contracts to power several thousand military trucks, Bradley fighting vehicles, and AS90 self-propelled howitzers. McCord heat-transfer components and systems went into a number of military vehicles, while Onan generator sets produced power for Allied efforts. Meanwhile, B and C engines continued to sell well, with demand climbing to 625 per day—accounting for 31 percent of 1990 engine revenues and 55 percent of engine unit shipments.[6] But rising small-engine sales still were a mixed blessing for Cummins. As part of the no-holds-barred effort to keep the Japanese offshore, B and C engines were still priced below cost. In these lines, for the time being, higher sales only meant higher losses.

The pincer-like recession showed no signs of abating, making necessary some drastic measures. On May 21, 1991, the Cummins board voted to cut the quarterly dividend by 90 percent (from 55 to 5 cents per share). In the company's long history, this was an unprecedented step, and it was one that Schacht and Henderson were loathe to take. But it accurately reflected the company's truly dire short-term prospects.

Off the Cliff with the 88NT

Cummins had surrendered its dominant position in the heavy-duty diesel market, slipping from a high of 60 percent in 1984 to 50 percent in 1989. Some observers saw this relative decline as expected, given the intensely competitive environment of the 1980s. And surely the company's new strategic direction played a role; the new focus on smaller engines naturally diverted attention and resources away from the making and selling of heavy-duty engines.

But the gradual decline of the early and mid-1980s turned into a free-fall. On top of its recent 10 percent loss, Cummins shed an additional 4 points in 1990, 8 points in 1991, and 3 points in 1992, leaving it with a mere 35 percent of the heavy-duty market.

What had happened? The major culprit was a faulty engine line introduced in 1988—the 88NT—which by this time was generating huge and growing warranty costs. Worse, word began to spread throughout the industry that the 88NT engine was a loser, leaving the door open for an opportunistic competitor (described below) to gobble up market share.

The 88NT's problems grew out of new diesel emissions standards imposed by the Environmental Protection Agency (EPA) in the mid-1980s. In the 1970s, the EPA focused on gasoline engines, declining to treat heavy-duty diesels as a separate class. By the 1980s, growing public awareness about engine emissions, combined with the rising prices of cleaner-burning new cars, compelled more and more Americans to question the diesel exception.

The first diesel regulatory standards were slated for 1987. For several years prior to that date, however, Cummins representatives lobbied strenuously (both individually and through involvement with the Health Effects Institute) for the EPA to develop emissions standards for the heavy-duty diesel industry. This was a principled stance, but it was also pragmatic. As early as 1982, internal memoranda within Cummins pointed out that although the EPA had not yet handed down definitive oxides of nitrogen (NO_x) and particulate emissions standards, existing standards for gasoline engines were getting progressively more stringent—so much so that if similar standards suddenly were imposed on diesels, Cummins would have a hard time meeting them within a reasonable time frame.[7]

Moreover, early hints of what a particulate standard might look like were ominous. A letter from Henry Schacht to Washington attorney (and former Nixon administration official) Elliot Richardson in mid-1982 laid out the company's growing concern:

> There is as yet no particulate standard for heavy duty engines. EPA has proposed such a standard for model year 1985. The first hearing before EPA on that proposal occurred only last week. It is generally acknowledged that the proposed particulate standard is simply not technologically feasible by 1985.[8]

By late 1984, Cummins and other diesel manufacturers still awaited regulatory attention from the EPA, and internal concerns about the company's ability to comply when the dreaded day finally arrived continued to grow. A

November 1984 internal memorandum cautioned that a 1987 effective date for new standards would pose "a severe problem for Cummins" at that point, and projected that "even with a major resources shift and a crash effort, we doubt our ability to meet this deadline *at best* without experiencing considerable reliability and durability problems."[9]

Finally, in March 1985, the EPA promulgated regulations for NO_x and particulate emissions for the diesel industry. These new regulations laid out a staggered compliance schedule, defining a series of ever-more-stringent standards to be adopted in 1988, 1991, and 1994. The dire predictions of many industry observers (including some within Cummins) had come true: The first benchmark—requiring a reduction in NO_x from 10.7 grams to 6 grams, and a reduction in particulates to 0.6, both by product year 1988—violated the Clean Air Act's own statutory requirement for a four-year window between imposition of new regulations and their implementation.[10] To put it mildly, these new regulations, and especially the schedule that drove them, posed a daunting challenge for the industry.

Members of the Engine Manufacturers Association (the relatively conservative trade group that looked after the industry's legislative interests) quickly filed a joint petition against what they considered to be the EPA's unreasonably compressed schedule for compliance. Their concerns were both case-specific and general. Not only did the offending schedule have to be undone, argued the engine makers, but the industry's legal right to a four-year development lead time had to be defended. Cummins' managers debated about what stance to take—continued cooperation with the EPA, or unaccustomed confrontation—and eventually decided to cooperate. Cummins informed the EMA that it would not join in the petition.[11] For its part, the industry association went forward with the case *sans* Cummins, perhaps unsurprised by the Indiana company's odd-man-out stance.

Meanwhile, Cummins still was obliged to develop an engine that met the new, stricter standard. If the EPA's new schedule stood, the new requirements would take effect on January 1, 1988—just two and a half years away. And even if the 1988 standards were stayed temporarily, the much stricter 1991 and 1994 emissions requirements looming on the horizon still would fully tax the company's technological capabilities. The test cells in the Tech Center shifted into a higher gear.

It took the courts a year and a half to rule in favor of the Engine Manufacturers Association (on November 7, 1986). The EPA then agreed to delay requiring the reduction of NO_x from 10.7 to 6.0 grams until 1990. For many manufacturers, this was welcome news indeed. "All our competitors heaved a big sigh of relief," Miller recalls, "and went back to their old product." But any celebrations within the industry were muted, because the reduction of diesel particulates required in 1988 still stood.

For Cummins, the legal ruling posed a new set of challenges. Paula Gustafson, a government-affairs specialist within the company, articulated these soon after the decision. "As a result of the Court's decisions," she wrote to her colleagues, "the industry is faced with having to meet a particulate standard in 1988, a NO_x standard in 1990, and more stringent revised NO_x and particulate standards in 1991." Taken together, this series of regulations threatened to have enormous impact:

> *Manufacturers will be faced with a significant increase in development, certification, and distribution costs if they choose to take advantage of the relaxation of NO_x standards. Instead of a single product line to meet all markets (49 states, California, and Canada) with certification in 1988, 1991 and 1994, manufacturers will be required to develop separate product lines for California and the 49 states in 1988 and conduct certification in 1988, 1990, 1991, and 1994.*[12]

The certification process was extremely expensive and time-consuming. Furthermore, in the eighteen-month interim since the offending regulations had been promulgated, Cummins engineers had made substantial progress toward modifying the heavy-duty engines and fuel systems enough to meet the new standards. Many of the changes already had been designed into the manufacturing process. As Jim Henderson recalls, "We had made all the necessary plans to go ahead and release, and we had gotten the tooling in place. If we *didn't* release, we were going to put our plants in real turmoil." And so, little by little, the question at Cummins became: Why *not* go ahead?

So go ahead they did. Cummins made an all-out commitment to its new technologies, launching the newly revised 1988NT and L10 engines in 1987. The next year, the company introduced four new or substantially revised engines (L, C, B, and A) and also unveiled significantly improved K, NH, and V903 models. It was an unprecedented plunge, and the Engine Company—apparently getting the jump on the competition—was proud of its accomplishment.[13]

The new NTs began to sell briskly, and helped push the company back into profitability in 1989. But the honeymoon ended quickly. Within six months of hitting the road, the 88NT engines began to experience significant problems, including excessive wear, sooting, and difficulties with the engines' "low-flow" cooling systems. Changes in the fuel system produced the most serious problem: heavy sooting, which in turn caused inordinate wear on the system.[14] Diagnosing reports from the field, Cummins engineers concluded that most of the 88NT's problems were likely to intensify with increased mileage. "When those engines started getting into trouble," Jim Henderson recalls, "they got into *huge* trouble."

The result was two kinds of losses. The first, of course, was cash, as Cummins found itself shelling out tens of millions of dollars in additional warranty costs. (In 1990 alone, the company paid an additional $41.3 million above projections for extended warranty programs.)[15] The second loss was in market share, as longtime Cummins customers left in droves. The money costs were painful, but the lost market share was potentially disastrous.

"The cost of failure is way up there on the scale, compared to what it used to be," Irwin Miller says. "The customer would tolerate your going through phase 1, 2, 3, and 4 on an engine in the '30s, '40s, and '50s. He won't do that anymore. He expects everything to run." When the NT engines did not run, customers balked—and in some cases, walked. "Some got very irate with us," Henry Schacht recalls. "They said, 'ABC: Anybody but Cummins.'"

Penske Goes for Broke

Two or three years earlier, a disaffected OEM or fleet operator with "ABC" ringing in his mind would have had few strong alternatives to Cummins. But by late 1989, engine customers found an unexpected suitor courting them in the marketplace: a newly rejuvenated Detroit Diesel.

It was singularly ironic that Detroit Diesel should be there to scoop up Cummins customers. Just a few years earlier—in the summer of 1985—Detroit Diesel's parent company, General Motors, had approached Cummins with a proposition. The Detroit giant was looking for two things: a buyer for Detroit Diesel, and an independent engine supplier to take that subsidiary's place. Cummins and Caterpillar were the two strong contenders.[16]

For Cummins, the offer was appealing, but had two major flaws. First, GM's asking price for Detroit Diesel seemed high. As a way to recoup some of that capital, Cummins came in with a less-than-competitive bid to act as preferred supplier to GM's Truck and Coach division. Second, as Cummins had learned from the White episode, there were antitrust implications to consider. But Schacht was assured by GM's Don Atwood (who had approached Cummins with the offer) that these problems could be resolved. And when Robert Stempel became GM's new president, Atwood introduced him to Schacht to demonstrate the firmness of the commitment.

Given this momentum, Schacht was astonished to pick up his newspaper one morning in 1987 and discover that auto-racing legend and entrepreneur Roger Penske had purchased Detroit Diesel—and at a discount price, to boot. Apparently Penske had gone directly to GM's CEO Roger Smith, who had not been involved in the Cummins negotiations, and cut his own deal.[17] According to Schacht, Penske picked up the diesel maker at a bargain-basement price:

*He got an absolutely sweetheart deal from General Motors. He bid a dime on the dollar—he bought it for significantly less than what we had offered, and no cash. He had no fixed costs. He rented the plant, and rented the labor. So he started with a cost structure that was very, very good for a UAW facility.** *

Penske entered the heavy-duty engine game in 1988 with two key technological advantages as well. First, his "Series 60" engine—designed almost entirely by a former Cummins engineer who had relocated to the Detroit area—was ready to go to market.[18] Second, Detroit Diesel offered full electronic controls over its heavy-duty engine and fuel system. Electronics in automotive applications were nothing new; automobiles had used them for years to enhance fuel economy and control emissions. But the development of electronics for trucks, a much smaller market, had lagged behind. Cummins had pioneered in this market by introducing a partially electronically controlled engine in 1987, and by marketing several highly successful electronic diagnostic and analytical tools as early as 1985. But Penske had purchased a company that had a fully developed, "full authority" electronic engine ready to go.[†] Given Detroit Diesel's precipitous slide down to a 3 percent market share, it had little to lose in taking the huge risk that electronics represented in the late 1980s.

Penske's opportunity arose, in a sense, from a marketwide failure of nerve. Nobody (neither manufacturers nor customers) wanted to take on the $2,000 premium before tougher emissions standards forced the adoption of electronics. Penske took the plunge. With a unique product in hand, he took advantage of his unusual financial structure to implement a bold pricing strategy. Whereas electronics typically added about $2,000 to the price of a heavy-duty engine, Penske offered his big Series 60 (a $14,000 model) for $12,000, rather than the $16,000 or so that Cummins expected.[19] "You get fuel consumption advantages with electronics," Schacht explains, "and where you don't have to *pay* for them, well, it just hit the market running."

Penske reinforced his pricing edge and technological advantage with a healthy dose of salesmanship and personal charisma. Many of Penske's marketing methods harked back to those of Cummins' original charismatic marketeers: Clessie Cummins and Paris Letsinger. Penske flew around the country peddling his engines personally. He won a number of heavy-duty customers over to the Series 60 by installing the engine in their trucks on a trial basis. He

---

*Jim Henderson also points out that GM agreed to keep all existing warranty liabilities—a huge advantage for Penske.

[†]"Full authority" means exactly what the phrase implies—that the electronics have complete control over the vital systems of the engine.

established 24-hour phone support lines to assist Series 60 owners, and sent Detroit Diesel staff out into the field to work with his newfound customers.[20]

By 1989, as the Series 60 began to take big bites of the market, Cummins was fighting a losing battle against two insidious forces. First, as noted, the 10- and 14-liter engines were experiencing a growing number of problems. And second, threats of takeover by Hanson and IEP were eroding the confidence of Cummins' customers. Cummins marketers and distributors were starting to hear a common theme, no doubt reinforced by Detroit Diesel's sales force: "Hey, we'd better try some of these Detroits, because you guys may be gone."[21] The net result of these converging trends was an astonishing turn-around. Detroit Diesel jumped from a 3.5 percent share of the heavy-duty market in 1988 to 21 percent in the first quarter of 1991, while Cummins slipped from 54 percent to 42 percent.[22]

Cummins faced a long road to win back the confidence and loyalty of the engine-buying public. Beyond that, it had to ensure that the deficient processes—both managerial and technological—hobbling the 88NT would not afflict future introductions.

Putting the Wheels Back On

How had it happened? In hindsight, Cummins' managers point to several key miscalculations—about technology, production processes, and the marketplace.

The technical shortcomings of the 88NT are still the subject of controversy. On one point, at least, there is consensus: The 88NT's injectors plugged up early and often. According to engineer Gary Nelson, the drive to lower emissions to meet the government's tighter standards led Cummins engineers to retard the timing on the engine. This led to a reverse flow of gases into the injector, which in turn caused injector carboning. Cummins had experienced this problem before in specialized circumstances—for example, in downhill performance with a Jake Brake engaged—but never under normal operating conditions.[23]

What is also clear about the 88NT is that Cummins engineers and managers had been lulled into a false sense of security. Whereas less familiar engine lines such as the B and C were tested exhaustively, the NT was not. This was mostly because the NT was considered to be a known technology. As Henry Schacht recalls:

> *With the Bs and Cs, we were terrified because we were jumping off the cliff. We had on both a belt and suspenders—we got it right. But all the lessons we had learned in the small Vs, in the introduction of the Bs and Cs, which came out of the learning experience of the 903, 555, etc., we didn't apply that to the '88. We knew it so well that we didn't*

apply the disciplines. We all were victims of that fact that this was another extension of the NT, which we had been doing forever.

But there were other factors as well. As described in Chapter 10, the Total Quality System (TQS) created by Cummins under the tutelage of General Systems and the Feigenbaums specifically addressed the challenge of new product introduction. The NPPD&I (new product planning, development, and introduction) protocol was nearly completed and was ready for use during the '88 introduction. When the decision was made to push ahead the 88NT's introduction on an accelerated schedule, however, Cummins made a serious mistake: It elected not to adopt the hard-won disciplines of NPPD&I and reverted to less disciplined habits. Another factor was the impact of the 30 Month Sprint, which altered many facets of the manufacturing operations. According to engineer Karl Kuehner: "It was the emphasis on cost-per-piece, and on cost reduction, that sank the 88NT."

Finally, there was disagreement at the very top of the organization about what kind of leadership was needed in this difficult period. In 1983, Cummins had promoted an ambitious and promising young manager named Michael H. Walsh—a former U.S. Attorney for the Southern District of California—from vice president of international and subsidiaries to executive vice president of operations and international. By the mid-1980s, Walsh was eager to take over operations. Jim Henderson had reservations about Walsh's ability to do the job—reservations that Henry Schacht did not fully share. But Walsh took over the operational reins on the NT and other engines. "Mike was a very, very talented guy," Henderson later observed, "but technology wasn't his strength. We did not have the right team on that product." Walsh left Cummins in mid-1986 and went on to a successful career as head of Union Pacific and later as head of Cummins' equity partner, Tenneco; but the NT continued on its ill-fated trajectory long after his departure.[*]

To tackle the turnaround of the heavy-duty engine—now dubbed the "N14"—Henderson tapped F. Joseph "Joe" Loughrey, the newly appointed head of Columbus operations. Loughrey had returned from a stint in the United Kingdom in 1986, and in 1987, as vice president of employee relations, had negotiated two labor union contracts in southern Indiana. At the end of 1987—a few weeks before the '88 engine's introduction—Loughrey took on responsibility for Columbus operations.

It was, in his words, a "pretty hair-raising" period. Problems with the 88NTs were burgeoning, warranty costs were escalating, and customer dissatisfaction was boiling over. Henry Schacht and other senior managers were

---

[*]Walsh departed Cummins to head Union Pacific Railway in 1986; in 1991, he left Union Pacific to take the top position at Tenneco.

busy fending off what they took to be takeover attempts. Amid this chaos, Cummins engineers were attempting to alter the stalwart NT engine more fundamentally than ever before. To further complicate matters, the DWU labor contract was up for negotiation. "Folks who were anywhere near assembly or test at that time," Loughrey recalls, "were more or less scared to death, depending on how close they were to the mad scramble. We're lucky to have survived it, given everything else that was going on at the time."

It was a tough juncture for Loughrey to enter the process: too late to change much, and too early to see the true dimensions of the avalanche of problems that was on its way. As soon as the avalanche struck, however, Loughrey took decisive action. After making personnel changes that he considered to be overdue, he announced to everyone involved in the 1991 product that *this* time, they would approach new product introduction in the way that had been specified jointly by Cummins and the Feigenbaums in the TQS system. As he recalls:

> We divided people into teams, called them into big sessions, and said, in effect, "Here's your group. Here's what we're expecting of you. We want you to go away and talk together, and then come back and tell us whether these expectations are real and realistic." So we drove it, in that sense. We used this project, even though it was already pretty far along, to demonstrate that we could and would use TQS.

To make the point perfectly clear, Loughrey appointed the acknowledged champion of TQS, Karl Kuehner, to head the engineering side of the N14. "Loughrey came to me," recalls Kuehner, "and said, 'OK, Kuehner, time to practice what you've been preaching.'"

Following the letter and spirit of the NPPD&I guidelines (which in effect create multiple feedback loops and go/no go decision points within the critical path of new-product development), Kuehner and his colleagues first fixed the most problematic components of the 88NT: oil coolers, pistons, and injectors. Then, step by step, they looked for ways to design the potential for new problems out of the N14 (later dubbed the "COMMAND" engine in marketing materials). One new tool that Kuehner called on was the "compatibility matrix," designed during the long TQS development process. Simply put, one axis of the matrix showed Cummins' capability at a given process. The other axis showed criticality of the process. How important was this particular process for the performance of the product, or the satisfaction of the customer? "What we said," explains Kuehner, "was that we would never go into production with something that was critical to the performance of the engine but was produced by an incapable process."

Both axes of the compatibility matrix called for increased product testing, and as a result, testing time on the new engine increased dramatically. Dyno testing at the Tech Center, for example, jumped from 15,000 to 95,000 hours. Engine Quality Audit testing in the plants increased more than five-fold—from 3,750 to 20,000 hours—and field-test distances were increased from 2 million miles to more than 5.5 million.[24]

Budget constraints were never far away. "I never felt like we had a blank check on resources," Kuehner recalls. "We were strapped, just like everybody else in the company." Compounding this constraint was the fact that engineering resources were spread over three tough challenges simultaneously: fixing the '88s, launching the '91s, and preparing for the not-so-far-off '94 launch.

The '91 launch took place on schedule. Kuehner, the day-to-day leader of the N14 trench warriors, wound up concluding that the launch was unsatisfactory. Fuel-system problems persisted through much of the introduction, and—after the fact—the new engine was faulted for being less fuel-efficient than its Detroit Diesel counterpart. "When I had to make a trade-off between reliability and fuel economy on that '91 engine," he explains, "I went with reliability every time. *Every* time!" Joe Loughrey, Kuehner's supervisor, disagrees with Kuehner's assessment. "It was a pretty terrific introduction," Loughrey says emphatically. After the experience of the 88NT, it seems, even an imperfect launch looked good.

Cummins was so determined to win back the favor of the marketplace that it not only announced a price reduction, but also enhanced its warranty coverage: up to two years/250,000 miles of "full coverage" and five years/500,000 miles of "major component coverage." As Henry Schacht explained to one OEM dealer, "This new warranty provides longer coverage for our mutual customers, and makes a strong statement about our confidence in the COMMAND engines."[25]

In most cases, customer and distributor loyalty had been badly shaken, but not destroyed. The challenge was to persuade all parties that the 88NT was the *exception*, in a much longer tradition of Cummins quality—a tradition that was embodied (once again) in the COMMAND engines. This marketing effort was greatly aided by the successful resolution of the Hanson and IEP episodes, which inspired confidence that Cummins was a dependable source of engines, in the game for the long term.

Within Cummins, confidence was growing as well. The company finally was on the threshold of introducing a sophisticated package of electronics into their product mix. As Detroit Diesel had discovered before Cummins, this new ingredient had the potential to change the competitive dynamic in dramatic ways. Moreover, as explained later in this chapter, management was convinced that it was finally beginning to build a companywide commitment to quality, and—just as important—that the rank-and-file were committed to helping Cummins compete in world markets.

Competing through electronics

Penske's leadership in electronics, in spite of its obvious disadvantages for Cummins, nevertheless helped educate consumers about the advantages of the new technology, to Cummins' long-term advantage. In fact, once Cummins applied the knowledge it had accumulated through a decade of work on electronics, it gained a competitive edge in the 1990s.

The first discussions of electronics within Cummins dated back to the early 1970s.[26] In this case, it was both Irwin Miller and Jim Henderson who foresaw the trend.[27] Soon after Karl Kuehner succeeded Phil Jones as the head of the Technology group in 1979, R&E head Bill Schwab (at Henderson's urging) asked Kuehner to pull together the company's first electronics group.[28] "Basically," Kuehner recalls, "we took the people who had been working on instrumentation kinds of electronics at the Tech Center—fixing oscilloscopes, and so on—and asked them to start thinking about getting electronics into our products."

Buying and Building

From that modest beginning, Cummins scaled up its commitment to electronics—and with this reemerged the perennial question of whether the company should develop the technology in-house or acquire outside competence.

In 1980, Cummins forged an agreement with Detroit-based Bendix to jointly develop an electronically activated fuel injector.[29] Within two years of start-up, the group had devised an electronically controlled unit injector, a sample of which Sir William Hawthorne, the board's leading technician, introduced to the directors in September 1982. The electronic injector, Hawthorne proclaimed confidently, "would be an eventual replacement for the PT."[30] At that same meeting, the board approved Cummins Engine Company's acquisition of the Diesel Engine Control Division of Bendix, located in Farmington Hills, Michigan.

Bendix engineers had worked for years in the automotive industry, and their experience was illuminating. Electronics were introduced in passenger cars in the early 1980s, and had substantially improved engine efficiency. By 1982, a number of companies (including, for example, Motorola) were producing electronics controls for purchase by auto manufacturers. Thus, Cummins could simply subcontract for its electronics. But this possibility raised several key questions. First, were electronics distinct and substantially separate from the engine, and therefore a commodity that Cummins could comfortably buy from an outside source? Or were electronics going to be an integral part of the engine, like a turbocharger, and therefore a component over which the Engine Company would want to exercise complete control? Or was there a middle ground?

The second key question concerned the "robustness" of the products then available on the market. Up to that point, all car manufacturers had taken great care to keep their electronics far away from the vehicle's engine—in the trunk, in the passenger compartment, but definitely not under the hood. This, as Jim Henderson explains, gave Cummins pause: "The diesel engine operated in a very different environment than passenger cars. If we relied on somebody like TRW or Motorola that supplied only passenger cars, we ran into a real possibility that vibration, harshness, and dirt, would be such that we would run into real failures." Equally compelling was the fact that Cummins could not afford to give up control of its fuel system. Putting fuel-system controls in the cab of a truck manufactured elsewhere meant, in a fundamental way, giving away the store. "For that reason," Karl Kuehner recalls, "we were hell-bent on engine-mounted electronics."

Building electronics in-house seemed to be the only viable option. That decision made, the Engine Company's push into electronics intensified. In 1982, it incorporated electronics into its product plan.[31] Over the three years that followed, Cummins management transformed that commitment—then more a statement of intent than a reality—into a real, free-standing organization.

The 1982 purchase of the Bendix unit gave Cummins access to technology, a crucial patent, a research facility in Farmington Hills, and the combined knowledge and experience of forty engineers. Those resources were greatly reinforced by the recruitment in 1983 of Robert S. Oswald, an engineer who had been a leader in electronics at Ford. "Bill Schwab and I were convinced that we had to move faster," Jim Henderson recalls, "and that led us to Bob Oswald."

Oswald was an interesting mix of engineer and entrepreneur, who fit well into the company's recently established "profit center" structure. Under this new approach, Cummins' components manufacturers were encouraged to think and act entrepreneurially, selling their products on the open market both as a way of making money and of "benchmarking" against the competition. (If Bosch began buying components from the Cummins electronics group, for example, that would be the best possible proof that Cummins was technologically expert.) Oswald was eager to lead an enterprise on these terms, and further argued that the new Cummins electronics entity should not only design, but manufacture, electronics components.

With the 1984 purchase of a 30 percent interest in Cadec Systems, Inc., Cummins added on-board electronic recording devices to its growing roster of products. Such devices, along with newly emerging electronic diagnostic systems, increasingly appeared to be necessary complements in building a full range of diesel engine electronic control and fuel systems.[32]

A year later, the U.S. Department of Transportation approved a Cadec on-board computer that recorded trip, load, and vehicle maintenance information as a satisfactory substitute for federally required handwritten logs. Although Cadec's work was not in the electronics mainstream—that is, it did not address directly the issue of engine or fuel control systems—the small company's success suggested that Cummins was able to spot and harness talent in this new field. In the three years following the initial Cadec investment, Cadec and Cummins introduced an array of electronic service and information tools for distributors and customers, including *Compucruise*, an electronic speed-control system designed to improve fuel economy and driving safety.[33] Cummins, satisfied with this progress, bought the remaining 70 percent of Cadec in 1986.

By the mid-1980s, the electronics movement at Cummins had gained significant momentum—so much so that the Engine Company formed Cummins Electronics Company, Inc. (CEL), in Columbus. "We intend to be the industry's premiere electronics-control design and manufacturing company," the parent company explained in its 1985 report to shareholders. Soon thereafter, Cummins closed the Farmington Hills facility and relocated its thirty-plus electronics engineers in a separate CEL facility in Columbus. The Engine Company hoped to benefit from this proximity, but also desired to create new jobs for some of its recently laid-off southern Indiana workers. DWU workers awaiting recall topped the list.[34]

These were welcome signs of growth and progress. But the increasingly independent electronics group faced a number of formidable challenges. First among these was the difficulty of the technical task at hand. The goal sounded simple enough: use electronics to improve upon the performance of the venerable PT fuel system.

That system, while remarkably versatile for its day, allowed for only one injection-timing setting. Once the hardware was designed, in other words, it always injected fuel at the same point in the injection cycle. This was far from optimal. A development engineer responsible for optimizing an engine along three key dimensions—emissions, performance, and fuel economy—would like to have different injection timings and different fuelings for a broad range of operating conditions. And this was what an electronically controlled engine promised. Full-authority electronics would give the designer a way to inject fuel precisely when it was needed, and in the precise amount needed. In this way, an engine could balance fuel economy, performance, and emissions control according to specific needs.

The exercise was far from purely academic. The EPA's newly promulgated emissions standards for 1988 and subsequent years presented a daunting and urgent challenge. There were few solutions in sight to meet those standards, especially without major sacrifices in engine efficiency. Electronics seemed the most promising of the solutions that were at hand, but it would be a hard-won victory. Ronald H. Temple was another electronics engineer who came to Cummins from Ford, and he found that the learning curve was steeper than he and his colleagues (who also had more experience with gasoline engines) ever expected. For instance, gasoline injectors typically run at a pressure of some 30 pounds per square inch, whereas diesels run at more than 20,000 pounds per square inch. Opening a diesel electronic injector therefore required dramatically higher voltage than opening its gasoline counterpart.[35]

Another issue was the sheer range and number of applications its electronic engines would have to accommodate. Cummins then served more than 170 vehicle OEMs (bus and truck manufacturers) and more than 1,800 industrial OEMs (manufacturers of bulldozers, cranes, rock drills, fishing boats, tugboats, generator sets, log skidders, and the like) around the world. Those OEMs cumulatively put out more than 3,500 types of equipment— or, accounting for size variations, something between 20,000 and 30,000 types of equipment. This staggering array of machinery operated under the widest variety of conditions imaginable, some of which were extremely harsh and demanding. As CEL's engineers gradually awoke to the enormity of the challenge facing them, they began to adjust their goals accordingly.

At the same time, the Engine Company's marketers and distributors were taking the pulse of their customer base, and were coming back from the field with a mixed message. Most engine buyers in the mid- to late 1980s acknowledged that electronics *eventually* would be needed to meet ever-stricter NO_x and particulate emissions standards. But most were betting that electronics would not be needed in the near term. And heavy-duty truck operators, as one Cummins engineer recalls, were a notoriously risk-averse crowd:

> *The only time the engine is turned off is the four hours at either end when they're loading on the trailers and checking the oil—otherwise they run these trucks 24 hours a day, seven days a week. They can't tolerate down time. They lose money. They don't want to try a new technology until it's proven, regardless of whether it's mechanical or electronic.*[36]

Electronics also were perceived to be *very* expensive. "The customer then would not pay for full-authority electronics," recalls Jim Henderson, "and there was the very real risk that if electronics failed, we would turn off the market. Therefore, we decided to take a very measured approach."

Cummins decided that rather than committing to a complete, full-authority electronically controlled fuel-injection unit, it would break down the introduction of electronics into smaller bites, beginning with an electronic road-speed governor and cruise-control unit. These devices would begin educating a skeptical customer base in the advantages of electronics. They also would ease the company into this new and risky universe.

Cummins introduced the "PACE"—an electronic governor and cruise control that yielded improvements in fuel economy of between 3 and 15 percent—in 1987, as an option on the L10 and NT engine lines.[37] PACE helped Cummins test the concept of the engine-mounted module. "If the PACE module failed," notes Karl Kuehner, "all you lost was road-speed governing and cruise control. You could still drive home."

The PACE electronic governor found a receptive market among over-the-road long-haul truckers, for whom gaining one or two miles per gallon could make the difference between loss and profitability. During 1988, Cummins sold more than 6,000 PACE units, thereby briefly capturing the right to boast that it had "more electronic diesels on the road than any competitor."[38] It seemed that the electronics revolution was finally taking hold in the marketplace, and that Cummins might well emerge in its vanguard.

But a second challenge was now coming into play: the company's legacy of hydromechanical thinking. It was not exactly that the Cummins engineering group was hostile to electronics. In fact, according to Karl Kuehner and others, there was almost universal agreement that electronics represented the wave of the future, and a good number of Cummins engineers in this time period were working on electronic and hydromechanical systems concurrently. But many of these designers were finding it very hard to think about engines and fuel systems in new ways. As Kuehner puts it:

> *Our error was that we designed electronics to replace hydromechanical functions in a one-to-one sort of way. So all of our efforts in those early days went toward making the fuel system do the same things it had done before, and simply adding things like variable timing. But it was a very narrow mindset. We were thinking that electronics just meant running the fuel system, when in fact today, electronics means much, much more.*

The Cummins electronics group, moreover, was sometimes unresponsive to urgent requests from within the larger organization. Technological obstacles, conventional mindsets, and an increasingly cumbersome bureaucratic process: All of these factors began to work to the disadvantage of the electronics group. Gradually, a "vendor-subcontractor" relationship emerged between the Tech Center and the electronics group. Engineers in the heavy-duty design group in the Tech Center would send over an internal purchase order for an electronic component with a new feature. (As explained above, the electronics group had been set up in a separate facility, away from the Tech Center, as a profit center.) As often as not, the Tech Center engineers would wait longer than they expected for the new component, and then find that they had been charged what seemed like an exorbitant amount of money by their "sister" unit.

This did not win friends for the electronics group. Joe Loughrey recalls this as a period when "we were building more and more of a wall between things electronic and things mechanical. . . . The wall was getting taller, and people were dealing with each other by throwing things over the wall. They were working with each other like separate companies. It was, "'Hey, *those* guys do *that* stuff. Go talk to them about it.'"

The troubled 88NT originally was intended to feature Electronically Controlled Injection (ECI), which was seen as a way of meeting the more stringent 1990s emissions standards.[39] But the ECI system fell behind schedule, and was deferred until the 1991 model.

This was precisely the juncture when the NT88's problems erupted and racing legend Penske launched his marketing blitz for the full-authority electronic Series 60. Confounding almost every industry observer, heavy-duty engine buyers took a chance on Penske and his electronic engine. Demand for Detroit Diesel's Series 60 engine rose by an astounding 62 percent in the first half of 1991.[40] The success enjoyed by Penske's company begat more success. Customers began to understand that electronic controls helped to meet ever-tightening emissions standards, and electronic engines gained credibility in the marketplace at a surprising pace. As a *Financial Times* special report on diesel technology explained:

> For the big producers, the preferred technological approach in the battle for ever cleaner engines is, "to deal with emissions at source—at the point of combustion and controlling what goes on inside the cylinder." Inevitably, therefore, the introduction of electronic fuel injection, allowing more precise control of the sequence—and consequence—of events at combustion, is an enormously important development for the diesel industry.[41]

During the difficult period that followed the launch of the 1988 engine line, Cummins increased its commitment to electronics. (CEL earned its first patent: on an air-heater system for internal combustion engines that was applied to B engines mounted in Dodge Ram Charger pickup trucks.)[42] Although there were no electronics on the 88NT, many of that engine's problems were fuel-system related, and solving those problems in the next generation of engines almost certainly would involve electronics. The electronics organization struggled against the clock to complete its contribution to the 1991 engine line, intended to include Cummins' first fully electronically controlled product.

The competitive need was pressing, and CEL urgently wanted to bring home some of the design and fabrication work then being performed by Motorola. But at the eleventh hour, the electronics group again came up short. Joe Loughrey, in charge of bringing out the '91 engine, finally concluded that CEL could not meet its deadline, and that the '91 electronics package would have to be designed primarily by Motorola.

Throughout 1990, Cummins introduced the 1991 line of COMMAND engines—the product that Loughrey's team hoped would win back customers turned off by the 88NT. COMMAND offered a choice of either standard hydromechanical, PT PACER (partially electronic), or CELECT (fully electronic) fuel-injection control systems. Henry Schacht—accomplished at making a virtue of necessity—began talking about Cummins' "dual approach" to fuel systems. Detroit Diesel only has one kind of fuel system to offer its customers, Schacht pointed out; we have *two*.

Initial returns were promising. The engines sold well enough to regain Cummins two percentage points of the heavy-duty market in 1991.[43] The tide, it seemed, had begun to turn, and CEL (with timely help from Motorola) had played a crucial role.

Electronics Meets Strategic Sourcing

CEL also had another project under way in the early 1990s that furthered the electronics revolution at Cummins: a collaborative research and development initiative conducted jointly by Cummins and its longtime customer Navistar. The two companies set up an entity called a "Product Alliance Team" (PAT), which took on a daunting assignment: to develop the perfect truck. The team first canvassed truck drivers and trucking company owners, asking what these two different "customers" wanted from their trucks and engines. The answers were not surprising. Both wanted reliability, but whereas drivers also emphasized performance, fleet owners demanded economy. But whereas higher performance and greater economy were more or less incompatible, in the context of the PT fuel system. As they had for decades, Cummins and Navistar either would have to frustrate one group or the other, or else strike a compromise—which of course risked frustrating *both* sets of customers.

Increasingly, the answer seemed to lie in electronics. As one Cummins engineer later phrased it: "Why don't we put *both* engines in that truck?"

The product that ultimately resulted from the team's efforts was an electronics package called "Extra Sensory Perception" (ESP). ESP comprised a host of integrated sensors that read and interpreted the conditions under which the engine was operating, as well as a software program that incorporated a number of specific "fuel maps" to react to driver actions. In time, the ESP system "learned" the driver's desired cruising speed, and consequently adjusted its "behavior" based on up-to-date road conditions.[44] For example, when the driver put the throttle pedal to the floor going up a hill, the engine sensors would assess a number of conditions, and—if all safety criteria were met and the environment was otherwise satisfactory—the computer would load a fuel map from memory that effectively converted the engine from 350 to 420 hp. Once the engine scaled the hill and started its descent on the other side, the computer would convert back to the more efficient fuel map.

By incorporating ESP into the CEL/Navistar prototype engine and putting it on the road, the designers found that drivers shifted to the higher horsepower engine only about 7 percent of the time. At all other times, ESP could run the engine at a horsepower that maximized fuel economy and minimized engine wear. Drivers were happy; owners were happy.

As a result of the success of the electronically controlled '91 engines, the PAT's progress, and other positive signs, Henry Schacht and Jim Henderson now were persuaded that electronics could thrive in the context of the Engine Company. In late 1992, in an effort to speed up the revolution, they moved CEL under the wing of Joe Loughrey, then group vice president of worldwide operations.

Loughrey had had his share of disagreements with the electronics group during the high-pressure 1991 engine introduction process. But through that experience, he also had gained an informed appreciation of the importance of integrating electronics into the larger company context. During the first six months of his tenure as head of electronics, he carried out a comprehensive study of the relationship between CEL and Cummins. A centerpiece of this study was a series of multiple interviews with the involved parties. Loughrey recorded their thoughts, ideas, and gripes, and used this information to create a composite picture of the situation. Whenever confusion or inconsistencies arose, he went back and sought clarification from the principals involved. And in the later iterations, he began "field-testing" a proposed course of action based on everything he had heard. As Ed Booth recalls:

> *He went back to them and asked, "Is this what you said? And if you said 'this, this, and this,' does that mean we should do these nineteen things?" He did that a bunch of times, until nobody would say "no" anymore. Then he said, "Okay, that must be how we're going to go forward then, right?"*

Loughrey's nineteen-step plan (dubbed the "nineteen points of light" by one insider) called for the gradual integration of Cummins Electronics into Cummins Engine Company. It was clear, Loughrey reported, that CEL had needed its independence at its birth to built momentum and credibility, especially vis-à-vis the outside world. But that isolation was now hindering the work of the electronics group by reinforcing an adversarial, "us-versus-them" environment. Under the new plan, electronics capabilities and CEL people were to be incorporated into Engine Company operations, for the ultimate benefit of the customer.

This shift mirrored a larger organizational move: away from the compartmentalized strategy of "every business on its own bottom" championed in earlier decades by John Hackett and others, and toward a more holistic approach to the overall business. And, reflecting another lesson learned during the 1980s, this shift was intended to focus the company more effectively on the needs of the *customer*.

This emphasis was reinforced by developments in the marketplace. Finally, the heavy-duty engine customer was demonstrating a wholehearted acceptance of full-authority electronic engines. The 1991 demand for electronically controlled CELECT model engines exceeded the supply. By 1992, more than half of the nearly 74,000 COMMAND engines shipped were equipped with CELECT electronic fuel injection. Cummins Electronics reported record profits in 1992, substantially based on those increased sales.[45]

In 1993, new edicts from the EPA brought still more good news for Cummins. The heavy-duty engine industry faced another substantial tightening of NO_x and particulate emissions standards. The government also announced that as of January 1996, emissions standards would be applied to a number of previously unregulated fields, including mining and power generation. Few companies were prepared to meet these new challenges—but Cummins was, thanks in large part to its massive investments in R&D and new technologies. (In the seven difficult years between 1986 and 1993, the company's investments in technological development more than doubled: from about $100 million in 1986 to just under $210 million in 1993.) Cummins was now positioned far better than many of its competitors in the emissions race, and this represented a formidable barrier to entry. As group vice president of marketing Roberto Cordaro put it, "No other manufacturer can match Cummins' investment in new technology without making the cost per engine prohibitive."[46]

Cummins' electronics engineers continued to develop customer-oriented products and services. In 1994, for example, they introduced INTELECT, a family of Windows-based integrated electronics software products incorporating service diagnostics and a management information-gathering capability.[47] This electronic tool was particularly effective for contemporary computer users, thanks to an architectural decision made by Cummins electronics developers back in 1984. They developed an alterable memory technology called E^2 P-ROM (or, Electronic Erasable Programmable Read Only Memory)—which stores and transfers information independent of a physical chip. The result: Rather than having to send a modified microchip to a truck on its route, new technology and upgrades for Cummins electronic engines could be broadcast to a worldwide network of service resources—the

Electronic System Data Network, or ESDN—including all Cummins factories, dealers, and service centers, as well a number of key customers. A truck receiving service at any of these locations could receive a near-instantaneous "upgrade" to the latest generations of software.

Through mid-1995, Cummins continued its move toward a full integration of electronics. At the same time, however, the company was pursuing a goal implied by the TQS "compatibility matrix" described above, and first articulated as a policy by Henry Schacht in 1992. Schacht argued that Cummins and other industrial companies in related fields ought to compete *selectively*, on the basis of their respective technological strengths, rather than competing on every technological front. In other words, engine makers should make engines, and co-venture with other businesses that made specific components with particular skill or efficiency. This philosophy was codified in the company's "Strategic Sourcing Policy," promulgated in 1993. The policy stated, in part:

> *Rapidly changing technology means that we must be willing to tap into the best sources of technology, internal or external, to offer our customers the best products. During this period, the demands on capital, management attention, and technical talent will be immense, and we cannot be distracted by competing with capable suppliers who are willing to partner with us.*
>
> *Our policy therefore is to focus our investments and resources on the design and manufacture of components that are BOTH STRATEGIC AND WHERE WE HAVE THE ABILITY TO BE COMPETITIVE with the best suppliers.[48]*

Inevitably, this logic was applied to electronics. In 1995, the company accepted a proposal from longtime electronics ally Motorola to take over the production of all electronic control modules for Cummins. (Motorola had been producing ECMs for Cummins for nine years, and then was producing about 55 percent of the ECMs used by Cummins.) At the same time, plans were announced to dissolve the formal entity of "CEL" and fold its technical functions back into the larger operation, with three-quarters of CEL's 620 Columbus-based employees being offered jobs elsewhere at Cummins.

This realignment, Cummins emphasized in its public statements, did not represent a retreat from electronics. (In fact, the entire Cummins product line was intended to be fully electronic by 1998.) Instead, it reflected the Engine Company's conviction that Motorola and other companies with broader competencies in electronic technologies would always dominate this particular niche, in part because they would always enjoy an economy of scale in electronics manufacturing that Cummins was unlikely to attain. Finally, a reintegration of electronic design skills into Cummins' worldwide operations was expected to accelerate their incorporation into new products.[49]

Cummins also asserted that it intended to stick with the concept of "Smart Power," which drew on lessons learned both in the electronics area and from the productive CEL/Navistar collaboration. This meant that Cummins engineers would look at the equipment holistically, as a basis for continuous improvement. For example, they would consider the air handling system as a whole, including the manifolds (intake and exhaust), the turbocharger, and the design of airflow in the head. Applying variable geometric principles for controlling turbocharger blades, developing infinite tunability on valves, using responses generated by drivers to fine-tune the combustion process—these and other design challenges would be tackled as part of a whole automotive package, or a new industrial application.

This holistic approach, moreover, would reflect a larger corporate push toward collaborative and team-based approaches to work—a shift that precipitated a revolution of its own among the Cummins Engine Company's work force during the early 1990s.

Manufacturing metamorphosis

The Cummins Engine Company looked very different at the beginning of the 1990s than it had even five years earlier. The massive restructuring that characterized the 1980s, and the successful move into new markets that followed, fundamentally changed the way the company did business.

In 1984, for example—the year Cummins introduced the B engine—the company sold a total of 4,400 Bs, accounting for 3 percent of total engine sales. By 1989, shipments of B and C engines topped 107,000, surpassing heavy-duty engine sales of 103,100 for that year. A year later, when the recession and the problems of the 88NT engine hit Cummins with full force, heavy-duty engine sales dropped by more than 20,000 units to 80,500. Meanwhile, sales of midrange engines rose to 123,500, thereby accounting for more than 58 percent of engine sales.[50]

For "Old Cummins," as Jim Henderson once described the company he had grown up with, there was bad news concealed within this good news. Both the changing external markets and the internal restructurings spelled trouble for the base business in southern Indiana. Not only were sales of midrange engines eclipsing heavy-duty engine sales, but even within the heavy-duty engine segment, the demand for L10 engines (manufactured at the Jamestown, New York, plant) was holding steady, while demand for the NH engines (manufactured at the Columbus plant) was slipping substantially. As in prior crunch periods, Cummins made deep cuts in its Columbus overhead and payroll to reflect these changes. Between 1980 and 1990, as part of its overall push for a competitive cost structure, Cummins reduced both floor space and manufacturing employment in Columbus by 30 percent.[51] But this time, things looked different. It looked as if the cuts would be permanent.

Many of the experiences of the Engine Company in the 1980s and early 1990s could be summarized in a single question: How can we make things better—at a higher quality level, and at a lower cost? The answer to this question emerged on multiple fronts; it was a slow and complex metamorphosis. It entailed a clear-eyed approach to the production process, as well as relearning and updating some earlier lessons about how to manage people.

Inventing CPS

The foundation for quality at Cummins was the company's tradition of attending carefully to the customer's needs, through a distribution system designed to keep the firm closely in touch with those customers. Customer satisfaction was absolutely vital to Cummins' "pull" marketing strategy. Cummins therefore "inspected quality in" to keep the customer happy.*

As the engine market became increasingly competitive, it slowly became clear that "inspecting quality in"—which was essentially a failure-driven process—no longer would suffice. Beginning in the early 1980s, therefore, Cummins made a conscious effort to improve its quality levels. Jim Henderson personally launched one homegrown initiative after another (the Achieving Paper, New Standards of Excellence, etc.) to try to push the organization to a higher level—especially after the true dimensions of the Japanese competitive threat became clear in 1983. The "Total Quality System" (TQS) initiative directed by the Feigenbaums in the mid- to late 1980s helped consolidate these efforts and transform them into a codified body of operational best practice.

In the later 1980s, Jim Henderson began to feel that a somewhat different approach was needed. As his company emerged from the trials of the 30 Month Sprint, it was more conservative, risk-averse, and bottom-line oriented than it had been in many years. The calamity of the 88NT only reinforced this mindset. If we don't take any risks—many at Cummins seemed to be saying—we can't get into any deep trouble.

Henderson disagreed. Into this gun-shy environment, he introduced his "Customer Led Quality" (CLQ) program, which attempted to focus the company's quality efforts on the needs of the customer. CLQ had five cornerstones:

---

*This was a common approach for industrial companies of the day. Cummins engineer Karl Kuehner recalls an entire Volkswagen ad campaign constructed around the theme of dozens of white-jacketed quality inspectors whose job it was to harass the production workers on behalf of the consumer.

comparative advantage, financial performance, profitable growth, responsible citizenship, and the development of people. Henderson recalls that in shaping this new corporate agenda, he deliberately led with the notion of comparative advantage. This he did in large part to overcome the emerging notion at Cummins that "being as good as the next guy" was good enough. "That's surely death for an independent engine producer," he explains. "You can't just be 'as good' in the eyes of the customer; you have to be better."

But how could Cummins make its customers perceive it to be better? One way would have been simply to go ask the customers what they wanted. But Henderson and his operations group suspected that their company was too hidebound in its practices—especially in its manufacturing practices—to be responsive. In part because of the stresses of the 30 Month Sprint, Cummins was having trouble delivering what it was already promising. (Henderson issued another of his informal white papers—the "Delivery" paper—in June of 1988 focusing specifically on this problem.)[52] How could Cummins promise more, if it could not deliver on earlier promises?

In late 1988 and early 1989, therefore, Jim Henderson, Joe Loughrey, and other senior operations executives toured all of the Cummins production facilities in an explicit effort to see who was doing what, in terms of cost, quality, and delivery. Their findings were both encouraging and discouraging. Loughrey recalls that the tour uncovered "what we came to call 'islands of excellence'—certain people in a specific area who had taken the initiative and done something great. But they were disconnected." After nearly a decade of pushing the quality boulder uphill, however, Henderson was impatient, and he soon decided that more drastic measures were needed. In the early months of 1989, therefore, he assembled a team of senior operations people from various functional backgrounds at his guest house in Columbus for a high-level summit conference.

Russ Bunio, for example, had a strong materials background, derived in part from years of experience at GM and with the Toyota production system at the celebrated NUMMI plant in Fremont, California. Dave Patterson, then the company's designated quality leader, also understood purchasing and "people" issues. Dave Hoyte understood the intersection of technology and production equipment. Mike Mitchell brought an international perspective. John Read, then head of the midrange product team that was responsible for the Rocky Mount operation, represented not only the perspective of a high-volume plant, but also of a joint-venture partner (Case). Henderson spoke his mind bluntly: Cummins needed an integrated approach to the production process—an approach that would let the company compete on cost, quality, and delivery on a worldwide basis—and needed it in a hurry.

Within a few months, responsibility for leading this team was assigned to Joe Loughrey, then still heavily involved with the 1991 engine launch.

Together, Loughrey and the other specialists-turned-generalists hammered out the first draft of what was intended to be a companywide blueprint for quality. They met with plant managers in July 1989 to review the first draft of their work, which was presented in the form of a series of related papers entitled "The Cummins Production System for Customer Led Quality" (CPS). Jim Henderson also addressed this group, and his remarks reflected the evolution of the company's thinking during the preceding half-decade:

> *We have a lot to learn from the Japanese. However, what Cummins wants to achieve is not a Japanese system. . . .*
>
> *We do not intend to take away the opportunity for innovation and trying new things in our plants, but we have come to believe firmly that we should move to more discipline and more uniformity in performing the "basics." With a common understanding of how we do the "basics," it frees us up to experiment and try new things in areas where we can improve. . . .*
>
> *We intend to train all of our employees in the key elements described in the paper—much like NSE training. This is a massive effort, and it will take us a while to accomplish. . . .*
>
> *What about cost reduction? We are not backing off the need for cost reduction, but it will now have a somewhat different focus. We will not rely exclusively on "cost per piece." . . . We believe through-put time is a more useful measure of cost in a flow-based manufacturing system, and we will add that to our measures.*

Henderson also laid out six interrelated fundamentals of the CPS initiative. First came *synchronized material flow*, starting with customer needs, which "pulled" appropriate materials through the plants. Next came *shorter lead times*, since lead times—Henderson noted disapprovingly—had been lengthening at several plants in recent months. Next came *product quality*, explicitly linked to TQS and NPPD&I. The fourth fundamental was the *improvement process*, which made continuous improvement a paramount concern. The fifth was the constant involvement of high-caliber technical talent from four disciplines—manufacturing engineering, materials, production engineering, and quality—in all aspects of production. (Henderson credited the Feigenbaums with hammering away at this point.) And finally, *people* were a critical factor. "It's possible to operate a system like the one I have just described," Henderson explained, "and treat people as if they were part of the machinery. That is not the Cummins way."[53]

Although Henderson took center stage at the July plant managers' meeting, it was Loughrey who orchestrated the effort and kept the pressure on the CPS team. Convinced of the value of deadlines, he established a demanding schedule for the working group and made them stick to it. The team revised its draft based on the plant manager's responses, and worked out the details of a training program between September and December.

The first CPS pilot was presented to managers in a five-day session during December 1989. Within a month, the training was substantially revised—mostly to inject urgency and raise the stakes for participants—and was offered again in January to teams from the Columbus Engine Plant, the Fuel Systems group, and the Jamestown plant. Break-out groups were organized by plant, and the last session was devoted to making a concrete plan for implementing CPS at each facility over the subsequent six weeks. Throughout the "seminar," Loughrey and his colleagues scrambled to develop concrete measures of progress at the plant level, because they had become convinced that such measures were indispensable to a successful quality program. These measures, still in a very rough form, were handed out on the last day of the program, and included both plant-level standards (percent of deliveries on time, defects reported by customers, etc.) and line-level measures (scrap, uptime, CPKs, etc.).

As usual, there was some skepticism among participants, some of whom felt that CPS was simply another short-lived scheme being handed down from on high. Loughrey attacked this interpretation head on:

> On the last day of that January training session, after hearing a lot of that kind of skepticism during the previous week, I stood up in front of the whole group and said, "Listen: If you want to interpret this as the 'program of the month,' you do so at your own peril. Because five years from now, we're all going to be together in southern Indiana celebrating the worldwide success of CPS." Everybody looked at me like I was nuts. But I just told them again: "You have to understand that we mean this."

Subsequent training sessions—the beginning of the "massive effort" promised by Henderson—began in March 1990. These continued throughout the next two years, until nearly all Cummins production employees had been steeped in the basics of CPS. Jim Henderson personally convened approximately two dozen of these training sessions, after which his presentation was videotaped for broader distribution. By 1993, the leadership at all thirty-eight Cummins plants had been through CPS training; and by 1995, more than 17,000 people—or 93 percent of Cummins' operations work force—had completed the training.[54]

Other companywide structures were put in place to reinforce CPS. The most important of these is the Plant Managers' Network, created in 1991, which brings together all plant managers twice a year. That model soon was extended to "network" the major functions of the plants—materials, manufacturing engineering, and so on—whose managers began to meet on an annual or semiannual basis. Gradually, the plant managers and functional heads refined the key objective measures, which were put in place on a worldwide basis.

Early returns on the CPS investment were encouraging. At the Columbus Engine Plant, the push-tube department reduced throughput time from ten days to one day, and improved its turns of inventory by 75 percent. At Diesel ReCon in Juarez, Mexico, fuel injector assembly time was reduced from six days to forty-one minutes, work-in-process inventory fell by 98 percent, and productivity improved 44 percent. The distance a cylinder head traveled in the São Paolo, Brazil, plant shrank by 3,000 feet, and throughput improved 32 percent. At Shotts, Scotland, a combination of innovations reduced throughput time for the average exhaust manifold from more than two weeks to a single day.[55]

Meanwhile flexible manufacturing practices were transforming the B and C engine plant at Rocky Mount, North Carolina. As described in Chapter 9, Rocky Mount (Cummins' joint manufacturing venture with Case) had begun operations in the expectation that it would achieve efficiencies through high-volume runs of a very limited number of engine types. But the nature of the B and C business—which involved manufacturing customized products for a huge variety of "distributor OEMs" (manufacturers of specialized equipment) necessitated a proliferation of specifications. This proliferation was made possible, and affordable, by the improved production practices of CPS. In 1986, Rocky Mount allowed only 400 customer specifications. By 1990, thanks in large part to the more flexible approach to manufacturing, this figure had increased to 1,700; by 1995, to 3,458; and by 1997, to 4,254.[56]

Joe Loughrey also had the satisfaction of seeing his implausible prediction come true. A little more than four years after the first full-fledged CPS training session in January 1990, Cummins hosted a companywide CPS anniversary celebration in Columbus (a part of its larger 75th anniversary during the April 1994 annual meeting) in which thirty-five plants participated.

Teams Come to Indiana

By the time CPS was being piloted in Columbus in 1989, Cummins already had the benefit of more than a decade and a half of experience with team-based work systems. The approach was tried first at the Charleston, South Carolina, and Jamestown, New York, plants, as described in Chapter 7. It was later extended to the B- and C-engine plant at Rocky Mount, North Carolina.

In the 1980s and early 1990s, several different streams in Cummins' production traditions converged. The principles articulated by Fred Herzberg that were first tested at Charleston were later updated—at Jamestown, Charleston, and elsewhere—and then encountered the discipline imposed by the Feigenbaums and TQS. These two streams then accommodated themselves to the CPS effort of the early 1990s. Meanwhile, shifts in the overall product line and the competitive environment created a greatly different context. But throughout these successive changes and overlays, Cummins maintained a consistent focus on *people* as a continuing concern of the corporation, and as the repository of its talents.

The first decade of experiments with team-based production systems—roughly 1972 through 1982—involved parallel efforts at Charleston and Jamestown. The Charleston experiment, as noted in Chapter 7, was an explicit effort to bring a highly diverse local work force into a team-based work structure. Jamestown proceeded on a very different track. Almost from the plant's inception, plant manager Dick Allison attempted to address some of the problems that were starting to crop up at Charleston. One step he took early on was to retain Richard E. Walton, a Harvard Business School-based specialist in workplace design, to help think through the challenges facing the plant. Walton's influential 1972 article in the *Harvard Business Review*, entitled "How to counter alienation in the plant," had caught the eye of Cummins' senior managers.

Walton drew heavily on his experience with the General Foods plant in Topeka, Kansas, then considered a model for team-based workplaces. Both at Topeka and Jamestown, Walton recalls, plant managers had to struggle to overcome the common wisdom of the day, which held that management's interest lay in "dividing and conquering" the work force. It was—and to some managers today, still is—counterintuitive to provide the means whereby workers could organize themselves into highly cohesive and functional groups. Walton considered Cummins to be among a tiny vanguard of American companies—including General Foods, Procter & Gamble, General Motors, TRW, Scott Paper, and General Electric—that were genuinely committed to restructuring the workplace.

Making teamwork pay for itself also was the focus of the next milestone in the evolution of the team concept, which came at Charleston in the early 1980s. Mark Chesnut, formerly country manager in Mexico, was picked to head Charleston in 1980. By that point, the team concept had evolved away from "long team" assembly (in which small groups assembled entire engines) to a number of specialized teams at various points on the assembly line: initial assembly, line assembly, up-fit, specialized machining teams for cylinder heads and injectors, and a number of product-oriented teams. It was a complex manufacturing process and a complex organizational culture, far removed from its origins seven years earlier.

Chesnut, gradually decoding this organization and culture, came to an unexpected conclusion: His plant seemed to be focused on teamwork for the sake of teamwork. Reflecting the status quo across Cummins at that time, the plant lacked a focused profit-and-loss statement and other key business measures. In the vacuum that resulted, Charleston's managers were relying on what appeared to be very soft measures of performance, such as the regularity with which they held team meetings, their relative ability to move people around the plant in response to shifting demand, and so on. This had serious, albeit disguised, consequences. As Chesnut recalls: "The piece that we had missed, in what Herzberg had been telling us, is that people feel good about serving the customer better than anyone else can serve that customer. . . . It wasn't that we weren't focused, but that we were focused too much on ourselves."

The new and relatively inexperienced plant manager pondered what to do about this odd state of affairs. He and his colleagues began working on a "logic" of the workplace that involved a sequence of four ideas: understanding, commitment, responsibility, and improvement. Only when someone *understands* the problem at hand will he or she be committed to solving that problem. Similarly, only when someone is willing to take *responsibility* for a problem will he or she act on that sense of commitment; and only that sense of personal responsibility can lead to improvement. This work gained a new urgency when, early in 1981, Komatsu complained strongly to Chesnut about the quality of K engines coming out of Charleston. This was a surprise, for Chesnut heard consistently that his plant's products and performance were fine. A trip to Japan quickly persuaded Chesnut that the Japanese were correct.

In the ensuing months, Chesnut and his colleagues hammered out a revised business "logic," this time beginning with the customer. The first phase of the Charleston logic was still "understanding," but henceforth, this meant an understanding of the needs of the customer. This meant getting his workers in direct contact with the customer.

At that point—mid-1983—a larger corporate need emerged. This was the same period in which Jim Henderson was touring Japanese plants and reaching his alarming conclusions about Cummins' uncompetitive manufacturing practices. Knowing of the ongoing efforts in Charleston to bring teams and world-class manufacturing standards together, he asked Chesnut to relocate to Columbus and head up the company's "organizational effectiveness" activities. To Chesnut, that meant making teams work better in a fast-changing context—defined both by the competition and by changes then going on within Cummins. The 30 Month Sprint, the Feigenbaum's TQS program, the "Customer Led Excellence Seminars" began in 1984—all had to be sifted and sorted for their "team" implications.

A big piece of that challenge was bringing some of the lessons learned at Charleston and Jamestown back to southern Indiana, where—despite layoffs—much of the work force was still based. This meant persuading the Diesel Workers Union to abandon some of the restrictive language and practices contained in its contract with the company, and experimenting with new approaches to the workplace. During contract negotiations in 1984, the union agreed to just such an experiment, which was formally dubbed the "Cooperative Effort." In exchange, the union received assurances that no jobs would be lost if the new team-based efforts increased the productivity of the Columbus-area plants.[57]

In a series of September meetings with the union, Jim Henderson went a step further. He personally promised the DWU's Rudy Baker that Cummins would try to help create new jobs to make up for positions that were lost as a result of more efficient work practices. Local employment, he told Baker, was very likely to go from 7,000 to 2,000 within the foreseeable future. Cummins would try to find 1,000 jobs for displaced DWU workers to minimize the pain.

Thus began a multiyear effort on the part of Henderson and others to deliver on this informal and unusual commitment. "We tried all kinds of things," Henderson recalls, "ranging from using our skilled tradespeople to do maintenance in the public schools to computer repair." For instance, the decision to bring electronics manufacturing to Columbus (over the objections of electronics head Bob Oswald) grew directly out of this commitment.

When Cummins laid off 550 Columbus-area employees in February 1985, therefore, the Diesel Workers Union registered no formal complaint. Then came a sharp business downturn in June, in response to which the company laid off 2,200 workers in July, of whom 1,054 were working in Indiana plants. Of those 1,054, the DWU estimated that at least 200 had been direct victims of productivity gains—a conclusion that management seemed to confirm when they announced that the cuts were permanent.

The *coup de grace* for the Cooperative Effort, however, came in September, when the Engine Company unexpectedly announced the *rehiring* of almost 600 of the previously laid-off workers. In isolation, this might have seemed like good news for the DWU. But in the larger context—jobs lost and not replaced, unprecedented swings in the size of the labor force, and mixed signals from management—the DWU found ample reason for anger and mistrust. In a strongly worded statement issued in October to its membership, the DWU bargaining committee announced that it was withdrawing immediately from the Cooperative Effort. "The Company has used our members to get the productivity gains," the union leadership wrote, "and spent all their energy on eliminating people's jobs and almost no energy on bringing in new work and work that is sourced out today."[58]

Conrad Bowling, later president of the DWU, recalls the union's thought processes at this time:

> *We'd had layoffs before and worked through them. What was different about this one was that there had been an agreement that if people contributed to continuous improvement, there would be no one elimi-*

nated for that contribution. Well, that implies that you ought to have a system in place to track that. There wasn't any system. People were involved with all kinds of effort to make machining more efficient, assembly more efficient, and so on. And then came the layoffs, right after so much had been done. When that happened, and there was no way to track why it had happened, there was a real fear on the part of the membership that we were being used.

In retrospect, this was a devastating blow to team building at Cummins. Mike Walsh—then head of Columbus operations—made the critical decisions regarding layoffs and recalls. But Henderson says that he and his other colleagues at the time share the blame equally for this disastrous unraveling. "We blew it," he says simply. "And by blowing it, we set back the effort in southern Indiana for the better part of a decade."

Unfortunately, the ups and downs of the mid-1980s were part of a larger, and more depressing, picture. The southern Indiana shop work force plummeted from more than 6,800 in June 1979 to 3,714 in 1989.[59] The closing of the Walesboro component plant in 1986 as part of the company's aggressive inventory reduction and cost-cutting push contributed substantially to the high layoff totals in southern Indiana. The few hundred jobs created at Cummins Electronics—part of Jim Henderson's commitment to bring new jobs to southern Indiana in exchange for the ill-fated Cooperative Effort—offset only a small fraction of the local jobs lost.

But in mid-1990, Cummins perceived an interesting opportunity to fill the employment gap in southern Indiana. The new opportunity grew out of the recently forged partnership with Ford, Tenneco, and Kubota. According to one of the terms of this new partnership, Ford chose Cummins to manufacture engines for their midrange applications—including a future line of medium-duty trucks, as well as a growing presence in the diesel-powered recreational vehicle market. These new applications, when added to Cummins' already booming midrange markets (at that point, the company counted over 800 customers for its midrange engines worldwide), pushed overall demand for B- and C-engine series beyond existing capacity.[60] When Ford signed on, it was clear that Cummins would have to open a new plant to meet midrange demand.

From the outset, the company made it clear that one criterion that would strongly influence its siting decision would be the relative willingness of the local work force to participate in team-based work systems. The evidence already was compelling that teams, when managed well, produced exceptional results. A 1989 Tuck School case study on team-based management practices at Jamestown, for example, had clearly highlighted the potential inherent in team-based work systems, concluding that team management had "become a way of life" and workers had "gained a unique power to influence substantially their own lives and that of the organization." And although the rigor of the Feigenbaum's Total Quality System (TQS) did not always mesh easily with Frederick Herzberg's ideas, the team-based concept had long since proven its value—especially to the workers. As one team manager at the Jamestown plant observed:

> *Just-in-time and all these new systems have substantially limited the amount of flexibility that the teams have in determining who works on what jobs, where, and when. Even so, it is amazing how committed my people continue to be. It took over ten years for them to learn that they can really take on more responsibility. They feel that at last they have real power. They are not going to give that up just because some new, complicated work systems are being introduced.*[61]

From the company's perspective, moreover, it wasn't even a close call: Plants in which the team system was in place were substantially more productive than those without it.[62] Successes at Jamestown, Charleston, and Rocky Mount convinced Cummins' managers that team-based work systems needed to be an integral part of all future manufacturing within the Cummins organization. In a traditional union setting, key decisions about employment—such as hiring, job placement, wages, and promotions issues—were determined largely by seniority. In a team setting, by contrast, they were determined on the basis of individual skills, education, and suitability to the requirements of a given position.

But would teams work in southern Indiana? By every conceivable measure, they would represent a radical departure from the status quo. Any new facility in southern Indiana—especially one being opened with the express intent of hiring workers already on layoff—necessarily would involve the DWU and OCU (Office Committee Union), and would revive any bitterness left over from the controversies of the mid-1980s. And behind these procedural questions loomed an even greater obstacle to success: The wage scale then in place at the main Columbus Engine Plant (CEP) was too high for the production of midrange engines, which had smaller margins and were therefore highly cost-sensitive.

At first, Cummins' managers assumed there was no way around this obstacle, and began to make plans for manufacturing midrange engines at the former Onan plant in Huntsville, Alabama. Huntsville soon would have excess capacity, in light of the company's decision to discontinue the A-engine series then being manufactured there. Senior managers from Columbus went down to Alabama to take a preliminary look at the Huntsville option.

Meanwhile, the DWU leadership in Columbus knew about the potential for expansion of midrange capacity, and were conducting some strategizing of their own. They were not coming to the question cold. For example, a few years earlier, the DWU already had tackled some of the complicated problems of negotiating contracts to respond to a changing work environment when it negotiated an agreement for laid-off workers to do production for Cummins Electronics. That contract allowed for work at a lower wage rate than at the CEP, and thus responded effectively to the pressure of foreign competitors.[63] Still, the CEL contract applied to only 100 people, and governed only electronics production. It would be quite a different matter, as both the union and company management knew, to negotiate a lower-wage contract covering a new engine manufacturing plant.

But in this same period, the Columbus work force witnessed a number of events that shook their confidence about the permanence of their jobs. In 1989, for example, the International Brotherhood of Electrical Workers (IBEW) and Columbus-based Arvin Industries crossed swords over a new contract. The IBEW went out on strike "all fired up," recalls DWU president Larry Neihart. But after several weeks with no progress toward a settlement, Arvin invited its workers to cross the picket line and go back to work. After several more unproductive weeks passed, Arvin simply broke the strike by hiring a new nonunion work force. Neihart recalls that this had a profound impact on the DWU membership: "Our people saw that happen to their neighbors, their relatives. People that had been there thirty-five years lost everything they had worked for. It certainly opened the eyes of our work force."

The point was that it was a truly different world out there. In the 1970s, the relentless demand for Cummins engines led to regular union/management deadlocks and relatively unsophisticated solutions. The default back then, Neihart says, was to "hire more people to throw at the problem, and cover the cost by raising the price of the product." But in the changed context of 1990, this was no longer an option, and shop workers knew it. The failures of the 88NT only exacerbated Cummins' competitive disadvantage in a very cost- and quality-conscious marketplace.

The opportunity in 1991 to expand midrange engine production required both Cummins and the DWU to look at their respective options in new ways. The company wanted to create new jobs in southern Indiana, but could not afford the established heavy-duty engine wage rates. Union leaders, for their part, wanted to protect the wage levels they had worked so hard to gain, but knew that inflexibility on this point would almost guarantee that no new manufacturing jobs would come to southern Indiana. According to Henry Schacht, a competitive cost base was "the first and foremost requirement of this decision." Compromise was needed, and it was compromise that led to a creative solution to the problem.[64]

One piece of the puzzle—the site—fell into place fairly easily. As all who had worked at Cummins in recent years were well aware, the former

Walesboro component plant sat vacant just a few miles down the road from Columbus. The factory had been on the market for a while, but it had not sold. Jim Henderson, for one, was just as happy that it hadn't:

> *It was fortuitous. I was the guy who went to Walesboro and met with all the people to tell them, "We're closing this plant, and here's why." I had always hoped we could reopen it in some way, to keep work in southern Indiana if we possibly could, because I had always told the union we were going to try to do that.*

The location was right, the size was right, and Cummins already owned it. Still, even with the attractions and advantages of this available site, manufacturing was still substantially more costly in Indiana than in Huntsville. To make Walesboro work, the DWU would have to agree to a number of significant changes. As Joe Loughrey recalls:

> *We said to the union, "Look. We're willing to talk to you about putting it here. But the economics are such that we need a whole new economic structure, and a whole new work system. And it* must *be a team-based work system, based on CPS principles and practices. And by the way, even if all of that comes together, it* still *might not come here, because state governments are involved, and we still have other options."*

As Loughrey implied, both Alabama and Indiana were bidding aggressively for the new plant. Eventually, Indiana's bid won out, providing Cummins with between $5 million and $6 million over three years—including between $3 million and $4 million for employment and training services—to bring jobs to Walesboro.

Of course, the DWU shared Henderson's desire to keep work in southern Indiana, and the union felt a particular obligation to its 1,200 members who were out on layoff with contractually guaranteed recall rights. When Cummins approached the union with a proposal to bring B engines to southern Indiana in early March 1991, the DWU was determined to find a way to nail down these new jobs. As Neihart put it, "You don't get a new engine family every day." After a round of back-and-forth on terms, the union presented a proposed contract to its members, who voted 1,722 to 630 in favor of the new plan. The company targeted a March or April 1992 opening date, and set to work preparing the plant.[65]

Looking back on this sequence of events, Henderson stresses the importance of management's decision to be entirely candid with the union throughout the negotiations. But he also credits the DWU's leadership with having the ability and courage to act in their membership's long-term interests.

"They were extraordinary," he says. "This was a period that confirmed my faith in Hoosiers."

The deal struck between Cummins and the DWU incorporated a number of fundamental changes, including a significant cut in starting salary for new hires to $8 per hour (compared with $14 at CEP). But equally important, the new contract permitted the full implementation of team-based work systems and CPS practices, which in turn sanctioned a whole host of related changes. For example, employees with contract-guaranteed recall rights would not automatically be hired into the new facility. Instead, they could choose to be included in a pool of applicants who would be selected based on their skill levels, as well as their ability and willingness to work in teams. Once hired, workers would be required to complete extensive training. The contract also gave the company the right to implement a "rings of defense" strategy commitment to employment stability during economic downturns, which employed various tactics (e.g., shorter work weeks) to avoid large-scale layoffs on the basis of seniority.

Just short of a year after the contract was signed—on March 17, 1992—production of the B series engines started at the Columbus Midrange Engine Plant (CMEP). During that year, the Walesboro site had been completely revamped under the supervision of CMEP manager Ronald Moore. The transformation had been wrought by workers representing almost every Cummins production operation. Walesboro's collaborative design process took many months to get right, but—according to Joe Loughrey—achieved an important corporate goal: "We've taken the best of what Cummins has to offer to establish a program at Walesboro."[66] The renovation (called a "stunning metamorphosis" by *Modern Materials Handling* magazine) incorporated ergonomic work stations, fed by automated electrified monorails interfacing with power and free conveyors. The result was a facility in which, commented Harold Steigerwalt, head of manufacturing engineering, "virtually everything about the way the plant operates, and will operate in the future, has been engineered according to the Cummins philosophy of Customer-Led Quality."[67] The new facility's white floors underscored that CMEP would not be diesel-making as usual.

The assembling and training of the CMEP work force was a second impressive accomplishment. From the pool of 1,200 laid-off workers, 150 had been chosen to be members of the several teams that would work as shop employees at CMEP. Once hired, these workers underwent 252 hours of rigorous training, including classes in the team concept of manufacturing, group dynamics, shop mathematics, the metric system, and quality control techniques. Every worker at CMEP assembled and disassembled a B-series engine at least fifteen times. These CMEP workers understood, moreover, that they were making a commitment to continuing education into the future, in the range of 80 to 100 hours a year.[68]

Throughout the training process, Cummins management, CMEP workers, and line workers from every Cummins U.S. engine operation improved and refined the team concept. The new system was built on four simple principles: flexibility (i.e., no "ownership" of specific work and few job classifications); skill-based performance system (promotions based on skill-attainment, performance, and teamwork); employment stability (the plant would do everything possible, including shutdown days and reduced work hours, to avoid layoffs); and competitive economics (benchmarking against comparable plants on costs, wages, benefits, and work rules). Managers, too, were required to be certified in key assembly functions—a type of training that had been required only of shop workers in other plants.[69]

The initial response among workers—all of whom had at least six years' experience working under traditional Cummins work rules—was enthusiastic. They appreciated the value of the extensive training program, and the resulting comprehensive understanding of the overall processes of the plant that they gained thereby. "I think I learned more in that period of time than since I started with Cummins," said one CMEP worker. "I personally guarantee the work we do here," volunteered another. "I don't think they can do anything in Japan that we can't do better."[70]

Gradually, CMEP won other kinds of endorsements, some of them quite telling. Late in 1992, for example, a number of workers at CMEP were issued recall options to return to the Columbus Engine Plant, or CEP (also known as the Main Engine Plant). Larry Neihart went to talk with them about the move, and what he heard finally convinced him that team-based work systems could really succeed:

> They said, "They wouldn't have to pay us what they're paying up at the Main Engine Plant, but if I could make another five dollars an hour"—and remember, these people took about a fifty percent pay cut—"I'd rather stay in this plant, because I like this work system."

Those who received the recall offer overwhelmingly accepted it, evidently because the higher wage level was an irresistible incentive. But their testimony in support of the new work system—and their willingness to make a financial sacrifice to stay within that system—illustrated an important point for union president Neihart. "People *did* feel restricted," he concluded, "and we had never paid attention to that."

Team-based management had proved itself over and over again outside southern Indiana; now, at CMEP, it had succeeded very close to home. (CMEP, says Jim Henderson, met every start-up goal that had been identified for it.) But could it be incorporated into Cummins' bastion of traditional work rules—the Columbus Engine Plant?

Labor Adapts to the Future

In late 1992, Cummins managers surveyed the growing number of Cummins manufacturing facilities worldwide that employed team-based management, and on balance they saw success for both the workers and the company. Workers felt much more control over what happened around them; they were pleased to have an opportunity to bring to bear knowledge gained through years of experience in refining manufacturing and process design; they valued the company's expanded commitment to training and education.. And the resulting improvements to manufacturing and process yielded faster through-put times, tightened inventories, decreased floor space, and higher productivity—all of which ultimately translated to lower costs and higher quality.

As they looked ahead to contract negotiations with the DWU in late 1992 and early 1993, Cummins management resolved that one of the Engine Company's highest priorities would be to convert the five facilities covered by that contract to team-based work systems. As Joe Loughrey, who had head-ed the contract negotiations that put team-based work systems into CMEP, subsequently told workers at the midrange plant in Walesboro, "This work system that we're putting in place here—we'll tweak it, and learn from it. Make no mistake, I'll be back. Because this is what we're going to want in all our plants."[71]

But the DWU membership had a long memory, and that memory included instances where past promises of positive change on the part of the company had led more or less directly to layoffs. The aftermath of the short-lived Cooperative Effort of the mid-1980s—which had scuttled team-based work practices in Columbus for almost a decade—still lingered. The introduction of efficiency measures and CPS principles in the early 1990s exacerbated the trend toward seemingly permanent layoffs for thousands in the DWU. According to DWU president Larry Neihart, one overriding directive from the rank-and-file was in the minds of DWU officials as they approached the 1993 negotiations: "The one thing people told us to say, real loud and clear, was, 'Don't ask us to help you if the result is going to be that we're going to get laid off.'"

Meanwhile, Joe Loughrey was responsible for worrying about management's negotiating stance—and he was finding plenty to worry about. It would be hard enough to get the DWU to agree to a team-based work system at CEP and the four other facilities up for contract renewal. But some sustained number-crunching had persuaded Loughrey that there was a second huge mountain to climb. In order to stay competitive, Cummins would have to win higher contribution rates to company health plans on the part of both active DWU members and retirees. If the Company failed to win concessions on both points, Loughrey saw only one option: "We were going to have to shrink southern Indiana production as fast as we could, and all new product was going to go somewhere else."

Loughrey knew that this round of negotiations would be difficult, and that it would most likely take more time than in previous years. He also knew that it was very important not only to tell DWU leadership and members what Cummins was thinking, but to do it in such a way that they truly understood the gravity of the situation. And there was only one person, Loughrey knew, whose credibility and integrity were absolutely beyond question. Accordingly, Loughrey enlisted the help of J. Irwin Miller.

Miller disliked the bleak scenario that Loughrey was painting, but he eventually agreed that the figures fully backed Loughrey's interpretation. Together, Loughrey and Miller devised a strategy. In mid-December 1992, at the Christmas party held by the DWU shop stewards, Miller addressed the group and explained the difficult situation they all faced. It would be hard to overestimate the impact of such a message, coming directly from Irwin Miller. Then in his early 80s, Miller had almost qualified for a sixty-year service award from the company. He was still a powerful presence, and the DWU knew him to be a fair and honest person, unquestionably committed to the economic health of southern Indiana. One might disagree with Miller's conclusions, but one could not impugn his motives.

Cummins and the DWU began negotiations that afternoon. The DWU had their own list of priorities, the top two being employment security and increased retirement benefits. Loughrey—who did not plan to participate directly in the negotiations—took advantage of his "outsider" status to open the first meeting with a statement of the company's goals. Very simply, Cummins needed a commitment from the union to move to team-based work systems, and to share in health-care costs. He told the group, "We don't have to have them all right now, but we must have them. And, if it helps any, we'll go for a longer contract."

With that, the two sides began negotiations. Not surprisingly, they soon discovered that reconciling their diametrically opposed positions, on issues that both sides saw as non-negotiable, was going to be extremely difficult. The DWU strenuously objected to the company's request to increase retiree participation in health-care costs—a point on which Cummins felt unable to compromise. During the next four weeks, discussions became progressively more heated and volatile. On January 31, the talks collapsed completely.

In retrospect, both Loughrey and Neihart identify that break in the negotiations as a turning point, although neither knew it at the time. Once the talks broke off, the union leadership encouraged their constituents to make their case directly to Cummins' senior management. This, in turn, gave management the opportunity to communicate directly with the rank-and-file, which they would not have been able to do during normal negotiations. The company set up small- and large-group question-and-answer sessions with workers and retirees, where they had a chance to meet face to face and talk through the issues. Meanwhile, Joe Loughrey personally received something like a thousand letters and notes—some of them irate, and almost all of them frank. He responded, he says, with equal candor:

> *I was pretty aggressive. To one letter I got from a pretty irate, very outspoken steward, I sent a very direct response. I don't know who it went to, but we know it was passed roughly 2,500 times in about 48 hours. It got around. So what really happened was that it became an opportunity for us to get as clear as we could with people about how we saw the choices.*

Face-to-face discussion with shop-floor workers also changed the way Larry Neihart thought about the negotiations. One incident in particular, he says, had a profound effect on him:

> *I had some of the junior people stop me. They knew that the big argument was whether we went with another three-year contract without employment security, or go with a longer contract with employment security, knowing that if we went with a longer contract we were going to make a lot of changes in the contract language.*
>
> *And I'll never forget a guy on the assembly line asked me which was my favorite. And I said, "Well, I've been here for a long time. I've been through three strikes to get this language in the shape we have. And everybody is pretty comfortable with the language the way it is. With a stroke of a pen, we can do away with twenty-five or thirty years of history of what we worked for in this union."*
>
> *"Mister," he said, "It's your job to make sure that I've got a paycheck and got a job. That's what you should worry about. Let me worry about the kind of work system this company puts in place." He said, "I've been laid off five times from this place. I can survive as long as I get a paycheck. I can't survive on unemployment."*

In their continuing discussions with workers, Neihart and other union representatives found that a significant percentage of the workers were not opposed to shifting to team-based work systems. Some openly endorsed such a move. They were a highly skilled and experienced work force, and they saw an opportunity to channel that experience into improving the work process, perhaps without unacceptably negative financial consequences.

The talks resumed after two or three weeks, and now seemed to be on very different footing. Still, the union remained determined to win concessions in the vital area of job security. And so, after canvassing the membership, union leaders came up with a highly unusual proposition, which they shared with their counterparts across the table. On April 24, 1993, DWU leaders invited union members to a meeting to discuss the details of a proposed contract. The response was positive, and a formal contract offer was soon forthcoming from management. Two days later, with more than 86 percent of the membership voting, the contract was approved by a vote of 1,948 to 694.

When Cummins and the DWU jointly announced the terms of their newly forged deal to the press, a number of people called the company asking whether there wasn't a major typographical error: Was it possible that the contract spanned *eleven* years?

In fact, it did, and the length of the contract was only one of many surprises. All union workers active on signing were guaranteed a job for the life of the contract, and would receive cost-of-living raises and improved retirement benefits. (They also received a $1,000 signing bonus.) In return, workers would participate in health-care costs. As for work rules, the union gave up the most restrictive contract language that created barriers to improvement efforts; and, most important, the DWU agreed to switch over to team-based work systems beginning on January 1, 1996. This included a commitment from the work force to undergo training, and revised seniority definitions to incorporate the completion of training and the acquisition of skills necessary to participate in the team system.

By any measure, it was a landmark agreement for Cummins and the DWU. Observers across the industrial landscape of America were impressed. As Jim Dworkin, associate dean of the Krannert Graduate School of Management at Purdue University, exclaimed to a reporter from the *Evening Republican*, "Wow! In my history of studying labor relations, eleven is the longest. I've heard of five or six years, but never eleven."[72]

Most outsiders wondered where the unusual idea had come from. The answer was that the union had proposed the long-term arrangement, and for very practical reasons. Layoffs had long been the bane of the union work force; negotiators made it their goal to protect members against job loss as much as possible. Members became eligible for retirement with thirty years' experience; and so, the goal would be to come up with a deal where active members were covered until they gained that eligibility. A full 600 of the 3,100 members to be covered under the contract were already eligible for retirement, and another 1,700 would have their thirty years by 1997.

Early on in the negotiation, Cummins had said it would be willing to enter a longer contract than the traditional three-year arrangement, and DWU leaders had debated among themselves the merits of proposing a six- or seven-year agreement. But during these debates, a key realization had struck them: Even the youngest member of the DWU work force being covered under the contract had at least nineteen years' experience. If the contract were to span eleven years, *everyone* would be eligible to retire by the next negotiation. It would be an unprecedented approach, but indisputably it would provide job security. If they could fashion an agreement that spanned eleven years *and* gained improved retirement benefits for the older work force, they would satisfy their basic requirements—and be prepared to make concessions on other points. They decided to pitch the idea to Cummins management.

The eleven-year proposal earned a surprised but receptive response. "That was longer than anything we were thinking about at the time," Loughrey recalls, "but we said, 'Hell, the logic makes sense, and it's salable to the folks.'" Cummins agreed in principle to the eleven-year deal with employment security, and in exchange gained a tentative commitment from the union to switch to team-based work systems in the five facilities covered by the contract. In the weeks that followed, working from these two basic assumptions, the two negotiating teams put the finishing touches on the agreement. But the eleven-year time frame was what opened the door to the deal, as Tim Solso recalls: "Unlocking the job security issue in southern Indiana instantaneously removed a dark cloud over everybody's head, and allowed everyone to collaborate in doing what was best for the company."

Design teams—each a mix of Cummins management, DWU leadership and rank and file, and at least one Office Committee Union (OCU) representative—next began planning how the team-based system would work at each of the southern Indiana sites where it was intended to be put into place. In 1996, three plants—the Main Engine Plant, now the "Columbus Engine Plant," or CEP; CIC; and the new Fuel Systems plant—made the transition to team-based, CPS-based practices. It remains to be seen how this change will affect the organization, but it appears that management and labor each believes that the other is committed to making it succeed. DWU head Conrad Bowling, for his part, points to the $600 million that the company has committed itself to investing in southern Indiana manufacturing between 1997 and 2000. And Jim Henderson says that the union's willingness to change the nature of work is the best guarantee for the future:

> *We are a manufacturing company. We manufacture a product in which the principal cost is material, not labor. If we made ping-pong balls, we might have to chase low wage rates around the world. But that's not what we do. We've realized, working with the DWU leadership, that it's possible to invest in your people and make them highly capable, doing high-content jobs. Both sides benefit in the process. People increase their value to the company, feel greater satisfaction in their work, and ultimately get paid more.*

Transitions: at home and abroad

In the early 1980s, Cummins—seeing trouble on the horizon—applied the economic screws to itself. In the late 1980s and early 1990s, the anticipated trouble (and then some) came, and the economic screws were applied from the outside. Finally, early in 1992, the recovery that Cummins Engine executives had promised a decade earlier finally started to show itself. Profitability returned—at first tentatively, and then decisively. The year 1992 presented payoffs on several of the Engine Company's long-term strategic decisions. The company's more diversified product line did, indeed, provide some insulation against cyclical downturn. The substantial investments in electronics and other emissions-related research placed Cummins at the forefront of emissions technology, at a time when domestic emissions standards were increasing in stringency, and the rest of the world was beginning to follow suit. Finally, Cummins' longtime international presence positioned it well to enter into a number of intriguing joint-venture opportunities.

After years of losses, Cummins climbed out of the depths in 1991. Losses shrank with each successive quarter, until the company finally put its head above water in the first quarter of 1992, declaring $5 million in earnings on sales of $881 million. And the news was even better than it first appeared. As one industry analyst observed, Cummins "has been able to show improved results over the last four or five quarters without any benefit from the economy and its main market."[73] In successive 1992 quarters, Cummins posted earnings of $18.8 million, $13.8 million, and $24 million. Ultimately, the company posted a net loss of $189.5 million for the year, due to a one-time after tax charge of $251 million associated with adopting several accounting changes with regard to retiree benefits.[74] Still, internal and external evidence confirmed that Cummins was on the comeback trail.

Analysts on Wall Street concurred in predictions of a bright future for Cummins. "Historically," wrote one, "they have had trouble delivering earnings to the bottom line, even in good times. That's changed in the last six quarters, and the Street is less skeptical. The earnings story is going to be quite good for a while." Another analyst advised that investors ignore the 1992 paper loss: "The parts that affect the true cash flow of the company are moving along very nicely." A third suggested that Cummins "finally seems to have turned the corner." *Business Week* celebrated Henry Schacht as "an executive to watch," and noted that "despite a sluggish economy, Cummins sales climbed" and that "Cummins' costly—and widely questioned—expansion into the midrange diesel business is finally paying off." Even the habitually skeptical Schacht declared: "The recovery is real this time."[75]

As 1993 progressed, those predictions were more than borne out. In the fourth quarter of 1992, Cummins reached a milestone when its sales exceeded $1 billion for the first time. The Engine Company was on a roll, and enjoyed four more quarters of record sales in 1993—all but the third of which exceeded $1 billion each. At year end 1993, Cummins declared more than $177 million in net earnings—the company's first annual profit since 1987.

Cummins' consistent improvement in the early 1990s was not lost on investors: The price of Cummins common nearly doubled to around $60 per share by April 1992. With occasional interruptions, it continued to rise until hitting a new record of $98.63 per share in August 1993. The following quarter, the directors split the stock 2-for-1, and boosted the quarterly dividend to 12.5¢ per share. On November 3, 1993, Cummins stock traded for more than $100 per share for the first time in the company's history.[76]

When asked how Cummins planned to leverage its hard-won profits, Jim Henderson responded that the company would go "on the prowl for acquisitions." Though he made reference to no particular targets, the *Indianapolis News* observed that the company's acquisition strategy in recent years had "largely consisted of joint ventures and other strategic alliances with overseas truck and engine manufacturers."[77] It was a good guess. More such joint ventures and alliances already were in the works. Henderson and others at Cummins knew that protecting and increasing the Engine Company's global presence—an institutional priority for nearly forty years—would be a critical component of success in the twenty-first century.

Global Reach

By 1993, the Engine Company made fully 44 percent of its sales outside U.S. borders. A determinant of Cummins' foreign success, in the 1990s and beyond, is likely to be how well the company's cumulative investments in research—and the advances in emissions and electronics technologies that have resulted—mesh with global needs. In 1992, Henry Schacht pointed to the decision to invest heavily in R&E as an important strategic advantage in non-U.S. markets. "Our research and engineering expenses tripled in the Seventies, and tripled again between 1980 and 1990," he observed. "We made a strategic bet that the rest of the world would go where the U.S. is on emissions standards, and that has come true."[78]

In an interview with a British trade journal, Schacht made predictions about the future state of the diesel trade:

> By the end of the century, there will be six major engine manufacturers, and all the present manufacturers will be in alliances, based on technology suppliers as a core. . . .
>
> People will have to make their arrangements before the snow melts in '94, to be ready for the rest of the decade. You can't imagine what my passport looks like![79]

Schacht's passport almost certainly recorded visits to China, Russia, India, Italy, Finland, Sweden, Japan, the United Kingdom, Germany, and Holland—among other places—representing the wide range of countries in which Cummins then had ongoing or imminent collaborations under way.

Some of those arrangements grew out of many years of relationship building. In February 1993, for example, Cummins entered into an agreement in principle with longtime competitor and collaborator Komatsu to jointly develop and sell diesel engines in Japan (building B series engines at Komatsu's huge Oyama plant) and in the United States (assembling engines at the CIC facility in Seymour, Indiana). In an astonishing turnaround from a mere decade earlier, China emerged as Cummins' third largest international market in 1993 (behind only the United Kingdom and Canada). Late in the year, Cummins negotiated successfully for license agreements with two plants in central China, whereby the Chinese would manufacture engines designed and engineered by Cummins, with the long-term prospect of joint ventures.[80] (This was a close approximation of the model that Clessie Cummins and W. G. Irwin had in mind for the Engine Company some six decades earlier.) And Cummins also found a unique opportunity to work collaboratively in India—the location of one of the Company's oldest and most successful international ventures—when it entered into a joint venture to produce B-series engines with Tata Engineering and Locomotive Co., Ltd., India's largest manufacturer of commercial vehicles.[81]

There are sure to be still more opportunities, some of which will arise in unexpected quarters. Economic reforms in (and eventually the collapse of) the Soviet Union, for example, made it possible for Cummins to enter into discussions about possible joint ventures with KamAZ—the world's largest truck manufacturer, and the first Russian company to privatize its operations.[82]

In both its ongoing and its new ventures, Cummins is seeking to move closer to the scheme sketched out by Henry Schacht in 1992, in which companies collaborate on the basis of proven technological strengths. To that end, Cummins has joined forces with Scania in Sweden to develop fuel systems; U.K.-based Cummins engineers have collaborated with Deutz to perfect a "pop-in/pop-out" engine with fully integrated radiator and hoses; and teams of engine designers from Cummins and the Finnish diesel maker Wartsila have merged parallel independent efforts to work together on an engine, hoping to be able to capitalize on synergies in manufacturing and marketing.

By this point, four decades after setting up its first overseas beachhead, Cummins has enough experience in international ventures to know they are unpredictable and prone to change. For example, the proposed KamAZ joint venture suffered an early setback when that company's truck factory was devastated by fire in May of 1993. Other potential partners are evolving just as quickly as Cummins, and not necessarily in the same direction as Cummins. As Tim Solso philosophically observes: "There is great possibility, and *variability*, in these deals. We look at them and see their potential, but only the future will determine what will happen."

A Changing of the Guard

On July 12, 1994, Henry Schacht stepped down as chief executive officer of Cummins Engine Company, and was succeeded in that position by Jim Henderson.* Concurrently, Solso assumed the position of chief operating officer from Henderson.

This transition had been a topic of discussion among Schacht, Henderson, and the Cummins board for nearly two years. One challenge faced by the company was the fact that Schacht and Henderson were relatively close in age, and—as Schacht told a *New York Times* reporter—"I felt the company should not face a double retirement and needed a phased succession." Schacht and Henderson considered Schacht's departure only another step in the long process of turning over the management of the company to a new generation.[83] Six months after this first transition, in February 1995, Schacht ceded his responsibilities as chairman of the board to Henderson as well; and Solso succeeded Henderson as president.

From its earliest days, Cummins usually has had the benefit of two strong figures at the helm: Clessie Cummins and W. G. Irwin through the early 1930s; J. Irwin Miller and his two presidents (Bob Huthsteiner and Don Tull) in the 1950s and 1960s; and Henry Schacht and Jim Henderson in the 1970s through the mid-1990s. Beginning in the Miller-Tull era, a natural division of labor emerged—with Miller as Mr. Outside and Tull as Mr. Inside—that was more or less recreated in the Schacht-Henderson era.

Traditions run strong at Cummins, but this is one tradition that is not likely to survive the most recent leadership transition. However Henderson and Solso (and their successors) divide up responsibilities, it is unlikely to look like any model Cummins has seen in the past. This is because, as Tim Solso explains, the leadership challenge has become so dramatically different:

> *When Henry and Jim figured out their respective roles, this was a $300–500 million company with essentially one product. It's now a $5 billion company, with half its sales overseas, with multiple products and markets. It's a much different management challenge.*

---

*After six months of semiretirement, Schacht became head of Lucent Technologies, the systems and technology company created by the AT&T divestiture in September of 1995. Schacht was a known quantity at AT&T, having been on its board since 1981.

When Jim Henderson conducted a videotaped interview with Irwin Miller in the spring of 1993, history was an inevitable focus of the conversation. Henderson has a keen interest in the history of the company where he has spent his professional life, and Irwin Miller embodies most of that history. But in response to one of Henderson's questions, Miller made a point of looking from the past to the future:

> *If you don't look out, you become an old business. You get to thinking, "We're seventy-five years old!" But it's very important that Cummins starts over every year. You learn the lessons from the past, but you don't fall in love with the past.*
>
> *We don't really know what the twenty-first century is going to be like, except that it's going to be very different from the past. The experience that we have is experience of a world that has disappeared. It's gone. It's not coming back. And that means we have to look forward.*[84]

Because Irwin Miller welcomes contradiction, the authors will devote the last chapter of this book to looking at the experience of Cummins. What is there in Cummins' past that will help the Engine Company—and other manufacturing concerns facing some of the same issues as Cummins—look forward with confidence, and operate with success?

13 | Cummins and the American Century

EARLY IN 1944, AS THE Cummins Engine Company approached its twenty-fifth anniversary, Clessie Cummins began a conversation with Spencer W. Curtiss, the Indianapolis-based advertising executive who then managed the Cummins account. The subject was a proposed book about the history of the company.

Clessie wanted to document the Engine Company's growth and development over the previous quarter-century. He was inspired by a conversation he had had in Washington, D.C., a year earlier with a professor from the University of Pennsylvania. This scholar had told him—in response to Clessie's engaging storytelling—that the Cummins history was one of the most fascinating accounts he had ever heard. Clessie eventually contacted Curtiss and encouraged him to pursue the idea. But the diesel-builder had an important precondition: "I made it plain that, so far as I was concerned, I would not O.K. anything that got very far away from the original story."[1]

J. Irwin Miller returned from his tour of duty in the Navy to find the history project under way. The first 150 pages of the draft arrived on Miller's desk in November 1944, and Miller had what he called a "violent" objection to the tone of the partial manuscript. The writing, in his estimation, was "straight advertising style," and didn't begin to do justice to the company's history. "The story of the Engine Company does not have to be glamorous or padded," he wrote to Clessie. The challenge was to find a suitable writer, and then turn that person loose on the subject:

> We would have to leave him free to poke fun at us and take cracks at us, if he wanted to. That wouldn't bother me, for that would make the story genuine, and the overall story is a good one and immensely to the credit of the people involved in it.

After reading the excerpt, Clessie agreed with Miller's assessment. "Knowing little about anything except ballyhoo," he wrote, "they did a poor job." Clessie had what he thought was a much better model in mind—a book about General Electric called *Men and Volts*—that he had shared with W. G. Irwin, who had died not quite a year earlier:

> *One thing I am sure of, and that is that this project would have met with the approval of your Uncle. He mentioned several times, after reading the General Electric book, that we could beat it, because all of the story of General Electric's development comes from many companies and sources, whereas ours is a complete job and from the one source.*

Although the book contemplated by Irwin Miller and Clessie Cummins in the 1940s was never completed, many people over the years have recorded their recollections and opinions of the Engine Company. One impulse, clearly, has been pride—pride in a story that is "immensely to the credit of the people involved in it." But a second impulse to share the Cummins story was the awareness that, unlike most companies, the history of Cummins was a "complete job." The Cummins story was largely uncomplicated by the mergers, acquisitions, and unravelings that complicate most corporate histories. Its products were developed internally, and its culture was homegrown. Wherever Cummins was, it had gotten there mostly on its own.

When Cummins reached its fiftieth anniversary in 1969—normally an occasion for nostalgia and retrospection—Irwin Miller wanted to carry forward only one lesson from the past. Look forward and prepare for the future, he told his colleagues on that occasion; that is the only way we will prosper.[2]

Another quarter-century has passed. In this chapter, the authors undertake to draw out a few additional lessons. We respect Miller's oft-repeated warning that companies should not fall in love with their histories. At the same time, we are convinced that a carefully considered past need not be a trap. We think it can provide useful insight to reflective practitioners who face challenges in the here-and-now.

Cummins' history now spans more than seventy-five years, and longevity itself is an accomplishment. But the significance of the company's story lies in how its has embodied—and deviated from—the main contours of American business history in much of the twentieth century. We have recounted in some detail what Cummins has done in this period. What lessons can we draw from that experience? And what do those lessons suggest for American manufacturing more generally, as it seeks a sharper competitive edge in the global economy?

Before we can answer these questions, we need to look once again at the broader context within which Cummins has done business.

Charting the American century

On the eve of World War II, publishing magnate Henry Luce printed an editorial entitled "The American Century." Sensing that direct U.S. involvement in the war was imminent, Luce—who was confident of Allied victory—began to envision the postwar world order. "The vision of America as the principal guarantor of the freedom of the seas, the vision of America as the dynamic leader of world trade, has within it the possibilities of such enormous human progress as to stagger the imagination," Luce proclaimed. "Let us not be staggered by it."[3]

The editorial attracted little attention, but postwar events soon validated Luce's vision. U.S. policymakers pushed aggressively to contain communism and promote capitalism around the globe. America's expanding power and national pride were fueled by a robust domestic economy. American industrial output soared, employment surged, and the nation's middle class grew rapidly.[4]

A half-century later, it is clear that the real American Century both began earlier and ended sooner than the one described by Luce. It spanned roughly the one hundred years between the 1870s and the 1970s. It began with the rise of giant industrial corporations, most of which followed a course charted by the nation's railroads before the Civil War. These new and powerful industrials (Standard Oil, Carnegie Steel, American Tobacco, Singer, and others) served national and international markets, consumed staggering amounts of investment capital, and grew through merger and vertical integration.[5] By the turn of the century, these giants dominated the U.S. economy and portions of the industrialized world, and they remained a dominant business model throughout the twentieth century.[6]

Seen from this perspective, the Cummins Engine Company came late to the American Century. It was born decades after the rise of big business in America, and did not itself become a big business until after the Second World War. Then came the last quarter of the American Century, which generated a level of broad-based prosperity that history had not seen before. Cummins itself embarked on a period of unprecedented growth, embodying these heady times: big trucks on wide highways, ever-higher speeds, rising horsepower, heavier loads, and longer distances. Cummins was a thriving company in a bustling economy.

Meanwhile, of course, American society was changing in fundamental ways, and business was changing along with it. The most significant aspect of this transformation was the emergence of a range of interests that began to impinge upon corporate agendas and strategies.

In the Gilded Age, John D. Rockefeller, embodiment of the old model, pursued profits single-mindedly. He worried very little about government regulation (which was weak), the treatment of workers (who had little power), or the general public (which more or less envied and hated him anyway). Business in Rockefeller's day meant minimal disclosure, far-reaching insider influence, harsh working conditions, nearly unchecked industrial pollution, and light tax burdens.[7]

All of this changed in the twentieth century, in part due to successive waves of regulation in the 1910s, 1930s, and 1970s.[8] Workers and consumers gained a voice—not only through legislation, but also through the formation of countervailing organizations. Business historians Louis Galambos and Joseph Pratt summarize the change in this way: "In [J. P.] Morgan's day a small elite in the business community had far more power than any businessperson . . . can exercise today. The business leaders of the 1980s do not command; they negotiate—with Congress, with organized labor, with federal and state agencies, with well-funded interest groups, all of whom constrain their choices."[9]

Organized labor and the federal government emerged as the two most important counterweights to business. Both were strengthened in the 1930s by the New Deal, which sanctioned collective bargaining and spawned an alphabet soup of activist federal agencies. In the late 1930s, when the workers at Cummins and many other companies first organized, union membership across the country surged. It continued to rise steeply after World War II. Meanwhile, the laws that were passed and the agencies that were created by the New Deal grew dramatically in size and importance after the war. The 1940s and 1950s marked the true birth of "big government" in America.[10]

The expansion and conduct of the federal government helped make the immediate postwar decades even more of a heyday for American business. Washington was now a major component of the economy—and a noncyclical one. Federal spending on social welfare chugged along, impervious to business cycles. So did military spending, as a result of the new state of permanent international hostilities known as the Cold War. The government employed more and more people, and spent more and more money: on interstate highways, dam building and flood control, education for veterans, and countless other long-term programs and projects.[11]

In the two decades following the Second World War, government played a paradoxical role in the economic affairs of the nation. On the one hand, the federal government assumed primary and active responsibility for the nation's economic health. On the other hand, policymakers had no clear guidelines for action. Exactly what level of unemployment was unacceptable? What rate of growth too slow? How much should the government spend to boost employment? Most of the time, this mixed bag of intervention and nonintervention worked. Up until the mid-1960s, the economy grew at a robust pace, while inflation remained under 2 percent and unemployment hovered around 5 percent. Democrats and Republicans came and went, but government policies changed only at the margins. Economic policymakers described their role as "fine-tuning" the economy.

Times were good. Many thought they would remain so forever.

The century ends

The American Century, as noted above, ended ahead of schedule. Some telltale signs of this reversal came in the military, social, and diplomatic realms: Vietnam, Watergate, and so on.[12] But the surest signs came in the crucial economic arena. In 1973, virtually all of the indices by which Americans charted their progress took a wrong turn. That year, real weekly wages—a key indicator of economic well-being—ended their long, steep, and steady postwar climb. After growing at an annual average rate of 2.9 percent between 1948 and 1973, weekly wages adjusted for inflation *fell* between 1974 and 1991 by an average of 0.9 percent per year. Median family income, which similarly had increased 2.8 per year from 1947 to 1973, rose and fell sporadically thereafter. And the overall productivity of the economy (as measured by nonfarm hourly output per worker), after rising 2.5 percent on average per year between 1948 and 1973, increased by a mere 0.7 per annum on average in the dozen years thereafter.[13] Clearly, this was the end of America's continuous postwar economic expansion.

In the media, the close of the American Century took the form of highly publicized struggles between U.S. firms and their foreign counterparts in the same industry sector—GM versus Honda, Motorola versus Siemens, Caterpillar versus Komatsu. These struggles came to be cast as morality plays, most of which had the same ominous outcome. Americans became uncomfortably accustomed to hearing of yet another industry—motorcycles, color TVs, VCRs, and so on—in which their nation seemed to be terminally uncompetitive. The automobile industry was a particular sore point. In 1980, total Japanese automobile output surpassed that of the long-dominant United States. By 1985, nearly half the small cars and nearly a quarter of the midsized cars sold in America were made in Japan.[14]

What went wrong? What happened, in such a relatively short span of time, to effect such a dramatic reversal of fortunes?

Some experts emphasize international macroeconomic shifts, such as the energy crisis and international exchange rates.[15] Others point to domestic federal policy as the chief culprit, whether in the form of the national security state (channeling resources into largely nonproductive military ends), the welfare state (shifting resources from investors to consumers), the regulatory state (hobbling the private sector with costly standards), or the voracious state (stifling savings and investment through heavy taxation). Still others blame organized labor for America's declining fortunes in recent decades: the allegedly excessive power of unions that supposedly saddle American industry with noncompetitive wage rates and cumbersome work rules. And finally, some argue that America's economic dominance in the early postwar years was unnatural and unsustainable. As Europe and Asia recovered from the devastation of World War II, a "correction" to the disadvantage of the United States was inevitable.

There is some truth in each of these interpretations. The authors' primary interest, however—especially as we have researched, pondered, and written the story of Cummins—has been the responsibility of management for U.S. industrial competitiveness. It is clear that American managers helped sow the seeds of their own decline.* They did so first in the expansionist 1950s, when they allowed their companies to become significantly bureaucratic—that is, depersonalizing, rigid, slow to innovate, and discouraging of creativity. Subsequently, other troubling undercurrents emerged as full-blown liabilities. One was a general preoccupation with the domestic market, at the expense of overseas growth. The second was an overreliance on financial performance measures. And the third was a misplaced belief in the transferability of management expertise across industries, and an over-reliance on management consultants, particularly in the new field of "strategy."

Based on the Cummins experience, we believe that America's business leaders should identify which levers are under their control—a group of tools that comprises organizational structure, corporate culture, relations with stakeholders, and so on. They should look hard at how and how well those levers have been applied, certainly beginning with their own companies' experiences, and perhaps looking to the experience of other companies—such as Cummins—for a broader frame of reference. And then, of course, they should *act* on that understanding.

We can distill our reading of the Cummins history into five lessons—lessons that are hard to learn, and all too easy to forget. They are:

- Cultivate and preserve organizational competence
- Compete in the long term
- Embrace change
- Identify and build relationships with all stakeholders
- Use values to drive the business

In the pages that follow, we will explore each of these lessons, and cite examples of how Cummins has learned and applied them. We will argue that for the most part, Cummins consistently practiced what legions of management experts now preach about how American business should compete in the next century—a century that is likely to be far less generous to the West in general, and the United States in particular. And for that reason, the Cummins story is a lesson for our times.

---

*"American managers," says Irwin Miller of this period, "became arrogant and cold-blooded, and they got caught."

Cultivate and Preserve Organizational Competence

Early in this century, one could have guessed a company's business from its name: General Motors. American Can. Otis Elevator. General Electric. Standard Oil. By the 1970s, this game was much more challenging: General Dynamics. United Technologies. Cooper Industries. ITT Corporation. Exxon. The traditional approach to business was to focus on a single product or product line. The Carnegie Steel Company, which dominated the steel industry in the late nineteenth century under hard-driving founder Andrew Carnegie, is a typical example. As Carnegie built his company into the world's leading producer of steel and steel products, he liked to quote Mark Twain's aphorism: "Put all of your eggs in one basket—and watch that basket!"

Carnegie's egg-tending differed dramatically from unrelated diversification, which emerged as a major trend in America after the Second World War. Spurred by falling rates of return, rising interest rates, and changes in government policy, an increasing number of companies in slow-growing industries began acquiring small, start-up firms in emerging industries. Often, the takeover targets were in fields completely unrelated to the parent company's business. But no matter (as the logic went). The parent company would supply not only capital, but also a set of generic managerial skills—from cost-control expertise to marketing savvy to sophisticated compensation systems—to transform the acquisition into an engine of economic growth. "We can manage anything," proclaimed a new generation of managers, many of whom held MBAs from leading business schools.

This new management philosophy peaked during the conglomerate mania of the 1960s. Textron, LTV, Litton, ITT, Gulf + Western, and other "darlings" of Wall Street gobbled up hundreds of firms, often in completely unrelated businesses. (Gulf + Western, as we have noted, briefly pawed at Cummins.) Companies like Textron managed massive empires from comparatively tiny corporate offices, staffed mainly by lawyers and number-crunchers. Theirs was a business of buying and selling companies, like stocks in a portfolio.[16]

The trend was exacerbated by the rise of management consultants in the same period. Equipped with new techniques for financial analysis and vastly expanded computational power, firms like Boston Consulting Group (BCG) developed schemes for analyzing business unit performance and setting strategy that gained wide currency. BCG's "growth share matrix," for example, classified business units as cash cows, stars, dogs, or question marks. Each category implied a strategy: Sell dogs, milk cows to feed stars, and so on. This kind of analysis, however, tended to wash out the specifics of the particular industry in time and context.[17]

The widespread overdependence on financial measures, consultants, and skills that were not easily transferable proved to be a weak foundation for U.S.

industry. Statistics eventually confirmed what some managers were beginning to suspect: Related diversified firms generally outperformed unrelated diversified conglomerations.[18] Worse, this loss of focus had come just as international competition began to heat up. Just when American managers most needed to think creatively about new markets and new technologies, they were seduced by short-term profitability.[19]

The central lesson to emerge from this debacle was about cultivating and preserving organizational competencies. Many of the firms that channeled resources into unrelated diversification did so at great cost to their core businesses, where they had been cultivating know-how and markets for decades. Manufacturing firms, in particular, tended to damage their hard-won capabilities when they plunged into service and unproven high-tech businesses, which were thought to be more future oriented. Skills and markets lost as a result proved to be extremely difficult to recover, especially in the hypercompetitive global marketplace that was emerging.

Organizational capabilities infuse all levels of an organization. They especially reside in the work force—the most important storehouse of formal training, experience, and nontransferrable functional knowledge. Firms that capture, preserve, and draw upon this know-how generally enjoy a competitive advantage. Japanese auto manufacturers, for example, have applied this lesson by implementing elaborate systems to reward assembly line workers for suggesting process improvements.

But organizational capabilities are difficult to build. The creation of a research and development organization, the training of a large skilled and semiskilled work force, and the construction of factories and distribution channels—these assets take years or decades to accumulate. Conversely, they are very easy to destroy, either gradually or abruptly and catastrophically. Firms that lose their focus destroy hard-won capabilities over time. Those that sell or shut down key business units do it overnight. "Core competencies," argue management scientists C. K. Prahalad and Gary Hamel, "are the collective learning in an organization, especially how to coordinate diverse production skills and integrate multiple streams of technologies." Not surprisingly, these experts warn against the "seductions of decentralization."[20]

American business can't turn back the clock to the days of single-business firms. *Related* diversification is a powerful competitive strategy, especially in industries (such as chemicals) where potential economies of scope are great. (It should be noted, too, that some *unrelated* diversified firms have performed well over time by defining their missions tightly.) At the same time, however, U.S. managers should recognize that know-how—at all levels within the firm—is hard to build up and easy to ignore. Certainly, general management skills are valuable to a firm's success. But what truly matter are the organizational capabilities specific to a firm's competencies—and by extension, to its products and customers.

Where does Cummins fall, on this spectrum of unrelated-to-related skill bases? For most of its past, Cummins has demonstrated an unusual degree of focus on core competencies. Apart from its short-lived forays into unrelated businesses (beef, banking, and skis) in the early 1970s, Cummins has remained in a single business. The company has remained dedicated to *engine* production, long after other loose engine producers had folded up their tents or joined forces with OEMs. By the 1970s, Cummins was the nation's sole remaining manufacturer of loose automotive diesel engines.

This focus came early to Cummins and gained momentum over time. The development of indigenous technical know-how began in earnest when Clessie Cummins and Hans Knudsen jettisoned the inferior engine-and-injection technology licensed from Hvid and began to develop their own designs. As these designs became more sophisticated, the prewar company's core competencies evolved away from cut-and-try metallurgy to hydromechanical engineering—but always toward the goal of making a better diesel engine.

When the Engine Company finally entered a period of robust growth in the early 1950s, it broadened its range of competencies in diesel making by internalizing the manufacture of one key engine component after another. From turbochargers, to pistons and crankshafts, to double-disc fuel systems and PT injection, Cummins expanded its core capabilities as rapidly as resources (human and financial) permitted.

The strategy worked. The PT fuel system, a proprietary invention, eventually contributed to Cummins' dramatic postwar success. But it is important to recognize that the PT's genesis lay far back in the 1920s. For decades afterwards, Clessie Cummins struggled to overcome a set of fundamental problems in diesel fuel injection. Combining insight with decades of acquired competence, he eventually made the needed breakthrough. Without this and related innovations, Cummins would have had to rely increasingly on its competitors for fuel-injection technology—and these were rivals who were likely to be as unwilling to license their own gems as Cummins was to license the PT. The stakes were unquestionably high. Borrowers of technology often find themselves standing outside the House of Innovation, their noses pressed against the glass as they peer wistfully inside.

Core competencies are shifting terrain. They change in response to, and help define, a firm's strategies, products, and markets. For most of its history, Cummins relied on its core product—the automotive diesel—to define its core competencies. As the automotive diesel evolved from a slow, heavy, smoke-spewing workhorse to a high-speed, compact, low-polluting power source, the expertise needed to manufacture automotive diesels migrated away from basic metal machining and toward advanced metallurgy, fluid dynamics, computer-aided design, electronics, and other advanced applied sciences. Cummins stayed with those developments, and often set the pace.

But as this product market began to mature in the 1960s and 1970s, Cummins began to think more broadly about its core competencies. Its intimate familiarity with heavy-duty trucking inspired the White merger attempt, as well as successful moves into trucking-related service and support businesses. Meanwhile, the company's know-how in high-speed diesels was applied to new, smaller classes of engines for trucks, construction equipment, and stationary generator sets. With the latter (and mainly through the acquisition of Onan), Cummins has moved from making engines for portable electric generator sets to producing complete gensets.

Identifying core competencies can be challenging. For Cummins, this has proven to be the case with electronic control systems. While increasingly essential in the trucking field—by bringing into harmony the control of engines, transmissions and drive trains, brakes, air foils, and other components—the manufacture of electronics demands know-how quite distinct from engine making. Is it an essential core competency for the Engine Company? Yes and no. It is absolutely essential to control the algorithms that run the fuel systems that run the engines. It is far less essential to manufacture the boxes that these algorithms put through their paces. Today, one in four R&E dollars at Cummins goes into the writing of software, a word that few at Cummins would have recognized several decades back.

Cummins may find it desirable to move beyond engines and controls to larger systems. But even if Cummins were to become a manufacturer of engine-and-drive-train combinations, or even a manufacturer of diesel-powered equipment other than gensets—two kinds of vertical integration that it has contemplated and rejected in the past—this still would be a well-defined mission in the context of the Fortune 500.

Compete in the Long Term

In the midst of Cummins' travails with Hanson, Will Miller—who played a central role in the struggle for corporate control—went to see *Other People's Money*, then being performed on Broadway in New York. The play (borrowing its title from a classic critique of rampant capitalism written by Louis Brandeis in 1932) inspired a popular film about the rough-and-tumble takeover battles of the 1980s. For Miller, the play struck a bit too close to home. "It was tough to take," he recalls.[21]

In the 1991 film version, Gregory Peck plays the head of an old New England manufacturing firm, New England Wire & Cable, that is about to be taken over. In the movie's climactic scene, Peck laments the fact that firms like his appear to be "worth more dead than alive." Retorts Danny DeVito (playing quintessential corporate raider Larry the Liquidator): "I didn't kill it; it was dead when I got here."

Not "dead," perhaps, but doomed. New England Wire & Cable was cash-rich and relatively free of debt, but—because business was in a slump—the company's stock price was down. If the firm could be dismantled and sold off piecemeal, it actually would be worth more dead than alive.

How did it happen? What had the stalwart Yankee company done to get itself into such straits? The answer is that it represented values and strategies that were out of date. But the values represented by Larry the Liquidator were no more effective. According to many observers, U.S. business had become so focused on the bottom line, and so subject to the pressures of Wall Street—home of liquidators—that it was failing to make desperately needed long-term investments in research and development, in new plant and equipment, and in training its work force. As a result, U.S. firms were turning out inferior and expensive products and undermining their own futures. This interpretation has been used to indict management (for siphoning off profits through princely salaries and benefits), the investment community (for investing in firms that generate short-term yields rather than those with solid long-term prospects), the federal government (for passing tax laws and relaxing antitrust policies so as to encourage a frenzy of non-value-creating mergers and acquisitions), and even organized labor (for seeking high wage scales instead of trying to cooperate with management to meet foreign competition).

Again, there is truth to all of these arguments, and they point to a formidable challenge, especially when viewed from an international perspective. In Germany, corporations are not permitted to file quarterly reports—an intentional effort on the part of the government to discourage short-term investor pressure. German banks work closely and cooperatively with leading German firms, in ways that would prompt antitrust actions in America. In Japan, the Ministry of International Trade and Industry (MITI) helps coordinate trade policy, finance, and technology development (among other functions) to promote the long-term competitiveness of selected industries.

Why the rash of mergers and acquisitions in the 1980s—the third such major wave in U.S. business history? The answer varies from company to company. In many cases, firms were spinning off unrelated acquisitions made in the previous decade or so. Some firms were simply victims of their times: well-managed companies caught in a squeeze during a sharp but temporary economic downturn, and made vulnerable by the availability of newly popular financial techniques and instruments (such as junk bonds and leveraged buyouts, or LBOs). But others were actively mismanaged, with depressed share prices resulting from management-induced inefficiency. In still other cases, top managers compensated themselves handsomely, while failing to reinvest for the long term.

According to some analysts, these restructurings brought certain specific benefits.[22] A hostile takeover or an insiders' coup (by means of an LBO) held the prospect of bringing new rigor and discipline to the firm. According to this view, an LBO transformed a small cadre of professional managers into highly leveraged owners, and thus motivated them to reinvest and think over a longer time frame. Moreover, the new high-debt structure compelled the firm to cut costs and increase efficiency. Indeed, if the leveraged firm continued to operate in its accustomed inefficient ways, it quickly collapsed under a mountain of unserviceable debt.

Since the prospective rewards generally were very high, these temptations were seldom resisted in the 1980s. The results were mixed. One study suggested that firms taken over through LBOs generally became more efficient than their industry peers.[23] On the other hand, many good companies were destroyed because—as it turned out—their profits couldn't be cranked up sufficiently to stave off the bondholders.

When it comes to poor financial performance, how long is too long? There is no easy answer. No firm is profitable every month, or every quarter. There are legitimate reasons for short-term losses: recessions, market shifts, new product launches, technological change, and new competition, to name a few.

The LBOs of the 1980s also prompted many to reconsider the "agency" question: Who works for whom, and for what reasons? And specifically, whose interests are represented by the top managers in a corporation? According to a growing number of experts, professional managers are not appropriately motivated to represent a corporation's long-term interests. Some have suggested that the only way to force managers to take the long view is to make them owners. But this is unrealistic in the context of today's giant corporations, whose largest individual shareholders typically control only a tiny fraction of the total shares outstanding. And even if this were a feasible strategy, it would hardly be a surefire one. Owners, too, have been known to opt for short-term profit over long-term growth.

The Cummins position on this matter has been remarkably consistent: The company has favored long-term investment over short-term returns. But as Irwin Miller, Henry Schacht, and Jim Henderson regularly have reminded us, Cummins doesn't take the long view solely (or even primarily) out of a sense of altruism. Instead, the company believes that the judicious sacrifice of short-term rewards will yield higher total returns in the long run.

In some ways, this runs against human nature. As board member Don Perkins, former chairman of Jewel Companies, Inc., comments:

> *For a company like Cummins, one of the real problems is that we human beings tend to think in annual terms. Take compensation, for example: Why do we think about compensation in annual terms? It*

would make much more sense to look at compensation over a period of
years. Similarly, Cummins has to think about the development part of
the product cycle as a multi-year commitment. So by definition, it
needs "patient capital"—that is, investors who understand long product
lead times. That's fundamental to the nature of the business.

The "patient capital" tradition at Cummins dates back to the company's unusual ownership structure at its founding. By any modern investor's standard, the Irwin-Sweeney-Miller family's support of Clessie Cummins' endeavors was irrational. And the family's support was doubly "irrational" because it went on for *so long*: seventeen years of losses, with one $10,000 check following another, until the first profits finally began to trickle in in 1937. The same $2 million invested elsewhere in the booming economy of the 1920s— or in the bargain-basement stock market of the 1930s—likely would have made W. G. Irwin and his family richer by an order of magnitude, in the short run.* Over the long run, however, Cummins proved to be one of the best investments in the family's diverse portfolio. Patience paid off—not for W. G., but for later generations. W. G. anticipated this outcome, and continued to make this and other long-term investments until the day he died.

The decade of the 1950s—the take-off period in Cummins' history—is worth reexamining in this light. As the economy began to boom, J. I. Miller called for reinvestment. Now was a time for sowing, not reaping, said Miller; and Cummins accordingly plowed profits into new facilities. A decade later, when it came time to scale up research and development—one of the purest manifestations of long-term thinking—Miller relentlessly pushed the company's managers to aim higher. In the new Tech Center, sixty-four test cells were not enough, argued Miller; but perhaps eighty-eight might do. Few could envision how this might pay off—until new environmental regulations began to show their teeth a few years later.

On the international front as well, Cummins has shown a sometimes surprising degree of patience. The ventures in Brazil in the 1970s and China in the 1980s seemed to grind along toward nowhere, until (after more than a decade, in the case of Brazil) they began to pay off. In these disparate cultures, time was needed to cultivate relationships and learn local laws and customs. That certainly was true in Japan, where Cummins established its first direct ties (with Komatsu) in 1961. Again, the real pay-off came decades later, when Cummins (unlike Komatsu's other American partners) was able to preserve its relationship with the Japanese firm. This was in part because Komatsu's man-

---

*In 1996, Will Miller—W. G. Irwin's great-grandnephew—did a back-of-the-envelope calculation and estimated that this original family stake in the business equaled $23 million in 1996 dollars (not counting any opportunity costs).

agers saw Cummins as an American company that took the kind of long-term view typical among Japanese manufacturers.

When the debate over American industrial short-sightedness was heating up in the 1970s, Cummins again took a long view of its future—and backed it up with $1.3 billion in capital investments. The restructuring launched by Henry Schacht and Jim Henderson in 1979 framed succinctly the great dilemma of that time. "How long must we wait?" investors asked, as the decade rolled by without profits (and as the dividend was cut). Meanwhile, Cummins (like Gregory Peck's New England Wire & Cable) began popping up on the computer screens of companies hungry for promising takeover targets. Why? Because the stock price was unnaturally depressed. Why? Because Cummins had been investing for the long term.

It took the better part of a decade, with considerable risk, but the long-term approach worked well for Cummins. The restructuring and investments of the early 1980s—complemented by a decade-long effort to raise manufacturing standards—yielded generous profits in the early 1990s. And typically, as soon as Cummins approached (in the early 1990s) the break-even point on its massive investment in midrange engines, it began a new round of capital investments in these engine families.

Embrace Change

By the standards of the 1970s and 1980s, American business in the 1950s and 1960s responded to change too slowly. But to be fair to the managers of that day, their context was radically different, and their businesses were held to very different standards.

The game accelerated in part because of larger economic forces. The "stagflation" of the early 1970s led economic policymakers to shift from fine-tuning to wholesale experimentation. President Nixon took America off the gold standard and embraced wage and price controls; President Carter launched large-scale deregulation. Meanwhile, the worldwide spike in energy prices exacerbated the economic slowdown. By the time Ronald Reagan entered the White House, economists were searching desperately for a solution to the stagflation trap. "Reaganomics" beat back inflation, but also launched the national debt into the stratosphere.

These domestic and international forces converged to make the 1970s and 1980s a period of extreme uncertainty and discontinuity. There was no telling from one month to the next which way energy prices or exchange rates were likely to go—or how economic policymakers were likely to respond to such changes. American government, purposely designed to prevent the centralization of authority, had always had trouble acting coherently. But by the late 1970s, according to Galambos and Pratt, "the costs associated with poor coordination of policy and weak leadership were higher than they had ever been."[24]

At the same time, margins for error were narrowing. International competitors, especially the Japanese, changed the rules of the game by placing a premium on efficient and low-cost production. And the market itself was changing. The computer-based information technologies born in the immediate postwar decades finally were having a major impact on the organization and operation of markets. As always, the trend was toward greater speed; but now the pace of change was accelerating geometrically. With nearly instantaneous market information, customers became more demanding than ever before.

For businesses engaged in the international marketplace, the world had become a much more uncertain and competitive place. This, in turn, put a premium on flexibility. Companies soon learned that they had to respond to shifting markets and new competitive threats *quickly*, or they might not get another chance.

Companies, though, are human organizations, with rigidities and historical momentum. The challenge was: How to capitalize on past experience while remaining limber and responsive?

In its formative years, Cummins Engine was responsive mainly because it was feeling its way. Clessie Cummins wanted to make the world's best diesel engines, but he wasn't sure for whom. Farmers? Construction equipment manufacturers? The government? Yacht owners? It took nearly two decades to hit upon the answer: diesels for big trucks. Even into World War II, when Cummins was a $25 million company, it continued to bear the personal stamp of its flamboyant co-founder. Clessie Cummins—always creative and inspiring, usually unpredictable—was constantly in search of new opportunities.

Time and size are what truly test a corporation's ability to respond to change. With success comes size, with size comes bureaucracy, and with bureaucracy comes formalism and a propensity for rigidity. Ways of doing business gain momentum simply because lots of people have been doing things that way for a long time. It becomes increasingly difficult to question assumptions and respond creatively to new challenges.[25]

When a Cummins bureaucracy began to establish itself after World War II, Irwin Miller prodded and cajoled the company's managers to take nothing for granted. "Obsolete your own product" became a clarion call. A man of relentlessly high standards, Miller rarely paused to celebrate accomplishments. In 1957—to cite only one of many examples—the chairman of the nation's leading producer of heavy-duty truck diesels remarked in the national press: "We have proceeded from one failure to another. Every engine at some point has been a turkey."[26] A clear-eyed view of both the possibilities and shortcomings of his company drove Miller to do better, and to demand the same from Cummins' managers. "I've never known anyone more alert to what is changing in the world," says board member and former University of Chicago president Hanna Gray, "nor more convinced that his company has to respond to these changes."

Miller has long served as a philosopher-statesman at Cummins. But he is hardly the sole source of its visions and guiding principles. For at least four decades, the values he has professed have been shared and reiterated by the company's cohort of top managers in a self-reinforcing cycle.

It helped that the circle was small. Until the 1960s, the company was led by a handful of dedicated functional heads, some of whom held important positions for decades: Dick Stoner in manufacturing, Ray Boll in marketing, and later Bill Schwab in R&D, among others. Among these men, trust was high and communication easy. At its top levels, therefore, Cummins resembled a family firm more than an impersonal corporation.

The agility that flowed from this management style was apparent in missteps and successes alike. What is striking about the 1970s experiments in unrelated diversification, for example, is how quickly Cummins retreated and recouped, realizing that it would be best to focus on its core business. This not only saved Cummins from making what could have been a large-scale strategic error, but also allowed it to divest the new ventures (as John Hackett proudly recalls) at a profit.*

Nowhere is Cummins' willingness to embrace change more apparent than in its encounter with Japanese diesel competition in the 1980s. True, company representatives early on the scene ignored warning signs and underestimated Japanese capabilities. But once Jim Henderson got a firsthand look at Japanese manufacturing methods, he called for a local revolution. The price cutting came at a most inopportune moment: just when Cummins' new B- and C-engine families were struggling for a foothold. The resulting 30 Month Sprint raised eyebrows—at home and on Wall Street—but it worked. The same could be said for the company's decisive response to Hanson PLC and Industrial Equity Pacific in the same decade.

As the margin for errors narrows for today's global competitors, this kind of agility will provide an increasingly important competitive advantage.

Identify and Build Relationships with All Stakeholders

No business competes alone. To be sure, a corporation is (strictly speaking) a self-contained entity—a legal construct created for a specified purpose, and required only to obey those laws that apply to it. Beyond these minimal obligations, a corporation theoretically could operate without regard to the needs of *any* parties.

In reality, every company is obligated to do much more than the bare minimum. No company would long survive, for example, if it ignored the

---

*It should be noted that Hackett remains convinced that Cummins could have made a go of it in most or all of its unrelated ventures, given adequate access to capital.

needs of its shareholders. In the early decades of the American Century, many companies operated on the assumption that their shareholders were the only constituency with a stake in the enterprise. The purpose of the business was to earn the greatest possible return for its owners. Any impulse beyond this most basic one was suspect.

Gradually, though, the circle of recognized "stakeholders" expanded beyond the shareholder base. It turned out that there were good business reasons for it to do so—and, increasingly, legal and regulatory incentives. Nevertheless, the expansion did not occur easily. Labor, for example, had to fight its way into the stakeholder circle. And, especially in the age of monopolies and oligopolies, customers had to struggle to assert themselves and to make sure that they weren't taken for granted.

Nor did the expansion occur uniformly. One element that strongly differentiates one company's history from another is the sequence in which new stakeholders are recognized, and the relative speed, skill, and enthusiasm with which they are embraced. Certainly, in the case of the Cummins Engine Company, this is an important distinguishing characteristic.

Over three-quarters of a century, Cummins identified seven key stakeholders:

- community
- labor
- government
- vendors
- distributors
- customers
- shareholders

A large measure of the company's success has come from its willingness and ability to internalize the interests of those stakeholders. Given the inevitable disparities (and, at times, contradictions) among those interests, this has been a difficult, often bewildering, task. But it is abundantly clear that in the era that follows the American Century—call it the Global Century—leading industrial corporations can do no less.

The first stakeholder acknowledged by Cummins, the community, is the one commonly recognized *last* by other twentieth-century corporations. As noted, the death of Joseph I. Sweeney on a riverbank in 1900 focused his mother (and by extension, the whole Irwin-Sweeney-Miller family) on the mission of providing jobs for young men in the community. "Had it not been for our desire to have a place to develop the young men around Columbus," W. G. Irwin wrote to Clessie Cummins in 1939, "we should not have taken the risks we did."[27]

The subsequent impact of Cummins on Columbus—a recurrent theme throughout this book—is almost incalculable. The economy of the city became inextricably intertwined with the fortunes of the company. (At times, Cummins took measures to *reduce* the city's dependence on the company, beset as the company was by larger economic cycles.) The city's architecture became an international attraction, thanks to the Cummins Engine Foundation's underwriting of architectural fees. A wealth of recreational resources, ranging from golf courses to employee-oriented parks, were made possible by Cummins. Open housing came to Columbus because of Cummins' (and in particular, Irwin Miller's) persistence. Schools improved inside and out. These are only a few examples among hundreds that could be cited.*

When Cummins appeared to be the target of acquisitive companies in the late 1980s, the company fought tenaciously to remain independent—at least to some extent to protect the community's interests as a stakeholder. By that time, scores of American communities had been eviscerated by the uprooting or shuttering of leading local industries. In spite of Cummins' growing international orientation, Columbus remained its chief center of employment—for production workers and managers alike. There was no reason to believe that a new owner would have kept the Engine Company in southern Indiana—nor, for that matter, even kept the company alive for very long.

Still another crucial lesson to emerge from recent economic history is the extent to which the fate of American business is woven inextricably with organized labor and government. It is an oversimplification to think of U.S. companies as competing against companies in Japan, Germany, or elsewhere. A parallel competition also occurs between two economic systems: each country's key institutions in business, labor, and government, and the nexus of relationships among them. Do they work in harmony or at cross-purposes? The answer says much about a nation's global competitiveness.

The history of the domestic steel industry illustrates the perils of ignoring this reality. Throughout the 1950s and 1960s, U.S. Steel exercised what was euphemistically called "price leadership," setting prices that were quickly matched by smaller producers in what amounted to a domestic cartel. This raised the ire of the Justice Department, which periodically threatened antitrust actions against Big Steel. Meanwhile, another arm of the federal government was pouring money into the war-devastated economies of Germany and Japan in an effort to turn those two countries into bulwarks against the spread of communism. But there was little concern on the part of the Washington, D.C.-based cold warriors about the structure of the steel industry within the former Axis powers. Cartels were sanctioned and legally

---

*Cummins' leaders are careful to point to the contributions made to the community by other Columbus-based companies with a tradition of community involvement, especially Arvin Industries.

enforceable in Germany, for example, and neither the U.S. steel industry nor the U.S. government perceived this internal contradiction in national policy. Both complained loudly and pointed fingers at each other, however, when the revitalized mills of Germany and Japan began to gobble up larger and larger shares of the world steel market.[28]

What is the best configuration of relationships? Comparative studies are revealing. Professor Jeffrey Hart of Indiana University found that among leading industrial nations, those in which business, labor, or the state held a dominant role did not perform as well as those that reflected more balance. Specifically, the strong position of organized labor in Great Britain, of business in the United States, and of the state in France proved to be less effective than Japan's labor-business accommodation and Germany's integration of corporate and state interests.[29]

The leaders of American business, government, and labor must do more than acknowledge their interdependence; they must agree on strategies and tactics for international competitiveness, and then they must present a unified front. Galambos and Pratt argue that the American enterprise system traditionally has lacked "effective integrative institutions."[30] Representatives from all three corners of the enterprise triad need to come together regularly and on many levels—not simply during contract negotiations or antitrust actions. There are simply too many opportunities to work at cross-purposes.

Cummins' recognition that its interests were interdependent with those of its work force came at the company's founding. As a means of creating local employment, the early Engine Company placed a high priority on the concerns of labor. But as a profit-seeking corporation, Cummins inevitably experienced tensions with its workers. The implicit paternalism of the early years, however well intended, had to give way to independent worker representation.

Labor-management relations at Cummins have been on the whole positive and cooperative. In the 1930s, rank-and-file workers voted to ally themselves with a company union rather than with the CIO. Management can be criticized (and indeed, criticizes itself) for losing touch with its work force during the late 1960s and early 1970s—but not for failing to respond when called to task by union members.

The new work systems instituted in many Cummins plants since the 1970s—systems that rely heavily on worker responsibility and input—illustrate the company's commitment to a true partnership with labor. The most eloquent expression of this philosophy, on both sides of the bargaining table, is the eleven-year contract signed in 1993. But this pact was only the culmination of years of relationship building between the two parties. By stabilizing labor-management relations, Cummins and the Diesel Workers Union have enabled the company to focus on the vital business at hand: producing and selling globally competitive products.

The challenge of global competitiveness greatly complicates the company-union relationship. As board member (and former Secretary of Defense) Harold Brown notes:

> *This has been put to a real test over the past fifteen years or so, because employment by Cummins in the southern Indiana region has been cut at least in half, and the salary scales for newer employees are substantially lower than was previously the case. That puts a real strain on the relationship. But with Irwin as its conscience, the company has agonized over each of those steps. It has listened to feedback from employees, and has made a real attempt to be fair, within the limits of fiscal prudence and fiduciary responsibility. And the commitment to put new jobs into southern Indiana that might have gone somewhere else is a real one.*

At the April 1997 shareholders' meeting in Columbus, the president of the Diesel Workers Union, Conrad Bowling, paid tribute to Irwin Miller, then stepping down as a board member after more than sixty years of near-continuous service to the company. In his brief comments, Bowling gave the union's perspective on Miller's contributions:

> *You were at the top of the company with lots of important strategic world issues vying for your attention, yet you always had time for those of us on the shop floor dealing with the issues of today's production. We could talk to you, and we knew you would listen. You came to our gatherings, and we knew that you cared.*

Toward the end of his remarks, Bowling presented Miller with a Diesel Workers flag signed by all the members of the union, and announced that Miller had been made an honorary lifetime member of the DWU. "Thank you," Bowling concluded, "and may God bless you for multiplying the talents you were given, and for helping others multiply their talents as well."

For three-quarters of a century, Cummins' relations with the state similarly have been far more cooperative than contentious. J. Irwin Miller publicly supported the expansion of federal power in the area of labor oversight and arbitration by supporting Section 7a of the National Industrial Recovery Act in 1933. National civil-rights legislation in the 1950s lagged behind the important private efforts of Miller and the policies and programs of the Engine Company to promote racial segregation and equal opportunity, and—according to Cummins insiders—when the Kennedys sought a politically safe way to push for black voter registration in the South, they turned to Irwin Miller for help.

Cummins did not shrink from lobbying to protect its interests when those interests were threatened by federal legislation. It moved strongly against efforts to tax away the differential between gasoline and diesel fuel. "Why tax a more efficient energy source into oblivion?" company officials asked pointedly.

For the diesel industry, environmental protection emerged as the most important area of expanded federal power. Cummins usually found itself in the enviable position of benefiting from tighter emissions standards, because its heavy investments in technology and its large size enabled it to meet such standards economically. But the record suggests that the company also cooperated because the cause was right: The harmful effects of unregulated pollution were obvious.

When the inevitable questions arose about fair standards governing diesel exhaust emissions, Henry Schacht proposed an innovative approach. The Health Effects Institute—an independent research entity with shared oversight and sponsorship from the Environmental Protection Agency and the diesel industry—in retrospect can be viewed as a model for business-government cooperation. This kind of mediating institution will be increasingly important to the American enterprise system, if it is to meet global competition in the next century.

In part because of the nature of Cummins' business, the company had to start acknowledging three other key players—vendors, distributors, and customers—as stakeholders in the 1930s. Of course, the company had bought and sold things well before this time. (Sears, the federal government, and Northwest Shovel were three customers who taught Cummins some painful lessons in the 1920s.) But it was the creation of the distributor network under Paris Letsinger's guidance in the early 1930s that really tied together Cummins' manufacturing and distribution systems—from purchased parts and subassemblies to showrooms to end users—into an interdependent whole. Cummins was absolutely dependent on the quality of the goods purchased from such suppliers as Golden Foundry and Atlas Crankshaft, because it was dependent on satisfied end users (who couldn't tolerate breakdowns) "pulling" Cummins engines through the distribution network. "We're in the business of selling engines to engine-makers," Irwin Miller commented with dry understatement to *Fortune* magazine in 1957, "which is surely not the smartest way to make a living."[31]

The evolution of the relationship between Cummins and its key suppliers mostly has to be inferred from hints in an incomplete historical record. It is clear, though, that Cummins took pains to help its vendors grow and improve their operations. The fact that Cummins complained bitterly to the federal government in 1941 about being denied access to these high-quality suppliers is illuminating. "In many cases," one memo noted, "our standards of manufacture, development, and research are responsible for the existence of such [high-quality] sources today."[32] And when Cummins offered to buy Atlas, its key crankshaft supplier, Atlas's president was unreservedly enthusiastic. "Over the years," he told the Cummins representatives, "you've been the ones who have made it possible for me to grow."[33]

Cummins sometimes forgot the lessons it learned, and had to relearn them in a hurry. One shock came in the late 1970s, when a series of bad report cards came in from vendors in the form of "corporate social responsibility balance sheets." What surfaced, in short, was a sense of antagonism and alienation on the part of key suppliers, who had been squeezed during Cummins' profound financial difficulties in the mid-1970s. "That ended up moving Cummins more toward the long-term partner relationship," recalls one manager, "that we later learned from the Japanese was the right way to do it anyway. But I think that effort gained us five years in getting away from the old-fashioned antagonistic relationships."[34] And in subsequent interactions with the Japanese—some collaborative, and some intensively competitive— Cummins learned a great deal more about respecting and giving a voice to its suppliers, whom it was increasingly inclined to view as partners.

Stakeholders are created in part when *self*-interest evolves into *mutual* interest. This collaborative spirit arose not only between Cummins and its suppliers, but also in the context of Cummins' relationship with small OEMs, a key component in the Engine Company's customer base. In the early postwar years, Cummins sold three-quarters of its engines directly to OEMs (and only one-quarter through its dealers). Cummins paid particular attention to the small OEM, who was most dependent on Cummins' technical expertise. "Over time," explains Ray Boll, "we came to have better technical capabilities in engine applications and operations than they did. So we were supplying a real service to these people. We knew that, and we worked at that awful hard."[35] And while the other components of Cummins' customer base (including larger OEMs and large fleets) had much greater leverage and "mobility"—that is, the ability to live without Cummins—the Engine Company struggled to transform these companies into "family members" as well. This took a literal form in the aftermath of the IEP episode, when Ford, Tenneco, and Kubota became significant owners of the company.

It is unusual to talk last about owners as stakeholders, but Cummins' history supports this odd sequence. For roughly the first third of its history, Cummins had only three significant groups of owners: the Irwin-Sweeny-Miller family, Clessie Cummins, and a small group of original investors who suffered through the company's worst years. Over time, this ownership mix changed only marginally. This was not because these owners were uniformly happy about the returns that the Engine Company provided on their investment. (Apparently, none were.) But for many years, an investment in Cummins meant a forced *re*investment in Cummins—for the alternative was dissolution.

As a result, a long-term view arose among the owners of Cummins. Clessie Cummins was the first significant owner to abandon the long-term view—not by choice, but by necessity—and the decision cost him dearly. "It seems clear that he sold the orchard just when the trees began to bear," one sympathetic observer later noted.[36] The phrase "patient capital" gained currency in subsequent decades, which subsumed the notion that people who owned Cummins stock should plan on seeing their most significant returns over the long run. Again, this posture was dictated in part by the nature of Cummins' business, and the markets in which it operated. In many cases, when the company looked cash-rich and capable of rewarding shareholders with increased dividends, it was actually preparing for one of two expensive near-term eventualities: a massive investment of capital for expansion, or a forced husbanding of reserves to ride out an economic downturn.

To summarize: Cummins has an unusual and distinguished history of identifying and embracing stakeholders as they have emerged over the decades. Stakeholders generally have had their voices heard, and their respective needs met. And the result, it seems fair to conclude, has been the creation of a key competitive advantage for the company.

Use Values to Drive the Business

Closely related to stakeholder considerations is the issue of values. It seems clear, based on Cummins' experiences in recent decades, that values can be an effective tool for driving a business forward.

Considerations of values in the business context are nothing new. One of the earliest arenas in which corporate America became self-conscious about values and social responsibilities was in labor relations. In the late nineteenth century, as family firms were eclipsed by large corporations in many industries, managers of large corporations began to offer a variety of non-wage benefits. These "employee welfare" programs could include everything from pension and insurance plans to safe and sanitary working conditions, from employee housing and medical care to educational and religious classes, company sporting teams, and employee outings. Welfare programs had many aims: reducing employee absenteeism and turnover, discouraging unionization, recreating a sense of "family" within a vast and bureaucratic organization, and bolstering the firm's public image. They combined altruism and self-interest. John Patterson, the president of National Cash Register and America's most ambitious welfare capitalist in the Gilded Age, justified his lavish welfare expenditures with the simple slogan, "It pays."[37]

But welfarism quite often was unpopular among workers because it was fundamentally paternalistic. (Indeed, some of the companies with the most elaborate welfare programs, such as Pullman, suffered the most violent labor uprisings.) The problem was that workers enjoyed little or no choice over which non-wage programs they would receive—and many would have preferred higher wages to paternalistically bestowed "benefits." In the 1920s, increasing average wages and the staunchly pro-business climate of the "Age of Normalcy" effectively ended the welfare movement. When hard times returned during the Great Depression, welfarism was neither attractive to workers nor affordable to employers. As unions gained membership and power, unionized businesses often defined themselves through how they negotiated with organized labor. This was a truer test of values than the paternalistic welfarism of the past.

Big business enjoyed broad public support during the great postwar economic expansion, and—not surprisingly—paid little heed to values and social responsibility as management tools. The primary task of business, nearly everyone agreed, was to make products and profits. This consensus disintegrated in the late 1960s and early 1970s. Beginning with the counterculture and spreading to the middle class, corporate America was criticized for depersonalizing its middle managers, befouling the environment, creating harmful products, operating dangerous workplaces, and discriminating against minorities. A wave of "New Social Regulation" addressed these issues and similar issues. Together, the protests and government interventions inspired a growing number of business leaders to reconsider their missions. As in the late nineteenth century, but on a much grander scale, many executives struggled with the challenge of how to do good and do well at the same time.

The shocks of the 1980s—blistering foreign competition and downsizing—intensified sensitivities about social responsibility across industrial America. By this time it was clear: Firms that mistreated employees, made poor products, or despoiled their communities did so at their peril. This broadening of the corporate mission to include broad social responsibilities, animated by a core of authentic values, was reflected in the language of business strategy making. In marketing, for example, the concept of selling was replaced with the "marketing concept," which emphasized customer needs, and in turn by the "societal marketing concept," which insisted that firms consider social externalities (such as the cost of waste disposal) in bringing products to market.

Many companies that began to take values and social responsibility seriously in the tumultuous 1960s, or the constraining 1970s, or the hard-bitten 1980s, faced a difficult transition. For Cummins, by contrast, the story has been one of continuity rather than forced adaptation. The prewar Engine Company—inclined by tradition to invest in its local community, promote an integrated work force, and take seriously the needs of its workers, customers, and suppliers—was an outlyer in American industry. Cummins, especially subsequent to Irwin Miller's arrival in the 1930s, has consistently viewed its values-driven policies as both good works and sound business. This is a view that has become much more the mainstream, as America's postwar economic expansion has slowed.

Most people who study Cummins conclude that its values are inseparable from the values of the founding Irwin-Sweeney-Miller family. (Old family sayings—such as "spell it, and let the other guy pronounce it"—have gradually evolved into company sayings.) Irwin Miller, in particular, has left an unmistakable stamp on the company. Most notably, he has insisted that Cummins both compete aggressively and scrutinize the ethical implications of its actions. "The thing I always admired about Irwin," says Franklin A. Thomas, board member and former head of the Ford Foundation, "was his wonderful combination of a tough, competitive business drive with a complete understanding of the context within which business should operate."

And, Thomas emphasizes, Miller's uncompromising stance in the realm of ethics has provided the company with an unusual competitive edge:

> *He has been an incredible magnet for talented people who are generally interested in improving human welfare. This is true at all levels of the company. I know that the board members, without exception, have been attracted to the company because of its breadth of vision. You had the sense that when you gave your time to this company, you gave it to more than just a narrowly defined business enterprise, but also to a philosophy of business that you could feel proud of.*

At certain points in history, the company's values have overlapped with larger social agendas, which in turn has helped to reinforce and advance key business imperatives. For example, Cummins' deliberate push to internationalize its operations in the late 1950s and early 1960s—by all accounts a practical business decision—was greatly aided by its determination to respect and reinforce local cultures. Young people who were inspired by the activism of the Kennedy era found themselves drawn to Cummins. As Jack Edwards, now an executive vice president, recalls:

> *To me, there is something symbolic about the fact that Cummins went international in the Kennedy era. There was almost this sense of, "Ask not what your country can do for you, but what you can do for your country." Cummins' going global was predicated on the fact that we could be responsible to our shareholders and our international stakeholders at the same time. And that's probably why Cummins attracted people like me, and [group vice president] Rick Stoner, and a few others*

*who had been in fact in the Peace Corps and really found a resonance
in those Cummins values, and wanted to do what was best for the
company, and what was best for the country, and didn't see any conflict
between the two.*

A clear value system also helps the organization cohere and keep its signals straight in times of crisis. During the Hanson and IEP episodes of the
late 1980s, for example, multiple temptations presented themselves to
Cummins' senior executives. Breaking up the company, or folding it into a
larger organization, could have made very wealthy men out of Henry
Schacht, Jim Henderson, and others. "But they had their *father* there," says
board member Don Perkins. "Irwin Miller was and is the father of things, in
so many ways. And there's no way they would have ever let him down."

Perkins' analysis underscores a critical challenge that Cummins has faced
in the last several decades: institutionalizing the values that initially were
embodied in one individual and his family. Other founding families have dis-
engaged from their companies, only to discover that the values that they
hoped were thoroughly inculcated in the company culture didn't long survive
the departure of key individuals. "Obviously, you can't institutionalize a person," comments board member Hanna Gray. "But from my perspective, the
next generation of executives are all people who have that sense of integrity,
and that sense of responsibility to the community as a whole."

Values are fragile, especially when they must be defended by hundreds or
thousands of people, representing many different cultures and upbringings.
Like core competencies, they are hard to build and easy to destroy. Cummins
finds it no easier to defend values than do other companies—but it has explicitly recognized the compelling ethical and practical reasons for doing so.

Maintaining focus and nurturing organizational competencies, embracing change, acting with a long-term view, building authentic relations with
stakeholders, and using values to drive the business: The failure to act in these
ways hurt many American firms and hobbled the U.S. economy in the later
twentieth century. In this conclusion, as well as through the rich details of a
longer story, we have described how one company followed these principles
more or less consistently, and benefited as a result.

Powerful in and of themselves, these principles take on a synergy when
practiced in combination. Core competencies flourish in a business environment oriented toward the long term. It is easier to understand and respond to
change when focused on a single business or small cluster of related businesses. Effective relationships with stakeholders, like core competencies, take
decades to build; and both facilitate an openness to change. Relationships are
inseparable from values. The list goes on.

One might conclude from this history that the Cummins experience is unique and unrepeatable. It is true that Clessie Cummins, J. Irwin Miller, Henry Schacht, and Jim Henderson (and many others among the vast supporting cast in this chronicle) were or are exceptional individuals; that Columbus, Indiana, is atypical of most Fortune 500 hometowns; and that the diesel engine business differs from many other manufacturing enterprises in significant ways. Nevertheless, there are many highly talented business leaders in America today, and plenty of U.S. manufacturing firms that face similar challenges. What matters are the principles. To be sure, history never repeats itself. But, as Mark Twain observed, sometimes it rhymes.

In the next century, the American companies that succeed very likely will look like Cummins in some fundamental ways. Such firms will be big businesses that act much like smaller ones. They will be of a size to capture economies of scale and serve world markets, but will be agile enough to respond to rapidly shifting markets and competitors. They will draw upon a circumscribed set of competencies, in which they will set world standards. They will be led by managers who stay a long time, who know the business intimately, who build strong ties to the work force and the community, and who plan carefully for continuity through succession. They will steer retained earnings into research and development, new plant and equipment, and other long-term investments. They will strive to collaborate with government policymakers and labor leaders in matters of strategic importance. They will reward loyal shareholders, and work to improve their local communities.

And, doing all of this, they will make good products and provide good jobs.

Acknowledgments

The authors would like to recognize those individuals and institutions who made this unusual book possible.

Henry Schacht, formerly the CEO of Cummins and now the CEO of Lucent Technologies, was the original driving force behind the project. His "partner" and successor as head of Cummins, Jim Henderson, inherited the project and put his full support behind it. (On this score, we were very lucky. Inherited book projects often meet a less happy fate!) Irwin Miller, an intensely private public figure, only gradually came around to supporting the effort. As his son Will explained to us, we were violating a central tenet of the Irwin-Sweeney-Miller family: "Spell it, and let the other guy pronounce it." But even before we overcame his resistance, Irwin Miller was unfailingly helpful.

We thank these three overworked individuals for their time—twenty-three formal interviews, at last count, as well as countless informal sessions—and for their unusual and unqualified willingness to let us pore over company and family records. In particular, Jim Henderson's determination to help us understand and depict accurately the struggles of the 1980s has made for a much better book.

We also want to pay special thanks to the members of the Cummins family who helped us. The late Don Cummins, in his nineties when we met him, talked with us for more than six hours, and loaned his records to the project. Lyle Cummins not only spent parts of two days with us in Oregon and made family papers available to us, but also lent his expert eye to the first half of the manuscript and made extensive suggestions about how to improve it. Lyle was scrupulously fair and open-minded in response to our interpretation of his father's complex relationship with the company that bears his name—and we hope we have lived up to his standard.

A complete list of interviewees is included as a separate appendix. Again, we thank all those dozens of people for their time and insights.

Pat Flynn, Karl Kuehner, Gary Nelson, and Bill Schwab (along with Lyle Cummins) were imposed upon to review the manuscript from a technical standpoint. Their responses underscored in our minds the fact that engineering is an art as well as a science.

The project outlasted one general counsel—Steve Zeller—and leaned heavily on a second, Mark Gerstle. We thank them both for ruling almost nothing out of bounds, and for letting the Cummins history speak for itself.

Our book consciously adopted a managerial and strategic perspective (as opposed to, for example, the rank-and-file viewpoint). But three past and present officials of the Diesel Workers Union sat for interviews: Conrad Bowling, Evan Bridgewater, and Larry Neihart. Bowling and Neihart also agreed to read the entire manuscript and give us their reactions. Their criticisms and suggestions give us some confidence that we have not misunderstood the union perspective, at least on the issues that struck us as critical.

If time had permitted, we would have spoken to every Cummins distributor, in part because they are full of lore, and in part because they love their work. Special thanks are owed to Syd Cook and Tom Shenk, Chuck Grace, Walter McCarthy, and Patrick McGahan. We hope that with their help—and Ray Boll's and Herschel O'Shaughnessey's—we have captured the flavor of the distributor network.

Records make a book like this possible. John Ferril (head of Retained Records) and Bill Poor (director of the Tech Center Library) guided us through the extensive records under their control. John Rowell, who went before us through the history of Cummins, also provided records and guidance.

Outside repositories gave us help as well. The Bartholomew County Historical Society shared its relevant records with us. (Thanks to Jean Prather, Laura Moss, and Frances Kenney.) The National Archive staff in Washington turned up valuable information on the World War II period. Linda Caldwell and Connie Tingle gave us access to the Irwin-Sweeney-Miller family papers. John Harmon and his staff at the *Columbus* (Indiana) *Republic* were very helpful in guiding us through their clippings and photo files. The true unsung hero of the research phase was retired Cummins employee Jim Rogers, who on his own initiative had photocopied every mention of Clessie Cummins and the Engine Company in the *Republic* dating back to the early 1900s, and shared that resource with us when we began our work. Incidentally, Rogers also has produced an astounding collection of hand-carved miniature wooden engines, which tell the history of Cummins in a very personal and compelling way.

Our colleagues at Kohn Cruikshank Inc., and particularly Patty Toland, helped us wrestle with papers, facts, and ideas for four years. Then the professionals at the HBS Press took over and got all these words into print. We thank Carol Franco for suggesting that we *not* shrink the manuscript down to human scale.

Projects like this depend on a small number of people in the subject company taking the book to heart. Without exception, book-tending is a labor of love. (It is in no one's job description.) At Cummins, there were three such people: Dick Stoner, Randy Tucker, and Margot Green. Without their willingness to open doors, ferret out information, interpret the corporate mood, crack the whip, suspend disbelief, criticize gently, and otherwise solve a succession of strange and unique problems, the book never would have been completed. Dick Stoner, in particular, made this book possible. Thanks, Dick.

Finally, we'd like to thank our respective wives—who became vicarious experts on diesels, manufacturing, and the weather patterns of southern Indiana—for bearing with us during the travel-intensive phases of this project.

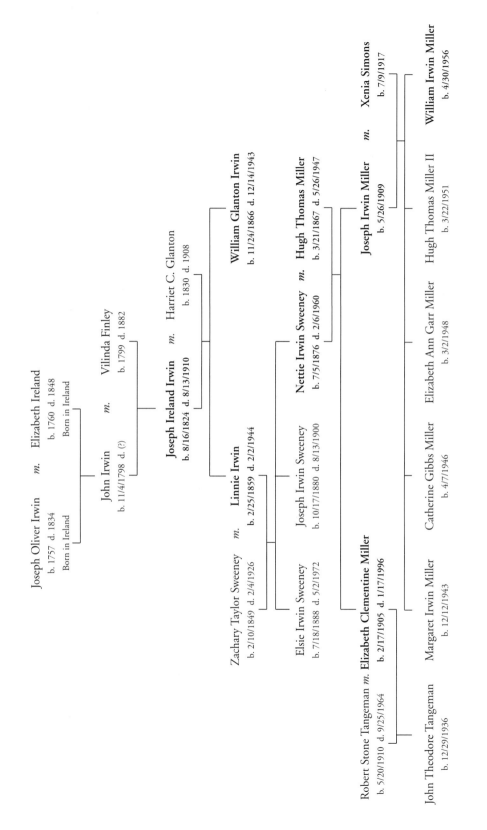

The Irwin-Sweeney-Miller family. Members with ties to the Cummins Engine Company are highlighted.

Note on Sources

This study is based primarily on several collections of correspondence and memoranda at Columbus, Indiana. The W. G. Irwin papers (on microfilm at Cummins headquarters) document a wide range of Cummins' activities through the early 1940s, particularly the key role played by the company co-founder and his dealings with Clessie Cummins and other early company managers. The J. Irwin Miller papers (in care of the Irwin Management Company) reflect Irwin Miller's wide-ranging interests and influence. These papers and microfilms contain a wealth of material about the Engine Company's history from the 1940s to the present, as well as the history of the Cummins Engine Foundation from the 1950s to the present. The Cummins-related correspondence of Henry Schacht, Jim Henderson, and other key company executives, as well as the "Problems Files" and similar management records cited often in the book, are stored either in a special room (known to the authors as "the bunker") or in the company's Records Center, both in the basement of the Corporate Office Building. In all of these collections, except the W. G. Irwin papers, documents are arranged in topical files.

The corporate headquarters, particularly the law department, also holds a variety of standard primary sources: board, executive committee, and shareholder meeting minutes; press releases; patent records; Planning Conference documents; and consulting and financial reports (such as the invaluable Annual Statistical Reports). Citations of these kinds of sources refer to Cummins documents, unless another company is specified. The Records Center also holds boxes of records on special topics, including the Health Effects Institute; selected facilities, products, and acquisitions; engine-build and warranty records; and so on.

The papers of Clessie Cummins reside in the private library of his son, diesel engine scholar C. Lyle Cummins, Jr., in Lake Oswego, Oregon. Sources from this collection, which Lyle kindly made available to this project, are duly attributed.

By mutual agreement of the authors, Cummins, and the Harvard Business School Press, citations are as inobtrusive and lean as possible.

References to letters, memoranda, and reports within Cummins do not include the names of files and collections in which they reside. But in most cases, these are self-evident (e.g., a letter from W. G. Irwin dated 1924 would be found in Irwin's papers). Similarly, interview dates, listed in the following section, are not repeated in the endnotes. When interviewees are quoted directly and identified in the text, no endnote is supplied. All interviews were conducted by one or both of the authors unless indicated otherwise.

Interviews

Following is a list of individuals interviewed formally by the authors in the course of our research. Many other individuals not named here answered specific questions, either in person, in phone conversations, or through correspondence. The authors are indebted to them all.

Barr, Bob
January 24, 1994

Boll, Ray
July 23, 1993
August 2, 1993

Booth, Ed
May 11, 1995

Bottorff, Mary
November 3, 1995

Bowling, Conrad
November 7, 1996

Bridgewater, Evan
June 4, 1994

Brown, Harold
May 15, 1997

Bush, Ben
June 23, 1994

Butler, Joe
July 22, 1993

Chesnut, Mark
September 20, 1996
November 1, 1996

Cook, Syd
November 10, 1993

Cummins, Don
October 6, 1993

Cummins, Lyle
November 8, 1993

Dick, Joyce Tull
February 27, 1995

Dietrich, Marion
June 24, 1994

Edwards, Jack
January 31, 1995
September 30, 1996

Farrar, Jim
October 22, 1996

Feigenbaum, Val
November 26, 1996

Grace, Chuck
June 1, 1994

Gray, Hanna
March 20, 1997

Hackett, John
February 23, 1994

Hamilton, Peter
July 22, 1994

Harrison, Tom
January 25, 1994

Hawthorne, Bill
July 18, 1994

Henderson, Jim
July 22, 1993
April 18, 1994

June 23, 1994
December 14, 1994
February 27, 1995
March 13, 1995
July 10, 1995
September 9, 1996
October 23, 1996
November 7, 1996
January 7, 1997
January 8, 1997
April 25, 1997

Husmann, Larry
September 6, 1994

Jones, Phil
January 4, 1995

Kelly, Jim
October 22, 1996

Kuehner, Karl
October 21, 1996

Loughrey, Joe
November 2, 1995
November 8, 1996

Mack, Maynard
October 3, 1995

Marston, Ted
January 30, 1995
September 30, 1996

McCarthy, Walt
June 1, 1994

McGahan, Pat
June 1, 1994

McGovern, John
September 6, 1994

McLachlan, John
October 23, 1996
November 7, 1996

Miller, Irwin
October 26, 1993
May 31, 1994
December 15, 1994
December 16, 1994
November 3, 1995
April 22, 1996

Miller, Paul
October 19, 1994
March 20, 1997

Miller, Will
September 6, 1994

Miller, Xenia
November 10, 1995

Muntean, George
May 31, 1993

Neihart, Larry
June 24, 1994

Nelson, Gary
March 24, 1995
October 1, 1996

Newlin, George
July 23, 1993
June 24, 1994

O'Shaughnessy, Herschel
February 1, 1995

Perkins, Don
March 21, 1997

Powers, Chuck
February 17, 1995

Rowell, John
July 22, 1993

Schacht, Henry
July 22, 1993
September 7, 1993
September 7, 1994
October 6, 1994

Schwab, Bill
September 30, 1993

Shaw, Stanley
January 24, 1994

Shenk, Tom
November 10, 1993

Solso, Tim
January 4, 1995
November 11, 1995

Stewart, Robert
July 22, 1993

Stoner, Dick
August 18, 1993
July 21, 1994

Tajima, Art
May 9, 1995

Tangeman, Clementine
October 28, 1993

Temple, Ron
July 11, 1995

Thomas, Frank
March 28, 1997

Tucker, Randy
January 25, 1994

Vujovich, Tina
November 8, 1996

Notes

Chapter 1

1. "The top 50 U.S. industrial exporters," *Fortune* (August 22, 1994).
2. Cummins' struggles in the 1980s, particularly its efforts on behalf of its work force, are well summarized in Robert Levering and Milton Moskowitz, *The 100 Best Companies to Work For in America* (New York: Plume Books, 1993), 83–88.
3. Henry Schacht speech to the Harvard Business School Club of Central Indiana, 3/11/70.
4. Rennie Atterbury III letter to Steven L. Zeller, 10/27/94.
5. Howard H. Stevenson interview, 8/14/95.
6. Tim Solso interview, 1/4/95.
7. J. Irwin Miller interview, 11/3/95.
8. See, for example, Charles R. Morris' excellent profile of the Cummins strategy, and its detractors, in his *The Coming Global Boom* (New York: Bantam Books, 1989).
9. See Robert S. Eckley's *Global Competition in Capital Goods: an American Perspective* (New York: Quorum Books, 1992), ch. 7.
10. Tom Shenk interview, 11/10/93.
11. John H. McArthur interview, 7/26/95.
12. See, for example, "The Cummins Engine Company in the Soviet Union," Harvard Business School Case #9-389-018, which includes a summary of Cummins' activities in South Africa in the late 1970s, and the company's 1/25/88 draft policy statement on South Africa.
13. Levering and Moskowitz, *The 100 Best Companies to Work For in America*, 88.

Chapter 2

1. Cummins Engine Company, meeting of incorporators and prospective stockholders, 2/20/19. The details of the company's organization are explored in greater detail later in this chapter.
2. Joseph A. Schumpeter, *Capitalism, Socialism, and Democracy*, 2nd ed. (New York: Harper & Brothers Publishers, 1947), 132. See also Schumpeter, "The Creative Response in Economic History," *Journal of Economic History* 7 (November 1947): 149–59.
3. Stephen S. Visher, *Economic Geography of Indiana* (New York: D. Appleton and Company, 1923), 95, 102; George Rogers Taylor, *The Transportation Revolution, 1815–1860* (New York: M.E. Sharpe, Inc., 1951), 25–26, 47–48; Clifton J. Phillips, *Indiana in Transition: The Emergence of an Industrial Commonwealth, 1880–1920* (Indianapolis: Indiana Historical Bureau, 1968), 224, 229.
4. Glen A. Blackburn, "Interurban Railroads of Indiana," *Indiana Magazine of History* 20 (September 1924): 221–26, 246–48; Fred B. Hiatt, "Development of Interurbans in Indiana," *Indiana Magazine of History* 5, March 1909, 122–23; and George W. Hilton and John F. Due, *Electric Interurban Railways in America* (Stanford: Stanford University Press, 1960), 26–27, 41–42, 279–80.
5. Hilton and Due, *Electric Interurban Railways*, 3, 208–51.

6. Howard H. Peckham, *Indiana: A Bicentennial History* (New York: Norton, 1978), 111–12; James H. Madison, *Indiana through Tradition and Change: A History of the Hoosier State and Its People, 1920–1945* (Indianapolis: Indiana Historical Society, 1982), 208.

7. Charles W. Boas, "Locational Patterns of American Automobile Assembly Plants, 1895–1958," *Economic Geography* 37 (July 1961) 218–30; Wallace Spencer Huffman, "Indiana's Place in Automobile History," *Indiana History Bulletin* 44 (February 1967): 11–44. See also Clessie L. Cummins, *My Days with the Diesel* (Philadelphia: Chilton, 1967), 39–40.

8. Madison, *Tradition and Change*, 30–32, 232; James H. Madison, *The Indiana Way: A State History* (Bloomington 1986), 274–75.

9. Bartholomew County Historical Society, "City of Columbus and Bartholomew County," one-page history on file at the BCHS, n.d.; Robert M. Taylor, et al., *Indiana: A New Historical Guide* (Indianapolis: Indiana Historical Society, 1989), 351.

10. BCHS, "City of Columbus"; BCHS, *History of Bartholomew County*, 141–45; Taylor, et al., *Indiana*, 351–52.

11. William Marsh, *I Discover Columbus* (Oklahoma City, Oklahoma: University of Oklahoma Press, 1956), 158–62; BCHS, *History of Bartholomew County*, 159–60.

12. BCHS, "City of Columbus"; BCHS, *History of Bartholomew County*, 158–61; Marsh, *I Discover Columbus*, 158–62; Taylor, et al., *Indiana*, 353.

13. Visher, *Economic Geography*, 174–81.

14. Visher, *Economic Geography*, 187.

15. Taylor, *Indiana*, 351, 353; BCHS, *History of Bartholomew County*, 159; Marsh, *I Discover Columbus*, 158; Visher, *Economic Geography of Indiana*, 182–85.

16. Gabriel E. Miller, *History of Bartholomew County, Indiana* (Chicago, 1888), 705.

17. Miller, *History of Bartholomew County*, 705; "Joseph Ireland Irwin," in *National Cyclopedia of American Biography*, vol. 33 (New York: J. T. White, 1947), 472; Irwin Family Tree, supplied to the authors by the J. Irwin Miller family. Although Miller states that Joseph Oliver Irwin first settled in Bullitt County, Kentucky, after the Revolutionary War, the *National Cyclopedia*, a less detailed and probably less reliable source on this matter, indicates the site as Westmoreland County, Pennsylvania, near Greensburg.

18. Richard H. Gemmecke, "W. G. Irwin and Hugh Thomas Miller: A Study in Free Enterprise in Indiana" (Ph.D. diss., Indiana University, 1955), 2.

19. BCHS, *History of Bartholomew County, Indiana*, 146.

20. Gemmecke, "W. G. Irwin," 11.

21. Gemmecke, "W. G. Irwin," 11.

22. *Columbus Evening Republican*, 8/14/1900.

23. David E. Harrell, Jr., "Disciples of Christ," in Mircea Eliade, ed., *The Encyclopedia of Religion*, vol. 4 (New York: Scribner, 1987), 364–66; David E. Harrell, Jr., "Restorationism and the Stone-Campbell Tradition," in Charles H. Lippy and Peter W. Williams, eds., *Encyclopedia of the American Religious Experience*, vol. II (New York: Scribner, 1988), 845–58.

24. J. Irwin Miller, "To the M5," typescript, n.d.

25. J. Irwin Miller interview, 10/26/93.

26. J. Irwin Miller interview, 10/26/93.

27. Gemmecke, "W. G. Irwin," 18.

28. *Columbus Evening Republican*, November 15, 1911; Gemmecke, "W. G. Irwin," 27.

29. Much of this section is based on Cummins, *My Days with the Diesel*. Supplementary sources are indicated.

30. Gemmecke, "W. G. Irwin," 209.

31. Fifty-three percent of white males in America were enrolled in school in 1900, sixty-one percent in 1910. The earliest years for which school retention rates are available are 1924–1925, when 7.4 out of 10 students finished the eighth grade. Retention rates have increased steadily every year since, suggesting a much lower rate in 1904. U.S. Bureau of the Census, *Historical Statistics of the United States, Colonial Times to 1970*, vol. 1 (Washington, D.C., 1975), 370, 379.

32. J. Irwin Miller interview, 10/26/93; Clementine Tangeman interview, 10/28/93; Don Cummins interview, 10/6/93.

33. Lyle Cummins interview, 11/8/93.

34. Gemmecke, "W. G. Irwin," 215.

35. *Columbus Evening Republican*, 4/16/15 and 12/26/16; Don Cummins interview, 10/6/93.

36. Gemmecke, "W. G. Irwin," 216–17.

37. *Columbus Evening Republican*, 1/7/26.

38. BCHS, *History of Bartholomew County*, 159; *Columbus Evening Republican*, 1/7/26; W. G. Irwin, untitled typescript history of the Cummins Engine Company, c. 1948. Hereafter cited as Irwin, "History."

39. Donald E. Thomas, Jr., *Diesel: Technology and Society in Industrial Germany* (Tuscaloosa, Alabama: University of Alabama Press, 1987), 4, 9–10.

40. Lynwood Bryant, "The Development of the Diesel Engine," *Technology and Culture* 17 (July 1976): 434–35; C. Lyle Cummins, Jr., *Diesel's Engine*, vol. 1, *From Conception to 1918* (Wilsonville, Oregon: Carnot Press, 1994), 308.

41. Bryant, "Development of the Diesel Engine," 439.

42. Bryant, "Development of the Diesel Engine," 434–35; Thomas, *Diesel*, 92, 201.

43. C. Lyle Cummins, Jr., *Internal Fire* (Lake Oswego, Oregon, 1976), 304.

44. The manuscript originally was published in German under the title *Theorie und Konstruktion eines rationellen Wärmemotors*; the English–language version came out in 1893. Bryant, "Development of the Diesel Engine," 435–36; Richard H. Lytle, "Introduction of Diesel Power in the United States, 1897–1912," *Business History Review* 42 (Summer 1968): 116–17.

45. Lytle, "Introduction of Diesel Power in the United States," 117; Bryant, "Development of the Diesel Engine," 439; Cummins, *Internal Fire*, 312, 314.

46. Thomas, *Diesel*, 201. On the rise of scientific theory in physics see Ronald Kline, *Steinmetz: Engineer and Socialist* (Baltimore: Johns Hopkins University Press, 1992). For a comparative overview of German industry and technical education see Alfred D. Chandler, Jr., *Scale and Scope: The Dynamics of Industrial Capitalism* (Cambridge, Mass.: The Belknap Press of Harvard University Press, 1990).

47. Bryant, "Development of the Diesel Engine," 432–33, 440; Lytle, "Introduction of Diesel Power in the United States," 117; Thomas, *Diesel*, 22–23, 33, 201–2; Cummins, *Internal Fire*, 321, 324.

48. Lytle, "Introduction of Diesel Power in the United States," 118; Bryant, "Development of the Diesel Engine," 440; Cummins, *Internal Fire*, 326–27.

49. Cummins, *Internal Fire*, 231; Lytle, "Introduction of Diesel Power in the United States," 116.

50. Cummins, *Diesel's Engine*, 230–34; Lytle, "Introduction of Diesel Power in the United States," 118–19; Thomas, *Diesel*, 21.

51. Lytle, "Introduction of Diesel Power in the United States," 119–20.

52. Bryant, "Development of the Diesel Engine," 442–43.

53. Thomas, *Diesel*, 24; Lytle, "Introduction of Diesel Power in the United States," 122.

54. Lytle, "Introduction of Diesel Power in the United States," 122–24.

55. Lytle, "Introduction of Diesel Power in the United States," 124–32; Cummins, *Diesel's Engine*, 298.

56. Lytle, "Introduction of Diesel Power in the United States," 132–41.

57. Lytle, "Introduction of Diesel Power in the United States," 141–42.

58. Thomas, *Diesel*, 35–36; Bryant, "Development of the Diesel Engine," 433.

59. Bryant, "Development of the Diesel Engine," 444. See also Thomas, *Diesel*, 203.

60. Bryant, "Development of the Diesel Engine," 443.

61. Bryant, "Development of the Diesel Engine," 445; Trevor I. Williams, *A Short History of Twentieth Century Technology* (New York: Oxford University Press, 1982), 164.

62. Williams, *Twentieth Century Technology*, 164; William Manchester, *The Arms of Krupp, 1587–1968* (Boston: Little, Brown and Company, 1968), 254; Thomas, *Diesel*, 205–8.

63. Lytle, "Introduction of Diesel Power in the United States," 134.

64. Cummins, *Diesel's Engine*, 385; Bryant, "Development of the Diesel Engine," 439.

65. In addition, the Brons engine differed from Diesel's later engine design in at least two significant ways: It did not operate at constant pressure and did not require air injection. Cummins, *Diesel's Engine*, 395.

66. Cummins, *Diesel's Engine*, 388–90.

67. It was then, with this move from Delfzijl to Appingedam, that the company took on the name N.N. Appingedammer Bronsmotorenfabriek.

68. Cummins, *Diesel's Engine*, 390–94.

69. Cummins, *Diesel's Engine*, 398, 400.

70. Cummins, *Diesel's Engine*, 398–400.

71. Shareholders' minutes, 4/21/25.

72. *Columbus Evening Republican*, 7/21/15.

73. Hans L. Knudsen, "History and the Development of Cummins Engine," typescript, n.d. Hereafter cited as Knudsen, "History."

74. Cummins, *Diesel's Engine*, 400.

75. Clessie L. Cummins, "History of the Cummins Engine Company, Inc. (to April 1939)," typescript, n.d. Hereafter cited as Cummins, "History."

76. Shareholders' minutes, 4/21/25.

77. Shareholders' minutes, 4/21/25.

78. *Columbus Evening Republican*, 5/26/19.

79. Cummins, *My Days with the Diesel*, 79.

80. Shareholders' minutes, 4/21/25.

81. Schumpeter, "Creative Response in Economic History," 152.

82. By coincidence, the Cummins organization meeting followed by a month a similar meeting in Indianapolis at which the Indianapolis Air Pump Company was born. This company—later called Noblitt-Sparks Industries Inc., and still later Arvin Industries Inc.—relocated to Columbus in 1931, and was a much more significant force in the local economy than Cummins for many years.

    Ed. L. Voelz, one of the original directors and incorporators, was not reelected. Cummins, Snider, Dunlap, Northway, and Richman were elected as directors at the first meeting, but resigned in February, at which time Bottorff joined the board. Meeting of incorporators and prospective stockholders, 2/20/19; board minutes, 2/21/19 and 3/4/19.

83. Irwin, "History."

84. Meeting of incorporators and prospective stockholders, 2/20/19; Cummins, *My Days with the Diesel*, 80.

85. Board minutes, 3/4/19 and 4/11/19.

86. *Columbus Evening Republican*, May 26, 1919; Cummins, "History."

87. Shareholders' minutes, 4/21/25.
88. Boris Emmet and John E. Jeuck, *Catalogues and Counters: A History of Sears, Roebuck and Company* (Chicago: University of Chicago Press, 1950), passim; Knudsen, "History."
89. Hercules Gas Engine Company prospectus, 1/1/20. The Hercules sales figure is for the year ending 5/3/19; John W. Rowell, "The way we were: making it in the '20s"; Cummins, *My Days with the Diesel*, 83. In his "History," Knudsen states that "Tippert [sic] and McMullen came to Columbus" to discuss the Sears contract with Irwin and Cummins. This account differs from Clessie's firsthand account and from evidence in surviving correspondence cited here.
90. Cummins, *My Days with the Diesel*, 83; Quentin Noblitt letter to W. G. Irwin, 10/14/19; Clessie Cummins letter to W. G. Irwin, 4/1/21; W. G. Irwin letter to Quentin Noblitt, 10/16/19.
91. W. G. Irwin letter to Quentin Noblitt, 10/16/19; board minutes, 10/25/19; shareholders' minutes, 11/7/19.
92. Shareholders' minutes, 1/21/20; T. E. Hallman letter to W. G. Irwin, 10/17/19; W.G Irwin letter to Vonnegut Machinery, 10/18/19; Atlas Drop Forge letter to W. M. Tippett, 12/22/19; W. G. Irwin letter to Atlas Drop Forge, 12/27/19.
93. *Columbus Evening Republican*, 10/28/19, 5/10/20, 8/14/20, and 12/20/20; board minutes, 6/5/20.
94. Cummins, *My Days with the Diesel*, 85; shareholders' minutes, 4/21/25; B. F. Watson letter to W. M. Tippett, 9/30/20.
95. B. F. Watson letter to W. M. Tippett, 9/30/20.
96. E. B. Blakely letter to W. M. Tippett, 9/30/20.
97. W. M. Tippett letter to W. G. Irwin, 10/20/20.
98. H. E. Daniel letter to W. G. Irwin, 4/21/21.
99. Cummins, "History."
100. Emmet and Jeuck, *Catalogues and Counters*, passim; Cummins, *My Days with the Diesel*, 84–85.
101. Cummins, *My Days with the Diesel*, 85–88; Emmet and Jeuck, *Catalogues and Counters*, 87.
102. Cummins, *My Days with the Diesel*, 86.
103. Shareholders' minutes, 4/21/25.
104. Emmet and Jeuck, *Catalogues and Counters*, 196–208; Harry N. Scheiber, Harold G. Vatter, and Harold U. Faulkner, *American Economic History* (New York: Harper & Row, 1976), 333–34.
105. Shareholders' minutes, 4/21/25.
106. Shareholders' minutes, 4/21/25.
107. Clessie Cummins letter to W. G. Irwin, 7/22/21.
108. Clessie Cummins letter to W. G. Irwin, 7/22/21; U.S. patent number 1,557,143, 10/13/25 (application filed 9/27/21).
109. Shareholders' minutes, 4/21/25.
110. Irwin "History."
111. Knudsen, "History"; Cummins, *Diesel's Engine*, 466.
112. Knudsen, "History."
113. Knudsen, "History."
114. Shareholders' minutes, 4/21/25.
115. J. Irwin Miller supports this interpretation in a 1967 report, in which he states that "once the Hvid license agreement was terminated, interest in OEDC languished." Cummins Engine Company, "Financial History," Document 3, 1/23/67.
116. J. Irwin Miller, "History and Present Operations of Cummins Engine Co., Oil Engine Development Co.," 10/31/41 in Cummins Engine Company, "Financial History," Document 5, Exhibit F.
117. Clessie Cummins letter to W. G. Irwin, 2/26/29.
118. Clessie Cummins letter to W. G. Irwin, 6/11/22.
119. *Columbus Evening Republican*, 6/23/22; Cummins, "History."
120. W. G. Irwin letter to Clessie Cummins, 6/13/21.
121. Gemmecke, "W. G. Irwin," 232; H. L. Knudsen interview with C. Lyle Cummins, Jr., 8/24/72; Cummins, "History"; Clessie Cummins letter to W. G. Irwin, 8/22/23.
122. Clessie Cummins letter to W. G. Irwin, 7/31/22; Don Cummins interview, 10/6/93; Knudsen "History"; H. L. Knudsen interview with C. Lyle Cummins, Jr., 8/24/72.
123. Gemmecke, "W. G. Irwin," 233–34; Cummins, "History."
124. Cummins, "History."
125. *Columbus Evening Republican*, 4/23/24.
126. Cummins, *My Days with the Diesel*, 96–97; Clessie Cummins letter to W. G. Irwin, 4/26/24.
127. Clessie Cummins letter to W. G. Irwin, 4/26/24; W. G. Irwin letter to Clessie Cummins, 5/1/24.
128. J. Irwin Miller memo on the "proposed recapitalization of Cummins Engine Company" to the Executive Committee, 9/29/45, OEDC historical file. See also Edwin Crouch's 9/2/47 memo entitled, "Preferred Capital Stock of the Company Issued Since Organization," OEDC historical file.
129. Clessie Cummins letter to W. G. Irwin, 8/24/25.
130. Clessie Cummins letter to W. G. Irwin, 8/31/25.
131. Thomas G. Marx, "Technological Change and the Theory of the Firm: The American Locomotive Industry, 1920–1955," *Business History Review* 50 (Spring 1976): 2–3.
132. *Columbus Evening Republican*, 1/7/26.

133. *Columbus Evening Republican*, 10/22/25.
134. The moving of equipment began December 21, 1925, and limited operations in the new facility probably began the following month. *Columbus Evening Republican*, 11/11/25, 11/18/25, 12/22/25, and 1/7/26.
135. W. G. Irwin letter to R. A. Millholland, 11/21/25.
136. R. A. Millholland memo to Clessie Cummins, 8/24/26.
137. Clessie Cummins letter to W. G. Irwin, 8/26/26.
138. C. Lyle Cummins, Jr., interview, 4/27/93; Gemmecke, "W. G. Irwin," 238.
139. Gemmecke, "W. G. Irwin," 239.
140. C. Lyle Cummins, Jr., interview, 4/27/93.
141. Frank Richman letter to Clessie Cummins, 8/9/26; Clessie Cummins letter to W. G. Irwin, 9/6/27.
142. Clessie Cummins letter to W. G. Irwin, 9/6/27.
143. Clessie Cummins letter to W. G. Irwin, 6/9/27; Cummins, *My Days with the Diesel*, 104–5; W. G. Irwin letter to L. M. Wainwright, 3/23/28.
144. *Columbus Evening Republican*, 1/26/27; Cummins, "History."
145. Clessie Cummins letter to W. G. Irwin, 1/1/26; Clessie Cummins letter to W. G. Irwin, 12/9/27.
146. *Columbus Evening Republican*, 5/28/29.
147. A. E. LeBlanc memo to Clessie Cummins, 12/28/28.
148. "Cummins Engine Company Sales and Profits; Irwin–Sweeney–Miller Advances," document on file in the Cummins corporate archive.
149. J. Irwin Miller memo to the Executive Committee, 9/29/45.
150. Clessie Cummins letter to W. G. Irwin, 8/28/28.
151. Clessie Cummins letter to W. G. Irwin, 7/24/28.
152. O. D. Treiber letter to W. G. Irwin, 9/28/27; W. G. Irwin letter to O. D. Treiber, 10/3/27.
153. Clessie Cummins letter to W. G. Irwin, 2/26/29.
154. W. G. Irwin letter to P. J. Shouvlin, 5/20/26; Clessie Cummins letter to W. G. Irwin, 12/1/26.
155. Clessie Cummins letter to W. G. Irwin, 8/26/27.
156. Clessie Cummins letter to W. G. Irwin, 8/27/29.
157. *Columbus Evening Republican*, 10/14/29 and 10/24/29.
158. Thomas, *Diesel*, 210; Marx, "Technological Change," 9; Cummins, *My Days with the Diesel*, 105–6.
159. *Columbus Evening Republican*, 5/26/19.
160. Thomas, *Diesel*, 211.
161. *Columbus Evening Republican*, 11/11/25.
162. Clessie Cummins letter to W. G. Irwin, 9/3/25.
163. Clessie Cummins letter to W. G. Irwin, 4/7/30.
164. W. G. Irwin letter to M. R. Denison, 4/15/30.
165. M. R. Denison letter to W. G. Irwin, 4/18/30.
166. Cummins, *My Days with the Diesel*, 112.
167. Cummins, *My Days with the Diesel*, 114–15.
168. Gemmecke, "W. G. Irwin," 225.

Chapter 3

1. Clessie L. Cummins, *My Days with the Diesel* (Philadelphia: Chilton Books, 1967), 8–9, 19.
2. Clessie L. Cummins, "History of the Cummins Engine Company, Inc. (to April 1939)," typescript, n.d. Hereafter cited as Cummins, "History."
3. James J. Flink, *America Adopts the Automobile, 1895–1910* (Cambridge, Mass.: MIT Press, 1970), 12–23.
4. Flink, *America Adopts the Automobile*, 25, 36–42.
5. Flink, *America Adopts the Automobile*, 42, 45; Robert Lacey, *Ford: The Men and the Machine* (New York: Ballantine Books, 1986), 55–61; James J. Flink, *The Automobile Age* (Cambridge, Mass.: MIT Press, 1988), 53.
6. Flink, *America Adopts the Automobile*, 47–49.
7. W. G. Irwin letter to Kent Cooper, 12/28/29; W. F. Brooks letter to W. G. Irwin, 12/31/29; John Rowell, manuscript of an unpublished history of the Cummins Engine Company, ch. 8, 3, Cummins inactive records; hereafter cited as Rowell, "History"; Cummins, *My Days with the Diesel*, 9–10.
8. *Columbus Evening Republican*, 1/4/30, 1/6/30, and 1/1/30; Cummins, *My Days with the Diesel*, 10–11. According to a *Columbus Evening Republican* story published 1/29/30, Clessie's traveling companions on the Indianapolis to New York trip were Knudsen and Don Cummins.
9. Cummins, *My Days with the Diesel*, 12–14; *Columbus Evening Republican*, 1/6/30.
10. Clessie's autobiography states he arrived at the hotel "exactly two minutes before 4 PM" (*My Days with the Diesel*, 14). But a more reliable, contemporary source is the *Columbus Evening Republican*, which published a detailed letter on January 30, 1930, written by Abe LeBlanc the week of Clessie's return.
11. Cummins, *My Days with the Diesel*, 14–15; William F. Sturm, "A Diesel Drives an Automobile," *Scientific American* (May 1930): 383.

12. Cummins, *My Days with the Diesel*, 15–17; *Columbus Evening Republican*, 1/8/30 and 1/29/30.
13. Cummins, *My Days with the Diesel*, 18–19.
14. *Columbus Evening Republican*, 1/22/30 and 1/30/30.
15. Cummins, *My Days with the Diesel*, 19–20.
16. Strum, "A Diesel Drives an Automobile," 383; Cummins, *My Days with the Diesel*, 22–23.
17. *Columbus Evening Republican*, 1/22/30.
18. Cummins, *My Days with the Diesel*, 24–27.
19. Cummins, *My Days with the Diesel*, 30–31; *Columbus Evening Republican*, 1/25/30 and 1/29/30.
20. Sturm, "A Diesel Drives an Automobile," 382–83.
21. *Columbus Evening Republican*, 2/27/30; Cummins, *My Days with the Diesel*, 111.
22. *Columbus Evening Republican*, 2/27/30 and 3/5/30; Cummins, *My Days with the Diesel*, 111; Cummins film archive, Communications Department, Cummins Engine Company corporate headquarters, Columbus, Indiana.
23. Cummins, *My Days with the Diesel*, 111–12; *Columbus Evening Republican*, 3/21/30.
24. Cummins, *My Days with the Diesel*, 116–17; *Columbus Evening Republican*, 1/21/31, 1/31/31, and 2/3/31.
25. Cummins, *My Days with the Diesel*, 117–18; *Columbus Evening Republican*, 3/31/31; "Rolled His Own," *Business Week* (March 11, 1931): 8.
26. *Columbus Evening Republican*, 3/31/31; Edward V. Rickenbacker, *Rickenbacker* (Englewood Cliffs, N.J.: Prentice Hall, 1967), 151, 153, 157.
27. *Columbus Evening Republican*, 2/17/31; Cummins, *My Days with the Diesel*, 119–20, 123.
28. Cummins, *My Days with the Diesel*, 120–23.
29. Cummins, *My Days with the Diesel*, 123–24; Wilbur Shaw, *Gentlemen, Start Your Engines* (New York: Coward-McCann, 1955), 140–43, 203; Brock Yates, *The Indianapolis 500: The Story of a Motor Speedway* (New York: Harper, 1961), 4–5, 10–11.
30. Cummins, *My Days with the Diesel*, 123–25. Clessie says they placed twelfth, but a couple of days after the race AAA officials rechecked the race results and set the diesel car back one place. *Columbus Evening Republican*, 6/2/31.
31. *Columbus Evening Republican*, 6/1/31; Cummins, *My Days with the Diesel*, 125–26.
32. James A. Thomas, *The Long Haul: Truckers, Truck Stops, and Trucking* (Memphis: Memphis State University Press, 1979), 15, 35; "An American Diesel-Engined Truck," *Scientific American* (February 1931): 123; Cummins, *My Days with the Diesel*, 128–29.
33. Cummins, *My Days with the Diesel*, 128–30.
34. Thomas, *The Long Haul*, 35; Cummins, *My Days with the Diesel*, 130.
35. Cummins, *My Days with the Diesel*, 130–32.
36. Cummins, *My Days with the Diesel*, 132–33; *Columbus Evening Republican*, 9/9/31.
37. *Columbus Evening Republican*, 11/19/31.
38. Cummins, *My Days with the Diesel*, 135–36; *Columbus Evening Republican*, 12/11/31, 12/16/31, and 12/23/31.
39. Cummins, *My Days with the Diesel*, 136–38.
40. Cummins, *My Days with the Diesel*, 139; *Columbus Evening Republican*, 12/19/31.
41. *Columbus Evening Republican*, 12/23/31 and 12/28/31; Cummins, *My Days with the Diesel*, 140–41.
42. Cummins, *My Days with the Diesel*, 142–43; *Columbus Evening Republican*, 12/28/31.
43. Harry Lindsey letter to W. G. Irwin, including lists of "Cummins Foreign [Patent] Cases, March 1930; Clessie Cummins letter to W. G. Irwin, 6/29/31.
44. W. G. Irwin letter to Harry W. Lindsey, 3/14/30, cited in Rowell, "History," ch. 8, 6.
45. W. G. Irwin letter to Charles T. Boyer, 10/29/31.
46. Senior Zerbi (Fiat, Torino) letters to W. G. Irwin, 11/11/31 and 12/17/31; W. G. Irwin letter to André Citroën (Paris), 12/28/1931; André Citroën letter to W. G. Irwin, 1/23/32.
47. A. J. Yeats letters to W. G. Irwin, 10/26/31, 11/12/31, and 2/6/32; W. G. Irwin to A. J. Yeats, 10/27/31.
48. A. J. Yeats letter to W. G. Irwin, 12/11/31; Flink, *The Automobile Age*, 252–58.
49. A. J. Yeats letter to W. G. Irwin, 10/26/31; W. G. Irwin letters to A. J. Yeats, 10/27/31 and 1/5/32.
50. A. J. Yeats letter to W. G. Irwin, 2/6/32; Cummins, *My Days with the Diesel*, 145.
51. Cummins, *My Days with the Diesel*, 145–46; *Columbus Evening Republican*, 4/13/32 and 7/6/32.
52. Cummins, *My Days with the Diesel*, 146–55.
53. Cummins, *My Days with the Diesel*, 150.
54. Cummins, *My Days with the Diesel*, 156; *Columbus Evening Republican*, 11/5/32.
55. Cummins, *My Days with the Diesel*, 156–57; *Columbus Evening Republican*, 11/12/32 and 11/14/32.
56. Cummins, *My Days with the Diesel*, 157–58.
57. Joseph Geschelin, "Cummins Diesel Test Bus makes Coast-to-Coast Trip," *Automotive Industries* (December 17, 1932), from unpaginated reprint.
58. "The Diesel Engine," *Science-Supplement* (October 21, 1932): 8–9; "The Triumph of the Diesel," *Popular Mechanics* (July 1934): 10–13; Phillip H. Smith, "Diesels Stride Ahead," *Scientific American* (December 1934): 285, 287; "Diesel into Auburn," *Time* (July 1, 1935): 24.
59. "A Bourgeois Engine," *Fortune* (June 1930): 64ff; "Diesels on Wheels, *Fortune* (December 1934): 106ff.
60. C. Lyle Cummins interview, 11/8/93.
61. "Diesel Sales Mount," *Business Week* (February 9, 1935): 24.

62. Albert J. Churella, "Corporate Response to Technological Change: The American Railway Locomotive Industry in the Twentieth Century" Ph.D. diss., Ohio State University, 1994, 69–90; "Diesels, 1938, and what's ahead for them," *Business Week* (April 16, 1938): 44.

63. W. G. Irwin letter to Fred W. Amend, 11/26/32.

64. John W. Rowell, "The 30s: From 50 engines a year to 50 a month," *Power Team* (July–August 1979): 5–7; Cummins, *My Days with the Diesel*, 159–60.

65. *Columbus Evening Republican*, 7/24/34 and 1/4/35.

66. Rowell, "The 30s," 6; "Diesel Sales Mount," 24; Stuart W. Leslie, *Boss Kettering* (New York, 1983), 267–70.

67. Rowell, "The 30s," 6; Cummins, *My Days with the Diesel*, 159.

68. Newell K. Chamberlin, "What about Diesel Power?" *Review of Reviews* (August 1935): 47; "Diesels, 1938, and what's ahead for them," 44; Thomas G. Marx, "Technological Change and the Theory of the Firm: The American Locomotive Industry, 1920–1955," *Business History Review* 50 (Spring 1976): 9.

69. Marx, "Technological Change and the Theory of the Firm," 9.

70. J. Irwin Miller interview, 10/26/93.

71. J. Irwin Miller interview, 10/26/93; Richard H. Gemmecke, "W. G. Irwin and Hugh Thomas Miller: A Study in Free Enterprise in Indiana" (Ph.D. diss., Indiana University, 1955), 331–33.

72. W. G. Irwin letter to H. C. Blake, 5/17/30.

73. Maynard Mack interview, 10/3/95.

74. J. Irwin Miller interview with Jim Henderson, 5/25/93.

75. Edward P. White telephone interview, 10/5/95.

76. Maynard Mack interview, 10/3/95. Miller's entry in the Yale 1931 yearbook also notes that "J. I. is planning to go into business after graduation."

77. J. Irwin Miller interview with Jim Henderson, 5/25/93.

78. "A Bourgeois Engine."

79. "The Use of Diesel Engines," *Science-Supplement* (November 6, 1931): 12–13.

80. Smith, "Diesels Stride Ahead," 287; "Diesels on Wheels," 114, 116.

81. "Diesel Sales Mount," 23.

82. "The Fortieth Anniversary of Diesel Power," *Science* (November 27, 1936): 497–98.

83. "Diesels, 1938, and what's ahead for them," 43, 46; "Diesels on Wheels," 106.

84. "Diesels, 1938, and what's ahead for them," 43.

85. "Diesels, 1938, and what's ahead for them," 45.

86. Meyer H. Fishbein, "The Trucking Industry and the National Recovery Administration," *Social Forces* 34 (December 1955): 171.

87. Thomas, *The Long Haul*, 3.

88. Thomas, *The Long Haul*, 27, 58–59.

89. Thomas, *The Long Haul*, 99; Anthony F. Herbst and Joseph S. K. Wu, "Some Evidence of Subsidization: The U.S. Trucking Industry, 1900–1920," *Journal of Economic History* 33 (June 1973): 417.

90. Harold Barger, *The Transportation Industries, 1889–1946: A Study of Output, Employment, and Productivity* (New York: National Bureau of Economic Research, 1951), 221–42.

91. Barger, *Transportation Industries*, 225–27; Fishbein, "Trucking Industry," 171.

92. Thomas, *The Long Haul*, 62–64, 92, 132–34.

93. Thomas, *The Long Haul*, 45–71.

94. William R. Childs, *Trucking and the Public Interest: The Emergence of Federal Regulation, 1914–1940* (Knoxville, Tenn: University of Tennessee Press, 1985), 52.

95. Thomas, *The Long Haul*, 102–8.

96. F. L. Paxton, "The Highway Movement," *American Historical Review* 51 (January 1946): 236–53; Thomas, *The Long Haul*, 37–41.

97. Herbst and Wu, "Some Evidence of Subsidization," 417–33.

98. Unless otherwise noted, the sources for this section are a typed reminiscence by Paris Letsinger, apparently derived from an interview with Waldo Harrison (hereafter cited as Letsinger, "History"); and John Rowell's unpublished history of Cummins Engine Company, Chapter X, "The breakthrough in trucks," which draws on Letsinger's oral history and Rowell's own research and interviews.

99. Paris Letsinger interview with John Rowell, n.d.

100. Ray Boll interview, 8/9/93.

101. Richard Meehan interview with John Rowell, n.d.

102. Letsinger, "History."

103. Letsinger, "History."

104. Smith, "Diesels Stride Ahead," 288.

105. "G.M.'s Diesel Plans," *Business Week* (May 1, 1937), 41; "G.M.'s Diesel Plans," *Business Week* (January 22, 1938): 18; "Fiddle," *Time* (January 31, 1938): 52; Reginald M. Cleveland, "The Diesel Broadens its Field," *Scientific American* (April 1938): 213–14.

106. John Niven letter to W. G. Irwin, 8/29/30.

107. Stanley Shaw interview, 1/24/94; John W. Rowell, "From the Depression to war, and how employees organized," *Power Team* (September–October 1979): 7.

108. See Robert S. McElvaine, *The Great Depression: America, 1929–1941* (New York: Times Books, 1984), 22–23; and Sidney Ratner, James H. Soltow, and Richard Sylla, *The Evolution of the American Economy*, 2d ed. (New York: Macmillan Publishing Company, 1993), 464.

109. McElvaine, *Great Depression*, 225–28, 258–59; Ratner et al., *Evolution of the American Economy*, 477–78.

110. Ratner et al., *Evolution of the American Economy*, 478; Melvyn Dubofsky and Warren Van Tine, "John L. Lewis and the Triumph of Mass-Production Unionism," in Dubofsky and Van Tine, eds., *Labor Leaders in America* (Urbana, 1987), 185–206.

111. The meeting, including the entire text of J. Irwin Miller's address referred to below, were reported in the *Columbus Evening Republican*, 5/22/37.

112. *Columbus Evening Republican*, 5/22/37; Stanley Shaw interview, 1/24/94.

113. *Columbus Evening Republican*, 5/27/37.

114. *Columbus Evening Republican*, 6/22/37 and 6/24/37.

115. See T. George Harris, "Egghead in the Diesel Industry," *Fortune* (October 1957): 268.

116. *Columbus Evening Republican*, 6/26/37 and 6/29/37.

117. *Columbus Evening Republican*, 6/30/37 and 7/1/37.

118. *Columbus Evening Republican*, 7/1/37, 7/7/37, and 7/8/37.

119. *Columbus Evening Republican*, 7/17/37.

120. *Columbus Evening Republican*, 3/17/38.

121. *Columbus Evening Republican*, 4/21/38, 8/13/38, and 10/15/38.

122. *Columbus Evening Republican*, 10/15/38; Miller reflected on his 1930s labor views two decades later in a speech at Dartmouth, "The Responsibilities of Management," reprinted in *Dartmouth Alumni Magazine* (March 1956).

123. Clessie Cummins letter to W. G. Irwin, 8/15/32.

124. Paris E. Letsinger memo to J. Irwin Miller, 11/7/37; Paris E. Letsinger letter to W. G. Irwin, 11/7/37.

125. Paris E. Letsinger memo to J. Irwin Miller, 7/2/37.

126. J. Irwin Miller, "Thoughts for Tomorrow's Managers," the third Lubbock Lecture on Management, delivered at Oxford University 5/9/83.

127. J. Irwin Miller memo to Clessie Cummins, W. G. Irwin, and V. E. McMullen, 4/6/36. This was one of the first substantive memos written by General Manager Miller.

128. J. Irwin Miller memo to Clessie Cummins and W. G. Irwin, 9/18/37.

129. Clessie Cummins letter to W. G. Irwin, 9/23/37.

130. Memo from the five named executives to C. L. Cummins and W. G. Irwin, 7/3/39.

131. Clessie Cummins letter to the five signatories of the precipitating memo, 7/21/39.

132. W. G. Irwin letter to Clessie Cummins, 7/24/39, C. Lyle Cummins private library. Evidently, Irwin's hand-written letters from Canada were not copied, since this letter is not represented in the Irwin microfilm.

133. C. Lyle Cummins interview, 11/8/93.

134. W. G. Irwin letter to Morris O. Johnson, 6/12/35.

Chapter 4

1. J. Irwin Miller, "History and Present Operations of Cummins Engine Co. [and] Oil Engine Development Co." in "Request for Closing Agreement" submitted to the Internal Revenue Service (n.d.).

2. Edwin G. Crouch and Merle H. Miller, "Request for Closing Agreement by Cummins Engine Company, Oil Engine Development Company, and their Stockholders," addressed to the Honorable Guy T. Hervering, Commissioner of Internal Revenue, 1941, 3.

3. W. G. Irwin letter to Stone, Webster, & Blodgett (New York), 11/9/38. Irwin again was standoffish in response to a similar inquiry a few months later. W. G. Irwin letter to David H. Jennings (Chicago), 2/10/39.

4. Jim Fritz interview, 7/4/94.

5. Edwin G. Crouch memo to J. Irwin Miller, 12/29/54.

6. W. G. Irwin letter to Ralph J. Heffernan (Pratt, Heffernan & Ramsayer), 11/23/40.

7. W. G. Irwin letter to Ralph J. Heffernan, 11/23/40.

8. J. Irwin Miller memo to file, 1/12/67.

9. For Clessie Cummins' version of this episode, see *My Days with the Diesel* (Philadelphia: Chilton Press, 1967), 177–82.

10. Cummins, *My Days with the Diesel*, 177–82.

11. Cummins, *My Days with the Diesel*, 177–82.

12. All dates and other facts in these two paragraphs are from the corporate minute books for this period.

13. Clessie Cummins letter to J. Irwin Miller, 9/8/42, C. Lyle Cummins private library.

14. W. G. Irwin handwritten note to J. Irwin Miller, 7/26/41, OEDC historical file.

15. W. G. Irwin, Linnie I. Sweeney, Elsie I. Sweeney, Hugh Th. Miller, J. Irwin Miller, and Elizabeth Clementine Miller letter to the Cummins board, 12/31/41, Cummins Engine Company, board minutes, 12/41.

16. Clessie Cummins letter to John Niven, 4/19/43, C. Lyle Cummins private library.

17. J. Irwin Miller interview, 5/31/94.
18. Clessie Cummins letter to John Niven, 4/19/43.
19. C. Lyle Cummins interview, 11/8/93.
20. Clessie Cummins letter to W. G. Irwin, 12/13/43, C. Lyle Cummins private library.
21. Xenia Simons Miller interview, 11/10/95.
22. Martin van Creveld, *Supplying War* (Cambridge, England: Cambridge University Press, 1977), 126–27.
23. Harry B. Yoshpe, ed., *Requirements: Matching Needs with Resources* (Washington, D.C.: Army Material Command, 1964), 26.
24. van Creveld, 194.
25. Bryan Perrett, *Desert Warfare* (Wellingborough, England: Patrick Stephens, 1988), 115.
26. *Columbus Evening Republican*, 12/8/41.
27. "Inventory Control" memo, unsigned, 1941.
28. "Purchasing Department Brief," unsigned, 1941, 1.
29. "Inventory Control" memo.
30. D. L. Buchanan (Hercules' Priorities Department) letter to James S. Adams (Automotive Section, Office of Production Management), 9/9/41.
31. F. E. Evans, "Engine Branch of Automotive Division, War Production Board," National Archives, War Production Board, record group 179, folder 631.404, 10/5/45.
32. "Requirements of engines and crankshafts submitted by Claimant Agency Representatives to the Automotive Division, War Production Board, December 1, 1942," National Archives, War Production Board, record group 179, folder 631.4025.
33. "History of the Internal Combustion Engine Business," 9/14/42, 3, National Archives, War Production Board, record group 179, folder 631.407.
34. War Production Board, Automotive Division, Annual Report for 1944, National Archives, War Production Board records, box 392, folder 053.108.
35. Evans, "Engine Branch of Automotive Division," 2.
36. "History of the Internal Combustion Engine Business," 5.
37. Norman Palmer (Cummins Engine Company) telephone conversation with F. E. Evans (WPB) in "Telephone Conversations by company," Cummins section, National Archives, War Production Board records, Automotive Division, box 390, folder 053.108C.
38. Evans, "Engine Branch of Automotive Division," Part IV, 3.
39. *Columbus Evening Republican*, 1/25/43.
40. Cummins, *My Days with the Diesel*, 184.
41. Transcript of Cummins' comments at the 10/7/43 Industry Advisory Group, National Archives, War Production Board, record group 179, folder 631.4005.
42. Comments at the 10/7/43 Industry Advisory Group.
43. "Summary Report of Subcommittee on Internal Combustion Engines," internal memo, 10/13/43, National Archives, War Production Board, record group 197, folder 631.402C. This is also the source for the data in the tables that follow.
44. C. Lyle Cummins telephone interview, 2/3/94.
45. "Army-Navy Production Award" memo to Clessie Cummins, 9/7/43, 4, National Archives, War Production Board, "Army-Navy 'E' Award" folder, cover labeled "Lock Box 551."
46. "Army-Navy Production Award" memo to Clessie Cummins, 9/7/43.
47. Robert Huthsteiner memo to Clessie Cummins, 9/7/43, 5.
48. Robert Huthsteiner memo to Clessie Cummins, 9/7/43, 6.
49. *Columbus Evening Republican*, 4/13/42.
50. *Columbus Evening Republican*, 11/16/42.
51. Robert Huthsteiner memo to Clessie Cummins, 9/7/43, 6.
52. A. G. Becker & Co., "Summary of Earnings" section in 1947 prospectus.
53. Irwin Miller general memo, 9/28/42.
54. Cummins Engine Company, board minutes, 12/21/43.
55. J. Irwin Miller letter to Clessie Cummins, n.d., C. Lyle Cummins private library.
56. J. Irwin Miller interview with Jim Henderson, 5/25/93.
57. J. Irwin Miller interview with Jim Henderson, 5/25/93.
58. J. Irwin Miller interview with Jim Henderson, 5/25/93.
59. J. Irwin Miller letter to Clessie Cummins, 4/3/44, C. Lyle Cummins private library.
60. Cummins Engine Company, board minutes, 5/18/44.
61. *Columbus Evening Republican*, 6/9/45.
62. Memo attributed to Clessie Cummins, 5/31/45, C. Lyle Cummins private library.
63. J. Irwin Miller letter to Clessie Cummins, 6/4/44, C. Lyle Cummins private library.
64. Harry W. Lindsey, Jr. (Davis, Lindsey, Smith & Shonts, a Chicago law firm) letter to Clessie Cummins and Irwin Miller, 7/2/45, C. Lyle Cummins private library.
65. J. Irwin Miller letter to Clessie Cummins, 1/1/46, C. Lyle Cummins private library.
66. Cummins Engine Company, board minutes, 1/22/46.
67. Cummins Engine Company, board minutes, 1/22/46.

68. Cummins Engine Company, board minutes, 4/1/47.
69. J. Irwin Miller note in margin of blind carbon copy of letter from K. W. Davis to Clessie Cummins, 6/21/47, forwarded by Davis to Miller July 1947.
70. George W. Newlin memo, 11/9/82, appended to "Financial History of the Cummins Engine Company," 1967.
71. George W. Newlin memo, 11/9/82.
72. *Business Week* (June 22,1946): 52.
73. *Popular Mechanics* (September 1945): 19.
74. "Marine Diesel Engines, May 1940–June 1945," National Archives, War Production Board, record group 179, folder 325.1243 ("Diesel Engines, Scheduling"), 5; and A. G. Becker & Company 1947 prospectus.
75. J. Irwin Miller interview, 5/31/94.
76. "Proposal for Expansion of Facilities of Cummins Engine Company," attributed to "Giffels and Vallet," but showing evidence of Irwin Miller's involvement; informally dated 1942.
77. J. Irwin Miller general memo, 9/28/42.
78. E. J. Bush (vice president of the Diamond T Motor Car Co.) memo to Robert M. Hatfield (special assistant to the Operations vice chairman), 3/14/45, National Archives, War Production Board, record group 179, box 34, folder "Automotive, Engines, Internal combustion."
79. J. Irwin Miller letter to Clessie Cummins, 11/20/45, C. Lyle Cummins private library.
80. J. Irwin Miller letter to Clessie Cummins, 5/6/47, C. Lyle Cummins private library.

Chapter 5

1. See John Kenneth Galbraith, *American Capitalism* (Boston: Houghton Mifflin, 1952), 63–83.
2. U.S. Bureau of the Census, *Historical Statistics of the United States, Colonial Times to 1970*, pt. 2 (Washington, D.C., 1975), 619, 711, 716.
3. Annual stockholders' meeting minutes, 4/4/50.
4. Annual reports for 1947 and 1958.
5. Edward W. Constant II, *The Origins of the Turbojet Revolution* (Baltimore: Johns Hopkins University Press, 1980), 57–58, 83–85.
6. Paris Letsinger interview with John Rowell, n.d.
7. Paris Letsinger memo to V. E. McMullen, 8/6/43, Problems File no. 27; J. Irwin Miller memo, annual board meeting minutes, 9/4/44; McMullen memo to the Executive Committee, 8/18/44, Problems File no. 27; Clessie Cummins memo to the Executive Committee, 5/15/45, Problems File no. 23; Huthsteiner and Knudsen memo to the Executive Committee, 12/3/46, Problems File no. 121.
8. Memos between H. L. Knudsen and D. B. Worth, Problems File no. 15; Bill Schwab interview, 9/30/93.
9. H. L. Knudsen memo to the Executive Committee, 3/31/47, Problems File no. 132; annual report for 1954.
10. H. L. Knudsen memo to Executive Committee, 3/31/47, Problems File no. 132; Bill Schwab interview, 9/30/93.
11. Bill Schwab interview, 9/30/93.
12. Bill Schwab interview, 9/30/93; *Columbus Evening Republican*, 6/24/47.
13. Joseph Butler interview, 7/22/93; Bill Schwab interview, 9/30/93.
14. Joseph Butler interview, 7/22/93; Sydney Cook interview, 11/10/93.
15. Bill Schwab interview, 9/30/93; Joseph Butler interview, 7/22/93.
16. Bill Schwab interview, 9/30/93; annual report for 1954.
17. *Columbus Evening Republican*, 2/2/50 and 5/13/50; John Rowell, "Back at the 500 . . . ," *Power Team* (January-February 1980): 9.
18. *Columbus Evening Republican*, 1/26/50; Griffith Borgeson, "Diesels at Speed: Cummins Diesel Records at Indianapolis and Bonneville," *Motor Trend* (December 1950): 19.
19. *Columbus Evening Republican*, 2/2/50 and 5/13/50.
20. *Columbus Evening Republican*, 5/11/50 and 5/13/50.
21. *Columbus Evening Republican*, 5/18/50, 5/20/50, 5/22/50, and 5/25/50; Borgeson, "Diesels at Speed," 31.
22. *Columbus Evening Republican*, 5/29/50.
23. *Columbus Evening Republican*, 2/2/50 and 5/29/50.
24. *Columbus Evening Republican*, 5/31/50; Borgeson, "Diesels at Speed," 31.
25. "The Car that Made Diesel History," *The Dependable Diesel* , vol. 6, no. 1, (1951): 4; Borgeson, "Diesels at Speed," 19.
26. Rowell, "Back at the 500 . . . ," 9.
27. *Columbus Evening Republican*, 1/17/52, 1/22/52, 4/21/52, 4/27/50, 5/28/50, and 5/29/50.
28. Robert Cutter and Bob Fendell, *The Encyclopedia of Auto Racing Greats* (Englewood Cliffs, N.J.: Prentice-Hall, 1973), 3–4; *Columbus Evening Republican*, 4/21/52.
29. *Columbus Evening Republican*, 4/18/52, 4/21/52, and 5/16/52.
30. *Columbus Evening Republican*, 4/26/52, 5/20/52, and 5/23/52; Wilbur Shaw, *Gentlemen, Start Your Engines* (New York: Coward-McCann, 1955), 311; Cutter and Fendell, *Encyclopedia of Auto Racing Greats*, 4.

31. *Columbus Evening Republican*, 5/19/52 and 5/22/52.

32. *Columbus Evening Republican*, 5/29/52 and 5/31/52; Cutter and Fendell, *Encyclopedia of Auto Racing Greats*, 4.

33. John Rowell, "And now: How some think it *really* was," *Power Team* (September–October 1981): 14.

34. Donald Davidson, "1952 Cummins Diesel Special," *Autoweek* (June 1, 1987); *Columbus Evening Republican*, 6/9/52; Cutter and Fendell, *Encyclopedia of Auto Racing Greats*, 4.

35. Don Cummins is quoted in Davidson, "1952 Cummins Diesel Special"; Shaw, *Gentlemen, Start Your Engines*, 311.

36. Annual reports for 1949 and 1950; Cutter and Fendell, *Encyclopedia of Auto Racing Greats*, 4.

37. Brock Yates, *The Indianapolis 500: The Story of a Motor Speedway* (New York: Harper, 1961), 68–69.

38. J. Irwin Miller memo to Robert Huthsteiner, 6/26/51, Problems File no. 199.

39. Memo [author unknown] to the Executive Committee, 9/13/45, Problems File no. 27; Robert Huthsteiner memo to the Executive Committee, 9/13/49, Problems File no. 149.

40. Robert Huthsteiner memos to the Executive Committee, 1/22/49 and 9/13/49, Problems File no. 149; Clessie Cummins letter to Don Cummins, 3/8/48, Problems File no. 143; Bill Schwab interview, 9/30/93; U.S. patent records for numbers 2,618,252, 2,652,041, and 2,661,729; R. A. Price memo to the Executive Committee, 2/21/47, Problems File no. 27; A. C. Bell memo to Don Cummins, 9/19/47, Problems File no. 143; George Muntean conversation with the authors, 5/31/94.

41. Joseph Butler interview, 7/22/93; Ray Boll memo to the Executive Committee, 2/16/50, Problems File no. 149; Lee Beck memo, 1/3/50, Problems File no. 143.

42. Robert Huthsteiner memo to Don Cummins, 2/19/48, Problems File no. 143; Robert Huthsteiner memo to the Executive Committee, 1/22/49, Problems File no. 149.

43. Robert Huthsteiner memo to the Executive Committee, 1/22/49, Problems File no. 149; special Executive Committee meeting minutes, 2/7/49, Problems File no. 143; annual report for 1950.

44. Ray Boll memo to Executive Committee, 2/16/50, Problems File no. 149; Lee Beck memo to the Executive Committee, 1/3/50, Problems File no. 143; Bill Schwab interview, 9/30/93.

45. Memos [author unknown] to Executive Committee, 7/2/52, Problems File no. 143; Bill Schwab interview, 9/30/93; memo [author unknown] to the Executive Committee, 6/6/50, Problems File no. 143; memo [author unknown] to Clessie Cummins, 1/23/51, Problems File no. 143.

46. "Cummins Fuel Systems - Early Fuel System History," including "The Exclusive Cummins Fuel Injection System," typescript report prepared by Cummins Engine Company Fuel Systems Department, n.d.; C. Lyle Cummins interview, 11/8/93.

47. "History of Development of the P. T. D. Pump by Clessie Cummins," typescript document, 7/2/54, JIMP. Patent attorney Lowell Noyes attested to the accuracy of this document in a letter to Don J. Cummins also dated 7/2/54, JIMP.

48. Harry W. Lindsey, Jr. (Davis, Lindsey, Hibben & Noyes) to Clessie Cummins, 5/24/1950, CLCP; "Cummins Fuel Systems"; U.S. Patent Office, patent number 6,670,725 (3/2/54).

49. U.S. Patent Office, patent number 6,670,725 (3/2/54); George Muntean discussion with the authors, 5/31/93; Merrill C. Horine, "Simplified Injection Systems," *Diesel Progress* (April 1955): 33.

50. George Muntean discussion with the authors, 5/31/93; U.S. Patent Office, patent numbers 2,727,498 (application date 7/6/50) and 2,727,503 (application date 2/25/53), both granted 12/20/55.

51. J. Irwin Miller letters to Clessie Cummins, 8/30/54, 10/18/54, 1/21/55, 2/11/55, 3/4/55, CLCP and JIMP; Clessie Cummins letters to J. Irwin Miller, 9/28/54, 1/13/55, CLCP; J. Irwin Miller, memos to file, 12/15/54, 2/1/55, and 2/24/55, JIMP.

52. Clessie Cummins letter to J. Irwin Miller, 10/18/54, CLCP; J. Irwin Miller letter to Clessie Cummins, 6/21/55, JIMP.

53. J. Irwin Miller letter to Clessie Cummins, 3/4/55, 4/19/55, and 6/21/55; J. Irwin Miller memo to file, 3/4/55, CLCP and JIMP.

54. Clessie Cummins letters to J. Irwin Miller, 9/28/54, 1/13/55, CLCP. Clessie's final resignation letter dated 8/28/57 is included in the Cummins board minutes for 9/24/57.

55. Much of this story comes from C. Lyle Cummins, who was interviewed several times by the authors, and who provided a copy of the 8/7/62 agreement. Company documentation regarding the second round of PT negotiations is scarce, but confirms a series of seven payments to Clessie Cummins extending to the spring of 1968.

56. Memo [author unknown] to Clessie Cummins, 1/23/51, Problems File no. 143.

57. Ray Boll memo to the Executive Committee, 10/9/51, Problems File no. 199.

58. *Columbus Evening Republican*, 5/29/54; C. B. Foster memo to regional managers and assistants, 4/5/54, Problems File no. 199; O. M. Savage memo to the Executive Committee, 7/21/54, Problems File no. 199; E. W. Wright memo to the Executive Committee, 1/8/54, Problems File no. 199.

59. E. W. Wright memo to dealers, 11/9/53, Problems File no. 199; Don Tull memo to Ray Boll, 9/18/53.

60. C. B. Foster memo to regional managers and assistants, 4/5/54, Problems File no. 199; John Rowell letter to distributors, 3/17/55, Problems File no. 199; Ray Boll memo to the Dealer Advisory Committee on the Introduction of the PT Fuel System, 6/24/54, Problems File no. 199; O. M. Savage memo to the Executive Committee, 7/21/54, Problems File no. 199.

61. E. W. Wright memo to dealer, 11/9/53, Problems File no. 199; T. B. Fulkerson memo to W. E. Bosley, "Progress Report on the PT Fuel System," 4/15/54, Problems File no. 199.

62. Ray Boll memo to the Dealer Advisory Committee on the Introduction of the PT Fuel System, 6/24/54, Problems File no. 199; *Columbus Evening Republican*, 5/29/54; Don Tull memo to Ray Boll, 9/18/53, Problems File no. 199.

63. William Mohr letter to dealers, 4/21/54, Problems File no. 199; Ray Boll memo to the Dealer Advisory Committee on the Introduction of the PT Fuel System, 6/24/54, Problems File no. 199; C. B. Foster memo to regional managers and assistants, 4/5/54, Problems File no. 199; Waldo Harrison memos to the Executive Committee, 7/20/54 and 1/20/55, Problems File no. 143.

64. See Arthur W. Judge, *High Speed Diesel Engines*, 5th ed. (New York: Van Nostrand, 1957); Karl W. Stinson, *Diesel Engineering Handbook*, 10th ed. (New York: Business Journals Inc., 1959); Horine, "Simplified Injection Systems," 33; "New Roosa-Master Model B Fuel Pump," *Diesel Progress* (April 1955): 54–55.

65. Alfred D. Chandler, Jr., *Scale and Scope: The Dynamics of Industrial Capitalism* (Cambridge, Mass.: The Belknap Press of Harvard University Press, 1990), passim.

66. *Columbus Evening Republican*, 2/9/48 and 8/4/48.

67. Annual reports for 1947–1949; board minutes, 10/18/46, 1/27/48, and 12/26/51.

68. Annual report for 1949; board minutes, 1/23/51; *Columbus Evening Republican*, 1/19/51.

69. Annual stockholders' meeting minutes, 4/4/50; annual reports for 1949 and 1950.

70. Board minutes, 8/22/50, 12/2/50, and 1/23/51; *Columbus Evening Republican*, 9/15/50 and 1/19/51.

71. *Columbus Evening Republican*, 6/1/51; board minutes, 4/24/51.

72. Annual report for 1951; *Columbus Evening Republican*, 9/5/53 and 2/8/54.

73. Board minutes, 10/4/55; *Columbus Evening Republican*, 1/13/56 and 6/30/56.

74. *Columbus Evening Republican*, 3/11/54.

75. *Columbus Evening Republican*, 3/11/54; board minutes, 9/28/54; Bill Schwab interview, 9/30/93.

76. Dick Stoner interview, 8/18/93; stockholders' meeting minutes, 4/3/56.

77. *Columbus Evening Republican*, 3/10/56, 6/26/56, 10/4/56, 3/20/57, 10/10/57, and 7/9/58.

78. *Columbus Evening Republican*, 3/10/56, 6/26/56, 10/4/56, 3/20/57, 10/10/57, and 7/9/58; annual report for 1950.

79. Board minutes, 10/24/50, 12/26/51, 10/21/52, and 10/28/52.

80. Board minutes, 9/28/54 and 1/28/58.

81. Board minutes, 10/18/46, 2/24/48, 3/23/48; stockholders' meeting minutes, 4/6/48 and 4/5/49.

82. J. Irwin Miller memo to the Executive Committee, 3/23/49, Problems File no. 45.

83. J. Irwin Miller memo to the Executive Committee, 3/23/49, Problems File no. 45.

84. Stanley Shaw interview, 1/24/94; Bill Schwab interview, 9/30/93; Dick Stoner's 2/7/64 speech to the AMA.

85. Board minutes, 3/27/56; stockholders' meeting minutes, 4/3/56.

86. Stanley Shaw interview, 1/24/94.

87. Alfred D. Chandler, Jr., *The Visible Hand: The Managerial Revolution in American Business* (Cambridge, Mass.: The Belknap Press of Harvard University Press, 1977), passim.

88. Stanley Shaw interview with John Rowell, n.d.; Stanley Shaw interview, 1/24/94.

89. Finley LeBar interview with John Rowell, n.d.; Stanley Shaw interview, 1/24/94.

90. W. M. Harrison and Dick Stoner memo to the board, included in board minutes, 1/28/58; Stanley Shaw interview with John Rowell, n.d.; Stanley Shaw interview, 1/24/94.

91. W. M. Harrison and Dick Stoner memo to the board, included in board minutes, 1/28/58; *Columbus Evening Republican*, 2/12/58.

92. W. M. Harrison and Dick Stoner memo to the board, included in board minutes, 1/28/58.

93. Stanley Shaw interview with John Rowell, n.d.

94. Dick Stoner interview, 8/18/93.

95. Dick Stoner interview, 8/18/93; W. M. Harrison and Dick Stoner memo to the board, included in board minutes, 1/28/58.

96. W. M. Harrison and Dick Stoner memo to the board, included in board minutes, 1/28/58; *Columbus Evening Republican*, 2/12/58.

97. *Columbus Evening Republican*, 5/12/58; board minutes, 1/28/58, 2/25/58, and 7/28/59; Dick Stoner interview, 8/18/93.

98. Pete Fritsch interview with John Rowell, n.d.

99. Dick Stoner interview, 8/18/93; Pete Fritsch interview with John Rowell, n.d.

100. Dick Stoner interview, 8/18/93.

101. John W. Rowell, "How Fleetguard got its start," *Power Team* (October 1992): 10; Dick Stoner interview, 8/18/93.

102. *Columbus Evening Republican*, 7/10/58; Rowell, "How Fleetguard got its start," 10; board minutes, 7/22/58.

103. Rowell, "How Fleetguard got its start," 10.

104. Rowell, "How Fleetguard got its start," 10; Dick Stoner interview, 8/18/93.

105. Clessie L. Cummins, *My Days With the Diesel* (Philadelphia: Chilton Books, 1967), 131.

106. See Robert Doughten, "Engine Brakes and Retarders," *Owner Operator* (January-February 1983): 29.

107. Lyle Cummins, an inventor in his own right, has also written extensively about the history of diesel technology. His most recent book, *Diesel's Engine* (Wilsonville, Ore.: Carnot Press, 1993) tells the story of the diesel from its inception to 1918. Cummins is now at work on a biography of his father.

108. C. Lyle Cummins, Jr., interview with the authors, 11/8/93.
109. From Clessie Cummins' 1/30/56 letter to Don Cummins, quoted in a 8/24/56 letter from Robert Huthsteiner to A. Donham Owen, Clessie's San Francisco-based attorney. These and other Cummins documents pertaining to the engine brake are from a legal file folder entitled "Agreement with C. L. Cummins dated 6/21/55," in the Law Department's collection.
110. Memo, 6/14/57, from D. Cummins to N. L. Reiners.
111. See, for example, the authors' 6/23/94 interview with Ben Bush, and their 9/6/94 interview with former purchasing heads Larry Husmann and John McGovern.
112. C. Lyle Cummins, Jr., 11/8/93 interview with the authors.
113. See "Downhill . . . in complete control!", an undated Jacobs marketing brochure circa mid-to-late 1961.
114. Syd Cook interview with the authors, 11/10/93.
115. Doughton, *Owner Operator*, 29.
116. J. Irwin Miller interview with the authors, 10/26/93.
117. Doughton, *Owner Operator*, 30.
118. See "Braking: Auxiliary brakes finally come into their own," *Fleet Owner* (July 1980): 88.
119. C. Lyle Cummins, Jr., interview with the authors, 11/8/93.
120. Letter, 6/20/62, from R. H. Wills to N. M. Reiners.
121. Ben Bush interview with the authors, 6/23/94.
122. Husmann and McGovern interview with the authors, 9/6/94; and R. A. Johnson's 5/8/80 memo to J. A. Henderson.
123. Larry Husmann and John McGovern interview, 9/6/94.
124. From an R. B. Bush memo, 2/3/81, to J. T. Hackett, on "Jake Brakes."
125. Tom Husmann and John McGovern interview, 9/6/94.
126. Syd Cook interview with the authors, 11/10/93.
127. Board minutes, 4/16/46.
128. Sydney Cook interview, 11/10/93.
129. Board minutes, 10/28/47.
130. Ray Boll interview, 7/23/93.
131. Ray Boll interview, 8/2/93.
132. From various records in Problems File no. 27.
133. Robert Huthsteiner memo to Paris Letsinger, 2/16/45, Problems File no. 5.
134. Leonard Beck memo to the Executive Committee, 12/11/46, Problems File no. 73.
135. From various memos (unattributed) in Problems File no. 8.
136. J. Irwin Miller memo to V. E. McMullen, 11/21/44, Problems File no. 9.
137. Robert Huthsteiner minutes on 10/30/44 meeting in Paris Letsinger's office, Problems File no. 10.
138. Robert Huthsteiner and Leonard Beck memo to the Executive Committee, 12/5/46, Problems File no. 74.
139. Robert Huthsteiner minutes on 10/30/44 meeting in Paris Letsinger's office, Problems File no. 10.
140. From various memos and notes in Problems File no. 77.
141. Norman Palmer memo to the Executive Committee, 1/31/46, Problems File no. 72.
142. Sydney Cook interview, 11/10/93.
143. Robert Huthsteiner memo to the Executive Committee, 1/4/51; J. Irwin Miller memo to Robert Huthsteiner, 1/6/51, Problems File no. 185.
144. Board minutes, 3/27/56.
145. Sydney Cook interview, 11/10/93.
146. Ray Boll interview, 8/2/93.
147. Sydney Cook interview, 11/10/93.
148. Ray Boll interview, 8/2/93.
149. Robert Huthsteiner memo to the Executive Committee, 3/13/45, Problems File no. 20.
150. T. Randall Tucker interview, 1/25/94.
151. J. Irwin Miller memo to the Executive Committee, 7/14/45, Problems File no. 38.
152. See Problems File no. 57 for copies of and revisions to the first three corporate policies, all written by Miller.
153. Paris Letsinger memo to the Executive Committee, 5/12/45, Problems File no. 6.
154. Annual stockholders' meeting minutes, 4/5/49.
155. J. Irwin Miller memo to the Executive Committee, 2/21/51, Problems File no. 71.
156. J. Irwin Miller letter to Clessie Cummins, 5/14/51, C. Lyle Cummins private library.
157. J. Irwin Miller letter to Clessie Cummins, 6/27/51, describing Waldo Harrison's appointment to the board of the Cotton & Woolen Manufacturers' Mutual Insurance Company of New England, C. Lyle Cummins private library.
158. *Columbus Evening Republican*, 6/29/57.
159. T. Randall Tucker interview, 1/25/94.
160. From the first issue of the (still unnamed) Cummins internal newsletter, 3/20/59.
161. J. Irwin Miller memo to the Executive Committee, 10/10/45, Problems File no. 53.
162. Board minutes, 2/24/53 and 5/25/54.
163. Board minutes, 10/23/51.

164. Robert Huthsteiner memo to J. Irwin Miller, 12/24/51, in board minutes, 12/26/51.
165. Board minutes, 12/26/51, 7/15/52, and 11/26/52.
166. Thomas Harrison memo to the board, 10/25/54, in board minutes, 10/26/54.
167. *Columbus Evening Republican*, 1/15/57.
168. Dick Stoner interview, 8/18/93.
169. Tom Harrison interview, 1/25/94.
170. Cummins publicity release, c. 1956.
171. *Columbus Evening Republican*, 2/9/59.
172. J. Irwin Miller letter and memo to W. G. Irwin, 8/1/38.
173. J. Irwin Miller letter to Clinton C. Johnson (vice president, Chemical Bank), 12/8/44.
174. Paris Letsinger memo to V. E. McMullen, Clessie Cummins, W. G. Irwin, and J. Irwin Miller, 4/25/43.
175. Clessie L. Cummins memo to W. G. Irwin, V. E. McMullen, Paris Letsinger, and J. Irwin Miller, 4/30/43.
176. *Columbus Evening Republican*, 7/12/51.
177. Stanley Shaw interview with John Rowell, n.d.; Stanley Shaw interview, 1/24/94.
178. *Columbus Evening Republican*, 7/12/51.
179. Seymour Dribben letter to J. Irwin Miller, 4/4/50.
180. Mira Wilkins, *The Maturing of Multinational Enterprise: American Business Abroad from 1914–1970* (Cambridge, Mass: Harvard University Press, 1974), 289.
181. Don Cummins interview with John Rowell, 2/21/78.
182. John W. Rowell's articles in the January/February 1981 and March/April 1981 issues of *Power Team*, a Cummins periodical, provide extremely useful background on Shotts.
183. J. Irwin Miller letter to Seymour Dribben, 4/7/55.
184. *Columbus Evening Republican*, 4/5/55.
185. For an explanation of SIE, see "Pathway to Prosperity," a twenty-first anniversary publication issued in 1958, designed and published by G. Shaw Leiper, Town Crier Publications, 23 Perth Road, Dundee. A roster of participating companies through 1958 is on page 34.
186. See, for example, the 5/11/57 issue of the *Manchester Guardian*, p. 11.
187. Dick Stoner interview with John Rowell, n.d.
188. See, for example, Percy Rugg's 1/16/58 letter to the "Capital Issues Committee" of the Treasury Chambers, in D. J. Cummins' "Government Negotiations Vol. 1" file.
189. Robert Barr interview, 1/24/94.
190. Dick Stoner interview, 8/18/93.
191. *The Dependable Diesel* (undated 1956 issue): 3.
192. *Highways and Bridges and Engineering Works* (May 22, 1957): 14.
193. *Motor Transport* (February 6, 1959): 7.
194. Robert Barr interview, 1/24/94.
195. Ray Boll interview, 8/9/93.
196. *Columbus Evening Republican*, 4/7/59.
197. J. Irwin Miller interview with Jim Henderson, 5/25/93.
198. "Making Customers Cry for It," *Business Week* (February 2, 1957): 51–52.

Chapter 6

1. *Columbus Evening Republican*, 2/29/60.
2. *Power-Team News* (May-June 1982).
3. John Hackett interview, 2/23/94
4. See, for example, Merle D. Yontz letter to Don Tull, 8/22/60.
5. Cummins presentation to the Chicago Security Analysts Society, 4/4/63.
6. Ray Boll interview, 7/23/93; Cummins Annual Statistical Report for 1960.
7. Dick Stoner interview, 8/18/93.
8. "Kennedy plans new railroad aid measure, orders Hodges to study transportation," *Wall Street Journal*, 8/4/61; "Rise in cost estimate for interstate roads will spark squabbling," *Wall Street Journal*, 12/10/64.
9. Cummins, untitled binder on diesel-differential lobbying efforts, c. 1965.
10. *Columbus Evening Republican*, 3/17/61.
11. *Columbus Evening Republican*, 1/23/69.
12. Much of this discussion, as well as the history of GM's efforts in this field, is drawn from a "Plaintiff's brief before trial," in an undated brief prepared for a trial (Civil Action #15859) in the U.S. District Court for the District of Maryland, in which Cummins sued General Motors and McCall-Boykin Truck, Inc., for alleged infringement of a V-engine patent issued to Neville M. Reiners on 11/12/63. (The suit was ultimately unsuccessful.) A second extremely helpful source is Ray Boll's 8/13/62 presentation to the Society of Automotive Engineers, entitled "The New Cummins V-Type Diesel Engines."
13. "Now it's compact diesel engines," *Business Week* (December 12, 1959): 142.

14. "New Engine Design Program" memo, 5/20/53, Executive Committee Problem File 151; Ray Boll letter to J. Irwin Miller, 9/15/53; J. Irwin Miller memo to Robert Huthsteiner, Don Tull, and Nev Reiners, 11/13/59; "General Motors sees expanded fields for new V-type diesel," *Business Week* (January 10, 1959): 54.
15. J. Irwin Miller memo to Nev Reiners, 11/20/59.
16. "Plaintiff's brief before trial."
17. *Diesel Progress* (issue unspecified) as quoted in *Power-Plus News* (October 29, 1962): 2.
18. *Time* magazine (from "this week") as quoted in *Columbus Evening Republican*, 9/26/61.
19. J. L. Wheeler memo to H. S. Kindle, 5/14/63.
20. J. Irwin Miller memo to Don Tull and Nev Reiners, 11/16/63.
21. *Power-Plus News* (June 15, 1964); *Columbus Evening Republican*, 9/22/66.
22. *Columbus Evening Republican*, 9/23/66; Peter W. Schutz (Director, Engine Division Planning), "Val/Vale Planning Report," 12/21/67, Box 58-6-23, labeled "President's Office 0514."
23. *Columbus Evening Republican*, 6/20/67.
24. W. H. Fox (sales manager) memo to Ray Boll, 2/16/50.
25. "Sale of concern to G.M. attacked," *New York Times*, 11/18/55.
26. See, for example, "Making customers cry for it," *Business Week* (February 2, 1957): 51.
27. Marion Dietrich interview, 6/28/94; *Columbus Evening Republican*, 8/29/61 and 2/5/62.
28. Henry Schacht interview, 10/6/94.
29. Marion Dietrich memo to Ray Boll, 1/29/62.
30. Annual report for 1961.
31. Annual report for 1963.
32 The 1962 McKinsey screening criteria are from a black binder prepared by R. E. Schroeder for the Policy-Planning Board's 5/23/68 meeting.
33. Dick Stoner memo to Don Tull, 12/11/62; "Perfect Circle holders approve sale of firm," *Wall Street Journal*, 5/16/63.
34. George Newlin memo to Don Tull, 2/1/62. Almost all materials relating to the White merger come from two sources: Ben Bush's legal records of the merger (in the Law Department's collection), and Marion Dietrich's business-related records of the merger (as yet unprocessed, in the care of Inactive Records).
35. "Effect of proposed increases to base engine prices," R. W. Franck memo to Don Tull, 1/29/63.
36. Legal File 100-1.
37. J. Irwin Miller undated memo, apparently an attachment to a Miller memo to Nev Reiners, Robert Huthsteiner, and Don Tull, 11/13/59.
38. "A brief history of negotiations," in an untitled black binder, most likely the back-up materials presented to J. P. Dragin by George Newlin at a 10/29/62 meeting in Cleveland.
39. George Newlin memo to Don Tull, Dick Stoner, Ray Boll, Sydney Cook, and John McKy, 5/19/60.
40. George Newlin interview, 6/24/94.
41. Untitled binder, 7/15/61, Marion Dietrich files.
42. Industry statistics can be found in the "Economic analysis of the proposed consolidation between the Cummins Engine Company, Inc., and the White Motor Company," submitted to Cummins by Jesse W. Markham and Eugene M. Singer, 9/63.
43. J. Irwin Miller interview, 12/14/94; binder dated 7/15/61, Marion Dietrich's files.
44. Waldo Harrison's notes on a 7/19/61 meeting between J. Irwin Miller, Waldo Harrison, and George Woods.
45. *Cleveland Press*, 1/16/62; "White Motor to make own diesel engines," *Metalworking News*, 4/30/63.
46. From George Newlin's minutes on the 5/27/63 meeting.
47. Waldo Harrison memos to Don Tull, 8/12/63 and 8/16/63.
48. "Heavy-duty, high gear merger," *Business Week* (October 5, 1963): 94.
49. *Columbus Evening Republican*, 9/25/63.
50. W. G. Hannan letter to Cummins, 10/7/63.
51. Chuck Hunter memo to file, 10/9/63; Glen Paschall (IRS) letter to Cummins, 12/16/63.
52. Untitled binder, 7/15/61, Marion Dietrich files; J. Irwin Miller interview, 12/14/94.
53. S. Chesterfield Oppenheim, "Legal opinion, evaluating the factors relevant to legal aspects and economic analysis of a merger of C and W, when judged by statutory standards and judicial interpretations of Amended Section 7 of the Clayton Act," submitted to Cummins 5/9/53.
54. Jerrold G. Van Cise (Cahill, Gordon, Reindel & Ohl) and Gerhard A. Gesell (Covington & Burling) letter to William H. Orrick, Jr., 9/25/63.
55. Sydney Cook interview, 11/10/93; Henry Schacht interview, 10/6/94.
56. Ben Bush memo to E. D. Tull, 10/4/63.
57. *Nation's Business* (October 1963).
58. William H. Orrick, Jr., letter to Gerhard A. Gesell, 2/27/64; "White Motor's sales, profits set highs in '63," *Wall Street Journal*, 2/27/64; annual report for 1963.
59. "Exhibit 1," c. 2/28/64, unlabeled black binder; Reece Hatchitt memo to Ray Boll, 3/9/64.
60. See Gerhard Gesell, "Memorandum for the White-Cummins file," 4/3/64.
61. J. Irwin Miller letter to Robert F. Kennedy, 4/6/64; *Columbus Evening Republican*, 4/25/64.
62. J. Irwin Miller and Don Tull, 6/26/64; Dan James letter to Ben Bush, 4/27/64.

63. Ray Boll, Nev Reiners, and Dick Stoner memo to J. Irwin Miller and Don Tull, 4/23/64; J. Irwin Miller memo to Dick Stoner, 4/9/64; *Columbus Evening Republican*, 9/10/64. According to this article, J. Irwin Miller bought the first 200 shares of Cummins stock that were traded publicly.

64. *Indianapolis Star*, 2/18/89. For more details on Schacht, see "Mr. Rust Belt," *Business Week* (October 17, 1988); and a similar story in *Indiana Business* (January 1989). For a company biography of Schacht, see *Power-Plus News* (July 1969).

65. See Paul Miller interview, 10/19/94; and George Newlin interview, 6/24/94.

66. Paul Miller interview, 10/19/94; Waldo M. Harrison memo to file, 2/11/64.

67. Henry Schacht interview, 7/22/93.

68. Henry Schacht memo to Don Tull, 12/11/64.

69. See, for example, Jim Henderson letter to an HBS staff member, 8/27/64.

70. Jim Henderson memo to J. Irwin Miller, 12/7/64.

71. Marion Dietrich memo to J. L. Keyes, 5/18/64.

72. J. Irwin Miller, "Why Cummins must lead," speech delivered at the Cummins National Distributors meeting, 5/19/64.

73. *Columbus Evening Republican*, 4/13/64 and 9/1/64. Details on Frigikar's early history can be found in "The Frigiking Division of Cummins Engine Company, Inc.," an undated Cummins brochure.

74. *Columbus Evening Republican*, 5/26/65.

75. Annual reports for 1965 and 1968.

76. Corporate Planning Department, "Policy-Planning Board Meeting #2," black binder, 3/68.

77. "Notes on meeting in Muskoka with R. F. Black and J. N. Bauman," two-page typescript.

78. J. Irwin Miller, "Opportunities of a changing decade," speech delivered at the Cummins national distributors' meeting in Chicago, 3/14/60.

79. Columbus *Evening Republican*, 3/21/63.

80. Annual report for 1963; *Power-Plus News* (November 1967; "Plaintiff's brief before trial"; N. A. Weil memo to Nev Reiners, 5/6/64.

81. J. Irwin Miller, "Why Cummins must lead."

82. *Columbus Evening Republican*, 1/13/65.

83. *Power-Plus News* (October 1965); *Power-Plus News* (September 1966).

84. *Columbus Evening Republican*, 5/4/66; *Power-Plus News* (September 1967).

85. Annual report for 1968.

86. Jim Henderson interview, 4/18/94; Philip Jones interview, 9/3/95.

87. Annual report for 1968.

88. J. Irwin Miller memo to Don Tull, 5/21/62; J. Irwin Miller memo to Dick Stoner, 6/27/62.

89. See Warren Snyder biography in *Power-Plus News* (March 28, 1962); and Nicholas Weil biography in *Power-Plus News* (July 23, 1963).

90. See, for example, Jim Henderson interview, 4/18/94.

91. *Power-Plus News* (November 11, 1965).

92. See, for example, "Notes on meeting in Muskoka."

93. Henry Schacht interview, 9/7/94.

94. Ben Bush interview, 6/23/94.

95. Reece Hatchitt memo to Robert Huthsteiner, 6/15/59; *Power-Plus News*, 6/17/60.

96. An extensive summary of S. L. Kirloskar's background is "Highlights and background on S. L. Kirloskar," 9/26/63, an attachment to F. R. Souza's memo, 9/26/63.

97. Ray Boll interview, 8/9/93.

98. D. G. Clodfelter memo to J. Irwin Miller, 11/6/61; Waldo Harrison memo to J. Irwin Miller, 11/14/61.

99. Carl Gossman and C. B. White memo to Reece Hatchitt, 3/23/60; Waldo Harrison and Reece Hatchitt memo to Don Tull, quoting Gossman, 5/17/60.

100. Waldo Harrison and Reece Hatchitt memo to Don Tull, 5/17/60.

101. Waldo Harrison memo to Don Tull, 1/29/60.

102. Waldo Harrison memo to J. Irwin Miller, 11/11/61.

103. Waldo Harrison memo to J. Irwin Miller; Reece Hatchitt telex to Ray Boll, 11/18/61.

104. The board minutes for the early years of Kirloskar-Cummins are retained in the Cummins Inactive Records area (Box 29-4-23).

105. *Power-Plus News* (July 26, 1962); Cummins presentation to the Investment Analysts Society of Chicago, 4/4/63.

106. *Power-Plus News* (October 29, 1962).

107. *Power-Plus News* (November 11, 1963).

108. Richard Stoner interview, 8/18/93; annual reports for 1965 and 1967; *Columbus Evening Republican*, 4/7/65.

109. Waldo Harrison memo to Don Tull, 8/13/63.

110. *Power-Plus News* (June 17, 1960).

111. Cummins board minutes, 7/26/60. The mislabeled "General Administration Kirloskar Chrysler Board Meeting Minutes" box (29-4-22) also contains information on Krupp. In particular, Folder 103 ("Krupp 103. Administration, background") is the source of most of this material.

112. Henry Schacht interview, 9/7/94; although H. Bromme's 1/24/68 memo and an article in the 7/29/68 issue of *Der Spiegel* suggest that Daimler-Benz soon had a much larger share of the market.
113. W. H. Opfermann memo to Ray Boll, 11/18/65.
114. Reece Hatchitt memo to Cummins' senior management, 6/17/63; board minutes, 5/22/62; *Power-Plus News* (June 17, 1960).
115. *Power-Plus News* (December 27, 1963); W. H. Opfermann memo to Ray Boll, 11/18/65.
116. Hamilton Goff "exhibits" supplement, 4/29/65, to his memo to Ray Boll, 4/21/65.
117. Berthold Beitz letter to J. Irwin Miller, 8/17/64.
118. W. H. Opfermann memo to Ray Boll, 11/18/65.
119. Ray Boll memo to Don Tull, 7/5/66; Cummins press release, 8/31/66; *Der Spiegel*, 7/29/68.
120. *Der Spiegel*, 7/29/68; H. Bromme memo to Henry Schacht, 1/24/68; Henry Schacht interview, 9/7/94.
121. Cummins Annual Statistical Report for 1970.
122. *Power-Plus News* (July 25, 1963); Henry Schacht interview, 9/7/94.
123. Unless otherwise noted, all material in this section is from Box 58-6-23, also labeled "President's Office 0514," in Cummins' Inactive Records. Labeling within this box is somewhat haphazard.
124. *Columbus Evening Republican*, 12/3/63.
125. *Columbus Evening Republican*, 3/4/66; *Economic Report of the President*, February 1986 (Washington, D.C.: Government Printing Office): 373.
126. Unsigned internal memo, 1/11/68.
127. Henry Schacht memo to Dick Stoner, 1/17/68.
128. Henry Schacht memo to Dick Stoner, 1/31/68.
129. George Rehfeldt memo to Dick Stoner, 3/18/68; George Rehfeldt memo to Henry Schacht, 3/26/68; annual report for 1968.
130. J. Irwin Miller (in London) memo to Don Tull, Ray Boll, Nev Reiners, and Dick Stoner, 7/14/64.
131. Jim Henderson interview, 4/18/94.
132. Paris Letsinger memo to the Executive Committee, 3/29/45; H. L. Knudsen memo to the Executive Committee, 4/27/45.
133. See J. Irwin Miller letter to John O. Ross, 8/10/63.
134. See, for example, *Columbus Evening Republican*, 10/2/62.
135. Annual report for 1967.
136. J. Irwin Miller letter to Eugenet E. Paul (school board chairman and Cummins' vice president for domestic subsidiaries), 11/13/63; *Columbus Evening Republican*, 8/4/65; J. Irwin Miller letter to Clarence E. Robbins, 9/11/64.
137. Randy Tucker memo to the Cummins Engine Foundation's board of directors, 11/13/63; *Columbus Evening Republican*, 6/8/66 and 6/20/66.
138. Walter N. Thayer memo to J. Irwin Miller, 6/12/68; George Newlin memo to J. Irwin Miller, 12/26/69.
139. Annual report for 1963; J. Irwin Miller memo to S. E. Lauther, T. R. Reed, Don Tull, and George Newlin, 7/12/63.
140. See the front page of the *Indianapolis Recorder*, 1/11/64.
141. J. Irwin Miller query scribbled on H. W. Abts memo to Dick Stoner, 1/15/64, which was the first "Corporate Negro Employment Status Report."
142. J. Irwin Miller memo to H. W. Abts, 3/17/64.
143. J. Irwin Miller speech, "Urban problems affect us all," quoted *Power-Plus News*, 2/68.
144. J. Irwin Miller letter to Mayor Eret Kline, 12/10/68.
145. Although this correspondence has not been located, this story was told to the authors by several interviewees. For an example of Miller holding a bureaucrat's feet to the fire, see his correspondence with the Mid-Mississippi Development District, 12/10/62.
146. J. Irwin Miller letter, 3/9/64, "Communications and telephone calls" file, Marion Dietrich's White Motors papers.
147. *Power-Plus News* (November 1967).
148. *Power-Plus News* (November 1967); "An inspired renaissance in Indiana," *Life* (November 17, 1967): 76.
149. *Power-Plus News* (November 1967); "An inspired renaissance in Indiana," *Life*, 76; "Skyline rises in a Corn Belt town," *Business Week* (November 18, 1967): 138; *Esquire* (February 1968).
150. Dick Stoner, during Ray Boll interview, 8/2/93.
151. Don Tull memo to J. Irwin Miller, 5/4/61.
152. Annual report for 1967.
153. Cummins Annual Statistical Report for 1970.
154. *Power-Plus News* (November 1967).
155. See the interesting letter from and interview with E. Don Tull, "Reorganization aimed toward company's profitable growth," and a Cummins organization chart (rarely made public), in *Power-Plus News*, 1/68.
156. *Columbus Evening Republican*, 10/13/69.
157. From Schacht's "Domestic Subsidiaries Strategy," written just before his promotion was made public.
158. "Cummins Engine sees record profit in 1969," *Wall Street Journal*, 10/16/69.
159. *Cummins Management Newsletter*, 9/27/68.
160. Annual reports for 1961 and 1969.
161. Cummins Annual Statistical Report for 1970.
162. Cummins Annual Statistical Report for 1970.

Chapter 7

1. Annual statistical report for 1970.
2. Henry Schacht memo to Don Tull, 6/24/69.
3. Jim Henderson interview, 6/23/94.
4. Henry Schacht's handwritten notes for his presentation to Cummins R&E personnel, 2/11/70.
5. Annual statistical report for 1970.
6. Jim Henderson interview, 6/23/94.
7. *Columbus Evening Republican*, 1/24/67 and 4/27/67.
8. See also John Hackett's memo to division managers and profit center managers, 3/19/69.
9. For the best summary of the five-year plan and the strategy that lay behind it see Henry Schacht memo to Don Tull, 6/24/69.
10. John Hackett memo to J. Irwin Miller, Don Tull, Dick Stoner, and Henry Schacht, 4/25/72.
11. Henry Schacht speech to the New York Automotive Analysts, 12/17/70.
12. The K2 history comes from a number of sources, including: *Power Team*, 1/73; Cummins management newsletter, 9/22/70; "Making skis on a Pacific isle," *New York Times*, 11/28/76; and "The ski moguls," *Seattle* magazine (November 1970).
13. John Hackett "K2 Corporation" memo, c. spring 1971.
14. "Skiing: The new lure of a supersport," *Time* (December 25, 1972).
15. "Making skis on a Pacific isle," *New York Times*.
16. Board minutes, 9/9/70.
17. J. Irwin Miller letter to H. W. Kirschner, 11/20/70.
18. John Hackett memo to J. Irwin Miller, 2/1/69; Henry Schacht interview, 10/6/94; John Hackett interview, 2/23/94; John Hackett memo to J. Irwin Miller, Don Tull, and Dick Stoner, 1/30/69.
19. John Hackett memo to J. Irwin Miller, Dick Stoner, and Henry Schacht, 5/22/72.
20. John Hackett memo to J. Irwin Miller, 2/22/72.
21. Annual report for 1970; John Hackett memo to J. Irwin Miller, 2/22/72.
22. John Hackett memo to J. Irwin Miller, 2/22/72.
23. John Hackett interview, 2/23/94.
24. *London Sunday Times*, 1/28/73.
25. Brendan McDonald letter to Ed Booth, 12/3/71.
26. Paul Berman report to John Hackett, 1/21/72.
27. Annual report for 1972; John Hackett memo to J. Irwin Miller, Don Tull, Dick Stoner, and Henry Schacht, 4/25/72; John Hackett memo to J. Irwin Miller, Dick Stoner, and Henry Schacht, 5/22/72.
28. *Power Team*, 11/72.
29. John Hackett interview, 2/23/94.
30. John Hackett memo to J. Irwin Miller, 8/9/71.
31. Annual statistical report for 1977; *Power Team*, 11/72.
32. Annual statistical report for 1970.
33. John Hackett memo to J. Irwin Miller, Don Tull, and Henry Schacht, 4/11/72; *Cummins News*, 2/71.
34. John Hackett memo to J. Irwin Miller, Don Tull, and Henry Schacht, 4/11/72.
35. *Columbus Evening Republican*, 2/6/70.
36. *Cummins News*, 4/71.
37. *Cummins News*, 2/70.
38. Henry Schacht presentation to Cummins shareholders, 4/7/70.
39. Marion Dietrich interview, 6/28/94.
40. Henry Schacht presentation to the international and domestic subsidiaries' DWU and Office Committee representatives, 5/8/68; annual statistical report for 1970.
41. Annual statistical report for 1970; John Hackett memo to J. Irwin Miller, 3/15/71.
42. *Cummins News*, 6/71; John Hackett memo to J. Irwin Miller, 3/15/71.
43. *Cummins News*, 6/71 and 6/72; John Hackett memo to Henry Schacht, 3/24/72; Marion Dietrich interview, 6/28/94.
44. Henry Schacht remarks at corporate planning meeting, 6/75.
45. Henry Schacht memo to J. Irwin Miller, 1/4/74; annual report for 1973.
46. Annual report for 1973; John Hackett memo to Henry Schacht, 3/24/72.
47. John Hackett memo to W. T. Hergenrader, 3/15/71.
48. John Hackett memo to all departments and division heads, 2/9/72.
49. Jim Henderson interview, 6/23/94; annual statistical report for 1977.
50. *Power Team*, 4/76; Henry Schacht remarks at corporate planning meeting, 6/75.
51. Annual reports for 1975 and 1976; "Making skis on a Pacific isle," *New York Times*.
52. Annual statistical report for 1977.
53. Annual statistical report for 1977.
54. *Power–Plus News*, 8/69 and 12/69; *Cummins News*, 2/70.
55. J. Irwin Miller memo to Jim Henderson, 4/29/74.

56. *Columbus Evening Republican*, 2/25/70. Henderson (whose executive-recruitment duties had taken him out of town frequently) was a virtual unknown in the Columbus community. The local paper mistakenly ran a picture of someone else along with the announcement of Henderson's promotion.
57. Jim Henderson interview, 1/8/97.
58. *Columbus Evening Republican*, 4/7/70 and 4/8/70.
59. *Cummins News*, 10/70; *Columbus Evening Republican*, 4/7/70, 4/8/70, and 7/15/72.
60. The figure includes a 100,000-square foot 1970 addition to the Atlas plant in Fostoria, Ohio, as well as office expansion in Columbus.
61. *Columbus Evening Republican*, 2/24/72; annual report for 1972.
62. *Power Team*, 4/74.
63. Henry Schacht memo to J. Irwin Miller, 12/3/73.
64. The Crane Carrier story is told in a series of letters in Miller's correspondence files, beginning with a J. Richardson Dilworth letter to J. Irwin Miller, 5/21/73.
65. R. L. Zeligson memo to T. F. Walkowicz, 5/14/73.
66. Henry Schacht memo to J. Irwin Miller, 2/27/74.
67. John Hackett memo to all "distributor owners," 7/15/69.
68. Henry Schacht memo to Dick Stoner, 8/20/69.
69. John Hackett memo to J. Irwin Miller and Henry Schacht, 10/2/72.
70. See, for example, Herschel O'Shaughnessey interview, 2/1/95.
71. *Cummins News*, 7/70.
72. *Columbus Evening Republican*, 11/1/71 and 9/13/72; *Cummins News*, 12/71; *Power Team*, 2/76 and 1/81.
73. *Power Team*, 2/76.
74. Henry Schacht memo to J. Irwin Miller, 5/3/73.
75. Larry Niehart interview, 6/24/94.
76. See, for example, Ted Marston interview, 1/30/95; and Henry Schacht interview, 10/6/94.
77. Jim Henderson memo to J. Irwin Miller, 11/18/70.
78. *Columbus Evening Republican*, 2/25/69 through 3/19/69 and 10/12/73.
79. Ted Marston interview, 1/30/95.
80. Jim Henderson interview, 12/14/94; *Columbus Evening Republican*, 5/12/71 and 5/15/71.
81. J. Irwin Miller memo to Jim Henderson, 7/7/71.
82. *Power Team*, 6/75.
83. *Columbus Evening Republican*, 12/7/70; Ted Marston interview, 1/30/95.
84. Specifics on the pre-strike negotiations are from a single sheet labeled "Background," but not otherwise identified. Judging from the final entries on the sheet, it appears to be information provided by the company to federal mediators in Washington in April 1972.
85. *Columbus Evening Republican*, 2/28/72 and 3/1/72.
86. Jim Henderson interview, 12/14/94.
87. See, for example, *Power Team*, 1/73.
88. See, for example, Lee Cross memo to Jim Henderson, 3/2/72.
89. All quotes and paraphrases from a folder entitled, "Minutes 1972 negotiations, outside sourcing," which contains the relevant meeting minutes.
90. "Minutes of the 47th negotiations session, March 21, 1972," from "minutes" folder.
91. *Columbus Evening Republican*, 3/17/72, and 3/21/72 through 3/24/72.
92. *Columbus Evening Republican*, 3/22/72.
93. Larry Neihart interview, 6/24/94; Ted Marston interview, 1/30/95.
94. This is the authors' interpretation of the contract language, but it is confirmed by (among others) Ted Marston, in his 1/30/95 interview.
95. *Columbus Evening Republican*, 4/3/72.
96. "Payboard regulations" internal memo, 2/21/72; *Columbus Evening Republican*, 4/8/72.
97. *Columbus Evening Republican*, 4/10/72.
98. Jim Henderson interview, 6/23/94; *Columbus Evening Republican*, 4/27/72.
99. Jim Henderson letter to Charles E. M. Rentschler, 5/2/72.
100. *Power Team*, 3/73 and 11/73; annual statistical report for 1977.
101. Henry Schacht memo to J. Irwin Miller, 5/23/72; Jim Henderson interview, 6/23/94.
102. J. Irwin Miller memo to Henry Schacht, 4/11/73.
103. See, for example, Ted Marston interview, 1/30/95.
104. *Columbus Evening Republican*, 6/30/72.
105. J. Irwin Miller memo to Henry Schacht, Jim Henderson, and Ted Marston, 4/28/72.
106. J. Irwin Miller memo to Henry Schacht, Jim Henderson, and Ted Marston, 8/22/72; J. Irwin Miller memo to Jim Henderson, 4/29/74.
107. See, for example, R. F. Richard memo to Jim Henderson, 6/16/69; J. Irwin Miller interview, 10/26/93; *Power Team*, 1/73; and *Columbus Evening Republican*, 4/3/74.
108. Frederick Herzberg et al., *The Motivation to Work* (New York: Wiley, 1959).
109. Herzberg, *The Motivation to Work*, 72, 132; M. Scott Myers, "Who are your motivated workers?" *Harvard Business Review* (January 1964): 73–88.

110. The firm's 6/25/70 report, entitled "Review of the Factory Job Evaluation Program," has not been located; but an 8/7/70 letter from the firm to J. A. Henderson summarizes its contents.

111. D. G. Prock and J. Longley memo to the Operating Team, 6/9/81.

112. Henry Schacht memo to J. Irwin Miller, 11/11/72.

113. Much of the Charleston history is taken from a D. G. Prock and J. Longley memo to the Operating Team, 6/9/81, and D. G. Prock memo to the Operating Team, 6/19/81.

114. J. Irwin Miller memo to Jim Henderson, 3/27/73.

115. D. G. Prock memo to the Operating Team, 6/19/81.

116. *Columbus Evening Republican*, 5/18/74.

117. D. G. Prock memo to the Operating Team, 6/19/81.

118. *Columbus Evening Republican*, 4/11/74. For background on the Jamestown plant, see binder labeled "Plant Selection, Jamestown, New York," in Box 40-1-14, Inactive Records.

119. "Plant Selection, Jamestown, New York."

120. *Power Team*, 11/79.

121. Ted Marston interview, 1/30/95.

122. Jim Henderson interview, 2/27/95.

123. Henry Schacht memo to file, 10/21/74.

124. *Power Team*, 1/75.

125. "Back to diesel basics at Cummins Engine," *Business Week* (July 25, 1977): 152; *Columbus Evening Republican*, 1/17/75 and 1/23/75.

126. *Power Team*, 4/75 and 12/76; *Columbus Evening Republican*, 1/28/75.

127. *Columbus Evening Republican*, 4/28/75; annual statistical report for 1977.

128. J. Irwin Miller planning letter, 3/18/70.

129. Tom Head memo to J. Irwin Miller, 8/29/72.

130. A key source for this section is the 1975 inventory study conducted by Jim Henderson and his colleagues, and circulated to Cummins' management team on 4/21/75.

131. Annual statistical report for 1982; Jim Henderson interviews, 6/23/94 and 9/23/96.

132. Henderson inventory study.

133. This story is seconded by financial officer John McLachlan, who—along with colleague Mike Jack—accompanied Henderson to the "Mater Mill."

134. Annual statistical report for 1975.

135. See, for example, J. T. Hackett's bemused memo to J. Irwin Miller, 12/9/74.

136. *Power Team*, 7/74.

137. Annual statistical report for 1977.

Chapter 8

1. Statistical annual report for 1977.

2. *Columbus Evening Republican*, 9/15/71; annual report for 1976; Henry Schacht speech to the annual "worldwide planning conference," 5/14/74.

3. John Hackett memo to J. Irwin Miller and Henry Schacht, 4/16/74.

4. Annual report for 1976; "Back to diesel basics at Cummins Engine," *Business Week* (July 25, 1977); statistical annual report for 1977.

5. John Hackett memo to Henry Schacht and Jim Henderson, 11/6/78.

6. Statistical annual report for 1977; *Power Team*, 12/74.

7. Henry Schacht interview, 10/6/94; annual report for 1977; "Vroom . . .Vroom," *Forbes* (July 15, 1977).

8. John Hackett interview, 2/23/94; statistical annual report for 1977.

9. *Power-Plus News*, 12/69.

10. *Cummins News*, 6/70.

11. Much of this background on federal air-pollution regulations in the late 1960s and early 1970s is taken from an excellent summary prepared for Cummins by the Washington-based law firm of Arent, Fox, Kintner, Plotkin & Kahn, submitted on 2/1/73, and titled "Federal environmental legislation: A review of major federal legislation regulating environmental pollution."

12. *Power-Plus News*, 11/69; *Cummins News*, 2/70.

13. Henry Schacht speech to the Harvard Business School Club of Central Indiana, 3/11/70.

14. Material on the early history of the EPA is from Marc K. Landry, Marc J. Roberts, and Stephen R. Thomas, *The Environmental Protection Agency: Asking the Wrong Questions from Nixon to Clinton* (New York: Oxford University Publishing, 1994).

15. *Power Team*, 9/97.

16. Henry Schacht speech at the national distributors sales meeting, 1/28/71.

17. See, for example, J. Irwin Miller planning letter, 3/18/70.

18. J. Irwin Miller's testimony is quoted in Robert Cahn, *Footprints on the Planet* (New York: Universe Book, 1978), 116.

19. "Auto firms shortsighted on pollution, critic claims," *Washington Post*, 3/27/72. The witness, J. Lee Rankin, said that Detroit manufacturers would meet the 1975 standards only if they were "literally forced to."
20. *Power Team*, 11/72.
21. Henry Schacht memo to J. Irwin Miller, 2/5/72.
22. See Cahn, *Footprints on the Planet*, 119–23, for an excellent summary of Cummins' role in the writing of the 1977 amendments to the Clean Air Act.
23. Henry Schacht, "Business and broader objectives," speech to the Conference on National Planning on Regulatory Reform, delivered by R. B. Stoner, 4/27/78.
24. Charles W. Powers memo to J. Irwin Miller, 10/5/76. The authors are greatly indebted to Charles Powers, former vice president of public policy at Cummins, whose personal recollections of and extensive files from this period greatly clarified Cummins' contributions to the Clean Air Act, as well as other issues. Powers' "A history of the Health Effects Institute from the viewpoint of an interested participant/observer," November 1991 (hereafter cited as Charles. W. Powers "History," is an especially useful and interesting case study of the joint efforts of the federal government and a besieged industry to find a *modus vivendi*.
25. See, for example, Cummins third quarterly report on clean air, 10/12/77, which defines the revised target as a 75 percent reduction in oxides of nitrogen by 1985.
26. Charles W. Powers memo to J. Irwin Miller, 10/5/76.
27. Cummins third quarterly report on clean air, 10/12/77.
28. Schacht speech, 4/27/78.
29. See Lawrence Susskind and Jeffrey Cruikshank, *Breaking the Impasse* (New York: Basic Books, 1987), 21.
30. Beginning in 1971, the federal government budgeted $15 million a year for research into internal combustion engines—a move that Henry Schacht, among others, thought was a waste of money. See Schacht speech, 1/28/71.
31. Charles W. Powers, "History"; R. J. Chalfant memo to the "CC list" of parties interested in air pollution at Cummins, 4/25/78.
32. W. T. Lyn and M. A. Zimmerman memo to the environmental "CC list," 5/4/78.
33. Charles W. Powers interview, 2/17/95; "A pollution cloud over the diesel car," *Business Week* (May 8, 1978): 39.
34. Charles W. Powers, "History."
35. Charles W. Powers, "History"; and various conversations at Cummins.
36. Chalfant memo to environmental "CC list," 4/25/78.
37. "A pollution cloud over the diesel car," *Business Week*; unattributed newspaper article attached to Randy Tucker memo to G. L. Olson, 6/28/78.
38. "Wage-Price Council criticizes EPA rules for diesel vehicles," *New York Times*, 4/23/79; *Arizona Republic*, 4/25/79.
39. Charles W. Powers, "History."
40. Paula A. Gustafson and Tina Vujovich memo to Peter Hamilton, 2/17/86, attached to a second memo to Hamilton, 5/8/86.
41. Charles W. Powers, "History"; Mike Brewer and Tina Vujovich memo to Henry Schacht, 11/12/84.
42. Henry Schacht memo to file, 1/19/79.
43. Thomas Murphy letter to Henry Schacht, 12/31/80.
44. Bill Schwab interview, 9/30/93.
45. Bill Schwab interview, 9/30/93.
46. Joe Butler interview, 7/22/93.
47. J. Irwin Miller memo to Henry Schacht, 10/19/72.
48. *Columbus Evening Republican*, 10/17/70; Joe Butler interview, 7/22/93.
49. See, for example, Henry Schacht memo to Don Tull, 8/16/71.
50. *Power Team*, 11/72.
51. Gary Nelson interview, 10/1/96; John Hackett interview, 2/23/94; *Columbus Evening Republican*, 7/20/70.
52. *Power Team*, 11/72.
53. *Cummins News*, 10/70, which gives details on both engines. Each engine was photographed, and the groups depicted in the two photographs reveal where Cummins was placing its bets. The VT-903 was surrounded by no fewer than seven Cummins vice presidents.
54. *Power Team*, 9/73.
55. Unless otherwise noted, the Holset story comes from the John Hackett interview, 2/23/94; and John Hackett's memo to J. Irwin Miller, 7/31/73.
56. John Hackett letter to Louis P. Croset, 9/20/73.
57. *Power Team*, 9/73.
58. *Power Team*, 4/75.
59. Tim Solso interview, 1/4/95.
60. *Power Team*, 1/80; J. Irwin Miller memo to Henry Schacht, 7/6/78; statistical annual report for 1981.
61. Phil Jones said 1969 in an interview published in *Power Team*, 4/75; but Karl Kuehner clearly recalls the project starting in 1968.
62. *Power Team*, 11/72.
63. Phil Jones interview, 1/3/95; *Columbus Evening Republican*, 11/26/71; Gary Nelson interview, 3/4/95; *Power Team*, 10/74.

64. Jim Henderson interview, 2/27/95.
65. *Power Team*, 11/72; Gary Nelson interview, 3/4/95.
66. *Power Team*, 4/79; "Automotive power," undated Cummins product brochure, c. 1977.
67. *Columbus Evening Republican*, 9/29/73 and 11/29/73; *Power Team*, 12/74.
68. *Power Team*, 6/75 and 12/76; Gary Nelson interview, 3/4/95; "A revved-up market for diesel engine makers," *Business Week* (February 5, 1979).
69. Jim Henderson interview, 1/8/97; Gary Nelson interview, 11/3/96; internal production and market share statistics.
70. *Power Team*, 12/76.
71. "Vroom . . . Vroom," *Forbes*.
72. Statistical annual report for 1982; Jim Henderson interview, 2/27/95.
73. Gary Nelson interview, 3/4/95; Jim Henderson interview, 2/27/95.
74. *Power Team*, 4/75.
75. One measure of the Rainbow engines' initial obscurity is their almost complete lack of a paper trail in company records. Their story is mainly reconstructed from oral interviews, particularly with Phil Jones, Bill Schwab, and Gary Nelson.
76. Bill Schwab interview, 9/30/93.
77. D. C. Harrison and M. Ogata "technical memorandum," 7/24/75.
78. See, for example, Jim Henderson memo to J. Irwin Miller, 9/20/73.
79. J. Irwin Miller memo to Jim Henderson, 9/18/73.
80. J. Irwin Miller memo to Jim Henderson, 9/18/73; Henry Schacht memo to J. Irwin Miller, 5/22/75.
81. "What powers Cummins," *Management Today*, 2/78.
82. *Columbus Evening Republican*, 12/18/71.
83. *Cummins News*, 6/70.
84. *Columbus Evening Republic*, 12/22/70.
85. See Margaret A. Nave letter to J. Irwin Miller, 1/21/71; and his response, 2/5/71.
86. J. Irwin Miller memo to Jim Henderson, 4/29/71.
87. J. Irwin Miller "planning memo" to Henry Schacht and others, 3/18/70.
88. This segment is derived from the foundation's annual reports (especially 1968 and 1971) and from a historical summary of CEF prepared by Cummins.
89. P. C. Sorenson memo to the CEF board, 1/23/69; *Columbus Evening Republican*, 3/25/75.
90. *Columbus Evening Republican*, 2/5/74.
91. *Columbus Evening Republican*, 10/17/75.
92. George Newlin memo to J. Irwin Miller, 4/11/78.
93. *Cummins News*, 6/72.
94. *Columbus Evening Republican*, 6/30/72.
95. "Companies must be good citizens," *Iron Age*, 8/23/76.
96. John Hackett memo to the Finance Division staff, 5/21/73; "Companies must be good citizens," *Iron Age*.
97. John Hackett memo to R. E. Brooker and J. P. Stanton. 2/18/74.
98. Henry Schacht memo to "all exempt personnel," 6/22/76.
99. Henry Schacht memo to "all exempt personnel," 6/22/76.
100. Charles W. Powers, "Using the Welfare Effects on Stakeholders as a Strategic Guide to Foreign Investment Decisions," undated paper, provided to the authors by Powers.
101. Charles W. Powers, "Using the Welfare Effects"; Charles W. Powers interview, 2/17/95.
102. "Cummins Engine: The role of corporate responsibility," *The Personnel Administrator*, 10/76.
103. Arthur Taylor (CBS president) letter to Henry Schacht, 6/13/74.
104. Statistical annual report for 1982.
105. "Outlook for heavy trucks," *Ward's Auto World*, 9/79; Henry Schacht memo to J. Irwin Miller, 6/22/79.
106. Statistical annual report for 1982.
107. Annual report for 1976.
108. J. Irwin Miller memo to Henry Schacht and Jim Henderson, 10/24/77.

Chapter 9

1. Annual report for 1979.
2. From Cummins documents cited in David B. Yoffie, "Cummins Engine Company in 1979," Harvard Business School case #9-387-066.
3. Robert S. Strauss (Special Counselor on Inflation to President Jimmy Carter) letter to Henry Schacht, 7/26/78; and Schacht's response, 9/27/78.
4. Statistical annual report for 1982.
5. Financial factbook, 1980; Henry Schacht letter to Robert S. Strauss, 7/26/78.
6. Inferred from data in the statistical annual report for 1982; and "A revved-up market for diesel engine makers," *Business Week* (February 5, 1979).
7. *Cincinnati Enquirer*, 4/8/79.

8. Henry Schacht letter to Franklin Thomas, 1/26/79; Henry Schacht memo to Jim Henderson, 4/26/79.
9. "A revved-up market for diesel engine makers," *Business Week*; Henry Schacht memo to J. Irwin Miller, 6/22/79.
10. *Power Team* (March 1980); "A revved-up market for diesel engine makers," *Business Week*.
11. Planning Conference, 4/78.
12. See Henry Mintzberg, *The Rise and Fall of Strategic Planning* (New York: Free Press, 1994).
13. Alfred D. Chandler, Jr., *Scale and Scope: The Dynamics of Industrial Capitalism* (Cambridge, Mass.: Harvard University Press, 1990), 1–46.
14. Annual report for 1979.
15. High fuel prices were noted frequently during this period in internal and external documents, often as the key factor in Cummins' planning. See, for example: Planning Conference, fall 1980; annual report for 1982; and Henry Schacht as quoted in Harold Seneker, "Fasten Seat Belts," *Forbes* (June 9, 1980): 43–44.
16. Daniel Yergin, *The Prize: The Epic Quest for Oil, Money, and Power* (New York: Simon & Schuster, 1991), 625; Richard H. K. Vietor, *Energy Policy in America since 1945* (Cambridge, England: Cambridge University Press, 1984), 269.
17. Seneker, "Fasten Seat Belts."
18. Statistical annual reports for various years; *Power Team* (October 1982).
19. Bill Schwab interview, 9/30/93.
20. Gary Nelson interview, 3/4/95.
21. Gary Nelson interview, 3/4/95.
22. *Power Team* (May/June 1981); *Power Team* (January/February 1982); *Power Team* (October 1982).
23. Jim Henderson interview with Henry Schacht, 2/27/95.
24. Henry Schacht interview with Jim Henderson, 10/20/94.
25. Henry Schacht interview, 10/6/94; Henry Schacht interview with Jim Henderson, 10/20/94.
26. John Hackett, "Corporate Strategy" memo, 12/10/79.
27. *New York Times,* 5/17/79; *Cleveland Plain Dealer,* 6/24/79.
28. The Case story is derived in part from the Jim Farrar interview, 10/22/96; and various interviews with Jim Henderson.
29. C. H. Wendel, *150 Years of J. I. Case* (Sarasota, Fla.: Crestline Publishing, 1991), 1–27; J. L. Keyes (Cummins Industrial Marketing) memo to J. Irwin Miller, 12/23/75.
30. Case-Cummins "Position Paper," 8/30/79.
31. Board minutes, 2/8/83; Jim Farrar, "B/C Series Time Line, Chrysler Program," 5/88.
32. Board minutes, 5/31/79; *New York Times,* 6/14/80; Executive and Finance Committee minutes, 5/15/80; Case/Cummins "position paper," 8/30/79.
33. H. A. Smitson, Jr. (vice president, Case-Cummins) memo to several executives, 4/9/80.
34. Press release, 12/10/80.
35. *Power Team* (November/ December 1980); *Power Team* (January-February 1982).
36. Case/Cummins "position paper," 8/30/79; *Power Team* (January-February 1982).
37. Board minutes, 2/12/80; annual reports for 1980 and 1981.
38. Tom Head memo to several executives, 5/7/80.
39. *New York Times*, 5/17/80, 2/26/82, 8/24/82, 9/3/82; annual reports, 1975–1982.
40. Tom Harrison interview, 1/24/94.
41. J. Irwin Miller memo to Jim Henderson, 7/21/73.
42. G. L. Olson memo to Henry Schacht, 7/1/77; Henry B. Schacht and Charles W. Powers, "Business Responsibility and the Public Policy Process," in Thornton Bradshaw and David Vogel, eds., *Corporations and Their Critics* (New York: McGraw-Hill, 1981), 29–30.
43. G. L. Olson memo to H. B. Schacht, 7/1/77; Tom Harrison interview, 1/24/94.
44. Kevin Roche letter to J. Irwin Miller, 12/23/77.
45. Jim Henderson memo to division and department heads, 10/2/81; L. P. Berman memo to J. Irwin Miller, 10/13/82; press release 10/14/82; *Columbus Evening Republican,* 10/14/82; memo [author unknown] attached to J. Irwin Miller memo to Henry Schacht and Jim Henderson, 3/30/82.
46. See for example: B. Randolph, "Minding its own business," *Forbes* (March 14, 1983); A. Bianco, "Cummins makes a comeback," *Business Week* (November 12,1984); Matt O'Connor, "Cummins cut headed off the Japanese," *Chicago Tribune,* 3/3/86; G. N. Smith, "The Yankee Samurai," *Forbes* (July 14, 1986).
47. Michael Schroeder, "The Quiet Coup at Alcoa," *Business Week* (June 27, 1988).
48. Schroeder, "Quiet Coup at Alcoa"; Jim Henderson interview, 7/10/95; Henry Schacht interview, 10/6/94.
49. Schroeder, "Quiet Coup at Alcoa"; Jim Henderson interview, 7/10/95.
50. Planning Conference documents, 9/78.
51. Board minutes, 12/11/79 and 2/12/80; Cummins 1981 annual report.
52. Cummins 1983 annual report.
53. Cummins 1985 annual report.
54. Cummins 1984 annual report.
55. Cummins 1986 annual report.
56. Tom Head memo to several executives, 5/7/80; Tom Head, "The Case/Cummins Project," *Power Team* (November/December 1980); Case-Cummins "position paper," 8/30/79.
57. From the 1/23/87 "B/C Executive Summary," from M. W. Howell and J. C. Read to the Engine Business Staff.
58. Case-Cummins "position paper," 8/30/79.

59. From the "Affiliated Enterprises Quarter 1, 1983 review," circulated on 4/17/83.

60. From a handwritten "B/C series time line, Chrysler program," prepared in 1988 by Jim Farrar.

61. From an undated internal Onan Engine history, faxed to Cummins in August 1989 to inform Cummins' Kubota background file.

62. John T. Hackett letter to D. K. Cross, 10/4/85.

63. First Boston Research progress report for Cooper Industries, Inc., 9/24/85, "Summary of New York meeting on McGraw-Edison Acquisition."

64. John T. Hackett memo to Jim Henderson and Henry Schacht, 10/9/85.

65. Cummins 1986 annual report.

66. For details of the proposed agreement, see John T. Hackett letter to David G. Bury, director of Hawker Siddeley, and Ronald N. Hoge, president of Onan, 12/10/87.

67. Cummins 1986 annual report.

68. Cummins 1991 and 1994 annual reports.

69. Henry Schacht memo to J. Irwin Miller, 2/3/74.

70. Henry Schacht memo to J. Irwin Miller, 2/3/74.

71. Much of this history is taken from Henry Schacht's draft memo to the board of directors, 11/20/74; and John Hackett's memo to Henry Schacht, Marion Dietrich, and Jim Henderson, 11/5/71. See also _Power Team_ (July 1974).

72. _Cummins News_, 12/71; Ben Bush interview, 6/23/94; Jack Edwards interview, 1/31/95.

73. _Columbus Evening Republican_, 1/3/75.

74. Ben Bush interview, 6/23/94.

75. _Columbus Evening Republican_, 12/20/72.

76. John Hackett memo to J. Irwin Miller, Don Tull, Dick Stoner, and Henry Schacht, 4/17/72; Henry Schacht draft memo to the board of directors, 11/20/74.

77. _Columbus Evening Republican_, 1/3/75.

78. _Power Team_ (April 1976); annual report for 1975.

78. Annual report for 1976.

80. John Hackett memo to Jim Henderson, 5/12/78.

81. Jack Edwards interview, 1/31/95; John Hackett memo to Ben Bush, 5/12/78.

82. Jack Edwards interview, 1/31/95; Reference Book, 1981.

83. John Hackett memo to Jim Henderson, 3/20/80.

84. Ben Bush memo to John Hackett, 7/31/80, quoting Pinheiro Neto, Cummins' lawyer in Rio de Janeiro.

85. See, for example, "In heavily burdened Brazil, buoyancy yields to despair," _New York Times_ (10/21/93).

86. This discussion of the Befiex program is largely taken from the Jack Edwards interview, 1/31/95.

87. Reference Book, 1981.

88. Meanwhile, in nearby Venezuela, political and economic turmoil was putting the entire Cummins operation in that country in jeopardy. See "Cummins Engine Company, Inc.: Black Friday," Harvard Business School case #9-586-122.

89. Cummins in 1988 stopped disaggregating data on individual countries in its financial reports, which makes apples-to-apples comparisons difficult.

90. The $70 million figure is taken from an 11/88 Cummins business profile of CUMBRASA, and is therefore relatively dependable; the $500 million figure is extrapolated, and may be somewhat low.

91. Jack Edwards interview, 1/31/95; "CUMBRASA Business Profile," 11/88; annual report for 1987.

92. See, for example, Tim Solso interview, 1/4/95.

93. _Columbus Evening Republican_, 8/23/75 and 10/3/75; annual report for 1975.

94. Jack Edwards interview, 1/31/95; John Hackett report to the board of directors, 12/11/79.

95. Reference Book, 1985; John Hackett report to the board of directors, 6/80.

96. John Hackett reports to the board of directors, 2/10/81 and 7/4/81; annual reports for 1980 and 1981; Reference Book, 1981.

97. Jack Edwards interview, 1/31/95.

98. Annual reports for 1984 and 1985.

99. Tim Solso interview, 10/4/95.

100. Annual reports for 1986 and 1987.

101. See, for example, "Westerners' joint ventures in China encounter bureaucratic delays, foreign-exchange blocks," _Wall Street Journal_, 3/18/85.

102. See, for example, "Firms doing business in China are stymied by costs and hassles," _Wall Street Journal_, 7/17/76.

Chapter 10

1. Geoffrey N. Smith, "The Yankee Samurai," _Forbes_ (July 1, 1986): 82.

2. Henry Schacht memo to several managers, 7/3/86.

3. _Power Plus_ (June 17, 1960); board minutes, 9/26/61; annual report for 1961; _Columbus Evening Republican,_ 11/16/61, 1/10/64, and 1/16/64; Ray Boll memo to Don Tull, 12/10/63.

4. Art Tajima interview, 5/9/95.
5. Art Tajima interview, 5/9/95.
6. Christopher A. Bartlett, "Komatsu: Ryoichi Kawai's Leadership," Harvard Business School case 9-390-037.
7. Art Tajima interview, 5/9/95.
8. Jim Henderson letter to John Hackett, 8/5/71.
9. "K Contract History Brief History" in M. A. Walsh memo to Henry Schacht, Jim Henderson, and John Hackett, 11/11/82; John Hackett letter to S. Sakuma, 12/17/74.
10. John Hackett letter to Marion Dietrich, 7/14/80.
11. S. H. Jenkins memo to Jim Henderson, 9/21/78.
12. W. T. Lyn and R. S. Lane memo to John Hackett, 6/9/80.
13. Bartlett, "Komatsu: Ryoichi Kawai's Leadership."
14. John Hackett memo to file, 6/18/80.
15. Will Miller memo to Henry Schacht and Dick Stoner, 8/17/81.
16. Bartlett, "Komatsu: Ryoichi Kawai's Leadership."
17. K. P. Singleton memo to Jim Henderson, Henry Schacht, and Carl Ahlers, 6/13/85.
18. Jim Henderson videotaped address, "A Message to Cummins Employees, August 1982."
19. Jim Henderson and other managers, report on "Japan Trip March, 1983."
20. Jim Henderson videotaped address, "A Message to Cummins Employees, August 1982."
21. Jim Henderson videotaped address, "Report on Japanese Engine Competition," 1984.
22. Jim Henderson videotaped address, "Report on Japanese Engine Competition," 1984.
23. Jim Henderson videotaped address, "Komatsu," March 1984.
24. Mike Walsh memo to Henry Schacht, 6/13/85.
25. Mike Walsh memo to Henry Schacht, 6/13/85; K. P. Singleton memo to Jim Henderson, Henry Schacht, and Carl Ahlers, 6/13/85.
26. Mike Walsh memo to Henry Schacht, 6/13/85; K. P. Singleton memo to Jim Henderson, Henry Schacht, and Carl Ahlers, 6/13/85; Jim Henderson telex to Shoji Nogawa, 5/24/85; Carl Ahlers memo to several Cummins executives, 6/14/85.
27. Jim Henderson videotaped address, "Report on Japanese Engine Competition," 1984.
28. *Business Week* (February 22,1988): 48.
29. Jim Henderson (taped) closing remarks at planning conference, 9/82.
30. "The 30 Month Sprint," undated summary in Jim Henderson's files.
31. Jim Henderson companywide announcement, 5/19/83.
32. B. J. White memo to Jim Henderson, T. L. Marston, and W. P. Snyder, 5/17/83.
33. Cost-reduction estimates are from John McLachlan; floor-space and payroll reduction estimates are Jim Henderson's.
34. Karl Kuehner interview, 10/21/96; Jim Kelly interview, 10/22/96.
35. J. Irwin Miller memo to Cummins management, 12/17/80.
36. The Achieving Paper went through many iterations, but its first recorded appearance is in the board minutes of 12/7/82, which state that Henderson described to the board the development of a paper entitled "Principles in Achieving a Productive Organization at Cummins."
37. From the "November version of the Achieving Paper," circulated to the Cummins planning staff on 11/4/83 by Jim Henderson.
38. See J. Irwin Miller memo to Jim Henderson and Henry Schacht, 5/5/83.
39. This and subsequent quotations are from the Armand V. Feigenbaum interview, 11/26/96.
40. Jim Henderson memo to file, 12/20/84.
41. Jim Henderson interview, 1/8/97.
42. Jim Kelly interview, 10/22/96.
43. K. P. Singleton memo to Jim Henderson, Henry Schacht, and Carl Ahlers, 6/13/85.
44. K. P. Singleton memo to Jim Henderson, Henry Schacht, and Carl Ahlers, 6/13/85.
45. Art Tajima memo to Mike Walsh, 12/22/83.
46. Art Tajima interview, 5/9/95; Mike Walsh memo to Henry Schacht, Jim Henderson, and John Hackett, 6/17/82.
47. Mike Walsh memo to Henry Schacht, Jim Henderson, and John Hackett, 6/17/82; J. Patrick memo to Mike Walsh, 3/10/82.
48. Henry Schacht memo to Jim Henderson and Mike Walsh, 1/27/86.
49. "Decision time in Peoria," *Forbes* (January 27, 1986).
50. "Decision time in Peoria," *Forbes* Robert Campbell memo to file, 6/24/86.
51. Henry Schacht memo to Jim Henderson and Mike Walsh, 1/27/86.
52. Henry Schacht memo to Jim Henderson, 11/3/86.
53. Henry Schacht memo to several managers, 7/3/86.
54. Ryoichi Kawai letter to Jim Henderson, 10/5/82; K. P. Singleton memo to Jim Henderson, Henry Schacht, and Carl Ahlers, 6/13/85; Art Tajima interview, 5/5/95.
55. Art Tajima interview, 5/5/95.
56. Robert Campbell memo to Jim Henderson and Henry Schacht, 6/8/87.
57. Mark Levett memo to Jim Henderson, 6/26/87.
58. Robert Campbell memo to Jim Henderson, 6/12/87.

59. Mark Levett memo to Henry Schacht, 8/26/87.
60. Robert Campbell memo to Jim Henderson, 3/10/87.
61. See, for example, Karel G. Van Wolferen, "The Japan Problem," *Foreign Affairs* (Winter 1986–1987), which was read and annotated by J. Irwin Miller and passed along to Henry Schacht.
62. Mark Levett memo to Henry Schacht, 8/26/87.
63. See, for example, the Henry Schacht memo to Jim Henderson and Mike Walsh, 1/27/86.
64. See Robert Campbell memo to file, 6/24/86; Henry Schacht memo to several managers, 7/3/86; Robert Campbell memo to the Strategy Committee, 7/21/86.

Chapter 11

1. "Mr. Rust Belt," cover story in *Business Week* (October 17, 1988).
2. See, for example, comparative sales data in "Strategy before Profits," *Financial Times*, 10/12/89.
3. The Hanson account draws in part on a deposition made by Henry B. Schacht on 1/30/96 and 1/31/96 in relation to Civil Action No. IP90-428-C T/G, United States District Court, Southern District of Indiana.
4. "An extraordinary gesture," *Indiana Business* (November 1989).
5. "Why Henry Schacht is Watching his Rearview Mirror," *Business Week* (January 9, 1989).
6. "Hanson's Meteoric Rise," *New York Times*, 3/5/89.
7. See, for example, "Cummins: Cautious Optimism about Future," *Indianapolis Star*, 1/24/89.
8. "Hanson 'Options Open' over Cummins Engine," *Financial Times*, 1/17/89.
9. For an explicit discussion of these issues, see E. W. Booth's remarkable 3/26/79 memo to H. B. Schacht on the subject of ownership and control of Cummins stock. Booth proposed that the company build a shareholder base that would represent a "network of accountability" — and whose members would keep each other honest.
10. Will Miller interview, 9/6/94.
11. See, for example, "Hanson, White and Cummins," *Forbes* (June 12, 1989).
12. "Columbus Firm Loses Favor on Wall Street," *Indianapolis Star*, 1/10/89; "Law Could Delay Takeover of Cummins," *Indianapolis News,* 7/28/89.
13. "Ivy League brainpower," *Indianapolis Star*, 2/19/89.
14. See, for example, "Cummins Seeks the Smooth Ride of Profitability," Louisville (KY) *Courier-Journal*, 4/17/89.
15. See "Columbus Firm Loses Favor on Wall Street" for recently departed Cummins chief financial officer John T. Hackett's perspective on the apparent takeover bid.
16. Jim Henderson interview, 7/22/93.
17. Henry Schacht interview, 9/7/94.
18. Henry Schacht deposition, 251.
19. Will Miller interview, 9/6/94.
20. Will Miller interview, 9/6/94.
21. Will Miller interview, 9/6/94.
22. Will Miller interview, 9/6/94.
23. Board minutes, 7/14/89.
24. "Millers Take Control," *Columbus Evening Republican*, 7/18/95.
25. "Cummins in Buyback Deal for Hanson Stock," *Financial Times*, 7/18/89.
26. "Cummins Attracts Second Foreigner; Stock Price Jumps," *Wall Street Journal*, 7/27/89.
27. Associated Press, Executive News Service, 7/18/89.
28. Standard and Poor, *PR Newswire*, 7/17/89, 12:57 EDT.
29. "Cummins Seen as Attractive Takeover Target," *Business Wire*, 7/17/89.
30. In the 7/23/89 edition.
31. "Family Pays $72 Million to Defend a Company," *New York Times*, 7/18/89.
32. For details on these two episodes, see Cummins Engine Company, Form 10-K, filed with the Securities and Exchange Commission 12/31/89, p. 8.
33. "Cummins Heirs Buy Back Hanson Stock," *Chicago Tribune*, 7/18/89.
34. Board minutes, 7/10/89 and 7/11/89; "Cummins Announces Stock Plan," *Columbus Evening Republican*, 7/11/89.
35. "Cummins Engine Strengthens Poison Pill," *Investor's Daily*, 8/10/89.
36. "Shareholders Group Calls Cummins Unfair," *Indianapolis News*, 7/14/89.
37. Associated Press, Executive News Service, 7/18/89.
38. Henry Schacht deposition, p. 308.
39. IEP, Schedule 13D, filed with the Securities and Exchange Commission 7/26/89.
40. From IEP/Brierley's filing under the Hart-Scott-Rodino Antitrust Improvements Act of 1976.
41. "Cummins Bid Not Hostile," *Columbus Evening Republican*, 7/27/89.
42. "Cummins Attracts Another Investor," *Chicago Tribune*, 7/27/89.
43. "Holder Boosts Cummins Stake; Stock up $1.625," *Wall Street Journal*, 9/20/89.

44. Much of this description, as well as Schacht's quotes, are taken from George J. Vlahakis' excellent series of articles in the *Columbus Evening Republican* in the week following the arrival on the scene of IEP.
45. "Who is IEP, Owner of 9.9% of Cummins?" *Columbus Evening Republican*, 8/6/89.
46. *Louisville Courier-Journal*, 7/27/89.
47. "Cummins Engine Strengthens Poison Pill"; "Cummins Engine Amends 'Pill' Plan," *New York Times*, 8/10/89.
48. David C. Wright letter to U.S. Justice Department, Antitrust Division, Office of Operations, 8/10/89.
49. "More Cummins Stock Acquired," *Indianapolis Star*, 9/20/89; "Holder Boosts Cummins Stake."
50. "IEP Takes Stake in Cummins to Limit," *Columbus Evening Republican*, 9/24/89.
51. "Cummins Hits Turnaround Roadblocks," *Wall Street Journal*, 9/25/89.
52. "Foreign Firm Adds to Stake in Cummins," *Indianapolis Star*, 9/23/89.
53. "Cummins to Cut Salaries by 5%," *Indianapolis News*, 9/28/89.
54. "Cummins Weathers Hugo," *Columbus Evening Republican*, 10/6/89.
55. "Wall Street's Patience Tried," *Financial Times*, 12/7/89.
56. "Was Brierley's Move on Cummins Dumb or Dangerous?" *Business Week* (March 19, 1990): 46.
57. "Cummins Sues Top Shareholder," *Columbus Evening Republican*, 1/26/90.
58. For details, see Cause No. IP90 063C, United States District Court, Southern District of Indiana, Indianapolis Division.
59. "Cummins Sues Top Shareholder," *Columbus Evening Republican*.
60. All details on these various suits and countersuits are from pages 8 and 9 of Cummins' Form 10-K, filed with the SEC on 12/31/89; and from "Was Brierley's Move on Cummins Dumb or Dangerous?"
61. "Probe of Investment in Cummins Requested," *Indianapolis News*, 2/1/90.
62. "Political Reinforcements: Cummins Wheels Out Big Guns in Battle with Hong Kong Investor," *Indianapolis Business Journal*, 2/5/90.
63. "Tougher Takeover Law Urged," *Indianapolis News*, 2/2/90.
64. "Industrial Equity Re-evaluates Stake in Cummins in Wake of Defense Moves," *Wall Street Journal*, 2/6/90.
65. "Lawsuit Attacks Cummins, Chief," *Indianapolis News*, 2/16/90.
66. "Lawsuit Attacks Cummins, Chief," *Indianapolis News*.
67. "Was Brierley's Move on Cummins Dumb or Dangerous?"
68. "Cummins Chief Becoming Riled," *Indianapolis News*, 3/14/90.
69. "Cummins Dissident Holds Court," *Indianapolis News*, 4/4/90.
70. "Cummins Dissident Holds Court," *Indianapolis News*.
71. "Cummins Sees Slow Growth, Hears Dissent," *Louisville Courier-Journal*, 4/4/90.
72. See, for example, "High-Stakes Cummins Bid Paid Off for One Investor, But Cost Another Millions," *Louisville Courier-Journal*; 2/20/91, "Cummins, Investor Reach Pact," *Indianapolis News*; 5/10/90, and "Cummins Engine, Biggest Holder Set Standstill Accord," *Wall Street Journal*, 5/11/90.
73. M. F. Brooks memo to Henry Schacht, 8/22/88.
74. Henry Schacht memo to file, 9/7/88.
75. Henry Schacht letter to R. Kawai, 10/9/89.
76. Henry Schacht memo to file, 11/6/89.
77. M. F. Brooks memo to senior Cummins executives, 4/20/89; unknown author's memo to Cummins senior executives, 8/19/89.
78. "Why Kubota Hitched its Tractor to Cummins," *Business Week* (July 30, 1990): 20.
79. M. F. Brooks memo to senior Cummins executives, 4/20/89; unknown author's memo to Cummins senior executives, 8/19/89.
80. "Onan Engine History," internal document, otherwise unidentified; *Engine Power Perspective*, 7/90.
81. See, for example, M. F. Brooks memo to Henry Schacht and Will Miller, 10/19/89.
82. Henry Schacht, memo to file, 11/6/89.
83. These emphases were confirmed in an interview with Kubota President Shigekazu Mino which appeared as an advertisement in the *Financial Times,* 9/10/90.
84. W. W. Gulden memo to Henry Schacht, Jim Henderson, Will Miller, and Peter Hamilton, 5/7/90.
85. H. B. Schacht letter to H. A. Poling, 8/10/90.
86. Details can be found in the Cummins Engine Company, Form 8-K, filed with the Securities and Exchange Commission, 7/26/90.
87. "Cummins: The Art of the Deal, The Shadow of Things to Come," *Engine Power Perspective* (July 1990).
88. "Cummins Deal Enthuses Investors and Analysts," *Columbus Evening Republican*, 7/22/90.
89. "Cummins: The Art of the Deal," *Engine Power Perspective*.
90. Henry Schacht letter to Tenneco, 5/1/90.
91. "Cummins Deal Enthuses Investors and Analysts," *Columbus Evening Republican*.
92. W. W. Gulden memo to Henry Schacht and Will Miller, 6/24/90.
93. Henry Schacht memo to file, 6/25/90.
94. Cummins Engine Company, Form 8-K, filed with the Securities and Exchange Commission, 7/26/90.
95. "Cummins: The Art of the Deal," *Engine Power Perspective*.
96. Cummins 8-K, filed with the Securities and Exchange Commission, 7/26/90.
97. "Deal Ends Family Role in Rescue Try," *Indianapolis News*, 7/16/90.

98. "Industrial Equity sues Cummins," *New York Times*, 2/16/90; "Purchase of Cummins Stake Looks Less Sacrificial Now," *New York Times*, 2/22/90; "Chief's Patient Vision Faces Test at Cummins," *New York Times*, 4/3/90; "Cummins Selling 27% Stake to 3," *New York Times*, 7/16/90. The second of these articles was the one to which the Millers took particular objection.
99. "Cummins Shares Rise by $3.125," *New York Times*, 7/17/90.
100. Henry Schacht interview, 10/6/94.

Chapter 12

1. Fact Book for 1993.
2. Annual reports for 1990 and 1991.
3. *Indianapolis Star*, 1/1/91; annual meeting reference book for 1991.
4. Annual report for 1990; annual meeting reference book for 1990.
5. *Columbus Evening Republican*, 12/31/90.
6. Business Update videotape for fourth quarter 1990; annual report for 1990.
7. See Mike Brewer and Christine Vujovich memo to Henry Schacht, 5/10/82.
8. Henry Schacht letter to Elliot Richardson, 7/10/82.
9. Mike Brewer and Christine Vujovich memo to Henry Schacht, 11/12/84.
10. Christine Vujovich interview, 10/20/94.
11. L. C. Broering memo to file, 4/9/85; Tom Head memos to Henry Schacht and others, 5/3/85 and 5/7/85.
12. P. A. Gustafson memos to many, 11/21/86 and 11/25/86.
13. Annual report for 1987.
14. *Columbus Evening Republican*, 4/8/90; Karl Kuehner, 10/21/96; Joe Loughrey interview, 11/2/95.
15. Annual report for 1990.
16. Henry Schacht interview, 10/6/94.
17. Henry Schacht interview, 10/6/94.
18. Jim Henderson interview, 1/9/97.
19. Henry Schacht interview, 10/6/94.
20. "Does Cummins have the oomph to climb this hill?" *Business Week* (November 4, 1991); "Racer's edge in Truck Engines," *New York Times*, 9/28/91.
21. Henry Schacht interview, 10/6/94.
22. "Cummins Attempts to Map Return to Profitability," *Wall Street Journal*, 5/20/91.
23. Gary Nelson interview, 10/1/96.
24. Business Update videotape for third quarter 1991.
25. Henry Schacht letter to Gareth Mitchell (Motor Truck Equipment Co., New Stanton, Pa.), 10/14/91.
26. The authors are indebted to Ed Booth, Ron Temple, Karl Kuehner, and Bill Schwab for their explanations of electronics and of the process of building an electronics capability at Cummins.
27. Ed Booth interview, 5/11/95.
28. Board minutes, 9/14/82.
29. John Hackett memo to Henry Schacht and others, with attached contract, 8/4/80.
30. Board minutes, 9/14/82.
31. Ron Temple interview, 7/11/94.
32. Annual report for 1984.
33. Annual reports for 1985 and 1987.
34. Annual report for 1985; Joseph Loughrey interview, 11/2/95.
35. Ron Temple interview, 7/11/95.
36. Ron Temple interview, 7/11/95.
37. Annual report for 1987.
38. Ron Temple interview, 7/11/95; annual report for 1988.
39. Annual meeting reference book for 1988.
40. "First company across the finish line," *Financial Times*, 11/8/91.
41. "Balancing act for producers," *Financial Times*, 11/8/91.
42. Patrick Shea of Cummins Electronics received U.S. Patent 4,944,260 for the "Air Heater System for Internal Combustion Engines," 9/90.
43. Annual report for 1992.
44. "Cummins Responds With ESP," *Mid-America Weekly Trucking* (November 6, 1992).
45. "Cummins comin' back," *Wards Auto World* (February 1992); annual reports for 1992 and 1993; fact book for 1993.
46. Ron Temple interview, 7/11/95; fact book for 1993; "Cummins introduces '94 line," *Columbus Evening Republican*, 7/6/93.
47. Annual report for 1994.
48. "Strategic sourcing policy: Total Quality System," 1993.
49. Joseph Loughrey letter "to all members of the company," 8/28/95.
50. Fact book for 1993.

51. Fact book for 1993; annual report for 1991.
52. Jim Henderson "Delivery" paper, first draft, 6/15/88.
53. All quotations and paraphrases are from "JAH Remarks to Manufacturing Conference, July 6, 1989," distributed by Jim Henderson to Joseph Loughrey, M. F. Mitchell, and J. C. Read, 9/30/89.
54. Anne E. Newman memo to Marjorie A. Freije, 10/7/96; "Cummins Production System Employee Manual," 1996.
55. Annual report for 1990.
56. From an e-mail to J. A. Henderson from Frank J. McDonald, vice president of worldwide midrange operations.
57. See, for example, Ted Marston letter to the OCU, 4/10/84.
58. DWU bargaining committee, "Announcement to membership," fall 1985.
59. Annual meeting reference books for 1988 and 1991.
60. *Columbus Evening Republican*, 3/25/91.
61. From a case study of the Jamestown plant by Robert H. Guest, professor emeritus at Dartmouth's Amos Tuck School, entitled "Team management under stress: Despite a massive overhaul in their manufacturing systems, the self-managed teams at a Cummins Engine Plant are alive and well," published in *Across the Board* (May 1989).
62. *Columbus Evening Republican*, 3/25/91.
63. *Indianapolis Star*, 5/21/89.
64. *Columbus Evening Republican*, 3/26/91. For much of the information about contract negotiations and the shift to team-based work systems, the authors are indebted to Joseph Loughrey and Larry Neihart.
65. *Columbus Evening Republican*, 3/25/91; *Indianapolis News*, 3/25/91; *Indianapolis Star*, 3/25/91.
66. *Columbus Evening Republican*, 3/17/92.
67. "We built a showcase out of a closed plant," *Modern Materials Handling* (December 1992).
68. *Columbus Evening Republican*, 3/17/92.
69. *Columbus Evening Republican*, 3/17/92; *Cincinnati Post*, 3/23/92.
70. *Indianapolis News*, 3/18/92; *Indianapolis Star*, 3/18/92.
71. Details and background on the negotiations that led to the Cummins/DWU 11-year contract in 1993 are from interviews with Larry Neihart, 6/24/94, and Joseph Loughrey, 11/2/95.
72. *Columbus Evening Republican*, 5/9/93.
73. *Columbus Evening Republican*, 2/16/92.
74. Annual report for 1992.
75. "A Diesel Maker's Comeback Route," *New York Times*, 6/11/92; *Indianapolis Star*, 10/20/92 and 2/12/93; "25 Executives to Watch," *Business Week* (April 5, 1993); "Cummins comes back," *CFO Magazine* (April 1993).
76. "A boom ahead in company profits," *Fortune* (April 6, 1992); *Indianapolis Star*, 10/13/95; Dow Jones News Service, 1/25/94 and 1/27/94.
77. *Indianapolis News*, 4/6/94.
78. "The Twelve Labors: To hell and back with Henry Schacht of Cummins Engine," *Financial World* (June 9, 1992).
79. *Truck* (November 1992).
80. *Indianapolis Star*, 1/20/94.
81. Transcript of Quarterly Update videotape for second quarter 1993.
82. "Savvy Russian Factory Manager Makes Profit," *Christian Science Monitor*, 11/20/91. For a concise history of Cummins' activities in the former Soviet Union through 1988, see "The Cummins Engine Company in the Soviet Union," Harvard Business School case #9-389-018.
83. "Some shifts in top posts at Cummins," *New York Times*, 7/13/94.
84. J. Irwin Miller interview with Jim Henderson, 5/25/93.

Chapter 13

1. The story of this first Cummins history is distilled from two letters: J. Irwin Miller to Clessie Cummins, 11/30/44; and Clessie Cummins to J. Irwin Miller, 12/12/44, C. Lyle Cummins private library.
2. 50th anniversary brochure.
3. W. A. Swanberg, *Luce and His Empire* (New York: Scribner, 1972), 257–58.
4. See Harold G. Vatter, *The U.S. Economy in the 1950s: An Economic History* (New York: Norton, 1963).
5. Alfred D. Chandler, Jr., *The Visible Hand: The Managerial Revolution in American Business* (Cambridge Mass.: Belknap Press, 1977).
6. Rondo Cameron, *A Concise Economic History of the World*, 2d ed. (New York: Oxford University Press, 1993), 228–31.
7. See Thomas C. Cochran, *Business in American Life: A History* (New York: McGraw-Hill, 1972), Part 3.
8. The reforms of the Progressive Era and New Deal are well documented; for an overview of the less documented reforms of the 1970s see David Vogel, "The 'New' Social Regulation in Historical and Comparative Perspective," in Thomas K. McCraw, ed., *Regulation in Perspective: Historical Essays* (Boston: Division of Research, Harvard Business School, 1981), 155–85.

9. Louis Galambos and Joseph Pratt, *The Rise of the Corporate Commonwealth: U.S. Business and Public Policy in the Twentieth Century* (New York: Basic Books, 1988), 2.

10. Galambos and Pratt, *The Rise of the Corporate Commonwealth*, 129–54; Louis Galambos, "By Way of Introduction," in Galambos, ed., *The New American State: Bureaucracies and Policies since World War II* (Baltimore: Johns-Hopkins University Press, 1987), 1–20.

11. Galambos and Pratt, *The Rise of the Corporate Commonwealth*, 129–83; Herbert Stein, *Presidential Economics: The Making of Economic Policy from Roosevelt to Reagan and Beyond*, 2d ed. (New York: Simon & Schuster, 1985), 65–87; and Robert J. Gordon, "Postwar Macroeconomics: The Evolution of Events and Ideas," in Martin Feldstein, ed., *The American Economy in Transition* (Chicago: University of Chicago Press, 1980), 101–33. For more on the advantages of predictability to the conduct of business, see Howard Stevenson and Jeffrey Cruikshank, *Do Lunch or Be Lunch* (Boston: Harvard Business School Press, 1998).

12. A detailed survey of the fragmentation of American society during this period is John Morton Blum, *Years of Discord: American Politics and Society, 1961–1974* (New York: W. W. Norton, 1991).

13. Wallace C. Peterson, *Silent Depression: The Fate of the American Dream* (New York: W. W. Norton, 1994), 32–42.

14. Davis Dyer, Malcolm S. Salter, and Alan M. Webber, *Changing Alliances: The Harvard Business School Project on the Auto Industry and the American Economy* (Boston: Harvard Business School Press, 1987), 128–29, 286.

15. The viewpoints summarized in this section can be found in scores of works on post-1945 U.S. business and economic history. Many of these arguments are discussed in Bernstein and Adler, eds., *Understanding American Economic Decline*, passim (but especially chs. 1–3); and Barry Eichengreen, "International Competitiveness in the Products of U.S. Basic Industries" (pp. 279-353) and other essays in Martin Feldstein, ed., *The United States in the World Economy* (Chicago: University of Chicago Press, 1988).

16. Alfred D. Chandler, Jr., and Richard S. Tedlow, eds., *The Coming of Managerial Capitalism* (Homewood, Ill.: R. D. Irwin, 1985), 737–75; Alfred D. Chandler, Jr., "The Competitive Performance of U.S. Industrial Enterprises since the Second World War," *Business History Review* 68 (Spring 1994); 16–20; Robert Sobel, *The Rise and Fall of the Conglomerate Kings* (New York: Stein and Day, 1984).

17. Richard G. Hamermesh, *Making Strategy Work* (New York: Wiley, 1986), 9–16; Arnoldo C. Hax and Nicholas S. Majluf, "The Use of the Growth-Share Matrix in Strategic Planning," in Arnoldo C. Hax, ed., *Readings on Strategic Management* (Englewood Cliffs, N.J.: Prentice Hall, 1984), 61–75; Christopher D. McKenna, "Do Consultants Really Matter: The Case of Lukens Steel," Hagley Museum and Library Research Seminar Paper 32 (February 8, 1996), 34, cited with the author's permission.

18. Gordon Donaldson, *Corporate Restructuring: Managing the Change Process from Within* (Boston: Harvard Business School Press, 1994); Frank R. Lichtenberg, *Corporate Takeovers and Productivity* (Cambridge, Mass.: MIT Press, 1992); Chandler, "Competitive Performance," 20–23.

19. Galambos and Pratt, *Rise of the Corporate Commonwealth*, 191.

20. C. K. Prahalad and Gary Hamel, "The Core Competence of the Corporation," *Harvard Business Review* (May–June 1990): 79–91.

21. Will Miller interview, 9/6/94.

22. See Harvey H. Segal, *Corporate Makeover: The Reshaping of the American Economy* (New York: Viking, 1994).

23. Lichtenberg, *Corporate Takeovers and Productivity*, 130–31.

24. Galambos and Pratt, *Rise of the Corporate Commonwealth*, 225.

25. See Alan M. Kantrow, *The Constraints of Corporate Tradition* (New York: Harper & Row, 1987).

26. "Making Customers Cry for It," *Business Week* (February 2, 1957): 51–52.

27. W. G. Irwin letter to Clessie Cummins, 7/24/39, C. Lyle Cummins private library.

28. Paul Tiffany, *The Decline of American Steel: How Management, Labor, and Government Went Wrong* (New York: Oxford Univesity Press, 1988), passim.

29. Some others scholars agree that Germany and Japan offer the two most promising models of political economy for the next century. See, for example, Hart, "A comparative analysis of the sources of America's relative economic decline," 231–39; and Lester Thurow, *Head to Head: The Coming Battle Among Japan, Europe, and America* (New York: Morrow, 1992).

30. Galambos and Pratt, *Rise of the Corporate Commonwealth*, 229.

31. "Egghead in the diesel industry," *Fortune* (October 1957): 167. This insightful article was written by T. George Harris, who got closer to Irwin Miller than any other journalist.

32. Unsigned "Purchasing Department Brief," 1941.

33. Dick Stoner interview, 8/18/93.

34. Jack Edwards interview, 1/31/95.

35. Ray Boll interview, 8/2/93.

36. George W. Newlin memo, 1967, included in "Financial History of the Cummins Engine Company," 11/9/82.

37. See, for example, Stuart D. Brandes, *American Welfare Capitalism* (Chicago: University of Chicago Press, 1976).

Index

About the Authors

JEFFREY L. CRUIKSHANK is a co-founder of Kohn Cruikshank Inc., a Boston-based communications consulting firm. He has written or co-authored numerous books on subjects of interest to managers, including *Herman Miller, Inc.: Buildings and Beliefs* (with Clark Malcolm); *A Delicate Experiment: The Harvard Business School 1908–1945*; *Breaking the Impasse* (with Lawrence E. Susskind); *From the Rivers: The Origins and Growth of the New England Electric System* (with John T. Landry); and *Do Lunch or Be Lunch* (with Howard H. Stevenson). He is currently working on a book about entrepreneurship in the United States in the post-World War II period.

DAVID B. SICILIA is assistant professor of history at the University of Maryland, College Park. A specialist in business, economic, and technology history, he is co-author of *The Entrepreneurs: An American Adventure* (with Robert Sobel) and *Labors of a Modern Hercules: The Evolution of a Chemical Company* (with Davis Dyer), the latter published by Harvard Business School Press in 1990. His current research focuses on the application of information technology in arts and humanities instruction and on the evolution of American business since 1945.